SOCIOLOGY
An Introduction

Third Edition

Earl R. Babbie

Wadsworth Publishing Company
A Division of Wadsworth, Inc.
Belmont, California

Sociology Editor: William H. Oliver
Project Coordinator and Designer: Detta Penna
Copy Editor: Joan Pendleton
Technical Illustrator: Li Greiner, Publishing/Art
Services
Photo Researcher: Lindsay Kefauver
Cover Designer: Russell Leong

Printed in the United States of America
1 2 3 4 5 6 7 8 9 10—87 86 85 84 83

**Library of Congress Cataloging in Publication
Data**

Babbie, Earl R.
  Sociology, an introduction.
  Bibliography: p.
  Includes index.
  1. Sociology. I. Title.
HM51.B16 1983   301   82-20081
ISBN 0-534-01366-X

**A study guide has been specially designed to
help students master the concepts presented
in this textbook. Order from your bookstore.**

ISBN 0-534-01366-X

PHOTO CREDITS

Prologue Charles Gatewood/Magnum Photos Inc.
2; Ken Heyman 7 left; Leo Hetzel 7 right; George W.
Gardner/Stock, Boston 8

Part One Owen Franken/Stock, Boston 10

Chapter 1 David Powers/Stock, Boston 12; Library
of Congress 16; Paul Popper 17 left; Elliott Erwitt/
Magnum Photos Inc. 17 right; Eve Arnold/Magnum
Photos Inc. 21; Historical Pictures Service 27

Chapter 2 Mark Godfrey/Archive Pictures 35; Snark
International 39; Library of Congress 41; Pamela R.
Schuyler/Stock, Boston 42; Alex Webb/Magnum
Photos Inc. 47; The Bettmann Archives 50; Hazel
Hankin/Stock, Boston 56; Wide World Photos 60

Chapter 3 Peeter Vilms/Jeroboam, Inc. 70; Jerry
Howard/Stock, Boston 72; Owen Franken/Stock,
Boston 87; Mike Mazzaschi/Stock, Boston 90; Har-
vard University News Office 98

Part Two Kent Reno/Jeroboam, Inc. 106

Chapter 4 Robert Azzi/Woodfin Camp & Associates 108; Levi, Europe 114 left; Bulloz 114 right; Rick
Smolan/Stock, Boston 116; Pennell Collection, University of Kansas Libraries 117; Elliott Erwitt/Mag-
num Photos Inc. 122 left; Lennart Nilsson/Black Star
122 right; Jeffrey Blankfort/Jeroboam, Inc. 123 left;
Jeffrey Blankfort/Jeroboam, Inc. 123 right; Field
Museum of Natural History, Chicago, Illinois 125;
Henri Cartier-Bresson/Magnum Photos Inc. 127

Chapter 5 Kent Reno/Jeroboam, Inc. 140; Ed Buryn/
Jeroboam, Inc. 144; Burk Uzzle/Magnum Photos Inc.
145: Bentley Historical Library, The University of
Michigan 148; Cornell Capa/Magnum Photos Inc. 153;
Ken Heyman 157; Peter Vandermark/Stock, Boston
159; Peter Menzel/Stock, Boston 162

Chapter 6 Peter Southwick/Stock, Boston 172; Bruce
Davidson/Magnum Photos Inc. 175; Peter Simon/
Stock, Boston 176 left; Bibliothèque Nationale 176
right; Michal Heron/Woodfin Camp & Associates 179:
Franziska Toennies Heberle 184; Western History
Collections, University of Oklahoma Library 185;
Richard Kalvar/Magnum Photos Inc. 190

Chapter 7 James R. Holland/Stock, Boston 201;
George T. Kruse/Jeroboam, Inc. 203; Wide World
Photos 208; Bruce Davidson/Magnum Photos Inc.
212

Part Three Tim Carlson/Stock, Boston 230

Chapter 8 Thomas Hopker/Woodfin Camp &
Associates 232; Courtesy of Harvard University
Archives 236; Eve Arnold/Magnum Photos Inc. 240
(continued after index)

A Note to the Reader

It seems ironic that prefaces—appearing first in a book—are almost always written last. Written at the completion of a major undertaking, they provide an occasion for reflection.

As I look back across the years I've spent writing this introductory textbook and revising it for its second and third editions, it occurs to me that I've been considering myself a sociologist for more than half my life. Yet this book represents my first attempt to shape all the miscellaneous bits and pieces of my chosen discipline into a coherent whole. In the course of writing, I have found a power and an excitement in sociology that I had not experienced before. That's what I want to share with you.

Part of my excitement about sociology stems from my practical concerns about the current and future state of the world. Like you, perhaps, I've grown increasingly disturbed about the many ways in which our world simply doesn't "work." War, prejudice, poverty, and pollution are only a few of my concerns. Whereas I once felt that such problems might be amenable to technological solutions, it is now clear that technology is not enough. There is no magical "superbomb" or "doomsday machine" on the technological horizon that will solve the problem of war. Nor is there a "clean" energy source about to be discovered that will solve the problems of environmental pollution forever.

Ultimately you and I are the source of the kinds of problems I've mentioned, and we represent the only possible solution to them. Our problems stem from the social agreements we and our ancestors have made for living together in groups; if we are to solve them—and survive—we need to understand those social agreements. This is the only way we'll ever succeed in creating the kind of world we want for ourselves and others.

I am presenting this third edition to you with the same confidence in our ability to handle our social problems as I had when I presented the first and second editions of the book. Shortly after the publication of the first edition, I had an opportunity to join about forty other people in making a commitment to bring about the elimination of world hunger within twenty years. In the five years since then, more than two million others have joined in that commitment, and my participation in The Hunger Project has been a new source of insight into the persistence of social problems and a source of inspiration for ending them.

Sociology is going to be increasingly important in the years to come. Physicists can develop nuclear power, but the decision to use that power for peace or war is the result of a social process. Chemists and biologists can develop effective methods of contraception, but a social process determines whether the methods are used. Without a firm sociological understanding of those social processes, we will end the human interlude on earth with a warehouse full of unused or impractical technological solutions.

My intention in writing this book has been to make the broad field of sociology accessible both to students who will go on to become sociologists and to those who will not. Sociology cannot fully serve all our interests in society if the field is understood only by professional sociologists. Thus, I have tried to provide a fundamental grounding in sociological points of view and findings appropriate both to further study *and* to responsible participation in society.

The Agreements Theme

The power and promise of sociology stem largely from the breadth of substantive and conceptual territory it covers. Ultimately, it subsumes all other sciences. However, sociology's breadth and diversity also present a problem to beginning students, who often have difficulty grasping and managing the field's many points of view, concepts, and research findings. Rote memorization often seems the only solution, since the logical scheme that holds all of sociology together is not always apparent.

The difficulty of understanding the diversity of sociology is at least matched by the difficulty of presenting it in lectures or textbooks. For teachers and authors, it has often seemed necessary to choose between (1) presenting a biased view of the field by focusing on a single point of view and/or subject area and (2) burying students under an avalanche of unconnected and often conflicting views and materials. It has never been a happy choice.

The chief contribution of this textbook—what excites me most about it—is the way in which this problem is handled. As a perpetual student of sociology and as a professor, I have found the notion of *agreements* to be an extremely effective device for organizing the field of sociology.

In briefest summary, this book presents sociology and human social life in terms of the agreements that people continually make, organize, break, and change. As we'll see, agreements are necessary for the survival of group life. Those agreements are created continuously through social interaction, and they are organized and perpetuated in the form of institutions. Social life, however, is as much a matter of disagreement as agreement. There is a continuing competition over *which* points of view will be established and institutionalized, and every institution becomes a source of dissatisfaction for some members of the society. Sometimes people simply break the agreements that dissatisfy them; sometimes they seek to change those agreements. Ultimately, agreements and disagreements are two sides of the same coin. There will be conflict, deviance, and social change as long as there are institutionalized social structures. The agreements theme provides a context for us to observe and understand all these different aspects of social life, and the Prologue will describe that context in detail.

It is not my intention to offer a new *theory* of society. The agreements theme is not intended as a competing point of view within sociology. Its chief value, I find, is as a context for existing theories and points of view, making it possible to look at all that the different views have to offer without choosing which is "true." Moreover, the agreements concept makes it easier to grasp the links among different points of view.

Special Features of the Book

In addition to providing an integrated and comprehensive introduction to the field of sociology, I wanted to explode some myths about higher education—myths that I've found troublesome. Chief among these is the myth that learning is painful, akin to the belief that for medicine to work, it has to taste lousy. Both as a student and as a teacher, I've found the most powerful learning experiences were also the most exciting and even fun.

A related myth suggests that Introductory Anything is by nature dull and lifeless. What ought to be a magical adventure in a field of newly discovered flowers gets dried into a dust bowl by this myth, and that seems a shame.

Finally, there is a myth that rich and complex ideas can only be presented in difficult, complicated language. I have not found this to be true in my own writing: Whenever I begin writing in clumsy and difficult prose, I have found it more a reflection of my own lack of understanding than of the complexity of the idea.

With an eye toward exploding these myths, it has been my intention to make this book both informative and enjoyable. I have wanted it to be simple and entertaining because I feel those qualities contribute to learning rather than detract from it. A number of special features of the book were created with that in mind.

Application and Analysis   In addition to presenting the essentials of each chapter topic, I have added a concluding essay that examines a special issue in more depth. For the most part, I have selected issues that are already familiar to you, through your daily life or through the mass media, and have shown how sociological points of view can add to your understanding of those issues.

Practicing Sociology   Each chapter ends with an opportunity for you to apply what you have learned in that chapter. In some cases, I have given you news stories to analyze; in other cases I've given you a set of social data. My feeling is that you can best learn about sociology by practicing the sociologist's skills.

Graphics   Sometimes concepts and information can be expressed more effectively in graphic form than in words. We have used photographs to bring life to concepts and events, as well as to show you sociologists past and present who might otherwise be lifeless names in footnotes. We have used a variety of charts, graphs, and diagrams to present information in an easily grasped form.

Glossary   A glossary in the back of the book defines and illustrates key sociological terms. These terms appear in boldface type in the text to signal that they are in the glossary.

Other student aids   There are previews and reviews throughout the book, aimed at keeping the specifics in perspective. Each of the book's five parts begins with an overview, and each separate chapter begins with a topic outline. Finally, each chapter ends with a summary and suggested additional readings. All these features aim to make sociology more easily grasped and held.

Student study guide   An excellent student study guide both reinforces the materials contained in the text chapters and creates opportunities to go beyond the text through a variety of projects and activities.

I want to conclude this preface by thanking you. If you are an instructor, I want to thank you for your willingness to share your experience of sociology with your students and for letting me participate in that process. It's truly an honor to take part in the education of the Meads, Parsons, and Marxes of future generations.

If you are a student, I want you to know that your willingness to take a look at sociology enables me to share something I enjoy very much. Every time I find a way to communicate an idea to you, I understand that idea better myself. In a sense, you teach me sociology at the same time I teach you. I enjoy it immensely and hope you do too.

Acknowledgments

In wrapping up the first edition of this book, I had a chance to recall the varied assistance and support I received from friends and colleagues around the country and I commented that it was "a humbling experience to review all the people who contributed to the creation of a book that has your name on the cover." I wanted to acknowledge everyone whose contribution had made the book substantially stronger and more useful. Ultimately, I acknowledged seventy-six people by name.

In revising the book for the second edition, scores of additional colleagues from around the country assisted in the updating and improve-ment of the book, and I acknowledged them in that book. What you have in your hands is very much a contribution to you from those hundred or so sociologists, though I won't reprint the entire list of names again here.

In revising the book once again, I had the good fortune of assistance and support from many of those who worked on the earlier editions, plus some new people. I'd like to mention a few of those whose assistance helped make the third edition what it is.

First, I want to acknowledge some groups too large to identify by individual names. Since the publication of the first edition, I have had the delightful job of teaching introductory sociology to several hundred students at the University of Hawaii and elsewhere, and that has had an importance for me that perhaps only another teacher/writer will understand. Every time a student in class has had the courage to raise his or her hand and say, "I don't understand what you meant by . . ." I have had to learn my own field a little better and to become more effective in communicating about it. I know how painful and embarrassing it is to participate in that fashion, and I want to begin by acknowledging every student who had the courage to do it anyway.

Second, three or four hundred students from around the country took the time and trouble to write to me to tell me what they liked or didn't like about the first edition. I am especially thankful that most liked it on the whole and said so (a little stroking now and then is definitely welcomed). At the same time, those students who were willing to write and say what they didn't like have participated directly and importantly in making the third edition better than the second.

As with the first and second editions, my faculty colleagues at the University of Hawaii and across the country have been a continuing source of stimulation and support. I have the feeling I've never met a sociologist I haven't learned something from.

I want to give a special thanks to Bonnie Summers, my assistant, for a variety of contributions too numerous to list. Most fundamentally, however, I want to thank her for being a true partner in the book and for teaching me how to accept support from others.

It has been my continued good fortune to write textbooks in partnership with a publishing house inhabited by people committed to the view that book making is an honorable trade. Nine times out of nine (so far), I have discovered everyone from editors to truck drivers acting with pride of personal ownership for the books they produce.

The first edition of this book represented the full realization of the special relationship that ought to exist between an author and editor. Steve Rutter, then the sociology editor at Wadsworth, was unquestionably the mold that editors should be struck from, a true magician and a full partner in the book. Not surprisingly, Steve was promoted to larger editorial responsibilities. Steve was ably replaced by Curt Peoples for the second edition and by Bill Oliver for the third. In all these experiences my awe and respect for what editors do have never stopped growing.

In the third edition, Bill has been assisted by many people at Wadsworth, in particular, Lauren Foodim and Susan Goerss. Detta Penna has been responsible for the overall production of the book.

Writing a textbook is an excellent exercise for learning to take guidance and criticism. Numerous colleagues around the country supported me in that fashion. In particular, Jeanne Gobalet (San Jose City College) and Jeanne Ballantine (Wright State University) were genuine partners in the book, advising on all stages and aspects of it. Others who contributed importantly to the shaping and tuning of the book include Henry Stewart, University of Richmond; Anson Shupe, University of Texas, Arlington; Terry Toazic, Middle Tennessee State University; Gretta Stanger, Tennessee Technological University; George R. Reinhart, University of Alabama, Birmingham; Frank A. Santopolo, Colorado State University; Joel C. Snell, Kirkwood Community College; S. Frederick Seymour, Northern Illinois University; Abraham Levine, El Camino College; Brent Bruton, Iowa State University; Richard G. Mitchell, Oregon State University; Eleen A. Baumann, Oregon State University; Norval D. Glenn, University of Texas, Austin; E. G. Maret, Texas A & M University; Bill Brindle, Monroe Community College; Roy E. Carter, Jr., University of Minnesota, Twin Cities.

It wouldn't be possible for me to put words together that would adequately describe the nurturance and support I received from my family during the writing of the book. My mother, Marion, my wife, Sheila, and my son, Aaron, all made it their own purpose to have the book turn out just the way it did; I couldn't have asked for more. In a broader sense, Sheila continues to pursue the difficult job of clearing away new spaces for me to expand into. No one could ask for a more powerful partner in life.

Finally, I want to acknowledge three people who shine especially brightly for me as models of how to live on this planet we share. First, Bucky Fuller introduced the notion of "Spaceship Earth," and by his personal example has shown that it's possible to be a member of the crew and not just a passenger. Bucky has served us all by dedicating a half-century of his life to asking and answering the question "What can the little individual do?" Second, Joan Holmes provides an equally powerful answer to Bucky's question. In 1977 Joan moved from a career as elementary school teacher to take total, personal responsibility for the elimination of death due to starvation on the planet by 1997. As executive director of The Hunger Project, she has since become a global spokeswoman for that objective. Lastly, my dear friend Werner Erhard continues to amaze and inspire me at every turn. Seven books ago I thanked Werner for adding excitement and satisfaction to my life. Since then, he has helped me see that I am the source of excitement and satisfaction in my own life and that I can contribute that to others as well. From Werner, I have discovered the special satisfaction of empowering others in the world.

Contents

Glossary

Bibliography

Index

To Aaron Robert Babbie:

Intrepid explorer,
he discovered a new world,
Took me to it,
and let me play there.

Prologue

Society
at a
Glance

A friend of mine was once asked by her five-year-old son, "What's astronomy?" Parents are accustomed to hearing that sort of question, so my friend gave a brief overview of astronomy. Then she asked her son, "Why didn't you ask your father? He's an astronomer." Her son replied, "I didn't want to know that much."

This book will probably tell you more about society and sociology than you ever wanted to know or will ever need to know. There's just a lot to tell, and that can present a problem for me, for your instructor, and for you. The problem is how *you* are going to manage, grasp, and hold all the information that will be sent your way.

In this prologue I propose to give you a *context* for the *content* that follows in the book. This prologue, then, presents the *whole* of society, and the rest of the book presents the many pieces. By having the whole first, you'll know how to fit the rest of the pieces together. Let's begin the construction of that context, starting with the most fundamental questions we might ask in order to grasp the nature of human social life.

What Do People Want Out of Life?

To understand why people do the things they do, including why they form certain kinds of societies and live together in certain ways, let's begin by asking what people want to get out of life. There are many answers to such a question, of course. Yet, if you observe people long enough and try to understand their behavior, four objectives keep coming up.

First, people seem to want *survival:* food, water, air, shelter, and so on. Much human behavior, then, can be explained in terms of people trying to get the things they need for survival.

The second thing people seem to want out of life is *comfort.* You can survive uncomfortably. Maybe one bowl of rice a day would keep you alive for some time, but you'd be hungry. Or a threadbare jacket may be enough protection for survival, but you'll still feel cold. By and large comfort seems to mean simply having more of what it takes for survival. So if one bowl of rice a day would keep you alive, ten bowls of rice would take away the hunger pangs.

The third thing that people seem to want out of life is *security*. In addition to survival and comfort right now, we seem to want some assurance that both survival and comfort will extend into the future. And, for the most part, security seems to be a function of having even more of what it takes for survival and comfort. If you had a warehouse full of rice, then you would know that you'd have enough for both survival and comfort in the weeks and years to come.

Beyond survival, comfort, and security, people seem to want *satisfaction*. I know you've had the feeling of satisfaction from time to time: perhaps when you completed a difficult task, when you were in love, or when you felt on top of the world for no apparent reason. Satisfaction is difficult to define and equally difficult to explain or find causes for. As we'll see throughout this book, people often seek the experience of satisfaction by amassing those things needed for survival, comfort, and security, though satisfaction doesn't seem to be a function of that accumulation. For many people, this search for satisfaction involves amassing money: a thousand dollars, a million, ten million, none of which seems quite enough.

In brief, then, these are four things that people seem to want out of life. When you observe

Some jobs are too big for an individual, yet working together can be a source of conflict as easily as cooperation.

people relating to one another, you can understand and explain a lot of what you see in terms of the attempts to get survival, comfort, security, and satisfaction. As we will see next, those goals of individuals provide a beginning explanation for the organization of group life.

The Advantages of Group Life

Long ago people found that living together in cooperative groups had important advantages for getting the things they wanted out of life as individuals. Cooperation brought strength, and it supported our ancestors in getting what was required for individual survival, comfort, and security.

If you are on your own in the jungle, for example, you can dig up roots to eat, pick berries, and maybe trap rats and squirrels. I can do the same as an individual. By cooperating, however, we can knock over a zebra. And Roast Rack of Zebra is a vast improvement over boiled rat. Instead of wearing fern capes, through cooperation we can have bearskin coats. I can chase the bears to you, and you can kill and skin them.

Or consider this. One annoying problem humans faced early in their history was that wild animals sometimes ate them in their sleep. Now you and I as individuals can stay awake only so long, but together we can handle the problem. I can keep watch from sundown to midnight, and your shift would be from midnight to sunrise. Cooperative group life supported many forms of security.

Quite aside from the things needed for survival, comfort, and security, however, relationships with others are an important source of satisfaction. Love, affinity, companionship, nurturance, camaraderie—all these are associated with the experience of profound satisfaction in life. Thus, group life can provide us with those things that we seem to want out of life *as individuals*.

The Costs of Group Life

Just as people have long recognized the benefits of group life, so they have been aware of the costs. First, it is usually necessary to divide up the booty through cooperation. Thus, although zebra is a vast improvement over rat, you and I have to split the zebra in half. We also have to share the work and responsibility. For me to enjoy the security of having you awake while I sleep from midnight to sunrise, I have to stay up until midnight and throw myself in the jaws of anything that starts to attack you.

Second, it is often necessary to *compromise* in cooperative ventures. Suppose that I like zebra, but you think deer is better. And suppose I can't stand the thought of killing anything with such soft, brown eyes. The result in such a situation might entail a compromise—eating pig, for example.

Finally, there are many "administrative overheads" in group life—certain requirements generated by "groupness" itself. For cooperation to work at all, for example, there have to be decision-making procedures and, perhaps inevitably, some form of leadership. Even in a democracy, somebody has to run the meeting and count the votes. Notice that when you and I were totally on our own—digging up roots, picking berries, and trapping rats—neither of us had to devote any energy to counting the votes. By the time we have formed a group of, say, fifty to one hundred people, it probably will require the full-time efforts of one member of the group to be the leader.

Being the leader probably doesn't seem like a bad job, but many of the jobs in the administration of group life are less pleasant and satisfying. Someone has to clean up the meeting hall. Someone has to take out the trash on Monday and Thursdays. By the same token, much of the power of cooperative group life comes through specialization, and some specialties are nicer than others. It may be fun to sit on the side of the river catching fish, but someone has to clean them, someone has to cook them, and someone has to wash up afterward.

To summarize, you and I want certain things out of life as individuals. We find that cooperating in groups assists us—as individuals—in getting what we want. Part of the cost is that we must share and compromise, though we probably come out ahead anyway. More subtly, however, other costs entailed in group membership often require that individuals do things that do not directly help them get what they want out of life. Taking out the garbage on Monday night, for example, does not directly give me survival, comfort, security, or satisfaction. My willingness to do it, however, supports the persistence of the group, and benefits from the group presumably make up for the sacrifice. One of the most fundamental questions in understanding human group life, however, is "How do you get people to do things needed for the survival of the group but of no direct benefit to them as individuals?"

Agreement and Alignment

The question posed above is not limited to humans. It applies equally to any "social animals"—any creatures who live in cooperative groups. Bees, ants, and other social insects, for example, provide interesting comparisons with human social life.

For a beehive to survive, each individual bee must each do its part. The queen must lay eggs, the drones must fertilize the queen, and the workers must do everything else: gather nectar, build the combs for honey, fight off intruders, and so forth. You may have asked yourself why anyone would choose to be a worker—slaving all day over a hot flower—rather than a drone, whose only job is to keep the queen pregnant.

The answer, as I'm sure you know, is that none of the bees chooses to be a worker, drone, or queen. They are genetically programmed to do what their instincts dictate, and collectively their instincts dictate behaviors that ensure the hive's survival, regardless of the consequences

to the bees as individuals. If a hive's laying queen is accidentally stepped on by a carefree sociologist cavorting in the forest, for instance, some of the workers instinctively begin laying eggs. Nobody is nominated to lay eggs, nobody is elected. They just do it. And if the hive is threatened, the bees instinctively attack and sting the intruder, even though they die in the process.

This kind of "natural" cooperation is called "alignment." I'll expand on the meaning of the term shortly, but for now think of it as individuals being "in line with one another," pointed in the same direction, so that what they do naturally as individuals supports the group goals. Thus, we might say that the social insects are aligned *by instinct* in that they are genetically wired to do jobs that are needed for the survival and success of the group.

But what about humans? Are we, too, genetically wired to behave in ways appropriate to the success of our group? Let's see.

Alignment among Humans

One of the newer schools of thought to arise around the topic of human behavior goes by the name of "sociobiology." At its base, sociobiology suggests that human group behavior can be understood in terms of biological and genetic processes. Edward Wilson, the best-known supporter of this viewpoint, defines sociobiology as "the systematic study of the biological basis of all forms of social behavior, including sexual and parental behavior, in all kinds of organisms, including humans" (1978b:2). Wilson's writings have provoked considerable controversy among social scientists—Wilson himself is a zoologist.

Although we are not going to deal with sociobiology in any depth, I want to spend a minute or so on it now, because the point of view it brings to bear on social behavior will be useful in setting up the questions that we'll be answering throughout this book. Recall that I asked a moment ago how we could expect individuals in a group to do those things that were needed for the survival of the group but were not necessarily to the advantage of the individuals themselves. Sociobiology offers an answer that is simple and direct: humans, like other social animals, are *genetically* programmed to behave appropriately for survival. But survival, in this instance, doesn't mean what you may think. Listen to Wilson's (1978a:2–3) explanation of the human mind and its grappling with the nature of physical reality:

> The human mind is a device for survival and reproduction, and reason is just one of its various techniques. Steven Weinberg has pointed out that physical reality remains so mysterious even to physicists because of the extreme improbability that it was constructed to be understood by the human mind. We can reverse that insight to note with still greater force that the intellect was not constructed to understand atoms or even to understand itself but to promote *the survival of human genes.* (emphasis added)

Thus, Wilson has offered an answer that needs little elaboration: you and I are genetically programmed to behave in ways that promote the survival of the genes that form the basic building blocks of humankind. Put differently, he suggests that human groups survive for the same reasons that bees and ants do. If that's so, there is little more to be said, other than to elaborate on the specific mechanisms by which it happens.

Sociobiology is essentially an extension of the Darwinian view of biological evolution. It has been criticized as *reductionistic:* attempting to reduce social behavior to a matter of biology alone. The sociobiological point of view is new, fascinating, and controversial. Undoubtedly, the controversy will grow hotter in the years to come, and I imagine that you will hear about it even if you do not continue to study sociology.

At this point, however, it has certainly not become widely accepted among sociologists. Instead, sociologists seek other answers to the question of why humans behave as they do—especially why they so often do those things that are required for the survival of the group, even when it doesn't benefit them directly and may even put them at a disadvantage. Even without assuming a genetic drive for the survival of our genes, we can nonetheless point to countless experiences of alignment among humans.

It's my guess that you've had experiences from time to time when it seemed as though you and some other person were "operating on the same wavelength." You may have been working on some project together, and it just seemed as though each of you knew what the other was going to do—it all seemed to flow together naturally. Maybe you've had that experience in sports or music. A few years ago, the University of Hawaii had a basketball team that seemed to operate on the basis of magic. In a surprise rush down the court, one player would hurl the ball in the general direction of the basket, and its path would "just happen" to coincide with the running leap of another team member. The "Fabulous Five" operated more as one person than five. They offered a great example of social alignment.

If you've ever been in love, you've probably had experiences of alignment with your loved one. Perhaps you can recall times when someone close to you did something nice for you when it wasn't necessary or expected, and there have been times when you did something nice for a loved one that you didn't have to do. You supported someone else in getting what he or she wanted, and in so doing you were demonstrating and preserving your experiences of the relationship. Cooperation is a natural expression of alignment.

Georg Simmel (1858–1918), a German sociologist, spoke of this latter form of alignment as *sociability:*

> Sociability has no objective purpose, no content, no extrinsic results, it entirely depends on the personalities among whom it occurs. Its aim is

nothing but the success of the sociable moment and, at most, a memory of it. . . . Wealth, social position, erudition, fame, exceptional capabilities, and merits, may not play any part in sociability. At most they may perform the role of mere nuances.(1908b:45,46)

The experience of alignment with someone else is a satisfying experience. You may feel good just recalling some of the times you experienced being aligned with someone. Moments of alignment are times when you feel "safe" with others. You feel it's safe to let your guard down, to just be yourself and do what seems natural and appropriate.

Now let's define alignment more carefully than before. *Alignment is a condition in which two or more individuals share the same common purpose, such that the natural and spontaneous behavior of each will support the other(s) in realizing their purpose.* The common purpose, in this instance, can be a group goal (such as our team winning the football game), an individual goal (one of us being elected president), or just being together and enjoying each other as described above by Simmel.

This definition of alignment requires that we have the *same* purpose. If you want to be president and I want to be president, we definitely do *not* have the same purpose, and we are not aligned. If you want to be president, and I want *you* to be president, then we have the same purpose and are aligned in that respect.

Take a moment now to notice what social life would be like if all of us were totally aligned with one another in all regards. It's hard to get a completely clear picture of such a situation, but some things come to mind readily. There would certainly be no conflict among people—no fistfights, murders, or wars. Moreover, in the situation of total alignment, there would be no need for laws, since everyone would just naturally do what was appropriate. In fact, there would be no need for planning sessions or leaders, since we would start out aligned on a common purpose.

You probably have mixed feelings about the situation I've been describing. Although it would certainly be nice to have an end to war and murder, the kind of *total* coordination/cooperation I've been describing seems somehow *unhuman*. You may have formed a mental image of humans scurrying about like ants and felt uncomfortable about it. Well, you can relax, since what I've been describing doesn't give a very accurate picture of human life as we know it. It's not a very accurate picture of Arab-Israeli relations in the Middle East nor of the political relations between Republicans and Democrats in the United States. In short, we do not act as though we were totally aligned on all things.

Enter Agreements

Even if we aren't *totally* aligned, the more pressing question is whether we are sufficiently aligned to support the survival of group life. If individuals were allowed to do absolutely what they pleased, what would happen? Would we get along, or would we go for each other's throats? That's one of the oldest questions in social philosophy. One of the best-known answers was given three centuries ago by British philosopher Thomas Hobbes (1588–1679).

Hobbes (1651:100) described the earliest human life as "continual fear, and danger of violent death; and the life of man, solitary, poor, nasty, brutish and short." In Hobbes's view, without the influence of a strong leader (whom he called the "Leviathan"), no social order could have arisen. Social thinkers have debated that basic issue ever since, and we still do not know for sure what the nature of human nature is. There are numerous theories but little agreement.

We do not know if humans are aligned sufficiently to get along and for human groups to survive. One thing we can know for sure, however: *we act as though we were not aligned.* As we pursue our examination of human societies in this book, it will be evident that the social

Some of the business of living together is handled through a natural alignment and cooperation . . .

. . . some aspects of social life must be coordinated by the establishment of intricate, detailed agreements.

arrangements we have created are based on the fundamental assumption that humans are *not* sufficiently aligned to promote the survival of society. Fearing the lack of alignment, then, *humans create agreements*.

"Agreements," as we are going to use the term in this book, are *attempts to generate and impose alignment*. Here's a simple example of what I mean. Suppose you and I both want succotash as our main meal. One way of producing the succotash would be for me to grow beans, for you to grow corn, and for us to share what we've grown with each other; each of us could then mix our beans and corn together, cook them, and have succotash. If we were aligned, in fact, we'd probably just throw both harvests together and cook up a common kettle of the stuff.

But what are the dangers of this system? Well, suppose I grow my beans and give you half—only to discover that you decided not to grow corn after all or, worse, that you grew the corn but refuse to give me any. If we were aligned on the common goal of succotash-for-all, that

wouldn't happen, of course, but how can I be sure of you? It is because of this uncertainty that we create an agreement. We generate a common goal of our both having succotash, then I agree to grow beans and turn over half, and you agree to do the same with corn. We make an agreement to share, because we aren't sure that each of us would do it naturally.

It is important to see that we not only have *generated* an agreement, but we also have *imposed* it upon ourselves. Now I have to turn over half my beans, and you have to turn over half your corn. In place of the natural spontaneity inherent in alignment, we have generated burden and obligation. In real life, our agreements take the form of *laws*, with specified punishments for breaking them.

Notice, then, that the very idea of agreement contains a contradiction in it. An agreement is an attempt to generate and impose alignment, but alignment by its very nature is spontaneous and natural. This contradiction is going to reappear throughout our examination of society. Over and over, we are going to see people generating social agreements aimed at promoting happiness and satisfaction, only to kill the possibility of satisfaction in the process.

Before turning to a more careful examination of agreements and how they operate, let's take a minute to review the series of steps that has brought us to this point:

1. Humans seem to want certain things out of life, such as survival, comfort, security, and satisfaction.

2. Long ago, people discovered that joining together in groups could promote the achievement of what they wanted individually.

3. Because of the advantages of cooperation, people came to depend on groups as a way of getting what they wanted.

4. Thus, the survival of the group became important in its own right.

5. Groups have certain requirements for survival; for example, they need administration.

6. To satisfy the survival needs of the group, individuals must do things not in their own interests as individuals.

7. The social insects handle this problem by being *aligned genetically*.

8. Sociobiology aside, humans don't seem to be genetically aligned to do what's needed for group survival.

9. Lacking total alignment, humans create agreements.

The remainder of this book is an elaboration on how humans make agreements and on the consequences of that process.

As we undertake a careful scrutiny of how agreements work, we are going to see that agreements constitute only part of the picture. Specifically, we'll see that we can't have agreements without also having *disagreements*. When people are totally aligned, that's all there is to it. When you and I are going in the same direc-

Our experience of social life is as much a matter of disagreement and conflict as of agreement and harmony. Agreement and disagreement are two sides of the same coin.

tion, pursuing a common purpose as a natural and spontaneous thing, it's difficult even to conceive of anything else. When we make an agreement to establish and impose "alignment," however, something else is not only possible, it is assured.

As soon as we generate an *obligation* to share our corn and beans, the grounds for resistance are generated in the same process. As long as I *have to* give you my beans, I can now *not want to*. As long as I was doing it as a natural, spontaneous, joyful thing, how could I not want to? I can disagree only if there's an agreement to disagree with.

"Society by agreement," then, is equally and inevitably "society by disagreement." As we'll see later in this book, some societies—such as totalitarian dictatorships—are less willing to tolerate disagreement than are others. Even where it is not generally tolerated, however, disagreement is an inevitable feature of society.

The interplay of agreement and disagreement, moreover, makes our life together eternally fascinating as well as challenging. My purpose is to share both the fascination and the challenge with you.

Part One

Sociology
as a
Discipline

1 **Sociology as Point of View**
2 **Theoretical Points of View**
3 **The Science of Sociology**

Sociology offers a way of looking at the world you live in. Using sociology, you'll be able to see familiar things in a new light. If you are majoring in sociology, this course and book will give you the fundamental grounding you need for advanced studies. If you are not majoring in sociology, you will add breadth to your general education, and you'll learn things about your society that will empower you in your everyday life.

Part One of this book will give you an initial grounding in sociology as a way of understanding social life. Once you complete these three chapters, you will be prepared to read and understand the materials contained in the rest of the book.

Sociology as Point of View   Sociology is the study of human social life—ranging from face-to-face interactions between two individuals up to the global relations among nations. The view sociology offers of those phenomena is importantly different from both common sense and other academic disciplines.

Chapter 1 will present you with the key concepts that make up the sociological point of view, and you'll understand the difference between sociology and other views of social life.

Theoretical Points of View   Sociology offers several different points of view for observing social life. Sometimes it is appropriate to focus on the ways people interact with one another and develop shared meanings in the process. Other times, it is more appropriate to see society as a system, composed of interrelated parts. Still other times, the appropriate focus is on the conflicts individuals and groups have with one another. Sociology allows you to bring all these points of view to bear on what you see going on around you.

In Chapter 2, you'll learn about the nature of theory in science, and you'll become familiar with three major theoretical points of view in sociology. You'll be able to apply those points of view to the materials that come later in the book.

The Science of Sociology   Sociologists use a set of scientific research methods, designed for rigorous observation and interpretation. You'll learn about many of the scientific techniques sociologists have developed for the purpose of studying social life. As you'll see, each different research technique has its special strengths and weaknesses.

Chapter 3 will prepare you to read and understand the sociological research reports described later in the book, and you'll also be able to read many of the research reports presented in sociological books and journals. In addition, you'll gain some idea of how you might do sociological research on your own.

1

Sociology as Point of View

What do all the following have in common: fist-fights, jury deliberations, the Equal Rights Amendment, labor unions, overpopulation, school busing, arms reduction talks, falling in love, television shows, computers? All are appropriate to sociological analysis.

Sociology is the study of human social life, ranging from the interactions that take place between two people, through small groups such as friendship cliques and large formal organizations such as General Motors, all the way to nation-states and international relations. All these are fair game for sociologists, and all have been and are being studied.

As C. Wright Mills (1959:132–3) pointed out, all manner of societies are appropriate subjects for sociology: "Byzantine and Europe, classical China and ancient Rome, the city of Los Angeles and the empire of ancient Peru." Sociology also addresses the varieties of social life within such societies. Mills continues:

> Within these worlds there are open-country settlements and pressure groups and boys' gangs and Navaho oil men; air forces pointed to demolish metropolitan areas a hundred miles wide; policemen on a corner; intimate circles and publics seated in a room; criminal syndicates; masses thronged one night at the crossroads and squares of the cities of the world; Hopi children and slave dealers in Arabia and German parties and Polish classes and Mennonite schools and the mentally deranged in Tibet and radio networks reaching around the world. Racial stocks and ethnic groups are jumbled up in movie houses and also segregated; married happily and also hating systematically; a thousand detailed occupations are seated in businesses and industries, in governments and localities, in near-continent-wide nations. A million little bargains are transacted every day, and everywhere there are more "small groups" than anyone could ever count.

Sociology deals with a broader, more fascinating range of topics than does any other academic discipline. The purpose of this book is to introduce you to sociology—to some of its research findings and, more importantly, to the conceptual framework that sociology provides for looking at the world. We'll be examining the same world you've been looking at all your life, but in a different way. This book introduces you to what sociologists "see" when they look at the world.

When I talk about the way a sociologist sees the world, I don't mean "vision" in the physiological sense. I mean that the sociologist experiences the world from a particular point of view. All of us experience the world through our personal points of view, and my intention in this book is to give you an opportunity to try out a new point of view, called sociology.

The sociological point of view can empower you with a special vision. It can let you see and understand things that might otherwise escape your notice or make no sense. Unfortunately, people sometimes have the idea that sociology is extremely complicated: a jumble of disconnected jargon. Actually, the many subtle concepts that constitute the sociological point of view are not too complicated for you to understand, and they fit together quite nicely into a powerful whole.

As I've indicated in the Prologue, the commonsense notions of **agreements** and **disagreements** provide a useful vehicle for understanding the many concepts sociologists employ in the study of human social life. Although agreements and disagreements are not a substitute for those concepts, students have found that the two simple notions highlight the order that exists in the sociological view as a whole.

When sociologists look at the world, they see the stated and unstated agreements that people make, and they see how those agreements are organized to produce orderly social relations. Just as important, sociologists also see the disagreements that exist. They see people breaking the agreements that others make and share, and they see agreements change. The domain of disagreement includes a wide range of social topics: for example, debates and arguments, gang wars, class and ethnic conflicts, and international wars.

In this chapter, I'll talk about points of view and agreements and disagreements, and in the process I'll describe what sociology is and what it isn't. By the time you finish this chapter, you should have a sense of what sociology is about.

The Nature of Agreements and Disagreements

Sociology—the study of human social life—can be approached as the study of agreements and disagreements people have in the course of living together on the same planet. It is the study of social harmony and conflict, order and disorder, persistence and change. In this section, I'll begin by defining the term **agreement** in more detail. I want to do that by looking at how agreements operate in the games we play, moving from board games and football to society. We'll see how our agreements affect our view and experience of reality, and how they ensure the survival of groups.

Agreements and Games

A number of social scientists have noted the similarity between social life and the games we play. The box entitled "Society and Game Theory" elaborates on this similarity. Games can also provide insights into the way agreements operate in social life.

The agreements in the games we play have four main characteristics. Knowing these characteristics will be useful to you as you try to understand how agreements operate in social life:

1. Agreements are *essential* in games.
2. Those agreements are often *arbitrary*.
3. Some agreements are more *appropriate* to the games than others would be.

SOCIETY AND GAME THEORY

Many observers have noted the similarity between games and life. George Herbert Mead (1934:151), for example, found value in examining the manner in which children assumed social roles for the purpose of playing a game. Not only did they have to learn the behavior appropriate to their own role, but they also had to learn what to expect from others who were playing other roles. As we'll see in Chapter 2, this latter issue was central to Mead's view of society.

More recently, the insights to be found in games have been formalized in what is called **game theory**. This approach to the study of social life is based primarily on decision making. Henry Hamburger (1979:3) identifies four key elements in game theory.

1. *Players.* Game theory begins by identifying those participants in the action who have an interest in the outcome and are able to make decisions.

2. *Choices.* Given a specific situation, what is the set of possible actions for each player?

3. *Results.* What are the likely consequences of the various actions available to each player?

4. *Preferences.* Among the possible results, what does each player prefer?

Because most of the actions available to players involve trade-offs, the decision-making process is one of perceived costs and benefits. Moreover, not all players have perfect knowledge in the matter, so they sometimes act on the basis of misconceptions.

If you think about it for a moment, you'll see that game theory could be applied to a wide range of social situations: labor-management negotiations, dating, the nuclear-arms race, classroom discussions.

Source: George Herbert Mead, *Mind, Self, and Society,* edited by Charles W. Morris (Chicago: University of Chicago Press, 1934). Henry Hamburger, *Games as Models of Social Phenomena* (San Francisco: W. H. Freeman, 1979).

4. Sometimes we begin to think that agreements represent "reality" rather than being just agreements, a process called *reification.*

Agreements Are Essential You can't have games without agreements. Some of the agreements are formally stated as rules, while others seem so obvious that they don't even have to be stated. You can't play craps without an agreement that rolling a 7 (on the first roll) is better than rolling a 2. Imagine a craps game in which you want rolling a 7 to win and I want it to lose.

Most games are based on an unspoken agreement that it's better to win than to lose. *That* agreement is so obvious that it doesn't even get written inside the cover of the box the game

comes in. Try to imagine a game of chess in which your strategy was to win and mine was to lose. It wouldn't be much of a game.

Agreements Are Often Arbitrary The agreements by which we play games are made up. They don't have to be the way they are. In Monopoly, for example, Boardwalk isn't of itself any more valuable than Baltic Avenue. You could play Monopoly just as well if all the players agreed to make Boardwalk less valuable than Baltic Avenue. We need some agreement, however, if we are to have the game, and we just happened to agree that Boardwalk would be more important.

Football would not be affected much if the playing field were 110 yards long instead of 100. Players could adjust to going a little farther for a touchdown. (Canadian football, incidentally, is played on a 110-yard field.) Some agreement on how far you must go for a touchdown is necessary, however, and Americans happened to agree on 100 yards.

Some Agreements Are More Appropriate than Others   Although the agreements involved in games are often arbitrary, some seem to work better than others. So, while football can be played as easily on a 110-yard field as on a 100-yard field, and while kids manage to play football in much less space, it probably wouldn't work to play football on a field 10,000 yards long. Having to run over 5 miles for a touchdown probably wouldn't work. At the least, football would become a less exciting spectator sport than it is now.

People Tend To Reify Agreements   Reification means making real or thinking something is real when it isn't. One of the strangest things about the agreements in games is that people often begin thinking they are real instead of just being agreements.

During the late 1970s and early 1980s, the game of *Dungeons and Dragons* was very popular in the United States. You may have played it yourself; you probably knew someone who did. Many parents were worried that their children were taking the game too seriously, and there were frequent newspaper stories about small groups of young people who had secluded themselves for days at a time for marathon sessions of *Dungeons and Dragons*. For many, injuries suffered by their fictional "character" were felt personally. People often forget they are only playing games.

Two Kinds of "Reality"

I've asked you to look at the place agreements have in games because these agreements have the same characteristics as those that operate in the rest of social life. First, they are essential.

Points of view regarding the exposure of the human body illustrate the changing of agreements over time. Consider our American progression from the "scandalous" exposure of the 1890s . . .

You couldn't have society as we know it without them. Imagine what your daily life would be like if you and others did not agree on what language to speak and which side of the road to drive on. Agreements are necessary in thousands and thousands of similar instances.

Second, the agreements that form the structure of your life in society are—like those in games—often arbitrary. Traffic flows as well with everyone driving on the left side of the road as on the right. Conversations can be conducted in French as well as in English.

Third, some of the agreements in your life are more appropriate than other possible ones. Societies operate more smoothly with an agreement that you shouldn't kill other people than they would if there were an agreement that killing was all right or an agreement that everyone *had* to kill one person a day.

Finally, in societies, as in games, people have a tendency to reify the agreements they make. Put somewhat differently, people reify the points of view that they have agreed on and begin

. . . through the cheesecake of the 1950s . . .

. . . to the more sensible cloth-conservation of today. While the American population has grown a great deal, the amount of cloth used in the manufacture of bathing suits has probably remained constant.

thinking that those points of view represent ultimate reality. Because the operation of armies requires clear systems of authority, for example, militaries have agreed that generals have authority over privates. Rather than regarding this as a logical arrangement for getting a job done, however, people tend to begin feeling that generals are really superior to privates. If the general and the private meet twenty years later when both are civilians, they are still likely to experience, to some degree, the earlier authority relationship that began as a logical agreement for getting a particular job done. The "private" will still defer to the "general," even though such deference would not be logically necessary in their new situation. Something similar often happens to people who first meet as professors and students.

If you look carefully at your own life, you should be able to see that you have reified countless agreements. You and I share an agreement, for example, that telling the truth is better than lying. That agreement makes a lot of sense because it makes communication easier. But suppose that you found out I had lied to you about something in this book. Would you merely say, "He shouldn't have done that because it gets in the way of communication," or would you feel that I was "really" wrong to have lied? Would you regard my lying as merely an inconvenience or also as immoral? Is "telling the truth" merely an agreement for you, or is it something more?

We have an agreement not to murder each other; and, like our agreement to tell the truth, it makes a lot of sense. Things would be pretty chaotic and disorderly without that agreement, and we probably wouldn't be able to live together in groups as we do now. But do you regard the agreement on murder as merely a convenient arrangement or as something more?

When you were a young child, you didn't feel that lying and murder were "really" bad. In your very beginning, you didn't feel they were wrong at all, and you didn't know about the agreements those around you shared. As you grew up, however, the agreements were taught to you. As you learned them, you had a tendency to think they represented something on the order of truth.

In a sense, you live in a world of two realities. Some things seem real to you because you experience them directly. Other things seem real to you because of the agreements you share with others, because you have reified the points of view you hold in common with those around you.

You may have had the experience of loving someone. You may not have been able to explain or justify the feeling; you just *knew* that you loved that person. You may also love your parents, but this may be because we have an agreement that we all should love our parents. If you've ever had doubts about whether you love your parents, if there have been moments when you hated your parents, you have probably felt guilty. We are *expected* to love our parents. That's the agreement we share.

I don't mean to suggest that you can't or don't have a direct experience of loving your parents quite aside from the agreement to do so. I'd simply like you to notice that some of the many things that seem "real" to you grow out of agreements you have learned from others and have later reified. It's often difficult to distinguish **experiential reality** from **agreement reality**, moreover, because they both "feel" real.

"Feeling" Agreements   Consider the following situation. Suppose you are visiting in someone's home and your host offers you a chocolate candy after dinner. You try one and find it tastes "really" good. You eat five or six of them. Then your host tells you that you've been eating chocolate-covered *worms*. You might very well throw up; you certainly wouldn't feel good. The feeling in your stomach would be very real, yet it stems from the agreement you share with others in our society that eating worms is awful. Realize also that people living in other societies around the world have agreements that eating bugs, worms, and grubs is okay—in some cases more than okay. The creatures are a delicacy.

For most Americans, snails are a lawn and garden pest. If you ever inspected one close up, you may have found it pretty disgusting. Yet for the French (and some Americans), snails *(escargot)* are a delicacy.

It was this variability of "reality" that led Peter Berger and Thomas Luckmann (1967) to examine what they called the "social construction of reality." For the most part, they addressed their attention to the shared reality of everyday life:

> I am alone in the world of my dreams, but I know that the world of everyday life is as real to others as it is to myself. Indeed, I cannot exist in everyday life without continually interacting and communicating with others. . . .
>
> The reality of everyday life is taken for granted *as* reality. It does not require verification over and beyond its simple existence. It is simply *there*, as self-evident and compelling facticity. I *know* that it is real. (1967:23; emphasis in original)

You and I *know* that worms are *really* terrible to eat. You feel the reality of it, the facticity ("factness") of it in your stomach and your throat. Yet, the way we know it is by agreement.

You live in a world of two realities. Both feel real, and they are often difficult to distinguish. Yet one is based on your own direct, personal experience of things and the other is based on the agreements you share.

"Seeing" Agreements   Agreements are powerful enough to affect what we see as well as how we feel. Several decades ago, Muzafer Sherif (1936) conducted a set of experiments that should cause you to take everything you experience and believe with a grain of salt. Sherif studied the development of group norms in regard to what are called "autokinetic effects."

In Sherif's experiments, a group of people were placed in a totally darkened room. Mounted on a far wall was a small, stationary point of light. I've pointed out that the light was stationary because if you were to sit in a totally darkened room, with no visible walls, floor, or ceiling to serve as a frame of reference, you'd eventually get the feeling that the point of light was moving around. That's what Sherif's experimental subjects experienced.

Besides signaling the experimenter whenever they saw the light move, the subjects were also asked to estimate the distance that it moved. Since the light was stationary throughout all the experiments, it's not surprising that estimates of how far it moved varied greatly. More surprising, however, was the discovery that whenever a group of subjects viewed the light together, they quickly reached an agreement as to the distance it moved, even though the initial estimates of different members of a given group disagreed greatly. By the end of each observation session, all members of the group were experiencing the same amount of movement. (Different groups, incidentally, arrived at quite different agreements.)

Notice how this discussion of experiential and agreement reality parallels the earlier discussion, in the Prologue, of alignment and agreement. Your experiences of alignment with someone fall within the realm of experiential reality. As I mentioned, you may experience loving your parents as a totally natural thing; you love them just because you love them. Or you may love your parents by agreement—because everyone is expected to love his or her parents. And either reality may be the source of pain for you if something bad happens to your parents. Again, agreement reality seems real; and that's important, as we'll see in the next section.

The Survival of Groups

The reality created by agreements is important in many ways. First, it makes group life possible. People seem unable to get along together in groups without agreements, although a wide variety of different sets of agreements is workable in this regard. The business of govern-

ment, for example, gets accomplished by democracies, monarchies, and totalitarian dictatorships alike. The exchange of goods and services gets accomplished through the use of money or direct barter. None of these would work, however, without an agreement on what system was operating.

Sociologists use the term **institution** to refer to the agreement system that organizes some general aspect of group life. Government is an example of an institution, as, more specifically, is democracy or monarchy. Democracy, then, is an institution made up of the agreements that govern political relations in America. Other major institutions that interest sociologists are the economy, religion, the family, and education. Each of these institutions is discussed at length in Part Four of this book.

To the extent that the institutions of a particular society remain unchanged, people are able to get along with each other in habitual ways. There are rules about the ways things are done, and everyone knows what to expect of everyone else. Voters in a democracy, for example, know that they will have an opportunity periodically to elect public officials, and politicians know that they must at least appear to represent the interests of their constituents. Business people in a capitalistic economy know that they can purchase goods at wholesale and sell them at retail, turning a profit in the process.

In a broad sense, institutions are made up of agreements about the ways in which people will get along with each other in a particular society. This does not mean that institutionalized agreements are necessarily "good"—racial prejudice, discrimination against women, and urban sprawl represent institutionalized agreements. All institutions represent the establishment of certain points of view and the denial of others. This means that in every society some people who have different points of view will disagree with the established ways of doing things. Sometimes these people simply break the agreements. Sometimes they try to set up new ones.

Since World War II in Poland, the centrality of the communist party in national policymaking has been an established agreement. Many Poles have disagreed with that, however, and the creation of the Solidarity union in 1980 crystallized that disagreement. Polish workers attempted to shift the base of power to the unions; and, as we'll see in Chapter 13, that action was regarded by the nation's leaders as a serious threat to the established order—and it was.

This, in overview, is the nature of the agreements and disagreements that provide the framework for our social existence. In a broader context, recall that this discussion began with the question of how we could expect individuals to do those things required for the survival of group life, especially when those things might conflict with individual self-interest. We saw that social insects handle this problem through a genetic alignment. Humans, while experiencing a degree of alignment with one another, don't seem aligned enough to guarantee the survival of society. Thus, we make agreements.

As this discussion has unfolded, you probably have been able to see how it applies to certain aspects of your life, and you may even have been aware of some of the issues before taking up this book. As you will see throughout this book, sociology deals with things very familiar to you. Yet it sometimes illuminates new aspects of that familiar world, because sociology offers a special point of view on things.

The View from Sociology

In a general way, **points of view** provide the basis for agreements and disagreements, so we can often understand aspects of social life through the points of view involved. At the same time, as I've already indicated, sociology itself is a point of view. For both these reasons,

it is important that you understand what points of view are and how they operate.

A point of view is a way of looking at things. What you see reflects your point of view. The accompanying cartoon illustrates how a person might look from three different points of view.

Although the three drawings in the cartoon are all of the same person, he looks different depending on whether we view him from the front, side, or back. Now ask yourself this: which drawing shows how the person "really" looks? Does he "really" look like the front view? The side view? The back view? Your answer has to be either "all of them" or "none of them." Each drawing portrays a point of view. Each presents the "real" view from a particular point, but nothing more.

Picasso, a founder of the artistic style called cubism, was once confronted by a critic who had just examined a Picasso painting entitled *Fish*. "It doesn't even look like a fish," the critic complained. "It's not a fish," Picasso retorted. "It's a *painting* of a fish." So, fish are fish; pictures are pictures; and one shouldn't be confused with the other. Every point of view gives you only a *partial* picture of whatever you are looking at. To see what's "really" there, you'd

have to be able to look at it without the distortion of a point of view.

Unhappily, however, points of view are like eyeglasses in a world where everyone needs glasses. Different glasses let you see different things, but you have to use some glasses—some point of view—to see at all.

You look at the world from many different points of view. So do I. Some of these points of view affect how we view physical objects, others affect how we behave, still others affect how we think and feel about things. You and I may see a sunset from the same point of view, or we may have different points of view. We probably see a course in introductory sociology differently.

For sociologists, the "point" or "place" from which people view things is *social* rather than geographic. If you and I "see" introductory sociology differently, it is because you are looking at it from a place called "student" and I am looking at it from a place called "sociology professor." Sociologists call these places **statuses** (more about them later in the chapter).

Human social life can be usefully examined by looking at the similarities and differences in people's points of view. Thus, for example, Karl Marx observed that workers had a particular point from which to view economic production and that capitalists had another. Marx then devoted most of his life to raising workers' awareness of their own point of view; this awareness he called "class consciousness."

What Sociology Is and Isn't

As I said in opening this chapter, sociology is the study of the agreements that people make, organize, teach, break, and change. It is also the study of the disagreements involved in the same processes. Some sociologists are chiefly interested in the processes through which agreements are continually being made and then remade because of disagreements. Others are more interested in the extent to which certain agreements are perpetuated. We'll look at different sociological points of view in Chapter 2.

What you see is a matter of your point of view.

Sociology is a science, a scientific study of agreements. As a science: (1) sociology aims at a rational, logical, systematic understanding of social agreements, and (2) it continually tests its understanding against careful observations of events in the world we seek to explain. Chapter 3 considers the scientific aspect of sociology in depth and some of the specific research methods sociologists use.

At this point, it will be useful to look at sociology as the study of agreements and disagreements that are involved in **social interaction** and social relationships.

Social Interaction

"Action" means pretty much what you think it does: action is something you *do*. Voting, talking, listening, selling, or being perfectly still are all actions. "Inter"action is what goes on between "actors." Typically each action is shaped somewhat by the actions that precede it, and each action in turn helps shape those that follow.

A tennis match is an excellent example of interaction. So is a conversation. Suppose that you and I are meeting for the first time. I tell you my name and hold out my hand. You tell me your name, shake my hand, and say it's good to meet me. I suggest that we sit down, and you agree, asking me what I do for a living. I respond. This is an example of interaction.

Of course, there's nothing to prevent you from interacting with a dog or a machine, and many people do. We use the term "social interaction" to make a distinction, to refer to interaction among human beings.

Social interaction doesn't need to be harmonious. A fistfight or a mugging is social interaction. The mugger points a gun at you, and you hold up your hands. The mugger demands your money, and you comply. If you refuse to hold up your hands or to hand over your money, your action will affect what the mugger does next.

Sociologists are interested in social interaction since agreements are formed through it. If you realize that the mugger wants you to hold your hands up, you've struck an agreement with regard to that intention. If you comply with the mugger's intention, you've made another agreement. If you refuse to raise your hands, the agreement-making process continues. In an important sense, social interaction is a matter of **communication**.

Many sociologists study how people communicate through interaction and how agreements are formed in the process. Some focus on what is being communicated, others on the actions involved; still others are primarily interested in the nature of the agreements and disagreements that are created. We'll look at these several points of view in Chapter 2.

Social Relationships

Agreements are formed in the course of social interaction, but this does not mean that no agreements existed before interaction. All interactions occur within a framework of preexisting agreements and are shaped by that framework. Language, for example, is a set of agreements; and all conversations occur within that set and are shaped by it. Even though we make new agreements about language (agreeing on a specific meaning for a key word we are using, for example), our interaction begins within a preexisting agreement framework. If the previous example of our meeting each other made sense to you, then we agree that when I say my name and hold out my hand, you are expected to say your name, shake my hand, and say you're pleased to meet me.

Sociologists are especially interested in how the agreements governing social interactions among people reflect their status relationships with each other. Social **relationships** are based on the social locations people have with reference to each other. Let me introduce the notion of "location" with a physical illustration.

Imagine for the moment that *you* are the only thing in the entire universe. There are no other people, no stars, no planets, nothing but you. Now ask yourself "Where am I?" Your answer has to be either "nowhere" or "everywhere." You simply can't have a location except in relation to something else. Now imagine that I also exist. Now *you* can be somewhere. You can be in front of me, in back of me, above or below me, near or far away. Where you are, however, has meaning only with reference to me: it is a matter of the relationship between us in space.

Now consider the question "Who am I?" Any answer you would give implies other people. We occupy *social* locations in relation to each other, too. You could be my parent or my child, but notice that you can't be a parent without reference to a child and you can't be a child without reference to a parent. That's true of all social relationships. You can't be a leader without followers; you can't be an employee without an employer; you can't be a student without teachers.

Sociologists use the term "status" to refer to the social locations people have in relation to each other. Statuses and status relationships are important to sociology because many of the agreements that govern social interaction refer to specific statuses. There are different sets of agreements about interactions between mothers and daughters, privates and generals, salesclerks and buyers, muggers and victims.

Different social statuses are also linked to different points of view. Your social location influences what you "see" just as your geographical location does. Imagine how differently a package of employee benefits (wage raise, retirement, and medical care, for example) "looks" to a worker, a stockholder, and a government economist. Physicians, patients, and insurance agents "see" major surgery differently according to where they are located in the network of social relations.

Many sociologists focus their attention on the ways in which statuses are organized in a group such as a society. Every status has a set of privileges and duties associated with it that define how individuals occupying that status should interact with individuals occupying other statuses. Sociologists use the term **role** to refer to what people do and are expected to do because of the statuses they occupy.

It is useful to look at the organization of roles and statuses because many of the lasting agreements in a group are those defining interactions between specific statuses. The concept applies well beyond the interactions of two people. A complex organization such as a corporation or a factory can be seen as the structuring of statuses: established agreements about interactions between workers and supervisors, planners and production people, presidents and boards of directors, and so forth. Some sociologists are primarily interested in examining the structure of statuses per se, and others are more interested in the kinds of social interactions that actually take place within the structures.

Sociology, then, offers special points of view from which to observe and "see" the world around you. Since sociology is often confused with other points of view, I'd like to make a distinction between it and some of them. There are, however, no rigid boundaries between them.

Sociology and Psychology

Psychologists study what goes on inside your head and adjoining parts of your body. They study such things as thinking and emotions. As a very general distinction, psychology deals with individuals, and sociology deals with what goes on *between* individuals.

Sociology and psychology have important things to say to each other, of course. How a person thinks and feels will affect the way he or she interacts with other people, and those interactions will affect how he or she thinks and feels. A special field called "social psychology," in fact, addresses the links between sociology and psychology.

The main distinction between psychology and sociology, then, is one of emphasis, with psychology emphasizing the personal and sociology emphasizing the interpersonal.

Sociology and Anthropology

Anthropology is a lot like sociology. Anthropologists also study social interactions and social relationships. Traditionally, however, anthropologists have studied preliterate peoples, while sociologists have studied what are called—sometimes erroneously—"civilized" ones. In recent years, this distinction between anthropology and sociology has grown less clear, with anthropologists paying more attention to modern, complex societies, and sociologists occasionally examining preliterate ones.

Anthropologists sometimes study aspects of social life that sociologists tend to ignore. Anthropologists, for example, are more concerned with *artifacts:* human products such as arrowheads, pottery, weavings, and other objects that people make in certain ways because of the groups they live in. Physical anthropologists study the physical characteristics of people, such as the width of their skulls and length of their arms. Archaeology, the study of past societies, is generally regarded as a subfield of anthropology.

Sociology and Economics

Economists study relationships and interactions among people also, but economics is more limited in scope than sociology. Basically, economists are interested in the exchange of goods and services, how people get what other people have. Economic exchange is important to sociology, too, but sociologists study *non*economic relationships and interactions as well. (In Chapter 2 we'll discuss exchange theory, which is an attempt to adapt the economic exchange model to social interactions and relationships.)

Sociology and Political Science

Political science is another specialized field, focusing on power relationships among people. Thus, political scientists study different kinds of governments (different ways of distributing power in a group) and the interpersonal processes, such as voting, war, and bureaucratic administration, through which power is exercised.

Power relationships are important to sociology, just as economic ones are, so political science and economics are both useful to sociology. By the same token, economics and political science have both profited from the theories and research of sociologists.

Sociology and Social Work

Many people confuse sociology with social work. Basically, the difference is this: social workers *help* people; sociologists study people. Sociologists aren't against helping people, and most

sociologists engage in helping people in many ways. It's just that sociology isn't about helping; it's about understanding.

At the same time, understanding people is often the first step toward helping them. Understanding social problems is the first step toward solving them. Sociology is applicable to the issue of helping, and sociological research is often specifically designed to improve social conditions. Too, the efforts of social workers often reflect the understanding that sociology provides.

Sociology Is Not Socialism

"Socialism" is an economic system in which the government, rather than private capitalists, owns the means of production (factories, raw materials, and so on). Some sociologists are in favor of socialism. Some are in favor of capitalism. Some favor something else altogether. Sociology is not a political or economic philosophy but a useful point of view for studying both socialism and capitalism. Sociological findings might be useful to both socialist and capitalist countries, and sociologists are active in both.

You should be especially aware of one link between sociology and socialism. Karl Marx, the founder of modern socialism, was a sociologist (among other things), and much of his work reflects a sociological point of view.

Is Sociology Social Reform?

Finally, sociology is different from social reform, though the relationship is controversial. Sociology is not necessarily about making the world a better place to live in—any more than sociology is social work—but proficiency in sociology would probably make you a more effective social reformer.

No one disputes that some sociologists *as citizens of societies* engage in efforts at social reform—fighting poverty, prejudice, war, and other social problems—just as others do not. In recent years, both within sociology and outside it, there have been heated debates over whether sociologists support or resist social reform in their activities *as sociologists*. Some people think that sociologists are out to restructure society—through socialism, for example. Others feel that the study of social order as it exists inevitably helps to maintain that order.

Besides the dispute over what sociologists *do,* there's disagreement about what they *should* do. An increasing number of sociologists have urged that sociology be practiced within a context of social reform, that it have the improvement of social conditions as its ultimate goal. They urge this course even granting disagreements about what would be "better" or "worse" conditions.

It is clear that sociologists can and do use their professional skills to change the society they live in. Sociology is potentially an instrument for social action, for social reform. As you can imagine, this potential has not escaped the attention of sociologists themselves, nor has it been only recently recognized.

Sociology typically addresses subjects that have day-to-day reality to members of society. Moreover, most people have personal points of view on such things, points of view that often reflect ideologies and are often reified.

When sociologists study and draw conclusions about such things as prejudice, religiosity, politics, education, and the family, they venture into areas in which everyone is an "expert." Were the world's most renowned sociologist to conduct the world's greatest research project and conclude that the nuclear family was dysfunctional for both society and individuals and urge legislation to ban it in the United States, it is unlikely that such legislation would even be considered seriously, let alone passed and enforced.

Here's a less extreme example. In Chapter 14, we'll see that sociological research on racial discrimination in education led to the creation of school busing programs across the country. This so violated established patterns that it provoked hostile and often violent reactions.

Sociologists, then, study things that most people already have strong personal feelings about. Sociological research often threatens people's personal values and ideologies. To make matters worse, sociologists are people with their own values. Can we be sure that sociologists can prevent their personal values from interfering with the scientific quality of their research and conclusions? This is something that has concerned sociologists themselves for a long time.

"Value-free" Sociology In 1918, the great German sociologist Max Weber addressed students at Munich University on the topic of "Science as a Vocation." In that talk, he stated a point of view that has figured importantly in sociology ever since. Weber was concerned about the great popularity of professors who took political positions that pleased students in the lecture hall, and he suggested that these professors were behaving improperly. Science, including sociology, needed to be "value-free" if it was to make its special contribution to society, Weber argued (Weber 1925a). In scientific research and teaching, the scientist needed to set personal values aside.

Few scientists would disagree with Weber's position that scientists should not allow their personal values to distort their research findings. Yet there is considerable disagreement on whether scientific activities can be totally free from personal-value influences.

No sociologist would be criticized for saying his or her research was aimed at achieving world peace. No one would condemn eradicating poverty as the motivation behind a research project. Sociologists also more or less agree that prejudice and bigotry are "bad." Glock and Stark (1966:xxi) candidly opened their study of anti-Semitism by saying, "Obviously our decision to undertake such a study was not dispassionate. If the churches, no matter how inadvertently, lead men to hate Jews, we mean to raise the alarm." Some sociologists and church people were displeased with the study's empirical findings and interpretations, but no one seriously questioned the propriety of using sociology to fight bigotry, just as nobody criticizes cancer researchers for being "against" cancer.

The question of personal values and professional scholarship is a complex one. In his 1961 presidential address to the Society for the Study of Social Problems, Alvin Gouldner (1962) criticized the Weberian view, referring to "the myth of value-free sociology." Gouldner suggested that it was simply impossible for a scholar's personal values to be totally divorced from his or her scholarship.

I have gone into the complications of this issue at length because the dilemmas it poses are not unique to sociology. Many physicists were rudely awakened by the atomic bombing of Hiroshima in 1945. Biologists have seen their discoveries used to lay the foundation for biological warfare. Statisticians see their findings used to promote and defend unwise and inhumane policies. Scientists from all disciplines have begun asking whether it is possible to be *just* a scientist.

A Useful Point of View

Throughout this chapter, I have repeated that sociology is a point of view with different, more specialized points of view within it. Points of view do not reveal the "truth," but some are more useful than others—in particular situations and for particular purposes. If you were interested in learning about cross-pollination in flowers, you would find biology a more useful point of view than poetry. A socialist point of view may convince you that your car broke down because of capitalistic greed and corruption, but taking a mechanic's point of view is more likely to get your car running again.

Sociology can be a very useful point of view. It can offer an understanding of things that other points of view do not provide. Let's look at one illustration.

For years it has been widely believed that the black American family was matriarchal—that is, dominated by the wife and/or mother. Empirical evidence has somewhat substantiated this belief. In a number of surveys, some black men and women have reported that their mothers made most of the important decisions while they were growing up and that their mothers were more powerful in family matters than were their fathers. Similarly, among some black couples, husbands and wives have indicated that the wives make most of the important decisions.

For years, political conservatives have used such evidence to support their belief in the weakness and submissiveness of black American males. Such supposed character flaws were used to explain why blacks fared so badly in American society.

Those with a liberal point of view, on the other hand, have taken the evidence as an indication of the ways in which the black American family has been weakened by discrimination, inhumane welfare regulations requiring fathers to desert their families to get government assistance for them, and other influences. These conflicting points of view have been expressed repeatedly in every possible medium of communication.

Notice how differently you might "see" the survey reports of female dominance in black families, depending on whether you were looking from a conservative or liberal point of view. There is another point of view, however—a sociological one.

Herbert Hyman and John Reed (1969) looked at the matter from a sociological point of view. To begin, they confirmed that the surveys did suggest that black women were more powerful than black men in family life. Then they looked at something others had overlooked: the answers given by *white* men and women in the same surveys. The answers given by white respondents were the *same* as those given by blacks! Thus, Hyman and Reed concluded, if black

Max Weber
1864–1920
Erfurt, Germany

Some Important Works
The Protestant Ethic and the Spirit of Capitalism,
trans. Talcott Parsons (London: Allen & Unwin,
1930 [1904–1905]).
The Sociology of Religion, trans., ed. Talcott Par-
sons (Boston: Beacon Press, 1963 [1922]).
From Max Weber: Essays in Sociology, trans., ed.
Hans Gerth and C. Wright Mills (New York:
Oxford University Press, 1946 [1925]).

With Durkheim, Weber is generally acknowledged to be one of the two founders of modern
sociology. Weber was born and brought up in a
literate household, and he enjoyed an excellent
education during the era of Bismarck's Germany.
Grounded in the German idealistic school, Weber
immersed himself in extensive historical studies, aiming at mastering the various fundamental issues of human social existence.

It would be foolhardy to attempt a list of
Weber's main contributions to sociology, though
such a list would include his classic and still-
useful study of bureaucracy, his representation
of the "ideal type" as a method of sociology, his
studies of the great religions (Confucianism,
Judaism, Hinduism) and his linking of religious
and economic ideas in his examination of the
Protestant ethic, and his examination of the various bases of authority in society (charismatic,
traditional, rational-bureaucratic).

Weber needs also to be acknowledged for laying groundwork for the development of sociological theory, and proponents of all the major
theoretical points of view (functionalism, interactionism, conflict theory) have found value in
Weber's work.

families were dominated by women, so were
white families. If this meant that black men
were weak and submissive, then white men were
equally weak and submissive.

In Chapter 3, we are going to look at some
of the characteristics of sociology *as a science*
that would lead sociologists to see things that
others might overlook. In that context, you will
be able to gain a clearer understanding of why
sociology can be a useful point of view for looking at the world around you.

Summary

Sociology is the study of human group life, and
this book will approach that study through an
examination of the agreements people make,

establish, teach, break, and change in the course
of finding ways of living together.

There are four main characteristics of the
agreements we make. First, they seem essential. If alignment is not sufficient for the perpetuation of group life, then it seems necessary
that we make agreements. Second, the agreements we make are often arbitrary: some other
agreements would work as well. Third, we can
see, nonetheless, that some agreements are more
appropriate than others. Finally, and most fascinating, we have a tendency to reify our agreements, to act as though they represent reality.

Ultimately, you and I live in two "realities"—
one based on experience and the other based
on agreement. Both seem very real, however,
and it is often hard to distinguish them.

Some of the building blocks of social reality

by agreement are status, role, relationship, and institution. A "status" is a social location that you occupy, such as student or Democrat or mother. A "role" is the set of behaviors expected of you by virtue of the status you occupy; for example, students are expected to study. "Relationships" link individuals through their statuses and roles. We speak of the father-son relationship, referring to the ways fathers and sons are expected to interact with one another, forming a social unit in the process. Finally, "institutions" are sets of interrelated agreements governing broad sectors of social life, such as family, government, economy, religion, and education. Most of your social life is experienced through the statuses you occupy and the roles you perform in your relationships with other statuses—all of it within general social institutions.

Sociology offers a point of view from which to observe and make sense of all this. As a point of view, it differs from such other academic disciplines as psychology, political science, economics, anthropology, and social work. Also sociology is not social reform, though sociologists differ among themselves on the degree to which they should or ought to influence the future course of society.

Sociology is an exciting window on the world, and I invite you to come along to learn how to look through it. In the next chapter, I'll describe some of the more specialized points of view that sociologists have developed for looking at social life, and you'll see that each reveals (and conceals) something a little different.

Important Terms

sociology
agreements
disagreements
game theory
reification
experiential reality
agreement reality

institution
points of view
status
social interaction
communication
relationships
role

Suggested Readings

American Sociological Association
  1977   *Careers in Sociology*. Washington D.C.: ASA.
  This little pamphlet provides a comprehensive picture of the various jobs that sociologists do in a modern society. In addition to seeing sociologists in conventional positions in university teaching, you'll see them at work in government, industry, publishing, and other sectors of the society.

Bart, Pauline, and Linda Frankel
  1976   *The Student Sociologist's Handbook, Second Edition*. Morristown, NJ: General Learning Press.
  A helpful guide for sociology students providing prac-tical information, sources, sociological literature, and advice.

Berger, Peter L.
  1963   *Invitation to Sociology: A Humanistic Perspective*. Garden City, NY: Doubleday
  This eminently readable little book offers an excellent introduction to the sociological point(s) of view. Berger illustrates the nature and utility of sociology within the context of day-to-day social life, showing how sociologists see a much different world than other people. Sociology, you'll see, can be practiced as a pastime as well as a profession.

Berger, Peter L., and Thomas Luckman
   1967   *The Social Construction of Reality*. Garden City, NY: Doubleday.
   A study in the "sociology of knowledge," this book explores what I have called "agreement reality" in depth. The book examines individuals' subjective experiences of reality, how those experiences are communicated through interaction and language, and how agreements on the nature of reality are established in the form of institutions.

Lee, Alfred McClung
   1978   *Sociology for Whom?* New York: Oxford University Press.
   This is a stimulating look at the issue of sociology and social reform by a recent president of the American Sociological Association. Lee is particularly concerned about the ways in which he feels sociology and sociologists are currently being used—in his view, unwisely and inappropriately. He sketches his vision of a humane sociology for the future.

Mills, C. Wright
   1959   *The Sociological Imagination*. London: Oxford University Press.
   A readable and engaging introduction to the sociological point of view in relation to social reform. Mills was not reluctant to say what he regarded as good and bad in his discipline.

Nisbet, Robert A.
   1966   *The Sociological Tradition*. New York: Basic Books.
   Focuses on historical development of the field of sociology, integrating key sociological concepts into the discussion.

Each chapter of this book ends with an analysis of some topic related to the chapter's focus. Since this first chapter introduced the field of sociology as a whole, it is reasonable to ask here whether it is really worth your while to pursue sociology for even one academic term. During the past decade, some thirty thousand students earned B.A.'s in sociology each year, alongside two thousand M.A.'s and six hundred Ph.D.'s (Dynes 1981:100). Every year around half a million students take the course you are now taking. Given all that, it is important to ask if the sociological point of view really makes a difference in the world. Does it matter? I'll return to these questions in the essay that concludes Chapter 20, but I want to raise them at the outset.

Several years ago, when I was chairperson of the Sociology Department at the University of Hawaii, one of my jobs was to lead a seminar for new graduate students, colloquially known as "Meet Your Local Professor." Each week, one or two of the department's faculty members would visit the seminar and talk about their professional pursuits and their views of the profession. The main purpose of the seminar was to introduce new graduate students to all the faculty.

To give the course some continuity, I developed a set of questions I asked each faculty member to discuss. The primary question was: "Is sociology worth it?" If we were to calculate all the costs our society pays in order to have sociology—faculty salaries, research grants, classrooms, offices, and laboratory equipment—could we honestly say that society got benefits from sociology equal to its costs? As journalist Anne Wyman (1982) stated the question in a newspaper headline: "Does Sociology Do Anybody Any Good?"

Some academic disciplines can justify their existence on the basis of concrete inventions or discoveries. While sociologists cannot point to a polio vaccine, the computer, or even Teflon, social research *techniques* such as public-opinion polling have really grown up and developed within sociology. Whether these techniques contribute to the quality of life could be debated, but they unquestionably represent an impact.

Sociological research *findings* have also had an impact on social life. To examine this, we need to distinguish between *basic* and *applied* research. Richard Berk (1981:204–205) contrasts them this way:

> Thus, [in applied research] one might help a given community address apparent increases in teenage vandalism, for instance, and apply whatever tools seem best suited to solve *that* problem. Any implications for large social science questions are of secondary concern.
>
> In contrast, basic research focuses first on some larger sociological question and then goes out into the world (or into the laboratory) to find an appropriate site in which to undertake the research. Any fallout for particular applications is, at best, a fringe benefit. In other words, the primary aim is to advance the current level of discourse *within the discipline.*

So, applied sociological research has the specific purpose of making a direct impact on social life. Basic research, however, often has practical consequences even though that was not the primary purpose of the research.

A great deal of applied sociological research is under way at any given time in American society. Some sociologists work on social problems such as crime and delinquency, poverty, or drug abuse—determining the nature of the problem as well as devising and testing solutions. Other sociologists work in industrial settings, solving problems of human relations that may get in the way of productivity, for example. Others work on morale, race relations, and similar issues within the military. Many sociologists are employed as demographers—researching population patterns and trends for governments, insurance companies, and others.

Berk and others have noted, however, that applied research has generally been regarded as a second-class citizen in sociology. Those in basic research have often looked down on those in applied research. And by extension, sociologists have often looked down on social workers much as theoretical physicists have often looked down on engineers as craftsmen rather than scientists. But basic researchers haven't necessarily kept their hands out of practical matters. Lewis Killian (1981:236) suggests they have been inclined in just the opposite direction:

> Reformist biases have been characteristic of sociology from its earliest days as a scholarly discipline and a would-be science. Of basic importance is what I believe to be the fact that, for all their claim to be scientists, most sociologists are at heart not only reformers but utopians. Some of them are self-conscious radicals "who look forward to a revolution in which not only the evils of the existing system will be swept away but evil itself will be diminished or abolished" (Killian 1971:281). Many others, particularly in these times, eschew the role of the revolutionary for that of the social engineer. They reflect a faith that progress can come through the Establishment if their expert advice is sought and heeded.

Moreover, sociologists have not only been reformers "at heart," but they have also acted on their feelings. Karl Marx not only researched the history of class struggle and the relations among different classes under capitalism, but he also set out to do something about the problems he saw. Jane Addams, best known for her social service activities at Chicago Hull House, offers a complementary example. Addams and her colleague, Emily Greene Balch, combined sociological scholarship and social action to deal with poverty, immigration, women's rights, aging, delinquency, and peace. Each was awarded the Nobel Prize for Peace (Addams in 1931, Balch in 1946), the only two American women to receive the prize. A great many, less dramatic, examples could be drawn from contemporary sociology and sociologists.

Sometimes, sociological research is commissioned as a basis for social action. Thus, for example, James S. Coleman's (1966) massive study of educational quality in America pointed to the impact of integrated schools on educational achievements among the poor. Coleman and his colleagues found that low-income students performed better when attending classes with middle- and upper-income students. One effect of Coleman's findings, as I indicated earlier, was the government policy of school busing. Unfortunately, since wealthy parents could avoid busing by sending their children to private schools, the policy has tended to combine poor whites and poor blacks rather than combining rich and poor. As you can see, corrective actions taken on the basis of sociological research do not always produce the results desired.

Often sociologists' contributions consist of pointing to existing conditions. This was the case, for example, with David Caplovitz's book, *The Poor Pay More* (1967), which exposed shabby retail practices that took advantage of poor people. In a different vein, David Riesman and his colleagues pointed to changing American values and behavior in *The Lonely Crowd* (1953)—indicating the ways in which Americans had shifted from being directed by inner values to being led by the opinions of others. William H. Whyte's *The Organization Man* (1956) zeroed in on a particular species of the "other-directed" American. More recently, Daniel Yankelovich (*The New Rules*, 1981) has offered an updated view of

Americans' values, based largely on public-opinion-poll results.

Perhaps sociology's most profound impact on society has been the idea that deviance is socially determined. Criminals and other deviants were once regarded as intrinsically bad people (whether from Satan, biology, or choice), but deviant behavior today is most often explained as a product of social environment. We speak of people as being the "victims of their circumstances." We take this view largely because masses of sociological research and analysis point to social environmental causes for all forms of deviant (and nondeviant) behavior.

This deterministic view has had implications for official responses to deviance. Thus we try to rehabilitate criminals rather than simply torture them. We attempt to cure alcoholics rather than punish them. Rather than blame poor people, we talk of the need to get to the "roots of poverty" in society and to change the conditions that produce poverty.

While this view is not shared by all Americans, it is pervasive throughout our society. It has been the basis for such social programs as welfare, unemployment insurance, and social security. Nor are government officials alone in holding the view. When the Gallup Poll asked a national sample of Americans in 1970, "Which in your opinion is more to blame for crime and lawlessness in this country—the individual or society?" Fifty-eight percent said society, 35 percent said the individual, and the remainder had no opinion (Gallup 1972:2273).

The deterministic view of deviance has had both positive and negative consequences. It has, on the one hand, produced a more humane response to deviance than was formerly the case. The torture rack and dunking chair are now gone, and capital punishment has been greatly retarded if not completely eliminated. At the same time, however, people rightly complain that criminals seem to have more rights than do their victims. We have frequently equated understanding crime with excusing it. Moreover, by making deviants the "victims" of their circumstances, we have often deprived them of the opportunity to improve their lot. In the case of poverty, for example, our social programs have often taught poor people that they are inferior—through no fault of their own, to be sure—rather than supporting them in overcoming their poverty.

I have concluded this discussion with the example of social determinism for two reasons. First, it illustrates that many of sociology's impacts on society are both subtle and profound. Second, it illustrates how the sociological impact—like the development of nuclear energy—can be a mixed blessing. Unless sociologists are consciously responsible for the potential power of sociology, it will not serve the interests of society as it should. Once you've mastered the fundamentals of sociology in the remaining chapters of this book, we'll return to this issue in the concluding essay of Chapter 20 and look at how such responsibility is to be exercised.

PRACTICING SOCIOLOGY

The preceding Application and Analysis essay asked the question "Is Sociology Worth It?" and suggested some answers to the question. Listed below are several social issues that concern Americans today. From what you know of sociology already, pick an issue that interests you and suggest some of the ways you think sociology could contribute to the resolution of that issue. Show how the sociological approach would differ from the way the general public (or segments of it) approach the issue.

Racial discrimination and prejudice in housing

The nuclear-arms race

Equal pay for equal work

Water pollution

Overpopulation

Violent crime in the streets

Inflation and unemployment

Effects of divorce on children

World hunger

Political apathy

2

Theoretical Points of View

In Chapter 1, I said that the sociological point of view actually encompasses *several* different points of view, none of which is *the* sociological point of view. If you'll picture a construction site in your mind, surrounded by a high fence containing several observation holes cut in it for sidewalk engineers, sociology represents several observation holes; and you'll have a different view of the construction from each hole. This chapter describes the several points of view that constitute sociology.

As you read this chapter, try to avoid identifying yourself with one of the theoretical points of view at the expense of others. I make this suggestion because students and professors alike often approach sociological theory the way they were taught to approach marriage: they seem to feel bound to pick the one theoretical point of view that's right for them and never stray. I'm urging you to treat sociological theory in a way that might be regarded as reprehensible in your sexual relationships. I urge you *not* to marry. Be promiscuous; play the field.

It is not only possible but even wise to approach sociological theory as I have suggested. If you can keep an open mind and avoid the temptation of theoretical marriage, you'll soon discover the value of having more than one point of view at your disposal. For though the different theoretical points of view portray social life differently, they do not necessarily contradict one another. They can complement one another.

Consider this homey illustration, and then we'll dive into sociological theory. Imagine a tree standing in the middle of a field. What do you think about that tree? How do you feel about it? If we were discussing this face to face, you'd probably say that to answer the question, you would need to know more about the tree. But . . . what would you want to know about it? Well, that would all depend on your point of view, wouldn't it?

Table 2–1 lists several points of view you might have in looking at the tree in the middle of the field. For each point of view, I've indicated how

Table 2-1

Points of View on a Tree

Point of view	Sees the tree as	Questions to ask; things to see
Lumberjack	Something to cut down	What kind of wood is it? How thick is the trunk? Is the tree leaning?
Carpenter	A source of building material	Is it hardwood or softwood? What kind of grain will it have? How many board feet in the tree?
Poet or painter	An object of beauty, strength, or symbolic of some other quality	What is the shape of the tree? What's the texture of the bark? What human emotions does it evoke? What patterns of light and shade does it create?
Ecologist	A component in the ecosystem	How much water and nitrogen does it consume? What are its by-products? Does its root structure hold the soil together and resist erosion?
Wheat farmer	An obstacle in the middle of the wheat field	How much wheat could be grown on the land covered by the tree? How long would it take to clear the tree away?
Sociologist	A place to hide in the rain	How long will it take to get there? Is it true what they say about trees and lightning?

you would see the tree. The lumberjack would see it as something to cut down, the poet as a thing of beauty, and so forth. In the third column in the table, I've indicated some things you might want to know or might notice about the tree, given a particular point of view. Notice how each point of view draws attention to aspects of the tree that might be totally overlooked by other points of view.

Notice also that these several points of view do not contradict one another, even though they may produce conflicting emotions or even conflicting lines of action. (The poet or the environmentalist might even challenge the lumberjack's ax to save the tree.) The carpenter's seeing the tree as lumber does not contradict or invalidate the ecologist's view of the tree as part of an ecosystem. Both are "true" or "real" even though they are very different from one another. In fact, the points of view are so different that they cannot contradict one another. If the poet says the tree is beautiful, for example, that does

not contradict the carpenter's view of it as potential lumber—nor would there be a contradiction if the poet said the tree was ugly! The theoretical points of view we'll be examining in this chapter have that same quality. They are very different from one another, and they provide very different pictures of social life, but they are not incompatible with one another. Let's see how that happens.

The Grounding of Sociological Theory

In reviewing early human intellectual history, it is difficult to separate what we would now recognize as sociological theories of society from social philosophy. For many of the early social thinkers, the questions of "what is" was inseparable from "what ought to be." Moreover, many of the earlier points of view were deeply embedded in religious beliefs, and explanations for the social order lay within the supernatural realm.

During the past two or three hundred years, however, this situation has changed dramatically. Theories of society have been shaped more and more by intellectual thought not influenced by supernatural concerns. We're going to look at the evolution of that shift, but first we'll take a moment to clarify some terms that are frequently misused.

Theory and Paradigm

People tend to use the term "theory" rather loosely in daily life. We often say "I have a theory about that" or "He was operating on the theory that the garbage truck would stop for a Mercedes." Thus, we use the word "theory" to mean a hunch or a suspicion—even a wish.

Theory means something more precise and more rigorous in science. A scientific theory is a comprehensive explanation for some sector of existence. It consists of (1) definitions of the elements making up the phenomenon to be explained, (2) a set of assumptions that will be taken as the starting point for the theory, and (3) a set of connected statements about relationships among the elements.

Later in this chapter, we'll look briefly at *exchange theory* as a sociological point of view. At this point, we can profit from some of George Homans's work (1971:23) in developing theoretical statements explaining the role of literacy in societies.

1. Men are more likely to perform an activity, the more valuable they perceive the reward of that activity to be.
2. Men are more likely to perform an activity, the more successful they perceive the activity to be in getting that reward.
3. Compared with agricultural societies, a higher proportion of men in industrial societies are prepared to reward activities that involve literacy. (Industrialists want to hire book-

keepers, clerks, persons who can make and read blueprints, manuals, etc.)
4. Therefore, a higher proportion of men in industrial societies will perceive the acquisition of literacy as rewarding.
5. And (by(1)) a higher proportion will attempt to acquire literacy.
6. The provision of schooling costs money, directly or indirectly.
7. Compared with agricultural societies, a higher proportion of men in industrial societies is, by some standard, wealthy.
8. Therefore a higher proportion is able to provide schooling (through government or private charity), and a higher proportion to pay for their own schooling without charity.
9. And a higher proportion will perceive the effort to acquire literacy as apt to be successful.
10. And (by (2) as by (1)) a higher proportion will attempt to acquire literacy.
11. Since their perceptions are, in general, accurate, a higher proportion of men in industrial societies will in fact acquire literacy. That is, the literacy rate is apt to be higher in an industrial than in an agricultural society.*

Ultimately, a comprehensive general theory of society would organize all aspects of social life in the rigorous, propositional form just illustrated by Homans. No one is near that achievement at this point, so this chapter cannot be about *the* theory of society. Indeed, this chapter will not be about theory, at least not within the rigorous definition I have cast for theory.

Instead, we are going to focus on some sociological **paradigms**. A paradigm is not a theory; intellectually it predates or lies behind theories. A paradigm is a point of view or frame of reference that determines what we will even consider in developing a theory. Paradigms are

---

*George Homans, "Reply to Blain," *Sociological Inquiry* 41 (Winter 1971):23. Reprinted by permission.

sometimes difficult to see because they are what we see *with* and determine how we see.

I have already illustrated the role of paradigms earlier in this chapter. The points of view that different people brought to bear on the tree in the meadow reflected their paradigms. When the carpenter saw the tree as a certain number of board feet of lumber, that illustrated the "carpentry paradigm." The "poetic paradigm," on the other hand, drew attention to totally different aspects of the tree, as did the other paradigms described.

Notice the fundamental nature of paradigms. Paradigms determine what is looked at and what sorts of relationship are seen. The lumberjack, for example, may develop a theory of tree felling, taking account of the height, girth, and tilt of the tree. Thus, the lumberjack might produce a formula to determine the best location for cuts to have the tree fall exactly where it is wanted. The ecologist, on the other hand, would be concerned with a very different set of elements, probably ignoring the degree of tilt, for example, but paying close attention to the tree's root structure.

In this chapter, we're going to examine three fundamental paradigms currently used in sociology. As a glimpse of what is to come, one of the paradigms sees social life primarily as a matter of interactions among individuals, the second sees mostly the organized rules of society, whereas the third focuses more on the conflicts that occur among individuals and groups. Before looking at the separate paradigms, however, let's consider two general influences on scientific theories and paradigms in sociology: Auguste Comte's *positivism* and Max Weber's *ideal types*.

Comte's "Positive Philosophy"

Auguste Comte (1798–1857) is frequently cited as the "father of sociology" for more reasons than his coining of the French term *sociologie*. He urged that sociology develop as a *science* similar to physics and biology, and he sug-

gested that such a development would represent a pinnacle in human intellectual achievement. Indeed, he referred to one of his own major works as "the greatest discovery of 1822."

Comte's primary influence arises from his "positive philosophy" or **positivism** (Lenzer 1975). Comte urged that social behavior be studied and understood logically and rationally and that rational/logical explanations be tested against empirical observations. In this, Comte was suggesting that sociology be modeled after the experimental method used in biology and other natural sciences. Comte also felt that the twin standards of empirical observation and logical understanding could make sociology a tool in the creation of a better society.

Comte recognized that biology had been separated from the religious point of view. He suggested that psychology would next be separated and that with the separation of sociology the emancipation of human reason from religion and superstition would be complete.

Comte's positivistic point of view has had a lasting influence on sociology. Sociology as a social influence could not have developed without an acceptance of positivism.

Weber's "Ideal Types"

There is another element in the development of sociological theory that was perhaps implicit in the views already examined, yet it was not formalized for sociology until early in this century. Theories of social behavior offer *approximations* of real life. Theories are more abstract and more general than the concrete details of day-to-day events. This aspect of sociological theory was best elaborated upon by Max Weber (1864–1920) in his discussion of **ideal types** (Weber 1925a).

Essentially, an ideal type is a model against which to compare the world we observe. The ideal type is intended to capture the essential qualities of a class of things we observe around us, even though it does not necessarily correspond exactly with any specific observation.

Auguste Comte
1798–1857
Montpellier, France

Some Important Works

A Discourse on the Positive Spirit (London: Reeves, 1903 [1844]).

A General View of Positivism (New York: Speller, 1957 [1848]).

System of Positive Polity (London: Longmans, 1875–1877 [1851–1854]).

Born into an aristocratic, Roman Catholic family, Auguste Comte was concerned over what he saw as the excesses of the French Revolution, and he feared for the stability of French society. He was to spend much of his life seeking ways of structuring a stable society. In the process, he founded the field of sociology as a scientific discipline.

Like a few of his contemporaries, Comte believed that society could be made the subject of scientific study, as were various aspects of the physical environment. He felt that the twin standards of empirical observation and logical understanding could reveal the workings of social affairs and could also be a tool in the creation of a better society. This orientation goes by the name "positivism."

Comte first called the application of positivistic philosophy to society *physique sociale*, "social physics." When that term became associated with a specifically mathematical approach to the study of society, Comte switched to the term *sociologie*, thereby establishing claim on the title "father of sociology."

Weber (1925a), for example, provided an ideal type for bureaucracy—a detailed description and explanation of bureaucracy as a form of social organization. Although his development of the ideal type reflected his observations of real-life bureaucracies, his purpose was not to incorporate all the details of each one. Rather, he sought to describe a "perfect" bureaucracy, thereby offering a model against which to compare and understand those bureaucracies we observe.

You should realize that by "perfect" bureaucracy, I do not mean to imply that you would *like* one that completely reflected the model. The terms "idealism" and "ideal type" in this context are based on the notion of "idea" and do not imply any kind of evaluation. You could, for example, construct an ideal type for dictators, murderers, or rapists without being in favor of them.

Think for a minute about the different kinds of professors you've come across during your studies. Perhaps some were warm and friendly, treating you more like a friend than like a student, and others were more formal, maintaining the traditional distance between students and professors. You could construct an ideal type for each kind of professor, describing the most significant characteristics of each. Those ideal types would be useful tools for you in summarizing your observations about professors in general.

Ultimately, ideal types describe what a society's agreements would be like if they were totally logical and rational, if society were totally understandable. Actual societies and social relations, then, can be understood as approximations of the ideal types.

Modern Paradigms of Social Life

Recall that when I initially asked you what you thought or felt about the tree in the field, it wasn't possible for you to give much of an answer without knowing more about the tree. And you needed some frame of reference in order to know *what* you wanted to know about the tree. Then we said that various points of view—or paradigms—would provide very different pictures of the tree in the field, revealing and concealing different aspects of it.

In the remainder of this chapter, we shall look at the three major paradigms modern sociologists have developed for the study of social life. They are *symbolic interactionism, social systems theory,* and *conflict theory.* The three paradigms offer fundamentally different views of what is happening in the world around you, and I expect you will find that each makes common sense and will no doubt accord with parts of your own experience. Taken together, they offer a fairly comprehensive sociological triangulation of the world we live in, for while the different paradigms portray social life differently, there is no contradiction among them. Each is complete unto itself and has potential utility when approaching any area of sociological concern. Let's take a look at each of them.

Symbolic interactionism looks at social life as a series of interactions between individuals trying to communicate with one another. Recall the last time you were introduced to someone new, and reconstruct the course your first conversation took as you learned about each other and established grounds for being together. Or recall the last time you were involved in the planning and execution of some social event, such as a double date, a construction project, or a study group. Recall the flow of events and interactions that event entailed. Formally defined, symbolic interactionism is the study of the process of social interaction that involves attempts to create and recreate shared meanings through the use of symbols.

A very different paradigm, **social systems theory**, focuses on the group rather than on individuals. For example, imagine the Oakland Raiders grinding out an eight-yard gain down the center of the field. Although one specific player carried the ball, you have a clear sense of the whole team achieving the advance, with each individual player contributing importantly to the group effort. Or imagine the Philadelphia Orchestra playing Beethoven's dramatic Fifth Symphony. We are so accustomed to the total effect that we sometimes forget that the sound we hear is actually a composite of individual instruments. In many of our experiences of social life, then, it makes sense to regard groups—even entire societies—as organic wholes, seeing individuals as parts of that whole. Besides being called social systems theory, this view of society as an organism is also known as **functionalism** and **structural-functionalism**. (In this book, I will use the terms synonymously, though I'll usually use "functionalism" for simplicity.) Using this paradigm, sociologists turn their attention to the ways in which the components of social systems are integrated and coordinated within the whole.

Finally, our common experience of living in society provides the third major paradigm in sociology, **conflict theory**. You may often feel as though you are being put upon or pushed around by others. Sometimes life seems to be little more than an attempt to gain domination over others or, at the least, to avoid being dominated by them. As we scan the headlines of any daily newspaper, we find evidence of this aspect of social life: murders, muggings, political corruption, unethical business practices, sexual discrimination, race riots, war. While functionalism tends to focus on coordination and cooperation in social life, **conflict theory** focuses on the strains, struggles and resistance so common in interpersonal and intergroup relations and interactions.

Each of these paradigms stresses a different, though complementary, aspect of social agreements. Symbolic interactionism deals primarily with the creation of agreements, social systems theory emphasizes their organization and integration, and conflict theory focuses on disagreement and the effort to replace and change existing agreements.

Please note that in making this translation into the terms of agreements and disagreements developed in Chapter 1, I am not suggesting a competing model for making sense of social life. The notion of agreements and disagreements is *not* another paradigm for organizing the study of society. Rather, it provides a *context* within which to hold the various paradigms of sociology. In this sense, it is not "better" than conflict theory, symbolic interactionism, or functionalism. It's not even in the same classification with them. It is simply an educational tool that I find useful, and I hope you will too.

With this caution in mind, we're ready to turn to a deeper examination of each of the three major paradigms. Let's begin with social life conceived as a series of interactions between individuals in search of common meanings.

Symbolic Interactionism

When people interact, they communicate through symbols—with words, actions, postures, gestures, and other signs—and in the process they form agreements with each other.

The sociological point of view called **symbolic interactionism** deals primarily with the communication of symbols through interaction. This orientation within sociology is most directly associated with the so-called Chicago school that was centered at the University of Chicago during the first part of this century. The key figure in that school was the philosopher and sociologist George Herbert Mead (1863–1931).

I'll begin with a review of the ideas Mead and others put forward to explain how our systems of social agreements were established. Then I'll turn to some of the contemporary symbolic interactionists in American sociology.

In the Beginning

A contemporary of Mead's, Georg Simmel (1858–1918), was one of the first sociologists to draw

George Herbert Mead
1863–1931
South Hadley, Massachusetts

Some Important Works
Mind, Self, and Society, ed. Charles Morris (Chicago: University of Chicago Press, 1934).
The Philosophy of the Act, ed. Andrew Reck (Chicago: University of Chicago Press, 1938).

Mead is an unusual figure in the history of sociology. Teaching as a sociologist and philosopher at the University of Chicago, Mead's ideas of society were largely developed in the process of extemporaneous lectures given to University of Chicago students between 1893 and 1931. Mead himself never published his work, and the volumes cited above were prepared posthumously by his students, working from their lecture notes.

Surely the most influential member of the "Chicago school" of the 1920s, Mead had a particular interest in the process through which society evolved. In his view, people created forms of social organization in the course of their interactions, addressing social problems. Interaction was the ultimate focus, with all large, established social institutions and societies having that as their origin. Mead examined the creation of shared meanings, symbols, and language as the basis for coordinated social life. He found that individuals' views of themselves (their "self"s) grew out of the same process that produced society. Indeed, Mead saw the individual "mind" arising in that same process.

attention to the simplest of social phenomena: small-group interaction. For Simmel, the organizations of religions, governments, economic systems, or whole societies were extensions of the process of interaction that could be observed between two people (a **dyad**) or among people in slightly larger groups.

Like Simmel, Mead felt that all the large-scale social phenomena we observe are the products of the interaction process, but Mead went even further. For Mead, our minds and our conceptions of our selves are also the products of interaction. Neither mind, self, nor society existed before interaction (Morris 1934).

To begin, Mead regarded interaction as inevitable among all species that reproduce through sexual union and whose offspring require parental care through infancy. However, three characteristics of the human mind, Mead said, make human beings unique among animals. First, they are able to assign symbols to represent the objects around them, giving those objects names and using those names in communication. Humans develop and use far more complex languages than animals. Second, humans can imagine what will happen if they pursue different lines of action in relation to the objects around them. They can imagine, for instance, what will happen if they punch a tiger in the nose or crash an Oakland Raider team party without actually doing either. Finally, humans seem able to choose appropriate actions from among those they have rehearsed in their minds.

Mead did not believe that our earliest ancestors actually possessed these abilities but rather that the abilities developed over hundreds of thousands of years. Without being able to explain exactly how they developed, Mead described what probably happened in the course of developing minds, selves, and societies.

Mead pointed to communication as being essential to the development process. People, like other animals, first communicated through gestures, a form of communication that pre-

dated language. You are already familiar with hundreds of different gestures: a dog's bared teeth, a cat's lick, a baby's smile. Gestures such as these seem to communicate to us directly, without having to be transformed into words or concepts. Other gestures can communicate directly too. We can guess that our earliest ancestors would not have had to possess very large brains to understand what someone shaking a fist and throwing rocks was communicating.

Communication through nonverbal gestures laid the foundation for the development of *language*. We don't know exactly how the first verbal symbols, the first words, were developed or what they were. Probably the first words were a lot like grunts and screams.

Over a very long time, a body of agreements on verbal symbols accumulated. There were

Sometimes we can communicate with one another without saying anything.

words to represent physical objects, emotions, and actions. A person not only could recognize an angry gesture but also could communicate about it orally, using a word for "anger." Different collections of people in different places developed words and languages distinct from one another's.

People were able to communicate verbally using a shared language. An individual could also communicate effectively with himself or herself, using words and the concepts that words expressed. In this fashion, people gained the ability to imaginatively rehearse possible courses of events. Through language, they could imagine not only possible actions but also how they and others might feel about those events. People were able to reflect on their day-to-day existences. Thus, people developed *minds*.

The combination of interaction and language, for Mead, was also necessary for the development of the **self**. With language, which allowed a person to mentally represent such emotions as anger, fear, and love, it was possible to include other people's mental states in the imaginative rehearsals of possible future events, anticipating how people would feel in various circumstances. In this sense, Mead spoke of a developing human ability to "take the role of the other," to take on someone else's point of view. It became possible to look at the world the way others saw it.

Think what might have taken place had you been one of our earliest ancestors, just beginning to look at the world from someone else's point of view. One of the first things you probably would have seen would have been yourself. That probably would have been the most profound thing to happen to you since you first looked into a pool of water and saw your face reflected in it. By looking at yourself from other people's points of view, you would have discovered that they regarded you as one of the objects in their environment, just as you regarded them as objects in yours. The more you looked at yourself through others' eyes, the

more you would have developed a consciousness of yourself, a self-image, or what Mead simply called your "self."

The full development of mind and self came, Mead said, when individuals were able to take the role of the **generalized other**, to recognize and look through the points of view that the members of the group generally shared. Besides learning that a particular neighbor was likely to hit you over the head with a club whenever possible, you could also learn that most members of your group felt such behavior was improper. In addition to learning that one person thought you were ugly and another thought you were pretty, you could also learn that most members of the group thought you were so-so.

Once an individual learns the point of view of the generalized other, that individual begins to govern his or her behavior by it. Having learned it is the general consensus of the group that the best hunter should get the most food to eat, most would try to excel in the hunt.

This body of group agreements was, for Mead, **society**, or "institutions," a term he seems to have preferred. Society developed out of interaction; and, once developed, it regulated the interactions that followed. Once you agree to something, you are bound by that agreement.

To summarize, George Herbert Mead attributed the development of our minds, our selves, and our societies all to the process of social interaction. Nonverbal communications through gestures led to the development of language. The combination of language with continued interaction made thinking possible. This, in turn, allowed us to "take the role of the other" and look at the world from other people's points of view. Finally, each individual learned the points of view that were generally shared by members of his or her group, and those shared points of view had the effect of at least partly controlling later interaction.

Mead could only speculate about the historical events that produced human minds, selves, and societies; but you can observe something similar to what must have taken place by watching young children develop. Watching them learn language and the other social agreements can offer insights into how it all began, and we'll return to that process in Chapter 5.

Other founders of symbolic interactionism include Charles Horton Cooley (1864–1929) and W. I. Thomas (1863–1947), and we'll look at their contributions to sociology later in the book. At this point, let's turn to the current status of this point of view and to some of the sociologists most closely associated with it.

Contemporary Interactionist Perspectives

Herbert Blumer (1900–), a student of Mead's at the University of Chicago, is generally regarded as the key figure in symbolic interactionism today. Early in his career, he studied such phenomena as crowd behavior (1939) to demonstrate the interactionist point of view in practice. More recently, he has become involved in elaborating interactionism as a paradigm (Blumer 1969).

In direct contrast to the social systems point of view, in which society is seen as relatively organized and fixed, Blumer regards society as an ongoing *process* of mutual adjustment among individuals. He acknowledges that people develop habitual patterns of behavior, but his primary attention is on the continual *creation* of those patterns as individuals define the meaning of situations, communicate, and interact.

Within the general interactionist paradigm, other sociologists have developed some more specific perspectives on social interactions. I want to briefly describe three of them to you: **exchange theory, role theory,** and **ethnomethodology**. I'll conclude the section with a discussion of the concept of **autopoiesis**, which is a relatively new concept and likely to have an impact on sociological thinking in the near future.

Exchange Theory

In economic relations, people exchange goods and services with one another, each hoping to profit or at least break even on the exchange. Over the years, a number of anthropologists and sociologists have suggested that a similar model might be used to explain social behavior in general. Exchange theory represents the adaptation of an elementary economic model to social relations. The theory suggests that when people interact, they do so with expectations that they will get at least as much out of the interaction as they put into it. To take a simple example, if I invite you to my home for dinner, I hope that my investment—in time and money—will be repaid to me by my pleasure in your company, future friendly relations between us, and perhaps an invitation to dinner at your house.

The sociologist most closely associated with exchange theory is George Homans (1910–). In his development of exchange theory, Homans (1961) has devoted most of his energies to two fundamental issues. First, he has set about specifying the various concepts involved in social exchange, such concepts as costs, investments, rewards, values, and profits. In this context, Homans has introduced the concept of "distributive justice": a "fair" profit for all parties to the exchange.

Homans has also sought to develop the fundamental axioms of social exchange in order to permit the derivation of a formal theory. The example of the theoretical reasoning about literacy, earlier in this chapter, shows Homans's exchange point of view. I have discussed exchange theory in the context of interactionism, since I think it is easier to grasp in those terms. As exchange theory has become more formally developed, however, some have regarded it as an example of social systems theory.

Peter Blau (1964) has made major contributions to the integration of exchange theory and functionalism. Beginning with exchange principles that can be observed in relatively small-scale interactions, Blau then shows how those same principles are reflected in the structure of society at large.

Role Theory

Some sociologists work within a theoretical view of social interaction that focuses directly on the concepts of role and status that were introduced in Chapter 1. For role theorists, social life is analogous to a play in the theater, a view anticipated by William Shakespeare in *As You Like It* nearly four centuries ago:

> All the world's a stage
> And all the men and women merely players:
> They have their exits and their entrances;
> And one man in his time plays many parts.
> (act 2, scene 7)

From the role-theory point of view, people are seen as occupying statuses in society, just as actors fill parts (roles) on the stage. A society's agreements are analogous to the script in a play. And just as different actors play a particular role a little differently, so people in society—though occupying the same status—behave somewhat differently, partly in response to differences in those with whom they interact. In role theory, a good deal of attention has been paid to the interactions and mutual expectations that shape the way roles are played (Biddle and Thomas 1966).

Erving Goffman is one of the foremost researchers in role theory. His analyses of interpersonal behavior provide illustrations of this point of view in use. Goffman is particularly interested in the ways we present ourselves to each other in our everyday interactions. He has applied role theory successfully, for example, in the study *Stigmas* (1963), showing how people cope socially with physical handicaps. He has employed the same technique in the study of behavior in mental hospitals (1961) and other settings.

Ethnomethodology

The final interactionist theory that I'll discuss is relatively new in sociology, although, like other theories discussed in this chapter, traces of its main ideas can be found throughout the history of social thought. As a sociological view, ethnomethodology is most closely associated with the work (1967) of Harold Garfinkel (1917–).

To understand this point of view, recall the way we have discussed "agreement" in this book. Two things agree if they are the same; thus, we may say that two people agree about something if their points of view on it are the same. In this sense, we have been looking in this book at some of the ways people agree and some of the ways they disagree.

In an important sense, however, people *never* agree totally. If you think for a moment of all the subtle nuances in your view of, say, the desirability of world peace—considering all the different international situations that can arise—you'll see how unlikely it is that *my* view of the matter is exactly the same as yours. Even though you and I both say we prefer peace, it seems certain that each of us means something different when we say it. We probably wouldn't even be able to agree on what world peace *is* or what it might look like if it existed.

The task of sociology, as seen from the ethnomethodological point of view, is to discover the processes through which people consciously or unconsciously *pretend* to agree. How do you and I come to the view that we feel the same way about world peace?

In the terms we set out in Chapter 1, ethnomethodology addresses the way people construct "agreement reality," their reified and shared view of the way things are. One way ethnomethodologists have sought to clarify the nature of agreement reality is through the violation of heavily reified agreements and the observation of people's reactions to such violations. Garfinkel's students have on occasion treated their parents like total strangers, openly cheated at games, and broke other unspoken agreements in an effort to learn more about those things people take for granted.

Autopoiesis

The interactionist view highlights a subtle but important aspect of society: it is *self-generating*. Society creates itself. Humberto Maturana (1980), a Chilean biologist and philosopher, has coined the term **autopoiesis** to represent the process of self-generation—noting there are many examples of this phenomenon. In language, for example, there are statements of fact which create the facts they report. "I apologize" is an example. When you say "I apologize," you have made that a reality. "I'm breaking my silence" is another example.

Human social life, as we've seen it operate in this discussion of interaction, is more than a passing set of events. It is a process that creates and perpetuates itself. Social institutions have as their first function their own continuing existence. The first job of families is to perpetuate family life, of religion to perpetuate religion. Each institution is structured to do that. Society didn't just come from somewhere: you and I keep creating it. We'll return to this in discussion of institutions in Chapters 4 and 7.

Some Special Applications for the Interactionist Point of View

In general, the interactionist pont of view is especially appropriate to *micro* (as opposed to *macro*) phenomena in social life. Because it is fundamentally addressed to the interactions among people and the generation of agreements in the course of interaction, it offers a special sensitivity to the sometimes subtle nuances of people being together face to face. It provides a special window in those agreements that are never written down, yet rule much of our lives.

Suppose, for example, that you were interested in the various strategies through which young men and women (of different social classes, perhaps) reach an agreement to have sex with one another. The interactionist perspective would illuminate the nature of the communication involved, how subtle hints were dropped and acknowledged, when subtlety was dropped, and so forth. Or to take something more pedestrian, suppose you wanted to know something about the conditions under which people will jaywalk across busy city streets. How do men and women differ, if at all? Does social class make a difference? Do jaywalkers attempt to gain agreement from others around them? Questions like this are clearly appropriate to the interactionist perspective, since it brings a special light to the evolving processes that go on between humans in their social encounters.

This special capacity of the interactionist point of view is evident in the research undertaken by sociologists working within it. In Erving Goffman's study of *Stigma* (1963), which he subtitles *Notes on the Management of a Spoiled Identity*, he presents a number of insights into the lives of people suffering from various physical and social handicaps: being crippled, blind, disfigured, or an ex-convict, prostitute, mental patient, and so forth.

As the subtitle of Goffman's book suggests, he was particularly interested in the ways stigmatized people handled their problems. To understand them, Goffman first had to assess the significance stigma held for interaction. Looking at the processes of social interaction yielded some delicate observations. For example, what do former mental patients and expectant unmarried fathers have in common? As Goffman notes (1963:48), their stigma is not immediately visible, as compared, let's say, with the stigma of being crippled or blind.

Certain characteristics put people at a disadvantage in society. This blind white man and sighted black girl both suffer disadvantages with which they must cope.

At the same time, a closer examination of common interaction situations shows the significance of various stigma to be an even more subtle matter. Here's how Goffman describes it.

. . . visibility must be distinguished from one of its particular bases, namely obtrusiveness. When a stigma is immediately perceivable, the issue still remains as to how much it interferes with the flow of interaction. For example, at a business meeting a participant in a wheelchair is certainly seen to be in a wheelchair, but around the conference table his failing can become relatively easy to disattend. On the other hand, a participant with a speech impediment, who in many ways is less handicapped than someone in a wheelchair, can hardly open his mouth without destroying any unconcern that may have arisen concerning his failing, and he will continue to introduce uneasiness each time thereafter that he speaks. The very mechanics of spoken encounters constantly redirect attention to the defect, constantly making demands for clear and rapid messages that must be constantly defaulted.*

Goffman's observations highlight the special insights to be gained from carefully examining the actual processes of social interaction. None of what he noted represents an "official" agreement that one might find written down as instructions for behavior.

---

*Erving Goffman, *Stigma*, ©1963, p. 49. Reprinted by permission of Prentice-Hall, Inc., Englewood Cliffs, New Jersey.

In a rather different social setting, the observation of social interactions and the shared meaning systems associated with them pointed Melford Weiss (1967:195–196) to some of the "religious" aspects of paratrooper training. As you read this account, try to imagine how you would ever have uncovered this religious aspect except through the observation of actual interactions or reading others' descriptions of such interactions.

> Paratrooper training is officially a secular affair. But certain superstitious practices which are interwoven show that, in the broadest sense, it is also a religious rite. From the beginning of the transition period the trainees are subjected to continuous periods of anxiety. Since they are all volunteers with a strong emotional investment in success, these stresses serve to bind them more closely to one another and to the group they seek to enter. So do the "magical" devices they learn to use to relieve anxiety. These include the wearing of charms and fetishes, such as a girl friend's picture above the heart, a pair of sweat socks worn on a previous successful jump, or a replica of the "trooper wings" placed inside a boot. . . .
>
> A paratrooper's training ends in a ceremonial climax. At the close of training it is customary in some military units to reenact the jumping procedure in a fashion symbolic of rebirth. Newly-qualified paratroopers are invited to a "prop blast" at the noncommissioned officers' club. There a wooden model of an airplane has been hastily rigged. The new initiates line up in jump formation inside the plane. They jump and land facing the jumpmaster, their instructor. He hands each a loving cup full of "blast juice." This must be quaffed within the count of "1000, 2000, 3000," the time between an actual jump from a plane and the opening of the chute. Failure to drain it to the dregs within the allotted span is called a "malfunction," the term for chute failure. The process must be repeated, perhaps three or four times, till success is achieved. Then the initiate is ritually one with his fellows.*

---

*Published by permission of Transaction, Inc., from *Transaction*, Vol. 4, No. 6. Copyright ©1967 by Transaction, Inc.

Notice how you could read the above passage as simply a description of paratrooper training. Or, if you were looking for the creation of shared meanings through interaction, you could see the quasi-religious process of creating group identity and solidarity.

Throughout this book, we'll be seeing more examples of the insights to be gained from the interactionist view in sociology. It's time to move on, however, and look at a very different perspective. My hope is that the contrast between the interactionist and *functionalist* points of view will dramatize the great breadth and robustness of the field of sociology.

Social Systems Theory

We have been focusing so far on the ways in which individuals interact with one another in the drama of passing events. Now let's step back from the trees to glimpse the forest, as seen through a lens called "social systems theory" or "functionalism." This point of view regards society as an organic whole, made up of interrelated parts. The two key and virtually inseparable components of this view are *system* and *function*.

System

The systemic view of society that we are going to examine has its roots at least partially in biology. During the nineteenth century, biologists began looking more clearly at the interrelations among the parts of biological organisms and began understanding the various parts in terms of their contributions to the total systems to which they belonged. Indeed, the parts really had meaning only within the context of the larger **system**.

The idea of "system" is an important one. Clearly, the human body as we know it is more than a mere collection of cells, tissues, bones, and organs. These different parts are *related* to each other, and they interact with one another. The lungs fill blood with oxygen, the heart pumps blood to the brain, the brain directs the lungs to fill with air again, and so forth. We say, therefore, that the body operates as a system. The term "system" refers to the interrelatedness and interaction of the parts.

Auguste Comte, who introduced positivism in sociology, was among those to see society as analogous to a biological system. Comte, in fact, sometimes went overboard in saying that society *was* an organism with a life of its own.

The organismic view of society has been a persistent one. British philosopher-sociologist Herbert Spencer (1820–1903), more restrained than Comte, went so far as to say that "society is *like* an organism," and he listed some of the similarities:

1. Both society and organisms can be distinguished from inorganic matter, for both grow and develop.
2. In both society and organisms an increase in size means an increase in complexity and differentiation.
3. In both, a progressive differentiation in structure is accompanied by a differentiation in function.
4. In both, parts of the whole are interdependent with a change in one part affecting the other parts. (Spencer, *The Social Organism*, 1860; quoted in Turner 1974:16)

Function

Spencer's description introduces the other main components of this view. Each of the parts in the system serves a **function** for the system as a whole. That is, each part has a consequence for or an impact on the other parts in the system and on the system as a whole. In a biological system, such as the human body, the heart serves the function of circulating the blood, the lungs the function of adding oxygen to the blood, and so forth. Similarly for social systems, the police serve the function of social control.

Functionalism was to become very important in anthropology, since it offered an explanation for many seemingly bizarre practices— for example, worshipping trees and practicing magic—among preliterate people. As anthropologists examined the functions such practices might serve for the social whole, they often found parallels in their own societies. Thus, for example, restrictions against killing or eating certain kinds of animals were often found to serve a religious function for a preliterate society, whereas religious functions are served by churches in more modern societies.

An important contribution to the functional analysis of preliterate religion was made by Emile Durkheim (1858–1917), an early functionalist in sociology and one of the most important sociologists to date. Analyzing ethnographic accounts of the Australian aborigines, Durkheim brought important insights to the understanding of *totemism*—a religious form in which a group of people (such as a tribe) identifies itself with a particular animal (say, the witchity-grub). In such a religion, the witchity-grub tribe would carefully avoid ever killing or harming its namesake and would generally treat it with reverence—*except* on special ritual occasions, when the totem would be killed and eaten!

Examining this bizarre practice, Durkheim concluded that it served the function of creating and solidifying group identity. The reverence shown to the witchity-grub represented the reverence felt toward the group, and ritually eating the grub on special occasions celebrated and symbolized the oneness of the group. Durkheim then extended this analysis to suggest that religions generally serve the function of creating and protecting the solidarity of what he called the "moral community." Thus, from the functionalist view, the local Episcopal church serves the same function in modern society as totemism did among the aborigines.

Like Comte and Spencer, Durkheim regarded society as an organism. He said it had a reality *as a system* and that the systematic whole should be the main focus of analysis, not the parts.

Emile Durkheim
1858–1917
Epinal, France

Some Important Works

The Elementary Forms of Religious Life, trans. Joseph
 Swain (Glencoe, Ill.: Free Press, 1954 [1915]).
Suicide: A Study in Sociology (Glencoe, Ill.: Free
 Press, 1951 [1897]).
The Rules of Sociological Method (Glencoe, Ill.: Free
 Press, 1950 [1895]).
The Division of Labor in Society (New York: Free
 Press, 1964 [1893]).

Along with Max Weber, Durkheim is generally
regarded as one of the two founders of modern
sociology. Though he and Weber lived during
the same era—in two neighboring countries—
there is no record of their having any contact
with one another or even knowing of each other's
work.

Durkheim is one of the primary spokesmen
for the functionalist, social systems point of
view in sociology. He regarded society—and
especially complex, modern society—as an
organic unit, analogous to living organisms. He
spoke in this context of modern society being
held together by an *organic solidarity,* in contrast
to the more mechanical solidarity of primitive
societies. He differed directly with Ferdinand
Toennies in this regard.

Thus, in his famous *The Division of Labor in Society* (1893), Durkheim examined the functional
interconnections of social statuses the way an
anatomist would trace the head-to-toe linkages
of parts in the human body.

Manifest and Latent Functions

Sometimes Durkheim's functional analysis produced startling conclusions. In *The Division of
Labor,* for example, he said that one of the functions served by crime was to *reinforce the agreements broken by the criminal!* It served this function by bringing the other members of society
closer together, by drawing attention to the
agreement, and by dramatizing the punishment that backed up the agreement .

This insightful observation points to another
aspect of functions: they need not be intended
or obvious. In recent years, we have discovered
a variety of *unintended consequences* of actions taken within the physical ecosystem (for
example, the use of DDT leading to the production of brittle eagle eggshells), and the
same is true of social life. Indeed, the unintended, not-obvious side of things is often
the most fascinating and sometimes the most
important.

In more recent times, Robert Merton (1957a)
has drawn attention to this subtlety of social
functions by distinguishing between **manifest**
(overt) and **latent** (hidden) **functions** of elements in society. The manifest function of
schools, for example, is education. One of their
latent functions is keeping young people out of
the job market for a number of years. Other
latent functions of schools include: freeing parents from child care so they can participate in
the labor force, providing athletes for professional sports, providing a communication vehicle for introducing young people to various fads
and gadgets, putting young people in touch
with potential spouses and developing their
sexuality.

The primary components of the social systems point of view, then, are system and function. But this is only the beginning. Let's look at some of the additional components.

Equilibrium

An essential characteristic of systems is **equilibrium**. The component parts of a system must be interrelated in such a way that the system will survive as changes in one component are "balanced" or "compensated for" by other parts. This simplest form of equilibrium, called "static equilibrium," has the effect of maintaining the existing system as it is.

A familiar physical mechanism will demonstrate the concept. In a house with central heating, governed by a thermostat, we have a system that functions to keep the temperature of the house constant. If the temperature begins to drop, the thermostat is designed to turn on the furnace and raise the heat to the desired level. Once the temperature has reached the specified level, the thermostat is designed to turn the furnace off.

In many ways, your body operates to maintain equilibrium. If you get too hot, you sweat (or perspire, depending on your upbringing), and that has the effect of cooling the surface of your skin. Economists have observed that economic systems have the same equilibrium-maintaining characteristic, for example, in the relationships among supply, demand, and prices.

Figure 2–1 presents the situation in a graphic form. The diagram depicts four variables: the *price* of some commodity, the *incentive to produce* it, levels of *production,* and the available *supply.* The types of relationships among these four variables are indicated by the capital letters, A, B, C, and D and the plus (+) and minus (−) symbols. Now let me explain what these notations mean.

A. The price that a commodity sells for affects the incentive to produce that commodity.

The plus sign beside the A in the diagram means that as price increases, so does the incentive to produce; and, conversely, if the price goes down, so does the incentive to produce the commodity.

B. The incentive to produce the commodity, reasonably enough, is positively related to levels of production.

C. Production, in turn, affects the supply of the commodity. The more produced, the more is available.

D. Notice that the link connecting supply with price has a minus sign associated with it. This means they are negatively related. If supply goes up, price comes down; if supplies are depleted, prices rise.

Taken together, this model represents a closed system that produces equilibrium. In system dynamics terminology, it forms a **negative feedback loop**. Although all the variables will fluctuate over time, the nature of the whole system is to stabilize rather than run out of control. To see how it works, run through a few cycles of the system: assume, for example, that supplies diminished. What would happen? What would happen next? And next?

Besides showing the relationship between price and supply, this model also allows you to see some possibilities for affecting the operation of the system from outside it. Prices can be affected by more than supply: by government price controls, for example. Similarly, the government could establish tax incentives to spur production. Production, in turn, is also affected by such things as the supply of raw materials and labor strikes. And supplies of a commodity could be greatly increased by foreign imports (or decreased by exports). The value of a detailed diagram such as this is the potential to fully understand and also to change a situation.

Not all systems stabilize, however; some generate **disequilibrium**. The much discussed

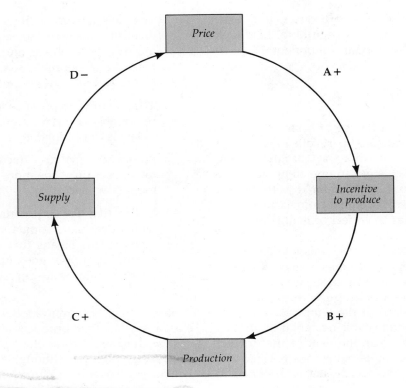

Figure 2–1 A diagram of economic supply and demand.

"wage-price spiral," as illustrated in Figure 2–2, is a perfect example.

Figure 2–2 includes five variables: the *cost of living, demand for higher wages,* the actual level of *wages, production costs,* and *prices.* As with the previous figure, we can start at any point; I've started arbitrarily where I've indicated point A.

A. As the cost of living increases, wage earners are more likely to demand higher wages, hence the plus sign. If the cost of living decreased (not likely) or stayed relatively stable, there would be less demand for raises.

B. As the demand for higher wages increases, the likelihood is that wages themselves will go up. It's obviously not a one-to-

one relationship, but its general structure is clear.

C. As wages go up, the cost of producing things obviously goes up.

D. Higher production costs are recouped through higher prices.

E. Higher prices directly raise the cost of living.

The point of this particular diagram is to illustrate a **positive feedback loop:** one that runs out of control rather than stabilizing. Now you have additional imagery to associate with the term "runaway inflation."

All feedback loops are either negative or positive, and complex systems are made up of a great many loops that interact with one another.

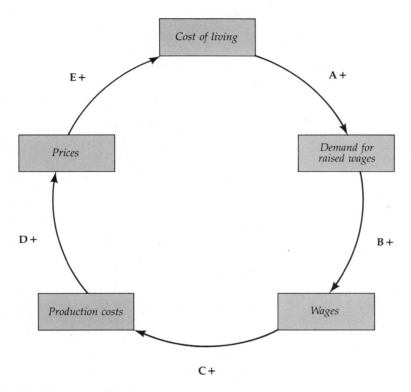

Figure 2–2 *A diagram of the wage-price spiral.*

Figure 2–3 represents a slightly more elaborate model of the relationship between college education and employment. It incorporates a feature that is very important in social systems, and one we'll pay special attention to in Chapter 18 when we look at the relationship between humans and the physical environment. The variables in the model are *jobs available for college graduates, number of college students, college graduates ready for employment,* and *upgraded job requirements.* The main loop of this system is found in A, B, and C.

A. As more jobs become available for college graduates, the incentive to attend college increases, and the number of college students increases.

B. With higher college attendance comes more college graduates ready for employment. Notice that I've added a box crosscutting this arrow. It signifies a *delay* in the process described. Thus although higher enrollments produce more graduates, it takes around four years for the effect to occur.

C. As the number of college graduates in the job market increases, the number of jobs available for college graduates decreases, since more and more jobs get taken.

In Figure 2–3, **A, B,** and **C** represent a negative feedback loop—but with a delay. The delay is significant. Imagine a year in which there are more jobs than college graduates to fill them:

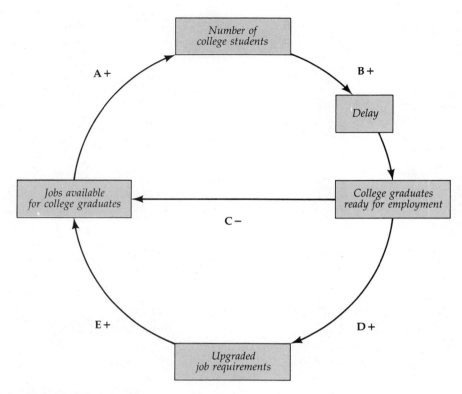

Figure 2–3 A diagram of the educational upgrading of occupations.

that situation would encourage students to go on to college. The next year, the shortage of college graduates in the job market would be just as bad and probably worse, since those who went off to school would still be there. That shortage of college graduates would provide even greater incentive for more students to go off to college. After a few years, the increased numbers of college graduates would begin appearing in the job market. Soon, the shortage would be filled, but a backlog of college students would continue graduating and looking for ever-scarcer jobs. By itself, this system would stabilize over time, though the delay would probably produce cycles of shortage and surplus.

Of course, this is no hypothetical illustration. Throughout the 1950s and 1960s, American youth were strongly encouraged to go on

to college and to graduate school because of the employment opportunities associated with higher education. During the 1970s, however, we began seeing surpluses in many fields. Too many students were trained as teachers, for example, and English Ph.D.'s were a glut on the market.

I've made the system in Figure 2–3 slightly more complex and realistic by adding another factor operating in the case of education and employment.

D. As the availability of college graduates increases, there is a tendency for employers to upgrade job requirements. Thus, a job that previously required a high school diploma now requires a bachelor's degree.

E. The upgrading of jobs creates an apparent but artificial increase in job opportunities for college graduates, thus creating a positive feedback loop that produces ever-greater numbers of college graduates.

Typically, when sociologists look at the matter of equilibrium in society, they find examples of balance rather than imbalance. The reason for this is simple. Societies that don't maintain a reasonable degree of equilibrium don't survive. Those that are around for us to study, therefore, have handled the issue to a large extent. Remember, however, that equilibrium in this sense does not mean "no change." All societies are changing constantly, but they must maintain their balance if they are to survive.

System Imperatives

The observation that systems operate so as to survive as systems has resulted in a persistent controversy in sociology and elsewhere. In the case of sociology, it has centered on the concept of **system imperatives**, sometimes called "functional imperatives." The term "system imperatives" refers to those things a system—such as a society—needs to survive.

Let's examine the concept itself first, and then we'll see why it has been controversial. Talcott Parsons, who has written most on this subject, has suggested that any system must accomplish four basic tasks or functions to survive as a system (1951). The letters A, G, I, and L have come to symbolize the four functions: adaptation, goal attainment, integration, and latency:

A Adaptation: The system must have the ability to get resources from the environment and distribute them. The *economy* is an example of adaptation in a society.

G Goal attainment: The system must have the ability to establish goals, set priorities, and move its parts toward achieving them. *Government* is an example of goal attainment in a society.

I Integration: The system must have the ability to achieve coordination and effective working relationships among its parts. The *laws* of a society are an example of the integration function of a society.

L Latency: The system must have the ability to maintain patterns of "proper" behavior by its components and to handle any strains or tensions that arise. *Religion* is an example of the latency function in society.

Unless a social system can satisfy each of these functions, Parsons suggested, it cannot survive. Since the social systems that sociologists study have survived, he continued, it makes sense to examine the ways in which different societies have performed the several functions.

David Aberle and his colleagues (1950:100–111) have approached the matter somewhat differently. They began by considering some condition that would result in the eradication of society; then they considered the prerequisites for system survival: (1) an adequate relationship with the environment, (2) provisions for sexual reproduction, (3) the differentiation and assignment of roles, (4) communication, (5) shared views of things, (6) shared values, (7) norms regulating the means to achieving the goals, (8) regulation of affective expression, (9) socialization, and (10) effective control of disruptive behavior.

Obviously, there are other ways of listing the requirements for system survival. Without worrying about which is "correct" (each has value), I think you can see the importance of knowing what it takes for a social system to survive. Nonetheless, this approach to sociology is a somewhat controversial one.

The danger some people perceive in the social systems view is that we may fall into the trap of thinking that those things that support system survival must be "good." Thus, some would warn, if the system of *apartheid* (total racial separation) currently in force in the Republic of South Africa supports the survival of that society, it could seem that apartheid must be a good

Aside from keeping bakers in business, what are some of the ways this wedding will contribute to the survival of society?

thing. Despite the possibility of unconsciously falling into that form of reasoning, you should be clear that social systems theory does *not* mean that. Nor does it mean that we must put up with distasteful arrangements just because they promote the survival of the system. As we'll see later in this book, and as you've seen many times in your life, it is possible to meet the needs for system survival in many ways, and the many societies that have existed have discovered numerous survival strategies. So what if monarchy supports the survival of a society? So does democracy.

So, there's no need to worry if sociologists say that discrimination against women has social functions and supports the survival of a stable economy and family system. That doesn't mean that sociologists think it's good or should be perpetuated. Indeed, seeing the functions served by an agreement to discriminate against women can be the first step toward eradicating the agreement. Unless we can make provisions

for the function currently served by the discrimination, we may be unable to replace the pattern.

Let's turn now to the structure of those patterns. Sociologists speak to this aspect of social systems as "social structure."

Social Structure

The persistent agreements of a society are organized so as to promote system survival. Even if the system itself cannot "act" in ways appropriate to its survival, the agreements that make up the system lead individuals to act that way. By and large, people obey the laws and customs of their societies, and generation after generation teaches those agreements to its children. In every society, some individuals assume a special responsibility for enforcing the agreements; and, in the process, they often resist the pressure to change.

A novelty item that you may be familiar with illustrates what I am saying about people resisting the pressure to change. It's a small black box with an on/off switch on top of it. If you flip the switch to the "on" position, a door opens on top of the box and a small mechanical hand reaches up to push the switch back to "off." Every time you flip the switch to "on," the little hand pushes it back to "off." This mechanical system is constructed to keep the switch in an "off" position.

Social systems theorists observe that the agreements of societies are "constructed" and organized to enhance their chances of survival, and we'll look further into that matter in the discussion of culture (Chapter 4) and in the examination of institutions (Part Four).

Some Special Applications of the Social Systems Point of View

We've already seen several examples of how the social systems point of view can influence and enlighten social research. In general, it is appropriate for examinations of the stable persistent aspects of society, though it is not limited to that. A few examples of social research may further illustrate this point of view.

Robert Merton, mentioned earlier, is a prominent functionalist in American sociology. Like Talcott Parsons, he has been concerned with the system imperatives that are the prerequisites for group survival. Whereas Parsons has been most concerned with highly general, overarching system needs, however, Merton has contributed importantly to sociology by urging that attention be given to the development of what he called "theories of the middle range" (Merton 1968:45ff.). Ultimately, Merton suggests, sociology must discover and document the principles of social order that exist among those aspects of social life that you and I see and deal with in our own lives.

Taking his own advice, Merton has examined various aspects of society—at the middle-range level lying between the microscopic view of the interactionists and the grand-theory level of Parsons and others—and sought to uncover the functions served by those aspects that seem to persist. For example, he has studied the political "machines" of large cities (1968) from a functional point of view.

Much of the work of *demographers* (see Chapter 18) reflects a social systems point of view. What will be the implications of changing a social norm regarding the "proper" age for people to marry? In the United States, for example, the average age at marriage has been getting steadily older, and we have generally decided that it's better for young people to delay marriage until after they've completed school and perhaps defined their career plans. But what are the implications of this for birth rates and population growth? Think about it for a minute and you'll see that it will *reduce* population growth by delaying the onset of childbearing and thereby shortening the overall period of childbearing. Such a discovery makes perfectly good sense within a systems viewpoint. Thus, the

point of view is particularly useful in showing how in a network the consequences and implications of specific events all fit together.

For the most part, the social systems view looks for the sources of order in society. Thus, systems theorists seek out the structures of agreements that create harmony and produce stability and persistence. Disagreement, chaos, and change represent the failure of social systems in this regard. Other sociologists, however, devote their chief attention to the sources of disorder, disagreement and conflict. What, they ask, produces the more turbulent side of social life? This is the realm of "conflict theory."

Conflict Theory

So far, we've noted that interactionists look at the world in terms of interpersonal communication and formulation of agreements. Structural-functionalists, on the other hand, focus on the orderliness of social relations in terms of organized and perpetuated agreements. Yet a third camp is made up of sociologists who see the world primarily in terms of conflict and power. In this section, you are going to meet four sociologists associated with **conflict theory** in sociology.

Karl Marx

The most important conflict theorist in the sociological tradition is the nineteenth-century German philosopher and economist Karl Marx (1818–1883). Marx is often associated with the German philosopher G. W. F. Georg Hegel (1770–1831), and Marx acknowledged being influenced by Hegel's thinking. Hegel saw human progress as a **dialectical** process: an idea (thesis) would be followed by its opposite (antithesis), with a synthesis eventually emerging from the struggle between thesis and antithesis.

Roman Catholicism, for example, contained the idea (thesis) that the relationship between

Karl Marx
1818–1883
Trier, Prussia

Some Important Works

The Communist Manifesto, with Friedrich Engels (New York: Appleton-Century-Crofts, 1964 [1848]).

Capital: A Critique of Political Economy (New York: Modern Library, 1906 [1867–1879]).

Both as a young scholar working to complete a doctorate by age twenty-three and throughout his life, Karl Marx carried a dual interest in abstract philosophical issues and in the concrete reality of day-to-day life in modern, industrial society. During his school years, he was intent on reinterpreting the dialectical philosophy of Georg Hegel. His criticisms of Hegel and of Christianity were to make a conventional academic career impossible, however, and Marx spent most of his life in political and philosophical exile.

Marx accepted the Hegelian view of human progress, but he argued that the dialectical process involved not ideas but economic conditions and relations. Thus, Marx's point of view on history is often called **dialectical materialism**.

Marx argued that all history was the history of **class struggle**: the conflict between economic classes, in particular between industrial workers and their capitalist employers. In contrast to the functionalist point of view, which focuses on the general stability of society, Marx applied Hegel's dialectic of thesis, antithesis, and synthesis to the struggle for dominance among economic classes.

Taking the class struggle as inevitable, Marx was especially interested in its dynamics. For him, a crucial aspect of these dynamics was the battle between classes for societywide acceptance of its opposing points of view. The dominant class attempted to promote and enforce a point of view that would justify its favored position in society. For the oppressed class to gain dominance, it needed to establish and gain agreement for an opposing point of view—first among its own members, then throughout society.

Out of his desire for social justice, Marx examined the process of communication whereby the members of an oppressed class became aware of the implications of their shared status and developed a unified "class consciousness" with a plan of social action. Marx recognized that as workers increasingly agreed among themselves about their true class interests and attempted to gain societywide acceptance for their point of view, the struggle would inevitably become more violent.

Marx had a special interest in the beliefs that composed what he called "false consciousness" and constituted a barrier to the victory of the working class. For Marx, the religious view that each individual's place in society is ordained by God was an example of a belief that is encouraged by the dominant groups in a society and used by them to keep oppressed groups "in their place." The medieval European doctrine

God and humans was to be mediated by the church and its clergy. Protestantism, among other things, represented a "protest" against that idea: offering the counter idea (antithesis) of a direct relationship between God and humans. In sixteenth-century England, these two points of view struggled for dominance, accompanied by considerable bloodshed. Ultimately, the Church of England emerged as a synthesis, containing elements of both religions.

of "The Divine Right of Kings" provides an excellent example of this pattern. Religion, for Marx, was an instrument of power in the hands of the rulers.

As a result of his studies of political economy, Marx became convinced that the great forces of history would move unavoidably in the direction of first socialistic, then communistic economic structures. His most important contributions in the realms of both ideas and action reflected that view. In *The Communist Manifesto*, Marx and lifetime collaborator Friedrich Engels sparked a revolutionary fire that was to spread around the entire planet, and *Capital* presented Marx's theoretical view and empirical research on political and economic history.

Marx's point of view focused on the historical struggle between societywide classes of people. Georg Simmel, another German sociologist, focused on smaller-scale conflicts.

Georg Simmel

Georg Simmel (1858–1918) had a greater interest than Marx did in the functioning of social systems, more akin to the point of view of social systems theorists. As I noted in the earlier discussion of symbolic interactionism, Simmel regarded the dynamics of small-group interaction as the foundation on which larger social phenomena were based. One facet of the disagreements that people have with one another that particularly interested Simmel was their varying levels of intensity. He found conflicts more intense when the people having the disagreements were emotionally involved and on intimate terms with one another. Disagreements among members of a tightly knit group were most intense and especially when the people having the disagreement felt it threatened the *group's* survival as opposed to affecting individual goals and interests only (Turner 1974).

Marx and Simmel shared the view that social structures produce conflicts and that conflict threatens the survival of social systems, but Simmel was also interested in the ways that conflicts could *support* the survival of social systems. Lewis Coser has elaborated on this latter view.

Lewis Coser

The work of Lewis Coser (1913–), sometimes called "conflict functionalism," might be regarded as an integration of the systems and conflict points of view. Coser (1956) regards conflict in part as a "signal" that the system needs readjustment and rebalancing, just as the cooling of air in a house signals the thermostat that it "needs" to turn the furnace on. Coser is best known, however, for his descriptions of the ways in which some kinds of conflict can support the survival and functioning of social systems. Here are some of his major conclusions:

1. Conflict between groups increases cohesion and solidarity *within* each of the groups.
2. Conflict draws attention to structural problems in a system and can stimulate innovative attempts to resolve them.
3. Frequent, unintense conflicts allow people to blow off steam and thereby avoid the buildup of tensions.
4. Conflicts between groups can clarify the perception of the agreements that the members of a particular group share.
5. Conflicts between groups can lead each to seek and form coalitions with other groups.

Ralf Dahrendorf

The contemporary German sociologist Ralf Dahrendorf (1929–) is one of those who has drawn renewed sociological attention to the Marxian view of social conflict as the struggle

Social disagreements, differing points of view, and the attempt of groups to dominate one another are of more than academic interest.

between parties seeking domination over each other. He has criticized the view that sees conflict as a functioning mechanism within basically orderly societies.

In Dahrendorf's (1959) reformulation of Marx's dialectical process, the organization and perpetuation of agreements involve what he calls **imperatively coordinated associations** (ICAs). In any social setting, Dahrendorf suggests, some participants have the power to impose their points of view on others. An ICA, then, is an association of individuals that functions harmoniously because some have the power to dominate others. The mutual cooperation of master and slave in an orderly fashion, for example, occurs only because of the power of the master over the slave. In contrast with Marx's focus on economic factors, Dahrendorf's attention is directed to "power"—economic or other.

Social conflict, in Dahrendorf's view, is the continuing competition for power to dominate,

to impose one's own point of view. It will persist as long as people occupy different positions and have different points of view. In short, according to Dahrendorf, conflict is inevitable. Moreover, social conflict operates dialectically: once a dominated class has gained the power to impose its point of view on others, the "others" begin the struggle for power. The box "Three Views of College Society" contrasts three portrayals of college life, from the conflict, functionalist, and interactionist points of view.

Some Contemporary Issues in Conflict Theory

Contemporary conflict theorists have focused on four major topics: the structure of elite domination, the consequences of elite domination, theories of revolution, and the structure of conflict.

The Structure of Elite Domination   What is the nature of elite domination in modern society? Who are the controllers and what are they doing to us? The most famous recent American work on this subject is C. Wright Mills's *The Power Elite* (1956). Mills argues that a small, loosely structured, but interpenetrating group of national leaders from high military, government, and business circles controls the key political and economic decisions in America. Ferdinand Lundberg in *The Rich and the Super-Rich* (1968), Gabriel Kolko in *Wealth and Power in America* (1962), and G. William Domhoff in *Who Rules America?* (1967) among others have attempted to ferret out the powerful and point out their decisions, their interconnections, and their consequences for American society.

A number of local-community studies uncovered a structure of control whereby a small group of rich and powerful persons decided what got done and what didn't in the towns where they lived. Whether it was the Ball family in Muncie or Coca Cola Corporation in Atlanta, a community power structure containing relatively few persons and families dominated local business, government, and social affairs. The basis of their influence was rooted chiefly in their control of major economic enterprises. These top business figures shared distinctive lifestyles and sets of interests. (See E. Digby Baltzell, *The Protestant Establishment*, 1964; the Lynds' *Middletown* series, 1929, 1937; and Floyd Hunter, *Community Power Structure*, 1953.)

Of course the study of elites has a long history and is not the sole province of conflict theorists. However, in general, conflict theorists have given the topic its most systematic attention and have found small, wealthy, and powerful conspiratorial groups who dominate political and economic decision making and maintain their position through manipulation, mobilization of resources, and encouragement of division and/or apathy among the most disprivileged sectors of the population.

The Consequences of Elite Domination
What are some of the dehumanizing conse-
quences of elite systems? Conflict theorists see unnecessary suffering and unhappiness among the powerless. In the elite-dominated societies, unnecessary poverty is generated and life chances are unjustly narrowed. More fundamentally, systems of elite domination have produced specialized industrial and bureaucratic work roles for wages that are dehumanizing and alienating.

In the disabling and diverse effects of elite-dominated societies, we begin to see why and how the poor are manipulated, dehumanized, and rendered politically impotent. Probably few have described this phenomenon more fully than Herbert Marcuse (1964:4, 5):

> The most effective and enduring form of warfare against liberation is the implanting of material and intellectual needs that perpetuate obsolete forms of the struggle for existence. . . . We may distinguish both true and false needs. "False" are those which are superimposed upon the individual by particular social interests in his repression: the needs which perpetuate toil, aggressiveness, misery, and injustice. Their satisfaction might be most gratifying to the individual, but this happiness is not a condition which has to be maintained and protected if it serves to arrest the development of the ability (his own and others) to recognize the disease of the whole and grasp the chances of curing the disease. The result then is euphoria in unhappiness. Most of the prevailing needs to relax, to have fun, to behave and consume in accordance with the advertisements, to love and hate what others love and hate, belong to this category of false needs.

Theories of Revolution   Elites and elite-dominated societies produce revolutionary dissatisfaction. When usurpation is recognized and discontent can no longer be quelled (usually because it can no longer be lied about), then the study of rebellion and revolution becomes the natural territory of the conflict perspective. The conflict theorists see structured inequalities in a system defined by scarcity as the basis for and recruitment field of conflicting groups.

But where are the lines of cleavage and who

THREE VIEWS OF COLLEGE SOCIETY

Different theoretical perspectives make us see events differently. Development of theory in a relatively young discipline such as sociology is always characterized by such competing orientations. Each seeks to find the "real" truth and the "real reality" of events. Let us illustrate the different realities that you would see if you looked at your college or university using the three main theoretical perspectives in sociology: functionalism, symbolic interactionism, and conflict theory.

With functionalism you would view your college as a system of interrelated roles: student, administrator, instructor, service roles, and the like. These roles would probably be seen as subsystems of the overall college system, and each of these subsystems would then be analyzed according to how it functions to meet the survival needs of the college. Instructors might be seen as meeting goal-attainment needs; administrators, integrative needs; students, adaptive needs; and so on. The college as a whole might then be viewed as a subsystem of the overall system of higher education in American society, and, in turn, the functions of higher education for meeting the functional requisites of the society in general might be assessed.

You would see your college much differently with symbolic interactionism. Interactionists are interested in how various people playing roles—students, teachers, administrators—define, interact in, and adjust to various situations. For example, a symbolic interactionist might examine your class in sociology by initially trying to understand the definitions of the classroom situation held by students and the teacher. Then, over the course of the term, the interactionist would examine the interaction between you and the instructor, noting your gestures, your assessments and reassessments of the situation, and your changed behavior. From observations of concrete patterns of symbolic interaction among actual people, the interactionist would attempt to develop laws of the basic processes of interaction that make human organization possible.

If you were a conflict theorist you would see your college (or any social unit) as a system of conflicting interests—usually, though not always, conflicting economic interests. You would analyze the different interests of different groups of participants: for example, students would be viewed as having one set of interests (getting diplomas and jobs), instructors another (instruction in their areas of expertise so that they can keep and justify their jobs), and administrators still another (maintaining order and control). These diverse interests would then be viewed as periodically coming into conflict. Students might be more interested, for example, in getting degrees and jobs quickly than in doing so in an orderly fashion. Such pressures might conflict with instructors' interest in maintaining a broad curriculum that would legitimate their areas of expertise. Thus, the conflict theorist asks these questions: How are the diverse interests of participants likely to come into conflict? What is the power of each conflict group? And how will conflict and its reconciliation create new arrangements, or social agreements?

Each of these theoretical views reveals a different picture of your college or university. Each gives only a partial picture, yet each draws attention to aspects of the situation that might be overlooked if you used one of the others. The best policy is to look at the situation through several points of view.

How would the three theoretical points of view present different descriptions of and explanations for a student demonstration in opposition to grading policies? Which of the three points of view would be the most *useful* in explaining how students form opinions of specific faculty members?

are the contending parties? Traditionally the answer to that question would have pointed us toward economic classes, but today it may also involve race, sex, or other interest groupings.

Conflict theories of revolution have been perhaps most fruitfully applied to the situation of the Third World. Sometimes colonized peoples have revolted against the small colonial elites

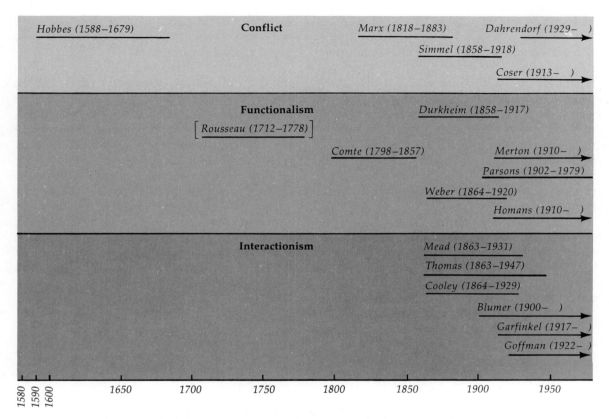

Figure 2–4 *Continuities in social theory, a summary of the development of the major sociological points of view—in the form of the lifetimes of major sociologists. Besides placing the sociologists in a time scale, I have grouped them according to general theoretical perspectives where appropriate. Thus, for example, I've grouped Hobbes, Marx, Simmel, Coser, and Dahrendorf as representing conflict theory. Rousseau has not been assigned to a group, and you should realize that many of the assignments are arguable. Nonetheless, I trust the diagram will allow you to bring a degree of order and continuity to the 400 years of social thought that have been covered in the chapter.*

dominating them and denying them national self-determination. At other times homegrown oligarchies (as in Iran and Nicaragua) have been the focus of rebellion. Considerable literature on how to win wars of liberation has come from these Third World experiences.

The Structure of Conflict   What is the structure of conflict? Until recently finding the answer has largely involved a choice between two models: either an evolutionary-change (growth)

model or a cyclical model. Modern thinking suggests that conflict may more fully resemble the theory of games, as mentioned in Chapter 1.

The most interesting games, from a conflict point of view, are those called "zero-sum" games. Here the objectives are so limited that only one side can win. If I win, you must lose. Politics offers a good example of this, but so does the struggle for jobs during times of high unemployment.

Summary

Our introduction to the major theoretical paradigms that sociologists have developed for organizing the study of social life is now complete. These different paradigms, I want to stress, do not need to contradict one another; they are merely alternative ways of organizing the examination of society. Furthermore, no one of these paradigms is "really" sociology or is "best." Each of the points of view is only a point of view, and none shows society as it "really" is.

There are two ways for you to look at the paradigms covered in this chapter. You can regard them as a burdensome mass of data to be memorized for examination purposes, or you can see them as an exciting, powerful set of tools to use in coming to grips with what is going on around you. In later chapters, we'll see how sociologists use these points of view to help make sense of society.

Rather than recounting the many details of the three paradigms discussed in this chapter, I want to summarize with a diagram. Figure 2–4 groups together most of the sociologists discussed, indicating when they lived so that you can get a sense of the historical development of sociology.

If you have mastered the theoretical points of view presented in this chapter, you will be able to grasp any of the ways of looking at things sociologically that will be discussed later in this book. Also, you are now halfway through understanding sociology as a *science*. The other half is composed of research methods, which we'll consider next—in Chapter 3.

Important Terms

theory
paradigm
positivism
ideal types
symbolic
   interactionism
social systems theory
functionalism
structural-
   functionalism
conflict theory
dyad
self
generalized other
society
exchange-theory
role theory
ethnomethodology

autopoiesis
function
manifest function
latent function
equilibrium
negative feedback
   loop
disequilibrium
positive feedback
   loop
system imperatives
dialectical
dialectical
   materialism
class, class struggle
imperatively
   coordinated
   associations (ICAs)

Suggested Readings

Coser, Lewis A.
1977   *Masters of Sociological Thought: Ideas in Historical and Social Context, Second Edition*. New York: Harcourt Brace Jovanovich.
Key figures in sociological history are looked at in their historical times. Their contributions to sociology today are discussed.

Etheredge, Lloyd S.
1976   *The Case of the Unreturned Cafeteria Trays*. Washington, D.C.: American Political Science Association.
This is a marvelous, tongue-in-cheek treatise on using different social-psychological theories to explain why some people don't bus their own dishes in a high-school cafeteria. I mention it because I think you'd like it; I'll justify it by saying that it illustrates the values of looking at a given phenomenon through several theoretical points of view.

Parsons, Talcott, et. al., Eds.
1961   *Theories of Society*. New York: Free Press.
This large, two-volume collection presents the major theoretical writings of social thinkers ranging from Machiavelli to the present. Editorial introductions by Parsons and the other editors place the selections in a contemporary, sociological context. Although you might not be inclined to read the entire collection from beginning to end (not a bad idea, though), it's an excellent place to explore further some of the theoretical ideas discussed in this chapter.

Stryker, Sheldon
1980   *Symbolic Interactionism*. Menlo Park, Calif.: Benjamin/Cummings.
An excellent overview of the history and current status of symbolic interactionism as a philosophy and sociological paradigm.

Turner, Jonathan H.
1974   *The Structure of Sociological Theory*. Homewood, Ill.: Dorsey.
This is an excellent presentation of the major theoretical points of view that were introduced in this chapter. Turner discusses the historical development of each point of view. Then he extracts the major theoretical propositions of each writer, making it possible for you to compare the implications of the different theoretical points of view in sociology.

Turner, Jonathan H., and Leonard Beeghley
1981   *The Emergence of Sociological Theory*. Homewood, IL: Dorsey Press.
Discusses concepts, models, and theories of early French writings, then other key historical figures in sociology including their basic works and origins of thought.

Turner, Jonathan H., and Alexandra Maryanski
1979   *Functionalism*. Menlo Park, Calif.: Benjamin/Cummings.
An excellent overview of the history and current status of functionalism in both sociology and anthropology.

Wallace, Ruth A., and Alison Wolf
1980   *Contemporary Sociological Theory*. Englewood Cliffs, NJ: Prentice-Hall.
Discusses functionalism, conflict theory, exchange theory, symbolic interaction, and ethnomethodology and key sociologists representing these approaches.

Wallace, Walter L., Ed.
1969   *Sociological Theory*. Chicago: Aldine.
Wallace begins with a discussion of what theory is and where it fits within sociology as a whole. Then he summarizes eleven (count 'em, eleven) major points of view. The remainder of the book is devoted to selections by representatives of each of the theoretical perspectives discussed.

Zeitlin, Irving M.
1981   *Ideology and the Development of Sociological Theory, Second Edition*. Englewood Cliffs, NJ: Prentice-Hall.
Reviews the context in which sociology emerged, especially as related to Marx's theory and writings. Chapters on Weber, Durkheim, and Marx.

In the Analysis and Application section of Chapter 1, I suggested that sociology has had an impact on people's views of deviance. Specifically, people have come to see deviance as a function of socioenvironmental factors instead of some innate defect or evil in the deviant. In this chapter, we have seen that sociology contains several points of view, so here let's examine how each of the main points of view reflects on deviance. Specifically, let's look at juvenile delinquency.

Though juvenile delinquency can be defined in various ways, the term fundamentally refers to crimes committed by young people, say under the age of eighteen. It is a major social problem for American society. In 1979, for example, about 3.5 percent of the U.S. population was sixteen or seventeen years old, yet that age group accounted for 11.3 percent of the 9.5 million people arrested for crimes that year. More specifically, they accounted for 25 percent of those arrested for motor vehicle thefts, 21 percent of those arrested for burglary, 19 percent of those arrested for vandalism, even 6.7 percent of those arrested for murder (Federal Bureau of Investigation, 1981:196).

Not surprisingly, many sociologists and others have sought to explain why young people commit crimes. The three major theoretical points of view discussed in this chapter suggest places to look for answers. Though we'll return to the topic of deviance in Chapter 11, let's preview the matter now.

The interactionist point of view suggests that some of the causes of delinquency can be found in people's interactions with one another. By and large, young people learn to commit crimes from their friends. Suppose you grew up in a social environment in which all your friends were stealing cars and breaking into apartments. Rather than seeing such activities as bad, your friends regarded them as a sign of being "cool" and grown up. If you refused to steal, you'd be called "chicken." Chances are, you'd join in with your friends.

In 1924, Edwin Sutherland coined the term *differential association* to describe this phenomenon. He suggested that much of people's behavior—including deviant behavior—could be explained in terms of the behavior patterns of those they associated with. It illustrates the sort of explanation you might arrive at if you took an interactionist view within sociology.

In more recent years, another explanation for delinquency has come from the interactionist view. Edwin Lemert (1951) suggested that some deviance can be traced, ironically, to the *labeling* of people as deviant. Suppose, for whatever reason, that the people around you all believed you were a thief; you found yourself called a thief and treated like one. Eventually, you might very well begin stealing. These then are some of the ways in which the delinquency might be explained in a context of social interaction.

The social systems point of view provides a very different picture of delinquency. For Emile Durkheim (1893), crime was a normal aspect of social life. It was not possible to have concepts of "good" behavior without corresponding "bad" behavior. Whereas the "good" was defined by the values and behaviors generally agreed upon in a society, crime was the violation of those agreements. Durkheim saw crime as inevitable. Moreover, he did not regard it as necessarily bad: the existence of crime, for example, reminded people of what the rules were. Beyond that, Durkheim recognized that "crime" was a source of social change, as in the case of Socrates' violation of his society's rules. Socrates' execution for religious heresy and "corrupting the youth" drew attention to the rules of the game in ancient Athens.

From the social systems view, one explanation for delinquency is improper socialization:

some young people do not learn the rules of society or at least are not instilled with a commitment to abide by those rules. We'll return to this issue in Chapters 5 and 11.

From this point of view, deviance can also be caused by social disorganization. Robert Merton (1957a), for example, said deviance is often a result of discrepancies in the structure of society. For example, if a society's values stress the importance of being wealthy, and some people are prevented—by race, education, or other background factors—from earning a good income, they will find other means for getting money. The discrepancy between goals and means is the problem here. Denied the accepted means to achieving the desired goal, those so denied will find other, "deviant," means. The social systems view suggests we should examine changes in rates of delinquency in relation to other trends in society, like inflation, unemployment, and so forth.

The conflict point of view suggests still another approach to understanding deviance. Conflict theorists see delinquency as a consequence of the struggle between competing interests in society. The youth in a deprived racial or ethnic group may organize a street gang in an effort to protect their interests and/or to get what they feel is owed them. Told they do not belong in "nice society," such young people may find the gang their only source of meaning, self-respect, and belonging (Balkan et al. 1980:72).

Sue Titus Reid (1982:111–112) suggests that the functionalist (social systems) and conflict views differ in their explanations of crime in three fundamental ways. First, the functionalists look for universal explanations for crime, whereas conflict theorists—especially the Marxists—stress the importance of specific historical conditions. Second, functionalists are particularly concerned with the system needs of society—challenged by crime—while conflict theorists are more likely to see society oppressing minorities. Finally, functionalists see crime as a deviation from society's value consensus, whereas conflict theorists see established values as the dominance of one group by another in society.

Notice that these differences are primarily matters of emphasis, not necessarily matters of fact. Much crime, for example, *is* produced by the structure of oppressive agreements in a society, *and* crime *is* a threat to society. Sociologists differ on which of these facts deserves the most attention, not on which is "truest."

We're going to return to delinquency and other forms of deviance in Chapter 11, but this introductory analysis should have pointed to some of the insights available through the various sociological points of view we've studied in this chapter. Notice that each point of view sheds both light and shadow on the matter. None gives a complete picture by itself. Yet, if you are willing and able to look from several vantage points, you can gain a real mastery of the subject.

PRACTICING SOCIOLOGY

The following story appeared in the June 14, 1982, *San Francisco Chronicle* (page 2):

MOSCOW—The Soviet police moved in yesterday to seal off the apartment where a fledgling independent disarmament group was planning to meet. The action came after the police had warned the group's members that their movement was provocative, antisocial and illegal.

The crackdown on the group, whose objective was to be as free of official control as disarmament movements in the United States and Western Europe, was accompanied by glowing accounts in the Soviet press of the huge protest Saturday in New York against nuclear war.

Tass reported that more than a million Americans marched in the demonstration and described this as an expression of "resolute disagreement with the U.S. government's policy of war preparations."

In Moscow, plainclothes officers turned away people trying to enter the apartment of Sergei Batovrin, a 25-year-old artist, where he and 10 other members of the unofficial movement had planned to gather.

An officer explained that the entryway was closed because of "police activity." It was not clear what had happened to Batovrin.

The group's members, in addition to Batovrin, include a doctor, a philologist, a dental technician, two mathematicians, two engineers and three physicists.

During the last two days, members of the group reported that they had been taken to police stations and warned against persevering. Batovrin told reporters he had been threatened with prosecution for violating laws against unregistered groups. He also said that he had been lectured against equating the Soviet Union and the United States as military powers "even while the American government supports Israeli aggression in Lebanon."

"The Soviet government and people are fighting for peace," Batovrin said he had been told in regard to his movement. "And this kind of activity can only be provocative and antisocial."

Other members reported much the same treatment.

A symbolic interactionist would be interested in differences in the interpretations made by Soviet authorities (including *Tass*, the government news service) of disarmament groups' activities in the U.S. and the U.S.S.R. Further, the interactionist would describe the crackdown as an example of the authorities' methods of imposing their interpretations on dissidents.

Write a few sentences analyzing the events reported in the *Chronicle* article from the functionalist and conflict perspectives. Also speculate about which perspective (symbolic interactionist, functionalist, or conflict) the protestors and the Soviet government would take.

3

The Science
of Sociology

All science is a matter of observing and making sense of what is observed. Both theory and research are involved. Theory provides the basic points of view from which to make sense of things; research provides ways of observing. Research also includes techniques for making sense of things.

In this chapter, we're going to examine some of the research methods used in sociology and see how they fit within the larger context of science in general. We'll begin with an overview of the nature of inquiry: human, scientific, and social scientific. In trying to understand the world, people sometimes make mistakes of reasoning and observation, and we'll see how scientists try to avoid these kinds of errors. We'll see what makes science "science."

Following the overview of inquiry, we'll look at two basic considerations involved in designing and undertaking—and even reading and understanding—sociological research. The first consideration deals with **conceptualization** and the second with **sampling**. Next, I want to touch briefly on three nonscientific considerations that figure importantly in research: logistics, ethics, and politics.

Once we have covered these scientific and nonscientific considerations, we're going to look at some popular methods of research in sociology: **field research, experimentation, content analysis,** and **survey research.** In each case, you should gain a general familiarity with the method so that you'll recognize it whenever you read about a study that used it. Beyond that, however, I want to impart a sense of the relative strengths and weaknesses of the different methods so that you'll be able to evaluate the studies you read about. You won't be trained to *use* the different methods, but you should be well prepared to begin learning how to do research after you have finished this chapter.

The materials I've mentioned so far are primarily concerned with preparations for observation and actual observing. The chapter concludes with a look at sociological analysis: how sociologists make sense of what they've observed.

The Nature of Inquiry

Inquiry seems to be a native human activity. From the time we are very young, we snoop around our environment, observing things and trying to understand them. At least in part this reflects a desire to predict what's going to happen. In particular, we want to be able to predict the consequences of our own acts. What will happen if I stick my finger in the shiny electric socket? What will happen if you pull the cat's tail?

We learn to predict even when our inquiring doesn't reflect a desire to do so. When you were a young child, you probably learned to predict what would happen if you wet your diapers while you were sitting in someone's lap or what would happen if you tried to crawl out into a busy street.

All of us learn the regular patterns of objects and events in our environment, and out of the specific patterns we observe we develop a more general understanding of how our universe operates. This understanding, in turn, helps us to predict future conditions—which helps us to survive.

Errors in Inquiry

In daily life, our attempts to find out and understand what's happening is often a fairly casual activity. As a consequence, we often make mistakes. Let's look at five common errors.

1. *Inaccurate observation* Sometimes we are simply sloppy in our observations, mistaking what we observe for something else or simply failing to observe what's there. Eyewitnesses at the scene of a crime, for example, often disagree in their descriptions of the criminal.

2. *Overgeneralization* The desire to *understand* what you observe can lead you to assume that specific events represent general patterns, even when they don't. If you were to meet a boisterous Albanian, you might assume that all Albanians were loud and rowdy.

3. *Selective observation* One danger of overgeneralization is that your satisfaction with the understanding you've developed may lead you, subsequently, to notice only phenomena that confirm your picture of how the world operates. If you've concluded, for example, that all politicians are liars, you may have a tendency to overlook the ones who don't lie.

4. *Deduced information* When you do observe something that contradicts your

Inquiry is a native, human activity. We observe. We experiment. We figure out.

ideas, you may be tempted to find new information to explain the discrepancy so that you can protect your understanding of the way things are. If you've concluded that all shopkeepers are crooked, for example, and one walks four miles to return your purse or wallet, your general picture of shopkeepers is threatened. One solution is to assume that the shopkeeper is attempting to gain your confidence so as to cheat you in a grand manner later on.

5. *Illogical reasoning* Sometimes we try to make sense of things in ways that make *no* sense. A common example of this is reliance on the idea that "the exception proves the rule." This idea is often used to protect prior conclusions that are threatened by disconfirming observations. There is simply no possible way that observing a friendly sociologist can "prove" that all the rest are unfriendly. What it "proves" is that *not all* sociologists are unfriendly; it might even suggest that there are several friendly ones.

These, then, are some of the pitfalls along the road to human understanding. What makes science special is that it offers safe routes around such pitfalls. Although people working as scientists can (and sometimes do) fall into the same holes as the rest of us, as scientists they share a number of agreements about how to observe and how to draw conclusions about what they observe. These agreements appear to offer protection against faulty observation and understanding. Let's look at what makes science different from everyday "common sense."

The Characteristics of Science

The first agreement that scientists share is that observation ought to be a careful and conscious activity, specific and recorded. Most of the time people observe things casually, sometimes nearly unconsciously. Try to remember, for example, what your sociology instructor was wearing during your last class meeting. Scientists—when they do research—carefully plan what kinds of observations they are going to make, choose a method of obtaining them thoughtfully, and report their findings in detail. A sociologist would not report that politically conservative people are generally more religious than politically liberal people, for instance, without telling exactly how political orientations and religiosity were measured and among whom.

A second agreement scientists share is that drawing conclusions from what is observed should be an equally deliberate process. I suspect that when you read the word "alcoholic," a picture that represents your general understanding of alcoholics comes to mind. Now ask yourself how you formed that picture. What were the specific observations that led you to your conclusions about alcoholics? If you're having trouble remembering exactly how and why you formed the picture you have, you're no different from most of us. Scientists, however, have agreed to form conclusions more carefully and consciously.

In forming their conclusions, scientists first seek explanations that will apply to more than the specific case under study. Thus, although a sociologist of religion might do research to discover why some Episcopalians are more religious than others, the major goal of the research would be to develop a general understanding of religiosity that would apply to Methodists, Catholics, Jews, Hindus, Buddhists, and all other religious groups. Ideally, such research would also explain why some people have *no* religion.

In developing an understanding of the way the world operates, scientists also seek **parsimony**: a combination of powerful explanation and simplicity. Let me give a practical illustration. If I could learn 1,328 specific things about you, I could guess with almost utter certainty whom you favored in the last presidential election. Moreover, if I could learn the same 1,328 specific things about anyone else, I could be equally certain whom that person favored. It would be more parsimonious, however, if I could achieve the same degree of certainty by knowing only two or three things instead of 1,328. When you shop around before making a purchase, you are trying to get the most value for the least expense. Scientists seek the same kind of "bargain" in terms of understanding.

A third agreement, and perhaps the most important one, that scientists share is that the process and results of their inquiries should be *public*. To return to your picture of an alcoholic, notice that you are under no obligation to tell anyone what you think about alcoholics; and, if you keep quiet about it, nobody can challenge the quality of your observations or the wisdom of your conclusions. The results of scientific inquiry are useless, however, unless they are communicated. Making the results public opens them to scrutiny by other scientists.

Opening your methods and results to public scrutiny permits *replication*, repeating of your study. When research methods are described in detail, other researchers are able to repeat or replicate the study, using all the same methods, to see if the same results are produced the second time. If two studies produce the same results, confidence in those results is increased.

Putting studies to the test of replication or, equally important, putting newly developed theories to the test of practice is called "empirical verification." It is the keystone in the agreements that distinguish science from nonscience. Whenever a scientist develops an understanding of how something operates, the next essential step is to *test* that understanding with additional observations. If you were to conclude that women are, on the average, more religious than men, your next step would be to undertake an empirical study—make observations—to test the accuracy of your conclusion.

These, then, are some of the agreements that scientists share—agreements that distinguish science from nonscience. You should realize, however, that scientists do not always behave the way I've described, just as nonscientists

sometimes *do* behave those ways. There is no magical dividing line between scientists and nonscientists. Even so, the characteristics we've been looking at do distinguish scientific inquiry from other forms of human inquiry. They are what make "science" special.

Science and Determinism

Another characteristic of science is different enough from those I've discussed to require special treatment. This characteristic is **determinism.** All science is based on a deterministic view of things, but this can present problems for people as they approach *social* science. Determinism conflicts with our implicit, personal feelings about **free will.**

The deterministic view assumes that some things are determined or caused by others. When asked why the moon doesn't fly off into space, an astronomer will tell you that the moon's orbit is caused by the gravitational pull of the earth. The astronomer wouldn't say anything about the moon's "desires" in the matter, and you probably wouldn't think to ask. How can it have any say in the matter?

But what about the scientific study of *human* behavior? Sociology and the other social sciences proceed from the same deterministic view that astronomy, physics, and biology do. Later in this book, for example, we'll ask why some people are more prejudiced than others. We'll look at some of the educational, religious, and economic "causes" of prejudice that sociologists have discovered. Nowhere in that discussion will we consider whether people "choose" to be prejudiced or not. Instead, we'll look at the factors that "make" people prejudiced, factors over which they have little or no control.

The deterministic view of human behavior implies that *you* have little or no personal say in how tolerant you are, how religious, how liberal or conservative, how hardworking or lazy. You have no control over any of the things that make up your image of who you are. This view assumes that people are totally determined in what they say or do when they study human behavior. You don't have to *believe* this assumption, but you should be aware of it in advance. Otherwise, as we look at various sociological attempts to explain and understand social life, it might become an unrecognized source of discomfort.

The Methods of Scientific Inquiry

In the preceding section we saw how science differs in general from ordinary human inquiry. In this section I want to be more specific in describing the ways in which scientists go about making their observations and forming their conclusions.

Two Kinds of Logic

Like nonscientists, but usually more rigorously, scientists use two distinct logical systems: **deductive logic** and **inductive logic.**

Deductive logic may be defined as reasoning that proceeds from general principles to particular cases. The classical illustration of deductive logic is the syllogism: "All men are mortals. Socrates is a man; therefore, Socrates is mortal."

Inductive logic works in just the opposite direction: the reasoning is from particular cases to general principles. Thus, you might observe that Socrates, a man, was mortal, observe a number of other men to be mortal, and conclude that "all men are mortal."

Let's see how these two different logical systems might be used in a research project. Imagine, for instance, that you are interested in learning whether there is a relationship between how much students study for a final examination and the grades they get on the exam.

First, you might begin by analyzing the matter logically. You might decide that the reason students study is to familiarize themselves with the course materials and that examinations measure familiarity with the course materials. You'd probably conclude that the more students study, the better their examination grades will be.

What I've just described is deductive logic; the conclusion you reached corresponds to a "general principle." In a research context, this general principle would serve as the basis for a **hypothesis,** an expectation about the way things are. You might hypothesize, therefore, that on a forthcoming examination students who study most will receive the highest grades and that the grades received will consistently reflect the amount of study.

Look now at Figure 3–1. Part *(a)* of section I ("Deductive Method") illustrates your hypothesis: the more students study for the exam, the better their grades on it. If you were conducting a research project on this topic, you would next collect data to test your hypothesis, an activity known, appropriately, as **hypothesis testing.** Part I*(b)* in Figure 3–1 represents the data that you might collect. Each point within the shaded area represents a single student. The position of a given point in relation to the horizontal scale tells you how many hours the student spent studying for the exam. The position in relation to the vertical scale tells you the grade that student received on the exam.

Notice that the "reality" in this example and your hypothesis do not exactly correspond. The two are shown together in part I*(c)* of Figure 3–1. Some students received higher grades than you would have predicted, given the hours spent studying, and others received lower grades. The "reality" roughly approximates your hypothesis, however. So you must decide whether the observations are "close enough" to the hypothesis for you to conclude that the general principle is an accurate summary of how things are.

The second approach you might take is illustrated in part II ("Inductive Method") of Figure 3–1. You might begin by observing the hours studied and the grades of the students in the course, doing this without any hypothesis link-

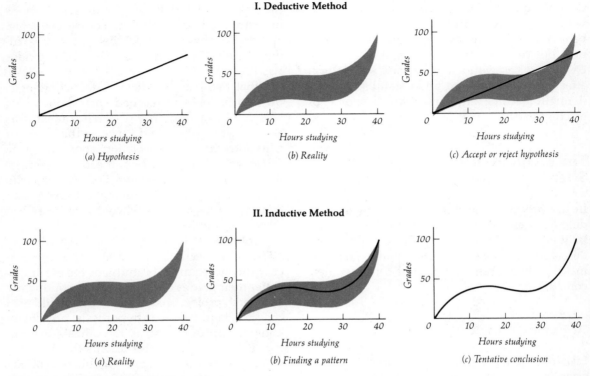

Figure 3–1 *Deductive and inductive methods.*

ing the two *(a)*. Using your observations as a base, you might look for a general pattern that will provide a reasonable summary of all those specific observations. The curved line shown in *(b)* is an example of the pattern you might find.

Notice what this pattern suggests about the relationship between studying and grades. Grades appear to improve with study among those who study between 0 and 20 hours. At that point, however, grades begin to decline somewhat with additional study—up to the point of studying 30 hours. Grades generally improve, however, for each additional hour spent in study above 30 hours. (Realize that this example is only *hypothetical*, not something you can use to govern your own study habits.)

Using the inductive method, you might frame a *tentative conclusion (c)* based on the pattern

best summarizing the observations you made. This then, is an example of working from particular cases to a general principle.

The Workings of Science

Science courses and textbooks tend to link "the scientific method" and the deductive system. They suggest that scientific research begins with contemplation and logical reasoning, is followed by the framing of hypotheses derived from that theoretical reasoning, and concludes with empirical tests of the hypotheses.

Although this is a useful model of how science operates, science doesn't always operate that way. Science is just as "scientific" when it follows an inductive rather than deductive pattern. Both approaches to scientific inquiry are legitimate and valuable.

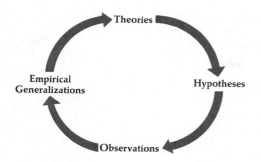

Figure 3–2 A more realistic image of science. Adapted from Walter Wallace, The Logic of Sociology *(Chicago: Aldine-Atherton, 1971).*

Walter Wallace (1971) has provided what seems to be a more realistic picture of how science operates. He sees science as a circle made up of theories, hypotheses, observations, and empirical generalizations (see Figure 3–2). The significant feature of Wallace's model is that scientific research can *start* anywhere. Furthermore, researchers may move around the circle many times. Observations are generalized; theories are framed suggesting hypotheses that form the basis for new observations; revised generalizations produce revised theories, and so forth. (For an example of an inquiry that seems to fit Wallace's model, see the box "Theory and Method in Durkheim's *Suicide*.")

Let's turn now to those attempts to explain and understand. I'll begin with a brief overview of the research process. Then we'll take a somewhat closer look at each of the separate steps in the process of clarifying and answering questions about social life.

The Research Process

Figure 3–3, p. 80, presents a simplified, schematic view of the social scientific research process. It presents an overview of the whole process before we launch into the specific components of research.

At the top of the diagram, I've represented interests, ideas, and theories as possible begin-

ning points for a line of research. The letters (A, B, X, Y, and so forth) represent concepts such as prejudice, anomie (a general feeling that things have little meaning), and so on. Thus, you might have a general interest in finding out what causes some people to be more prejudiced than others, or you might want to know some of the consequences of prejudice.

Alternatively, your inquiry might begin with a specific *idea* about the way things are. You might have the idea that working on an assembly line causes anomie, for example. I have put a question mark in the diagram to indicate that you aren't sure things are the way you suspect they are.

Finally, I have represented a *theory* as a complex set of relationships among several concepts: social class, prejudice, and education, for example. Notice, moreover, that there is a possible movement back and forth across these several possible beginnings. An initial interest may lead to the formulation of an idea, which may be fit into a larger theory, and the theory may produce new ideas and create new interests.

Any or all of these three beginning points may lead to empirical research as a way to answer your questions. The purpose of such research can be the exploration of an interest, the testing of a specific idea, or the validation of a complex theory. Whatever the purpose, however, you have a variety of decisions to make, as indicated in the remainder of the diagram.

Conceptualization You may have general ideas about the meanings of concepts such as prejudice or anomie, but to do research on them, you'll have to specify your definitions of these concepts—to conceptualize them. One aspect of this process is to create *variables* out of the concepts—specifying the kind and range of variation that interests you. As the diagram indicates, conceptualization is (usually) done early in the research process

Operationalization Having specified the concepts to be studied and having chosen the research method to be used, you must create

THEORY AND METHOD IN DURKHEIM'S *SUICIDE*

A classic sociological illustration of the complex interplay of theory and method is Emile Durkheim's pioneering study of suicide. In *Suicide* (1897), Durkheim's purpose was to investigate whether or not anything could be learned by considering suicide not just as a set of isolated, individual acts but as a social phenomenon tied to conditions in modern society.

As the preliminary step in his inquiry, Durkheim carefully delineated the object of his study. Suicides, he said, were those deaths that occurred through an action on the part of the victim which he or she knew would eventuate in death. Durkheim next assembled the available data on suicide and calculated the rate of suicide (number of suicides per unit of population) for various European countries over time. He noticed that these varied significantly from country to country and fluctuated over time in regular patterns, although they had generally been rising from the 1840s to at least the 1870s. What could explain these variations in suicide rates? This was the problem Durkheim set himself to explore.

Durkheim began his investigation of the causes of suicide by suggesting hypotheses about possible nonsocial causes. He considered, for example, whether the rate of suicide varied with the tendency to insanity in a given population, or with climatic differences. In each case, he found that the suicide rate did not vary (or correlate) with these factors, and thus could dismiss these hypotheses.

Having eliminated nonsocial causes, Durkheim deduced that variation in the suicide rate must depend on social factors. He compared the rates of suicide in different areas with the religious affiliations of their inhabitants and found that, in each instance, areas that were predominantly Protestant had higher suicide rates than areas that were mainly Catholic. Durkheim then reasoned that what differentiated Protestantism from Catholicism was the greater degrees of free inquiry and spiritual individualism that Protestantism permitted.

Were learning and inquiry responsible then for the rising rates of suicide? This hypothesis, Durkheim showed, had to be rejected because Jews in Europe, whose level of education was highest among religious groups, had generally the lowest rate of suicide. The reason for this difference, Durkheim suggested, was that among

concrete measurement techniques. *Operationalization* refers to the concrete steps or operations researchers use in measuring specific concepts.

Population and Sampling   Besides refining concepts and measurements, you must decide *who* or *what* to study. The *population* for a study is that group (usually of people) about whom you want to be able to draw conclusions. The population might be all college students in America, marriages, or cities. Researchers are almost never able to study all the members of the population that interests them, however. In virtually every case, then, you must choose a *sample* of subjects for study. Notice in the dia-

gram that decisions about population and sampling are related to decisions about the research methods to be used.

Choice of Research Method   As we'll see shortly, the variety of research methods available to the social scientist includes experiments, surveys, and field research. Each method has strengths and weaknesses, and certain concepts are more appropriately studied by some methods than by others.

Observations   Having decided what to study among whom by what method, you are now ready to make observations—to collect data.

Jews the pursuit of learning tended to make Jewish society more cohesive, whereas among Protestants it tended to promote schisms. What these religious differences showed, he tentatively concluded, was that religion curbed suicide to the extent to which it integrated individuals into a cohesive society with a set of common beliefs and practices.

Could what Durkheim had found about religious society and suicide be generalized to include other sorts of social groups? Through a chain of reasoning and hypothesis testing similar to his consideration of the effect of religious affiliation on the rate of suicide, Durkheim demonstrated that the rate of suicide tends to vary inversely with the extent of the individual's integration into family life and political society. From these investigations, Durkheim induced a more general explanation of suicide. Suicide was more likely to occur, he theorized, when integration into group life was so weak that the aims of the individual tended to take precedence over those of the group. The type of suicide that arose from this "excessive individualism" he called "egoistic suicide."

Durkheim went on to hypothesize two other forms of suicide, altruistic and anomic. "Altruistic suicide" arose, Durkheim argued, when the social group took on a reality so much greater than the persons who composed it that they were willing to die in its cause. Anomic suicide, by contrast, arose when the normal equilibrium of society was disturbed and the customary restraints on individuals were loosened. Individuals, released from the bonds of tradition, became more susceptible to insecurity and despair, and thus more likely to commit suicide. The reason the rate of suicide had risen over the nineteenth century, Durkheim suggested, was that industrialization had undermined the values and the institutions of traditional society but had failed to put anything in their place.

Durkheim did not actually prove his theory about the social causes of suicide, but his investigation shows how the interplay of theory and method in sociological inquiry can both advance our understanding of society and provide a rich soil for new hypotheses to take root. Do you think that Durkheim's theory could ever be proved? Based on Durkheim's study, what might be some useful questions to ask about contemporary suicide trends?

Source: Emile Durkheim, *Suicide: A Study in Sociology,* trans. John A. Spaulding and George Simpson (Glencoe, Ill.: Free Press, 1951 [1897]).

Data Processing Depending on the research method chosen, you will have amassed a volume of observations in a form that probably isn't easy to interpret. The data processing often involves the classification of observations into categories and the recording of the categorized data on punch cards or computer tapes.

Analysis Finally, you manipulate the collected data for the purpose of drawing conclusions that reflect on the interests, ideas, and theories that initiated your inquiry. Notice that the results of your analyses feed back into your initial interests, ideas, and theories. In practice, this feedback may very well represent the beginning of another cycle of inquiry.

After this preview of the overall research process, let's examine each component in a little more detail. We begin with the process of conceptualization.

Conceptualization

"Concepts" are pictures in your head, vague mental images that summarize the observations you make. Concepts categorize observations. I cannot know with certainty what your concepts look like , and you cannot know with certainty what mine look like. Yet concepts are an essential part of communication and interaction. To communicate with each other, you

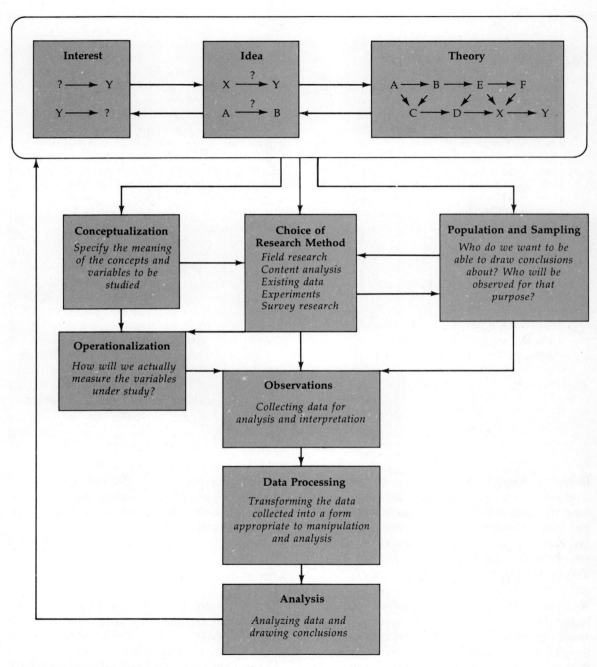

Figure 3–3 The research process.

and I agree to associate certain terms with our concepts, with our mental images.

"Conceptualization" is the process of refining and specifying exactly what we mean by the terms we associate with concepts. It's a process of clarifying our ideas so as to make the design of a research project possible. If I told you that young people don't know enough to vote intelligently, you'd probably be offended. But if I specified that by "young" I mean people under one year old, I would have communicated my meaning more clearly, and you'd probably agree with my assertion (and not be offended).

Sociologists frequently use terms that people already associate vague mental images with, so careful conceptualization in designing research is all the more important. You probably have some mental picture that you associate with the term "liberalism," for example, and it is very likely different from mine. If I were to undertake a study of liberalism, ultimately reporting my findings on why some people are more liberal than others, it is unlikely that the observations I based my study on would correspond exactly to your conception of what "liberalism" means. For my study to have meaning for you, then, I need to specify what I mean by the terms I use. Even if you disagree with my definition, you'll at least know what I mean by my research conclusions and what my observations mean to you.

It is essential to realize that none of the terms we associate with our mental pictures has a "real" meaning. My concept of "liberalism" is no more "correct" or "incorrect" than yours. The closest we can come to the "real" meanings for terms are the *agreements* we make for the purpose of communication. "Liberal," after all, is only a word that we agree to use in summarizing certain observations. Our agreement is a concession we make in the interest of communication. The process of conceptualization is a further concession, in that we specify an even narrower range of observations in the interest of even greater communication.

Attributes and Variables Sociologists typically deal with two kinds of concepts: attributes and variables. Attributes are characteristics of people or things. Some attributes are "tall," "heavy," "blue," "upper-class," "four-year-old," and "male."

Variables are logical sets of attributes. Gender, for example, is a variable composed of two attributes: "male" and "female." "Color" is a variable composed of such attributes as "red," "blue," and "green." "Social class" is a variable composed of such attributes as "upper-class," "middle-class," and "lower-class."

The relationships among attributes and variables are at the core of the two goals of scientific research: description and explanation. Scientists *describe* the way things are by reporting the distribution of attributes on a particular variable. We describe the "sex composition" of a population, for example, by telling how many men and women there are in that population. Scientists *explain* why things are the way they are by noting **correlations**—"co-relations"—among variables, by noting that certain attributes of one variable typically appear in the presence of certain attributes of other variables. Thus, for example, we note that the attribute "liberal" appears more often with the attribute "young" than it does with the attribute "old." We say that "liberalism" and "age," as variables, are related to each other. Making sense out of the observation that some people are more liberal than others, then, involves, in part, the matter of age. We'll look at the process of description and explanation in more detail near the end of the chapter.

Operationalization

Operationalization is an extension of the process of conceptualization, specifying the meanings to be associated with certain attributes and variables. In my research project, the most explicit way I can tell you what I will mean by the terms "liberal" and "conservative" is to detail the operations I will undertake in classifying people as liberal or conservative. "Operationalization" is the process of determining the operations I'll use.

I might decide, for example, to base my **operational definition** of political orientations on such specifics as the political party people identify with, whom they have voted for or whom they prefer, or their attitudes on specific political issues. Although the definition I choose will inevitably lack the "richness of meaning" that you (and I) associate with the terms "liberal" and "conservative," my definitions will at least be clear to us both. The use of operational definitions in sociology, then, is one aspect of the characteristic of explicitness that I discussed earlier.

In general, conceptualization and operationalization are processes by which sociologists prepare to measure what they observe. Let's discuss now *what* they observe.

Sampling What To Observe

Sociologists and other social scientists have a problem. Much of what we do is based on observations—we observe and make sense out of what we observe—yet it is impossible to observe everything relevant to a particular investigation. Suppose, for example, that you want to discover how people decide which way to vote on election day. It would be simply impossible for you to observe every voter in the process of reaching a decision. And the decision-making processes of the few voters you did observe might be different from those you didn't observe.*

_____

*Notice that this is less a problem for physical scientists. The chemist who wants to study the properties of carbon, for example, doesn't need to worry about "which" carbon is observed: all carbon is the same. Because of the heterogeneity of people, however, the social scientist cannot study whatever person is convenient and assume that all other people will be like the one studied.

Typically, we want to draw conclusions—descriptive and explanatory—about a "population," a large group or class of people, such as "all Americans," "Nebraska teenagers," or "naval officers." Since we are unable to observe all members of the population in question, we select a sample for actual observation and analysis. We select some members of the population and try to make our selection so that those we *do* observe closely resemble those we do not. The term **representative sample** refers to a sample that has the same essential characteristics as the population from which it was selected. The technique of the representative sample is used by political pollsters like Gallup and Harris. It accounts for their ability to interview 1,500–2,000 voters across the nation and predict with uncanny accuracy how some 80 million voters will vote on election day.

Scientific sampling is based ultimately on **random selection,** a process most commonly illustrated by flipping a coin. Random selection gives all members of a population an equal chance or probability of being selected into the sample. This, in turn, ensures that those who *are* selected will closely reflect the characteristics of the total population from which they were drawn. Although actual sampling methods can be complex and almost never involve flipping coins, the fundamental logic is the same as what I've described.

The probability sampling methods used by social researchers today are the result of a long history of trial and error. Let's look at a little of that history.

Some Milestones in Social Sampling

Sampling in social research has developed hand in hand with political polling—because, no doubt, political polling is one of the few opportunities social researchers have to discover the accuracy of their estimates. On election day, they find out how well or how poorly they did.

President Alf Landon   You may have heard about the *Literary Digest* in connection with political polling. The *Digest* was a popular newsmagazine published between 1890 and 1938 in America. In 1920, the *Digest* editors mailed postcards to people in six states, asking them whom they were planning to vote for in the presidential campaign between Warren Harding and James Cox. Names were selected for the poll from telephone directories and automobile-registration lists. Based on the postcards sent back, the *Digest* correctly predicted that Harding would be elected. In elections that followed, the *Literary Digest* expanded its polling operations and correctly predicted the outcomes of presidential elections in 1924, 1928, and 1932.

In 1936, the *Digest* conducted its most ambitious poll: 10 million ballots were sent out to people listed in telephone directories and on lists of automobile owners. Over 2 million people responded, giving Republican contender Alf Landon a stunning 57-to-43 percent landslide over incumbent President Franklin Roosevelt. The *Digest* editors (1936a: 6) modestly cautioned:

> We make no claim to infallibility. We did not coin the phrase "uncanny accuracy" which has been so freely applied to our Polls. We know only too well the limitations of every straw vote, however enormous the sample gathered, however scientific the method. It would be a miracle if every State of the forty-eight behaved on Election day exactly as forecast by the Poll.

Two weeks later, the *Digest* editors knew the limitations of straw polls even better. They were spared the miracle of all forty-eight states voting exactly as forecast: voters gave Roosevelt a third term in office with 61 percent of the vote, the largest landslide in history. Landon won only 8 electoral votes to Roosevelt's 523. The editors were puzzled by their unfortunate turn of luck.

Part of the problem surely lay in the 22 percent return rate garnered by the poll. The editors (1936b: 7) asked:

Why did only one in five voters in Chicago to whom *The Digest* sent ballots take the trouble to reply? And why was there a preponderance of Republicans in the one-fifth that did reply? . . . we were getting better cooperation in what we have always regarded as a public service from Republicans than we were getting from Democrats. Do Republicans live nearer to mail-boxes? Do Democrats generally disapprove of straw polls?

Certainly part of the answer to these questions lay in the lists from which the *Digest* selected the sample: telephone subscribers and automobile owners. Such a sampling design would select a disproportionately wealthy sample, especially coming on the tail end of the worst economic depression in the nation's history. The sample effectively excluded poor people, and the poor people predominantly voted for Roosevelt's New Deal recovery program.

President Thomas E. Dewey   The 1936 election also saw the emergence of a young pollster whose name was to become synonymous with public opinion. In contrast to the *Literary Digest*, George Gallup correctly predicted that Roosevelt would beat Landon. Gallup's success in 1936 hinged on his use of **quota sampling,** about which I'll have more to say later in the chapter. For now, you need only know that quota sampling is based on a knowledge of the characteristics of the population being sampled: what proportion are men, what proportion women, what proportions are of various incomes, ages, and so on. People are selected for the purposes of matching the population characteristics: the right number of poor, white, rural men; the right number of rich, black, urban women. The quotas are based on those variables most relevant to the study. By knowing the numbers of people with various incomes in the nation, Gallup selected his sample to include the right number of respondents at each income level.

Gallup and his American Institute of Public Opinion used this quota sampling method to good effect in 1936, 1940, and 1944—correctly picking the presidential winner in each of those years. Then, in 1948, Gallup and most political pollsters suffered the embarrassment of picking New York Governor Thomas Dewey over incumbent President Harry Truman. A number of factors accounted for the 1948 failure. First, most of the pollsters stopped polling in early October despite a steady trend toward Truman during the campaign. Second, many voters were undecided throughout the campaign, and they went disproportionately for Truman when they stepped in the voting booth. Finally, and more important for our present purposes, Gallup's failure rested on the unrepresentativeness of his samples.

Quota sampling—which had been effective in earlier years—was Gallup's undoing in 1948. Recall that this technique requires that the researcher know something about the total population (of voters in this instance). For national political polls, such information came primarily from census data. In 1948, however, a world war, producing a massive movement from country to city, had radically changed the character of the American population from what the 1940 census showed. City dwellers, moreover, were more likely to vote Democratic, hence the rural-urban unrepresentativeness also underestimated the number of Democratic votes.

In 1948, a number of academic researchers had been experimenting with **probability sampling** methods. By and large, they were far more successful than those using quota samples. Today, probability sampling remains the primary method for selecting samples for social science research .

President Ronald Reagan   In November 1980, Ronald Reagan was elected president of the United States with 50.8 percent of the popular vote, as against 41 percent for Jimmy Carter and 6.6 percent for third-party candidate John Anderson. This election outcome was widely regarded as an "upset" for political pollsters—none of whom had predicted such a wide margin for Reagan. How far off were the polls?

In his final preelection poll—based on interviews conducted October 30 through November 1—Gallup reported the following outcome:

	Final Gallup Poll (%)	Actual Voting (%)
Reagan	47	50.8
Carter	44	41.0
Anderson	8	6.6
Other	1	1.6
	100%	100.0%

When George Gallup released his findings on November 2, he warned that political polls could give only an estimate of probable election outcome, not a precise prediction of the results. He pointed out, moreover, that in all the final election polls since 1936, the latest estimate had been off by an average of 2.4 percentage points. As things turned out, the 1980 poll was off by 3.8 percentage points, somewhat more than the average (Ladd and Ferlee 1981: 15).

Whether you feel the 1980 Gallup "error" was large or small, there's one other aspect that you ought to find a little startling. In 1980, nearly a hundred million Americans voted (U.S. Bureau of Census 1982: 3). How many interviews do you suppose the Gallup organization conducted in order to come within 4 percentage points of the actual result? Fewer than two thousand. At the least, this fact should indicate the importance and power of probability sampling in social research.

Some Nonscientific Aspects of Scientific Research

Most of the remainder of this chapter is devoted to the various aspects of *doing* research. We'll look at some of the ways sociologists collect data and what they do with what they collect: how they process, analyze, and interpret data. But first I want to draw your attention briefly to some nonscientific aspects of research that are nonetheless important to its conduct.

If you fully understand the logic and techniques of scientific research, then you will be able to design research projects that are scientifically excellent. And yet, you might never be able to conduct the research—because of nonscientific considerations that prevent it. In this section, I want to mention three such considerations: *logistics*, *ethics*, and *politics*.

First, I'm sure you can imagine that it is often simply not feasible to do what would appear to be the best conceivable study. To understand public opinion in North Korea, for example, you might decide to send a staff of one hundred interviewers into that country to select a sample and interview Koreans about their attitudes and opinions. You will not succeed, however, since North Korea (at this time) is not accessible to American researchers, so your interviewers will be turned back at the border (if not before).

Or consider this: a certain part of homosexual behavior in America occurs among strangers meeting in public toilets, an activity sociologists (taking their lead from the gay community) call "tearoom trade." Suppose you wanted to study this behavior. I suppose you could go on a field trip to public toilets and interview people. "Excuse me, sir. Are you here to engage in homosexual activities with strangers?" Imagine the likelihood of success in that instance. The people you wanted to study would run for the hills, and people who came there merely to use the facilities would call the police and have you arrested.

The point of these two examples is that often it is not feasible to do a study in the way that might otherwise seem most logical to you. Common logistical constraints include money, time, access to what you want to study, and the impact of your study on what you are studying.

I chose the tearoom example for an additional reason. Suppose that you did want to study the tearoom trade. How would you go about it? Sociologist Laud Humphreys (1970) set his study up this way: he began visiting public toilets where he suspected homosexual activity was taking place, and he began volunteering to act as a lookout for those wanting some action. He had discovered that "lookout" was an acceptable, even important, position to occupy, so he took advantage of it. By pretending to want only to watch the others in action, to be a voyeur, he placed himself in a position to make sociological observations.

As you'll see shortly, this form of research is called "field research" or "participant-observation," and researchers using this method must decide whether or not to reveal their identities as researchers. Humphreys chose not to, reasoning that announcing himself as a sociologist would have made his study impossible. In deceiving those he was studying, however, Humphreys was criticized by others who felt his research was "unethical." If he could not conduct the research without lying to people, some said, he should not have done the research in the first place. That particular debate still rages among sociologists, and it illustrates the fact that ethical concerns are another consideration that must be handled in the design of research.

If you wanted to conduct research on how people react to emergencies such as automobile accidents or theater fires, it would be obviously unethical to go out and create the situation. As inefficient as it might be, you'd have to wait around for the real thing to happen on its own, or—as we'll see in the case of experimentation—you might be able to create a *simulated* (make-believe) emergency to study.

Finally, political considerations often enter into the picture, as the North Korean example suggested. This aspect of sociological research was dramatized during the 1960s when a group of social scientists was hired by the U.S. government to study revolution and counterrevolution in Latin America. "Project Camelot," as it was called, seemed like a good idea at the time, yet it aroused considerable fear and hostility from sociologists, who said that the project would be used by the military to squelch Latin American revolutions. The sociologists, they said, were contributing their sociological expertise to the maintenance of dictatorships in other countries. As a result of the furor created, the project was canceled (see Horowitz, 1967).

As we turn now to some of the popular data-collection methods used by sociologists, you should bear these three nonscientific considerations in mind. Ultimately, practical research is a compromise reflecting many influences—but it is one of the things that makes research a constant challenge.

Modes of Observation

Just as sociologists have a variety of different theoretical points of view, they also have several methods for observing people and other aspects of society. The method a sociologist uses depends mainly on what he or she wants to know. In this section, I am going to describe three major research methods used in sociology—field research, experiments, and survey research—and I'll mention some additional ones more briefly.

Field Research

If you want to study how people behave during a riot, the most obvious way to do so would be to pick the riot of your choice and watch it unfold. Similarly, if you're interested in student-faculty interaction in the classroom, you could go to a class and watch students and faculty interact. Field research is as simple as that—almost.

Field research is fundamentally a matter of going where the action is, and you begin your observations by planning where and when you can be in the presence of what you want to study. If you are studying a new religious group, you should find out when and where they have meetings. Go there. See what happens.

This research method is sometimes referred to as **participant-observation,** and that name points to one of the key decisions a field

researcher needs to make.* Will you *participate* in what you study or will you only observe? Either decision has strengths and weaknesses. Participating directly in what you study (getting a job as a coal miner, for example, to study coal mining) can give you insights that might escape you otherwise. On the other hand, personal participation can interfere with the scientific "detachment" that seems essential to analytical observation. This is a common problem for anthropologists who speak of field workers "going native."

If you decide to participate directly in what you study, you face another decision. Do you identify yourself as a researcher to those you will study? Again, there are reasons to support either conclusion. Concealing your identity—saying you are just another coal miner, for example—encourages those you are studying to act "naturally." They might change their behavior if they knew they were being studied. Some kinds of behavior, moreover, can't be studied if you identify yourself as a researcher. On the other side of the issue, however, many object that the deception involved in hiding your identity is unethical and should not be allowed.

The issue is complex. If you act as and become accepted as a full participant in whatever you are studying, there is a good chance that you'll shape the events under study. When Leon Festinger and his colleagues (1956) pretended to be full members in a small Midwestern group that believed flying saucers were about to make contact with a few chosen earth people, they were frequently asked what they felt the group should do next. Should the group try to recruit more members or just lie low until the saucers came? This was a problem for the researchers, since they were largely interested in the conditions under which the group attempted to recruit members.

---

*Raymond Gold (1969) has examined these issues in detail and has suggested there are four roles the field researcher might play: "complete participant," "participant-as-observer," "observer-as-participant," and "complete observer."

The steps involved in *doing* field research are largely a matter of refined and sharpened common sense. If you were to undertake field research on a topic—understanding the popularity of a new religious sect, for example—you'd want to begin by finding out all you could about it. You'd want to study books and articles written about the group and about any similar groups. If there were people familiar with the group, you'd probably want to talk to them, learning as much as you could before beginning your own direct observations.

Once in the field, you'd probably want to interview participants. If you've identified yourself as a researcher, you can conduct the interviews in that context. If you've pretended to be a participant yourself, you can still conduct interviews in a conversational form.

Note taking is the backbone of field research. Observing is not enough. You need to record what you observe. Styles of note taking vary from individual to individual. Shorthand is useful if you have that ability. If conditions permit, you may be able to tape-record at least the audio portion of what you're observing, devoting your note taking to the visual. As you review and reinterpret what you've observed, your

research is likely to gain focus: as you begin to discern what appear to be important patterns, you will focus your attention on those things in later observations. This aspect of your research is not that different from the procedures a good detective or newspaper reporter follows, except that you'll bring a sociological point of view to the subject.

Among the methods available to sociologists, field research has some special advantages. More than any other method, this one allows you to study social life in its natural habitat. In that respect, it can offer you a very comprehensive picture of what you want to study. By being there you can *sense* things that would be totally lost in doing an experiment or making a survey.

Field research also has disadvantages. It is generally less rigorous and less precise than other methods. A survey, for example, can determine, say, voter intentions with considerable accuracy and precision, something that cannot be accomplished in field research. Also, as you begin to focus your attention as a field-research project unfolds, you run the risk of reaching a premature conclusion and failing to observe other things of equal or greater importance.

Undoubtedly, the quality of field research improves with practice, and practicing it is relatively inexpensive and easy. As you read this discussion, it may have occurred to you that you've been doing field research all your life. You may not have been as consciously rigorous as sociologists are, but you were doing field research all the same. You have also been engaging in the next mode of observation we shall discuss.

Experiments

All of us experiment copiously in our attempt to understand the world around us. All adult skills are learned through experimentation: eating, walking, talking, riding a bicycle, swimming, and so forth. Students learn how much

Observation and recording what you've observed are fundamental to social science. This young man is learning about times and events which are otherwise unrecorded.

studying is required for academic success through experimentation, and that's how professors learn how much preparation is needed for successful lectures.

Basically, experiments involve (1) taking action and (2) observing the consequences of the action. In preparing a stew, for example, we add salt, taste, add more salt, and taste again. In defusing a bomb, we clip a wire, see if the bomb explodes, and clip another.

Scientific experiments are like the ones we carry out every day, but they are much more carefully planned and rigorously controlled. A classical scientific experiment has three major components: (1) an **independent** and a **dependent variable,** (2) **experimental** and **control groups,** and (3) **pretesting** and **posttesting.** Let's look at each of these components in turn.

Experiments typically test the effects of one variable on another: the effects of an independent variable on a dependent one. If you want to find out, for example, whether a movie dealing with black American history reduces prejudice among those viewing it, prejudice is the dependent variable. The movie is an experimental stimulus and whether or not people see the movie is the independent variable. The question to be answered by the experiment is whether the independent variable (seeing the movie or not seeing it) has an effect on the dependent variable (prejudice).

The independent variable, then, is one whose variations are accepted as given and not requiring explanation. In the earlier example of hours spent studying and the grades received on an exam, the number of hours spent studying (the independent variable) is treated as the *cause* in the cause-effect pattern under study. The grades received are the dependent variable, inasmuch as the grades "depend" on the number of hours spent in study. In the cause-effect pattern, the grades are the effect.

The "experimental group" is a group of people (called "subjects" in experiments) who are exposed to the experimental stimulus. In the present example, the black-history movie is shown to the experimental group. The "control group" is made up of subjects who are similar to the experimental group in all respects except one: they are *not* exposed to the experimental stimulus.

A typical method for measuring the effects of an experimental stimulus is the use of pretesting and posttesting. Measurements of the dependent variable are made before and after the experimental stimulus is administered. In the present example, you might give a questionnaire to all subjects in both the experimental and control groups to determine their levels of antiblack prejudice. If the members of the two groups are similar to one another, the average level of prejudice in the two groups should be about the same. Then you show the movie to members of the experimental group only. Afterward, you measure prejudice among all members of both groups. If the movie reduces prejudice, you expect to find a reduction in the level of prejudice in the experimental group but not in the control group.

Control groups are especially important in experiments because they pinpoint the effects of the experimental stimulus. Suppose, for example, that you had been conducting an experiment on the black-history movie in April 1968, working *without* a control group. You had measured your subjects' prejudice, shown them the film, and arranged to remeasure their prejudice a week later, on April 10, say. In the posttest, you might have discovered a dramatic reduction in antiblack prejudice, but you'd be unable to tell how much of that was due to the movie and how much was due to the assassination of Martin Luther King, Jr., on the day before the retesting. Had you been using a control group, however, the amount of reduction in prejudice among them would have allowed you to determine the independent effects of the movie.

Control groups also guard against the effects of the experiment itself. Very often people modify their behavior and attitude just because they are participating in an experiment. In the famous "Hawthorne" study to be discussed in

Chapter 8, it was found that worker productivity in an assembly plant was affected more by the fact that the workers were being studied than by any of the steps taken to improve productivity.

Evaluation Research   Studies of worker productivity also point to a more general issue, concerning the growing use of experimental methods to evaluate innovations in the real world. **Evaluation research** is the name associated with an increasingly important type of social research in connection with social experimentation. Whenever new social programs are put into effect, social researchers may be asked to evaluate their impact and success. Such situations are essentially large-scale experiments within natural social settings (Moursund 1973).

Suppose, for example, that a prison warden wants to experiment with home visits as a way of improving inmates' morale and hastening their rehabilitation. A sociologist might be invited to study the innovation and evaluate its effectiveness. Prisoners might be divided into experimental and control groups, with the former permitted home visits. In a comparison of the morale and rehabilitative progress of the two groups, the sociologist could assess whether or not the program achieved its objectives.

In recent years, evaluation research has been growing faster than any other research method in sociology. Indeed, most major social programs are now being accompanied by provisions for determining whether they achieve their purposes. For example, when the New York judiciary experimented with an expanded program of releasing people without bail while awaiting trial, the Vera Institute (Ares et al. 1963) created the now-famous Manhattan Bail Project to find out whether expansion of the release program resulted in more people skipping town to avoid standing trial. They found the program did not create that problem. By the same token, when the federal government moved to supplement its Head Start program with a "Middle Start" program, sociologists Milton Yinger,

Kiyoshi Ikeda, Frank Laycock, and Stephen Cutler were engaged to study and evaluate the program as it took place (Yinger et al. 1977).

I have discussed evaluation research at this point, since it follows the basic logic of the experimental model. At the same time, you should realize that evaluations often utilize surveys and the other methods to be discussed shortly.

Experiments have both advantages and disadvantages. The primary advantage lies in the researcher's ability to control the variables under study. If you are interested in the effects of a black-history movie on prejudice, the experimental method allows you reliably to rule out the effects of other variables.

The chief disadvantage of the experiment is its artificiality. (Natural experiments are an exception, of course, but they cannot be greatly controlled.) Human behavior is studied under "unnatural" conditions for the purpose of learning about human behavior in general. The persistent danger is that what is learned in the laboratory will not apply in the world outside it.

Let's turn now to what is probably the most popular research method in sociology. If you browse through the research reports in a sociological journal, you'll find that they are based primarily on survey research.

Survey Research

Surveys have a long history if you take into account their similarity to **censuses.** For thousands of years, people have sought to describe and understand populations by asking standardized questions of individual members. A census involves all members of the population. The term "survey," in contrast, typically implies a "sample survey." Using methods we have already discussed in this chapter, a usually large sample (hundreds or thousands) is selected from a population, those in the sample are questioned, and their responses are analyzed for

The telephone has made the collection of some social science data far more feasible than before.

the purpose of describing and understanding the larger population.

We've already discussed survey research several times in this chapter. Public-opinion polling—such as political polls—are a form of survey research. Also, the discussions of probability sampling apply more directly to survey research than do the other methods we're examining.

Survey research is probably the most commonly used research technique in sociology. When Richard H. Wells and J. Steven Picou analyzed articles published in the *American Sociological Review* between 1936 and 1978, they found surveys used in 67 percent of the studies involving empirical research. During the period 1965 to 1978, surveys accounted for 80 percent, indicating an increase in the method's popularity over time (Wells and Picou 1981:115). Let's see some of the elements in this popular method.

The questioning in a survey can take one of two forms. Interviewers may contact the respondents (either face to face or by telephone), read the questions, and record the answers. Or respondents may be asked to read and complete "self-administered" questionnaires.

A variety of information can be collected in surveys. Respondents may be asked to provide routine information about themselves—such as age, sex, race, education, and income—that can be brought together in a composite description of the population. Many surveys tap people's attitudes, opinions, and beliefs. Quite aside from sociological studies, this type of survey research is used in political polling, consumer-product marketing, and other similar endeavors.

Writing good questions for a survey is more complicated than you might think. First, you need to decide what you want to know and in what form. Then, bearing in mind who will be questioned, you must frame your questions so that they are likely to be understood and get the information you need. Survey research is an undertaking in which the "customer" is always right. If a respondent misunderstands a question and gives a useless answer, you lose regardless of how stupid you may feel the respondent is.

Sometimes questions are constructed in an open-ended format. A question is posed and the respondent gives an answer in his or her own words. You might ask, for example, "What do you consider to be the most important problem facing the United States today?" More frequently, perhaps, closed-ended questions are asked. These are questions to which respondents are given a limited number of responses to choose from. Figure 3-4 presents a portion of a questionnaire used in a self-administered survey of medical-school faculty members.

The chief advantage of survey research is uniformity. Hundreds or thousands of people carefully sampled from a population answer the same question. Often the respondents even answer using a uniform set of responses. This uniformity makes it possible to draw general conclusions about the whole population.

The Teaching Physician

Instructions

Either pen or pencil may be used to complete the questionnaire. Please disregard the small numbers and letters next to each question; these are for the use of IBM tabulating machine operators.

In the first section, we would like to learn something about your interests and opinions regarding a number of issues which concern the medical profession in general and medical schools in particular.

Part I. Professional Interests and Opinions

1. While some medical students find it more natural to view each patient as an individual person, others are more likely to perceive him as an example of a disease entity. Do you feel the overall medical school experience at the school where you teach has any effect on the way students ultimately view patients in this regard?

   01 8/a ☐ Yes, it creates a shift toward viewing the patient as an individual person.
       b ☐ Yes, it creates a shift toward viewing the patient as an example of a disease entity.
       c ☐ No, there seems to be no effect.

2. Do you feel medical school training *should* encourage either or both of these views, or do you feel the issue is irrelevant to medical training?

     9/a ☐ It should encourage a view of the patient as an individual person.
       b ☐ It should encourage a view of the patient as an example of a disease entity.
       c ☐ It should encourage both views equally.
       d ☐ The issue is irrelevant to medical training.

3. When students have their first prolonged contacts with particular patients, do you feel there is generally a greater tendency for them to become overly involved with their patients, or a greater tendency to remain overly detached?

   10/a ☐ There is a greater tendency to become overly involved.
      b ☐ There is a greater tendency to remain overly detached.
      c ☐ Both seem to occur about equally.

Figure 3–4   Example of a self-administered questionnaire. Source: Earl Babbie, Science and Morality in Medicine *(Berkeley, Calif.: University of California Press, 1970). Copyright ©1970 by the Regents of the University of California; reprinted by permission of the University of California Press.*

Surveys also have the advantage of being relatively efficient ways for collecting large masses of information, another benefit of standardizing the inquiry. By standardizing the inquiry, however, surveys overlook the subtle varieties of attitudes and conditions that exist for people. The respondent who protests that none of the standardized answers is a satisfactory one presents a problem for survey research. Realize, of course, that this problem is handled by the use of open-ended questions—but at the cost of reduced standardization.

Survey research, like field research and experiments, represents a compromise. Each method I've discussed has its special strengths and weaknesses, as I've tried to illustrate in Figure 3-5. With research methods, as with theoretical points of view, a combination of approaches is more effective than reliance on only one in investigating an aspect of social life.

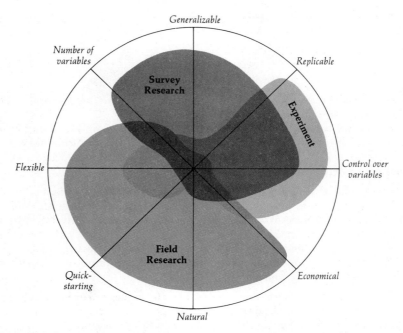

Figure 3–5 An overview of the strengths and weaknesses of three research methods. Terms are defined as follows: "generalizable"—extent to which the results of a specific study can be assumed to apply to social behavior in general; "replicable"—extent to which a specific study can be repeated exactly by another researcher; "control over variables"— degree to which a researcher can determine which specific variables have which effects; "economical"—how inexpensive the method is to use in general; "natural"—extent to which the method offers an observation of social behavior in its natural setting; "quick-starting"—speed with which a study can be designed and launched using the method; "flexible"— extent to which the researcher could modify a research design if appropriate in mid-study; and "number of variables"— the number of variables that can be measured and analyzed effectively in a given study.

Other Modes of Observation

Aside from survey research, field research, and experiments, sociologists sometimes use other techniques of observation. I want to conclude this section by mentioning three of them briefly.

Historical Research   Some sociological research involves examinations of historical records. The earlier discussions of Marx's study of economic forms provide an example. Among other things, you'll recall, Marx concluded that religion was determined by economic structures. Max Weber disagreed.

Without denying that economic factors could and did affect other aspects of society, Weber argued that economic determinism did not explain everything. Indeed, Weber said, economic forms could come from noneconomic ideas. In his research in the sociology of religion, Weber examined the extent to which religious institutions were the *source* of social behavior rather than mere reflections of economic conditions. His most noted statement of this side of the issue is found in *The Protestant Ethic and the Spirit of Capitalism* (1905), and we'll examine that study in Chapter 15.

In arriving at this interpretation of the origins

of capitalism, Weber researched the official doctrines of the early Protestant churches, studied the preachings of Calvin and other church leaders, and examined other relevant historical documents.

In three other studies—originally published in 1934—Weber conducted detailed historical analyses of Judaism (1952) and the religions of China (1951) and India (1958). Among other things, Weber wanted to know why capitalism had not developed in the ancient societies of China, India, and Israel. In none of the three religions did he find any teaching that would have supported the accumulation and reinvestment of wealth so basic to capitalism—strengthening his conclusion about the role of Protestantism in that regard.

Content Analysis Sometimes sociologists study human communications as a way of learning about people (Holsti 1969). They analyze the content of such things as books, newspapers, poems, songs, paintings, and radio broadcasts. To determine the key news issues of the 1960s, for example, G. Ray Funkhouser (1973) pursued two lines of inquiry. In one, he examined public-opinion polls to see what people said were the most important issues for them. In the other, he undertook a content analysis of three major newsmagazines. He selected a sample of issues of each; then he measured the amount of space devoted to different news issues. As it turned out, the two methods produced strikingly similar rankings of issues, headed—as you might have guessed—by the Vietnam War.

Researching Existing Data With the exceptions of content analysis and historical research, so far in this section I've been talking about collecting data that involve direct contact between the researcher and those he or she studies. Sometimes, however, sociologists concentrate on analyzing data that have already been collected by someone else, perhaps for some other purpose. This procedure is called **secondary analysis.** There are three main reasons why sociologists may choose this method of inquiry.

For one thing, no one person or group of persons can do all the basic research necessary to describe whole societies, much less compare whole societies. For instance, in his epic study of human societies, Gerhard Lenski (Lenski and Lenski 1978) was able to bring together masses of data describing hundreds of preliterate and modern societies only by relying on materials initially compiled by others.

Another reason why sociologists sometimes rely on the primary research of others is that the costs of research in terms of money and time can be very great. Suppose that I have conducted a large-scale survey for a particular purpose. I analyze my data and report my results. Quite possibly I will have collected data that would be useful to you in examining some other topic. Rather than conducting a survey of your own—costing both money and time—you can obtain a copy of the data collected in my survey and reanalyze them for your own research purpose (Hyman 1972).

As this secondary analysis has become more popular in sociology and other social sciences, "data libraries" have been established around the nation. Sets of computer cards or magnetic tapes containing the data collected in surveys are filed and stored the same way that books are handled in a conventional library (Nasatir 1967).

The third main reason why sociologists sometimes depend on the research of others is that the people under study may not be available for observation. The classic example of this use of existing sources is Emile Durkheim's (1897) study of suicide. From a painstaking and ingenious analysis of suicide rates in different countries compiled from official government statistics, Durkheim was able to draw conclusions about the motivations of individuals.

The analysis of compiled, government (and other) statistics about a society often takes the form of **social indicators** research. Just as economic indicators tell about the state of economy, a wide range of social indicators—crime rates, hospital admissions, population growth, literacy, educational levels—can tell us about the condition of the society. Sociologists often track such indicators over time, noting trends, and also use such data as the bases for explaining conditions.

These, then, are some of the many facets of sociological observation. I'll conclude the chapter with a discussion of some ways sociologists *analyze* what they observe in their search for understanding.

Data Analysis

With the exception of field research and historical studies, most sociological research involves the collection and analysis of quantitative data, information transformed into numbers. In this concluding section, I want to cover some of the logic and techniques involved in quantitative-data analysis.

Descriptive Analyses

Description is a fundamental purpose of much social research. In data analysis, description involves determining the distribution of attributes that make up a variable. For example, "male" and "female" are attributes making up the variable "sex." And so a population can be described in terms of the numbers of men and women.

Percentages often replace numbers in sociological descriptions. Pursuing the above example, we might simply report that, say, 53 percent of a given population are females.

Averages are also used in description. Rather than reporting the numbers or even percentages of a population who are of particular ages, we might report that the mean age is 24.7 years. To arrive at the mean, we shall add all the individual ages and divide that total by the number of people.

Descriptive analyses are sometimes deceptively simple in appearance. The interpretation of "the simple facts" can make a great difference in conclusions. Here's an example.

In 1964, Daniel Patrick Moynihan, then an official in the Department of Labor, wrote a memorandum called "The Negro Family: The Case for National Action." Among other symptoms of strain on black family life, Moynihan pointed to what he saw as a pattern of matriarchy: husbands and wives had, he asserted, reversed roles within American black families.

At first glance, statistics seem to bear Moynihan out. Consider, for example, the answers black respondents gave to a Gallup-poll question in 1951: "When you were growing up, who was the most important influence on you—your father or your mother?" Of those who answered, 73 percent said that their *mother* was the more important influence. Surely this supports Moynihan's assertions about the matriarchy of the black family. Or does it? That figure—73 percent—takes on a rather different meaning when we discover that virtually the same proportion of whites (69 percent) gave the same response (Hyman and Reed 1969).

This example illustrates a general difficulty: It is hard to know what to make of many statistics unless you have something to compare them with. Let's look at some of the comparisons sociologists make.

Explanatory Analyses

Most sociological analyses of data go beyond description, seeking to explain. Although it might be interesting to know what percentage of a population consider themselves very happy, a sociologist would be more interested in learning what causes happiness and unhappiness. Why are some people happy while others are not?

Subgroup comparisons are an intermediate step between description and explanation. The observation that young people appear happier than old people suggests that something about age is relevant to happiness. From a sociological point of view, we would say that the two variables "age" and "happiness" are related to each other. Particular attributes of one variable are associated with particular attributes of another variable.

Notice that although sociologists may observe people, those people are seen primarily as the "carriers" of attributes, and it is the relationship between the attributes of different variables that we seek to discover in the **explanatory analysis** of data. Thus, we might look for the relationship between age and happiness, religion and prejudice, education and income, and so forth. People in such studies are the units of analysis: they are units that can be described in terms of the variables under study.

How to Read a Table   Explanatory analyses are often presented in the form of percentage tables, as shown in Table 3–1. In order to construct, read, and understand a percentage table, you must recall the earlier distinction made between cause and effect, respectively. Let's look at the sample table to see how it works.

These data are taken from a Gallup poll conducted in April 1978 to learn something about contemporary Americans' values and their hopes for the future. In addition to learning about Americans in general, the researchers wanted to learn about differences among subgroups of the population, such as different age groups. To find out, respondents to the survey were asked whether they would welcome certain changes in values. One of those, presented in Table 3–1, concerned sexual freedom.

Five steps are involved in creating and understanding a table like this one:

1. Identify the independent and dependent variables.

Table 3-1

Example of an Explanatory Analysis

Here is a social change that might occur in coming years. Would you welcome it or not welcome it?

| | Age of respondents | | |
	18–29	30–49	50 and older
More acceptance of sexual freedom:			
Welcome	54%	28%	11%
Not welcome	37	64	79
Don't know	9	8	10
	100%	100%	100%

Source: The Gallup Poll, April 21–24, 1978 as reported in *World Opinion Update* 2, no. 4 (July 1978): 94.

2. Note that the cases have been divided into subgroups based on the independent variable.

3. Describe each of the subgroups in terms of the dependent variable.

4. Compare the subgroups with one another in terms of the dependent variable.

5. Interpret the meaning of those comparisons.

The first step, then, is to identify the independent and dependent variables. In this case, *age* is the independent variable and the *attitude about sexual freedom* is the dependent variable. Put differently, in the causal relationship we are examining, age is the cause and attitude the effect. That is, differences in attitudes could be *caused by* differences in age.

Once we have identified the independent variable, we are ready for the second step: grouping respondents in terms of that variable. In this case, we have separated the survey respondents into age groups: 18–29, 30–49, and 50 and older. Then, the third step is to *describe* each subgroup in terms of the *dependent* variable. In this case, to describe the attitudes of the 18–29-year-old group, we find that 54 percent say they would welcome more sexual freedom, 37 percent would not welcome it, and the remaining 9 percent say they don't know how they would feel. Then we describe the next group: the 30–49-year-old group. Notice that their distribution of responses is different. Finally, we describe the oldest group.

Now we are ready for the fourth step in the explanatory analysis. We compare the distributions of responses given by the subgroups. The easiest way of doing this is to select a particular attribute of the dependent variable and examine its frequency in each subgroup. Looking at the attribute "welcome the change," we see that 54 percent of the 18-to-29 group say they would welcome more sexual freedom, 28 percent of the 30-to-49 group said that, and 11 percent of the oldest group said so.

The fifth step involves interpreting the comparison we have just made. The different subgroups gave different answers, but how would we summarize the difference? A typical way of saying it would be "The young people were *more likely to welcome* a greater acceptance of sexual freedom than were the older ones." Another way of saying it is " Support for sexual freedom decreases with age." That is, as age increases, support for sexual freedom (as indicated in these data, at least) decreases. Still another way of saying it would be "Age and support for sexual freedom are negatively associated with one another."

Explanatory analyses are not limited to two variables, however, and sociologists often engage in more elaborate and complex ones. I don't want to get into anything too complicated at this point, but let me give you an example of a slightly more involved analysis.

Table 3–2 presents an analysis of three variables. In this 1975 survey by the National Opinion Research Center in Chicago, respondents were asked: "If your party nominated a woman for president, would you vote for her if she were qualified for the job?" This attitude,

then, could be a dependent variable that you might want to explain; why might some people say they would vote for a woman candidate while others say they would not? What are some independent variables that might make a difference?

In this instance, the researchers suggested two variables that were worth looking at: sex and education. They expected women to be more supportive than men and educated people more supportive than the uneducated. Table 3–2 shows the data that reflect on both of these possibilities simultaneously. Here's how the table was created: first, the respondents were subdivided in terms of *both* independent variables. Then each subgroup was described in terms of support for the woman candidate. All that done, we can now read and interpret the table.

To simplify the presentation here, notice that I have given you only one attribute of the dependent variable: the percentages that said they *would* be willing to vote for a woman for president. What do these data tell you? First, they confirm the suspicion that increasing education would result in more support for a woman president, since increased education is generally related to more liberal political and social attitudes. As you read across the two rows in the table, you will find that support for the

Table 3-2

A Three-Variable Explanatory Analysis

"If your party nominated a woman for president, would you vote for her if she were qualified for the job?"

	Amount of education received		
	Not a H.S. graduate	*H.S. graduate*	*College graduate*
% yes among:			
Men	70%	83%	91%
Women	64%	82%	88%

Source: E. M. Schreiber, "Education and Change in American Opinions on a Woman for President," *Public Opinion Quarterly* 42, no.2 (Summer 1978): 178.

woman president increases with education among both men and women.

Now here's a surprise. What do the data tell us about the relationship between sex and attitude? Contrary to what you might have guessed, men at each educational level are more willing to vote for a qualified woman as president than are women themselves, though the differences are relatively small. This example illustrates something else about sociological research that we will see again and again throughout this book: things are not always as we expect or assume them to be.

This brief introduction to reading tables is intended to do two things for you. First, it should give you some sense of the logic of explanatory analyses in sociology. And, second, it should give you a beginning ability to read the kinds of tables that will be presented from time to time throughout the text.

Research and Theory

I began this chapter by saying that science involves observing and making sense out of what you observe, and I indicated further that both theory and research addressed these objectives. Though I have covered theory and research in separate chapters, it's important to realize how intertwined the two are in sociological inquiry. Let me give you one illustration of this.

Often, something that makes good sense simply doesn't turn out to be so. This was true when Samuel Stouffer and his colleagues (1949) set out to study morale among soldiers during World War II. Stouffer's group began by considering three factors for testing that might reasonably be expected to affect a soldier's morale. First, the researchers suggested that promotions would surely affect morale—that soldiers serving in units with slow promotion rates would have low morale, and those in units with fast promotion rates would have high morale. Second, they felt that soldiers' educational lev-

els would affect their morale—specifically that those with the most education would resent being drafted, but those with the least education wouldn't be upset by it. Finally, the researchers felt that since segregation and discrimination were still legal in the South and since the lot of black people in the South was far worse than in the North, it stood to reason that black soldiers who were sent to training camps in the North would have higher morale than those kept in the South.

At first glance, these expectations seem so obviously reasonable that you may wonder why the researchers even bothered to test them. But when Stouffer and his colleagues probed these issues, they found each of their predictions wrong.

First, they found that soldiers serving in the Military Police (MPs), which had the slowest promotion rate in the army, were *more* likely to say the promotion system was fair than were those assigned to the Army Air Corps, which had the fastest rate of promotion. Second, soldiers with the *least* education were most likely to say they should have been deferred; those with more education said it was fair for them to be drafted. Finally, there was no difference in the levels of morale of black soldiers in northern and southern training camps.

Among the research team, there must have been a strong temptation to set the findings aside for "further study" later on. After all, the failure to substantiate three expectations that seemed so obviously reasonable could call into question the quality of their research. Stouffer was not one to set such things aside, however. Confident of his ability to observe scientifically, he turned his attention to making sense of his observations. Could he find theoretical grounds for the surprising findings?

Stouffer found the answer to his puzzling observations in work being done by Robert Merton and his colleagues at Columbia University. In their attempt to understand the links between groups and individuals, Merton's group had arrived at the notion of *reference groups:*

Samuel Stouffer
1900–1960
Sac City, Iowa

Some Important Works

The American Soldier (Princeton, N.J.: Princeton University Press, 1949–1950) (4 vols., with various co-authors).

Communism, Conformity, and Civil Liberties (Gloucester, Mass.: Smith, 1963 [1955]).

Social Research to Test Ideas: Selected Writings (New York: Basic Books, 1962).

Probably no one has done more than Sam Stouffer to establish quantitative research methods in modern sociology. Trained as a graduate student in the "Chicago school," Stouffer earned a fellowship in England where he studied under Karl Pearson and R. A. Fisher, the two men most responsible for the development of statistics for use in the social sciences.

Stouffer returned to the United States, where he devoted his career to the use of sociological research in addressing real social problems. His substantive interests included family stability, migration, mass media, and fertility. He is best known for two major research activities. First, he created a research bureau in the U.S. Army during World War II, pulling together a first-rate team of social scientists to do social research in support of the war effort. Second, during the McCarthy era of the 1950s, Stouffer did a major study of mass support for civil liberties in America. All in all, Stouffer exemplifies the best in social inquiry: he was a master puzzle-solver who would have held his own with Sherlock Holmes and Inspector Gideon.

those groups that an individual uses as a barometer for judging how well or poorly he or she is doing in life. As a full professor, for example, I am likely to evaluate my university parking assignment (to go directly to the important stuff) in comparison with the assignments of other full professors—who would, in this instance, constitute my reference group. You, on the other hand, would be likely to judge your parking assignment in comparison with those of other students. You'd thereby decide if yours was a *relatively* good or bad one, and I'd do the same. Looked at logically, the notion of reference groups makes it possible (1) for me to have a better parking assignment than you, (2) for you to feel you had a great assignment, and (3) for me to think I'd been cheated. All this led Merton and his colleagues to speak of *relative deprivation*, as distinguished from one's objective circumstances.

As Stouffer reconsidered the relationship between promotion rate and morale in light of Merton's work, the mystery dissolved. Obviously, the MPs were comparing themselves with other MPs, while the air corpsmen compared themselves with other air corpsmen. If you were an MP, you would receive few if any promotions, but neither would anyone else in your unit. When asked by researchers whether you felt the promotion system was fair, you'd likely respond that it was, since it seemed to treat people equally. If you were an air corpsman, however, no matter how often you had been promoted, you would be able to point to some less deserving person in your unit, who had been promoted faster than you. As a result, you would be likely to say that the system was unfair. The idea of relative deprivation and reference groups made sense of the seemingly nonsensical findings.

In the case of education and attitudes toward being drafted, the same thing happened. Imagine for a minute that you are a newly enrolled college student who gets drafted into the army shortly after the war begins. Although you might not be thrilled at being inducted into the army, you wouldn't feel singled out because all of your friends in college would be suffering the same fate. Asked whether it was fair for you to have been drafted, you'd probably tell the researchers that it was. Now imagine, however, that you dropped out of school before high school and are working in a filling station when Uncle Sam sends his invitation. Who would compose your reference group in this instance? Stouffer suggested that people tend to have friends similar to themselves, especially in terms of characteristics such as educational level. If you had little education, then it was likely that your friends had little education and would probably be working in factories, on farms, or in similar jobs. Now here's the tricky part. In World War II, many young men who were working in factories and on farms were deferred from the draft because their jobs were considered essential to the war effort already. Thus, Stouffer suggested that because young draftees with little education would be likely to have many friends who were deferred, they would tend to feel discriminated against.

Finally, reference-group theory offered the answer to the puzzle of why black soldiers had as high morale in southern training camps as in northern camps, despite the greater discrimination and prejudice against them in the South. In this instance, objective deprivation and relative deprivation seem to have canceled each other out. Here's how the relative deprivation seemed to operate. If you were a black soldier being trained in the South, you were indeed subject to the southern system of segregation and discrimination; but, as a soldier, you would have received a little more respect, better pay, and better living conditions than black civilians in the South. Thus, in comparison with black civilians—your reference group—you would

have been doing relatively well. In the North, with less objective discrimination, you would have been doing *relatively* worse! The black civilians around you would have been working on assembly lines, often earning overtime pay; and, when you spent your weekends slogging in the mud at camp, they would be out enjoying the benefits of the less-segregated North. Thus, you would have found yourself doing *relatively* poorly in the North, as contrasted to doing *relatively* well in the South.

This illustration should give you some idea of the interplay of theory and research in sociological inquiry. Often we make a mistake in seeing these two concerns as separate and unrelated to one another. I'd like you to leave this chapter, however, seeing yourself as someone who approaches social life with the joint and intertwined purposes of observing and making sense of what you observe.

Summary

In this chapter, we have seen the scientific side of sociology, and what distinguishes sociology from more casual observations of social life. First, we say that there are several common mistakes that people make in their observations of the passing scene. Sometimes they simply are inaccurate, sometimes they overgeneralize from what they see, sometimes they see only what they want to see, sometimes they make up information to explain things, and sometimes their reasoning isn't all that logical.

Science offers some protection against these errors. First, science is based on an agreement that observation should be a careful and conscious activity. That cuts out many errors. Second, drawing conclusions is to be equally careful and conscious. That handles a lot of illogical reasoning. Finally, science operates within the context of a commitment to publicness. Everything is to be open and aboveboard so that the mistakes you overlook will be caught by your colleagues.

Another way science differs from everyday inquiry into social events is in its implicit grounding in a deterministic point of view. Explanatory science, if it is to explain the causes of behavior, must assume that behavior is caused and that it is caused by forces over which the actors have little or no control. Thus, whereas you and I live our lives with an experience of free will and choosing from among alternatives, the scientific view suggests that we are determined.

Two fundamental logical models are used in science. The deductive model involves reasoning from general principles to concrete events, as in the framing of hypotheses based on logical theory. Inductive logic, on the other hand, involves the creation of general principles from a mass of concrete observations. Science proceeds through an alternation of deduction and induction.

The research process involves several interrelated operations. "Conceptualization" is the specification and refinement of concepts. "Operationalization" is an extension of this, involving the creation of methods for observing and measuring concepts. "Sampling" has to do with the selection of subjects for study—in such a fashion that what is learned from observing the sample will also tell us something about the population at large.

In addition to scientific concerns of careful observation and logical reasoning, actual research is shaped by nonscientific considerations such as logistics, ethics, and politics. Each of these can rule out certain types of research projects, and the constant challenge of social research is the design and execution of studies that satisfy all these criteria.

Much of the substance of research is to be found in observation or data collection. We saw that there are several popular methods used by sociologists.

Field research involves going to the natural setting in which that which we want to study is happening. Sometimes the field researcher participates as a member of what is happening,

and the term "participant-observation" is often used in reference to such research.

Experiments represent a very different approach to observation. Where field research studies social life in its natural setting, experiments often involved "unnatural" settings, bringing subjects into the laboratory, for example, to be examined under controlled conditions. At the same time, natural experiments study natural events, approximating the control of variables through logical manipulations rather than actually controlling what happens. Also, evaluation research uses the experimental method to assess social programs, particularly to find out if the programs are accomplishing their goals and objectives.

In survey research, data are collected by asking people questions—either through self-administered questionnaires or interviews. Surveys usually reach people in their natural circumstances, though the questioning process is somewhat artificial. Of all the methods examined, however, survey research is the best in terms of accurately describing characterisitcs of a population.

In addition to these three methods of data collection, we looked at some of the ways in which sociologists can study issues through the examination of existing data. All in all, you should have seen that there are many roads to discovery in sociology; and the best inquiry, in fact, is one that takes advantage of several of those roads.

Finally, we have looked at some of the ways in which sociologists analyze the data they collect, relating that to the earlier issue of sociological theory. In that sense, it was my intention for Chapters 2 and 3 of this book to move in a circle. Both theory and research are necessary for a comprehensive understanding of social life.

Important Terms

conceptualization
sampling
field research
experimentation
content analysis
survey research
parsimony
determinism
free will
deductive logic
inductive logic
hypothesis
hypothesis testing
correlations
operational
  definition
representative
  sample

random selection
quota sampling
probability sampling
participant-
  observation
independent variable
dependent variable
experimental group
control group
pretesting
posttesting
evaluation research
censuses
secondary analysis
social indicators
descriptive analysis
explanatory analysis

Suggested Readings

Babbie, Earl
  1983   *The Practice of Social Research*. Belmont, Calif.: Wadsworth.
This lucid, up-to-date, charming, witty, and generally wonderful (you thought maybe I'd say it was lousy?) introduction to the logic and methods of social-science research pursues in more depth the materials covered in this chapter . My intention was to present the basic logic and ideal techniques of sociological inquiry in a context of research realities, showing the compromises that have to be made.

Cole, Stephen
  1976   *The Sociological Method, Second Edition*. Chicago: Rand McNally.
Shows how to apply scientific method in the analysis of human behavior.

Madge, John
  1962   *The Origins of Scientific Sociology*. New York: Free Press.
Madge describes several classic examples of sociological research, representing a variety of methods. In addition to gaining familiarity with the specific studies, you should gain a more comprehensive view of the potential for sociological inquiry. The biographical quality of Madge's presentation makes this a fascinating and engaging book.

Stouffer, Samuel A.
  1962   *Social Research to Test Ideas*. New York: Free Press.
I've suggested this collection of articles by a giant of sociological research for inspirational as well as educational purposes. No one exemplifies the sociologist as detective better than Stouffer. Addressing a variety of research topics, this book illustrates the manner in which a sociologist transforms an interesting idea or puzzling question into a strategy of observation and interpretation.

Wallace, Walter L.
  1971   *The Logic of Science in Sociology*. Chicago: Aldine-Atherton.
This is an excellent presentation of scientific inquiry as a cyclical process involving theories, hypotheses, observations, empirical generalizations, and back to theories. As Wallace demonstrates, scientific inquiry can begin at any point on the circle and goes round and round thereafter. Here's an excellent antidote to the view of science as a routine, lock-step undertaking.

In this chapter, you've gotten your first taste of the mathematics of sociology. From time to time in the book, we'll be looking at some sociological research findings expressed in the form of tables like those I've introduced in this chapter. While this book does not require any extensive mathematical background, I want to talk a little about the problems students sometimes have with this aspect of sociology.

Over the course of teaching research methods which involve at least a small amount of statistics, I've been struck by the very large number of students who report that they are "simply no good at math." To accommodate for this defect, I have increasingly limited the amount and difficulty of statistics to be covered in the course. But no matter how simple the statistics, I've found a large number of students unable to master them—they all report the *congenital math deficiency syndrome* (CMDS). Just as some people are inherently tone-deaf and others unable to learn foreign languages, I've found about 90 percent of the college students I've taught to be suffering from CMDS. Some of its common symptoms are frustration, boredom, and drowsiness. I'm delighted to report that I have finally uncovered a major cause of the disease and have brewed up a cure. In the event that you may be a sufferer, I'd like to share it with you.

You may be familiar with the story of Typhoid Mary, whose real name was Mary Mallon. Mary was a typhoid carrier who died in 1938 in New York. Before her death, she worked as a household cook, moving from household to household, causing ten outbreaks of typhoid fever. Over fifty people caught the disease from her, and three of them died.

The congenital math deficiency syndrome has a similar cause. After an exhaustive search, I've discovered the culprit, whom I'll call Mathematical Marvin, though he has used countless aliases. If you suffer from CMDS, I suspect you've come in contact with him. Here's how you'll recognize him.

Take a minute to recall your years in high school. In particular, I'd like you to recall that person in your class who was generally regarded by your teachers and your classmates as being a "mathematical genius." Getting As in all the math classes was only part of it; often the math genius seemed to know math better than the teachers did.

If you now have that math genius in your class in mind, let me ask you a few questions. First, what was the person's sex? My guess is that he was probably male. Most of the students I've asked in class report that. But let's consider some other characteristics:

1. How athletic was he?
2. Did he wear glasses?
3. How many parties did he get invited to during high school?
4. If he was invited to parties, did anyone ever talk to him?
5. How often did you find yourself envying the math genius, wishing you could trade places with him?

I've been asking students (including some adult classes) these questions for several years, and the answers I've received are amazing. Though the agreement has not been unanimous, a clear profile of Marvin emerges. He is usually unathletic, often either very skinny or overweight. He usually wears glasses, and he seems otherwise rather delicate. During his high school years, he was invited to an average (mean) of 1.2 parties, and nobody talked to him. His complexion was terrible. Finally, I have found almost nobody who ever wanted to change places with him: he was a social misfit, more to be pitied than envied.

If the person you are thinking of squares at all with this description, it seems certain that you've been infected by Mathematical Marvin and rendered mathematically impotent. Beware! Marvin has been known to wear a disguise, and you may have gone to school with him during one of his adventurous periods.

Here's the point of my report on Mathematical Marvin (there *is* a point). As I've discussed Marvin with my students, it has become increasingly clear that most of them have formed a subconscious association between mathematical proficiency and Marvin's unenviable characteristics. Most have formed the conclusion that doing well in math and statistics would turn them into social misfits, and they have regarded that as too high a price to pay.

While I've treated this situation lightly in the preceding discussion, it is no laughing matter for many students. Many are seriously hampered in their career aspirations by what sociologists have called *math anxiety*. In fact, a number of sociological studies have addressed the problem.

Many people have commented on the relationship between gender and math. It shows up, for example, in occupations that require mathematical training. In 1978, only 13 percent of the nation's 83,323 life scientists (biologists, medical researchers, and agricultural scientists) were women (U.S. Bureau of Census 1981a: 9) . Only 8 percent of the nation's 129,918 physical scientists (chemists, physicists, and astronomers) were women (U.S. Bureau of Census 1980b: 7).

Lest you conclude that these differences are biological, social-research findings indicate not. Maccoby and Jacklin (1972) found no significant differences in the math abilities of boys and girls before adolescence. At that point, however, girls begin surpassing boys in verbal abilities and lagging behind in spatial and math abilities.

Sheila Tobias, an expert in this field, suggests that cultural stereotypes excluding women from math may account for women's performances from adolescence on. In one study of elementary math textbooks, two-thirds of the people pictured were boys or men, and the girls and women were frequently shown in insulting situations. For example, a housewife is shown in front of a table bearing a dozen cans. She is scratching her head, and the caption of the drawing reads, " It is hard to tell how many cans are here. How many cans are here?" (Tobias 1978: 85). Tobias continues:

> In another survey of math textbooks published in 1969, not one picture of a girl was found and the arithmetic problems used as examples in the book showed adult women having to ask even their children for help with math, or avoiding the task entirely by saying, "Wait until your father comes home." (Tobias 1978: 87)

Tobias suggests that the adult differences in math ability and participation among men and women result from "math avoidance" by women. She reasons (1978: 78):

1. Each year math gets harder and requires more work and commitment.
2. Both boys and girls are pressured, beginning at age 10, not to excel in areas designated by society as outside their sex-role domain.
3. Girls now have a good excuse to avoid the painful struggle with math; boys don't.

As a result, the stereotype is perpetuated that women are just no good at math, despite powerful evidence to the contrary. Lynn M. Osen's history of *Women in Mathematics* (1974) details both the profound contributions of women throughout the history of mathematics and the often-brutal discrimination women have suffered in that regard. Be clear, however, that both men and women have generally accepted the stereotype. Olsen (1974: *ix*) reports that "Many women in our present culture value mathematical ignorance as if it were a social grace . . ." Many observers have noted that math ability is generally regarded as unfeminine.

Gender is not the only, nor the most powerful factor related to math ability, however. Ethnicity and social class are both more powerful predictors of math ability, according to Lucy Sells (1982). Sells analyzes 1979–1980 data published by the California State Department of Education. While ethnicity is not reported in the original publication, Sells notes that data are presented separately for students fluent in English and in another language, thereby permitting an approximate test of ethnic differences. Sixth-graders fluent in English and an Asian language averaged above the 90th percentile (scoring better than 90 percent of those studied). Those fluent in English and Spanish averaged in the 14th percentile.

These differences are reflected in the racial and ethnic characteristics of America's scientists. Compare the 1978 racial/ethnic composition of America's natural scientists with the 1980 composition of the U.S. population, as shown in Table 3–3.

These data indicate clearly that non-Hispanic whites and Asians are overrepresented among the nation's scientists and that blacks and Hispanics are underrepresented. Why is that the case? Sociological analyses suggest the differences are not racial or ethnic per se.

Table 3-3

Ethnicity and Scientific Occupations

	1978 physical scientists	1978 life scientists	1980 population
White			
Non-Hispanics	92.3%	93.7%	76.8%
Hispanics	1.1	1.2	6.4
Blacks	1.7	1.8	11.7
Asians	4.1	2.3	1.5
Other races	0.6	0.7	3.6

Source: These data are taken from U.S. Bureau of Census 1980a, 1981a, and 1981. "Asians" includes Pacific Islanders in the population data.

The California data analyzed by Sells indicate that social class is an even stronger predictor of math ability. For example, sixth-graders whose parents are executives, professionals, or managers average in the 90th percentile on math ability. By contrast, those whose parents are unemployed or unskilled average in the 10th percentile. Sells concludes that family circumstances are powerful determinants of math ability. In particular, parents' expectations for their children's performance strongly affect teachers' expectations, and both sets of expectations affect the students' actual performance.

As you can see, therefore, mathematical ability is far more complicated than you might have imagined. It's an example of the sort of topic sociologists study, and I hope this presentation may give you some insights into your own situation.

PRACTICING SOCIOLOGY

Here are two percentage tables dealing with voting in the 1980 election. Read both tables and write a paragraph on each, explaining what it tells you. Include suggestions about *why* voting patterns vary with education and income.

	% Who voted	% Who didn't vote
EDUCATION:		
0–8 years	43	57
9–11 years	46	54
12 years	59	41
13–15 years	67	33
16 or more years	80	20
INCOME:		
Under $5,000	39	61
$5,000–$9,999	49	51
$10,000–$14,999	55	45
$15,00–$19,999	60	40
$20,000–$24,999	67	33
$25,000 or more	74	26

Source: U.S. Bureau of Census, *Voting and Registration in the Election of November 1980* (Washington, D.C.: Government Printing Office, 1982), p. 3.

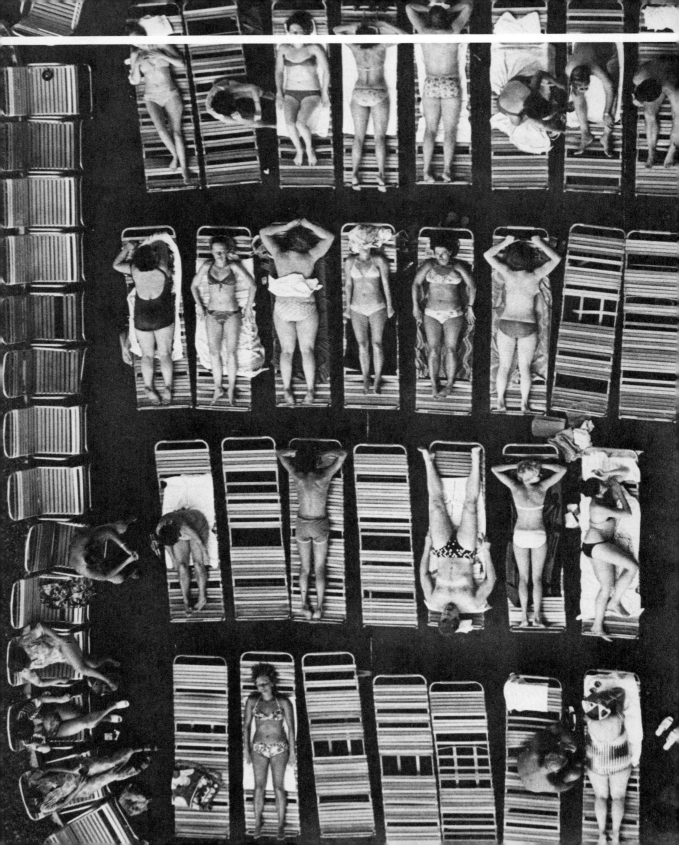

Part Two

The Organization of Social Life

One way of understanding the nature of social life is through an examination of the ways social agreements are created and structured. This also explains why different societies are organized differently.

In Part Two, you'll learn about the elements that make up a society's culture and how individuals come to share that culture.

Culture and Society Culture includes the symbols, beliefs, values, and behavior patterns that the members of a society share. Some cultural patterns are shared across several societies. At the same time, every complex society includes groups of people who share cultural patterns that differ from the main culture of that society.

In this chapter, you'll learn to recognize the various components of culture. You'll see how they relate to one another to integrate life in a society, and you'll also see how conflict is created.

Socialization No one has a culture at birth; it must be learned. Socialization is the process of learning the cultural patterns of a particular society. It has two functions: the society's culture is passed from generation to generation, and individuals learn how to live within their society.

You are going to see several ways in which socialization operates in a society, including the issue of who teaches whom. You'll see how you formed your most fundamental beliefs and values, as well as your conception of who you *are*.

Groups A good deal of human social life centers on groups. Groups control the way individuals behave, and they are also a vehicle for individuals to express themselves and relate to one another.

This chapter will show you the variety of groups people form, and you'll learn some of the things sociologists have discovered about the dynamics of behavior in groups.

Organizations and Institutions Organizations are structured groups, such as corporations, universities, or government agencies. Participants in organizations have specified statuses and roles. Institutions are sets of agreements governing some broad sector of life, such as religion, economy, or government. As such, institutions provide a context within which organizations operate.

In addition to examining organizations and institutions in general, we are going to focus on two organizational forms in some detail. Bureaucracy is an organizational structure that touches many aspects of your life. Voluntary associations are organizations that people create in order to work together in some common purpose, ranging from hobby clubs to social reform organizations.

4

Culture and Society

Throughout Part One, I pointed to a number of ways in which the agreements people make influence how they live together and interact with one another. In this chapter, I want to take a broader view, looking at how the many agreements people share are organized and interrelated so as to provide a comprehensive framework within which social life occurs.

Culture is a general term sociologists, anthropologists, and others use to refer to the whole collection of agreements that the members of a particular society share. It includes all the shared points of view that define what's true and what's good and what kinds of behavior people can expect of one another. To put this another way, culture includes those ways of thinking, feeling, and acting that the members of one society simply take for granted, but which might seem very strange to an outsider.

To get a sense of all I'm including when I speak of culture, I'd like you to do two short exercises. After you've finished reading these instructions, I first want you to close your eyes and imagine a hundred or so prehistoric cavemen and cavewomen, a collection of small, unrelated families. Imagine that none of the families has ever seen other human beings before. They've just been wandering through the forest and the plains looking out for their own survival. In the picture you create, have all the families suddenly converge on the same water hole and discover each other. Notice what happens when they meet. Those are the instructions for the first exercise. Close your eyes for a couple of minutes, do the exercise, notice what goes on when the people meet, and then come back here.

Welcome back. I'm glad you escaped safely. They can be a pretty rough bunch, those human beings. I can't guess exactly what you saw, of course, but there was probably quite a bit of confusion and fear, with possibly some excitement and attempts to communicate as well.

Now for the second exercise I'd like you to look at the people around you or remember the last time you were with a large group of people.

You will probably notice that all the people around you are speaking the same language. They're not just using the same words to stand for the same physical objects, but they're also communicating some pretty complex ideas. Notice the ways they are dressed. Given all the possible states of dress and undress, the similarities you see will probably be greater than the differences. Notice how people meet each other, say "hello," and perhaps shake hands. Think about the things the people around you eat and drink. How do they move around? What do they do for entertainment?

Compared to the picture you had of that sudden meeting at the water hole, the people around you must seem pretty orderly. Given the range of possibilities of ways people *could* behave, the people around you are remarkably similar to one another. The similarities in the ways people around you think and act reflect the fact that they share a common culture.

You are living in a sea of cultural agreements. The fact that you can read this book is a matter of agreements as to the meaning of the words I've used and an agreement that a book is something to keep words in. The fact that you wear clothes when you go out of the house (as well as the kinds of clothes you wear), the fact that you don't punch everybody you see on the street, the fact that you say "hello" to people and ask them how they are even if you don't really care—all these things make up the culture you share with those around you. Many of those agreements seem so natural, so "right," that you probably don't even think about them.

If you reflect, you'll see that there's no obvious reason for the existence of many of the agreements that make up your culture. Why do men wear ties when they dress up, for example? It doesn't make any sense at all if you think about it. To find out how real that agreement is though, try getting into a fancy restaurant without a tie—*if you're a woman, that is.* If you're a woman you don't need a tie, of course. Of course? Why? What sense does *that* make?

Young children frequently regale the adults around them and add to the stock of "family stories" by asking "why" about matters that adults find obvious and don't question. Why can't the family dog eat dinner at the table with the rest of the family? Why can't you tell someone he or she has a funny-looking nose? Why can't you take off all your clothes when it's hot?

Every generation of children draws attention to the discrepancies between the world of direct experience and the agreement reality that has become reified in their society. We laugh at children, however, and they soon learn they can't "belong" until they participate in the reality shared by everyone else. Generation after generation, children give in and learn to take for granted what "everybody knows."

Sociologists are more persistent. We've learned, for example, that what "everybody knows" is one society is very often different from—even contradictory to—what "everybody knows" in another society. Sociologists are unwilling to accept agreement realities as true and obvious.

The sociological view of culture also draws attention to and clarifies the existence of disagreement in any society. Although a society's culture represents the generally agreed-on patterns of living together, some people in any society disagree with some aspects of that culture. They have different points of view. Rather than seeing such differences as weird or antisocial, sociologists look at the ways in which such disagreements can themselves become shared and structured and actually define a separate culture—or *subculture*—within the larger society. A later section of this chapter will focus on subcultures.

This chapter discusses the different aspects of culture that I've mentioned. I'll begin with an overview of the historical or evolutionary development of societal types. This will illustrate a variety of cultures as totalities. Having done that, I'll zero in on some of the separate components of culture. Then we'll take a look at how cultural agreements are organized and related to one another. We'll see that cultures are more than mere "collections" of agreements: they are systematically interwoven so that the "whole" hangs together.

Types of Societies

Throughout this book, I will make references to different forms of societies that exist and have existed. It will be useful for you to have a clear picture of the range of variation at our disposal in that regard, so I want to say a word or two about some broadly different forms now. I will rely heavily on the excellent analyses provided by Gerhard and Jean Lenski in their *Human Societies* (1978). The Lenskis discuss four major types of societies: *hunting and gathering, horticultural, agrarian,* and *industrial.* Let's look at each of them briefly.

Hunting and Gathering Societies

As the Lenskis point out, the hunting and gathering form of society is unique in that it spans the entire history of humankind on the planet. It is the earliest form of societal organization, and there are hunting and gathering societies scattered around the world today: the Pygmies and Bushmen of Africa, the Australian aborigines, and some Eskimos offer living examples of this way of life.

The defining characteristic of this form of society is to be found in its name, indicating the source of sustenance for the society's members as well as the activities in which they spend most of their waking hours. And yet there is more to note about hunters and gatherers. First, they tend to be *nomadic*, moving from place to place in search of things to hunt and gather, abandoning those places that have been picked reasonably clean. This nomadic pattern means that they have few physical possessions, which would slow them down in their search for food.

Both the economic base and the need for mobility place a limit on the size of communities, and the Lenskis report that most contemporary hunting and gathering communities are no larger than twenty-five to forty members. This has implications for other aspects of culture and the experiences individuals have of that culture. Living in a small, preliterate tribe surely supports a greater sense of the links between humans and the rest of nature. Not surprisingly, religious and magical rituals are aimed in that direction. Isolated hunting and gathering societies must be relatively self-sufficient economically; they cannot depend on trading with other communities, though that may occur on occasion.

Kinship, the Lenskis point out, is fundamental in the organization of hunting and gathering societies. Everything is done in families. Family members cooperate in the hunt, and they share food with one another. One's place in the community is importantly a function of kinship. Education occurs in families. Though hunting and gathering societies still exist today, they have been on the decline during the past nine thousand years of human history, yielding to the forms of society we'll examine in the following sections.

Horticultural Societies

Around 7000 B.C., a significant shift in social organization began to occur among communities in the Middle East. Groups who had subsisted through hunting wild animals and gathering wild crops began to settle down. In place of hunting, they began *herding* animals; in place of gathering fruits and vegetables, they began learning the art of *cultivation.* Archaeological evidence points to such horticultural communities in Asia Minor, Palestine, elsewhere in the Middle East, and also in China, Britain, and other points on the globe. It is clearly a stage of development that was independently experienced many times over.

A significant aspect of this shift was the decline of nomadism. People began building and living in permanent and semipermanent houses, instead of in caves and skin tents. Now they could accumulate possessions such as large tools, bowls, and pottery. Larger and denser populations became possible, thereby transforming the nature of social relations. In horticultural communities such as ancient Jericho trade began and trading centers arose.

Another significant difference separating hunting and gathering from horticultural societies was the rise of social inequality and stratification. Although there was a degree of inequality even in the earlier societies (the leader versus the followers), the range of difference was small. Since no one had possessions, for example, there could be no real economic inequality. With more established settlements, with homes and possessions, with herds and gardens, it became possible for some people to do better than others. The Lenskis tell us that two classes arose in Chinese horticultural society, for example: a small warrior nobility and a mass of common people.

Horticultural societies exist today in New Guinea, in the Amazon area of South America, and in various other locations. These living horticultural societies make it possible for us to see other aspects of that stage of social development. Kinship is still important, but kinship systems are more complex, involving more relatives. Ancestor worship tends to be important in horticultural religions. With things to inherit, lineage becomes important. Finally, both the archaeological record and contemporary examples point to the appearance of warfare—essentially unknown among hunting and gathering societies.

Agrarian Societies

With the rise of horticultural society, people had begun to manipulate the environment to make it somewhat more fruitful than it naturally was. Nonetheless, they still seem to have been coaxing and cajoling a nature that was still very much in command of how things turned out. With the appearance of great agrarian societies in Egypt, Mesopotamia, and elsewhere, humans took charge in an unprecedented way. Even though they settled in one place in horticultural societies, they were always prepared to move on—and often they did so—if things didn't turn out. In agrarian society, however, people made a commitment to stay and make the land pay off.

Technological developments abounded in this period. The plow, for example, made a deeper cultivation possible, adding to the kinds of crops that could be grown and fertilizing the soil in the process. In particular, with the invention of irrigation, agriculture became more intensive, more extensive, and more productive. The most significant offshoot of this was that a substantial portion of the population was released from agricultural activities altogether, and a variety of new social statuses arose.

Religion flourished, and with it the advent of priesthoods. Political systems became more complex, and rulers multiplied. As the state grew, leaders sought ever larger empires, and warfare became increasingly important. Armies were needed, and still more people were employed outside of food production. Many crafts arose, and writing was invented and improved. Monetary systems appeared, and social stratification became more pronounced—with the development of ruling and priestly classes.

No development was more important to the evolution of contemporary society than that of occupational specialization, represented in several of the above-mentioned developments. The Lenskis report these examples:

In the larger urban centers, occupational specialization reached a level that surpassed anything achieved in simpler societies. For example, a tax roll for Paris from the year 1313 lists 157 different trades, and tax records from two sections of Barcelona in 1385 indicate a hundred occupations. The clothing industry alone contained such specialized occupations as wool comber, wool spinner, silk spinner (two kinds), headdress maker (seven kinds, including specialists in felt, fur, wool and cotton, flowers, peacock feathers, gold embroidery and pearls, and silk), and girdle maker. Though such specialization could be found only in the largest cities, smaller cities often had forty or fifty different kinds of craftsmen, and even small towns had ten or twenty. In addition to craft specialists, urban centers contained specialists in government, commerce, religion, education, the armed forces, and domestic service. The list should also include specialists engaged in illegal occupations, since they were a normal part of urban life in advanced agrarian societies.*

Industrial Societies

I'll have little to say about modern, industrial societies at this point for a couple of reasons. First, you are already familiar with them, since chances are very good that you have spent most of your life living in one. Second, we will focus on industrial societies throughout the book as we examine various aspects of social life. I trust that the brief descriptions of earlier forms of society will have given you a sense of where we have come from, to better understand where we have come to and perhaps to see where we are headed.

In many ways, our contemporary social forms are extensions of past developments. Stratification systems have grown more complex, and they extend to greater extremes. Occupational and other specialization has certainly continued to grow. Warfare has grown ever more fierce and destructive. And as we'll see throughout the book, industrialized societies have produced issues of their own, unantici-

pated in earlier societies, just as the future may hold developments we do not dream of today. Let's shift our focus now from the historical to the analytical and delineate the components of culture as sociologists see them.

The Components of Culture

Historically, what sorts of things have people of a common culture shared? Sociologists usually subdivide these agreements according to whether they involve symbols, beliefs, values, norms (expectations), sanctions (rewards and punishments), or artifacts. First, we'll explore each of these central components of culture—symbols, beliefs, values, norms, sanctions, and artifacts—and then we'll look at how they are related to one another.

Symbols

One of the most important things that people of a particular culture share is a common set of **symbols.** A "symbol" is a representation of something else that can communicate information in shorthand form. The dove, for example, is a symbol of peace; the cross, a symbol of Christianity. The cross may symbolize Christianity for two people even though they have different feelings about Christianity itself.

Symbols that represent emotion-charged ideas can themselves evoke high emotions. National flags, the swastika, the star of David, and the hammer and sickle can evoke strong positive feelings in some people and strong negative ones in others. There are "dirty words" that titillate some people and horrify others; "dirty names" have the same effect. Racial epithets can spark a riot.

I chose not to give examples of "dirty words" so as not to offend you or other readers. I am less reluctant to say *merde* in this book, however, because I know that most English speakers don't associate *any* meaning with that col-

---

*Gerhard Lenski and Jean Lenski, *Human Societies: An Introduction to Macrosociology* (New York: McGraw-Hill, 1978), p. 194.

Much symbolism is limited to a single culture. This Levi's ad, for example, might not mean much to you. If you were French, however . . .

. . . you'd probably recognize it instantly as a recreation of the well-known (among the French) La Marseillaise sculpture at the Arc de Triomphe de l'Etoile in Paris.

lection of letters, let alone feelings of offense. Some French speakers, however, would be horrified. They would not be particularly offended by the word *kukai*, a Hawaiian word meaning the same thing. The point is that symbols don't mean anything in and of themselves: they symbolize things only by agreement.

As we noted in Chapter 2, a "language" is a symbol system, with words representing objects, actions, feelings, and other aspects of our experience. Because we agree on a symbol system called the English language, it is possible for me to communicate with you through this book.

The language you speak is more a part of your experience of things than you may realize. As Edward Sapir (1960) has suggested, languages both reflect and shape the ways people think, act, and feel.

I'm sure you've already heard about language differences relating to the number of different words Eskimos have for distinguishing among kinds of snow, the number of different kinds of parrots distinguished by some tropical peoples, and so forth. Since the purpose of language is communication, it is not surprising that specific languages will reflect what people have to communicate about. At the same time, however, our languages influence the experiences we want to communicate.

A particularly fascinating view of the impact of language comes from studies of bilingual people. In one such study, S. Ervin-Tripp (1964) interviewed Japanese-American women in both English and Japanese. The interviews, separated by a period of time, were identical in content, but the answers the women gave were different. Asked to complete the sentence "I will probably become . . . ," one respondent replied "housewife" when the interview was conducted in Japanese and "teacher" when it was conducted in English. Similarly, when asked to complete the sentence "When my wishes conflict with my family . . . ," she replied "it is a time of great unhappiness" in the Japanese-language study and "I do what I want" in the English-language study. What can we conclude about the way this woman "really" felt about career and family matters? About all we can conclude is that her feelings depend on the language she was speaking at the time and the culture it represented for her.

Our languages are deeply woven into our experiences of the world. Consider such mainstays of "reality" as time and space. When I mention "time," you probably think of calendars, clocks, years, days, hours, minutes, and seconds. Most Westerners tend to view time as something linear that can be broken into chunks—chunks that can be assigned, scheduled, invested, spent wisely, or wasted. This view of time is not universal, however, as different languages indicate.

Edward Hall (1959) reports that the Sioux Indians have no words for "time," "late," or "waiting." The Sioux, like other American Indians and other peoples around the world, live in the present, doing what they feel is appropriate to the moment. Things happen when they happen and take as long as they take. This orientation to time has contributed to countless conflicts between the Indians and the white American majority.

In a more recent analysis, Stephen Marks (1977) has drawn attention to our fundamental assumption of scarcity in regard to time. For modern Americans, time is a limited quantity—something to "spend," to "save," or to "invest." Such concepts have no meaning for other cultures, such as the Eskimos. However, we can create the *experience* of scarcity, Marks suggests, as "a function of arbitrary cultural agreements and priorities":

> When social institutions in a complex society become segregated from each other (such as modern families and work-places), *then* time becomes experienced as universally scarce, since so many of one's activities will isolate one from so many of one's role partners to whom some time is "owed." (1977:928)

Notions of space, especially what it symbolizes in interpersonal relations, differ from society to society. In his discussion of the "silent language," Hall notes the difference in the ideas of North Americans and Latin Americans about how much distance should separate two participants in a conversation (Hall 1959:164):

> In Latin America the interaction distance is much less than it is in the United States. Indeed, people cannot talk comfortably with one another unless they are very close to the distance that evokes either sexual or hostile feelings in the North American.

Hall recounts episodes in which Latin Americans move close to North Americans in conversation, only to have the North Americans back away. The moving close is misinterpreted as aggressive and the backing away is misinterpreted as cold and unfriendly. The implicit symbolism of interpersonal distance, although deeply ingrained in each, is different in the two cultures. Even the facial expressions that you and I take for granted reflect cultural agreements. Symbols, then, are a part of culture. They represent agreements that are shared by mem-

of the universe is an agreement among millions of people around the world.

All this illustrates a fact about beliefs. Some people have agreed to beliefs that directly contradict the beliefs other people have agreed to. As you look around you, you'll find both agreements and disagreements about what is true.

The beliefs of one culture can seem completely foolish to people of another. During World War II, the American military built airstrips on tiny islands throughout the Pacific in order to facilitate the shipment of men and supplies to the battlefront. Natives of these islands observed the construction of the airstrips and, subsequently, observed the landing of airplanes carrying tons of cargo.

Once the war was over and the troops had left, anthropologists discovered that the natives on many of the tiny islands were building airstrips! Not only that, they expected airplanes to begin arriving with supplies for them. These "cargo cultists," as they came to be known, believed that building airstrips caused great birds to come out of the sky bearing gifts. You may think their belief strange. That's another thing about beliefs: the ones you don't share can seem pretty silly. When the anthropologists told them that the airplanes weren't going to land, the cargo cultists thought the anthropologists were stupid.

Some people believe that the number 7 is lucky and that 13 is unlucky. Some people believe it's bad luck to have a black cat cross your path or to walk under a ladder. Some people believe that Libras and Cancers always spell trouble for each other. Some people believe that peace is better than war. Some people believe that the different races are equal in human value. Another thing about beliefs is that they don't seem at all silly if you happen to share them.

Between 1939 and 1945, approximately 6 million Jews were murdered because members of Adolph Hitler's Third Reich agreed that Jews were inferior human beings who represented a threat to the purity of the Nazi super race. Some beliefs are absolutely dangerous.

Some cultural differences are so great as to be almost inconceivable. How do you suppose these New Guinea islanders include this helicopter in their systems of beliefs? How do you include poltergeists, faith-healing, and time-travel in your set of beliefs?

bers of one society, but that vary across societies. Let's turn to some other components of culture.

Beliefs

Beliefs are agreements about what's true in the world. By definition, beliefs are views that have been reified. Every culture contains many broadly shared statements about what is true, and those beliefs form a foundation for the rest of the culture. Some beliefs are held across cultures.

The belief that a single God exists is shared by Christians, Jews, Muslims, and others around the world. The belief that there is no god also is widely shared. The belief that thousands of gods exist is shared by hundreds of millions of Hindus and others. The belief that "godness" or the godhead pervades all creatures and objects

Values are no casual matter. We are often willing to kill and be killed in defense of our agreements about what's better or worse than something else.

Beliefs, to review, are views about what's true, typically in the form of agreements that people share. People also disagree about what's true. If you agree with a belief, it seems very *real* to you. Beliefs are, by definition, *reified* agreements. As you'll recall from Chapter 1, reification is the process through which people treat as "real" things that are only agreements.

Usually beliefs don't appear in isolation but rather as parts of belief systems. For example, physicists believe that all matter is composed of molecules. They believe that molecules are composed of atoms, and they believe that atoms are composed of electrons, protons, and other subatomic particles. These beliefs exist within

a context of beliefs about electromagnetic attraction, centrifugal and centripetal forces, and countless other related beliefs.

Social beliefs also occur as systems. Communists believe that the excesses of capitalism will generate revolutions among the disgruntled masses. They also believe that revolutions by the masses result in socialist governments and that those socialist governments will eventually "wither away," leaving a classless, communist society.

All of us share agreed-on belief systems. One belief supports another, just as one hand washes the other. As we shall see shortly, moreover, beliefs are linked to other components of culture.

Values

Values are agreements about what's good. Some of the values of American society are freedom, equality, individual achievement, and human dignity. While most Americans agree with these values in a general way, the values themselves do not always mesh with one another. Historically, in our culture, as Seymour Martin Lipset (1963) has pointed out, there has been a conflict between the values of individual achievement and social equality. Some people feel it is better to permit people to achieve the full extent of their potential even though inequalities are inevitably created in the process. Other people prefer that everyone have all the necessities of life rather than allow some people to accumulate more than they need. Thus, the values of achievement and equality are inevitably in tension with one another, since achievement implies the opportunity to be unequal.

In a very general way, conservatives and Republicans in American society have tended to favor the value of achievement over that of equality, whereas liberals and Democrats have favored equality. This is why Democrats are more likely to support programs such as welfare and unemployment benefits, whereas Republicans are more likely to support less regulation for business. Realize this is a gross generalization and does not apply to all Democrats and Republicans. Nonetheless, you'll see evidence of this basic value difference between the two parties in political speeches, Congressional voting, and so forth.

Values influence other aspects of a culture in countless ways. Democracy is based on the value of self-government. Monarchy is based on the value of hereditary leadership. Peace is based on an agreement that it's bad for people to kill each other. War is based on an agreement that it's all right to kill to get what you want. (Notice that you can't have a war unless *both* sides agree to this, even if one side only feels that it's all right to kill to get peace.)

Like beliefs, values are usually no casual matter. Values, by definition, are statements that some things are *better* than others. People are willing to kill over whether democracy is better than monarchy or whether peace is better than war.

Values are often reified, just as other kinds of agreements are. Peoples of any culture tend to believe that the things they think are good are "really" good. If you feel peace is better than war, you probably don't regard this as a simple matter of personal preference. You feel peace is "really" better, and you probably have hundreds of reasons to back up your point of view. That's because values also appear as components in larger systems of values. If you share the values of human life, dignity, and freedom, these values support your view on the value of peace over war.

Values are related to beliefs. As a general rule, values are justified by beliefs. For example, our American value of democracy is often justified by the belief that all people are the equal children of God. For some people, then, the preference for democracy is based on a belief about what's true, and the value seems to flow logically from the belief. Notice that monarchy is sometimes justified by the belief that God has specially chosen the monarch to rule.

Looking at the relationship between beliefs and values from the other direction, we see that values *specify* beliefs. The belief that all people are the equal children of God doesn't, by itself, say anything about what's good or bad. A value specifies what is good if one's belief is true. In this case, the value of equal representation in government specifies the "best" kind of political structure if the belief that all are the equal children of God is true.

Norms

How do norms function as a component of culture? **Norms** are agreements about what is generally expected of members of a particular culture. Norms typically describe the kinds of behavior we expect of one another. In the United States, for example, driving automobiles on the right side of the road is the norm. In England, by contrast, the norm is that automobiles will be driven on the left side. In India, the norm is that people will not kill or eat cattle, while in most countries, beef is eaten freely when available. In poker, the norm is that the person to the left of the dealer bets first, and the betting proceeds in a clockwise direction from there. In Chapter 1 I said you couldn't have games without rules. The rules I talked about were norms.

It sometimes takes some digging to grasp the source and function of specific norms. The Indian prohibition against eating beef, for example, often seems irrational to outsiders. Cattle are allowed to roam untouched in the cities and countryside of India while millions of people starve. Why are cows considered sacred symbols of life in India, and why do so many Indians refrain from eating beef? Anthropologist Marvin Harris (1977) has a theory which accounts for these cultural peculiarities.

Archaeological records indicate that beef was not always taboo in India. As population became denser and arable land grew more scarce, however, agriculture had to become more intensive: it was essential that cows and oxen be available for plowing the fields, or else it was not possible to grow enough food. Harris suggests the cow was made into an object of veneration to remove temptation. If crucial to food production, the cow was also the most readily available food source in times of hunger. By venerating cattle, Indians prevented their slaughtering, and the long-term continuation of the food supply was ensured.

The cultural taboo against slaughtering cattle and the veneration of the cow came not out of some explicit collective agreement, Harris argues, but out of the life experience of millions of individual farmers. The lesson of experience was, and still is, brutally simple: those farmers able to resist the temptation to slaughter their cattle for meat are more likely to survive and pass on their farms to their children than those who can't resist. Harris states the case this way:

> Under the periodic duress of droughts caused by failures of the monsoon rains, the individual farmer's love of cattle translated directly into love of human life, not by symbol but by practice. Cattle had to be treated like human beings because human beings who ate their cattle were one step away from eating each other. To this day, monsoon farmers who yield to temptation and slaughter their cattle seal their doom. They can never plow again even when the rains fall. They must sell their farms and migrate to the cities. (1977: 147)

Whatever their origins, norms fit into the cultural whole of the society in which they exist. Norms are related to values the same way that values are related to beliefs. Values justify norms just as beliefs justify values. For example, the norm that says no one shall drive over 25 miles per hour on neighborhood streets is legitimated by the value of traffic safety, the value of preserving human life. If you were to protest the inappropriateness of the norm to an arresting officer, he or she would probably respond with this justification. From the arresting officer's point of view, by violating the norm, you are violating the value.

Looking at the relationship from the other direction, norms specify values. Neither beliefs nor values say anything directly about how we should behave. Norms specify what we should expect in behavior if what's good is good and what's true is true.

Beliefs legitimate values, which then legitimate norms; and norms specify values, which then specify beliefs. Why are you going to the library tonight instead of going to a movie? Because going to the library is one of the things you are expected to do if you feel education is good. Why do you feel education is good? Because you believe that education will set you free, perhaps, or make you happy or rich. Here's a simple diagram of the relationships among beliefs, values, and norms.

$$\text{BELIEFS} \xleftarrow[\text{Specify}]{\text{Justify}} \text{VALUES} \xleftarrow[\text{Specify}]{\text{Justify}} \text{NORMS}$$

Like beliefs and values, the norms of a given culture can conflict with each other and with the culture's values and beliefs. Countless norms of inequality have persisted alongside the American value of equality throughout our national history. Both formal and informal norms have denied equal treatment to women and to racial and religious minorities. The norms of free speech and free assembly—embodied in the Bill of Rights—have existed side by side with laws making it a crime to "conspire to advocate" certain ideas.

Like beliefs and values, norms can be reified. We begin to think that the ways we've *agreed* people should behave are the ways they "really" *should* behave. If you feel there is "really" something wrong with walking naked down the street, you've reified a norm shared in American culture. Realize, however, that many people around you have reified that norm, so you'd better keep the agreement. What happens when you don't keep your agreements is the topic we'll turn to next.

Sanctions

The existence of a norm specifying how you should behave is not in and of itself enough to ensure that you will behave that way. The elements in a culture that ensure the keeping of these agreements are called **sanctions** by sociologists. There are both positive and negative sanctions: rewards and punishments. Some norms have stronger sanctions than others, and sociologists often try to figure out why.

Sanctions function to teach you the norms of your culture and to ensure that you keep them once you've learned them. Positive sanctions reinforce and encourage behavior that

William Graham Sumner
1840–1910
Paterson, New Jersey

Some Important Works
Folkways: A Study of the Sociological Importance of Usages, Manners, Customs, Mores, and Morals (New York: Dover, 1959 [1906]).
Essays of William Graham Sumner, eds. Albert Keller and Maurice Davie (New Haven: Yale University Press, 1940 [1881–1910]).

Like many of the early American sociologists, sociology was a second career for Sumner, who first served as an Episcopal minister in New York and New Jersey. He shifted to sociology upon his appointment to Yale University in 1872, where he taught for the next thirty-eight years.

In 1899, Sumner set about writing an introductory sociology textbook, based primarily on the lecture notes amassed in ten to fifteen years of teaching. The more he got into writing the text, the more central he found the notion of custom, mores, or—to take the term he coined—"folkways." Finding the notion had not been presented to his satisfaction in the existing literature, he diverted from the textbook to write a separate piece on folkways. It was to become his best-known book.

For Sumner, folkways were to society as habits were to individuals. They were patterns of interaction and structure that built up and persisted over years of coping with social situations. Eventually, they became more reified and coercive. Sumner, therefore, set about studying the ways in which agreements were formed and crystallized.

maintains the norms, and negative sanctions discourage behavior that violates the norms. Praise, displays of affection, and good things to eat are positive sanctions sometimes used in training children in normative behavior. Spanking, scolding, and withdrawal of love are examples of negative sanctions.

Artifacts

Finally, we shall consider the dimension of culture known as **artifacts**—the physical productions of a society. Examples of artifacts include such diverse things as handwoven blankets, pottery, abstract art, musical compositions, high-rise buildings, religious objects, and beer cans.

Beliefs, values, norms, and, sometimes, artifacts—like symbols—both compose culture and reflect it. People transform their physical environment in countless ways, leaving behind traces of their having been there. The ways we transform the environment and the nature of the artifacts we produce reflect the agreements we share. American factories dramatize the contemporary value of efficiency, just as the feathered headdresses speak plainly of the traditional Indian's belief in harmony with nature.

Cultural artifacts are sometimes referred to as the *material culture* of a society. Symbols, beliefs, values, norms, and sanctions constitute the nonmaterial culture.

Ideal and Real Culture

The *ideal culture* of a society comprises its "official" beliefs, values, and norms. Very often, however, this differs from the society's *real culture*. In the United States, for example, we have an official commitment to equality, yet in practice we discriminate against racial and ethnic minorities, the elderly, women, and others.

Another expression of our ideal culture is to be found in the Boy Scout Law. Officially, we would probably agree that we prefer people who are trustworthy, loyal, helpful, friendly, courteous, and so forth. At the same time, contemporary Americans tend to be suspicious of those who seem to be "too" virtuous. In fact, we ridicule those we regard as "holier than thou."

Ethnocentrism and Cultural Relativity

When we reify the agreements that make up our culture, we lose sight of the fact that agreements are only agreements and start thinking they represent some kind of ultimate reality. We tend to see people who disagree with us as more than just different: they seem *wrong*. Sociologists call this tendency **ethnocentrism.**

Ethnocentrism is the reification of one's culture. Extreme ethnocentrism can even blind us to the fact that other people have different agreements; we assume that everyone everywhere must be pretty much like us. When confronted with indisputable evidence that someone disagrees with them, ethnocentric people can experience amusement, concern, or even violent rage. On the one hand, ethnocentrism promotes group identity and solidarity; at the same time, however, it is a source of prejudice, hatred, and war.

Cultural relativism is the opposite of ethnocentrism. It is based on the recognition that different peoples have different sets of agreements. You can drive on the right side of the road in America and recognize that it is ultimately no more correct than driving on the left side. You can value equality over achievement while recognizing that it is ultimately no more valuable than achievement. Sometimes you can step back from your beliefs and see them as merely different from other people's beliefs.

Without a heavy dose of cultural relativism, you might ridicule the seemingly bizarre practices reported by Horace Miner (1956) in his classic analysis of body ritual among the Nacirema. This contemporary tribe, he reports

People do many of the same things in all societies, but their styles differ. Differing styles are a source of ethnocentrism.

(1956:505), has "an almost pathological horror of and fascination with the mouth, the condition of which is believed to have a supernatural influence on all social relationships."

> Were it not for the rituals of the mouth, they believe that their teeth would fall out, their gums bleed, their jaws shrink, their friends desert them, and their lovers reject them. . . .
>
> The daily body ritual performed by everyone includes a mouth-rite [that] consists of inserting a small bundle of hog hairs into the mouth, along with certain magical powders, and then moving the bundle in a highly formalized series of gestures.

Strange as the mouth rite of the Nacirema might seem to you, it makes perfectly good sense to the members of that tribe. Indeed, the high priests associated with the mouth rite—among the wealthiest members of Nacirema society—could probably persuade you of the wisdom of the rite, but only if you could rise above your ethnocentrism and Miner's backward spelling habits (look again at the word "Nacirema" if this comment doesn't make sense).

If I've presented ethnocentrism as a "bad" thing, there's another side to the matter. As we'll see more clearly in Part Three, reification and ethnocentrism can be functional for society. In general, societies survive best when people keep the agreements making up their cultures, and they're more likely to do that if they believe that their points of view are really true, really the best. But as a sociological orientation, cultural relativism is more functional than ethnocentrism because it allows you to seek understanding of cultures different from your own without blinding prejudices.

As we'll now see, a cultural relativist orientation can also help us understand the cultural configurations of our own society.

Subcultures

We have been talking so far about a particular society's culture as if everyone shared its agreements. Such unanimity of belief is of course a rare occurrence, especially in a large society such

Conformity is not limited to any one subculture; agreement within a group is what gives it its special identity, distinct from that of other groups.

as our own. For this reason, when sociologists look at a particular society, they often speak of the society's "dominant culture" in reference to its *generally* shared agreements. But in addition to the dominant culture, any large, complex society is likely to include several **subcultures,** sets of agreements shared by specific subgroups in the society.

During the 1960s, Americans witnessed the rise of a special subculture in their midst: it was often called the "counterculture." Composed mostly of young people (largely college students), this subculture was primarily characterized by social and political attitudes. Its politics were leftist, sometimes revolutionary, with an emphasis on participatory democracy. It was pro-civil rights and antiwar. Socially, the counterculture was permissive on such issues as sex and drugs. In its attitudes, manner of dress, hairstyles, music, and behavior, the counterculture repesented an explicit challenge to the culture of Middle America. While the counterculture generally faded away during the 1970s and 1980s, many of its elements were incorporated into the mainstream culture. Men began wearing their hair "fashionably" longer, for example, and beards became generally popular.

The early 1980s saw the emergence of an American subculture called "preppies," generally representing the opposite of the counterculture. "Black culture," including black jargon, afro haircuts, black heroes, African dress, and so forth, constitutes a subculture in America today. Many American cities have gay subcultures.

Subcultures develop whenever people occupying certain statuses in a society have shared experiences quite different from those of others in the society. Out of these experiences, people create agreements—through interaction—about what is true, good, and expected. Among immigrant groups, subcultures may be a continuation of their earlier cultures. The subculture of Jewish immigrants to America contained the languages, occupational preferences, religious beliefs and practices, food preferences, and family values that had characterized them in Europe before immigration.

Sometimes the experiences shared by members of a subgroup make the dominant culture of their society seem irrelevant or oppressive. For people deeply mired in poverty, for example, the values of education, hard work, and thrift seem grossly inappropriate if they have any meaning at all. What hand one's fork should be held in while cutting one's chateaubriand has little relevance for one who has no meat to eat.

Even though the dominant culture of a complex society often contains elements from its several subcultures, it usually reflects primarily the subculture of a dominant group in it; that is, it often reflects the domination of one subgroup over others, as we discussed in Chapter 2 when we examined conflict theory. The respective groups can be based on economic status, religion, race, ethnicity, or any number of other factors.

The English language, for example, is one of the most widely shared elements of American culture. Its dominance in America was hardly achieved democratically. If we were to trace the ultimate national ancestries of all of today's Americans, we'd find that only about 20 percent of us come originally from purely English-speaking people. English as an element in the dominant culture, then, represents the domination of one subculture over others in America. Similarly, the persistence of capitalism as the dominant economic form through our national history has sometimes involved the suppression, imprisonment, and execution of those Americans who preferred something else.

When sociologists speak of the "dominant" culture in a society, then, you should remember two things. First, the elements of that culture are probably not shared equally by all members of the society. Second, the dominant culture probably represents the domination of one subgroup over others. With these distinctions in mind, let's now look more deeply into the general cultural agreements of a society and how they are related to its social structure.

Culture and Social Structure

An agreement that a primitive tribe's survival depends on hunting is likely to produce a view that the best hunter is the most important person in the tribe. An agreement that the gods intervene in every aspect of the tribe's daily activities suggests that the priest is the most important member of the tribe. Either of these agreements, moreover, would probably produce further agreements on how people should act toward the hunter, the priest, and other members of the tribe.

Sociologists use the term **integration** to refer to the extent to which norms, values, beliefs, and other elements of culture are consistent with one another, and we haven't found a totally integrated culture yet. The extent to which a culture *is* integrated, however, explains why social life is as orderly as it is.

Many of the agreements making up a culture govern behavior by specifying social relationships. As we noted in Chapter 1, social relationships refer to one person's social "locations" in terms of others. Mother-daughter is an example of a social relationship, and every culture contains some agreements about the ways in which mothers and daughters should interact with one another.

Like many cultural agreements in general, the agreements governing interactions in different social relationships are interrelated. The agreements governing mother-daughter interactions are related to the agreements governing father-daughter interactions, for example.

Social structure is a term sociologists use to refer to persistent patterns of social relationships and the interactions expected in those relationships. The term "structure" reflects the organized character of those relationships and interactions.

Social structure is the primary concept that sociologists use to understand the agreements that make up culture. In this section, we'll look at the basic elements of social structure as the sociologist conceives them.

The Concepts of Status and Role

Everything I've said so far seems to indicate that the agreements making up a culture govern the interactions of *people*, but that's not totally accurate. They specify the relationships among social *locations*. People get involved only because

Ralph Linton
1893–1953
Philadelphia, Pennsylvania

Some Important Works
The Study of Man: An Introduction (New York: Appleton, 1936).
The Tree of Culture (New York: Knopf, 1955).

Linton was a cultural anthropologist who had an important influence on anthropology and other social sciences during the second quarter of the twentieth century. At a time when the functionalist perspective was particularly strong in anthropology, Linton kept alive an emphasis on historical development, the part played by individuals, and such factors.

He is most remembered by sociologists for formalizing the terms "status" and "role." A "status" was a social position individuals might occupy—carrying with it certain rights and duties—and "role" was, in Linton's phrase, "the dynamic aspect of status," the behaviors expected of people by virtue of the statuses they occupied.

Sociologists use the term **status** to represent a social location and the term **role** to represent the behavior that cultural agreements prescribe for a status. Ralph Linton, an anthropologist, defined and distinguished status and role this way (1936: 114):

A status, as distinct from the individual who may occupy it, is simply a collection of rights and duties. . . . A *role* represents the dynamic aspects of a status. The individual is socially assigned to a status and occupies it with relation to other statuses. When he puts the rights and duties which constitute the status into effect, he is performing a role.*

Status   A status, then, is a position or a location that a person may occupy. Here are some statuses that are very familiar to you: student, professor, woman, man, old person, tall person, minister, judge, police officer, criminal, Buddhist, employer, Democrat. Any term you might use to describe or identify yourself or someone else is probably the basis for a status.

Some of the statuses you occupy are called **ascribed statuses.** These are statuses that you don't have to "earn." "Female" and "male" are ascribed statuses. Your race and your age are ascribed statuses. Probably your nationality is an ascribed status for you, if you were born into it. Other statuses you occupy are **achieved statuses,** meaning that you have to do something to occupy them. "College student" is an achieved status; so is "professor" and "parent."

It is often a matter of agreement whether a particular status is achieved or ascribed. Take the example of "head of state." "President of the United States" is an achieved status, whereas "queen of England" is ascribed. And, similarly, the relative weight of ascription and achievement can shift over time. Not long ago, a number of occupations in America were very solidly

they occupy those locations. In a sense, there are no cultural agreements specifying how *you* should behave, only how a student should behave, how an American should behave, how a young woman, young man, friend, enemy, son, or daughter should behave. Your behavior is governed by agreements only as you occupy social locations.

*Ralph Linton, *The Study of Man,* © 1936, renewed 1964, p. 114. Reprinted by permission of Prentice-Hall, Inc., Englewood Cliffs, New Jersey.

sex-linked by agreement: police officer, nurse, barber, secretary, engineer, flight attendant. Although no one was born a nurse, for example, men were effectively born "never-nurses." Now these statuses are beginning to lose their ascriptive element, becoming a matter of achievement regardless of sex.

Everybody occupies a large number of statuses. Which of the statuses mentioned in this section do you occupy? Try thinking up some other statuses you occupy. In a sense, your identity—who you are—is the collection of statuses you occupy. I'll have more to say about this in Chapter 5.

As we've already noted, individuals occupy statuses in relation to other statuses. Most statuses directly imply one or more other statuses. "Wife" implies "husband." "Teacher" implies "students." "Pitcher" implies "catcher" and "batter." The fact of relationship makes possible the dynamic aspect of status, which is role.

Role   If your status is a description of who you *are,* the role associated with that status describes what you *do* because of who you are. "Student" is a status. The role of a student is all the things students are expected to do: going to class and to the library, reading, learning, taking examinations, writing papers. Roles are sets of agreed-on expectations we have about the behavior of people who occupy the statuses associated with those roles.

The roles we perform also create points of view. Corporate executives, for example, are expected to earn large profits for their stockholders; union leaders are expected to get large raises and fringe benefits for their members. It is hardly surprising that they bring different points of view to contract talks.

Some of the roles associated with statuses have developed gradually over centuries of interaction. The expectation that restaurant customers will tip waiters and waitresses is a familiar example, as is most etiquette. Other roles are the results of specific agreements by specific people at specific times. For example, when

they drafted the United States Constitution, the founding fathers agreed that if the president of the United States dies in office or resigns, the vice-president should assume the duties of president.

Interestingly, however, the founding fathers did not specify whether the vice-president would occupy the status of "president" or "*acting* president." This issue was still unresolved in 1841, when President William Harrison gave his inaugural speech in the rain, caught pneumonia, and died a month later—becoming the first president to die in office. Harrison's vice-president, John Tyler, to the unhappiness of many, simply declared himself to be the president, not the acting president. His decision was not successfully challenged, and a new agreement was born.

Since people play many roles, they very often experience what sociologists call **role conflict.** The different statuses you occupy frequently demand conflicting behavior of you. Your role as "friend," for example, may involve going to the movies tonight, but your role as "student" may involve studying; and you experience role conflict when your parents expect you to come home for their wedding anniversary the week before finals.

Even when your different roles don't conflict, you may experience what sociologists call **role strain.** A single status that you occupy can carry more role expectations than you seem able to handle. The status "leader" very often produces role strain. So does the status "college student." By the same token, a single status may have conflicting roles. Wives, for example, may have difficulty doing piles of dirty laundry, holding down a regular job, *and* being beautiful, charming, and witty.

Sometimes role conflict can be resolved through compromise: you fly home for the *day* of your parents' anniversary, for example. Often, however, you must choose between one role and another, choosing to keep one set of agreements while violating another. In extreme cases of role conflict or role strain, you may

Sometimes it seems as if more is expected of you than you can possibly deliver. Sociologists refer to this as "role strain."

resolve the situation by choosing to leave the status you occupy. If you find you simply cannot keep all the agreements expected of a college student, for instance, you may drop out. In any case, your performance in one role can affect the other roles you play.

Violating the role associated with a status while still occupying the status can have a variety of consequences. You may find yourself removed from the status against your will. Or you may find yourself trying to change the role associated with that status. This happened in 1955, for example, when a black woman in Alabama chose to violate the agreement that persons occupying the status "black" should give up their seats on the bus to persons occupying the status "white."

Social Organization

From a sociological point of view, the statuses you occupy and the roles associated with those statuses describe who you are, and they have an important effect on what you do. Status and role have another function for sociologists: they make it possible to understand how social interactions are organized. Chapter 7 will examine *organizations* and *institutions* in depth, but I want to introduce you to those concepts here.

Social organizations—a factory, for example—are composed of statuses, and they operate through roles associated with those statuses. "Lathe operator" is a status you might find in a factory, and the role associated with that status describes the ways a lathe operator is expected to behave. The role describes agreements regarding interactions with other lathe operators, foremen, and other statuses in the factory.

Or consider the structuring of families—more specifically, for example, the relationships between husbands and wives. All societies have agreements about how husbands and wives relate to one another, yet they differ from one society to another. In traditional Japanese and Chinese cultures, for example, wives were extremely submissive in their relations with their husbands. Among the Hopi Indians of the American Southwest, just the opposite was true. Wives totally dominated their husbands. Finally, in contemporary, white, middle-class American families, husband-wife relations are more egalitarian. Despite cultural differences such as these, however, you should note that status relations are structured and organized in all societies.

Institutions

We've seen how some social-interaction patterns are woven together into concrete social organizations such as a family or a factory. Some aspects of social life may be seen in terms of more general structures called "institutions." An "institution" is a relatively stable and integrated set of symbols, beliefs, values, norms, roles, and statuses relating to some aspect of social life. "Religion," for example, is an institution that attempts to answer the ultimate questions of existence. A particular church is a social organization composed of statuses and roles, but religion in general is an institution.

A given family is a social organization, but "the family" in general is an institution. A given factory is a social organization, but "the economy" is an institution. Other institutions of interest to sociologists include education, government, medicine, the military, and science. Chapters 13 through 16 examine some of these institutions in detail.

Institutions are important to sociological analysis since they contain systems of beliefs, values, and norms that govern the activities of specific social organizations. Thus, although no two families are exactly the same, the institution of the family in American culture repre-

---

An Overview/Summary of Social Structure

1. A status is a position of social location that you can occupy. It is a place from which to view and participate in social life. It is the basis of your interaction with others and your identification within the group.

Examples: student, professor, mother, plumber, Republican, agnostic.

2. Statuses are linked to one another by roles: the dynamic aspect of status, describing what you are expected to do by virtue of the statuses you occupy. Often, we speak of the linking of statuses by roles as the "relationship" that exists between the statuses.

Examples: Professors are expected to lecture; students are expected to take notes.

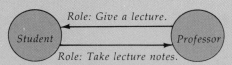

3. A social structure is a persistent set of statuses linked to one another by roles in such a way as to create a new entity in addition to the statuses and roles themselves. Thus, "mother," "father," "son," "daughter," "brother," "sister," "husband," and "wife" are all statuses—connected to one another by role expectations—that constitute a new social whole called "family."

Examples: family, company, team, bureaucracy.

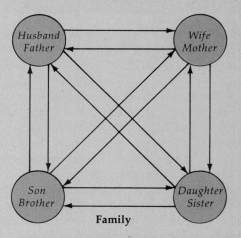

Family

4. A social structure is an *analytical* entity. It is like the blueprint for a house rather than the house itself; it doesn't have any people in it. A concrete social structure with real people in it is an organization. Put differently, a social structure is an organization "in theory," while an organization is a social structure "in practice."

Examples: General Motors, the Smith family, the Harlem Globetrotters.

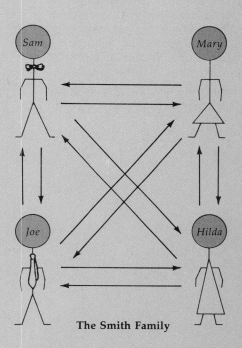

The Smith Family

5. A social structure is a *static* arrangement, a schematic snapshot that freezes a portion of social life in its potential for interaction and life. A social system is a social structure with *process* and *change* added. Thus, a social system is a social structure in action—with component parts changing, affecting one another, and maintaining a relative balance and persistence among those components and for the whole as well.

6. Individuals and organizations are governed in their actions by more than status relationships, however. They operate within an overarching umbrella of agreements that we call culture. Some of the components of culture are:

beliefs	agreements about what's true
values	agreements about what's preferred

$e = mc^2$

norms	agreements about what's expected
sanctions	agreements about the enforcement of the other agreements
symbols	shared representations of things

7. The components of culture come in coherent bunches, moreover. They are organized and linked to one another in systems of mutual support. For example, norms are *justified* by values, which in turn are justified by beliefs.

belief "God created all people with equal worth."

Justification | "It makes sense, therefore, that all citizens should be able to participate in government."

value "Democracy is the preferred form of government."

Justification | "Democracy can work effectively only as long as people actually participate."

norm "Citizens are expected to go to the polls and vote."

8. The corollary to 7 (above) is that (a) norms *specify* the implications of values and (b) values *specify* the implications of beliefs. A belief in and of itself tells us nothing about what's good or expected. A value, however, describes what would be preferred if what the belief says is true were true. The norm, in turn, describes what we ought to do if we hold as preferable that which the value says is preferable.

9. Coherent portions of a culture deal with separate portions of social life. For example, one interconnected set of beliefs, values, norms, and other elements of culture deals with the structure and functioning of family matters. Another set deals with religious affairs. These broad sets of agreements, including those dealing with relevant statuses and roles, are called institutions. The five major institutions that sociologists most often discuss are family, religion, education, economy, and government. Each of these institutions deals with a set of problems that must be handled for social life to persist with reasonable stability.

10. Organizations operate against a contextual backdrop provided by institutions. While most organizations are primarily governed by a particular institution, all institutions have an influence throughout social life.

Examples: The Smith family is an organization structured and operated in accordance with its culture's institutional agreements pertaining to family—for example, agreements having to do with monogamy and with the nuclear family.

General Motors is an organization operating in accord with the prevailing capitalist agreements that make up the American institution of economy.

11. A society is a social system with people living in it, sharing a common culture.

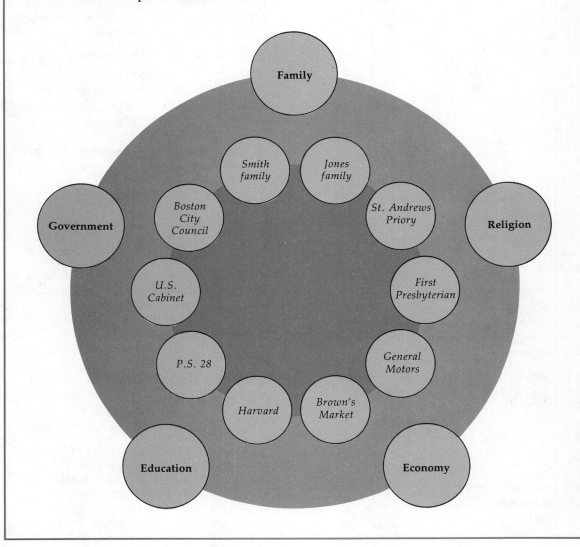

sents broadly shared agreements about what families should be and do. That individual families are expected to provide for the welfare of their young members is a part of family as an institution, even though individual families do this differently and to different degrees.

The preceding discussion of social structure—including roles, statuses, organizations, and institutions—should have expanded your understanding of the *social systems* view that we discussed in Chapter 2. (The box "An Overview/Summary of Social Structure" will help you to review the points we have been making.) Sociologists using that point of view are particularly interested in the functional interrelationships among the different elements of social structure of culture.

These same sociologists help us to see the remarkable persistence of institutions and cultures once they are established. Why cultures persist and how they change (a general interest of those who take the conflict perspective) is the subject of the next section.

Cultural Persistence and Change

In this final section, we're going to look directly at the most fundamental quality of institutions: *persistence*. Similarly, we speak of the culture of a particular society only because that culture persists generation after generation. Then, once you've seen the doggedly persistent quality of culture, we'll shift gears and take a preview of the ways in which it *changes*, a topic that will be examined in more detail in Chapter 20.

Stability in Culture

In discussing the lasting power of cultures, sociologists sometimes use the concept of **institutionalization.** "Institutionalization" is the process by which the agreements people make are organized and perpetuated. Let's look at the

major reasons why institutionalized agreements tend to persist.

One reason cultural agreements tend to persist is because of the force of habit or custom. As the American psychologist and pragmatist William James once suggested, "Habit is . . . the enormous fly-wheel of society, its most precious conservative agent" (1890:121). Through custom and force of habit, some agreements, once established, persist long after the conditions that made them reasonable and functional have disappeared. Other agreements persist through habit and custom even when they have no apparent reason or function at the outset. For instance, when Handel's great *Messiah* was first performed in the mid-eighteenth century in London, the king of England was in attendance. As the rousing "Hallelujah Chorus" began, the king rose to his feet and remained standing throughout the chorus. Nobody has ever figured out why. Evidently, no one thought to ask him, but in eighteenth-century England you didn't remain seated when the king stood up. Everyone in the audience rose and remained standing throughout the "Hallelujah Chorus," and two centuries later people who've never heard that story jump to their feet as soon as the chorus begins.

Institutionalized agreements also tend to persist because they offer a degree of predictability and security in the face of what might otherwise be chaotic and uncertain group existence. Group participation in such agreements, moreover, enhances the warm feelings of belonging and identity. You may have experienced this if you were ever in an audience standing for the "Hallelujah Chorus," and you've probably had other experiences of it, too.

Comfort and security of habit are not the only reasons why institutionalized agreements persist, however. Vested interests exert pressure also. For example, those who profit most from a particular economic system—whether capitalist, socialist, or other—are the most active supporters of its continuation. People who hold political power in a society support the maintenance of the political system that gives them power. To a large degree, then, institutions persist because those who are in the best position to effect changes often have the least interest in doing so.

Another reason why institutionalized agreements persist is that social institutions have been constructed to support their own survival. Institutions such as the family, education, and religion are composed of agreements governing broad areas of social life. For an institution to function, people must know and keep its agreements. Each institution is thus structured to serve the function of **socialization,** which is the teaching and learning of agreements.

As we will see in Chapter 5, socialization is most effective when agreements are **internalized**—that is, when people take agreements inside themselves and make them a part of their personal feelings and sentiments. Internalization, in turn, is most effective when the agreements are reified, when people lose sight of them as merely agreements and regard them as representing reality and truth.

Once the agreements making up an institution have become reified, the die seems cast. Who would consider changing truth or reality? Those who have reified and internalized the agreements during their own socialization within an institution become the socializers of the next generation, and the institution persists.

As we begin to look more closely into the structure and operation of institutions in Part Four of this book, it will become ever more apparent to you that social institutions have been structured to promote their own survival. Actually, the first job of any institution is to perpetuate itself, since it can't do its other jobs if it doesn't survive. The dilemma we'll keep seeing is that the survival needs of the institution very often conflict with the other jobs the institution was designed to handle.

In the struggle for survival, institutions operate through the force of habit, the power of internalization and reification, and the vested interests of those who profit most directly from the institutions. Finally, it will become clear how extensively institutions have been linked to one another so that each institution supports not only its own survival but also that of other institutions. Thus, for example, families send their young off to schools with instructions to behave, the schools teach children that it is important to respect their parents and instill patriotism to the government, which pays the cost of the schools through taxes contributed from families, and so on.

Cultural Change

As important as it is for you to see the remarkable persistence of cultural form, there is always a danger in stressing that aspect. The danger is that you will come to think of culture as fixed and immutable; but, in fact, cultures are always in a state of flux and change (as we'll see in more depth in Chapter 20).

Cultures are constantly in a process of change because people are continually finding new ways of doing things. Take a moment to consider the social changes brought about by the invention of television. How has it affected the communication of news events? How has it changed patterns of entertainment? Look at how differently families now interact. And television is only a single example. Consider the impact of such innovations as writing, inoculations against diseases, the internal-combustion engine, powered flight, and computers. And realize further that a particular culture is changed not only by its own innovations but also by innovations appearing anywhere on the globe—through the process of *diffusion.* In fact, anthropologist Ralph Linton has estimated that 90 percent of the elements of any current culture are a result of diffusion. Here's a sample of what Linton had to say about "The Culture of a Solid American."

Our solid American citizen awakens in a bed built on a pattern which originated in the Near East but which was modified in Northern Europe before it was transmitted to America. He throws back covers made from cotton, domesticated in India, or linen, domesticated in the Near East, or silk, the use of which was discovered in China. All of these materials have been spun and woven by processes invented in the Near East. He slips into his moccasins, invented by the Indians of the Eastern woodlands, and goes to the bathroom, whose fixtures are a mixture of European and American inventions, both of recent date. He takes off his pajamas, a garment invented in India, and washes with soap invented by the ancient Gauls. He then shaves, a masochistic rite which seems to have been derived from either Sumer or ancient Egypt.*

Second, although the persistence and stability of cultural agreements depends on harmony among people, realize that people are not always harmonious with one another. Often they fight. They disagree. And out of their struggles with one another come new agreements. Recall from Chapter 2 that Marx saw the history of society as the result of just such a dialectical process, and you don't need to be a Marxist to see the countless examples of that in your own daily life.

Finally, the environment within which we operate our societies is continually changing, partly on its own and partly by virtue of what we do to it. This constitutes another source of inevitable change. If, as many scientists suggest, we are about to enter another ice age, can you imagine the kinds of changes it is going to produce? Or, on a shorter-term scale, notice the adjustments that have been made to the depletion of various natural resources, to the pollution of the land, air, and water, and to the various other changes we have imposed on the physical environment.

In short, I want to leave you with a paradox. On the one hand, the most salient quality of

culture is its persistence. It is organized to perpetuate itself, and culture would be of no consequence were it not for its persistence and stability. On the other hand, however, we can see that culture never stands still; it is constantly in a state of flux. If you can hold both of those views simultaneously, you are in a good position to continue your examination of social life.

Summary

In this chapter, we have examined the composition and structure of the basic agreements that govern social life: *culture*. The chapter began with a review of social evolution spanning tens of thousands of years, from hunting and gathering societies to horticultural and then agrarian societies, concluding with modern, industrial societies.

Next, we examined some of the components of culture. "Beliefs" are agreements about what is true. "Values" are agreements about what is preferred, and "norms" are agreements about what is expected. "Symbols" are representations that communicate agreed-on meanings. "Languages" are complex symbol systems that both reflect and shape the rest of social life. "Institutions" are sets of interconnected agreements governing some broad area of life, such as family and religion.

"Cultures," then, are the shared systems of meanings and the ways of living that characterize different societies. And different societies do indeed have different cultures. Since people have a tendency to reify their agreements—to hold them as more real than they are—cultural variations are a potential source of puzzlement, conflict, and hostility. "Ethnocentrism" is the view that your group's culture is superior to others, whereas "cultural relativity" refers to a tolerance of other cultures, a recognition that cultures differ without necessarily being better or worse than each other.

Whereas a culture is the shared way of life for a society, most complex societies are made

*Ralph Linton, *The Study of Man*, © 1936, renewed 1964, p. 326. Reprinted by permission of Prentice-Hall, Inc., Englewood Cliffs, New Jersey.

up of subgroups, each sharing a set of subcultural agreements. In the United States, for example, ethnic and racial groups provide illustrations of this, as does the "youth subculture."

The study of culture is, in part, also the study of social culture, and we looked at the many elements of structure. "Statuses" are locations or social positions that people occupy for the purpose of interaction, and "roles" are the agreed-on rules for behavior associated with statuses. Some statuses, called "ascribed statuses," are assigned at your birth; others are achieved.

The linking of statuses by roles creates networks of social relationships. The term "social structure" is used in reference to persistent patterns of social relationships. For example, "family" is a social structure comprising statuses such as "father," "mother," "son," and "daughter" plus the roles describing the kinds of behavior expected to occur between the statuses. Organizations are social structures, fleshed out with real people. Thus, "basketball team" as an analytical concept is an example of social structure, whereas the Harlem Globetrotters team is an organization.

A "social system" is a social structure, with the additional element of process. In a social system, the components are interconnected in such a way as to promote the stability and long-term survival of the whole. Systems are characterized by a balancing of parts in their interactions with one another. Finally, a "society" is a social system with people living in it, sharing a common culture.

For the most part, the chapter focused on the persistence of culture and social structure. As we saw near the end, however, this is but a part of the picture. While persisting, culture is also constantly changing. Sources of change are to be found in innovations, in conflict, and in physical-environmental changes.

In Chapter 5, we are going to return to the individual sometimes lost in extended discussions of social structure and culture. In doing that, however, our attention will be on how individuals fit into groups and—in particular—how they learn where they fit.

Important Terms

culture
symbols
beliefs
values
norm
sanctions
artifacts
subculture
ethnocentrism
cultural relativism
integration

social structure
status
role
ascribed status
achieved status
role conflict
role strain
institutionalization
socialization
internalized

Suggested Readings

Benedict, Ruth
   1961   *Patterns of Culture*. Boston: Houghton Mifflin.
   Benedict uses examples from several societies to describe the effect of culture on social structure and personality.

Freud, Sigmund
   1930   *Civilization and Its Discontents*. Trans. Joan Riviere. Garden City, N.Y.: Doubleday.
   Here's another oldie-but-goodie. Within the context of

psychoanalytic theory, Freud portrays social life as an endlessly unsatisfying struggle between the aggressive and self-destructive drives of individuals and the need for order if society is to exist. The creation and maintenance of order, moreover, frustrates individuals, requires countless renunciations of desires, and produces guilt. Freud did not have a particularly optimistic view of individuals and society.

Harris, Marvin
 1974   *Cows, Pigs, Wars and Witches: The Riddles of Culture.* New York: Vintage Books.
Here's a fascinating trip into some of the seemingly bizarre cultures that people have put together across time and around the world. In addition, the author offers insightful and stimulating ideas about the meaning and sources of puzzling practices.

Harris, Marvin
 1977   *Cannibals and Kings: The Origins of Culture.* New York: Random House.
Uses an ecological perspective to explore origins and evolution of culture, arguing available resources shape characteristics of a culture.

Lenski, Gerhard, and Jean Lenski
 1978   *Human Societies : An Introduction to Macrosociology.* New York: McGraw-Hill.
This is an excellent presentation of the evolution of human societies. Rich in both archaeological and ethnographic data, it offers a valuable supplement to what we know about modern industrial society—plus offering an historical vantage point from which to view where we've come to and who we've become.

Liebow, Elliot
 1967   *Tally's Corner: A Study of Negro Streetcorner Men.* Boston: Little, Brown.
This very readable account of aspects of black subculture in America shows patterns of day-to-day interactions against the backdrop of interrelated subcultural agreements. Liebow's humanistic portrayal of life in the blighted inner city (Washington, D.C.) illustrates one of the ways people create a set of social agreements appropriate to the situation they find themselves in.

Mead, George Herbert
 1934   *Mind, Self, and Society.* Ed. Charles Morris, pp. 227–336. Chicago: University of Chicago Press.
Mead's discussion of society is the classic interactionist statement of institutionalization. Beginning with the social organization of insects, Mead examines the part played by communication, interaction, and self-discovery in the creation and recognition of social institutions. In addition, Mead examines the issue of social conflict and looks at the obstacles to the "ideal society."

Roszak, Theodore
 1969   *The Making of a Counter Culture.* New York: Doubleday.
Growing out of the protest movement of the 1960s, Roszak's examination draws attention to those aspects of contemporary American culture that were the targets of opposition and reform. It highlights a number of fundamental issues regarding human social existence that lie behind particular cultural forms.

Sapir, Edward
 1924   "Culture, Genuine and Spurious." *American Journal of Sociology* 29:401–29.
The sociological view of culture derives largely from the research and writings of anthropologists, since the study of very foreign forms of social life draws attention to the most implicit agreements in our own culture. This classic discussion of culture by a great anthropologist remains insightful and useful for those just approaching sociology today.

Slater, Philip
 1976   *The Pursuit of Loneliness, rev. ed.* Boston: Beacon Press.
Discusses some characteristics of American culture which cause discontent and unhappiness for some individuals.

Weber, Max
 [1925] *The Theory of Social and Economic Organization.* Trans.
 1964   A. M. Henderson, Talcott Parsons, pp. 363–86. New York: Free Press.
In his discussion of "The Routinization of Charisma," Weber expands on a point touched on in this chapter. Some of society's institutionalized agreements have their beginnings in the ideas and actions of special, charismatic leaders. How is it that those agreements are perpetuated long after the death of their originators? This is the question addressed by Weber.

Yankelovich, Daniel
 1981   *The New Rules: Searching for Self-Fulfillment in a World Turned Upside-Down.* New York: Random House.
Yankelovich suggests that a period of economic prosperity allowed Americans to focus their attention on a search for "self-fulfillment," but that problems were created in terms of social relationships. Moreover, later economic conditions require another shift in our culture.

Even acknowledging subcultural differences, people generally have overall pictures of the cultures characterizing the various nations of the world. We have no doubts that the cultures of England, China, and Ghana are quite different from one another.

By the same token, we have images of what the residents of various societies are like—*in general*. Thomas Hartshorne (1971:10) puts the matter this way:

> How often we find ourselves saying or thinking or hearing, "That's just like a Swede," or, "What else would you expect from a German?" We have even arrived at a sort of informal folkloric consensus concerning dominant national traits: Englishmen are staid, Germans militaristic, Frenchmen avaricious and amorous, Italians volatile, Spaniards haughty, the Japanese inscrutable, and so on. And there are many who insist, "There's just something about an American; you can always spot one in a foreign country."

Images such as these are called "stereotypes," and I'm sure you realize they do not have a particularly high standing in science. Such gross generalizations cannot possibly apply to all the millions of people composing a large society. And yet, just as we feel we can give a general characterization of a society's culture, it seems to follow that the members of one society are generally different from the members of another. Thus, while all the English are not staid, that characteristic seems more typical of the English than of other peoples. While they are bothered by stereotyping, social scientists have maintained a fascination with what is called *national character* or *modal personality*.

The study of national character has waxed and waned throughout sociology's history, because there are numerous methodological problems. First, no one has the resources to conduct rigorous, comparative studies of all the world's societies, ranking each in terms of the personality variables that make up national stereotypes. Instead, different scholars study different societies and create their own overall characterizations. And those who try to compare these studies have to remember that different scholars may use quite different standards. Second, the characteristics that make up a national profile are generally impressionistic, rather than based on rigorous data analyses. Finally, national character assessments must be based on only portions of the societies characterized, since any complex society contains great differences among its ethnic, religious, social-class, and age subcultures. Thus, when Geoffrey Gorer (1967) set out to describe English national character, he pointed out that his analysis referred only to the middle and urban working classes.

Quite aside from methodological concerns, national character studies can also set the stage for international bias and discrimination, just as racial stereotypes produce prejudice and discrimination against racial minorities. "Yet," as the eminent sociologist, David Riesman (1967:37), asserts, "something would be lost if the area of inquiry signified by 'national character' were abandoned because of the criticisms which our scientific superegos can bring against its more ambiguous uses."

From some perspectives, national character studies can be seen as profoundly important. During World War II, for example, policymakers in the United States had great difficulty getting a clear picture of how the Japanese would react to various situations. Ruth Benedict, a noted anthropologist, summarized the questions being asked near the end of the war:

> Crises were facing us in quick succession. What would the Japanese do? Was capitulation possible without invasion? Should we bomb the Emper-

or's palace? What could we expect of Japanese prisoners of war? What should we say in our propaganda to Japanese troops and to the Japanese homeland which could save the lives of Americans and lessen Japanese determination to fight to the last man? . . . When peace came, were the Japanese a people who would require perpetual martial law to keep them in order? (1946:3)

Benedict's classic *The Chrysanthemum and the Sword*, based on library research and the interviewing of Japanese Americans and others provided the answers needed by policymakers. When the book was translated into Japanese after the war, it was generally regarded as accurate by the Japanese themselves. Among other things, Benedict explained why captured Japanese soldiers were so willing to cooperate with their captors: from their cultural point of view, they were already dead. Capture cut them off from their society as much as death would have.

Numerous national character studies have been undertaken by sociologists and other social scientists. For example, a special issue of *The Annals of the American Academy of Political and Social Science* (March 1967) provided social scientific assessments of national character in the United States, Canada, Brazil, Mexico, England, France, Sweden, Russia, Israel, India, Japan, and China. In it, Gilberto Freyre (1967:57) reports "the core of Brazilians' character comprises spiritual volition, adventurousness, and poetical vision." Michael Maccoby (1967:67) tells us that "When Mexican intellectuals describe their national character, they almost invariably see themselves as a nation of liars, destructive power-seekers, suffering, resentful women, and boasting predatory men." Reino Virtanen (1967:82) describes the French as "a peasant, artisan, *bourgeois* type of character, sociable but not hospitable, preferring a settled existence, and inclined to fall into routine." The Swedes

have a "strong nationalistic bias," Gösta Carlsson (1967:93) tells us, and they exhibit an "emotional coldness and distance together with stress on achievement and work rather than the warmth of interpersonal relations." These are but a few examples of the conclusions offered in national-character studies. In Chapter 20, we'll see another aspect of this concept. Though a process called "modernization," the cultures of many societies are becoming more and more like each other.

I have pursued the issue of national character in concluding this chapter since it offers a slightly different perspective on culture. The two are merely different sides of the same coin, and the problems of studying one are often found for the other. We'll complete this discussion with a look at some of the research that has been devoted to American national character.

Scholars have been looking at and writing about American character throughout our history. When the French aristocrat, Alexis de Tocqueville visited the new republic during its early years, he recorded his observations in the classic, *Democracy in America* (1835, 1840). He was especially impressed, for example, with Americans' inclination to take charge of the problems that confronted them, organize voluntary groups, and set about solving those problems.

When Robin Williams (1959:338–340) examined contemporary American society, he pointed to the following dominant values:

1. "Achievement" and "success"
2. "Activity" and "work"
3. "Moral orientation"
4. "Humanitarian mores"
5. Efficiency and practicality
6. "Progress"
7. Material comfort
8. Equality
9. Freedom

10. External conformity
11. Science and secular rationality
12. Nationalism-patriotism
13. Democracy
14. Individual personality
15. Racism and related group-superiority themes

	(Rank order)	
	Men	Women
A world at peace	1	1
Family security	2	2
Freedom	3	3
A comfortable life	4	13
Happiness	5	5
Self-respect	6	6
A sense of accomplishment	7	10
Wisdom	8	7
Equality	9	8
National security	10	11
True friendship	11	9
Salvation	12	4
Inner harmony	13	12
Mature love	14	14
A world of beauty	15	15
Social recognition	16	17
Pleasure	17	16
An exciting life	18	18

Williams was careful to point out that not all Americans shared the values he enumerated; certainly the values were not shared equally by all members of the society. His criteria for identifying the "dominant" values included: extensiveness (the proportion of people sharing the value), duration (how long the value had persisted), intensity (seen in the severity of sanctions, for example), and the prestige accorded the "persons, objects, or organizations considered to be bearers of the value" (1959:382–383).

Williams' assessments, like those of other students of American character, were qualitatively derived, based on impressions. In contrast, Milton Rokeach (1973) set out to measure central values quantitatively. In 1968, a national sample of Americans was asked to rank eighteen values with 1 being the most important and 18 the least important of the values listed. Their responses, shown separately for men and women, are shown in the table, next column (adapted from Rokeach, 1973:57).

Except for women rating salvation much higher than men, and men rating a comfortable life much higher than women, their ratings of the eighteen values are strikingly similar.

Data like these offer a picture of Americans' values at a particular point in time. Other scholars have been particularly interested in shifts in those values. David Riesman's classic *The Lonely Crowd* (1953) suggested that individuals in America were shifting from a reliance on their own judgment ("inner-directedness") to a conformist bending to the views of those around them ("other-directedness"). Three decades later,

pollster Daniel Yankelovich (1981) saw another trend expressed in public-opinion data. During the 1960s, Yankelovich reported, a substantial minority among Americans had turned their attention to "self-fulfillment" and realizing their human potential. For some of those, their concern had resulted in a selfishness—a narrow view of "doing their own thing"—which created problems in their relations with their families and others around them.

It is worth noting that both Riesman and Yankelovich saw these shifts in values—shifts in American culture—as being linked to economic factors. For Riesman, the shift from inner- to other-directedness was partly a result of the growth of "service industries" in which more and more people earned their livings by interacting with others instead of by producing physical goods. Other-directedness was also fostered by the permissiveness of the modern, urban family, which gave peer groups and the mass media more impact on young people. In Yankelovich's analysis, the focus on selfish needs and desires was only possible in the expanding economy of the 1960s, becoming less viable during the economic stagnation of the 1970s and 1980s.

My intention in these comments has been to give you a sampling of some concerns scholars have explored and continue to explore in the domain of culture. As you can see, culture is no distant and abstract concept; it is immediate and vital to our daily lives.

PRACTICING SOCIOLOGY

To get a first-hand view of life in a white working-class neighborhood in Washington, D.C., Joseph Howell (1973) moved into a depressed neighborhood on Clay Street. As he got to know his neighbors, he began to see aspects of that subculture generally unknown to academic researchers.

The quotation below is from Howell's interview (1973:277–278) with a twenty-two-year-old mother, Bobbi, married six years to a man whom she describes as usually drinking a six-pack or two of beer on his way home from work, arriving "so drunk he don't know what he's doing." Bobbi feels trapped in her marriage and longs for excitement, like the thrills and excitement her twin sister finds with a motorcycle gang. She notes that the gangs are rough, too.

Like when Denny was killed—that was over a year ago. Well, just this fall, his brother was killed. You might have read about it in the papers. He and a member of another gang were drinking at the same bar, and they were both getting sort of high. Denny's brother is sort of religious. The other guy was saying something like "goddamn," and Denny's brother, he asked him to quit cussing, quit using God's name that way, that he believed in God. And the other guy, he just pulled out a gun and blew Denny's brother's brains out. Killed him right then and said, "If you're so goddamn religious, let's see if *you* rise again in three days." That's what I mean when I say it's sort of rough.

Write a paragraph analyzing the beliefs, values, norms, and sanctions of the Clay Street subculture. Contrast the subculture with mainstream American society.

5

Socialization

William James once described the world of the newborn baby as "a blooming, buzzing confusion." Jean Piaget's extensive observations of newborns seem to support that view, leading him to conclude that "in the first weeks of life the universe is not really cut up into objects, that is, into things conceived as permanent, substantial, external to the self and firm in existence . . ." (1954:5).

It would appear that you and I came into this world making no distinctions between ourselves, our bodies, and the rest of our environment. We apparently experienced an undifferentiated reality in which our own arms, legs, and cries were no less a part of the whole than were walls, cribs, parents, and the sound of a truck passing by. We certainly did not share the symbols, beliefs, values, and norms of those around us—but we learn.

"Socialization" is the process by which people learn the agreements of the group. It has two key functions. First, through socialization individuals gain social identities, their sense of self as discussed by Mead and as reported in Chapter 2 of this book. Second, through socialization a society's agreements are transmitted from one generation to the next.

Since socialization shapes your view of who you *are*, I want to begin the chapter with a discussion of the persistent debate over the effects of heredity and environment in personal development. The remainder of the chapter will examine the environmental influences in more detail.

Socialization and personal development are topics of special interest to psychologists, and we'll look at some psychological theories that have been influential in framing sociological points of view. Socialization is largely a matter of status and role for sociologists, so we'll reexamine these concepts to see how they shape the sociologist's view of socialization. Then we'll look at some mechanisms of socialization and its "agents"—the people and groups who socialize with each other.

For the most part, this chapter focuses on the socialization of children. Socialization is *not* limited to children, however, and later in the chapter we'll look specifically at adult socialization and "resocialization."

The chapter concludes with an examination of the implications of socialization for society. How does it create continuity, harmony, and order, on the one hand, and how does it foster disruption and change, on the other?

Heredity and Environment

One of the oldest debates in the study of human beings has revolved around the relative contributions of hereditary and environmental factors to development. Is a person primarily the reflection of his or her genetic heritage—what he or she was born with—or primarily the reflection of what happens after birth, during the growing-up process? This is sometimes referred to as the "nature-nurture" controversy.

There is truth in both positions, of course. We are inescapably the products of our genetic heritages. Born humans, we cannot simply flap our arms and fly. Many of our characteristics— such as sex, race, and eye color—are determined at the moment of conception. And if we are born male, we simply cannot conceive and bear children of our own. Some aspects of who we are, then, are clearly a function of genetics.

We also possess characteristics that are unquestionably a matter of upbringing rather than biology. You were not born speaking the language you now speak, for example. You were not born feeling the way you do about politics, religion, and sex. Nor did your biological makeup determine how you would turn out in these regards. All these characteristics developed as you grew up and were influenced by your environment. They are a matter of agreements: agreements that were a part of your culture before you were born and agreements that you had a hand in making during your lifetime.

Other aspects of who you are seem to reflect important components of both genetics and environment. Intelligence is a good example.

The interplay of heredity and environment has been demonstrated by studies of IQ-similarity among different pairs of children. A greater IQ-similarity is found, for example, between identical twins (born of the same egg) than between fraternal twins (born at the same time but of different eggs). Even identical twins who were raised apart in different families had greater IQ-similarities than fraternal twins who were raised together. This would point to the influence of genetic factors (Erlenmeyer-Kimling and Jarvik 1963).

Studies of foster children, however, point to the importance of environmental factors. These studies (for example, Erlenmeyer-Kimling and Jarvik 1963, Jones 1946) show IQ-similarities between children and their foster parents, who are biologically unrelated to them. Genetics aside, then, children raised by high-IQ parents tend to have higher IQs than those raised by low-IQ parents. Intelligence can only be a product of *both* heredity and environment.

The question of which personal characteristics are more a matter of genetics and which more a matter of environment is a subject of continuing research, and new discoveries are being made continuously. Most researchers would agree, however, that we are born with certain genetic limitations and potentials, and environmental factors determine the extent to which we realize our potentials. A well-nourished person with "tall" genes, for example, will grow taller than an undernourished person with "tall" genes.

As we turn now to the first function of socialization, the creation of social selves, we'll focus only on environmental factors. The sociological point of view sees who you are as a function of your culture and your experiences within it. Sociologists do not deny the influence of biological factors; they simply deal with the environmental side of the coin.

The Creation of Social Selves

Have you ever thought about how you became the person you feel you are? The sociological answer to this involves your culture and the social experiences you have within that culture.

Introductory sociology and psychology students are often asked to complete an exercise that requires them to give ten or twenty answers to the question: "Who am I?" (Kuhn and McPartland 1954). They give a variety of answers, as you might imagine, and many of their answers are like the following: a student, a woman, a Japanese American, a Jew, an athlete. Take a moment to think about all the answers you might give. I know you can't actually exhaust the possibilities, but you can probably get a sense of what it would be like to do so. You'd have to use all the applicable family statuses you occupy: daughter, sister, niece, aunt, granddaughter, sister-in-law, and so on. All your school and occupational statuses would have to be included: sociology major, junior, honors student, future professor, and so on. Similarly, you'd have to run through all your physical and psychological characteristics: short, cute, blond, youthfully mature, emotionally stable, and so on. All your religious, political, and other beliefs and values would also have to be expressed.

My purpose in asking you to do this exercise is to see if you have a sense of who lies behind all the statuses you might use to describe yourself. You may have a sense of being someone—or just a sense of *being*—that can't be given a descriptive name. For the purpose of this discussion, I want to call that your **self.** Now let's isolate your self a bit more.

Let's suppose that one of the answers you would have given in the exercise was "sociology major." Now imagine that you changed your major—to psychology, let's say. I know that you would still experience yourself as the same self even though you switched your major from sociology to psychology. You would have the

experience of continuity of the same being through that change.

Now let's consider a more drastic change. Let's suppose you had a sex-change operation. You would still experience that continuity of your self. Obviously, if you used to be a man and now you're a woman, that's a bigger change than switching your major from sociology to psychology. Just about every aspect of your life would be changed, yet your inner sense of self would weather the shift. Take a minute now to think back on some of the major changes that have actually happened to you, and you'll see what I mean about a sense of continuity. What you experience as being the same through all those changes is what I mean by your self.

You may recall that we touched on the concept of self in the Chapter 2 discussion of George Herbert Mead's ideas about the creation of mind, self, and society through social interaction. For Mead, however, the self had two aspects: he called them the "I" and the "me." Your "me" represents your social side, you as a social object. The "me" is your collection of social statuses. But Mead recognized that people also experience something more than their statuses, and he used the term "I" to represent your *subjective* side, you as subject rather than object. Mead's "I" represented your experience as a chooser and willful actor in your interactions with others. For purposes of clarity in these discussions, we'll continue using the terms "self" and "status."

Now we're ready to look at how socialization figures into our sense of self. What do you suppose selves do when they get together? Suppose we could somehow isolate your self and my self from all our statuses; what would we do when we got together? It's as impossible to express the answer to that as it is to describe the sense of self that's left over once you've described all the statuses you occupy.

Now let's see how human beings handle the dilemma of what to do when they come together. Suppose you and I are at a party one night, and we happen to meet at the punch bowl. Since it's empty at the time, each of us decides to wait

Your social identity is a product of who others think you are and how you fit into the network of social relationships in society.

Figure 5–1 Two selves and a mask.

Figure 5–2 Two masks confront each other.

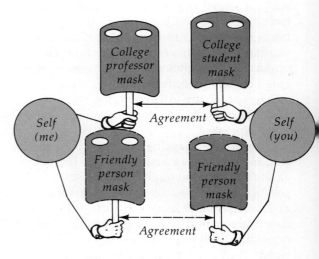

Figure 5–3 The plot thickens.

for it to be refilled. So there we are, two strangers, stranded together at the punch bowl. Each of us takes a sudden interest in fingernails and shoes, and we begin staring at all the other guests but each other. Finally, I can no longer bear the discomfort of just being there with you, so I say "Hi."

Figure 5–1 is a schematic illustration of what has happened: I have thrust a mask in front of myself, concealing my self from yours. The mask is titled "friendly person," the shorthand label I've chosen to represent the kind of person who'd say "hi" to a stranger at a party.

What do you do? Figure 5–2 illustrates your response. Rather than face the discomfort of having your naked self exposed to me, you hold up your own mask. You, too, choose a "friendly person" mask.

What happens next? Probably I would ask that most common party question in Western civilization: "What do you do?" That's consistent with my "friendly person" mask. Suppose you reply, "I'm a college student." Notice that you have now held up another mask. Now I set about rushing through the clothes closet of my mind searching for a mask that would be appropriate to the mask you've just held up. Finally, I locate one. "Hey, what a coincidence! I'm a college professor." Figure 5–3 illustrates where all this has gotten us.

Notice what a relief there is in the process of holding up masks like that. Even the discovery that I'm a professor is better than having to stand there simply being with me. That's because you know something about how professors and students interact. You might not have been able to give much of an answer to the question of what two selves would do if they bumped into each other, but you *know* how to behave with a professor. You should be properly respectful. When the punch bowl is filled, you'd insist that I got some first. You'd hang on my every word, soaking up the wisdom in everything I said. Right?

Suppose our conversation continues. I mention something about growing up in Vermont, and you exclaim, "I used to spend summers in Vermont!" Now we've lifted two more masks, and we know how those masks are supposed to interact with each other. Notice that I just said we know how the *masks* are supposed to interact, because that's really the process I've been describing and diagramming. In an important sense, you and I aren't interacting at all. Rather, we are the puppeteers, maneuvering our masks around in previously prescribed ways. The enduring aspect of human society is, in a sense, the complex set of interconnected agreements prescribing the proper interactions between and among the masks (social statuses) that people hold up to conceal their selves.

You can see this masquerade enacted openly among children. "I'll be the detective and you be the murderer;" or "I'll be the doctor and you be the patient." Once they've agreed on the masks they'll use, the children know how to interact with each other. As they get older, the game changes somewhat. ("I'll be the Grand Inquisitor and you be the religious heretic.") The

In a way, social life is really the interaction of masks that we put on and take off. We can learn a lot about that process from watching children, who aren't as adept at it as we are.

most significant difference is this: the young children know they're playing with masks. Put differently, children are able to occupy social statuses for the purposes of interacting, whereas adults feel obliged to move in and live there.

Socialization is involved in this masquerading in two ways. First, it is the process through which we learn which of the millions of masks we are allowed to use; and, second, it is the process through which we learn the agreements linking masks with one another. When you were very young, for example, you didn't know that college students were supposed to be respectful of their professors. In the remainder of this chapter, we are going to look at the way in which socialization accomplishes these two purposes.

Sigmund Freud

Sigmund Freud (1856–1939) was an Austrian neurologist and physician who is best known as the founder of psychoanalysis (Freud 1909). As Freud probed into the minds of patients who had come to him in search of relief from emotional distress, he became aware of a bizarre mental life previously little noticed. He found that patients had countless thoughts and memories that were hidden below the surface of their conscious awareness. In particular, Freud became interested in those childhood experiences that had been hidden in the dark recesses of what he began calling the "unconsciousness." Increasingly, he found "repressed" sexual desires and fantasies to lie at the base of adult emotional disorders. Unconsciously holding in such feelings resulted in various psychological problems. Making patients aware of those repressed thoughts and memories often alleviated their disturbances. But why, Freud asked, had such thoughts been hidden and repressed in the first place?

Freud eventually came to regard personal development as a struggle between two powerful forces. One of these forces was made up of the pleasure-seeking drives and instincts that all humans share, including the pleasure of being nursed at the mother's breast and other bodily pleasures. Freud referred to this aspect of the individual, representing all the inborn tendencies to seek pleasure, by the term "id."

Set against this inherent tendency to seek pleasure were the demands of society. Freud recognized that societies could not survive if all individuals followed their pleasure-seeking instincts without restraint. Thus, Freud suggested, each individual also had a "superego." The superego was an internalization of all the beliefs, values, and norms that ensure group survival, the result of a process we now know as "socialization."

What Freud (1927, 1930) saw as a continuing combat between the individual and society, he also saw internalized within each person as the id and the superego. Mediating between these powerful forces and influenced by them was the "ego," Freud's term for your sense of who you are. Freud's psychoanalytic theory, then, offers one view of the influence of society in the development of individuals.

Ultimately, Freud's significance for sociology does not hinge much on the specific things he had to say about id, ego, and superego. Rather, he was important in that he opened up a new realm of human existence that was previously concealed. He pointed the way toward an arena that others could probe for answers to the nature of our social selves. Many followed Freud's lead. One of the more prominent was his student Erik Erikson.

Erik Erikson

Erik Erikson (1902–) used Freud's idea as the basis for his own view of eight lifetime developmental stages. In each of the stages the ego faces a crisis (Erikson 1963).

In the first stage of development—in earliest infancy—the child must develop a sense of hope that forms a foundation for all later development. This sense of hope grows out of the basic trust in its parents that the infant may develop. Parental responses to the child can either foster trust or hinder it, promoting a sense of basic mistrust.

In succeeding stages of development, the child may develop a sense of autonomy (versus shame and doubt), initiative (versus guilt), industry (versus inferiority), and in the fifth stage of development, identity (versus role confusion). Erikson says of the fifth stage (1963:261): "The sense of ego identity, then, is the accrued confidence that the inner sameness and continuity prepared in the past are matched by the sameness and continuity of one's meaning for others."

With the onset of adolescence, we pull together the lessons and discoveries of childhood to form a picture of who we are, a picture that we compare with the pictures other people seem to have of us. The fifth stage is a difficult time, since it is also a period of significant physiological and social changes. In this stage we may be thrown into confusion.

The crisis faced during young adulthood, the

sixth stage, in Erikson's view is one of intimacy versus isolation. Having established our *selves* as individuals, we enter into intimate relationships with others or remain apart. Largely, this stage centers on the formation of love relationships, and young adults must balance the risk of being hurt in making a commitment to a relationship against the lonely protection of refusing to make such commitments.

In the next stage, spanning young adulthood and middle age, Erikson speaks of the crisis between generativity versus stagnation. Generativity includes the ideas of productivity and creativity, including the production of new generations of children. At the final stage of old age, Erikson sees a crisis involving ego integrity versus despair. This is a time when a person reviews his or her life and prepares for death. Such a review may produce a sense of value, worth, and kinship with past generations, or it may result in "the feeling that the time is now short, too short for the attempt to start another life and to try out alternative roads to integrity" (1963:269).

Let's turn now to a rather different psychological view of how selves develop. In contrast to the psychoanalytic views of Freud and Erikson, the next one to be examined centers on cognitive development: how children learn the nature of the physical and social reality into which they are born.

Jean Piaget

An internationally renowned child psychologist, Jean Piaget (1896–1980) has spent his career in direct observations of child development.

As I mentioned at the outset of this chapter, according to Piaget's research on newborn babies, we begin life with absolutely no sense of our selves. We begin as observers of a multidimensional motion picture, having no sense of the distinction between the observer and the observed. As Piaget suggests (1954:xii), newborns are ironically "self-centered" for

beings with no sense of self: "It is precisely when the subject is most self-centered that he knows himself the least, and it is to the extent that he discovers himself that he places himself in the universe and constructs it by virtue of that fact."

To find out who you are, then, you must separate yourself from your environment, and Piaget has examined in detail the process through which this occurs. Much of his research centers on the manner in which children learn the nature of physical reality: learning, for example, that objects don't really disappear when they are out of sight. Piaget has examined the series of stages through which children learn such things.

During the first stage of development, children have difficulty learning the concept of individual people separated from their contexts. Children do not automatically equate "Mother in the kitchen" with "Mother in the bedroom." Piaget notes in this regard the trick adults play on young children, saying, "Go up to my room and see if I'm there." Young children often fall for this, not recognizing that the person talking to them is the same one they are being sent to look for.

During the intuitive stage (from two to seven years), children expand their understanding of the physical and social worlds, influenced by their growing ability to communicate with others through language. Increasingly, they experiment with the points of view of others, although they often do so clumsily.

As Foss reports (1973:19):

One of Piaget's earliest and most useful concepts is that of egocentrism in thinking—an inability to see the world from anyone else's point of view. Egocentrism of most kinds extends well beyond the fifth year. A child is asked how many brothers he has. "Two, Paul and Henry." And how many brothers has Paul? "One, Henry."

Eventually, children develop a greater ability to take on the point of view of others, making it possible for them to see themselves the way others would see them. As they become less egocentric, they become able to recognize the existence of the person—themselves—standing behind their own point of view.

George Herbert Mead

Notice how closely Piaget's studies of children mirror George Herbert Mead's theory of self-development as discussed in Chapter 2. We discover ourselves by taking the role of the other, eventually developing a sense of the "generalized other"—how we are seen by other people in general.

Mead was particularly interested in the functions of play and games in the development of social selves in children. In unstructured play, Mead saw children imitating the roles of others around them, acting like their parents or teachers, for example. Organized games, however, took this process one step further.

> The fundamental difference between the game and play is that in the latter, the child must have the attitude of all the others involved in that game. The attitudes of the other players which the participant assumes organize into a sort of unit, and it is that organization which controls the response of the individual. The illustration used was of a person playing baseball. Each one of his own acts is determined by his assumptions of the action of the others who are playing the game. What he does is controlled by his being everyone else on that team, at least in so far as those attitudes affect his own particular response. We get then an "other" which is an organization of the attitudes of those involved in the same process. (Mead 1934:153–154)

Charles Horton Cooley

George Herbert Mead's notion of the generalized other in reference to the development of our awareness of how people regard us was elaborated by one of his colleagues: Charles Horton Cooley (1864–1929). Cooley suggested that

Charles Horton Cooley
1864–1929
Ann Arbor, Michigan

Some Important Works
Social Organization: A Study of the Larger Mind (Glencoe, Ill.: Free Press, 1956 [1909]).
Social Process (Carbondale, Ill.: Southern Illinois Press, 1930 [1926]).

A member of the "Chicago school," Cooley brought a number of wide-ranging interests to his study of society. Like George Herbert Mead, he sought to uncover the links between the working of the human mind and the nature of massive social structures. Like many sociologists before and after him, he was as motivated by a desire to create a better society as he was motivated to understand what existed.

Despite a variety of contributions to the field, Cooley is most remembered for two terms having to do with face-to-face interaction: the "primary group" and the "looking-glass self." In the close-knit "we feelings" of the primary group, Cooley saw a hope for the structuring of humane relations on a broader scale.

those around us—the people who provide the elements that make up our sense of the generalized other—act as mirrors, providing us with a picture of who we are socially. He called what an individual sees in the mirror of the generalized other his or her **looking-glass self:**

A social self . . . might be called the reflected or looking glass self:

"Each to each a looking-glass
Reflects the other that doth pass."

As we see our face, figure and dress in the glass, and are interested in them because they are ours, and pleased or otherwise with them according as they do or do not answer to what we should like them to be; so in imagination we perceive in another's mind some thought of our appearance, manners, aims, deeds, character, friends, and so on, and are variously affected by it.

A self-idea of this sort seems to have three principal elements: the imagination of our appearance to the other person; the imagination of his judgement of that appearance; and some sort of self-feeling, such as pride or mortification. (Cooley 1902:184)

If you imagine that others regard you as beautiful, you come to have that same regard for yourself. If you think others see you as a thief and a scoundrel, you take on that self-image. In this view, then, who you think you are is a matter of who you think other people think you are.

To empirically test this notion of how we develop our self-conceptions, Miyamoto and Dornbusch (1956) undertook a study of the self-conceptions of several groups of college students. Each student in each group was asked to evaluate himself or herself in terms of (1) intelligence, (2) self-confidence, (3) physical attractiveness, and (4) likableness.

Since all the members of a given group (sororities and fraternities) knew each other, every person was also asked to evaluate all the other members of his or her group in terms of the same four characteristics. Then they were asked to guess how their group would evaluate *them*.

The researchers compared individuals' self-images with their perceptions of group evaluations and with the group's actual evaluations. In the majority of cases, students correctly perceived how their group saw them.

Their self-conceptions corresponded closely with the group evaluations as well, thereby supporting the notion of the looking-glass self as a source of self-identity.

In his autobiography (1965) Malcolm X told how, since he got better grades than any of the white students in his class, he had come to regard himself as a bright student. He began thinking he would become a lawyer. To his great disappointment, he found that even a trusted white counselor saw him primarily as a "nigger" and encouraged him to pursue a trade as a carpenter. Malcolm X found his looking-glass self directly contrary to his own growing sense of who he was. Individuals can also rise above their looking-glass selves to shatter and finally reconstruct the images others have of them.

The ideas of generalized other and looking-glass self point to the critical role other people play in your development of a self-image, a sense of who you *are*. At the same time, these ideas can be misleading because they seem to suggest that we are simply products of what others think of us. Actually, none of us has *one* self-image that sums up all that we think we are. As William James (1842-1910) observed, a person has "as many social selves . . . as there are distinct groups of persons about whose opinions he cares" (1890:294). Let's turn now to this more complex state of affairs and the ways in which sociologists view it.

Status, Role, and Identity

From a sociological point of view, then, you might see yourself—your social self, that is— as the collection of statuses you occupy. Recall from Chapter 4, however, that the statuses you occupy have meaning only in terms of other, complementary statuses. You can't be a parent without children, for example, or a teacher without students.

Your social self, in terms of your statuses, is a function of your interactions with people occupying complementary statuses. The peo-

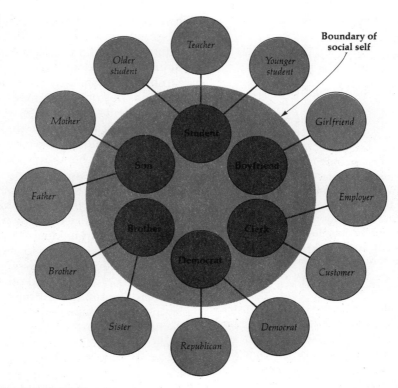

Figure 5–4 A social self as defined by statuses.

ple occupying those statuses constitute count-less looking-glass selves for you. Robert Merton (1957b) has used the term "role set" in reference to those complementary statuses. He defined the term as "that complement of role-relationships in which persons are involved by virtue of occupying a particular social status" (Merton 1957b:110).

Figure 5–4 is a graphic illustration of a person's social self as defined by the statuses that person occupies and the role sets that give those statuses meaning. The small circles represent statuses, while the large circle encloses the set of statuses that constitute the person's social self.

The lines connecting statuses represent the roles that define and condition the interactions between those statuses. If you are a student, there is a set of agreements relating to the interactions between students and teachers. The ways you are expected to behave in interactions with your teacher are also a part of who you are. "You" are a person who is respectful to teachers and obeys their instructions, for example.

Your social self, then, is the social web spun out of the statuses you occupy and the roles you play. Cooley made the case for this point of view in 1902 when he wrote that "individuals" as well as the groups they belong to were "an abstraction unknown to experience." He elaborated on the point as follows:

"Society" and "individuals" do not denote separate phenomena but are simply collective and distributive aspects of the same thing.

. . . Through both the hereditary and the social

factors in his life a man is bound into the whole of which he is a member, and to consider him apart from it is quite as artificial as to consider society apart from individuals. (1902:1–3)

Figure 5–5 presents this sociological view graphically. Despite its apparent complexity, the illustration is grossly oversimplified. One oversimplification is that it presents only a tiny fraction of the statuses and roles that make up the social selves of real individuals. And, for any given status, only a tiny fraction of the complementary statuses forming its role set have been shown.

Another oversimplification is that the agreements describing relations between a pair of statuses are never as explicit and precise as I may have implied. To pursue an example already introduced, you may disagree about students' respecting and obeying teachers. Regardless of how you feel about it, it's clear that not all students and not all teachers share your view. Even when there is a very broadly shared set of agreements about the behavior expected of those occupying a given status, someone who does not share those agreements may choose to violate them. You may disagree with your instructor on the appropriateness of holding all questions until the end of class and choose to violate the agreement by asking one in the middle. Doing this may subject you to negative sanctions, you may end up changing the agreements, or both. The mere fact that you occupy the status of student, then, doesn't totally determine how you behave in relation to others. Other factors complicate matters still further.

In your real-life interactions with other people, it is unlikely that you actually limit your behavior or your expectations of the behavior of others to that appropriate to single, specific pairs of statuses. You are likely to respond to several of the statuses another person occupies, and your actual behavior is likely to reflect many of your own different statuses. When you are sitting in class, you may define your relationship with your instructor as primarily one

of professor and student. If you are a political liberal, however, something your instructor says or does may strike you as politically conservative, and a part of your definition of the situation takes on a political coloring. Something else your instructor says or does may start you thinking: "What does a woman (man) know about that?" When you finally ask a question in class, your feelings and actions may reflect several different status relationships.

Different people occupying the same status have different ways of performing the role associated with that status. Whether you are basically relaxed or tense or whether you are basically quiet or aggressive will affect the "kind" of student you are, how you behave as a student, and ultimately, all the statuses you occupy will affect the way you perform the roles associated with individual statuses.

In summary, then, your social statuses and roles govern your behavior, but not totally. Moreover, the set of statuses you occupy is unique. Although you may share each of your statuses with other people—there are other students, for example—and may have several statuses in common with some people, there is no one else in the world who occupies exactly the same set of statuses that you do. Your statuses make your social identity unique at the same time that they weave you into the cultural whole.

Socialization, then, provides you with a set of identities that allow you to be a part of the whole. Ensuring that you are part of the cultural whole of your society leads to another important function of socialization. I've already mentioned it earlier. Now let's look at it in detail.

The Transmission of Culture

The second major function of socialization is the transmission of culture across generations within a society. In learning those agreements that lie at the base of who you are, you also

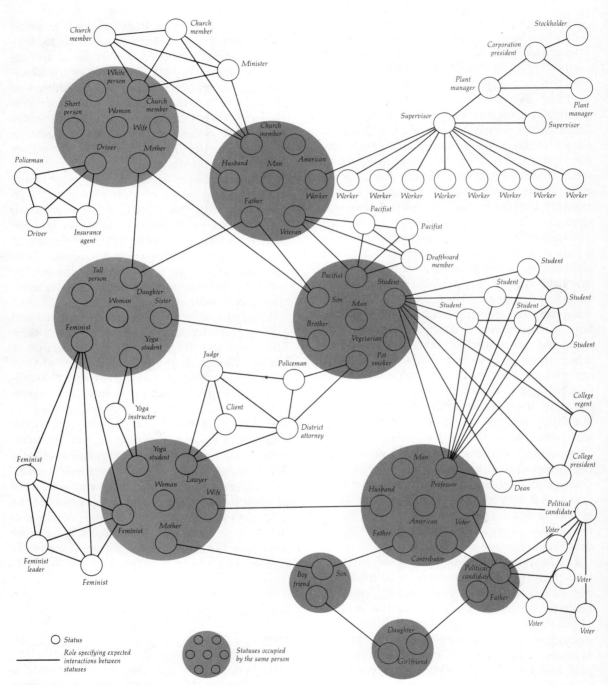

Figure 5–5 A sociological view of the world.

At the same time that socialization provides individuals with social identities, it accomplishes the transmission of agreements from generation to generation.

learn the agreements that make your society what it is.

Socialization, as the transmission of culture, involves a process called **internalization,** as we noted in Chapter 4. The survival of society and the perpetuation of its agreements is more fully assured when the new generation of members takes those agreements within themselves. Typically, this requires the reification of agreements. Children come to feel that the beliefs shared by those around them are really true, the values are really good, and the behavior specified by norms is really proper.

Socialization is most successful when people "feel" the agreements of their society. Suppose you stole something from a store and nobody ever found out about it. Would you feel guilty nonetheless? If you would, that indicates your internalization of the norm against stealing and the value of honesty that lies behind it.

Some aspects of culture are internalized through formalized instruction, but a great deal occurs in an informal, almost unconscious manner. We are going to look at both kinds of socialization in this section. To do that, I want to organize the discussion around the different kinds of agreements that constitute culture—symbols, beliefs, values, and norms.

Symbols

All symbols are a social creation, and they must be learned. Christian children learn the symbolism of the cross, just as children among the Australian aborigines learn to revere their clan's totemic emblem, the witchity-grub. American children learn the national symbolism of the stars and stripes, just as Russian children learn of the hammer and sickle.

The most important set of symbols to be transmitted in any culture, of course, is its language. Like other symbols, language must be learned. No child is born speaking his or her "native" tongue. How this learning occurs, however, is the subject of much current controversy.

In the view of the school of psychologists called "behaviorists," language learning, like socialization in general, takes place entirely through a process called "selective reinforcement." This term simply refers to the use of positive and negative sanctions—rewards for behaving the way your parents or other authority figures want you to behave and punishments for behaving contrarily. As explained by the leading behavioral psychologist B. F. Skinner (1953), we learn to speak by being rewarded (with an approving word, a smile, perhaps a piece of candy) for making sounds that are increasingly like those of the language spoken by people around us.

A radically different view of language learning is offered by linguist Noam Chomsky (1957, 1972). Our language is simply too complicated for anyone to learn totally from scratch, Chomsky and his followers argue. Take a moment, for example, to see how you would go about explaining the significant difference between these two strikingly similar sentences:

Jimmy is eager to please.
Jimmy is easy to please.

Even young children learn and grasp the different meanings without the necessity of lengthy explanations. How can they do that? Chomsky suggests it's because human languages all follow a basic universal grammar and that each of us is born with a genetic facility for it. This position is in striking contrast to conventional social science, yet Chomsky makes a compelling case, one that has had an enormous impact within the discipline of linguistics.

Beliefs

A society's agreed-on beliefs—views about what's real and true—are also learned through socialization. Sometimes children learn the beliefs of those around them by merely observing what they say and how they act. But many beliefs are specifically taught—by parents, peers, teachers, and others. That's how children learn about Santa Claus, the Easter bunny, and the tooth fairy.

Some shared beliefs appear to grow directly out of experience. Young children learn about gravity long before they can be told about it. Every time they get off balance, they have a direct experience of gravity, and they learn a set of behaviors appropriate to it. Only later do they learn about the *concept* of gravity.

Values

In Chapter 4, we noted how agreements about what's good or preferred vary from society to society and how the values of a given society constitute an important part of its special character. Sociologists and anthropologists have found some societies to be basically warlike and others more peaceful. Some, like traditional China, have a special reverence for the past, while others, like the United States, are more oriented to the future. Some societies place religious values above economic ones, and others do just the opposite. Whatever the values of a given society, it is essential to the society's survival that those values be passed from one generation to the next.

Jean Piaget has written (1965), "All morality consists in a system of rules, and the essence of all morality is to be sought for in the respect which the individual acquires for these rules" (p. 13). In his observations of moral learning among children, Piaget concludes there are "two moralities." The first consists of the child's unilateral responsibility to obey adults. Later, however, children adopt a view of morality based more on a sense of cooperation, reflecting a greater degree of individual intention and choice.

Another researcher interested in the moral development of children is Lawrence Kohlberg (Kohlberg and Gilligan 1971). Kohlberg traces six stages. In the first two, "preconventional," stages, children conform to expected behavior, first out of fear of punishment, then out of a recognition that "proper" behavior can be traded for favors. Not until the third stage (around age thirteen among American children) do they begin associating "proper" behavior with general notions of right and wrong, seeing the values that lie behind norms. By stage four, children are learning specific moral rules, such as "It's wrong to lie," completing what Kohlberg calls the "conventional" level of moral development. In the two final, "postconventional," stages, children (becoming young adults) gain insight into some of the moral disagreements around them and, finally, develop some notions of universal values such as justice, human dignity, and human rights.

By posing specific moral problems for children—and asking what's right or wrong—Kohlberg's empirical research has shed light on the development of morality in children and youth. Suppose a man needs money to buy life-saving drugs for his wife and can get the money only by stealing. What should he do? Using typical answers given by American, Chinese, Mexican, Turkish, and other children of different ages, Kohlberg has been able to describe the developmental patterns characterizing different cultures. All the children studied appear to progress through all the sequential stages, however.

Norms

From the beginning of your life, you began learning about the patterns of expected behavior agreed on by those around you. You did this by acting and by observing the consequences of your actions. During the first months of your life, you learned, for example, that crying usually caused someone to come and pick you up. You learned that smiling and cooing when people were around attracted their attention and often resulted in displays of warmth and affection.

As you learned what actions would get you the things you wanted and what actions would get you things you didn't want, you were learning about the role of a baby. You learned how to act the part of a baby, even though you didn't realize it at the time, and the process of role playing has continued and will continue through your life.

As a baby you also observed the ways in which other people behaved, not only in relation to you, but in relating to each other as well. You noticed how your parents behaved, for example. Some psychologists (Bandura 1969) feel that much of socialization takes place through observational learning.

Once you gained sufficient skills in moving around, talking, and manipulating things, you began a process of imitation, reflecting what you observed in the behavior of others around you. You began acting out the same behaviors you witnessed in others, most notably your parents. No one is certain *why* children imitate. Piaget, for example, suggests that imitation is a drive in *all* children, simply a given. Other psychologists disagree.

Whatever the reasons for imitation, it is extremely common in children. A father picks up a hammer and pounds a nail, then sees his young child attempt the same act with no understanding of the purpose of pounding nails. A mother may take her child for a drive in the car only to find the child later sitting on the floor making engine noises and steering an imaginary car.

When imitation takes the form of a child's acting out the role behavior of someone else, sociologists use the term **role taking.** The term derives from Mead's "taking the role of the other," as discussed in Chapter 2. Much role taking involves social interaction, as when children play house or cops and robbers. On the basis of their observations of how adults occupying their various statuses behave, the children interact in ways they feel reflect the "significant" aspects of adult role behavior. Probably every parent has been embarrassed on learning what aspects of his or her behavior children consider significant. Swearing is an example.

Role taking often serves as preparation for actual role playing and is sometimes called **anticipatory socialization.** As children we imitate the behavior of adults we observe, and what we observe and imitate very often carries over into our behavior once we become adults. Historically, the period given over to anticipatory socialization was much shorter than it is today in industrial societies.

Philippe Aries (1962) has pointed out that the children who lived during medieval times in France, for instance, did not go through a long period of anticipatory socialization; instead, they were thrust into the midst of adult life from a very early age. In the medieval period, socialization occurred primarily through the child's active participation in the adult world. Indeed, the whole notion of separate stages of childhood and adolescence as we conceive them did not exist then. From about the age of seven, children were considered adults in miniature. At about that age they were usually sent to live with a relative or to board in a stranger's house to do service as apprentices.

Formal schooling in this period was confined mainly to budding clerics. For most of the population, education occurred through service—working as an apprentice in a printer's shop, for instance, or as a helper in a relative's family. The transmission of culture took place not through formal instruction in the home or school, then, but through practice and through the commingling of children and adults—in the streets, in shops, in taverns and brothels, in workrooms, and in densely populated houses.

The more regulated patterns of socialization familiar to us today began to take shape about the fifteenth century, according to Aries. Religious and other reformers argued that formal education should be extended to the middle classes and that the young should be kept quarantined from what they saw as the corrupting power of adults. At about the same time, parents began to take a new interest in their children's education and in keeping them closer to home. Children began to be viewed as a breed apart, in special need of protection and systematic instruction in becoming civilized. Out of this new relationship between parents and children came a more private and regulated family life, with concern for the child at its center, and a subsequent decline in the vigorous public life of the Middle Ages. With the recognition of childhood, the development of formal schooling, and a more intense and separate family life, the context of our form of socialization was established.

Anticipatory socialization, as it operates today, has many obvious functions. It permits us to grow into statuses gradually by practicing role behavior long before it is expected of us. Observational learning through role taking can also be dysfunctional in that we may not understand the reasons behind what we observe and imitate. Thus, a child may try eating a cigar, having misunderstood why it was put in an adult's mouth.

Sanctions

Aside from observation and role taking, much socialization of norms involves selective reinforcement, which we discussed earlier. Sanctions can take many forms. Positive sanctions, or rewards, include kind words, displays of affection, special treats, money, special privileges, and a variety of other good things. Negative sanctions, or punishments, also vary: angry words, the withdrawal of affection, the withdrawal of privileges and treats, a whole host of unpleasant things.

You can probably recall examples of both rewards and punishments from your own childhood, and both continue to operate in your life today. The grading system for this course, for example, represents a combination of the two.

The kind of socialization sanctions and the relative balance of rewards and punishments vary from culture to culture, as Robert Wernicke (1974:21) describes:

> In many cultures, reward may mean a smile, a hug, an affectionate word; punishment a frown, a spank, a sharp reproof. American parents frequently reinforce good behavior with material gifts such as money or a transistor radio or a TV set for a youngster's bedroom. A favorite punishment is withdrawal of privileges—use of the family car, permission to go to a party. Russians are more apt to withdraw love. A Soviet mother who considers promptness essential may say to her tardy son, "You've disobeyed me again. Now I don't feel like finishing the chess match we began yesterday; I don't even like to look at you."

In Communist China, punishment is considered an ineffective tool for socialization; a young child struggling to draw the elaborate characters of Chinese calligraphy finds that his mistakes are ignored and only his best work is noted. Crow

Indians, on the other hand, emphasize punishment, and behavior the culture finds unacceptable is publicly ridiculed; a whole camp may come alive at night with shouts of derision directed at some unfortunate offender.

Let's turn now to a specific form of role and status socialization, found everywhere around the world.

Sex Typing

Every known culture makes some distinctions regarding the roles expected of men and women. Traditionally in America, boys have been socialized to take on paying occupational statuses, while girls have been socialized primarily for the household statuses "wife" and "mother." And, generally speaking, boys have been encouraged in aggressiveness, while girls have been encouraged to be submissive. Although there have been radical changes in these patterns of socialization in recent years, the old patterns remain strong.

Interestingly, though all cultures make some distinctions between the expected behaviors of men and women, different cultures differ greatly in the distinctions they make. Among the Tchambuli tribe of New Guinea, the kinds of behavior expected of men and women are just about the opposite of what has traditionally been expected of men and women in America. Women are dominant, impersonal, and aggressive, whereas men are more submissive and emotionally dependent. Margaret Mead, who studied (1935) the Tchambuli, also studied the Mundugumor tribe and found both men and women to be dominant, impersonal and aggressive. Among the Arapesh, the third tribe studied by Mead, both men and women were submissive and dependent.

Although differences exist across cultures in sex-typed socialization, a few patterns appear to be common, as an examination of child-rearing practices in 100 preliterate cultures shows

Margaret Mead
1901–1978
Philadelphia, Pennsylvania

Some Important Works
Sex and Temperament in Three Primitive Societies (New York: Morrow, 1935).
Coming of Age in Samoa (New York: Morrow, 1928).

Probably the best-known cultural anthropologist in the United States, Margaret Mead's examinations of social life reached from preliterate societies of Oceania to modern, complex society. Many of her earliest studies focused on the process and problems of growing up—"coming of age." Her very popular books on life in preliterate societies drew attention to the fact that established, Western patterns were but one set of alternative social forms, and throughout her life she was an enemy of reification and stagnation. In her later years, when she could have rested comfortably on her accomplishments, she argued for alternative forms of marriage that she felt were more appropriate to the times in which we live.

(Barry, Bacon, and Child 1955). In those cultures where data were available on training for "nurturance," the quality of being helpful toward younger brothers and sisters and other dependent people, 82 percent taught nurturance primarily to girls. The remainder taught it equally to boys and girls. None taught nurturance primarily to boys. In 85 percent of the cultures, as another example, the value of "self-reliance" was taught primarily to boys, 15 percent taught the value equally to both boys and girls, and none taught it primarily to girls.

Sex-typing has received increased popular interest in America in the context of women's liberation. In Chapter 10, we'll return to this issue and see some of the many ways children are taught that being male is superior to being female.

Agents of Socialization

We have been examining the manner in which a young child is shaped according to the dictates of other people. The child's beliefs, values, behavior, and even self-identity, we have seen, are largely a function of what *others* believe, value, expect in the way of behavior, and see as the child's identity.

Who are those "other people" who wield such an influence over you from the time you are born? Who tells you what to believe and value, how to behave, and who you are? The accurate, though perhaps unsatisfactory, answer is "everybody around you."

Some people seem to have more influence than others, however. Sociologists often use the term "significant others" in reference to those people whose opinion you value. Clearly, your significant others are vitally influential in your socialization. At the same time, certain general classes of people have special influence in the socialization process, and we call them "agents" of socialization. Let's look briefly at four important agents for socializing children: family, peers, schools, and the mass media.

Family as Socializers

The members of your family surely had the earliest influence on your socialization. (By "family," I mean the people who brought you up,

even if they weren't your biological mother and father.) That's not surprising since you spent most of your time with them and were dependent on them for your survival.

Whatever your family's religious beliefs, they probably became yours when you were young. Whatever their language or dialect, it became yours. You learned and shared in their racial prejudices or their lack of prejudices. You learned their version of what love is and how to express it. However much your beliefs and values may now differ from those of your family, you will never totally escape what you learned at home as a child.

Peers as Socializers

Your **peers** are people who are like you. They are people who occupy the same statuses you do. If you are a college student, for example, your classmates are your peers. If you are a nurse, your peers are your fellow nurses. Since you have many statuses, you have many peer groups, and since you change statuses over time, your peers keep changing also.

During childhood, peer groups are particularly important socializing forces. After a review of the research that has been done on the influence of peer groups, Boyd McCandless (1969) concluded that peers are more powerful socializers than either teachers or siblings. Only parents are more powerful.

Psychologists Mussen, Conger, and Kagan (1974:515) describe the socializing role of childhood peer groups in this way:

The peer group provides an opportunity to learn how to interact with age-mates, how to deal with hostility and dominance, how to relate to a leader, and how to lead others. It also performs a psychotherapeutic function for the child in helping him deal with social problems. Through discussions with peers the child may learn that others share his problems, conflicts, and complex feelings, and this may be reassuring. . . . Finally, the

Socialization tells us who we are and where we fit in the social scheme of things. This both offers us opportunities and puts limits on our opportunities.

peer group helps the child develop a concept of himself. The ways in which peers react to the child and the bases upon which he is accepted or rejected give him a clearer, and perhaps more realistic, picture of his assets and liabilities.

Childhood peers can have a lasting influence in creating your picture of who you are. Before they learn what may or may not properly be said, children are often candid reporters of a culture. If you grew up handicapped in any way or just looked a little different from your peers, for example, it is unlikely that adults told you directly that it was something to be ashamed of, even though they may have felt that way. Your childhood peers would have told you

directly that your nose was too big, that you were too skinny, or that you were the shortest kid on the block.

Schools as Socializers

Schools are charged with the formal task of passing on many of a culture's symbols, beliefs, values, and norms. Instruction in language and in mathematics is one way in which two symbol systems are passed from one generation to the next.

Schools also play an important role in the transmission of beliefs. Thus, American schools today teach children that the earth revolves around the sun just as earlier schools taught that the sun revolved around the earth. As we've seen a number of times in this book, agreements about what is true change over time, and the schools have the function of teaching children the current agreements of their society.

In addition, schools transmit cultural agreements regarding values and norms. As is the case with symbols and beliefs, the agreements to be transmitted change. The function of the schools, however, is to assist students in learning whatever agreements exist at a given time.

Schools sometimes reinforce or extend the socialization received in the family. Children begin learning language in the family, for example, and the schools carry language instruction even further. Sometimes, however, schools modify or undo the socialization received in the family. This is likely to occur whenever the family's agreements are different from those of the main culture.

Methods of socialization vary considerably from one society to the next. One of the most important instances of this in the modern world is the difference between the socialization of schoolchildren in the Soviet Union and that of schoolchildren in the United States.

The prime agent of socialization for the young in the Soviet Union is the "children's collective," according to Urie Bronfenbrenner (1970), an

American social psychologist who observed many Soviet schools between 1960 and 1967. From their earliest years in school, Soviet children are organized into collectives. Each class represents a detachment of a community youth organization, and within each class, children are organized into different groups or "links." These groups differ from American peer groups in a crucial respect. Whereas in the United States the youth peer group usually develops outside of, and often in opposition to, adult society, children's collectives in the Soviet Union always involve adult guidance of some sort.

In Soviet schools, Bronfenbrenner notes, emphasis is placed on three things—work, "socialist competition," and collective evaluation and discipline—each illustrating a dimension of the Soviet citizen's collective upbringing. Unlike most American schools, Soviet schools promote useful work and the learning of work skills for all children. Children are encouraged to perform services for the community and are integrated from an early age into the tasks of maintaining the school. An adult work group, such as a group of workers at a local factory, may help organize activities for a class and provide students with guidance, just as each class is expected to help bring up a group of younger children.

"Socialist competition" involves competition between groups—between links in a classroom, for instance, or between different classes. Soviet children are rarely singled out to be rewarded as individuals; instead, they are usually given rewards as a collective. When individuals are praised or faulted, Bronfenbrenner says, this is usually done within the group context. Children are praised, for instance, for helping another in their group or blamed for letting the group down.

Soviet schoolchildren are usually evaluated weekly by their collective, under the supervision of the teacher. Individuals are taught to put the needs of the group over their personal desires, and members of the group are encour-

aged to praise and constructively criticize each other's progress. Discipline is also meted out by the group when necessary, with the teacher nearby to keep it from getting out of hand. As in Soviet child rearing generally, the primary emphasis is on positive sanctions. When punishment is handed out, it does not consist of physical abuse but of censuring or withdrawing of affection.

What are the results of this socialization "in the collective, by the collective, and for the collective," to use the words of the guiding spirit of Soviet education, Anton Makarenko? According to Bronfenbrenner, Soviet children tend to be more conforming than their American counterparts, but less delinquent, aggressive, and antisocial.

Given the power of the school as socializer, it is no wonder that education has been a focus of numerous controversies in America. Some parents have protested racism and sexism in school textbooks. Others have objected to sex-education courses, and some have insisted that the Biblical doctrine of Creation be taught alongside evolution in science classes.

Mass Media as Socializers

In recent years, considerable concern has been expressed over the role of the mass media—especially television—as a socializing agent for young children. In their entertainment function, for example, the media portray various aspects of life: family, work, adventure. Their power in this regard is tremendous. As actor David Carradine has said, "We as the movie makers, have the power to do anything. We can make our characters live or die, triumph or fail" (quoted in Kilday 1975:127).

Recognizing this form of moviemaker omnipotence, many people have protested the entertainment industry's portrayal of sex and violence in everyday American life. Serious resistance to the portrayal of violence is recent, but resistance to the portrayal of explicit sexual activities and the use of sexual language has been evident for some time. Sociologists and other social scientists have been involved in both controversies.

The findings of social-scientific research on the consequences of pornography and television violence have clashed with agreements on those topics. When the National Commission on Obscenity and Pornography reported there was no evidence linking sex crimes to exposure to sexual materials, President Nixon condemned the report as "morally bankrupt" (Chaffee and Petrick 1975).

When, on the other hand, the United States surgeon general's million-dollar, three-year study of violence on television concluded that it had an adverse effect on American society—encouraging violence and dulling sensitivities to the violence of others—NBC-TV President Robert Howard was moved to suggest that "research does not replace common sense" (*TV Guide,* June 14, 1975, p. 6). Edith Efron (1975:22) argued against the report by saying that "the social sciences are not true sciences."

Perhaps one of the most telling arguments against violence on television has come from science-fiction writer and scientist Isaac Asimov. While noting that violence was a requirement for survival in early human history, Asimov (1975:31) suggests all that is past.

> We've got to get rid of violence for the simple reason that it serves no purpose any more, but points us all in a useless direction.
>
> The new enemies we have today—overpopulation, famine, pollution, scarcity—cannot be fought by violence. There is no way to crush those enemies, or slash them, or blast them, or vaporize them.

Regardless of how people feel about the merits of sex and violence on television and in the other media, all are more or less agreed on the power of the media to *create* implicit pictures of reality.

Commercial advertising creates "reality" in many subtler ways than simple product propaganda. It implies values, for example. Mouthwash commercials suggest that people with bad breath are somehow beyond the pale, out of it. Detergent commercials suggest that clean laundry has high moral value. Commercials also create pictures of social life and stereotype social statuses. Women are often portrayed as having no social function outside the kitchen, nursery, and laundry. Men are portrayed as totally inept in those areas, being superior in the things that "matter." Increased public objection has changed these portrayals somewhat in recent years; but, as this is being written, the unsuspecting viewer of an evening of television programming and commercials would come away believing that women are basically inferior to men.

Finally, the mass media provide some of the most important role models in modern life. Superstar entertainers, the tough cops of shoot-'em-up dramas, and other popular characters—real and fictional—become the ideal we sometimes aspire to.

Socializing the Socializers

While a father and mother are teaching their baby what it means to be a baby, the baby is teaching its parents what being a father and or a mother means. At the same time your professor is showing you what it means to be a student, you are showing him or her what it means to be a professor. There's a story about a man visiting a dude ranch and asking, "Do you have a horse I can try? I've never ridden before." The answer was, "Sure, try this one. He's never been ridden before, so you can learn together." Socialization is like that in one sense. We are all learning together, from each other. Moreover, socialization never stops, no matter how old you get, as we'll now see.

Adult Socialization and Resocialization

Socialization happens to adults as well as to children. Every time you interact with someone, you are being further socialized by that person, and you are socializing him or her. When you buy something in a store, you learn a little more about being a customer, and the salesperson learns a little more about being a salesperson. You may not have noticed it, but your understanding of the role of customer probably changed a little in the process.

Some societies, like ours, have formal schools for adults that further socialization. A "liberal education" in college, for instance, is explicitly designed to put students in touch with their cultural heritage. Vocational and professional schools are examples of training for specific (occupational) roles. On-the-job training programs sponsored by many large corporations also illustrate socialization into occupational roles.

Military boot camp is a perfect example (if you're not going through it) of adult socializa-

tion. Socialization of trainees involves their being taught the beliefs, values, and norms of the military. Trainees are drilled in the specific behaviors expected of military personnel in various roles.

Military training also is an example of **resocialization,** the *un*learning of agreements previously learned and their substitution by new ones. Trainees must unlearn many aspects of their civilian socialization. The Amerian civilian value of equality, for example, does not fit well with the military rank structure and the special privileges and duties associated with senior and junior ranks. During the Vietnam War, the military established special programs to resocialize returning veterans: the purpose was to reorient them to civilian life in America.

Adult socialization and resocialization is not always a smooth and harmonious process. Countless soldiers and sailors have refused to accept the agreements of military life, for instance. Some have refused to obey orders; others have deserted. From time to time, sailors have mutinied. In some instances, the only result has been the punishment of the

While they are enormously powerful processes, socialization and resocialization seldom succeed completely. The individuality that falls through the cracks is part of what separates us from the social insects.

"offenders." In other instances, things have been changed. American enlisted men today, for example, enjoy many privileges unheard of a decade or two ago. None of these changes would have occurred without disagreement.

When adults change statuses, their resocialization often includes subtle changes in their points of view. Seymour Lieberman (1963) found this to be the case, for example, in a study of industrial workers. Comparing the attitudes of workers recently promoted to the position of foreman with those of a control group of similar workers, Lieberman found the new foremen to be more pro-management and anti-union.

The effects of promotion on attitudes were even more telling when Lieberman examined long-term occupational patterns. Studying workers' attitudes in three different years, he was able to detect the changing points of view of particular workers. Those promoted to foremen were more critical of the union than they had been before they were promoted. Some of those promoted, however, were later demoted. These became less critical of the union after demotion.

Socialization and resocialization have been operating throughout your life and will follow you to the edge of your grave. Senior citizens learn that many of the behaviors expected of them earlier are no longer appropriate. The elderly couple who gets drunk at a party and starts dancing wildly will likely be regarded as a pitiful sight rather than as a happy spectacle of people enjoying themselves. Aging parents may learn that their children no longer expect or want them to offer guidance on child rearing. We'll look into the agreements surrounding old age in more detail in Chapter 10.

Socialization and Social Change

If the preceding discussions have made socialization seem like a force for stability and the perpetuation of the status quo, that's only a part of the picture. Social scientists have often warned against the danger of oversimplifying the process and impact of socialization on the creation of social identities and the "standardizing" of social affairs. Dennis Wrong (1961), for example, has cautioned against accepting an "oversocialized conception of man," pointing out that there is far more uncertainty and variation in the way people turn out than a simplified view of socialization would indicate. In part, the explanation for variations lies in the complexity mentioned by James earlier. In part it reflects the limits to malleability in humans—we can be bent only so far. And also, socialization fails to be totally effective because it is not done consistently. Put differently, one reason we do not grow up to be total robots is that we are not trained by total robots. Finally, the novelty of all new situations, Wrong argues, militates against routinized behavior patterns.

This caution against the "oversocialized" view extends even further, however. In a variety of ways, socialization also produces social change, disrupting and destroying the status quo.

Before World War II, black Americans had been socialized to a set of agreements that placed them in an inferior, second-class status in American society. The need for fighting men, however, was color-blind, and the same demands were made of blacks as of whites. In the military, moreover, blacks were socialized to a greater equality with whites than they had experienced in civilian life. Once the war was over, the socialization to equality couldn't be undone, and the experiences of returning black soldiers were undoubtedly influential in shaping the militancy of the civil rights movement and the black power movement that followed.

In general, the resocialization inherent in wars usually results in social change. During World War I, for example, a popular song was entitled, "How You Gonna Keep 'Em Down on the Farm (After They've Seen Paris)?"

Socialization can also result in social change whenever a group's "official" culture differs from what actually goes on in the group. Sociologists often speak of society's having an "ideal culture" (the *stated* beliefs, values, and norms) and a "real culture" (the *actual* state of affairs in day-to-day life). Many Americans have been personally troubled by the discrepancy between their childhood socialization of internalizing the stated American value of peace and their later resocialization in terms of the frequent wars we engage in. The peace movement that paralleled the Vietnam War is an example of what can happen when an attempt is made to socialize people into contradictory points of view. Or consider the conflict generated by the value of human equality and the second-class status of women in America, resulting in a liberation movement we'll examine further in Chapter 10.

These latest examples notwithstanding, socialization is basically a conservative process. It aims at the perpetuation of agreements, the maintenance of the status quo. Maintenance of the status quo is accomplished, moreover, by building many of those agreements into our very conceptions of ourselves.

We have constructed our societies to perpetuate what we have constructed. Notice that we are not saying anything about the appropriateness of the perpetuated agreements to the needs, desires, or aspirations of individual members of those societies. As Piaget (1965:13-14) has said,

> Now, most of the moral rules which the child learns to respect he receives from adults, which means that he receives them after they have been fully elaborated, and often elaborated, not in relation to him and as they are needed, but once and for all and through an uninterrupted succession of earlier adult generations.

Summary

"Socialization" is the process of teaching and learning the agreements of society. It serves two interconnected functions. On the one hand, individuals learn how they fit into the rest of the society they live in. And, on the other hand, the agreements making up a society's culture are passed on from generation to generation.

To understand how people turn out in the ways they do, it is necessary to examine the relative contributions of heredity and environment. Although sociology deals primarily with environmental factors, sociologists recognize they both play a part. Heredity provides limits within which environmental experiences produce their results.

"Social identity" includes the social statuses that you occupy and the roles you perform appropriate to those statuses. Socialization is the process of learning which statuses you occupy and the roles associated with those statuses. Lying outside those statuses may be an experience of *self* as something more fundamental, but your social interaction occurs through the medium of statuses.

Interaction through statuses is analogous to masks talking to one another. I discover what statuses you occupy, and you learn mine. If we have learned patterns of interaction appropriate to the coming together of those statuses, we use those patterns in dealing with each other.

How do you learn what statuses you occupy? George Herbert Mead said that you discovered your social identities from the "generalized other," that fictional average of all the opinions and views of those around you. Charles Horton Cooley pursued this idea by suggesting that the generalized other formed a mirror in which to see yourself, in which to see what Cooley called the "looking-glass-self."

Sociologists are not alone in their interest in how people form social identities. Sigmund Freud pointed to the powerful part played by unconscious emotions and desires in the shaping of social beings. Whereas the "id" represented primitive drives, people had to learn and submit to the agreements of the group, incorporating in themselves what Freud called the "superego." Out of the confrontation of the id with the demands of society came the "ego," the person's sense of social identity. Freud's insights showed a fertile arena for investigation. One of his students, Erik Erikson, has done considerable research into the stages of development that mark the individual's long-term life cycle, from childhood to old age.

Jean Piaget has also contributed importantly to our understanding of human development. Among other things, Piaget has studied the manner in which children form their ideas of "reality." As he shows, the stages in which they construct the reality of their world are important to the construction of their reality of themselves.

The second major function of socialization is the transmission of culture. Each new generation in a society is taught the agreements that distinguish that society from others. Much of this function involves the process of "internalization," in which individuals move the enforcement of agreements inside themselves. Thus, you may find there are many agreements you would keep even if no one checked up on you.

The transmission of culture involves symbols, beliefs, values, and norms, and sociologists have studied various aspects of these. Lawrence Kohlberg, for example, has been particularly interested in the moral systems that children learn in different cultures—both cultural variations and apparent universals in the stages of moral development.

Socialization occurs in many ways. Imitation is one. "Role taking" involves the acting out of behavior appropriate to a status that you don't actually occupy, as when a young child pretends to be a doctor. Much role taking, however, is a form of anticipatory socialization—learning role behavior that is appropriate to statuses you may later occupy.

In all cultures, a differentiation is made between men and women and the role behavior considered appropriate to each. *What* is expected varies from culture to culture, but the process

of socialization into these agreements occurs in all. This is called "sex typing."

Socialization is carried out by various "agents." Chief among these are family, peers, schools, and—in modern societies—the mass media. Agents of socialization teach people the general agreements of the society; they tell people what statuses they occupy and what role behavior is appropriate to those statuses. Ultimately, however, socialization is a subtler process than that—indeed, all of us are socializing each other, as students socialize teachers into "teacher behavior" and teachers socialize students into "student behavior."

Socialization is not something that happens only to the young, therefore. Indeed, sociologists often speak of "adult resocialization," a process associated with the lifelong shifting from one status to another, requiring an unlearning of previous learned role behavior and its replacement with new behavior.

Finally, although socialization is fundamentally a conservative process—lending support to the persistence of established agreements—it often serves as a source of change in society. In part, this results from the conflicting agreements that exist in any complex society. Thus, for example, women are taught both that they are equal to men and that they are second-class citizens. Out of this conflict has arisen an important social movement that is changing patterns of interaction and the many agreements that lie behind them.

In these latest two chapters, we have seen some of the power of stability and persistence in society. In the examination of culture, you should have come to appreciate how solidly entrenched agreements can become, and in this chapter we have looked at the ways in which those agreements are anchored within the very identities of humans.

Important Terms

self
looking-glass self
internalization
role taking

anticipatory socialization
peers
socialization
resocialization

Suggested Readings

Bronfenbrenner, Urie
  1973 *Two Worlds of Childhood: U.S. and U.S.S.R.* New York: Pocket Books.
  Here's a comparative view of the socialization process, dealing with two modern, industrial nations set apart by significant social and political differences.

Douglas, Jack, *et al.*
  1980 *Introduction to the Sociologies of Everyday Life.* Boston: Allyn and Bacon.
  Treats experiences of people interacting in concrete situations, using sociologies related to experiencing, observing, understanding, describing, analyzing, and communicating.

Elkin, Howard A. and Gerald Handel
  1972 *The Child and Society: The Process of Socialization, Second Edition.* New York: Random House.
  Discussion of the socialization process, concentrating on childhood and written from a sociological perspective.

Erikson, Erik H.
  1963 *Childhood and Society.* New York: Norton.
  Erikson's classic statement of the eight stages of ego development is cast in a broader context of socialization and its consequences for the individual and society. A number of cross-cultural and individual case studies are presented to illustrate Erikson's view. This is an easily readable, insightful, and important book.

Gordon, Thomas
  1975 *Parent Effectiveness Training: The Tested New Way to Responsible Children.* New York: New American Library.
  This is an applied book, written for parents who find themselves in the front lines of socialization. The PET system of child rearing, centered around children learning to take responsibility at a young age, has been very popular in recent years. Even if you are not now raising children of your own, you will find insights into the socialization process.

Gould, Stephen Jay
  1981 *The Mismeasure of Man.* New York: Norton.
  A recent and comprehensive analysis of the IQ controversy. Gould's study places IQ testing in a historical context of human mismeasurement.

Koller, Marvin R. and Oscar W. Ritchie
  1978 *Sociology of Childhood.* Englewood Cliffs, NJ: Prentice-Hall.
  Reviews theories and research on socialization in the first 12 years of life.

Maccoby, Eleanor E. and Carol N. Jacklin
  1975 *The Psychology of Sex Differences.* Palo Alto, CA: Stanford University Press.
  Review of existing literature on sex differences between girls and boys which can be attributed to socialization versus inborn traits.

Mead, Margaret
  [1928] *Coming of Age in Samoa.* New York: New American Library.
  1949
  Often the socialization process is seen most clearly in the case of agreements that are unfamiliar to you. Margaret Mead's classic examination of adolescence and the learning of sexual norms in Samoan society provides an excellent illustration of this assertion. While the problems of adolescence and of socialization are fundamentally the same in early Samoan society and in the modern United States, the manner in which those problems are handled is very different in many respects.

Meyer, John
  1978 "The Effects of Education as an Institution," *American Journal of Sociology* 83(1):55–77.
  In this chapter, I have presented the school as a socialization agency, passing on the agreements established in society. Later in this book, we are going to see that education can also present a challenge to the established agreements, and this article will give you a review of that side of the issue.

Piaget, Jean
1954   *The Construction of Reality in the Child.* Trans. Margaret Cook. New York: Basic Books.
Piaget is without peer in the careful and detailed observation of childhood learning. In this book, Piaget chronicles the painstaking process through which young children make sense of the physical world in which they live, learning the permanence of objects, causation, movement, and other concepts that adults take for granted.

Rosow, Irving
1974   *Socialization to Old Age.* Berkeley: University of California Press.
Analysis of socialization into aging and aged role in society as contrasted to other social roles.

Skinner, B. F.
1953   *Science and Human Behavior.* New York: Macmillan.
Skinner's view of operant conditioning is one of the most controversial in the current literature on socialization. This report of his research on the power of positive sanctions in shaping behavior among animals lays the theoretical foundation for his more recent and even more controversial book, *Beyond Freedom and Dignity* (New York: Knopf, 1971).

APPLICATION AND ANALYSIS / SOME IMPLICATIONS OF HEREDITY VERSUS ENVIRONMENT

Early in this chapter, I raised the age-old issue of heredity versus environment, sometimes referred to as the "nature-nurture controversy." Lest you regard that issue as "purely academic," I want to conclude this chapter by pointing out the real-life consequences of theories and research on the question of whether people turn out to be what they were born to be or what they learn to be.

Stephen Jay Gould (1981) places the current IQ controversy in a lengthy historical context. The determination to measure and rank human ability dates back at least to ancient Athens. In *The Republic,* Plato presents Socrates' view that all citizens must be assigned to live their lives in one of three classes: rulers, auxiliaries, and craftsmen. Socrates informs Glaucon that it will be necessary to create a myth for the people to believe:

> Citizens, we shall say to them in our tale, you are brothers, yet God has framed you differently. Some of you have the power to command, and in the composition of these he has mingled gold, wherefore also they have the greatest honor; others he has made of silver, to be auxiliaries; others again who are to be husbandmen and craftmen he has composed of brass and iron; and the species will generally be preserved in the children. . . . An Oracle says that when a man of brass or iron guards the State, it will be destroyed. Such is the tale; is there any possibility of making our citizens believe in it?

In Plato's account, Glaucon answers Socrates, "Not in the present generation; there is no way of accomplishing this; but their sons may be made to believe in the tale, and their son's sons, and posterity after them." As Gould points out, Glaucon's prophesy has proved true. The myth has been accepted down through the centuries. As Gould (1981:20) summarizes:

. . . the basic argument has not changed: that social and economic roles accurately reflect the innate construction of people. One aspect of the intellectual strategy has altered, however. Socrates knew that he was telling a lie.

In American history, the question of whether social status was a mere reflection of innate ability—human superiority or inferiority—has often revolved around the issue of race. Black slavery was largely justified by the assertion that blacks were biologically inferior to whites. Even with the emancipation of the slaves, it was still widely believed that blacks were inferior. Lincoln, among others, held that view. The "liberal" position was that even inferior people deserved the rights of citizenship.

Most of Gould's analysis concerns, not the prejudices of laypeople, but the part played by scientists in maintaining the myth of white superiority. Anthropological evidence was sometimes falsified to suggest that blacks were genetically similar to apes and chimpanzees.

During the nineteenth century, the thesis of white superiority hinged largely on the measurement of human skulls. The larger the brain cavity, it was assumed, the greater the intelligence. A mass of anthropological data showed whites to be thusly superior to blacks and Native Americans. Later reanalyses of the data, however, point to either sloppy science or worse. Gould reports a common tendency to set aside small skulls of whites and large skulls of nonwhites in calculating averages. When such biases are eliminated, Gould finds no racial differences.

Like the size of brain cavities in skulls, the weights of brains have also been treated as evidence of superior intellect. This proved a troublesome thesis, however. On an individual basis, the brains of acknowledged geniuses often weighed in below those of convicted mass murderers. More damaging, however, was the discovery that several nonwhite groups had larger brains than whites. Gould (1981:87) quotes a leading scholar of the time in dismissing the validity of brain size as a measure of superiority: "Eskimos, Lapps, Malays, Tartars and several other peoples of the Mongolian type would surpass the most civilized people of Europe. A lowly race may therefore have a big brain." Notice the circular reasoning here. Since we know whites are superior, we can see that brain size is not an adequate test of whether whites are superior.

During this century, the issue of intellectual superiority or inferiority has hinged largely on IQ tests. A fundamental issue, as we saw early in the chapter, has concerned whether intelligence was a matter more of heredity or of environment. Realize that the thesis of racial superiority depends on intelligence being inherited rather than a matter of environment.

As I indicated earlier, much of the research on this topic has involved the study of twins, with particular attention paid to their later-life IQs. As you'll recall, twins raised apart have greater IQ-similarities than found among non-twins raised apart, suggesting the importance of heredity, while children raised together—all else being equal—have greater IQ-similarities than children raised apart, pointing to the importance of environment.

Suppose for the moment that heredity was in fact more important than environment in determining intelligence. Aside from matters of race, what would be some implications of that discovery? Certainly it would have important implications for education. If students arrive at school with immutably different potentials, it would make no sense to try bringing them all to the same educational level by the end of their schooling. If heredity were the key to intelligence, it would make sense to identify levels of intelligence early and then provide different educational programs for the "bright" and "dull" students. This reasoning has, in fact, been put into practice.

The most prominent educational psychologist of this century in England was Sir Cyril Burt, knighted by King George VI for his research in the field of heredity and environment. His most noted research concerned the study of IQs of identical twins raised apart. In numerous studies conducted before his death in 1971, Burt demonstrated a powerful consistency in findings which showed heredity to overshadow environment. So impressive were Burt's findings that he served as a government advisor to the British school system during the 1940s. As a consequence of Burt's research and advice, children were given IQ tests at age eleven, and their scores were then used to place them in one of three different educational tracks—reflecting their native abilities. While it was argued that placement in the "slow" track meant that a student would leave school less well educated than if he or she were placed in another track, that argument was muted by the assertion that such students were genetically incapable of handling more demanding materials.

"Tracking systems" have been the focus of controversy in American schools, also, as we'll see in Chapter 14. But Burt's findings have had other implications as well.

If intelligence—as measured by IQ—was a function of genetics, then perhaps IQ tests would show that blacks were less intelligent than whites. This possibility was given scientific support in 1967, when Nobel Laureate engineer, William Shockley (1967), publicly urged the American scientific community to undertake research on the relative intelligence of blacks and whites. Two years later, the issue was brought to scientific and popular attention by one of Sir Cyril Burt's American students, Arthur Jensen. Writing in the *Harvard Educational Review,* Jensen (1969) reported significant differences in the IQs of blacks and whites.

Jensen's findings were hotly contested in both scientific and nonscientific communities. Scientists raised numerous methodological issues. Chief among them was the white, urban, middle-class character of most IQ tests. Ehrlich and Feldman (1977:71) report:

> While most existing IQ tests seem to show that urban and suburban children score better than rural children of the same age, it is possible to construct a test using items of general information that favor rural children. In 1929, psychologist Myra Shimberg made up two information tests—one favored urban schoolchildren, the other favored rural children. Children from the cities were better at answering questions such as "How can banks afford to pay interest on the money you deposit?" while rural children did better on items such as "Of what is butter made?" "Name a vegetable that grows above ground," and "How often do we have a full moon?"

To demonstrate the white middle-class bias of standard intelligence tests, Adrian Dove, a social worker in the predominantly black Watts district of Los Angeles has constructed a "Chitling Test of Intelligence." Here are some of the items in the test:

T-Bone Walker got famous for playing what?
    (a) Trombone
    (b) Piano
    (c) "T-flute"
    (d) Guitar
    (e) "Hambone"

A "Gas Head" is a person who has a _____
    (a) Fast-moving car

    (b) Stable of "lace"
    (c) "Process"
    (d) Habit of stealing cars
    (e) Long jail record for arson

If you throw the dice and "7" is showing on the top, what is facing down?
    (a) Seven
    (b) "Snake eyes"
    (c) "Boxcars"
    (d) "Little Joes"
    (e) Eleven

(quoted in Ehrlich and Feldman 1977:72)

Clearly, middle-class whites, who do well on standard IQ tests, would probably have trouble with the "Chitling" test. No one would suggest they were unintelligent, however, since the information asked for in the test is simply not a part of their cultural socialization. Yet those who would do well on the "Chitling" test might do poorly on the standard IQ tests—for the same reason. In case you are "culturally deprived," the answers to the above questions are (d), (c), and (a).

As Ehrlich and Feldman (1977) point out, however, the Shockley/Jensen controversy had immediate reverberations throughout American society. Jensen's findings were seized upon by racists and were used to justify opposition to integrated schools by people who had opposed them long before the findings were published.

In 1974, an astounding revelation further complicated the debate. Sir Cyril Burt was back in the news, this time in a bad light. Leon Kamin, writing of *The Science and Politics of IQ* (1974), had scrutinized Burt's policymaking research. In part, Kamin raised questions about Burt's methodology. For example, Burt's research reports did not provide sufficient details to permit a careful evaluation. Then, there were cryptic remarks about modifications and adjustments to the data. Students' IQ scores were often reviewed by the students' teachers, and if the teachers felt a particular student's scores might not accurately reflect the student's abilities, that student was retested, a questionable procedure at best.

As the final straw, however, Kamin noted that the consistency of Burt's findings was altogether *too* consistent. In study after study, *exactly the same* correlations were reported—something extremely unlikely. The growing conclusion was that Burt had simply made up his findings!

Further research revealed that some of Burt's co-authors, as well as scholars who had written positive reviews of his work, didn't even exist. Evidently, Burt had made them up as well. During his lifetime, however, he was so powerful a figure that few dared challenge him. With many of Burt's papers later destroyed, it seems unlikely that we will ever know for sure how much of his research on IQ was genuine and how much was a fraud. The subsequent revelations by Kamin and others, however, have called into question all his contributions to the nature-nurture controversy.

The debate over the relative impact of heredity and environment continues. And with it continues the policy debate over race, education, and related matters.

PRACTICING SOCIOLOGY

Ling Yang writes the following in the Communist Party weekly *Bejing Review* regarding the arrival of television in the People's Republic of China:

There is a program entitled *Across the Land*, which spotlights the scenic beauties and special features of various places in China. A special weekly program *Round the World*, has featured, among other things, the agro-industrial complexes in Yugoslavia, a new type of hospital in West Berlin, the music center in Sydney, off-shore oil drilling in Mexico, and different cultural customs in the world.

Culture of Foreign Countries has been running since New Year's Day. The first of the series was an American film about the Louvre, and proved to be a hit. Other programs include *On the International Scene, Science and Technology, Hygiene and Health, Advice on Everyday Living*, and *Cultural Life*—the last dealing with literary and artistic endeavors. Still others provide a glimpse of sports overseas, such as surfing, canoeing, and frisbee. . . .

Advertisements are new in China's mass media. They appeared only after the elimination of ultra-leftist influence in the course of resuscitating the economy and culture. Thanks to these advertisements, many products have found a brisk market.

In what ways might Chinese television differ from U.S. television? What would you need to know about Chinese society to assess the potential effects of television on patterns of socialization and resocialization there?

Source: Ling Yang, "China's Television Explosion," *Bejing Review*, reprinted in *World Press Review*, May 1981:59.

6

Groups

Implicit in much of what has gone before in this book is the group aspect of human existence. Our involvement in groups is so fundamental, in fact, that instances of people living in total isolation from groups are unusual enough to warrant attention. Just being in and participating in groups hardly seems to deserve attention.

In this chapter, we are going to look at the various aspects of group life that will be useful for you to know in your full understanding of social life. We'll begin by defining the term "group." We'll see that sociologists have something fairly precise in mind when they use the term, and we'll see some of the things that are similar to groups but are not considered groups in sociology. We will then examine some types of groups that sociologists have found especially important: dyads, triads, in-groups, out-groups, reference groups, and primary and secondary groups.

Following this introduction to the taxonomy of groups, we'll see where groups fit into the bigger picture of society. There has been a long-term trend toward societies based on rather impersonal, superficial groups and group encounters, and we'll see some implications of this trend. The remainder of Chapter 6 is devoted to the research sociologists have done on the dynamics of small-group interactions. We'll see how much power a group can have over individuals, the consequences of group size, composition, structure, and leadership, among other things. We'll see how people (or groups) form coalitions in order to further their own interests, often at the risk of being swallowed up by their partners.

You should finish this chapter with a well-rounded understanding of the ways in which groups operate and how they fit into the larger society. This understanding will prepare you for the study of larger organizations in Chapter 7.

What Is a Group?

The term **group** is used in everyday language in a variety of ways, reflecting many meanings. We speak of a "group" gathered at a bus stop and the "group" that used brand X toothpaste. We also speak of "groupies," people who follow rock-music stars around. In this section, I want to spell out some of the meanings sociologists usually associate with the term and then look at some different types of groups.

Sociologists have not exactly agreed on the most appropriate definition of group. For Dwight Sanderson (1959:133), a group is

> Two or more people between whom there is an established pattern of psychological interaction; it is recognized as an entity, by its own members and usually by others, because of its particular type of collective behavior.

Theodorson and Theodorson (1969:176) agree that groups are a plurality of people with shared identity and feelings of unity. In addition, they suggest groups have "certain common goals and shared norms." They continue:

> A group is further characterized by direct or indirect communication among its members, standardized patterns of interaction based on a system of interrelated roles, and some degree of interdependence among members.

Werner S. Landecker (1964:295) begins his definition of group with a focus on structure: "a definition of group must refer to an integrated social structure rather than a mere category of individuals." Thus, when sociologists define "group," they usually distinguish it from a **category** and an **aggregation.** A "category" is a set of people who share a characteristic. Examples include black Americans, blue-eyed people, and all those who used brand X toothpaste. Members of a category don't necessarily know each other. They belong to the same category merely because they share a characteristic.

An "aggregation" is a gathering of people in the same physical location. People gathered at the bus stop are an example, as is a theater audience. Members of an aggregation need not know one another or interact with one another, and there is no expectation that they'll ever gather together again.

After a review of sociological definitions, Charles S. Palazzolo (1981:19) concluded that any definition of group must include "interaction." While it should be noted that Palazzolo's analysis was consciously from a symbolic interactionist point of view (recall Chapter 2), most definitions do include that element.

While sociologists clearly do not agree on the most appropriate definition for the term "group," these are among the most common elements found in formal definitions:

1. *Shared interests.* Members of a group agree in some degree on values, norms, goals, and so forth. For example, the members of a PTA share a belief in the desirability of "quality" education, and they may agree on the means for achieving it.

2. *Interaction.* Members of a group usually interact or communicate to some extent among themselves because of their membership in the group. Thus, members of a family interact because of their membership in the family.

3. *Identity.* The members of a group must have a sense of membership in or of belonging to that group. At some level, the group constitutes an element in the individual's definition of who he or she is. A group is, in some degree, a *union* of individuals, and it is useful to consider the notion of *"reunion"* in this context. Class reunions, for example, reflect the group identity characterizing the graduating class. It is unlikely that you'd contemplate or wish for a reunion of the crowd that gathered to watch a suicide attempt.

An aggregation is a gathering of people in the same physical location. They may not know each other nor will they necessarily meet again.

4. *Structure.* Unlike categories or aggregations, groups have structure—agreed-on relationships among statuses. The structure present in a group may be either formal or informal *or* explicit or implicit.

The strictest sociological use of the term "group" covers a broad variety of collectives. Examples of groups include a family, a bureaucratic office, a high-school graduating class, a Communist-party cell, a sociology-department faculty, and a political-party caucus within a legislature.

Formal definitions notwithstanding, sociologists use the term "group" quite loosely. Although Hispanic Americans, strictly speaking, are a social category, we refer to them as a minority *group*—despite the fact that they lack social structure and do not all interact with one another. Our discussions of "in-groups," "out-groups," and "reference groups" later in this chapter illustrate other variations from the formal definitions.

Do not conclude from these comments, however, that the formal definitions of group have no value. In fact, the common elements we've been discussing point to the ways in which individuals impact on one another in their social existence. However defined, groups are important for two major reasons. First, they provide an important part of an individual's social identity. Your sense of who you *are* is largely a function of the groups you belong to. Second, they are a key to understanding much social behavior. Many sociologists have studied the dynamics of interaction within groups—particularly small groups—thereby gaining insights into social interaction more generally. Further, the behavior of individuals within society is largely a function of their membership in particular groups. I'll be elaborating on each of these points through the rest of this chapter and the next.

Types of Groups

Having defined groups and characterized them at the most general level, I now want to display some of the variations among types of groups. We'll look at some of the ways sociologists have distinguished groups in the course of understanding their contributions to social life.

Dyads and Triads

Let's start with the question of how large a group has to be to be a "group." One person clearly is not a group, but are two people enough? This is not as simple a question as you might imagine.

Georg Simmel (1858–1918) was one of the earliest scholars to pay close attention to very small groups, arguing that all of society could be understood as an extension of the interaction between individuals. He (1908b) introduced the German term *zweierverbindung* liter-

A zweierverbindung is something more than two individuals; it is also a single unit. (Fortunately, it is also a dyad *when translated into English.)*

Georg Simmel
1858–1918
Berlin, Germany

Some Important Works
Conflict and the Web of Group Affiliation, trans. Kurt Wolff (Glencoe, Ill.: Free Press, 1955 [1908]).
Sociology, trans., ed. Kurt Wolff (New York: Free Press, 1964 [entitled *The Sociology of Georg Simmel*] [1908]).

A contemporary of Durkheim and Weber, Simmel was generally well known in sociological and philosophical circles during his lifetime. In the succeeding years, his influence in sociology has been greatly overshadowed by both Durkheim and Weber.

In sociology, Simmel's interests were diverse and many. He often immersed himself in the most fundamental issues of human nature and social interaction. In his later years, his writings on such topics were often mystical, speaking of a life force that transcended physical reality while manifesting itself in societal structures. On a very different subject, his writings on the functions of social conflict are as valuable today as they were seventy years ago.

ally translated as "union of two," and fortunately translated into English as **dyad,** a two-member group.

Simmel felt that the dyad is the most elementary social unit, having an existence and reality that transcends the existence and reality of individuals. Still, Simmel recognized that the existence of a dyad was dependent on the membership of each individual, either one of whom could terminate the group by withdrawing.

The group as a reality apart from individuals becomes more apparent and persistent when a third member is added, Simmel argued: "The dyad, therefore, does not attain that super-personal life which the individual feels to be independent of himself. As soon, however, as there is a sociation of three, a group continues to exist even in case one of the members drops out" (1908b:123).

Sociologists use the term **triad** for groups of three; and, as Simmel suggested, the triad dif-

fers from the dyad in two important ways. First, each member of a dyad recognizes that the "groupness" depends directly on his or her continued membership. The members of a triad, on the other hand, recognize that the group has a reality that extends beyond their individual membership in it. When two people make agreements with each other, each recognizes his or her part in making the agreements. The agreements shared by members of a larger group appear to have more substance, more "reality," since the group itself has a reality which transcends the individual members in it.

The second important distinction between dyads and triads is a variation on the first: triads have a greater survival potential than dyads, making them more significant in the overall structuring of societies. Simmel was particularly interested in the "immortality" of larger social groups, how groups themselves continue forever although the membership changes.

Consider the following example. Suppose three people—A, B, and C—form a very exclusive wine-tasting club. Here's what might happen to the club over time:

Events	"Elite Wine-Tasting Club" Members				
Club founded	A	B	C		
A quits the club		B	C		
D joins the club		B	C	D	
B quits the club			C	D	
E joins the club			C	D	E
C quits the club				D	E
F joins the club				D	E	F

Note that the membership of the club has changed completely. None of the original members still belongs, yet the "Elite Wine-Tasting Club" has never died. If you think about it, this is by no means an artificial situation.

The survival of social units is one of the critical elements in society. The United States Senate as a social group has survived for two hundred years, even though its membership has changed totally. Despite the continuous changing of membership, the Senate is still the Senate.

In-Groups and Out-Groups

Earlier I said that a sense of "belonging" is an element in defining groups. The sense of belonging is also important to another distinction that sociologists make, that between **in-groups** and **out-groups.**

Most simply put, an "in-group" is a group you belong to. Since membership in a group is a status, and statuses define your social identity, your membership in an in-group contributes to the social definition of who you are. Whether you belong to an exclusive country club or are a member of an impoverished urban neighborhood, such membership is a part of your social identity.

In-group membership has no meaning, however, unless there are *non*members, people who do not belong to your in-group. In-group membership takes on social significance to the extent that the nonmembers belong to distinct groups of their own, groups that are in some degree in competition with yours.

An in-group is composed of people you refer to as "we"; an out-group is made up of people you call "they." The "we feeling" that characterizes in-groups has implications for both the individual and the society. I have already mentioned that your own social identity is partly based on the groups you belong to. "We" includes "I," as illustrated by Rudyard Kipling in the poem "We and They."

Father, Mother, and Me
Sister and Auntie say
All the people like us are We
And every one else is They.

All good people agree,
And all good people say,
All nice people, like Us, are We
And every one else is They.

In-group membership affects your personal feelings as well as your identity. Many of your in-groups are likely to provide you with feelings of support, loyalty, and even affection. This occurs across a range stretching from family membership to nationality. Because an in-group is typically based on shared points of view, you may feel more comfortable interacting with members of your in-groups than with other people. This is all the more true to the extent that you have reified the points of view that your in-groups share. Perhaps you have experienced the discomfort of visiting people whose food preferences seemed strange and bizarre to you.

From a societal point of view, in-groups and out-groups provide important bases for both stability and conflict. Within-group cohesion and solidarity keep knots of people bound together in persistent groups, whereas between-group tensions and conflict provide a continuing source of stress, strain, and change. Consider, for example, the team spirit within an athletic team, and the sometimes fierce competition between teams. Notice how often the two go hand in hand.

Often, defining who is in and who is out of the group is the basis for inhumane actions, as when West Coast Japanese Americans were herded into detention camps during World War II. During the same war, the Nazis excluded Jews from the human species, and the Japanese took essentially the same approach to the Chinese. Earlier in our own history, white Americans essentially excluded Native Americans from the human species. Once a group of people has been defined as outside the in-group of human beings, even the most basic, shared agreements regarding the relations of humans are suspended, and atrocities often follow.

You may already have noticed a similarity between this discussion and an earlier one on *ethnocentrism* in Chapter 4. The two are intimately connected. In analyzing ethnocentrism and in-group/out-group relations, all students seem to agree on four propositions, according to Levinen and Campbell (1972). First, a chief source of ethnocentric conflict seems to be competition over scarce resources. Second, groups seem to return hostility for hostility, escalating

the conflict. Third, the characteristics that distinguish one group from another get exaggerated into stereotypes, thereby making existing differences seem greater than they really are. Fourth, in general, the more complex a society is, the more likely is ethnocentric conflict between groups.

Reference Groups

In Chapter 5 we discussed Cooley's concept of the looking-glass self, suggesting that we learn who we are by seeing ourselves reflected in the eyes of others. Certain groups and social categories around us also provide us with the standard against which we evaluate ourselves. These are called **reference groups,** as you may recall from an earlier discussion.

Reference groups operate in two ways. First, they can provide a measure of how well or poorly we are doing. For example, would you regard a grade of B as a "good" or "bad" grade in this course? Your answer is likely to reflect the grades your friends are receiving in their courses or the grades other students in this course receive or both. If you received the only B in the course and everyone else did worse, you'd think that B was a good grade. If everyone else got an A, you'd take a much different view of your B. We tend to judge ourselves in comparison with other members of our groups.

Comparing ourselves with others lays the foundation for what sociologists call **relative deprivation,** another term we discussed briefly in Chapter 3. We experience deprivation whenever our situation seems worse than that of those we compare ourselves with—regardless of the objective circumstances. Stouffer and his colleagues (1949), you'll recall, found soldiers in World War II judging their situations almost exclusively in comparison with others they identified with. Thus, for example, the less educated soldiers were likely to resent being drafted because many of their friends had been

Our reference groups are those people we compare ourselves with to determine how well we're doing.

deferred, whereas the more educated accepted the draft as fair since most of their friends had also been drafted.

Second, reference groups can be composed of people whose opinions we respect, providing a somewhat different standard for us. Suppose you are the best dancer in your college and want to become a professional ballet dancer. Your dance teacher and those around you might reasonably regard your stature as a dancer to be great. If your reference group is the Bolshoi ballet company, however, you are likely to have a low regard for your abilities.

Reference groups have an important socializing effect in providing goals for us to work toward in our personal development. Very often we attempt to gain membership in the reference group, whether it is the Bolshoi ballet, an exclusive "jet set," a university faculty, or a streetcorner gang.

Sociologists use the concept of reference groups to help explain differences in behavior.

Robert Merton (1957a), who has written extensively on the subject of reference-group theory, provides a good example. In his study of personal influence within a small eastern seacoast town, Merton found that some residents confined their interests largely to the small town in which they lived, giving little thought to national and world issues. These people were the "locals." Other residents, the "cosmopolitans," took a much broader view. Clearly, the "locals" and the "cosmopolitans" had different reference groups.

A similar observation has been made about university faculty members. Some tend to identify primarily with their own campuses; others identify primarily with their national profession. A "local" professor would value being appointed to an important campus committee, but a "cosmopolitan" would take greater pride in being asked to address a national convention. The reference group, then, is another way in which the sociological point of view can organize and clarify familiar aspects of social life.

Primary and Secondary Groups

Now I want to turn to a distinction between types of groups that has interested sociologists for a long time. Basically, this interest grows out of the observation that some groups are characterized by warmth and intimacy while others are more detached and casual.

Take a minute to make a mental list of ten or so groups you belong to. Which of those groups are the most "important" to you? How easily could you drop your membership in each of those groups? Disowning the family you grew up in would probably be pretty traumatic, but you should be able to drop out of your local PTA more easily. This difference is one that distinguishes **primary groups** and **secondary groups.**

The Oneida Community: A Primary Group with a Difference

Most primary groups are, almost by definition, quite small. There are exceptions, however. One of the most remarkable of these was the Oneida Community, a group of from two to three hundred people who lived together under one roof from 1848 to 1881.

The Oneida Community, located in Oneida, New York, was founded by John Humphrey Noyes, a visionary, radical preacher. The son of a congressman from Vermont, Noyes believed that men and women could lead perfect, sinless lives on earth if conditions were right. For Noyes, these conditions included separation from contemporary society and abolition of private property, marriage, and the upbringing of children solely by their biological parents. In the place of these institutions, Noyes and his followers established a communal life in which primary relations were maintained by submerging the individual in the group. Paradoxically, Noyes's discouragement of the formation of small, exclusive primary groups within the larger community allowed primary relations in the community as a whole to flourish.

In Oneida, daily life was designed to encourage the interaction of everyone with everyone else. All members lived together in a huge "Mansion House," with separate rooms for each adult, many communal spaces, and adjoining facilities for the children. Community members worked together, too. Very few jobs were any particular person's province. Instead, most work was rotated, the constellations of men and women working in any given area changing frequently.

Oneidan children, after an initial fifteen-month period in the care of their mothers, were brought up collectively. They knew who their biological parents were (usually) but were discouraged from forming exclusive attachments to them. Instead, they were taught to look upon all adults in the community as their parents. For adults, not only was marriage disallowed, but also were long-

Primary Groups

In 1909, Charles Horton Cooley drew attention to a special type of social group, and his characterization has remained near the heart of sociology ever since. He called this kind of group the *primary group*, saying: "By primary groups I mean those characterized by intimate face-to-face association and cooperation. They are primary in several senses, but chiefly in that they are fundamental in forming the social nature and ideals of the individual" (1909:23).

Cooley went on to say that primary groups were characterized by a "we feeling" and that individual members of primary groups personally identified with the group and group goals. He said that the intimate association in a primary group creates a feeling of "wholeness" with the group that "involves the sort of sympathy and mutual identification for which 'we' is the natural expression."

The family is an example of a primary group. Although you may grow away from your parents, sisters, and brothers as you get older, there is a sense of identification and belonging that you can probably never escape fully.

Families are not the only primary groups, however. A clique of close friends is also a primary group, characterized by intimacy and identification. You share many of your innermost feelings and most personal experiences with them and they with you. Each of you is important to the others, and the joy and sadness that one of you experiences affects the others to some extent.

Cooley was careful to caution that primary-term exclusive relationships. The Oneidans practiced group marriage. Through a go-between, any man could ask any woman to sleep with him; and, if she consented, they were all set. It was the intermediary's task to ensure that no particular couple slept together too often.

A sense of belonging in the group was fostered in a number of ways. Community members shared similar philosophical and religious beliefs; and, as a condition of membership, they all agreed that Noyes was God's representative on earth. Group members also shared a consciousness of their difference from the outside world, a strong sense of "in-group." Outsiders looked upon them as scandalous and erotic, a point brought home to them by the regular visits of the curious.

Another important way in which Oneidans developed a sense of group belonging was through their political life. Although Noyes was the undisputed leader and the final arbiter of all important issues, everyone was involved in the political life of the community on a daily basis. There were nightly meetings of the entire group, in which every aspect of communal life was discussed and members were encouraged to voice their criticisms and personal grievances.

The Oneida Community was able to maintain this primary-group atmosphere for almost two generations, with no major disagreements. From all indications, the members lived happily. In 1881, however, the group decided to disband in the face of crusades by moral reformers, signs of internal dissension, and the resignation of Noyes, who, already in his seventies, fled to Canada to escape arrest on morals charges for his participation in this unorthodox community.

I've discussed the Oneida at some length to give you the full flavor of primary group relations on a grand scale. For the most part, however, large groups are characterized by a different group experience.

Source: William M. Kephart, *Extraordinary Groups: The Sociology of Unconventional Life-Styles* (New York: St. Martin's, 1976).

group relations are not always friendly and harmonious. You may fight with members of your primary groups, verbally and even physically. When you do, though, you are likely to feel the unhappiness more deeply than you would after a fight with other people. Willard Gaylin stated the case succinctly when he said (1978:121), "The kindness of strangers can touch all our hearts . . . but only those we love can hurt us."

Primary groups are usually based on shared points of view. You and the members of your primary groups are likely to agree on many aspects of life. Even when you do not actually discuss those agreements, you have a "sense" of agreement that runs deeper than words. Herein lies the basis for the feeling of "wholeness" with the group. For an unusual example of a primary group, see the box "The Oneida Community: A Primary Group with a Difference."

Secondary Groups

Although Cooley never spoke of "secondary groups" as such, the contrast between them and primary groups was implicit in his writings on the primary group, and subsequent sociologists have added this term to the discussion of social groups. *Secondary groups* are characterized by more segmented and more specialized relations. They lack the intimacy and feeling of belonging that characterize primary groups. While primary and secondary groups actually represent the ends of a continuum rather than neatly separated types, it is nonetheless useful to examine their distinguishing characteristics.

Your sociology class is probably a good example of a secondary group. Although your class meets periodically, you interact with one another, and the class is somewhat structured by statuses and roles, it is unlikely that you experience the kind of intimacy and belongingness that characterizes your experience of your family. Other secondary groups would include large political parties, large corporations, government bureaus, and the like. Chapter 7 will deal extensively with secondary groups.

A Schematic Model of Primary and Secondary Relationships

Charles Palazzolo (1981) has offered an excellent schematic model of the difference between primary and secondary relations. His model is based on Joseph Luft's (1969) "Johari Awareness Model."

Luft has suggested that interactions can be usefully understood by looking at four aspects of each actor in the interaction. The four quadrants in the Luft model (see Figure 6–1) can be described as follows:

1. *Open:* Those things you bring to an interaction—feelings, motivations, and behaviors—which you are aware of and which you make available to others.
2. *Blind:* Those things which others can see in you but which you are unconscious of.
3. *Hidden:* Those things you are conscious of but which you conceal from those you interact with.
4. *Unknown:* Those things you bring to the interaction that neither you nor those you interact with are aware of.

If you think about the awareness model for a moment, you'll be able to think of situations

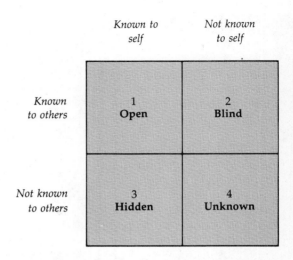

Figure 6–1 The Johari Awareness Model. From Of Human Interaction *by Joseph Luft. By permission of Mayfield Publishing Company. Copyright © 1969 by The National Press.*

in which you emphasize your "open" quadrant—really opening yourself up to those you are interacting with—and situations in which you more cautiously emphasize your "hidden" quadrant. In fact, you can probably think of people you know who generally emphasize one or the other of the quadrants.

Figure 6–2 presents Palazzolo's model of primary and secondary relationships. In "primary relationships," the two actors interact through enlarged "open" quadrants. This would be the case if two good friends are sharing their innermost thoughts and feelings with one another. In a "secondary relationship," the interaction involves more of the actors' "hidden" quadrants. An example of this interaction might be the time a stranger knocked on your door to sell you a magazine subscription.

Palazzolo's use of the Johari awareness model should help you distinguish between primary and secondary groups operating in your life. The applicability of the distinction far exceeds everyday matters, however.

Cooley wasn't the only sociologist to draw a

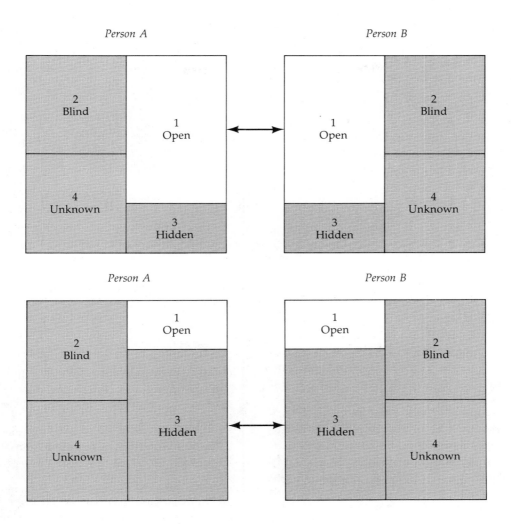

Figure 6–2 A Model of Primary and Secondary Relationships.
   A. Primary Relationship
   B. Secondary Relationship
Source: Adapted from Charles S. Palazzolo, Small Groups: An Introduction, *(New York: D. Van Nostrand, 1981), pp. 126–127.*

distinction between two types of groups. Two European sociologists, Emile Durkheim and Ferdinand Toennies, had also noted and written about the distinction made by Cooley, although the time lag between initial publica-

tion and translation into English delayed the impact of their ideas on American sociology. In the next section, we'll see how they used this distinction to characterize the changes being wrought by the Industrial Revolution.

The Trend Toward Secondary Relations

Cooley's distinction between primary and secondary groups can be seen not just as a way of classifying groups but also as a way of characterizing two types of social relationships. It is in this latter sense that Durkheim and Toennies made a distinction analogous to the one made by Cooley. What both of these European sociologists saw taking place around them was the growing predominance of secondary groups and the relations they entailed, which were transforming the nature of modern life. The conclusions they drew from the analysis, however, were quite different.

Toennies: Gemeinschaft and Gesellschaft

Ferdinand Toennies (1855–1936) was a German sociologist, born into a well-to-do peasant family. He attended the University of Tubingen and received his doctorate when he was twenty-one.

As soon as Toennies completed his doctorate, he returned home and began what was to become his classic work, entitled *Gemeinschaft und Gesellschaft,* later translated as "community and society." In it, Toennies scrutinized two human orientations to social life that had been noted by countless writers at least from Plato onward.

Toennies characterized the two orientations in many ways, but at base he pointed out that some social relations seem to occur *naturally*— what Cooley was to call "primary relations"— while others seem more artificially constructed—what we've called " secondary relations." The former relations he called those of **gemeinschaft,** the latter, those of **gesellschaft.**

The prototype for gemeinschaftlike relations was the family. The order found in family life seemed to flow naturally, without the necessity for discussion, negotiation, or explicit agreements. Each member did what was appropriate

Ferdinand Toennies
1855–1936
Oldenswort, Schleswig
(now West Germany)

Some Important Works
Community and Society, trans., ed. Charles Loomis (East Lansing, Mich.: Michigan State University Press, 1957 [1887]).
Custom: An Essay on Social Codes (New York: Free Press, 1961 [1909]).

Certainly best known for introducing the terms *gemeinschaft* and *gesellschaft,* Toennies was a contemporary of Durkheim. He crossed intellectual swords with Durkheim and Durkheim came away the victor in terms of subsequent influence.

Toennies wrote of the steady shift from closely knit, small-town and rural "communities," to large-scale, complex, industrial "societies," generally favoring the former, at a time when most intellectuals were rosy-eyed about the "progress" of bigger and better. As a result, Toennies's ideas were not well received, and he was essentially ignored.

to the survival and proper functioning of the family as a unit. Toennies saw an organic *unity* in the family akin to the unity you find in your own body. Family members did not need to negotiate their interactions with one another any more than your own heart and lungs negotiate how they will interact. The parts of your body cooperate with one another *naturally*, and Toennies suggested that families and other gemeinschafts operated on the basis of a "natural will."

The prototype for gesellschaftlike relations Toennies found in commerce. Buyers and sellers needed to form explicit agreements to carry out their relations. Each operated from his or her own self-interest, those self-interests clearly conflicted, and it was necessary to create commercial transactions that would be relatively satisfactory to each party.

In contrast to the natural will that family members shared in common, Toennies spoke of the "rational will" that individuals possessed and exhibited. Human beings were also capable of logical calculations and figuring out how to get what they wanted out of life. This rational will, Toennies suggested, lay at the basis of gesellschaft relations.

Toennies summarized these two orientations to social life by saying that gemeinschafts were "organically integrated," whereas gesellschafts were "mechanically integrated."

Toennies went on to apply this distinction in a much broader context. Granting that all individuals engaged in both gemeinschaftlike and gesellschaftlike relations, and that all societies contained both types of relations, Toennies pointed out that different societies had a different balance of the two. Some societies—such as preliterate tribes and small, rural towns—were primarily characterized by gemeinschaft relations, whereas others—such as large, modern cities and nations—were tipped in the direction of gesellschaft relations.

Toennies saw a trend in modern society toward increasing predominance of gesellschaftlike relations, and he lamented many aspects of the change. Modern society was organizing and distorting what was spontaneous and natural in gemeinschaft relations, and the patterns of social life were thus becoming "gradually devoid of substance until they are mere ways of speech or phraseology" (1887:107).

Toennies's obvious preference for gemeinschaft over gesellschaft did not sit well in an

"You the one who ordered the gesellschaft?"

age of awe over industrial and urban progress. In its first edition, his book was largely ignored. One critic, however, took the book's message seriously and made his disagreement explicit.

Durkheim: The Division of Labor

In contemporary sociology, the French sociologist Emile Durkheim (1858–1917) is far better known than Toennies. In 1889, Durkheim wrote a review of Toennies's classic for the *Revue Philosophique*. After criticizing the book as "very laborious," Durkheim noted his many agreements with Toennies:

> Like the author, I believe that there are two major types of societies, and the words which he uses to designate them indicate quite well their nature. . . . like him, I admit that gemeinschaft is the first to develop and that gesellschaft is the derived end. Finally, I accept his general guidelines of analysis and the description that he makes for us of gemeinschaft.
>
> But the point where I part company from him is with his theory of gesellschaft. (1889:1198)

In particular, Durkheim objected to Toennies's characterization of gesellschaft relations as "mechanical." Durkheim was unwilling to consider modern society as in any way inferior to earlier social forms. Durkheim wrote:

Now I believe that all the life of great social agglomerations is as natural as that of small aggregations. It is neither less organic nor less internally activated. Beyond purely individual actions there is in our contemporary societies a type of collective activity which is just as natural as that of the less extended societies of former days. (1889:1198)

To prove his point, Durkheim wrote *The Division of Labor in Society* (1893), which has become one of the classics in sociological literature. In it, he described the manner in which complex, modern societies develop ever-greater specialization of work roles. In place of the earlier "jacks-of-all-trades," Durkheim shows how each individual in modern society becomes a specialist and comes to depend on others in meeting his or her needs.

A chief concern of Durkheim's—and the one that most concerns us now—is his view of the manner in which all the many specialists were coordinated and integrated into a whole society. Recall that Toennies described this as "mechanical solidarity." Following out his earlier objection, Durkheim simply reversed Toennies's terms: he said modern societies were characterized by *organic* solidarity while simpler ones were characterized by *mechanical* solidarity!

Modern societies, Durkheim argued, ought to be seen as single organisms—as the human body is an organism. At a time when popular sentiment favored modern society, Durkheim's reversed terminology was accepted and Toennies's was forgotten. In this startling move, Durkheim also created a problem for sociology students ever since. ("Let's see, mechanical solidarity is what characterizes the groups that *don't* have machines.")

The debate over the net "goodness" or "badness" in the evolution of modern society has survived both Toennies and Durkheim. Although the recent environmental movement in the United States and elsewhere has tipped the balance more in the direction of the view taken by Toennies, people still disagree today.

There is one thing people do not disagree about, however. Everyone recognizes that significant changes *have* occurred and that the changes continue unfolding with each passing day. Many social interactions that typically were "intimate, face-to-face relations" a century ago in America, for instance, are now more typically secondary relations. Where most Americans used to buy groceries from neighborhood grocers who were personal friends as well as shopowners, today's shopping patterns are more likely to involve large supermarkets where the shopper may never have met the checkout clerk before. Family physicians have been increasingly replaced by medical clinics in which patients may see a different physician each time. In higher education, mass lectures have increasingly replaced small classes.

The study of social groups in society, then, involves both small groups such as families and friendship cliques and large, more impersonal organizations. Research on group dynamics has touched both aspects. The remainder of this chapter will report on some of the things sociologists have learned about small-group dynamics, and Chapter 7 will focus on large, formal organizations and on what some have called "organizational society."

Small-Group Dynamics

As I've suggested, sociologists have long been fascinated with what goes on when a few folks get together to interact with one another: playing cards, carrying on a discussion, negotiating a purchase, and so on. This fascination has led some sociologists out into the field, lurking around card games, discussions, and so forth.

It has led other sociologists to bring human groups into the laboratory for controlled scrutiny. "Small-group research" refers to the controlled examination of small-group interactions. Typically, the researcher recruits individuals for the study, combines them into a group, gives them a task to perform, and observes what happens under various conditions. In this section, I want to give you a sense of the topics that sociologists and social psychologists have pursued both in the field and in the laboratory. We'll look at such things as group size, composition, structure, cohesion, and leadership. Let's begin with an examination of the power groups have to affect individuals.

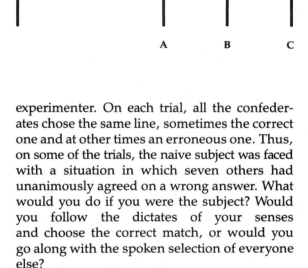

A   B   C

The Power of Group Judgments: The Asch Experiment

Everyone has experienced the power that groups can have in swaying our judgments about ourselves and the world. We already discussed this in terms of Mead's "generalized other" and Cooley's "looking-glass self" in determining our self-images. But what are the limits to this power of groups to influence our perceptions? In trying to answer this question, the social psychologist Solomon Asch (1955) constructed one of the most famous experiments in small-group research.

Asch's initial experiment went like this: each person in a group of eight men was asked individually to match a given line with one of three others of clearly different lengths and then announce his decision to the group. For example, which of the three lines to the right in the figure,—A, B, or C—is the same length as the line on the left?

If you picked C, you'd be correct. So far, the experiment would seem pretty trivial. In the Asch experiments, however, there was a catch. Unknown to the real subject, seven of the eight people in the group were confederates of the experimenter. On each trial, all the confederates chose the same line, sometimes the correct one and at other times an erroneous one. Thus, on some of the trials, the naive subject was faced with a situation in which seven others had unanimously agreed on a wrong answer. What would you do if you were the subject? Would you follow the dictates of your senses and choose the correct match, or would you go along with the spoken selection of everyone else?

On two-thirds of the trials, Asch found, the fifty male college students who were the subjects of the experiment resisted the group's pressure, but on the remaining one-third of the trials, they went along with the erroneous perceptions of the group. (For comparison, subjects in a control group, who were not subjected to group pressure, matched the lines correctly on virtually every trial.)

Individuals varied widely in how they responded to the pressure of the group. Some didn't succumb to the pressure at all, whereas others caved in on almost every trial. Among those who resisted, some appeared confident and unperturbed by the group response, but others appeared anxious and increasingly embarrassed by their deviation from the group consensus.

Among the "yielders," most subjects were aware that their answers contradicted the way they actually saw the lines. One subject said afterward that had the other members of the group appeared less confident, he would have answered in accord with his perceptions. Based on follow-up interviews with the subjects, Asch suggested that most of the yielders fell into two categories—one composed of those who, in the face of group pressure, came to believe that their own perceptions were wrong, and the other composed of subjects who answered in accordance with the group because they feared appearing different from or inferior to the others.

In later trials, Asch varied the conditions of the experiment to learn more about the nature of group conformity. For instance, when there were two naive subjects in the group rather than one, Asch found that the error rate was cut by two-thirds. And when one of the confederates consistently answered correctly, the error rate dropped even further. In other words, the introduction of just one other potential dissenter into the group undermined the hold of the majority. To Asch this demonstrated how crucial it is that we have at least some human support for the formulation of our perceptions.

Asch also varied the size of the group. The pressure to conform was virtually absent when only one other person was matching the lines with the subject. In groups of three, when the two confederates answered erroneously, the power of the group began to be felt. Group pressure reached its full force with the subject and three confederates. Further increases in group size didn't significantly change the extent of the pressure, as measured by the rate of matching errors.

The Asch experiment demonstrates the power groups have on the individuals in them. Later research has examined the nature of interactions among members of groups. Let's look at some of the variables that seem to influence our behavior within groups.

The Size of Groups

We have already seen some reasons why group size is important. Simmel pointed out that a dyad ceases to be a group if one person drops out, whereas triads have more survival power. And the Asch experiments showed that group size had an impact on the conforming behavior of individuals. A. Paul Hare, a researcher who has examined the influence of size on how groups work, has identified (1981:705) five steps involved in a group getting work done:

1. Members need to define the situation and agree on the rules to be followed in addressing it.

2. They search for relevant facts and resources needed to solve the problem they face.

3. They establish a division of labor and build a group solidarity.

4. Leadership is exercised and decisions are made.

5. Finally, the issue of commitment is addressed as the group works out who will do what in carrying out the decisions reached.

This process is strongly affected by the size of the group. As Hare reports:

Usually in a small group, of five members, there is enough time to explore in some depth the opinions and feelings of each member of the group and to take them into consideration when reaching a group decision. But with a group several times as large, say 20 or 30 members, there is a tendency to consider the opinions of only the most vocal and high-status members and to use some form of majority decision, sometimes leaving a dissatisfied minority that is nevertheless supposed to remain committed to the group goal. (Hare 1981:705)

Hare suggests that large groups can operate more like small groups if a consensus model is used in place of majority rule. Thus, all group decisions must be based on unanimous consent. This works, however, only if all members are willing to be honest in their participation. There must be a full opportunity for people to express their views, without concern for who has the "right" or "wrong" view, and no one can give in simply to reach agreement. Ultimately, whatever decision is reached, each member needs to be willing to support that decision as though he or she had been the first to think of it.

Coalitions

Another aspect of "microgroup" life that has interested sociologists is the formation of temporary or permanent partnerships called **coalitions.** Individuals usually enter into coalitions for the purpose of gaining advantages that they could not enjoy as individuals. Such coalitions, moreover, are formed in opposition to someone else.

Theodore Caplow (1920–) has done the most extensive theoretical work (1959,1969) on this subject in recent years. Caplow has been especially interested in the formation of coalitions in connection with creating power, asking which two members of a triad would most likely form a coalition against the third member.

The simplest example of coalition formation involves three individuals who have different amounts of some resource such as money, strength, or political power. Suppose two relationships exist initially: (1) A has more power, say than B, who, in turn, has more than C, and (2) A has less power than the combined power of B and C. Under these conditions, we might expect B and C to form a coalition against A.

Repeated experiments on coalition formation, however, show the matter to be more complicated. Shaw (1976:102–105) summarizes the main contemporary theories on the subject.

The "minimum resource theory" suggests that people will form coalitions in such a fashion as to create the smallest combination of resources—people, money, or other resource—that gets the job done. This is the B + C coalition mentioned above. Notice, however, that other coalitions—A + B and A + C—*could* have been formed. In fact, A might wish such a coalition to avoid domination by B + C. But neither of these alternative coalitions is reasonable from B's or C's positions. In the B + C coalition, B gets to be the "senior" partner, instead of being the "junior" partner in A + B, and C is more nearly an equal partner in B + C than would be the case in A + C.

The contrasting "anticompetitive theory" suggests that persons will form coalitions with a main concern for creating equality among the partners to the coalition—thereby providing an equal sharing in the rewards that result from joining together. In the above situation, we would expect B to form a coalition with either A or C, whoever came closest to being an equal partner. Since most of the support for this theory has derived from studies limited to female subjects, Shaw (1976:105) suggests that women are more likely than men to seek equality within their coalitions.

Finally, Shaw suggests an "utter confusion theory," which holds that, because so many factors enter into the calculation, coalition formation is ultimately unpredictable. Although some orderliness is apparent under controlled experimental conditions, it tends to disappear under real-life conditions.

Before leaving this topic, I want to remind you that coalitions represent much more than logical exercises and laboratory experiments. Hear how John Gittings (1981:19) points this out in *South*, a newsmagazine representing the point of view of the Third World:

As US-Soviet detente collapses, the leaders of the West make their pilgrimages to Peking and welcome China's new alignment. But is it really in China's own interests, or ultimately even in the interests of world peace? One recalls the international background of George Orwell's gloomy vision of 1984: Three superpowers dominate the world, two ganging up on the third to wage war. The alliance periodically breaks down as one or the other changes side, but the war continues regardless. Today's situation falls short—as yet—of war, but it embodies the same crude use of triangular diplomacy as a device by which A + B can combine against C.

As we shall see throughout this book, many of the dynamics of small groups can be seen to operate on large-scale organizational, societal, and even international levels.

The Composition of Groups

Another factor that determines the nature of interaction within a small group is the group's *composition*—who makes up the group. Are they all men, all women, or mixed? Are they homogeneous or heterogeneous in age, social class, and various other characteristics?

M. E. Shaw (1976:235) has summarized some of the more consistent findings that have emerged from a great many experiments on this aspect of small-group interaction:

1. Other things being equal, groups composed of members having diverse, relevant abilities accomplish group tasks more effectively than groups composed of members having similar abilities.

2. Members conform more in mixed-sex groups than in same-sex groups.

3. Racial heterogeneity tends to create interpersonal tension that is reflected in the feelings and behaviors of group members.

4. Groups whose members are heterogeneous in personality profiles perform more effectively than groups with homogeneous personality profiles.

In this context, researchers have been especially interested in different degrees of *compat-*

ibility among group members and the degrees of *cohesion* created. Researchers have found that the more compatible group members are and the greater their cohesiveness, the higher their productivity and effectiveness in task performance is likely to be. Moreover, compatibility and cohesion seem to produce member satisfaction also.

Measuring Interaction

The measurement of interaction is fundamental to much small-group research. Very often, we want to describe how members of a group act toward one another under various circumstances. Are they friendly or hostile, cooperative or competitive? Robert Bales's (1950) **interactional process analysis** (IPA) schema describes twelve classes of actions that he found critical to understanding small group interactions. Bales's IPA is presented in Figure 6–3. As you can see, Bales has categorized the types of interaction and indicated the problem areas they address.

Using the IPA, small-group researchers observe groups in action, noting the chronology of interactions. For example, Person X asks Person Y for an opinion (8) about what the group is addressing. Y responds (5), but Person Z

Much can be learned about organized social life through the study of small-group interactions.

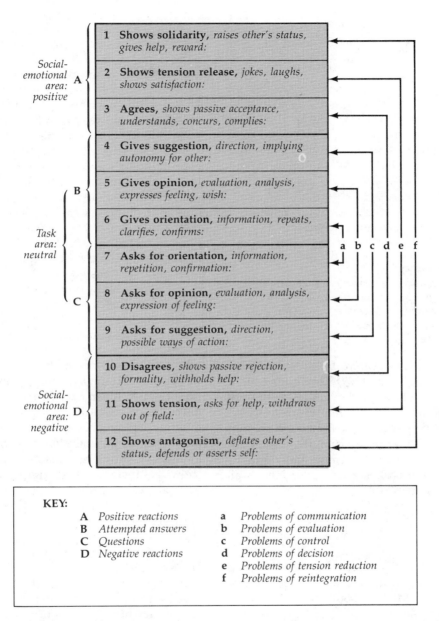

Figure 6–3 *Interaction Process Analysis Categories. Reprinted from* Interaction Process Analysis *by Robert F. Bales.*
By permission of The University of Chicago Press. Copyright © 1950. The University of Chicago Press. Source: Reprinted
from Charles S. Palazzolo, Small Groups: An Introduction, *(New York: D. Van Nostrand, 1981), p. 159.*

jumps in to disagree (10) with Y's opinion. X comes to Y's defense (1), and Y jokes (2) "Take it easy. We don't want to upset the sociologists who are watching us."

Bales and others have used this system for years, and they have amassed a great deal of data on small-group interaction. Palazzolo (1981:167) summarizes some of what researchers have learned about the effects of group size on interaction:

As the size of the group increases:

Showing tension release increases emphatically
Giving suggestion increases emphatically
Showing solidarity increases somewhat
Giving information increases (if dyads are excluded from this category)
Showing tension decreases emphatically
Showing agreement decreases
Asking for opinion decreases
Giving opinion decreases (if dyads are excluded from this category)

In more recent research, Bales and collaborator Stephen Cohen (1979) have suggested a "System for the Multiple Level Observation of Groups" (SYMLOG) which classifies behavior along three dimensions: (1) dominant/submissive, (2) friendly/unfriendly, and (3) instrumentally-controlled/emotionally-expressive. Any given action, then, is coded on all three dimensions.

Leadership

Leadership has been one of the most studied aspects of small-group interactions. According to the research of Bales (1950) and others, there are two basic leadership "styles"—"task-oriented" and "expressive." Task-oriented leaders focus their attention on organizing group members to get a job done, whereas expressive leaders mostly attend to the interpersonal relations among group members. Issues like this are, of course, relevant to day-to-day work situations, with organizational leaders leaning in one or the other direction.

Which leadership style do you suppose is best? Fred Fiedler (1981) reports that neither style is superior to the other. Different situations seem to call for different leadership styles. When the work to be done is highly structured and repetitive—assembly line work, for example—leaders do well to pay attention to their subordinates' emotional needs. This is less critical in situations where the job itself provides challenge and satisfaction; there, task-oriented leadership is more appropriate.

This conclusion, which makes sense on the face of it, suggests that leaders should tailor their leadership styles to the individual situations in which they find themselves. Unfortunately, few people seem capable of changing their style that easily, and studies of organizational leaders show most don't even know how their subordinates view them.

Sociologists have been particularly interested in understanding who becomes a leader in informal small-group interactions. On the whole, people with high status tend to run things in most small groups and in small-group experiments. If some participants are known to have a high status in society—represented by a title, academic degree, or similar credentials—they are generally looked to by other group members to provide the leadership. Jury studies show, for instance, that high-status members have a greater influence than other members on a group verdict.

Some researchers see the tendency of higher-status people to take the lead in small groups as part of a more general process called "status generalization." "Status generalization" refers to our tendency to assume that a person's relative standing in one situation should have some bearing on his or her standing in another situation (Webster and Driskell 1978). In the case of juries, for example, executives and professionals are presumed to be better judges of legal issues, better judges of character, and simply better judges—period.

These, then, are a few of the topics that sociologists have examined in the study of small-group dynamics. You may find small-group dynamics particularly interesting since it focuses on something very close to you. You should be able to observe some of the things you've been reading about if you pay attention to your own participation in small groups during the next day or so.

We need to leave this topic and move on now, but I want to be sure that you realize we have only scratched the surface here. We've said next to nothing, for example, about the influence that different *tasks* have on the flow of interactions. We've scarcely touched on the impact of personal characteristics and have mentioned the element of cohesion only in passing—two topics that have been studied extensively. What I've had to say about leadership merely points you in the direction of what has been done. Still, I think it is useful for you to have this beginning contact with small-group research, especially as we turn now to bigger things—that is, bigger groups.

Summary

In this chapter, we have examined a fundamental building block of organized social life—the group. As we saw at the outset, sociologists have something fairly specific in mind when they speak of "groups." The chief characteristics are: (1) shared interests, (2) interaction, (3) a common identity, and (4) some degree of structure. These characteristics, then, distinguish a group from a "social category" (such as dog owners) or an "aggregation" (a gathering, such as an audience).

There are many different ways of examining groups and their impact on social life. First, we tend to organize our view of and response to group life in terms of "in-groups" (those we belong to) and "out-groups" (those we don't belong to), and we saw that this "us/them" approach to things can generate prejudices and malice.

Reference groups are another important side of group life. Essentially, "reference groups" provide us with a vehicle for evaluating ourselves. Some reference groups are made up of those we identify with, and we compare our lot in life with that of our peers, creating the possibility for experiencing relative deprivation, even in the presence of plenty. Our reference groups are made up of those we look up to and whose opinions we respect.

One of the more persistent distinctions sociologists and others have made concerns primary and secondary groups. Charles Horton Cooley described "primary groups" as those intimate, face-to-face groups about which we experience a definite sense of "we feeling." The family is a prototypical example. "Secondary groups," on the other hand, are more casual and superficial in the interpersonal experience they produce. Typically, members of a secondary group know and experience only limited aspects of each other—having to do perhaps with a member's function in the group. The members of your sociology class constitute a secondary group, though there may be small primary groups contained within it.

The distinction between primary and secondary groups actually reflects something bigger in society and in sociology. Stepping back to take a broader view, you will see that the development of society—from the simple to the complex—corresponds with a growing predominance of secondary groups, with more of our life involved in secondary relationships. In contrast with the small town where everyone knew everyone else in depth, most of our relationships in a modern society are more fleeting and superficial.

Two sociologists—among many—who have examined this difference were Ferdinand Toennies and Emile Durkheim. Toennies gave the German names *gemeinschaft* and *gesellschaft* to the two forms of social organization, translated respectively as "community" (where primary relations predominated) and "society" (characterized more by secondary relations.) Toennies saw the former as more "natural" and said it was held together with an "organic solidarity," whereas modern society was more artificial, requiring a "mechanical solidarity" to persist. Durkheim disagreed with Toennies in the evaluation of the two forms, and he argued that modern, industrial society—with an intricate division of labor—was more of an "organism," thus reversing Toennies's use of the terms "mechanical" and "organic solidarity."

Because the two forms of group life—intimate, face-to-face interactions versus more distant and casual relations in larger organizations—are both important aspects of social life, sociologists have studied both. The remainder of Chapter 6 was devoted to some of the research done on small groups, whereas Chapter 7 is about formal organizations.

Small-group research involves the controlled examination of interaction in small groups, typically conducted in a laboratory. Under such controlled conditions, researchers are able to get a close look at the dynamics of group life at an intimate level.

The size of groups is an important determinant of interactions. At the lowest level, what Simmel labeled the "dyad"—consisting of two people—is the smallest group. The "triad" (three or more) differs significantly from the dyad in that it has an existence that transcends the participation of a specific member. That is, someone can drop out and the group persists, whereas a dyad is dependent on the continued participation of each member.

Beginning at this level, sociologists have devoted considerable attention to the process of "coalition" formation, the creation of partnerships for the purpose of dominating others or avoiding their domination. Several strategies have been observed, and they can be seen in operation among individuals in face-to-face relations among nations.

The composition of groups—in terms of the characteristics of its members—also affects group dynamics. In terms of accomplishing tasks effectively, for example, diversity seems more functional than similarity, both in terms of abilities and in personality types. Racially mixed groups tend to generate some tensions, whereas groups mixed by gender produce more conformity than is found among all-male or all-female groups.

Group leadership has also been researched extensively. One of the more persistent findings in this regard has to do with the extent to which members of small laboratory groups grant respect and leadership to members who have (or are said to have) high social status in real life. This observation has important real-life connotations in such situations as jury deliberations.

It's time now to expand our focus on group life to encompass bigger things. In Chapter 7 we are going to take a look at formal organizations: such things as large corporations, bureaucracies, voluntary associations, and so forth. By the time you complete Chapter 7, you will have seen how thoroughly you and I are group-oriented in almost every aspect of our day-to-day life.

Important Terms

group
category
aggregation
dyad
triad
in-group
out-group
reference group

primary group
secondary group
gemeinschaft
gesellschaft
coalitions
interactional process
 analysis

Suggested Readings

Blalock, Hubert M. and Paul H. Wilken
1979 *Intergroup Processes: A Micro-Macro-Perspective.* New York: Free Press.
Looks at how people evaluate probabilities based on exchange theory perspective.

Borgatta, Edgar F., and Paul Morgan Baker, eds.
1981 "Small Groups: An Agenda for Research and Theory." *American Behavioral Scientist*, May/June.
This entire issue of the journal is addressed to small-group research. Among other things, it brings you up to date on what is known regarding leadership, coalitions, performance, group structure, size, and characteristics—plus describing the history of this approach to the study of social life.

Caplow, Theodore
1969 *Two Against One: Coalitions in Triads.* Englewood Cliffs, N.J.: Prentice-Hall.
I touched on this briefly in the chapter, and you might like to pursue it further. Caplow's analysis demonstrates the dynamic process of group formation. Though he focuses on a specific type of group (the coalition), the logic of creating purposeful partnerships can provide more general insights into the foundation of group life.

Hare, A. Paul
1976 *Handbook of Small Group Research.* New York: Free Press.
This handbook lays out the field of small-group research in comprehensive detail. Hare provides a good tour through the topics that concern researchers in this field as well as presenting the findings derived to date.

Hyman, Herbert, and Eleanor Singer, Eds.
1968 *Readings in Reference Group Theory.* New York: Free Press.
The reference-group concept has received far more detailed attention in sociology than could be presented in an introductory chapter such as this. The Hyman-Singer collection of articles on the topic illustrates the many directions that sociologists have taken in the elaboration and application of this fertile idea.

Nisbet, Robert
1970 *The Social Bond.* New York: Knopf.
The threads which hold society together are explored from a sociological perspective.

Nixon, Howard L.
1979 *The Small Group.* Englewood Cliffs, NJ: Prentice-Hall.
Discussion how small groups work and are structured.

Palazzolo, Charles S.
1981 *Small Groups: An Introduction.* New York: Van Nostrand.
This provides an up-to-date and comprehensive summary of small-group research. Palazzolo brings together a variety of theoretical viewpoints, research methods, and empirical findings.

Shaw, Marvin E.
1976 *Group Dynamics: The Psychology of Small Group Behavior.* New York: McGraw-Hill.
Shaw has created a powerful and interesting compendium of findings arrived at by small-group researchers. His organization is particularly useful: he summarizes all the research dealing with a particular topic, and each chapter concludes with a listing of plausible hypotheses to be drawn from previous research.

Weber, Max
[1925] "Bureaucracy." In *From Max Weber: Essays in*
1946 *Sociology,* ed., trans. H. H. Gerth, C. Wright Mills, pp. 196–244. New York: Oxford University Press.
This work is a classic in two regards. First, it is a classic statement on the nature of bureaucracy. Second, it is a perfect illustration of the "ideal type" method of analysis discussed in Chapter 2, thus making it a wise investment of time and energy for the serious beginning sociologist (or for anyone else who wants to know why bureaucracies turned out the way they did).

The North Carolina jury took only seventy-five minutes to find Joan Little not guilty of killing her jailer, who (she stated) had tried to assault her sexually. The defense team had spent ten days in July 1975 to question 150 prospective jurors in an effort to find a panel it considered sympathetic to the young black woman's plea of self-defense. The ten-day examination—similar to others involving significant political and social issues—was the culmination of the nine-month-long Joan Little Fair Trial Jury Project, an undertaking that cost nearly forty thousand dollars, most of it spent on a seven-member team of professional sociologists, psychologists, and pollsters. The project involved over a thousand telephone interviews, the use of a computer to correlate attitudes and demographic data, and detailed questioning of prospective jurors—with a psychic and body-language expert on hand to be sure that nonverbal clues would not be missed—in order to decide which jurors to remove from the panel through challenges. (Van Dyke 1977:ix)

Thus, Jon Van Dyke begins a recent examination of jury-selection procedures. What Van Dyke describes is increasingly common in the modern American system of justice. It's a far cry from what you may have seen on late-night Perry Mason reruns, and it's also a far cry from the jury system that we Americans inherited from English legal tradition.

Harry Kalven, Jr., and Hans Zeisel (1976:360) say of the jury's beginnings: "Originally, the jurors were neighbourhood witnesses who passed judgement based on what they themselves knew." While such a system might have made sense in very small villages, population growth and urbanization made it unworkable. Eventually, then, a model was developed in which the jurors would know nothing of the case initially, and they would reach their verdict based on evidence presented to them in court. So the criterion for a "good" juror shifted from having personal knowledge and conclusions

regarding the case to having *none:* now jurors were to be clean slates, ignorant of the case and impartial. This model was exported to the American colonies and later embodied in the United States Constitution.

Kalven and Zeisel (1976:361) report that the jury system has never been successfully established outside the Anglo-American orbit. In England, moreover, it is now limited to specific types of cases; "thus, the United States has emerged today as the home of the jury system for both criminal and civil cases. Some 120,000 jury trials are conducted there annually, more than 90 percent of all jury trials in the world."

The intention behind the jury system is to place the issue of guilt or innocence in the hands of a panel representing a cross section of the community. In practice, however, several factors militate against that ideal. We can see this in the process of jury selection.

The process begins as the court creates a list of eligible jurors. In many jurisdictions, this list is simply the list of registered voters or those who voted in the latest election. Elsewhere, the jury commissioner makes a personal selection. Clearly, this latter method is open to all sorts of bias and certainly does not insure that juries will represent a cross section of the community. Even where voter lists are used, representativeness is not assured, however; many minority groups, as well as the poor, are underrepresented among voters. This is a matter of real concern for minority victims and defendants alike. The black man who rapes a white woman, for example, does not fare as well as the white man who rapes a black woman. This is not the only form of bias in jury selection, however. Van Dyke (1977:25) reports that:

In four-fifths of the federal districts surveys in 1971, blue-collar workers had fewer seats on juries than they would have had if they had been represented in proportion to their presence in the population. Three out of every ten federal districts underrepresented these workers by more than 20 percent—which would seem to be a "substantial" amount.

Increasingly, sociologists have been called into court to testify as to the demographic makeup of communities and the lack of representativeness in juries. This is only the beginning of the process, however.

When a particular case is ready to be heard, some forty or so prospective jurors are called to report to court. Once there, they are questioned individually—first by the judge and then by the prosecution and defense attorneys—to determine if there are any reasons why they cannot hear the case impartially. If grounds are uncovered which suggest a prospective juror cannot hear the case impartially, he or she will be challenged "for cause." In addition, each side has a certain number of "peremptory challenges," requiring no reason. All of this means that the attorneys have a good deal of control over who is excluded from the jury—and neither side is interested in creating an impartial panel. Each side wants a jury biased in its direction.

Over the years, a good deal of conventional wisdom has developed over how different types of people behave on juries. Butchers and barbers, for example, are thought to be harsher than other people, so defense attorneys avoid them. Van Dyke (1977:152–153) quotes from a book prepared by a Texas assistant district attorney for the training of prosecutors:

III. What to look for in a juror.

   A. Attitudes

     1. You are not looking for a fair juror, but rather a strong, biased and sometimes hypocritical individual who believes that Defendants are different from them in kind, rather than degree.

     2. You are not looking for any member of a minority group which may subject him to oppression—they almost always empathize with the accused.

     3. You are not looking for free thinkers and flower children.

   B. Observation is worthwhile.

     1. Look at the panel out in the hall before they are seated. You can often spot the showoffs and the liberals by how and to whom they are talking.

     2. Observe the veniremen [jurors] as they walk into the courtroom.

       a. You can tell almost as much about a man by how he walks, as how he talks.

       b. Look for physical afflictions. These people usually sympathize with the accused.

     3. Dress

       a. Conservatively, well dressed people are generally stable and good for the State.

       b. In many counties, the jury summons states that the appropriate dress is coat and tie. One who does not wear a coat and tie is often a non-conformist and therefore a bad State's juror.

     4. Women

       a. I don't like women jurors because I don't trust them.

       b. They do, however, make the best jurors in cases involving crimes against children.

       c. It is possible that their "women's intuition" can help you if you can't win your case with the facts.

       d. Young women too often sympathize with the Defendant; old women wearing too much make-up are usually unstable, and therefore are bad State's jurors.

In recent years, as indicated in the opening quotation regarding the Joan Little case, sociologists and other social scientists have been engaged as consultants in the selection of jury members. Sometimes, it has been possible for researchers to survey the panel of prospective jurors before their appearance in court. More typically, surveys of representative samples within the community have made it possible for the researchers to determine how different kinds of people may behave if seated on the jury.

In one Chicago civil case, a young man was being tried for an auto accident in which a teenage girl was left a quadriplegic. The main question was how much money the jury would award the victim; the award was expected to run in the millions. The victim's attorney arranged for a community survey in which 713 Chicago residents were presented with the essential facts of the case and asked how they would vote. An analysis of the survey results produced a set of guidelines for the attorneys in the jury-selection process. Lori Andrews (1982:66) reviews some of that advice:

> They found that young, unmarried renters with incomes under $15,000—people who have high hopes for their own futures—would be good jurors [for the victim]. Also good bets were older, lower-income, blue-collar workers who did not have such fabulous futures themselves, and thus could sympathize with the girl. The *worst* jurors, according to the survey results, would be successful people who enjoy a good life: "They look at Sue's predicament differently, feeling that it is just a matter of putting a price tag on Sue's loss, which in most cases is less than they would put on their own life and their children's."

Social scientists have been involved in many other aspects of the jury-trial process. Andrews (1982:67) continues:

> Today, social scientists stand ready to advise attorneys on how to be most persuasive in every phase of a trial. Experts in marketing, communications, social psychology, and other disciplines are now available to tell attorneys not only how to choose a jury but whether to ask for a jury at all, how best to phrase their legal arguments, and even how they can hide or accentuate their own personality traits—all in an attempt to influence the verdict.

Besides their involvement in actual trials, sociologists have also studied and commented on the jury system in general. For example, they have studied the jury deliberation process. Much of the small-group research discussed earlier in this chapter is relevant to the process through which juries reach their decisions, and some studies have addressed the jury process specifically. While it is no longer legal to tape real jury deliberations—some early studies did that— a variety of methodologies have been developed.

In one massive study, Kalven and Zeisel (1966) surveyed the judges who presided over 3,576 jury trials, asking them how they themselves would have decided the cases. In 78 percent of the cases, the judges would have rendered the same judgment as the juries did. This finding led the researchers to question whether the expense of jury trials could be justified.

Sometimes researchers have interviewed jurors after their verdict was reached, asking about the deliberation process. And, finally, a variety of simulation techniques have been used. Mock juries, composed of college students or a sample drawn from the community, have been asked to deliberate real cases. In some cases, they have been given transcripts of the trial, other times they have heard the case through audio or video tapes. The problem with mock juries, however, is that they do not operate under the same pressure as real juries. Nonetheless, the observation of mock juries has produced some insights into the small-group dynamics at work.

Sociologists have also contributed to innovations in the jury system. Some critics have suggested that twelve jurors are more than enough for the job to be done, and six-member juries have been experimented with. Hans Zeisel (1971) has shown, however, that smaller juries are less likely to be representative of the community than are twelve-member juries. He concludes further that the smaller juries would result in more guilty verdicts. Walbert (1971) agrees with Zeisel, basing his conclusion on studies of group pressure and conformity in small-group research.

Numerous other studies have been conducted on the implications of smaller juries, and the issue is likely to be researched further in the years to come. I've presented this research overview to show you some of the ways that the sociological study of groups has real-life implications.

PRACTICING SOCIOLOGY

On June 22, 1982, a jury in Washington, D.C., found John W. Hinckley, Jr., not guilty of attempting to assassinate President Reagan, by reason of insanity. The next day, two jurors said they wanted to find Hinckley guilty but gave in to pressure.

[Maryland T.] Copelin, 50, an elementary school food service director, and Nathalia L. Brown, 31, a machinist for a local utility company, said during an emotional joint press conference that they held out as long as they could, but finally yielded to the arguments of other jurors.

"Till the day I die, I'll believe he's guilty," Brown said. "My conscience wasn't clear—that's why I called this press conference. I felt he was guilty. I argued and argued the case. But trying to fight 10 other people was hard. My nerves were so bad, I just gave up."

From what you've learned about small group dynamics, comment on this report. What factors—aside from being outnumbered—might have contributed to the two jurors giving in?

Sources: San Francisco Chronicle, June 23, 1982, p. 6. *Time*, July 5, 1982, pp. 22–27.

7

Organizations and Institutions

In Chapter 6, we saw that humans appear to have a natural tendency to join together in groups. We are a gregarious species, and the history of humans is unavoidably a social one. In this chapter, we are going to move beyond simple "groupness" and the small group to more formal and complex forms of social life, from primary to secondary groups. As we are going to see, humans have a tendency not only to form groups but also to regularize, routinize, and systemize their groupness. This is a general theme that will recur in this book.

This chapter deals with **organizations** and **institutions**. Organizations, as we'll see, are a type of group—specific social structures organized around a purpose. Institutions, on the other hand, are the contexts within which organizations function. Thus, for example, capitalism is an institution: a set of agreements about economic affairs in a society. General Motors is an organization, structured and operating in accordance with those agreements.

This chapter begins with a brief look at the characteristics of organizations such as size, subdivision, specialization, structure, and system. The purpose here is to sketch the elements of organizations, just as we began the previous chapter by sketching the elements of groups in general. We'll examine the notions of *formal* and *complex organizations*, and we'll see some of the factors that determine the structure of organizations.

Having introduced organizations, I will deal in more depth with two quite different, though not mutually exclusive, forms of organization. First, we'll look at *voluntary organizations* in order to see how extensively we have organized our interests and concerns in modern society. Then we'll zero in on the most formal of organizational forms: *bureaucracy*. As you'll discover, sociologists have been particularly interested in bureaucracy, as the extreme example of secondary-group relations. We'll look at the chief characteristics of bureaucracy, at its main advantages, and at some of its problems.

The chapter then turns to an examination of the various methods of organizational leadership that have evolved over the course of developing ever more complex and larger organizations, chiefly in business and government.

We'll conclude with an examination of institutions, setting the stage for a more in-depth study of the major institutions of society in Part Four.

Characteristics of Organizations

It has been said that we are an "organizational society": we are typically born in organizations (hospitals), educated in them, married in them, work in them all our years, and finally die in them. Richard Hall (1977:24) distinguishes our experience of organizations from unorganized interactions:

> When the captain of the defensive platoon of a football team shouts "Pass!" both the linemen and defensive backs react immediately in their stance and their entire approach to the play. When an item to be charged in a department store costs more than $100, the clerk routinely calls the credit office to check the credit of the prospective purchaser. Both these illustrations involve routine learned behavior. Although the learning has taken place in a direct-interaction situation, the actual behavior takes place without mental reference to the interaction process. It has become a type of learned stimulus-response mechanism, with the intervening interaction variable deleted as a consideration. Much behavior in organizations is of this type. The organization trains, indoctrinates, and persuades its members to respond on the basis of the requirements of their position. This response becomes quite regularized and routinized and does not involve the interaction frame of reference.

Organizations, then, are a form of social group structured in relation to a purpose, with the individual members occupying statuses and acting out specified roles relevant to that pur-

pose. As a member of an organization, your behavior does not reflect John Brown or Mary Smith as much as it represents "clerk," "Vice-president for Marketing," "lathe-operator," or whatever status you happen to occupy within that organization. Moreover, when you interact with an organization from the outside, you will be regarded as the status you occupy in relation to the organization: "customer," "robbery suspect," and so forth.

Later in this chapter, we will see that not all behavior that occurs within an organization is in accordance with the specific statuses people occupy, yet this does not diminish the tremendous power organizations have over our lives and the events of our society. Philip Selznick (1952:22–23) spoke of the "organizational weapon" in describing a main strength of Bolshevism and quoted Lenin to illustrate the point:

> Let us take a modern army, here is a good example of organization. This organization is good simply because it is flexible, because it knows how to impart a single will to millions of people. Today, these millions sit in their various homes at the different ends of the country. Tomorrow a mobilization order is issued and they gather at appointed places. Today, they lie in trenches sometimes for months at a stretch. Tomorrow, in a prearranged order, they march forward to storm the enemy. Today, they perform miracles in evading bullets and shrapnel. Tomorrow, they perform miracles in open battles. Today, their advance posts lay mines under the ground; tomorrow, they cover dozens of miles in accordance with instructions from flyers in the air. That is what you call organization, *when in the name of one object, inspired by a single will, millions of people change the form of their intercourse and their action, the place and methods of their activity, their weapons and arms, in accordance with the changing circumstances and demands of the struggle.*

Or from the other end of the political spectrum, here is the organizational vision of Alfred Krupp, Hitler's chief munitions maker during World War II:

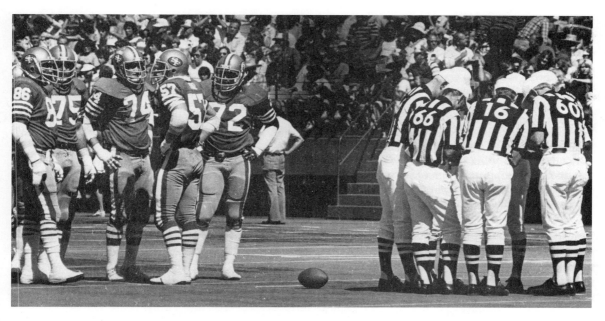

In a formal organization, individuals have specific functions to perform within the whole unit. Some are supposed to stomp, some to gouge, and others to crush.

What I shall attempt to bring about is that nothing of importance shall be dependent upon the life or existence of any particular person; that nothing of importance shall happen . . . without the fore-knowledge and approval of the management; that the past and the determinable future of the establishment can be learned in the files of the management without asking a question of any mortal. (quoted in Gouldner 1954:179–180)

As both of these quotations indicate, organizations are much more than mere collections of individuals. They represent a powerful force in society and, like most powerful forces, they can be used to support people's well-being or to stamp it out. Organizations make it possible for people to cure diseases, to explore the universe, and to enjoy comforts on earth. Organizations also make it possible for people to fight wars, to enslave millions, and, potentially, to destroy the planet. Clearly, it is worth your while to know something about how organizations operate.

Characteristics of Formal Organizations

Although many social groups "just happen," organizations are typically the result of conscious human creation. Sociologists use the term **formal organization** to identify an explicitly structured social group, having formal rules, roles, and objectives. A school is a formal organization, as is a business firm. Formal organizations are composed of social statuses, linked to each other and to the objectives of the group through formally specified rights and duties. The term **complex organization** is often used interchangeably with "formal organization," though it usually carries an additional connotation of size and intricacy.

Large corporations, modern armies, government agencies, hospitals, and library systems are all examples of complex organizations. The large, modern university is another good example of a complex organization, and we can use it to illustrate the central characteristics of this social form. Here's an overview of those characteristics. We'll explore some of them in greater depth in the section on bureaucracy.

Size   In sharp contrast to small, face-to-face, primary groups, complex organizations usually comprise hundreds, thousands, or even millions of members, many of whom obviously never see one another. A modern university often employs thousands of employees, for instance, and serves a clientele numbering in the tens of thousands.

Subdivision   Complex organizations comprise many different departments, bureaus, and agencies. Academics constitute only part of a university, for example. Other portions are responsible for such matters as maintaining the physical plant, accounting and record keeping, health, security, and housing and feeding. The academic portion of the university is subdivided into colleges of arts and sciences, medicine, law, education, social work, engineering, and others. Research institutes may be housed within colleges or may exist separately. Academic colleges, like the college of arts and sciences, are further subdivided into departments such as sociology.

Even academic departments are often subdivided into sectors. In a sociology department, for example, some faculty may be chiefly involved in "demography" (the study of population—see Chapter 18), others in deviance and corrections (see Chapter 11), and still others are interested primarily in research methods.

Specialization   Corresponding to the subdivision of the organization into departments, bureaus, and the like, the individual members have specialized functions to perform. Thus, university employees include not only faculty members, but also administrators, secretaries, physicians, electricians, plumbers, custodians, lawyers, and so forth.

Structure   The subdivision and specialization characterizing complex organizations is, however, more than mere segmentation: all the various parts are woven together in a structured fashion. In particular, most complex organizations have hierarchical structures for the flow of control and communication. In a statewide university system, for example, the president may oversee several campuses. Each campus, in turn, may be headed by a chancellor or provost, who watches over the deans, who rule the colleges that make up the campus. The deans also oversee the chairpersons, who head the various departments.

At each level, there may be assistants, associates, and "vices." The president has vice-presidents to handle special aspects of the presidency. Vice-chancellors, associate deans, assistant chairpersons, and the like fill out the administrative hierarchy.

System   Finally, complex organizations operate through systematic routines. To change from one course to another, for example, you must follow established procedures, visit the proper offices, see the proper officials, fill out the correct forms, and collect the proper signatures. If you fall down a flight of stairs on the way to your sociology midterm exam, swallow your number 2 pencil, or otherwise incapacitate yourself, you can be assured that your situation will fall within some set of established rules.

Clearly, organizations differ greatly in all the respects we've been examining. Sociologists have devoted considerable attention to the source of those variations.

Determinants of Organizational Structure

Richard Hall (1977) identified four basic factors that are involved in how organizations come to be structured: size of the organization, the technology it employs, the environment in which it is located, and the choices of its management. Sociologists currently disagree over which of these factors is most important.

Most research on the subject (summarized by Hall) indicates that *size* is a prime determinant: the larger the organization, the greater the number of subdivisions, levels of hierarchy, and specialized tasks it is likely to have. This increasing differentiation suggests that more money will need to be spent and more persons employed in coordinating all these functions. But research surveys show that these administrative costs generally aren't proportionately as great for large organizations as for small ones. Although the evidence for medium-sized organizations (those that employ between 700 and 1,400 persons) is contradictory, the image of the large organization as being top-heavy with administrative personnel seems distorted.

Other sociologists view *technology* as the key determinant of organizational structure. According to Joan Woodward (1965), organizational structures tend to differ depending on whether the technology of the plant is geared toward mass production (machine-made clothing, for instance), unit production (the building of a yacht or custom house, for instance), or process production (such as the refining of oil). She found that technology affects structure in crucial ways—the number of levels in the management hierarchy, the number of subordinates supervisors have under them, and the ratio of managerial personnel to other employees.

Charles Perrow (1970), another sociologist who emphasizes the role of technology, suggests that most crucial for organizational structure is the kind of "raw material" that the firm uses in its work—"raw material" being anything from iron ore to people on welfare. Organizational structure will differ, he argues, depending on the number of exceptional cases that occur in production and on the nature of the solutions found to handle these cases. For example, in an auto plant the number of exceptional cases is few and the means of solving them is fairly clear, so supervisors and technical people are likely to have relatively little power and latitude for decision making. In a research and development firm, where there is little routine and where the solutions to exceptions are varied, both supervisors and technical people are likely to have much more power and latitude in order to operate efficiently.

Other studies show that the cultural and physical *environments* can have important effects on organization structure. To use Hall's example of a cultural difference in structure, the United States relies more on written documents than Britain does. This cultural difference is reflected in the structure of organizations in the two countries. Highly competitive organizational environments are more likely to emphasize written rules, required reports, tighter controls, and fewer innovations than in less competitive situations.

Finally, Hall notes that *choice* plays a role in organizational structure as well. After all the executives of the organization ultimately choose the structure. Although these leaders work within the constraints of organizational size, technology, and environment, their decisions, interests, and strategies sometimes vary considerably.

Voluntary Associations

Voluntary associations are groups formed by individuals sharing a common set of interests. A professional association such as the American Sociological Association is an excellent example. It was organized in 1905 by a group of professors and others engaged in sociological teaching and research. They felt they would gain something working together and meeting occasionally to discuss their common interests. A great many other voluntary organizations have been organized around occupations: American Medical Association, American Bar Association, American Dental Association, and so on.

The Dilemma of Success

Voluntary associations offer a special opportunity for observing the dynamics of organizational life, since many have grown from small, informal groups to large, complex organizations. Here's an example typical of many national voluntary associations.

The Christmas Donation Project was created in 1972 in San Francisco. That year, the employees of a small firm, along with family and friends, spent Christmas Day delivering gifts to patients in San Francisco hospitals, and they joined together for Christmas dinner that night. The experience was so rewarding that they resolved to make it an annual event. The second year, four hundred volunteers visited two thousand confined children and adults on Christmas Day.

In 1974, the project spread to Los Angeles, New York, and Honolulu, and more people participated. The following year, the project was renamed The Holiday Hospital Project and expanded to include visits during Hanukkah as well as on Christmas. As in earlier years, the volunteers chipped in to buy simple gifts such as socks, perfume, small toys, and the like. The project continued to spread geographically and to grow in each locale.

In 1980, the project was formally established as The Holiday Project, a nonprofit charitable corporation in California, with local committees in seventy-seven communities across the nation, plus affiliated committees outside the United States. That year, 30,000 volunteers visited 242,000 people in 1,144 hospitals, prisons, convalescent homes, detention centers, and similar institutions. Cash contributions now totaled $130,000 and another $100,000 was donated in goods and services by businesses. The project was coordinated nationally by a paid executive director and was overseen by a board of directors.

In 1981, four governors and twenty-nine mayors proclaimed a "Holiday Project Day." Some 38,000 volunteers in 114 communities visited 207,000 people in 1,781 institutions, while cash and in-kind contributions exceeded half a million dollars.

Besides its tremendous growth in size, the project has been transformed organizationally. In 1972, the volunteers met informally, chipped in a few dollars each, and chose a few hospitals to visit. Someone volunteered to buy the presents, and the group got together for a gift-wrapping session, sang Christmas carols, visited the hospitals, and met later for a potluck dinner.

Nine years later, the local experience was much the same, but the structure of the organization was very different. The executive director was assisted by a staff of volunteers in the national office. Two part-time national coordinators, operating out of New York City, held weekly conference calls with nine regional coordinators who were in weekly communication with their local committee chairpeople. Each local committee included a lawyer, an accountant, a media professional, and others responsible for enrollment, fund-raising, institutional contact, and gift-wrapping. This organizational complexity reflected several factors.

First, the participants in the project across the country wanted to see their activities expanded. They wanted more and more shut-ins visited, and they also wanted to share the experience of participating with others. To accomplish this, a national office was needed to make contacts in new cities and to provide assistance and guidance in the organizing of new committees. In addition, a national office—representing tens of thousands of volunteers—had more leverage in attracting media attention and gaining business and governmental support.

Second, a formal national structure could insure that anything calling itself "The Holiday Project" would be true to the original intention of the project: individuals sharing the experience of the holidays with others. By legally "owning" the name of the project and officially chartering new committees, the national office could prevent it from becoming commercialized—like Santa Claus—and could protect it from fraudulent individuals.

Finally, the project became more formal in response to government regulations. As a legally incorporated charity, The Holiday Project is required to file financial reports with the State of California. How much money was collected, and how was it spent? The purpose of such reports is to protect the public from fraudulent "charities." With tens of thousands of volunteers across the country collecting and contributing, however, adequate record-keeping became a real challenge. The national office had to establish standardized reporting procedures for each local committee, so that all the local records could be combined at year's end to prepare a national accounting to the state.

As with any large voluntary association, perhaps, these organizational requirements established by the national office seem to conflict with the intentions that originally sparked the organization. The first group of volunteers needed no one's permission to begin; they simply did what seemed appropriate. Today, a group of individuals wishing to start a Holiday Project committee would need to comply with the national guidelines and gain official approval from the board of directors. Whereas the first volunteers simply threw some money in a hat and bought presents, each contribution must now be recorded, and receipts must be kept to document all purchases.

Any successful voluntary association will face the problem of an apparent conflict between the interests of the national office and the local chapters. This division is usually clearest in matter of finance. In organizations that are sustained by annual dues from members, one of the most delicate issues becomes how much of the money goes to support the national office and how much to support the activities of the local chapters. Locally, the expenses include telephones, postage, office supplies, perhaps office rent. Nationally, the expenses are those of any formal organization, including staff salaries. The potential for conflict and for resentment is ever-present.

There are other dimensions to the local/national division. In the case of The Holiday Project, the "work" of the organization must ultimately be done at the local level—people visiting hospitals and other institutions. In other organizations, however, this is not so clear. Consider an organization like Zero Population Growth (ZPG), dedicated to handling the problem of overpopulation. Much of ZPG's work has been done by local chapters engaging in public education at the local level. At the same time, much of the work—on national policies such as immigration, abortion, tax exemptions for dependents—is more appropriately addressed at the national level. In such situations, conflicts may arise over where the greatest effort (and resources) should be directed.

So the organizational growth of a voluntary association is a two-edged sword. On the one hand, the establishment of a formal, national office can contribute enormous power to the pursuit of the original intention, even when the "work" of that intention occurs locally. A national office can print up materials for local use, provide seed money to new chapters, handle the requirements of incorporation and accounting. At the same time, the requirements and the tendencies of formal organization provide a constant strain in the direction of separating the association's original intention from its later success.

When people are dissatisfied with the structure of society, they often join together in voluntary associations to bring about change.

Unlike business ventures, voluntary associations do not have a profit-making purpose; though, as we'll see, finance is an important element in their operations. As Jacquelyn Hochban (1981:546) points out:

In general, nonprofit organizations are so called either because their revenues do not exceed costs (i.e., there is no profit) or because the excess of revenues over costs to the organization does not return to owners or investors, as in for-profit organizations, but is instead put to use to further the service or other nonmonetary goals of the organization.

The Purposes of Voluntary Associations

Some associations have a charitable or altruistic purpose. Examples include the American Cancer Society, Big Brothers of America, Cousteau Society, Greenpeace. A specific concern, such as ending world hunger, can be the focus of a

great many voluntary associations, some with slightly different emphases within the whole job. Thus, to name but a few, Save the Children focuses its attention on the plight of children around the world; Bread for the World deals mostly with the political aspects of hunger; The Hunger Project generates a context of individual commitment. The general task of providing emergency aid is carried out by many associations such as Cooperative for American Relief Everywhere (CARE), OXFAM, Catholic Relief Services, UNICEF, and others.

Many voluntary associations have a political focus. The Democratic and Republican parties are clear examples, as are the Socialist Workers Party, the Communist Party USA, the American Independent Party, and countless others past and present. The American Civil Liberties Union (ACLU), Common Cause, and others are organized for specifically political purposes though they are not political parties.

Perhaps the greatest number of voluntary associations are organized around hobbies. Consider this abbreviated sampling: Baker Street

Irregulars (Sherlock Holmes lore), Beer Can Collectors of America, Manuscript Society (autographs), American Numismatic Association (coins), American Philatelic Society (stamps), Deltiologists of America (postcard collectors), U.S. Parachute Association, Playing Card Collectors, Puppeteers of America, Soaring Society of America (gliders and sailplanes), Lovers of the Stinking Rose (garlic fanciers), Sweet Adelines, Inc. (female barbershop quartets), Tattoo Club of America, Voicespondence Club (cassette pen pals), The Friends of Wine (perfect way to end the list).

So far, I have mentioned only a handful of the thousands of national voluntary associations. Every state, community, and neighborhood has more of its own. Community associations organize to protest the building of a highway, and others organize to demand its construction. Associations form to support voluntary abortions, and others form to oppose them. Wherever and whenever people share a common interest, they are likely to form a voluntary association in support of that interest.

Voluntary associations serve two functions. First, and most obvious, they provide a vehicle for sharing common interests. The American Contract Bridge League, for example, is a vehicle for getting people together to play bridge. Your local chamber-music society is a vehicle for people to listen to chamber music together.

Second, in America at least, voluntary associations act as potent political forces. Often the interests that association members share are affected by governmental actions, and the association is a vehicle for affecting those actions. The National Association of Manufacturers, for example, seeks legislation favorable to industry. Gays organize to gain and protect rights for homosexuals, and the American Legion seeks legislation favorable to veterans.

The box entitled "The Dilemma of Success" describes the organizational history of an American voluntary association. In particular, you'll see some of the problems that accompany success.

A Potent Force in America

Many writers have commented on the importance of voluntary associations to American democracy. Alexis de Tocqueville (1835, 1840) saw them as our protection against totalitarianism, saying "The danger that faces democratic governments is the passivity of the populace; the tendency for individuals to abandon their personal responsibility for social actions." William Kornhauser (1959) saw voluntary associations as a critical intermediary between the people and government. Whereas government may seem distant from the private individual, the voluntary associations are easily accessible and have an impact on government. In short, voluntary associations are one of the ways in which individuals have found they can make a difference in modern society.

Table 7–1 reports the membership levels in various kinds of voluntary associations in America in 1978.

In 1974, the Census Bureau found 23.5 percent of the American population were engaged in volunteer work. What do you suppose all this free service was worth? The Census Bureau valued it at *over 67 billion dollars* (U.S. Bureau of Census 1980c:519). A 1981 Gallup Poll found 29 percent "involved in any charity or social service activities, such as helping the poor, the sick or elderly" (*Public Opinion* 1982a:21).

Since 1981, American voluntary associations have received heightened public attention, because the Reagan administration sees them as a way to reduce government expenses. As the president explained on September 24, 1981:

> The truth is we've let government take away many things we once considered were really ours to do voluntarily out of the goodness of our hearts and a sense of community pride and neighborliness. I believe many of you want to do those things again, want to be involved if only someone would ask you or offer the opportunity. Well, we intend to make that offer.
>
> We are launching a nationwide effort to encourage our citizens to join with us in finding where

Table 7-1

Membership Levels for Different Types of Voluntary Associations, 1978

	% Population who are members
Church-affiliated groups	36
Farm organizations	4
Fraternal groups	10
Hobby or garden clubs	9
Labor unions	15
Literary, art, discussion, or study	9
Nationality groups	3
Political clubs	3
Professional or academic societies	13
School fraternities or sororities	4
Social service groups	14
Service clubs	8
Sports groups	20
Veterans' groups	7
Youth groups	9
Any other groups	10

Source: U.S. Bureau of Census, *Social Indicators II* (Washington, D.C.: Government Printing Office, 1980c), page 521.

need exists and then to organize volunteer programs to meet that need. We have already set the wheels of such a volunteer effort in motion.

Simply put, a variety of government services would be terminated, thereby cutting government costs. This would result in reduced taxes, making possible increased individual and corporate contributions to private, nonprofit organizations. Those organizations would then be in a position to provide social services once provided by the government. As this is being written, the government cuts are being made, but the appearance of substantially increased individual and corporate contributions remains an open question.

As we've seen, voluntary associations can be small and informal, or they can be formally structured. In this next section, we are going to delve further into the *formality* and *complexity* of complex, formal organizations. Nothing reveals this aspect better than *bureaucracy*—the epitome of secondary-group relations. We are going to examine the essential characteristics of bureaucracy, see its advantages as a form for conducting social life, and look at its shortcomings and quirks.

Bureaucracy

Bureaucracy is a word that people use frequently, commonly distinguishing among several types of bureaucracy: "stupid bureaucracy," "petty bureaucracy," "bungling bureaucracy," "damned bureaucracy," and worse. For most people, "bureaucracy" means long lines, red tape, impersonality, forms, and frustrations, although bureaucracies don't have to have all these characteristics.

From a sociological point of view, "bureaucracy" is simply one way in which social statuses and social relationships are organized. Max Weber (1846-1920) did the earliest comprehensive analysis (1925a) of this form of organization, and his observations are still generally applicable to today's bureaucracies.

Weber saw the following as the key characteristics of bureaucratic organization:

1. Jurisdictional areas are officially fixed and generally governed by the rules. The required regular activities of the organization are specified as official duties. The structure of authority in the organization is clearly spelled out, as are the means by which each member of the organization is to fulfill his or her official duties.

2. The organization is structured hierarchically, with specified levels of authority. Like a pyramid, the organization has fewer people at each higher level of authority, ending with a single person at its head.

3. The organization is managed largely through the preparation, maintenance, and use of written files.

4. Those holding positions in a bureaucracy are specially trained for their jobs.

5. The fully developed bureaucracy requires the full working capacities of those holding positions in it. Administration is a full-time job. In this regard, Weber contrasted modern bureaucracies with earlier enterprises in which management was treated as a secondary activity.

6. All of the organization's official activities are governed by formalized rules, and knowledge of the rules constitutes a special skill.

In summary, bureaucracies engage in the business of "administration," and they do so through officially specified agreements regarding status relationships and role expectations. The bureaucracies of Weber's day were very different from the governmental and business organizations that preceded bureaucratization.

Advantages of Bureaucracy

Weber felt bureaucracy to be technically superior to other forms of organization in the same fashion that machine production is technically superior to handwork. Bureaucracies are faster, more precise, clearer, more certain, more effective, and more efficient than nonbureaucratic organizations.

In addition, Weber saw an advantage in the continuity of bureaucracies and their files. Individual members of a bureaucracy can come and go, but the structure of statuses and the written records of past activities give the organization a life of its own that outlives the service of individual bureaucrats. The continued functioning of the United States civil service in spite of the frequent changing of politically appointed offi-

cials is an illustration of this feature of bureaucracies. Bureaucrats tend to continue performing their specified duties regardless of personnel changes above, below, and around them.

Weber cited the technical expertise of members of a bureaucracy as another advantage of this form of organization. Only in a bureaucracy is it possible for people to develop extreme competence in very narrow specialties and for all those special skills to be coordinated into a productive organizational effort.

Disadvantages of Bureaucracy

Weber's description of bureaucracy, although accurate, differs greatly from the common opinion of bureaucracy among Americans today. Most criticized of all are government bureaucracies. Especially galling is the feeling that our tax dollars pay people intent on causing us trouble. Paying to have an Internal Revenue Service sometimes seems like giving your wicked stepmother an allowance.

Allen Barton (1980:29–30) outlines the interrelated causes of problems in the American government bureaucracy:

(a) a patronage-based party system has led reformers to impose rigid rules on personnel policies and contracting

(b) the lack of either scientifically based or market-based measures of performance likewise causes the political leadership to impose rigid rules of procedure on the bureaucracy. . . .

(c) the rigidity of rules thus created contributes to the weakness of rewards and penalties to top management

(d) weak reward systems reduce the motivation to do a good job, and are thus a major source of inefficiency and lack of innovation

(e) rigid rules themselves are also a direct source of inefficiency, lack of innovation, and unresponsiveness to public needs, even for those who are motivated to do a good job

Organizational leaders may come and go, but bureaucracy perpetuates itself.

(f) development of professional norms of service and craftsmanship, which might motivate doing a good job even in the absence of economic rewards, is discouraged by rigidity of rules, weakness of reward systems, and the political environment of patronage politics and pressure-group representation

(g) weakness of professional norms of service and craftsmanship contributes to inefficiency, lack of innovation, and unresponsiveness

(h) the bias in the political representation system toward narrow, highly organized interests makes the bureaucracy unresponsive to public needs.

One of the major complaints lodged against both public and private bureaucracies is that they are frequently inefficient. Ironically, the very aspects of bureaucracy that make it generally efficient often make it extremely unwieldy and inefficient in particular cases. Bureaucratic efficiency is achieved largely through standardized procedures, which seems to work well when the situations to be handled are also standardized. But when something out of the ordinary happens, the system breaks down.

You have probably had more than one experience in which a clerk or official, simply using common sense, could have solved the problem you presented simply and quickly, but who instead sent you running from department to department or forced you to correspond for months over a trivial matter.

My wife and I took a trip outside the country, and we used a credit card for many of our expenses. By prior arrangement with the credit-card company, we kept careful records of our expenses and sent in a payment each month, even though we were far from home and didn't receive bills. After the trip, we found that the company had failed to bill us for $85 worth of our purchases. Ever honest, I wrote to the company, asking that my account be corrected.

Now I'm sure that had I complained about being charged too much, my letter would have found a departmental home in the company. But evidently they had no department to handle complaints from people who felt they had not been charged enough, because I received no answer. I wrote again, saying that I would not use my card again until the account had been corrected. Still no answer. Finally, I cut the credit card into little pieces and wrote a hostile letter demanding that my account be canceled and the $85 charge be made. I enclosed the tiny pieces of cut-up credit card.

Several months later I received a form letter thanking me for my continued use of the credit card and for being such a loyal customer—evidenced by my resubscribing for another year. Enclosed was a credit card for the new year and a statement indicating a credit balance of $73! They had deducted twelve dollars from the account to cover the cost of another year's membership. I now realized that I could look forward to another six ($73 ÷ 12 = 6+) years of credit-card renewals with no correction made to the account. So, in desperation, my wife and I went on a small-scale shopping spree and charged $73 worth of merchandise to the account. I then cut up the new card and mailed it to the company with a rather personal suggestion as to where they might file it, and—at last—the matter was closed.

Democracy and Bureaucracy

Probably one of the problems Americans have with bureaucracy—particularly government bureaucracy—is that it is undemocratic. When you deal with the government bureaucracy from the outside, you scarcely feel like an equal partner in government, let alone the tax-paying employer of government. As if to highlight the point, bureaucrats are appointed, not elected. The complex issue of democracy is also relevant within bureaucracies, both public and private.

One problem of bureaucracy has been its tendency to consist of so many layers that the people at the bottom and the people at the top may as well be on different planets. Every new idea has to go up the hierarchy for approval and then back down again (generally coming back so stretched, distorted, reinterpreted, shaved, or bloated that the originator of the idea does not recognize it).

Because operations are so centralized, the people at the lower level soon lose any initiative they have. To make matters worse, they are watched closely by their supervisor, who is watched closely by his or her supervisor, and so on up the line.

The "height" of a bureaucracy—measured in levels—is related to its "width"—measured in the average number of subordinates under a supervisor. In bureaucracies where each supervisor has a "narrow span of control" (relatively few subordinates), a greater number of levels are required to accommodate the entire enterprise. Few levels are required if each supervisor is responsible for a large number of subordinates. There are "tall, slim" bureaucracies and "short, fat" ones, as illustrated in Figure 7–1. Such structural differences appear to have implications for people's experiences within them.

We might well expect, for example, that supervisors would be more authoritarian and autocratic in bureaucracies where they had fewer subordinates, since it would be relatively easy to watch and control people under them. That's what Peter Blau (1966, 1968) assumed when he began his study of finance agencies and personnel agencies. To his surprise, he discovered the opposite to be true.

Blau found that the more levels in an organization, the more decentralization there was in decision making. Agencies with many levels were more likely to delegate decision making to lower levels of the organization.

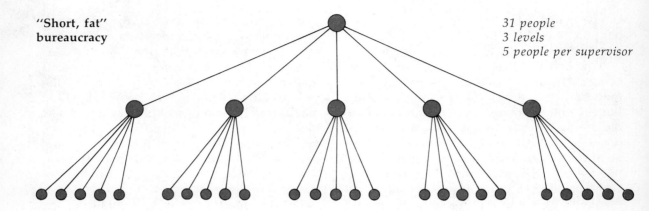

**"Short, fat"
bureaucracy**

31 people
3 levels
5 people per supervisor

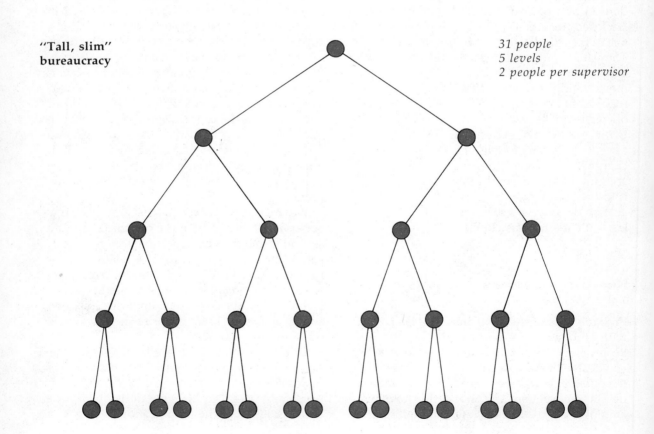

**"Tall, slim"
bureaucracy**

31 people
5 levels
2 people per supervisor

Blau also noted that "tall, slim" organizations used computers more and required college degrees of more of their personnel. He found some evidence that they had more complex and sophisticated outputs. Apparently, each boss and his or her small number of well-trained subordinates worked closely together on a fairly egalitarian basis solving complex problems, while the routine work was done by machines.

In the squat, traditional bureaucracies, one boss watched over many subordinates who did routine work, and this surveillance could have been quite authoritarian. It may even be that the boss wanted to keep all control, so he or she wouldn't appoint a couple of lieutenants and delegate some authority to them.

This interpretation of Blau's findings was bolstered by some other studies. One researcher in a large hospital found the span of control was narrow where the work was complex, non-routine, and required many skills (such as in open-heart surgery), but the span was broad where the work was simpler and more routine (for example, "on the assembly line" in obstetrics).

More striking, because the researchers were dealing not only with span of control, but also with other aspects of bureaucracy, such as standardization, specialization, and formalization, were two studies in England. Derek Pugh et al. (1968), John Child (1972), and two research teams studied a large number of industrial firms and found that the more bureaucratized the organization, the greater the decentralization of decision making. Ponder that for a minute. The more bureaucratic the firm, the more discretion it gives to lower-level personnel! Perhaps the squat, fat organization with few levels of authority, little specialization of functions, few rules, and little standardization of materials and tasks was not so "democratic" after all. However, the basic issue of democracy within formal organizations is a more complex one than this suggests.

Notice some of the other characteristics of those organizations that granted lower-level authority—measured by the authority to hire, fire, and spend money without higher-level approval. The organizational goals and priorities were already quite clearly spelled out. There were standardized procedures for handling many situations, and the degree of organizational structure controlled the information available to people. In situations like that, efficiency is increased by giving people considerable latitude in using their skills, experience, and training. Given the prior set of structural controls, it is likely that people will use their talents in the interests of the organization.

Efficient, modern bureaucracies, then, are more "democratic" in some sense. People are not closely watched and directed in their every action. They enjoy relatively greater freedom—within a narrow range of possibilities. We should not assume from this, however, that the workers in such organizations would be allowed to vote on whether the organization should be producing nerve gas, mislabeling its goods, or destroying the environment. Only at the top of the modern bureaucracy is there room for that kind of discretion.

The Internal Dynamics of Formal Organizations

In this section, we'll see how the nature of bureaucracy fosters certain aspects of personality. Then we'll look at how people in bureaucracies respond to the pressures and constraints upon them, and finally we'll look at changing patterns of compliance and control in American formal organizations.

Bureaucracy and Personality

Many people have written of the negative effects of bureaucratic organizations on the lives of individuals within them. Perhaps the most popular book on this topic was William Whyte's *The Organization Man* (1956). One of the classic sociological examinations of this issue was Robert Merton's essay, "Bureaucratic Structure and Personality," which appeared in his book *Social Theory and Social Structure* (1957a).

Noting that bureaucracies are primarily characterized by formal, written regulations, Merton further noted bureaucratic officials were largely evaluated (for promotion, for example) in terms of their "strict devotion to regulations" (1957a:200). The safest course for any bureaucrat is unswerving enforcement of the formal rules. If deviation from the rules results in disaster, the bureaucrat will be blamed; if irrational obedience to the rules results in disaster, however, the rules are to blame. The sure way to avoid making bad decisions is to make no decisions at all.

Blind obedience to regulations, Merton observed, produces "timidity, conservatism, and technicism" in officials and makes bureaucracies incapable of adapting readily to new or special conditions: "Thus, the very elements which conduce toward efficiency in general produce inefficiency in specific instances" (1957a:200).

Primary Groups in Secondary Settings

An outside observer armed only with Weber's ideal-typical portrait of bureaucracy and with stereotypes about bureaucratic behavior, might assume that social relations within formal organizations were pretty simple and mechanical. Merton and others have noted, however, that despite the appearance of robotlike obedience to regulations, detached objectivity, and bureaucratic impersonality, formal organizations have a human underbelly. For one thing, bureaucracies are frequently the scene of struggles for power and control. For another, every bureaucracy and other secondary group is the scene of informal primary-group relations, which often means that the real social relationships within a formal organization are more complex than they first appear. Even when they function within groups formally structured around secondary-group relations, people still establish patterns of primary relations and form primary groups.

Let's take an example that should be familiar to you. Your sociology class is a secondary group, most typically characterized by secondary relations. The main agreements governing behavior in the class reflect the specific purpose of providing instruction in sociology. In most classes, however, small groups of friends form. You get to know some of the other students in your class and develop the "intimate, face-to-face relations" that characterize a primary group.

Primary groups often form within other formal organizations as well. If you were a clerk working behind one of the hundreds of identical desks in a large insurance company, it is likely that you would join in a small group of friends. If you were in the military, you would probably be part of a similar primary group. Most soldiers have groups of "buddies."

The primary groups that form within formal organizations usually seem totally irrelevant to the formal agreements of the organization and its functions. In practice, however, they often support the official activities. In a classic study of the German army during World War II, for example, Edward Shils and Morris Janowitz (1948) found the strong primary relations among German soldiers to have been a critical factor in their morale and effectiveness. Ideological commitments to Nazism seemed largely irrelevant: rather, the German soldier was committed to supporting the soldiers in his unit, his friends.

At the same time, primary relations can be dysfunctional for the secondary group. Such primary groups can hold sets of agreements among themselves that conflict with those of the secondary group. A classic example of this was revealed in an important series of studies of Western Electric workers earlier in the century. During the late 1920s and early 1930s, F. J.

Roethlisberger and W. J. Dickson undertook studies of industrial behavior in the telephone "bank wiring room" of the Western Electric Hawthorne Works in Chicago. Out of these studies (reported in the book *Management and the Worker*, 1939) came an appreciation of the significance of primary relations in secondary groups. In particular, Roethlisberger and Dickson discovered an informal agreement as to the "rate" of work that a worker was expected—by the members of his primary group—to accomplish during a given period of time. "Rate setting" was totally a function of primary-group agreements: it was not an official policy of the organization. This does not mean that it was not enforced, however. "Rate busters" were severely sanctioned by their fellow workers. The consequence of the informal agreement was to keep production lower than it might otherwise have been. Rapid workers were unwilling to outproduce the members of their primary group, thereby casting their friends in a bad light and possibly causing them to lose their jobs. And, if my high level of production may cost you your job today, someone else may be my undoing tomorrow. To avoid that, then, the workers created a mutual-protection system where no individual was a threat to others.

Primary groups within organizations often represent alternative lines of communication and authority. Weber characterized bureaucracies as having specified command structures, spelling out who could give what kinds of orders to whom. Primary relations often conflict with that. Suppose, for example, that you are an office supervisor in a large company, and one of your office workers asks to have a day off on Friday to go to the beach with her boyfriend. You deny the request, basing your decision on the proper functioning of the office. Later, you receive instructions from the head office to grant the requested day off because the president's son is the boyfriend in question. You have witnessed an example of how primary relations within a secondary organization can conflict with formal command structures.

Sometimes, however, the alternative lines of communication and authority can serve the organization's ultimate interests. I've already commented on the disadvantages of bureaucratic rigidity. Primary relations are often a remedy. They permit people to work around incompetent supervisors, for example, and they can make needed information and other resources available when the formal agreements get in the way of getting the job done. Most military units have at least one person who knows how to "get things." If the unit has orders to paint its building, for example, and other orders prohibit their being issued paint, such a person will know someone in the supply office, and the paint will appear.

Compliance and Control in Organizations

We have seen that patterns of association in formal organizations are more complex than one might suspect looking only at the Weberian model. For related reasons, patterns of compliance and control in formal organizations aren't simply matters of the official delineation of rights and duties either.

No matter how clearly and rationally the rights and duties of statuses in an organization are laid out, it is never enough to ensure that they'll be adhered to. Nor is this the case for bureaucracy alone; it applies to all aspects of social order. As Jean Jacques Rousseau (1762:2) said of brute force over two centuries ago: "The strongest—unless he transforms force into right and obedience into duty—is never strong enough to have his way all the time." Once the rights and duties have been laid out, subordinates have to have a reason for going along with their assignments, and managers have to present some justification or incentive to get subordinates to follow orders.

In observing a wide variety of organizations, Amitai Etzioni (1975) has found three primary types of compliance on the part of the individuals within those organizations. They are *coercive*, *normative* and *utilitarian*.

Coercive compliance means what you think it does. Members of an organization do what they are supposed to do because they have to. Clear examples of this form of compliance can be found in prisons and certain mental hospitals. Prisoners do not stay in their cells by choice but because of the bars and the locked doors. They do not return to their cells after a meal out of preference alone but only in preference to the punishment they would receive for refusing.

Other organizations—particularly voluntary associations such as churches and clubs—operate on the basis of moral acceptance of the organization's agreements of performance. Etzioni calls this **normative compliance.** What keeps a churchgoer from taking a fistful of money out of the collection plate as it passes? No threat of imprisonment or torture is even necessary. Political parties, colleges, professional associations, and many other organizations must depend primarily on normative pressure to ensure compliance of members.

Utilitarian compliance, for Etzioni, refers to payoffs. People do what they are supposed to do because they get paid for doing it. This is obviously important within economic organizations.

Etzioni points out that all organizations probably depend on more than one form of compliance in order to function. In the modern college, for instance, much of what you do as a student is a matter of normative compliance. Thus, you are likely to be relatively polite to your instructors and fellow students and to be relatively quiet in class and in the library because you accept these agreements about how to behave. There is, however, a utilitarian component to this, since you expect your normative behavior to result in good grades. And, finally, there is an element of coercion also, because you recognize that certain forms of deviant behavior—cheating on exams, for example—could result in dismissal from school.

In the concluding essay of this chapter, we'll return to the issue of motivating the participants in an organization, with particular reference to American and Japanese managerial styles. At this point, however, I want to shift gears and examine the context within which organizations function in a society.

Institutions

So far in this chapter we have seen some of the ways in which organizations operate in society. We've seen how voluntary associations can start out small and informal and then grow into complex, formal organizations. We've seen the pros and cons of bureaucracy and have examined some of the internal dynamics that occur within large organizations. Now I want to turn our attention to different level of analysis: to the **institutions** that are the context within which organizations exist and function.

As defined in Chapter 4, an institution is a relatively stable and integrated set of symbols, beliefs, values, norms, roles, and statuses relating to some aspect of social life. In this sense, religion is an institution and, more specifically, so are Hinduism and Roman Catholicism. St. Patrick's Church on Main Street, on the other hand, is an organization. Higher education is an institution, but Harvard is an organization.

It is worth noting that people often refer to certain organizations as institutions. Harvard, the nation's oldest and most prestigious university, is often referred to as an institution. The same is sometimes said about Disneyland and about Harry's Bar and Grill. Football team mascots—Army's mule and Navy's goat—are sometimes called institutions.

While sociologists would not apply the term institution in any of these cases, such uses are not altogether off base. When people say that Harvard or Harry's Bar and Grill is an institution, they often also say it "has become a tradition." It's something that is always there, something you can depend on. This is sometimes the sense that an institution is a part of the background against which life's events occur.

This last aspect of the common usage of the term institution is very close to the sociological usage. Institutions are never "what's happening," they are the contexts within which things happen. Let's see how institutions get established in the first place.

Institutionalization

Sociologists use the term "institutionalization" to refer to the process through which the agreements people make are established, organized, and perpetuated. Often we refer to a particular agreement becoming institutionalized—that is, established and perpetuated—and it is also the process whereby institutions are formed.

Let's begin this discussion with an example of institutionalization that reflects a conscious and deliberate act. When the American founders forged an alliance among the several colonies, they created an electoral college through which representatives of the new states could meet and select a president. It was a reasonable arrangement, reflecting the nature of the initial alliance.

The electoral college became institutionalized. It was written into the Constitution, and later generations of Americans ratified the agreement by electing their presidents through the electoral college system.

Many Americans argue today that the electoral college is outdated, that it is no longer appropriate or functional. We are no longer an alliance of semiautonomous states, they point out. We are a nation and should elect the president directly. Moreover, the present system allows one person to be elected president over an opponent who actually received more votes. For example, do you recall President Samuel J. Tilden? In 1876, Tilden received 4,284,020 votes for president, compared to 4,036,572 for his opponent, Rutherford B. Hayes. Hayes, however, received 185 electoral votes to Tilden's 184.

Several presidents have earned the office with fewer than half the votes cast, including Lincoln (40 percent in 1860) and Nixon (43 percent in 1968) (U.S. Bureau of Census 1960:682, 1979a:496). Yet the electoral college system persists.

Persistence of Patterns

Once established, institutionalized agreements often persist long after the conditions that made them reasonable and functional have disappeared. In part, this happens through habit and custom. Sometimes, they take on different meanings. Thus, we are told that handshaking began as a demonstration that two people were weaponless. Similarly, knights had a ritual of lifting their visors as a gesture of trust, and men have been tipping their hats ever since—until they pretty much gave up wearing hats.

The sources of institutionalized agreements are numerous, as are the reasons for their persistence. Given that so many of our agreements occurred pretty much by chance, why do we stick to them so doggedly? In part, there is simply a degree of comfort and security in knowing that things are going to be the same as they've always been. You and I can predict how each other is going to act, as long as we don't keep changing the patterns. At the same time, such long-standing patterns can prompt feelings of identity and belonging, even linking us with other generations.

Comfort, security, and identity are not the only reasons why institutionalized agreements persist, however. Vested interests exert pressure also. For example, those who profit most from a particular economic system—whether capitalist, socialist, or other—are the staunchest supporters of its continuance. People who hold political power in a society support the maintenance of the political system that gives them power. The clergy are hardly disinterested in whether religion survives.

Everything that's been said so far is essentially a description of **tradition:** customary patterns of behavior. Institutions are more than mere tradition, however.

Institutions and the Requirements of Group Life

In the discussion of the social systems point of view in Chapter 2, we saw that every society must deal with certain general problems of group life. Societies have survival needs. For a society to persist over time, for example, there must be some provision made for *replacement:* since all members of a society die eventually, they must be replaced by new members. Fortunately, humans have both the ability and the drive for sexual reproduction, so we have the potential for solving the problem. Institutions integrate individual and group needs. Thus, the family insures that individuals' sex drives are expressed in such a way that the society's need for replacement is satisfied.

Replacement, however, is more than a matter of producing babies. A newborn infant is hardly a replacement for a deceased brain surgeon. The new members of society must be fed and nurtured until they can care for themselves, and they must be socialized if they are to be functioning members of their society. Thus the need for replacement requires some coordination of sexuality and socialization. This coordination, moreover, is facilitated by the sexual partners and their offspring living together in the same house, hut, or cave. If you continue this line of reasoning—as we'll do in Chapter 16—you'll find other functions that naturally fit together with those we've been discussing.

Notice how the various system survival needs of society relate to the needs of individuals. Everybody needs a place to live, sleep, and eat. Individuals seem to have some degree of need for sexual expression, and babies need to be fed, nurtured, and socialized.

As an institution, family represents the relatively stable and integrated set of symbols, beliefs, values, norms, roles, and statuses by which a society structures the issues of sexuality, reproduction, socialization, residence, and related aspects of social life.

We could repeat the above exercise for other sets of individual and group needs. For example, every society must make provisions for transforming the raw materials of the physical environment into food, shelter, and other things that individuals need to survive. Sociologists use the term "economy" in reference to the institution which accomplishes that. For the most part, sociologists speak of five major institutions of society: family, economy, education, government, and religion, and each of these will be examined in Part Four.

Institutional Forms

In a sense, an institution represents a problem area without specifying how the problem will be solved. If you think about any of the problems we've considered so far, you'll see that each could be handled in several ways. In fact, those problems *have* been handled in many different ways by different societies. The problems associated with economy, for example, have been solved through barter, capitalism, socialism, communism, and other methods and combinations.

The point of these most recent comments is to indicate that there is no definitive list of the institutions making up a society. Within a fairly broad range, the question is whether it is useful to treat a particular social structure as an institution. So within capitalism, for example, it sometimes makes sense to treat banking, professional athletics, and the labor-union movement as institutions—in that each represents a relatively stable and integrated set of symbols, beliefs, values, norms, roles, and statuses relating to some aspect of social life.

Institutions as the Context for Organizations

Institutions are a set of agreements; organizations put those agreements into practice. Thus capitalism includes a fundamental agreement on the private ownership of property. General Motors is an example of that agreement put into practice. General Motors' property—land, factories, equipment, cars, trucks—belong to the stockholders. Where socialism is the established institution, automobile-manufacturing firms belong to the state.

There are two important implications of this relationship. First, you can understand the behavior of organizations by understanding the institutional agreements within which they operate. If business firms often seem to be "only out to make a profit," that's because profit making is a fundamental principle of capitalism.

Second, institutions offer a more powerful leverage point for social change than do organizations. By challenging the institution of racial segregation in the South, Martin Luther King, Jr., and the civil rights movement of the 1950s and 1960s brought about far more social change than just the integration of the Montgomery bus system. By establishing consumer rights as an institution in American society, Ralph Nader accomplished far more than just auto-safety improvements at General Motors. By changing the institutions of a society, it is possible to affect the practices of all the organizations operating within those institutions.

The Persistence of Institutions

All this is not to say that institutional change is an easy matter. As we've seen, institutions are the backbone of society's survival and are not changed casually. Institutions are inherently conservative—resistant to change. Indeed, it might be said that the first job of any institution is to perpetuate its own survival.

The organizations governed by an institution devote much of their efforts to the perpetuation of that institution. Thus, families teach children the values of family life, just as schools teach that education is valuable.

The various institutions of a society are linked to one another in a network of mutual support. After all, it is the families who surrender their children to the schools. The economy provides money, through taxes, to government to be used to pay for the schools, and the schools train children in the general and specific skills required for productive participation in the economy. Once they enter the work force, they will earn money to support their own families and begin training their children in the same patterns they learned. Everything is so interconnected that a threat to one institution is usually a threat to others as well.

As you continue in this book, you should develop a growing awareness of the enormous power of institutions over your life. You should also came to recognize them as two-edged swords. Institutions, after all, make group life possible, yet institutions also restrict individual freedom. This dilemma is one that has concerned thinkers throughout history, and the issue is still very much alive today.

Summary

"Formal organizations" are explicitly structured social groups, having formal rules and objectives. The term is often used interchangeably with "complex organizations," though the latter carries additional connotations of size and intricacy.

Formal, complex organizations differ from small, face-to-face groups in many ways. First, they are typically larger, ranging up into the thousands and more. Second, they are characterized by subdivision—being broken into separate departments, bureaus, and agencies. Third, specialization follows hand in hand with subdivision, as the different subgroups of the organization have special jobs to do. As mentioned above, organizations are explicitly structured: they have a clear, overt organization of relations among individuals and offices. Finally, formal organizations are structured so as to create a dynamic process; in the terms of an earlier chapter, they are systems as well as structures.

"Voluntary associations" are secondary groups organized around a set of shared interests. The PTA is a good example; so are Greenpeace, the American Legion, and the Democratic party. Some voluntary associations are formed for the purposes of advancing an interest—such as home computers, stamp collecting, or frisbee flinging—and others seek to achieve social reform; still others seek to prevent social reform.

"Bureaucracy" is a special form of organizational structure: the epitome of secondary-group relations. As such, it holds a special interest for sociologists. The key elements of bureaucracy are specialization, hierarchy, and explicit rules governing interactions and specifying authority. As we've seen, bureaucracy has many advantages and potential advantages as a vehicle for getting some of the business of society accomplished. Standardization of procedures can make administration more efficient, faster, more precise, and so forth. Through the separation of positions from those occupying them at any given time and through the maintenance of office files, bureaucracies also provide for organizational continuity.

As many have pointed out, bureaucracies have a negative side as well. Ironically, many of the potential advantages of bureaucracy are cited as things bureaucracies do *not* accomplish. Thus, bureaucracies are criticized for being inefficient, slow, imprecise, and so forth. These many failings of bureaucracies will be examined again later.

In the examination of bureaucracy, we looked specifically at the intersection of individuals and organizations. We found, for example, that all complex impersonal organizations seem to develop informal primary-group networks within them. Sometimes those informal networks actually support the formal purposes of the organization—and sometimes they thwart those purposes. Finally, we examined the interplay of individual personality and participation in bureaucracies.

Institutions are the context within which organizations operate. They are fundamentally conservative—functioning to perpetuate themselves—and they are linked in such a way as to support each other.

Important Terms

organization
institution
formal organization
complex organization
voluntary
   association
bureaucracy

coercive compliance
normative
   compliance
utilitarian
   compliance
tradition

Suggested Readings

Kanter, Rosabeth Moss
1977   *Men and Women of the Corporation*. New York: Basic Books.
Analyzes the role of sex stratification in the corporation, how it pervades the organization and influences interaction between members at different levels.

Knoke, David, and James R. Wood
1981   *Organized for Action: Commitment in Voluntary Associations*. New Brunswick, NJ: Rutgers University Press.
Looks at role of voluntary associations in policy-making and politics, factors affecting membership, and sources of organizational effectiveness.

Likert, Rensis, and Jane Likert
1976   *New Ways of Managing Conflict*. New York: McGraw-Hill.
Here is an excellent and thorough examination of modern management techniques, based on the Likerts' extensive research on styles of leadership and the results produced. This is the latest and most up-to-date report on *system 4 management*.

Olsen, Marvin E.
1978   *The Process of Social Organization, Second Edition*. New York: Holt, Rinehart and Winston.
Analysis of social structure, processes which operate and social systems which make up society.

Ouchi, William G.
1982   *Theory Z*. New York: Avon.
In this national best-seller, Ouchi discusses the nature of Japanese management and its applications in America.

Perrow, Charles
1979   *Complex Organizations*. Glenview, Ill.: Scott, Foresman.
Here's an excellent, up-to-date examination of complex organizations as seen by an insightful sociologist. Perrow examines the key features of complex organizations and their historical development, as well as the development of the study of such organizations. In addition to the analytical examination, the book contains numerous examples to round out your understanding of this form of social group.

Pfeffer, Jeffrey
1981   *Power in Organizations*. Marshfield, MA: Pitman Publishing.
Reviews work on power in organizations and attempts to develop sociological theoretical perspective on topic.

Weber, Max
[1925a]   *From Max Weber: Essays in Sociology*, trans., ed.
1946   Hans Gerth and C. Wright Mills. New York: Oxford University Press.
Many of the essays contained in the volume are relevant to an understanding of organizational structure, but Weber's classic description of bureaucracy is probably as useful to students today as when it was first written.

Weiss, Carol H., and Allen H. Barton, eds.
1980   *Making Bureaucracies Work*. Beverly Hills: Sage.
This collection of articles examines the many problems facing bureaucratic organizations and reports on experiments to solve those problems.

Earlier in the chapter, we saw that organizations vary in their methods of gaining compliance from their members. Over the years, there have been many different theories about how to gain compliance from the employees of business firms. In this concluding essay, I want to look at some of the various management theories that have been used.

Until well into the twentieth century, most discussions of industrial leadership focused on the heroic qualities required of leaders as they struggled with one another for dominance in the marketplace. The prototype was the "captain of industry" fighting a Darwinian struggle for the "survival of the fittest." The common worker was not considered at all or was looked down upon. To illustrate the latter point of view, Charles Perrow (1979:61) quotes from the popular essay "A Message to Garcia," written in 1899 about an American lieutenant who overcomes all odds to deliver a message from President McKinley to General Garcia in Cuba:

> We have recently been hearing much maudlin sympathy expressed for the "downtrodden denizen of the sweatshop" and the "homeless wanderer searching for honest employment," and with it all too often go many hard words for the men in power.
>
> Nothing is said about the employer who grows old before his time in a vain attempt to get frowsy ne'er-do-wells to do intelligent work; and his long patient striving with "help" that does nothing but loaf when his back is turned. In every store and factory there is a constant weeding-out process going on. No matter how good times are, this sorting continues, only if times are hard and work is scarce, the sorting is done finer—but out, and forever out, the incompetent and unworthy go. It is the survival of the fittest. Self-interest prompts every employer to keep the best—those who can carry a message to Garcia.

This harsh view of industrial relations dominated organizational thinking until about the 1930s, when Chester Barnard, Elton Mayo, and others began to see that organizational compliance was more than a matter of simple coercion. Reinhard Bendix (1956:296) summarizes the new view as follows:

> People are tractable, gullible, uncritical—and wanting to be led. But far more than this is deeply true of them. They want to feel united, tied, bound to something, some cause, bigger than they, commanding them yet worthy of them, summoning them to significance in living.

Though demeaning of workers, this view represented a turning point in industrial management, from an emphasis on coercive and utilitarian forms of compliance to more of an emphasis on normative forms. Organizations, as Barnard argued in his *The Functions of the Executive* (1938), were by their very nature cooperative ventures and could enhance the self-fulfillment of individuals while advancing organizational goals at the same time. For as workers were encouraged in diligence, honesty, and loyalty to the organization, so the organization itself prospered.

In stark contrast to the contemporary thinking, Barnard said that organizations were "moral" enterprises. Their purpose was not profit, not power, but *service*. Indeed, unless organizations served a larger, legitimate purpose for society, Barnard suggested, they could neither prosper nor survive. Within this view, service of individuals—workers as well as executives—within such organizations was moral behavior.

It is easy to dismiss such arguments by this telephone company president as attempts to dupe workers into doing the executive's bidding. Yet such dismissal misses an important point. Barnard was sincere in what he said, and his book had an important impact on the nature of organizational relations in industry and throughout society. If workers were enjoined to be loyal and cooperative, executives were urged to treat workers as human beings and as partners in the undertaking.

If workers were to be considered as something more than beasts of burden, their many human dimensions needed to be taken into account. Most obvious, perhaps, was the matter of working conditions. Though it could be argued, in the long view, that improved lighting, heating (or cooling), and other creature comforts of the workplace would ultimately improve production and profits, such measures were also regarded as correct in their own right.

Moving beyond simple safety and survival, improving the *morale* of workers became a matter of interest and a goal of the modern organization. More attention was given to the *social* aspect of organizations, as places where social life took place. Through studies like those of the Hawthorne plant that we've already noted, industrial leaders began to recognize that the workplace was an important source of primary relations for workers and that the time spent with fellow workers on the job constituted a major part of their waking existence.

In this new view of work relations advocated by people like Barnard and Mayo, which has become known as the "human relations movement," the role of social science grew ever greater. Both sociologists and psychologists were brought into industry to illuminate the nature and motivations of the humans working there. In part, social research pointed to the correlates of morale and productivity—the famous Hawthorne studies mentioned earlier are an example. In part, the social research was aimed at developing more effective leadership techniques. More specifically, this research was aimed at showing managers how best to manage the activities of others.

The human relations movement in business has gone though fads and phases, as different experts have offered various surefire techniques for effective management. Some of these have paid off; others have not. Company athletic leagues and teams, pension and profit-sharing programs, college scholarships for employees' children, and the like are the fruits of the movement.

The recognition of organizational members as human beings with human responses to things has nowhere been more carefully elaborated than in the work of Rensis and Jane Likert. The Likerts's four systems of organizational leadership provide a systematic review of the ground we have covered so far.

In examining methods for organizational leadership, the Likerts (1976:20) cite four underlying motives of employees: the desire for physical security, economic motives, the desire to achieve and maintain a sense of personal worth and importance, and the desire for new experience.

The Likerts identify four management systems that have tapped these motivations quite differently. In his earliest work (1961), Rensis Likert called them the "exploitative authoritative," "benevolent authoritative," "consultative," and "participative group" systems. In his more recent works, he simply uses the numerical notations 1, 2, 3, 4. The four systems attempt to engage the four underlying motives as follows.

System 1 (exploitative authoritative) depends mainly on the desire for physical security for success, though it also makes a moderate use of economic motives and may touch slightly on the desire for personal worth in the form of increasing status and power. The manner in which the motives are aroused is also distinctive in this form of management: they are aroused primarily through fear, threats, and punishment.

System 2 (benevolent authoritative) comes closer to Etzioni's utilitarian model, depending mostly on economic motives—with less use of physical security and status concerns to ensure compliance. In system 2, the emphasis shifts to rewards, though punishment—threatened and real—still plays a part.

System 3 (consultative) is a management strategy in which employees are partially involved (or consulted) in the operation of the organization. The desire for physical security is essentially satisfied, and extensive economic rewards are offered, but more attention is paid to employees' desire for personal recognition and the sense of real contribution to the organization as motivating factors.

System 4 (participative) has come to represent the Likerts's major contribution to organizational theory. System 4 fulfills the employee's desire for physical security and engages economic motives by linking them to the employee's sense of personal worth and desire for new experience. In this system, employees help set organizational goals and evaluate the efforts to achieve them. Ideally, all members of the organization experience themselves as partners in the organization, sharing in its successes both economically and physically. Profit-sharing programs, for example, are designed to break down the traditional labor-management adversary relationship, and employees can experience a new pride in a job done successfully as well. In our society, some of the voluntary associations mentioned earlier in the chapter best exemplify the system 4 type of management.

As a management strategy, system 4 contrasts most directly with system 1. In system 1, participants in the organization operate within a model where one person's gain is another's loss. For me to be successful in this system, you must be unsuccessful. (I referred to this earlier in the book as the "zero-sum model.") In system 4, by contrast, participants in the organization see that either all win or all lose. The success of the organization is experienced as a personal success for all its members. And the good leader is one who supports them all in seeing that. Table 7–2 shows other contrasts between system 4 and system 1.

To a contemporary American, the Likerts's description of system 4 sounds consonant with our fundamental democratic and humane beliefs and values. What's more compelling, however, is that the Likerts's conclusions, presented in Table 7–2, are based not on ideological interests but on empirical studies of organizational operation.

Douglas McGregor, in *The Human Side of Enterprise* (1960), coined the terms "Theory X" and "Theory Y" in reference to these two fundamental management techniques. Management expert Peter Drucker (1974:231–232) summarized the two theories as follows:

Theory X—the traditional approach to worker and working—assumes that people are lazy, dislike and shun work, have to be driven and need both carrot and stick. It assumes that most people are incapable of taking responsibility for themselves and have to be looked after. By contrast, Theory Y assumes that people have a psychological need to work and want achievement and responsibility. Theory X assumes immaturity. Theory Y assumes fundamentally that people want to be adults.

Drucker goes on to caution that McGregor's position may be misleading. Agreeing that Theory X management no longer works in American business, he warns that Theory Y does not necessarily work either. In a powerful insight, Drucker sees the danger that Theory Y man-

Table 7–2

Organizational Leadership: Likert's System 1 versus System 4

System 1	*System 4*
Attitudes usually are hostile and counter to organization's goals.	Attitudes are strongly favorable and provide powerful stimulation to behavior implementing organization's goals.
Marked conflict among motivational forces, weakening motivation to achieve organization's goals.	Motivational forces in support of the organization's goals generally reinforce each other in a substantial and cumulative manner.
Members feel little or no inclination to take initiative in the best interests of the organization.	Much initiative in the interest of the organization.
High-level management feel responsible for achieving organizational goals; rank and file do not.	All members of the organization feel responsible for achieving organizational goals.
Widespread distrust among members of the organization—both between levels of structure and among members at same level.	Cooperation, mutual trust, and confidence in one another.
Lower levels feel no responsibility for communicating accurately to upper levels.	Subordinates feel responsible for initiating communications upward of all relevant information.
Decision making separate from implementation, hence no real incentive to implement.	Decision makers are also implementers, hence real commitment to implement decisions.
An informal structure arises that often works against the formal structure and the achievement of organizational goals.	Informal structure is the same as the formal one, and hence supports the organizational goals.

Source: Adapted from Rensis Likert and Jane Likert, *New Ways of Managing Conflict* (New York: McGraw-Hill, 1976), pp. 20–26.

agement is but Theory X in more sophisticated clothing: seeing workers as psychologically weak and susceptible to psychological manipulation by management. Saying that "psychological despotism is basically contemptuous," Drucker (1974:244) concludes, "The work relationship has to be based on mutual respect."

For Drucker, as for the Likerts, effective modern management needs to reflect a true partnership between workers and managers. The workers must recognize that their own success is inseparable from that of their company.

In his 1974 opus on *Management*, Drucker made occasional, comparative references to Japanese management styles. Seven years later, that contrast produced a national bestseller for William G. Ouchi when he added *Theory Z* (1981) to American management's lexicon. Ouchi (1981:48–49) contrasted Japanese and American organizations as follows:

Japanese organizations	vs.	American organizations
Lifetime Employment		Short-term Employment
Slow Evaluation and Promotion		Rapid Evaluation and Promotion
Non-Specialized Career Paths		Specialized Career Paths
Implicit Control Mechanisms		Explicit Control Mechanisms
Collective Decision Making		Individual Decision Making
Collective Responsibility		Individual Responsibility
Wholistic Concern		Segmented Concern

Most observers of Japanese industry eventually use the term "family" in describing the work experience. As Ouchi's contrast above indicates, Japanese workers tend to work for one company throughout their life. The workers experience a lifetime commitment to the company, and the company has a similar commitment to the worker. Such companies are not merely a place to earn a living—many provide housing, medical care, social activities, and so forth.

On the job, Japanese workers feel a genuine responsibility for the company's success; their feelings are reflected in the popularity of "Quality Control Circles." During the years following World War II, the Union of Japanese Scientists and Engineers grew concerned over the inability of professionals to discover and remedy all the problems of industrial production and quality. Their solution was to involve the workers. In 1950, an American statistician, W. E. Deming, was brought to Japan to deliver seminars on scientific methods of studying and determining production problems.

Ultimately, Quality Control Circles were formed by two to ten workers in a firm. Each team engages in research on production problems—addressing both quality and efficiency. When problems are identified, the team then works out solutions. If the team itself is in a position to implement the solution, it does so. If the solution is more far-reaching, the team makes a proposal to management. In December 1979, there were 100,000 Quality Control Circles officially registered with the Union of Scientists and Engineers, and it was estimated that another million unregistered circles were operating in Japanese businesses. Did they suggest many solutions? The average circle produced *50 to 60 implemented suggestions per worker per year* (Ouchi 1981:223–224).

American managers have taken special notice of Japanese management methods in recent years, because of the meteoric advances of Japanese firms in such areas as automobile production and electronics. In contrast to American industry, Japanese competitors are cost-efficient and produce products of extremely high quality. More than one American executive has attempted to copy Japanese management techniques.

Some critics, like Thomas Weyr (1982) have warned against the Theory Z "quick fix" which the Japanese techniques seem to offer and suggest that Japanese management techniques are inseparable from Japanese culture. Ouchi (1981:54–55) is mindful of the cultural differences.

The Japanese have had to develop the capacity to work together in harmony, no matter what the forces of disagreement or social disintegration, in order to survive. . . . Subordinating individual tastes to the harmony of the group and knowing that individual needs can never take precedence over the interests of all is repellent to the Western citizen. But a frequent theme of Western philosophers and sociologists is that individual freedom exists only when people willingly subordinate their self-interests to the social interest. A society composed entirely of self-interested individuals is a society in which each person is at war with every other, a society which has no freedom.

In his research, Ouchi (1981:57) finds a number of American organizations that have naturally developed a Theory Z management style (he identifies Japanese management as Theory J): "IBM, Procter & Gamble, Hewlett-Packard, Eastman Kodak, the U.S. military. These organizations, all commonly thought to be among the best managed in the world, were identified by our respondents as having the same characteristics as Japanese companies!"

The final chapter of Theories X, Y, and Z is yet to be written. It should be clear, however, that the sociological study of organizations is vitally important to our daily lives in our nation and on our planet.

PRACTICING SOCIOLOGY

Writing in the *Harvard Business Review*, Charles Handy says:

> Legislation and public opinion are increasingly pushing management to change its concept of its responsibilities. Instead of finding labor to do the work that is needed, management will be urged to find work to fill the hands available. "If tires don't sell anymore," the laid-off workers said as Dunlop closed its tire factory at Liverpool in 1979, "management ought to find something for us to make that *will* sell." If, after all, management has always regarded its physical assets as capital in search of an outlet, why not its human assets as well?

Assume you are a business executive, who holds the Theory X point of view. Write a paragraph in response to this quotation.

Now repeat the process, assuming you are a business executive who holds the Theory Y point of view; finally write a paragraph to respond as a Theory Z executive would.

Source: Charles Handy, "Through the Organizational Looking Glass," *Harvard Business Review*, January/February 1980, p. 119.

Part Three

The Problem of Inequality

The structuring of social life is fundamentally a process of structuring inequalities.

Part Three examines some of the major dimensions along which inequality is structured: race, ethnicity, age, and sex. In addition, we're going to look at some of the ways in which individuals and groups break with the established agreements of their society through crime and other forms of deviance. We'll also see how people collectively change the agreements of the society.

Social Stratification Social stratification is a ranking of people in terms of wealth, prestige, power, and other rewards of social life.

As you'll see, it sometimes makes sense to view stratification as a matter of separate social classes: for example, lower class, middle class, and upper class. Other times, it is more useful to regard stratification as a continuum reaching from high to low social status.

Racial and Ethnic Relations Many of the inequalities in social life are based on racial- or ethnic-group membership. American history is, in part, a history of prejudice and discrimination against racial and ethnic minorities.

In this chapter, you'll learn about the reasons for and dynamics of prejudice and discrimination in a society.

Inequalities of Age and Sex Age is an important basis for status in any society, because people of different ages are treated quite differently. Certain age groups, such as the elderly in America, are the victims of prejudice and discrimination. Women are another minority group in America, even though they constitute a slight majority numerically.

We will examine the life experiences of people at all age levels, from young to old. Then we'll see the many ways in which women are discriminated against.

Deviance and Social Control You will have become aware by now that the structuring of agreements in society are a source of dissatisfaction for many people. Deviance, the breaking of established agreements, is often the result. Social control represents the forces in society which keep people from breaking agreements and punish them when they do.

You're going to learn that deviance, broadly defined, is widespread throughout society. In fact, all of us are deviants to a degree. Still some people are more dramatically deviant than others, and we'll see why. In addition, we'll see how social control operates, including the problems it sometimes creates.

Collective Behavior and Social Movements Sometimes people join together to change the agreements of a society.

We're going to examine the causes of collective behavior and social movements and also their impact on society.

8

Social Stratification

You've probably had a direct personal experience of what we might call "human worth." That experience probably cropped up unexpectedly in the context of seeing a person treated as if he or she were not worth much. Maybe once when your classmates were making fun of a kid for having torn and dirty clothes, you felt that they were being cruel and unfair. Maybe you read about someone dying, someone poor, unknown, and unimportant, and you felt that at some level every human being is worth the same as any other.

You've probably had an experience of feeling that some people were worth more than others. When sides were being chosen for a game, you may have wanted desperately to be picked by the "right" side. You've experienced either the pride of being friends with the most popular child in school or the sadness of being passed by and ignored. Even now, you undoubtedly have a sense of some people around you being more important than others. And, just as surely, you wonder from time to time where *you* fit into the ranking of who's who and who isn't. Other people wonder, too, as we'll see.

This chapter will examine the many faces of social inequality. Regardless of whether people were created equal, they typically live in a state of inequality. In every society, some people are more powerful than others, some have more of the good things than others, some can do things others cannot, some can be what they want to be while others cannot. I'll limit the discussion of inequalities to those within one society, and the concluding essay of this chapter will look at inequalities *between* societies.

Sociologists use the term **social stratification** to refer to the organization of inequality in society. In geology, "stratification" refers to the appearance of layers of different kinds of rock, one on top of another. To sociologists the word means the same thing, except that different kinds of people rather than rocks are layered one on top of another. The layers, in sociology as in geology, are called "strata."

Our discussion will begin with an examination of several different sociological views of social stratification. In particular, we'll examine the differences between conflict and functionalist views of stratification and the difference between **strata** and social classes.

Next we'll look in some detail at the many different dimensions of stratification, the different bases for stratifying people and groups of people. We are going to see that different societies have different agreements regarding proper ways to rank people. Then we'll examine some of the ways in which sociologists measure social status.

Different social classes are sometimes regarded as subcultures within a society, each with its own agreements about what is true, good, and proper. We'll look at how those different sets of agreements conflict within a society. We'll also examine the consequences of social stratification—why it makes a difference whether you live out your existence in one stratum or class rather than another.

The chapter concludes with an examination of social mobility, movement from one stratum to another. Your membership in a particular stratum or class is a matter of agreement. In looking at mobility, we'll see how agreements can be changed.

Points of View on Stratification

In this section, our examination of the ways sociologists and other social thinkers have looked at stratification should give you an idea of how the notion of stratification has developed over time and an idea of how it stands now.

Early Social Theorists

Stratification has probably existed among human beings ever since the first time one cave dweller beat another into submission. The first, prehistoric, agreement that one person was superior to another was probably created with a club or rock. We have been using clubs, rocks, and subtler devices ever since.

Throughout most of our history, humans have assumed that inequalities among people were the result of natural or divine ordination. When Plato and Aristotle set about designing ideal societies, for instance, they devoted the greater part of their attention to the unequal distribution of power and privilege: the proper arrangement of affairs among rulers, common people, and slaves.

In the century before the American and French revolutions, Jean Jacques Rousseau (1712–1778) and other social thinkers began to suggest openly that social stratification was more arbitrary than had previously been assumed. Rousseau (1750:101), for example, concluded that there were two kinds of inequality: one natural and the other the result of agreements.

> I conceive that there are two kinds of inequality among the human species; one which I call natural or physical, because it is established by nature and consists in a difference of age, health, bodily strength, and qualities of the mind or of the soul; and another, which may be called moral or political inequality, because it depends on a kind of convention, and is established, or at least authorized, by the consent of men.

The same century in which Rousseau wrote those words witnessed the reigns of kings George III of England and Louis XVI of France, neither of whom demonstrated a "natural" ability to rule over the affairs of others. Each enjoyed his high social rank by virtue of earthly agreements that God had ordained in him through family descent. Each was said to rule by "divine right."

Rousseau, along with Voltaire, Montesquieu, and others, drew attention to the fact that the conventions placing one person in a position superior to others were only agreements—not ultimate truths—and thus could be changed. Bloody revolutions in America, France,

Russia, and elsewhere have flowed from that realization, and many basic agreements have been irrevocably altered.

Still, stratification among people persists. Sociologists have explained why inequality continues to persist and how stratification works in societies like our own by using conflict theory and functional theory. Let's look at what each point of view has to contribute to our understanding of stratification.

Conflict Theory and Stratification

You may recall from the discussion in Chapter 2 that Karl Marx saw human history as the history of "class struggle," in which the exploited classes sought to overthrow their exploiters. In Marx's view, a **social class** is a group of people who share a similar relationship to the economic system of a society. Because of this similar economic relationship, Marx argued, people of a class tend to develop similar ideas about society, similar patterns of interaction, and similar lifestyles.

The system of economic capitalism, Marx thought, established two distinct classes of people: those who owned the means of production (the bourgeoisie) and those who were forced to sell their labor to the owners of industry (the proletariat). It was Marx's belief that through a series of economic crises and increasing organization by the proletariat, capitalism would eventually be overthrown and replaced by a socialist state, which, in turn, would evolve into a truly egalitarian, or "classless," society.

Although most modern conflict theorists disagree with many of Marx's political beliefs, they, like Marx, are interested in the problem of inequality from the point of view of individuals and subgroups, as Gerhard Lenski (1966) has pointed out. Where functionalists focus on the needs of society, conflict theorists focus on the needs and desires of individuals. Lenski goes on to say:

Conflict theorists, as their name suggests, see social inequality as arising out of the struggle for valued goods and services in short supply. Where the functionalists emphasize the common interests shared by the members of a society, conflict theorists emphasize the interests that divide. Where functionalists stress the common advantages which accrue from social relationships, conflict theorists emphasize the element of dominion and exploitation. Where functionalists emphasize consensus as the basis of social unity, conflict theorists emphasize coercion. Where functionalists see human societies as social systems, conflict theorists see them as stages on which struggle for power and privilege take place. (1966:16–17)

Thus, Ralf Dahrendorf (1959), a contemporary conflict theorist, stresses the importance of "class" over "strata," favoring the analysis of distinct groups rather than positions located on a continuous hierarchy of status. Unlike Marx, who focused almost exclusively on economic factors, Dahrendorf sees an inevitable conflict between the interests of those giving orders and those subjected to them.

While the conflict theory point of view on social class makes a lot of sense and probably reflects much of what you have observed about stratification around you, not all sociologists see things that way. The functionalist point of view, discussed in Chapter 2, offers another way of examining stratification.

The Functionalist View of Stratification

In 1940, the American sociologist Talcott Parsons published "An Analytical Approach to the Theory of Social Stratification." This article, which appeared in the *American Journal of Sociology,* laid the groundwork for a functionalist point of view on stratification. Parsons said that stratification was a matter of "moral evaluation." Noting that societies have systems of values, Parsons suggested that a person's relative standing in the society reflected the extent

Talcott Parsons
1902–1979
Colorado Springs, Colorado

Some Important Works

The Social System (New York: Free Press, 1951).
The Structure of Social Action (Glencoe, Ill.: Free Press, 1937).
Societies: Evolutionary and Comparative Perspectives (Englewood Cliffs, N.J.: Prentice-Hall, 1964).

Generally regarded as the primary creator of the social systems view in modern sociology, Talcott Parsons was, at the time of his death, considered the "dean" of American sociology by friend and foe alike. Beginning with his enormous 1937 examination of "a group of recent European writers—chiefly Durkheim, Weber, Alfred Marshall, and Vilfredo Pareto"—Parsons devoted his professional life to the attempt to create a general theory of society. He is the chief founder of "grand theory" in modern sociology.

Although he will be remembered chiefly for his theoretical work on the social systems view of society, Parsons also brought a special insight to a variety of concrete social situations: the distinctions between business and the professions, the nature of the doctor-patient relationship, the structure of the school class, family relations, the superAmericanism of "hyphenated-Americans," to name only a few.

Parsons's lifetime goal of creating a general field theory for sociology comparable to Einstein's contribution to physics had not been achieved at the time of his death. He had, nonetheless, influenced American sociology more fundamentally than any contemporary or predecessor.

to which his or her characteristics and achievements corresponded to those values.

According to Parsons's view, in a society that places a special value on physical strength, the stronger members will be accorded higher status than will the weaker members. In societies giving religion a special importance, we can expect those occupying religious positions to be accorded the higher status. In a society such as the United States, where economic achievement is a central value, persons with wealth are accorded high status.

Building on the work of Parsons, in 1945, Kingsley Davis and Wilbert Moore published what is now the classic statement of the functionalist view of stratification. In "Some Principles of Stratification," they described the functions of stratification for societies and argued that stratification was both universal and inevitable.

The functionalist view of stratification is based on three observations about positions in a society. First, some positions seem more important than others for the stability and survival of a society. The king, for example, seems more important than any individual commoner. Second, some positions are more easily filled than others because of the skills and training required by the roles associated with those statuses. For example, potentially more people can perform the role of street sweeper than the role of physician. Third, some roles are less "pleasant" than others in terms of the time, physical effort, and working conditions entailed. More is required of corporation presidents than of clerk-typists, for example.

For a society to function effectively, or at all, statuses must be filled—particularly the "most important" statuses—with people qualified and willing to perform the roles associated with them. Social stratification systems, by providing unequal rewards in the form of money, prestige, deference, and privilege, ensure that statuses will be filled and roles performed. Social stratification systems provide **incentives.**

From the functionalist point of view, then, the corporation president receives more money, prestige, deference, and privilege than a secretary because the president (1) is more important to the corporation and to the larger society, (2) possesses the relatively scarce skills and qualities needed for the position, and (3) devotes more time and effort to the job and suffers more emotional strain from it (or is expected to).

Socioeconomic Status (SES)

The functionalist point of view portrays stratification in a society as a more or less continuous ranking from low to high. To measure how people rank on this overall hierarchy, sociologists attempt to combine the several dimensions they consider relevant into a single measure. Typically, they do this by creating an index of **socioeconomic status (SES),** an overall summary of where individuals stand in the social pecking order. The particular methods used to create this index vary from study to study, but a simplified example will illustrate the process involved.

Table 8–1 describes the construction of an SES index based on two variables: income and education. Suppose for the moment that we have conducted a survey and wish to characterize the survey respondents in terms of their socioeconomic status. Each respondent is given a score (see Table 8–1) reflecting his or her income

Table 8–1

Hypothetical Measurement of SES

Income	Score	Education	Score
Under $5,000	0	0–8 years	0
$5,000–7,499	1	9–11 years	1
$7,500–9,999	2	12 years	2
$10,000–19,999	3	13–15 years	3
$20,000 or more	4	16 or more years	4

Composite Socioeconomic Status

Low ⟶ High

0   1   2   3   4   5   6   7   8

and another score reflecting his or her level of education. The higher the income or education, the higher the score. The scores assigned on the two variables are then added, with the result that people are ranked from 0 to 8.

In this example, a person who earns $4,000 a year and has completed six years of school is scored 0 overall. Someone who earns $8,000 a year and has fourteen years of school is scored 5 overall. In such a system very different patterns of income and education can produce the same overall score. For example, a person who earns more than $20,000 a year and has a sixth-grade education is scored 4 overall, as is the college graduate who earns less than $5,000 a year. Such cases are the exception, however, and as we shall see when we examine the relationships among the different dimensions of stratification, combining scores generally yields useful social stratification classifications.

Measures of socioeconomic status have two important functions for the sociological study of stratification. First, they permit studies of the factors that seem to produce high or low status. Second, they permit studies of the consequences of different status levels, a topic that we will examine later in this chapter.

Two Views of Stratification in Review

As we've seen, sociologists employ two distinct points of view in examining social stratification. These points of view—social class and socio-economic status—are shown graphically in Figure 8–1.

Conflict theorists see society as divided into discrete social "classes," separate subgroups with different lifestyles and competing interests. For instance, a strong case could be made that those who own or control the corporations of the United States form a "class" separate from those who own little property and who do routine, low-paying work. Studies of families such as the Rockefellers and DuPonts, who own and control the nation's wealth, suggest that they have much in common with each other but little in common with many of the employees of the companies they own. Elite, property-owning families tend to associate with each other, and people who do blue-collar or low-level white-collar work are more likely to form friendships with each other than with corporate lawyers or Wall Street investment bankers. Members of the elite are likely to send their children to private schools, belong to exclusive country clubs, and vote Republican; factory workers are more likely to send their kids to public schools, go for their swims at the "Y," and vote Democratic. At work, the corporate owners are likely to want to keep complete control for themselves and to pay their employees as little as possible, whereas people in subordinate positions are likely to want higher wages and opportunities to have at least a limited say in company policy.

Functionalist sociologists see people ranked in a more or less continuous hierarchy from the bottom to the top. The term "socioeconomic status" (SES) has often been used in reference to this view. Functionalists point out that both the bank teller and the local bank president work for a living, and that it is not unheard of for the teller's son to marry the president's daughter or for the teller's son to become an executive

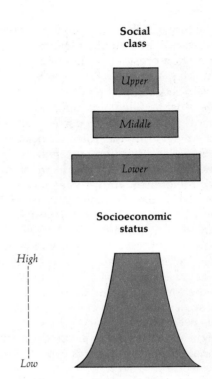

Figure 8–1 *Two views of social stratification.*

himself someday. Furthermore, these sociologists may argue that both the teller and the executive share an interest in keeping the bank running smoothly. They may both go to the same church, belong to the same fraternal organization, and vote Republican. In general, adherents of the status-continuum point of view suggest that people of different strata do not form cohesive subcultures, that political differences often are not dramatic and not sharply etched, particularly in comparison with the countries of Europe or the Third World, and that there is substantial movement between strata for individuals.

Social class and socioeconomic status both provide useful pictures of social stratification in America and other societies. Depending on why you are studying stratification, one point of view might be more appropriate than the other.

Dimensions of Stratification

In the preceding discussions of different sociological points of view, I have touched on a number of the different dimensions of stratification: the qualities according to which people are stratified. This section examines various dimensions of stratification more fully. Whereas Marx saw social stratification almost exclusively as an economic matter, Max Weber suggested there were *three* major bases of stratification: the economic order, the social order, and the political order. In Marx's view of capitalist society, economics and politics were intertwined. Weber analytically separated wealth from power. He also distinguished stratification that involved the distribution of honor, prestige, and deference.

Weber used the term "class" to refer to economic stratification. Like Marx, he considered ownership of property to be the primary index of economic position. Weber used the term "party" to refer to political power, recognizing that some people enjoy high standing in society because of their political activities and affiliations, regardless of whether they own property. Finally, he used the term "status" to refer to honor, prestige, and deference (Weber 1925b).

In the rest of this section we will take a more comprehensive look at the different ways people have created to rank themselves and others. We'll consider the dimensions already mentioned and expand the list considerably. Some of the bases for stratification are **ascribed statuses** (family, age, sex, race) while others are **achieved statuses** (possessions, occupation, education, power).

Family and Kinship

In many societies, your social standing would be based largely on your status within the kinship and family system. Newborn children take on the social status held by their parents. Children of rich parents become "rich children" automatically—even at an age when they think money is just another thing to put in their mouths. Being born into a royal family would give you high social standing that would probably stay with you throughout your life. Less dramatically, being born into a "good family" in a small American community is likely to give you high social status as long as you remain in that community, unless you do something objectionable enough to contradict your high standing.

Age, Sex, Race

In some societies, such as traditional China and Japan, social stratification is related to age. The elders are especially revered and typically exercise more political power than do the young. Sometimes this reflects the view that experience provides greater wisdom in the ways of the world. And where authority is based on tradition, the elders of society have more direct knowledge of how things have "always been done."

Modern industrial societies do not typically grant high status to the old. In the United States, for example, the opposite is true. We value youth and generally resist growing old. Hairpieces, face-lifts, and "age-spot" removers are all evidence that high social status does not come with age. I'll have more to say about this in Chapter 10.

Sex and race are also frequent bases for social stratification. In some societies, women have higher status than men; in others, the opposite is true. The relative status of different racial and ethnic groups also varies from society to society. We'll see how race functions as a basis for stratification in the discussion of caste later in this chapter and in Chapter 9, and we'll look at sex in Chapter 10.

While Americans are created equal in principle, we are created unequal in practice. At birth, each of us inherits the social status of our family.

Possessions

Money, and lots of it, is perhaps the dimension of stratification that comes to mind most readily for most of us. In American society and in many others, people are ranked socially on the basis of how much wealth they have. Although money is not everything, all other things being equal, being rich is considered better than being poor.

The valuation of wealth is not a universal agreement. Indeed, wealth is negatively valued in some societies. Among the Navaho Indians of the American Southwest, for example, the wealthy tribe member is sometimes viewed with suspicion. Often it is suspected and rumored that one's wealth was obtained through witchcraft—a very real possibility within the Navaho point of view.

A somewhat more complicated pattern is found among some Indian tribes in the Canadian Northwest. Wealthy families are expected to give lavish parties —called "potlatches"—that deplete their wealth. Status appears to be gained in proportion to the lavishness of the potlatch. Wealth gains status for a family only through its destruction.

Property, such as landholdings, stocks, and bonds, is also a part of one's wealth. Other possessions can symbolize your social standing, too. The agreements on what objects symbolize high social rank, however, vary from place to place and from time to time. Automobiles, shrunken heads, color television sets, seashells, and early-edition comic books are each important possessions among some groups.

For a college professor, books are an important symbol of high status. Those he or she has written come first, followed by those in which he or she is mentioned. Beyond that, new books symbolize the professor's up-to-date interests, old ones symbolize how long he or she has been a scholar, and a diversity of books indicates a wide-ranging intellect.

We might well consider friends, associates, and memberships in groups as "possessions," as they bear the same relationship to one's social standing as objects do. Belonging to an exclusive country club symbolizes your exclusiveness. Having important and powerful friends suggests that you are important and powerful.

Occupation

Occupation is another critical determinant of social standing in many societies. Some examples are obvious: kings rank higher than stable cleaners, corporation presidents higher than mailing clerks. When you try to make sense of less gross status distinctions among occupations, however, the matter becomes murkier. As Hauser and Featherman (1977:xix) have pointed out, "There is nothing hierarchical in the concept of an occupation, which merely invokes the differentiation of work from other activities and a certain division of labor among those who work."

Even though jobs are not intrinsically ranked from low to high, people in diverse cultures value the occupations of their societies differently. As Hauser and Featherman continue, "there is an almost universal and moderately consistent hierarchy of occupations, which is expressed in variables like the educational requirements for occupational entry, the typical level of remuneration, and the esteem with which occupational incumbents are held by the public" (1977:xix).

Of the three indicators of occupational status mentioned, the first two—educational requirements and amount of pay—are relatively easy to determine. But what prestige do people accord

various occupations? For the United States, two major studies have addressed this question since World War II.

In 1947, a group of researchers at the National Opinion Research Center (NORC) in Chicago undertook a study of the social status that Americans granted different occupations (Reiss et al. 1961). This study, named the "North-Hatt study" for Cecil North and Paul Hatt, has become a classic and much-cited resource in American sociology. The 651 people in the national sample were presented with a list of ninety occupational titles and asked: "For each job mentioned, please pick out the statement that best gives *your own personal opinion* of the *general standing* that such a job has." Five choices were provided: excellent, good, average, somewhat below average, and poor. The researchers then tallied the answers given for each occupation and ranked them according to their overall ratings.

Sixteen years later, in 1963, another team of NORC researchers repeated the 1947 study to see what changes had taken place in the way Americans rank occupations (Hodge et al. 1964). They found virtually no differences, despite the many changes that have taken place in American society. The results of the two studies are presented in Table 8–2.

Amazed by the consistency of agreements on occupational-prestige ratings between 1947 and 1963, the researchers then turned to a study conducted in 1925. Many fewer occupations were rated in that earlier study, but the overall rankings corresponded very closely to the 1947 and 1963 findings. Thus, the informal agreements on the prestige of different occupations survived nearly forty years, a catastrophic economic depression, World War II, and great social change in America.

Education

Education is an important aspect of social stratification, epecially in developed societies. All

Table 8-2

The Prestige of Selected Occupations in America

Occupation	1963 Score	1947 Score	Occupation	1963 Score	1947 Score
U.S. Supreme Court justice	94	96	Farm owner and operator	74	76
Physician	93	93	Undertaker	74	72
Scientist	92	89	Newspaper columnist	73	74
State governor	91	93	Policeman	72	67
Cabinet member in the federal government	90	92	Radio announcer	70	75
			Insurance agent	69	68
College professor	90	92	Carpenter	68	65
U.S. representative in Congress	90	89	Manager of a small store in a city	67	69
Chemist	89	86	Local official of a labor union	67	62
Lawyer	89	86	Mail carrier	66	66
Diplomat in U.S. foreign service	89	92	Railroad conductor	66	67
Dentist	88	86	Traveling salesman for a wholesale concern	66	68
Architect	88	86			
Psychologist	87	85	Plumber	65	63
Minister	87	87	Automobile repairman	64	63
Member of the board of directors of a large corporation	87	86	Barber	63	59
			Machine operator in a factory	63	60
Mayor of a large city	87	90	Owner/operator of a lunch stand	63	62
Priest	86	86	Corporal in the regular army	62	60
Civil engineer	86	84	Truck driver	59	54
Airline pilot	86	83	Clerk in a store	56	58
Banker	85	88	Lumberjack	55	53
Biologist	85	81	Restaurant cook	55	54
Sociologist	83	82	Singer in a nightclub	54	52
Instructor in public schools	82	79	Filling-station attendant	51	52
Captain in the regular army	82	80	Dockworker	50	47
Accountant for a large business	81	81	Night watchman	50	47
Owner of a business that employs about 100 people	80	82	Coal miner	50	49
			Restaurant waiter	49	48
Musician in a symphony orchestra	78	81	Taxi driver	49	49
			Farmhand	48	50
Author of novels	78	80	Janitor	48	44
Economist	78	79	Bartender	48	44
Official of an international labor union	77	75	Soda-fountain clerk	44	45
			Sharecropper	42	40
Railroad engineer	76	77	Garbage collector	39	35
Electrician	76	73	Street sweeper	36	34
Trained machinist	75	73	Shoe shiner	34	33

Source: Selected from data presented in Robert Hodge, Paul Siegel and Peter Rossi, "Occupational Prestige in the United States, 1925–63," *American Journal of Sociology* 60 (1964):290. Reprinted by permission of The University of Chicago Press. Copyright © by the University of Chicago.

other things being equal, a college graduate in America has a higher social standing than does a person with no education. Part of the high ranking of scientists, college professors, and public-school instructors in Table 8–2 reflects the education associated with those occupations.

The high social standing associated with education is by no means limited to contemporary American society. Indeed, scholars were accorded very high standing among the ancient Hebrews (as also among modern Jews), and the contemporary Japanese have a higher regard for education than Americans do.

Religion

Persons occupying religious statuses are accorded high social standing in many societies, particularly in societies where religion is the most important aspect of life. In predominantly Roman Catholic countries, for example, cardinals, bishops, and priests have high social standing. So do "shamans" (religious medicine men) in many primitive societies, the Hindu saints of India, Shinto priests in Japan, and many others.

Even in the United States, where economic values are stressed, religious leaders generally have high social standing. In Table 8–2, for example, ministers and priests are ranked higher than many people in occupations that usually yield much more money.

Power

Bertrand Russell said power was the key concept in social sciences, analogous to the importance of energy in physics; and Dahrendorf sees it as the main dimension of stratification.

Some power comes as a part of occupying certain social positions, such as political office. We spoke of authority in this context as "legitimated power." Authority is also granted outside of government, as in the case of business executives or religious leaders. Material goods can be a source of power, aside from considerations of authority. "Money talks" is one way in which this sociological observation is sometimes expressed.

Although, of course, not all sociologists agree with Russell's and Dahrendorf's pronouncements, few would deny that people are often ranked according to the power they have. Generals rank higher than privates, corporation presidents higher than clerks, and kings higher than commoners. Their power is undoubtedly a part of the reason why Supreme Court justices and other government officials were ranked high in the list presented in Table 8–2. Agreements granting some people more authority than others are always subject to challenge and change, however.

Stratification as a System

In 1980, Americans earned about $1.7 trillion in personal income, which works out to about $7,670 per person. Of course, not all the members of American society shared equally in those earnings. Some got well over "their" $7,670, and some got much less. In fact, as Figure 8-2 shows, the poorest one-fifth of American families received just 5.1 percent of the total, while the richest one-fifth of families received 41.6 percent (U.S. Bureau of Census, 1981d:15).

The degree of uneven distribution in annual income may strike you as a lot or a little: essentially the highest paid one-fifth of families earns twice as much as they would if everyone earned the same. But the lowest fifth got only one quarter what they would have gotten in an even distribution. More striking, however, is the distribution of accumulated (including inherited) wealth. While such data are harder to come by, the U.S. Census Bureau (1980c:471) has published figures for selected years between 1958 and 1972. With little variation across that period, the wealthiest 1 percent of the population owned just over one-quarter of the personal wealth of

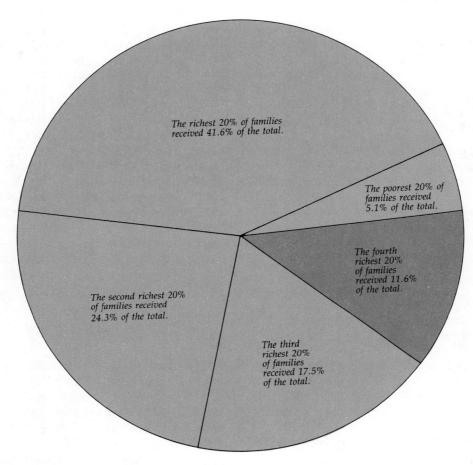

Figure 8–2 The distribution of 1977 income among families in America. Source: U.S. Bureau of Census, Money Income and Poverty Status of Families and Persons in the United States, *Washington, D.C., 1981, p. 15.*

the nation. In 1972, for example, 1 percent of the people owned 25.9 percent of the $3.5 trillion of personal wealth.

Why is wealth distributed unevenly in American society? As we shall see, it results from the stratification *system* in which the several dimensions of social status are interwoven. In other words, a person who ranks high on one dimension tends to rank high on others, too. In this section, we'll look at the three most important connections in our society—those between income, occupation, and education.

Relations among Dimensions

The relationship between income and occupation should need no documentation. Persons employed in professional and technical jobs receive far higher incomes than do those in manual labor, and the impact of unionization has not erased this general pattern. The relationship among stratification variables only begins here, however.

Education and income are also related—in a circular fashion. By and large, persons with the

<table>
<tr><td colspan="3">Table 8-3</td></tr>
</table>

Table 8-3

Median Money Income, by Sex and Education, 1978

	Men	Women
Elementary school:		
less than 8 years	$5,600	$2,700
8 years	7,500	3,100
High school:		
1–3 years	8,600	3,300
4 years	12,300	5,000
College:		
1–3 years	12,500	5,200
4 years	17,400	7,800
5 or more years	21,000	11,100

Source: U.S. Bureau of Census, *Statistical Abstract of the United States* (Washington, D.C.: Government Printing Office, 1980), p. 152.

Table 8-4

Relationship between Education and Occupation among Americans in March 1977

Occupation group	Percent with four or more years of college
Professional, technical, and kindred workers	61.1
Managers and administrators, except farm	22.5
Sales workers	8.8
Clerical and kindred workers	6.7
Craft and kindred workers	7.5
Operatives, except transport	1.6
Transport-equipment workers	2.0
Laborers, except farm	1.2
Private household workers	1.1
Service workers, except private household	2.8
Farm workers	6.3
All occupational groups	15.1

Source: "Educational Attainment of Workers, March 1977," *U.S. Bureau of Labor Statistics Special Labor Force Report 209,* 1978.

most education earn the most money, and children from wealthy families are more likely to get advanced education than are those from poorer families. Table 8-3 presents the average 1978 incomes for men and women with different levels of education. Notice how consistently income increases with more schooling and the amount of difference education makes: men with five or more years of college earned an average of $15,400 more in 1978 than those with less than eight years of elementary school. Education also affects women's incomes—though less dramatically than men's—and you'll notice that women earn less than men at every educational level.

Now let's look at the schooling received in families with different income levels. In 1978, the Bureau of the Census reported that among families with income under $9,000 in 1977, 23 percent of the members between eighteen and twenty-four years of age were enrolled in college. This percentage increases steadily as family income rises. Among families with incomes of $27,000 or more, 60 percent were enrolled (U.S. Bureau of Census 1978a:164).

To round out your review of the interrelationships among income, occupation, and education, Table 8–4 presents the percentages of people in several occupational groupings who have completed four or more years of college. The differences are dramatic, ranging from 61.1 percent among the professionals and technical workers to less than 5 percent among most blue-collar occupations.

These three dimensions of stratification, then, are closely related to one another. Persons who would be judged as having high status on one dimension are likely to appear high on the others as well. These dimensions are related to other aspects of status as well. Income, for example, is related to possessions to a greater extent than

Table 8-5

Family Income and Possessions, 1974

Income	2 or more cars	Color TV	Percent of families owning Washing machine	Freezer	Air conditioner
Under $3,000	6.2	31.6	50.7	50.7	29.6
$3,000–4,999	8.8	40.6	55.4	55.4	37.7
$5,000–7,499	15.6	50.4	62.6	62.6	43.5
$7,500–9,999	23.1	57.8	68.5	68.5	48.8
$10,000–14,999	36.8	67.4	77.2	77.2	53.7
$15,000–19,999	50.1	78.1	85.3	85.3	60.5
$20,000–24,999	60.1	80.2	86.0	86.0	63.0
$25,000 and over	67.2	84.4	89.2	89.2	69.0

Source: U.S. Bureau of Census, Statistical Abstract of the United States, 1978, p. 474.

you might imagine. Table 8–5 presents some data on income and possessions as of 1974.

Status Inconsistency

In our discussion of the connections between different dimensions of stratification, it's important to note that we've been talking only about *tendencies*, not about associations between dimensions that always hold. When you rank high according to one dimension but not others, sociologists use the term **status inconsistency.** This means that your social standing may be quite different according to different sets of agreements. For example, you would have an inconsistent status if you were very wealthy but had little education, or if you were very well educated but poor. Many ministers, teachers, and "self-made" millionaires have inconsistent statuses.

Notice that inconsistent statuses create problems for both those occupying them and those interacting with people who occupy them. Ranking within a stratification system—like social statuses in general—provides guidelines for interaction. We may, for example, offer deference to those ranking higher than us. Ambi-

guities regarding who ranks higher or lower make unclear the "proper" patterns of interaction, and people may come together with conflicting expectations as to their relationship and interactions.

The notion of status inconsistency offers one explanation for the beginning of the women's liberation movement; women began to realize that they were not allowed to compete in the same world of work as men. Many of the women who participated in the beginning of the women's movement had high levels of education. These women expected their educations to lead to good jobs with prospects and pay equal to the prospects and pay of the jobs their brothers and husbands were getting. Instead, they found themselves working as secretaries or permanent "assistants." The jolting recognition of the gap between reality and beliefs about democracy led to anger, demonstrations, and demands.

At the same time, researchers found that the dimensions of stratification are not related in the same way for women as they are for men. High income goes along with high occupational status for men, but women's income rises much more slowly as occupational status goes up. The same thing is true for education: more education gives men greater income increases than it gives women, as Table 8–3 shows. In spite of laws and court cases upholding equality of opportunity for women, few changes seem to have occurred since the beginning of the women's movement. We'll return to this issue in Chapter 10.

Social Classes as Subcultures

We have been looking at social stratification as if it were a continuous hierarchy of strata. In this section, we'll return to the point of view that sees social classes within a society as more or less discrete groups.

The definition of membership in particular social classes is often unclear and ambiguous, but sociologists do examine the different orientations and lifestyles that generally characterize the different classes. To the extent that social classes have special sets of agreements, they might be examined as subcultures within the same society. Children and adults socialized in terms of the class's shared agreements further consolidate their membership in that class.

The Study of Social Class in America

During the 1920s and on into the 1940s, a number of American sociologists undertook in-depth community studies of social stratification in which they used the concept of social class. Their aim was to determine how stratification related to other aspects of Middle American social life.

Robert Lynd and Helen Lynd (1929, 1937), for example, chose to look at Muncie, Indiana, which they subsequently called "Middletown." Examining stratification primarily by way of economic and occupational factors, the Lynds identified two classes: the "working class" and the "business class." The latter included pro-

Robert and Helen Lynd
Robert: 1892–1970
Helen: 1896–
Robert: New Albany, Indiana
Helen: LaGrange, Illinois

Some Important Works
Middletown (New York: Harcourt, Brace, 1929).
Middletown in Transition (New York: Harcourt, Brace, 1937).

Though they were also independent scholars, Robert and Helen Lynd will always be most remembered as the husband-wife team who brought a sociological perspective to bear on Muncie, Indiana—thereby revealing the social structure of Middle America in the 1920s and 1930s. The Lynds's study of "Middletown" represented the application of anthropological field methods to the examination of a modern society, and many scholars were to follow in their steps.

Aside from their sociological careers, Robert was active in the publishing field, and both Lynds were committed to using their sociology to understand and improve the quality of social life. The sociopolitical commentary of the Middletown books probably accounts in part for their broad popular success.

Photograph of Helen Lynd not available.

fessionals such as physicians and lawyers. The Lynds were especially interested in the ways that social status was reflected in the social life of the community. In general, they found that schools, churches, and other institutions and

Table 8-6

Warner's Typology of American Social Classes

Class	Characteristics
Upper-upper (UU):	Wealthy individuals whose wealth came to them through inheritance over the course of several generations; the "old rich."
Lower-upper (LU):	Newly wealthy individuals; those from modest or poor backgrounds who had made their own fortunes; the nouveau riche.
Upper-middle (UM):	Typically professional people and managers who, although not wealthy, were financially quite comfortable.
Lower-middle (LM):	Lower-level white-collar workers such as clerks and secretaries.
Upper-lower (UL):	Upper-level manual, blue-collar workers, such as skilled craftspersons.
Lower-lower (LL):	Lower-level manual, blue-collar workers, such as unskilled laborers and domestic servants; also includes the unemployed poor.

Note: "Jonesville" was a relatively new community and Warner found few (and maybe no) residents who could be considered upper-upper there. (Warner, 1949)

associations were unofficially segregated by status. Identifying the "business-class" churches and the "working-class" churches, for example, was a simple matter.

Perhaps the best known and most influential of the American community studies of class was W. Lloyd Warner and associates' (1949) examination of Morris, Illinois, which Warner called "Jonesville." For Warner, social class was pri-

marily a matter of agreement on the part of those living in a society: "By class is meant two or more orders of people who are believed to be, and are accordingly ranked by the members of the community, in socially superior and inferior positions" (Warner 1941:82).

Appropriate to this point of view, Warner sought to discover the social-class standing of community members by asking others in the community. Through studies in Jonesville and elsewhere, Warner developed an elaborate typology of American social classes. These are presented in Table 8-6.

The study of social classes in America has remained a lively interest among sociologists. Though they may differ in their pursuits of the topic, and though they have gone far beyond the descriptions of classes provided by Warner and others, there is an undeniable continuity in the point of view that looks to differences by social class for a key to the structure and process of society at large. Let's look now at some of the differences sociologists have discovered.

Politics

The classes in America have quite different agreements regarding politics and government. In large part, this reflects their manner of participation in these institutions. The middle and upper classes tend to be the most conservative politically and the most likely to be Republicans. Members of these classes are much more likely than members of the lower classes to be involved in politics and government, serving in official positions or working behind the scenes. Their motives range from feelings of dedication to the well-being of their country as a whole to feelings of dedication to their own well-being.

Members of the working class tend to be more liberal on economic issues and are more likely to be Democrats. They are more likely to feel that politics should be an instrument of social change because they are not doing as well with the status quo as are the upper and middle classes. Traditionally, many among the working class have been alienated from politics altogether. They have been less likely to believe that government will do anything in their interest, and they are less likely to vote on election day. In recent years, however, the working class has been changing radically in its attitudes toward politics. Labor unions and racial-ethnic movements have increased both the political participation and the political effectiveness of the working class in America.

In many ways, the political point of view of the very poor is an extension of that of the working class. The very poor tend to be the most alienated from politics in general and are the least likely to participate in the political process. They are more likely to regard government as belonging to someone else and as an instrument of their oppression. During the late 1960s, however, the poor became more active in politics and government, at least for a brief period, partly because of the organization of welfare recipients. When poor people *are* politically active, their point of view tends to be the most radical of all the social classes, calling for the most far-reaching kinds of social and political change.

The preceding comments have dealt mostly with social class and political *economics*. In general, the white-collar portion of America is economically conservative while the blue-collar portion is economically liberal. This is not to suggest, however, that economic orientation extends as neatly to other issues. When racial discrimination, abortion, and other issues of social change are being considered, a very different pattern appears. The white working class and the white poor have tended to be the most conservative with regard to legislation aimed at ending racial discrimination, for example. Similarly, the working and lower-middle classes provided much of the strongest support for the continuation and acceleration of the war in Vietnam.

Religion

As a general rule, white-collar religion in America is relatively reserved and ritualistic, while blue-collar religion is characterized by more emotional fervor. The lower classes have a greater tendency to reify religious beliefs, values, and norms than do the upper classes, and blue-collar religion is generally more fundamentalist and dogmatic. In large part, this difference reflects the educational component of social class. Education, as we will see in Chapter 14, is a natural enemy of dogmatic religious belief, especially through the impact of scientific discoveries on traditional religious beliefs.

Upper-class people are also more likely to be church members than are persons in the lower classes, and the churches they belong to are more likely to be the "right" ones: Unitarian, Episcopal, Congregational, and Presbyterian. Members of the lower classes are more likely to join the Baptists, Missouri Synod Lutherans, or one of the many fundamentalist sects. Higher church membership among the upper classes partly reflects their greater participation in all aspects of society.

Speech

The great majority of Americans speak English as their native language, yet members of different social classes speak it very differently. The fact that people *communicate* their class when they speak has been demonstrated in a number of studies. In one experiment, for instance, people from different social-class backgrounds were asked to tell familiar children's stories or to count from 1 to 20 into a tape recorder. Groups of judges—typically college students—were then asked to guess the social class of the speakers when the recordings were played. The judges' estimates consistently corresponded very closely to the speakers' actual social-class back-

Social status is reflected in all aspects of life. Just from what you can see of these houses and yards, what educated guesses can you make about other aspects of the occupants' lives?

grounds. Even when all the speakers were themselves college students, their speech betrayed their family backgrounds (Ellis 1967).

Class and Societywide Agreements

We have discussed just a few of the many differences that characterize the American social classes as subcultures. I want to bring up one additional point, however. The different sets of agreements that classes have are more than merely "different." While reading about speech differences, you may have found yourself thinking that the upper class speaks what is considered "good English" while the lower class speaks what is considered "bad English." The upper-class version of English is dominant.

Most simply put, the agreements of the upper classes tend to be the formal agreements of the society. Functionalists and conflict theorists agree on the existence of this tendency, but they disagree strongly as to its meaning. In Parsons's view of stratification as a "moral ranking," people receive high social status to the extent that their conditions and behaviors reflect the general values of the society. The conflict point of view is very different: the upper classes, through their greater power and greater control of the institutions of the society, *impose* their own class agreements on everyone else.

In elaborating on this latter view, Seymour Martin Lipset (1968:160) states, "To a very large degree, lower classes throughout history have acceded to the societal values that define them as being, in various aspects, inferior to those of higher status." We have already seen in the preceding two chapters how this takes place—through socialization into the agreements of the society. And socialization is all the more effective to the extent that people are brought to reify and internalize those agreements.

Consequences of Social Stratification

As you might imagine, sociologists have debated whether social stratification, as it operates in a society such as ours, is good or bad. The functionalist point of view tends to see stratification as generally beneficial for the functioning of society—as essential, in fact—and as inevitable anyway. The conflict point of view suggests that our current stratification system has more problems than value. Marxian conflict theorists, moreover, feel that it would be possible to develop a society without stratification, the "classless society" envisioned by Marx.

Sociologists will probably never agree on whether stratification is ultimately good or bad. Even so, it is possible to note some of the consequences of the American stratification system that most sociologists would agree ought to be corrected. It is obvious that people at the bottom of the stratification system often lack the necessities of life: food, shelter, and adequate clothing. Other consequences of stratification are not so obvious.

The poor have more mental and physical health problems than do other Americans, according to a variety of studies. The poor are more likely to be classified as mentally ill; they are more likely to be admitted for hospital care (rather than being cared for at home); and, when they are released from care, they are more likely to suffer relapses.

The relationship between mental illness and social class is a particularly complicated one, since scientists disagree about what constitutes mental illness. You'll see in Chapter 11 that it ultimately boils down to a violation of society's agreements. And as we've seen in this chapter,

---

Poverty and Nutrition in America

There are many consequences of social class in America. Studies by the U.S. Census Bureau found substantial differences in the daily consumption of nutrients among individuals in families below the official poverty level and those above it. Here are some of the differences they found.

Daily average (mean):	Below poverty level	Above poverty level
Calories	1,817	2,021
Protein (grams)	68.76	79.11
Calcium (mg)	782	882
Iron (mg)	10.70	12.13
Vitamin A (I.U.)	4,381	4,821
Vitamin C (mg)	72.05	88.53

Source: U.S. Bureau of Census, *Statistical Abstract of the United States: 1978* (99th edition) (Washington, D.C., 1978) p. 125.
Note: These data represent average daily nutrition intakes during 1971–1974.

---

it is the rich and powerful, far more than the poor, who determine what the agreements of society shall be.

The relationship between social class and *physical* health is perhaps less ambiguous. One aspect of the relationship is to be found in the hazards involved in working-class occupations. Mining, for example, couples the danger of sudden death with the less apparent hazard of lingering respiratory diseases. More recently, we have become aware of the asbestos poisoning that workers have been subjected to for decades. All this is not to say that middle- and upper-class occupations have no physical health dangers; indeed, there has been increasing concern lately regarding stress as a debilitating—even fatal—ailment. Nonetheless, the poor are exposed to more danger.

Some of the consequences of low social status are obvious; some are not. What are some of the hidden disadvantages to be faced by this young boy as he grows up in New Mexico?

The lower classes also have an experience of war different from that of other Americans. Leo Srole and his associates (1962) have shown that the lower classes were more likely to be rejected by the military draft. Other research suggests that those who do enter the military suffer a higher casualty rate (Hoult 1974), possibly because the officer corps is drawn primarily from the middle and upper classes.

Ironically, the lower classes—with less money to spend—often pay more for the things they buy than do the upper and middle classes (Caplovitz 1967). Even when they buy a particular item, such as a television set, the poor are likely to pay more for it than those who have more money to start with. For instance, when they lack the money to buy something outright, the poor are forced to buy on installments, and the interest rates are often outrageously high (and hidden). The poor are also often the tar-

gets of fraud because their predators assume that they will not know how to seek official redress or protection. The box "Poverty and Nutrition in America" (on page 251) reports still another consequence of poverty.

The Functions of Poverty

Thus far, I have been talking as though poverty were something that everyone would deplore and seek to alleviate. As a general principle, perhaps, people agree that it would be better if no one had to suffer the more tragic aspects of impoverishment. Why, then, hasn't poverty been eliminated in the world's wealthiest nation? One central reason, sociologist Herbert Gans (1971) has suggested, is that poverty serves some "positive functions for the society as a whole and for the nonpoor in particular." Here is a summary of the thirteen main functions Gans has uncovered:

1. As long as there are poor people, there will always be someone to do the "dirty work" of society.

2. Since the poor must accept low wages, the wealthy can "afford" luxuries —such as domestic servants—that might otherwise cost too much.

3. The presence of the poor provides work for those who take care of them—ranging from police and social workers to loan sharks.

4. Poor people provide a market for inferior goods—such as spoiled food—that would otherwise be thrown away.

5. The poor can be held up as bad examples to justify and strengthen the social norms of hard work, thrift, and the like.

6. The poor can provide a fantasy life for those who must abide by the norms of society—offering a vicarious thrill of uninhibited sex, drugs, and so forth.

7. The poorest classes provide a source of cultural elements that may be later adopted by the more affluent. For instance, the blues, spirituals, and rock-and-roll all originated among the black poor.

8. As mentioned earlier in discussing relative deprivation, having poor folks around makes everyone else feel more affluent.

9. As a specification of (8) above, the rise in status of most immigrant groups has been made possible in part by the arrival of new immigrants—below them in the stratification system.

10. The poor provide a justification for the charitable paternalism of the old aristocracy in a society, giving them a chance to demonstrate their superiority to those who must work for a living.

11. The poor take up the slack created in times of social change. They give up their homes to urban renewal, for example, making it possible for a city to get a face-lift.

12. They create a degree of political stability through their present support of the Democratic party in the United States.

13. In capitalist countries like our own, the poor also offer some protection against the threat of socialism. To the extent that opponents can argue that the benefits of socialism would accrue mostly to the poor—describing them as lazy, dishonest, and generally deviant—the mass of the society will not look favorably on socialism.

These, then, are some of the social functions presently played by poverty in America. In his analysis, Gans went on to point out many ways in which these functions could be handled through alternate means. Rather than report the solutions Gans found, however, let me suggest that you take a moment now and see what alternatives you can think of.

The Perpetuation of Inequality

One major problem of social stratification systems is that inequalities tend to be perpetuated across generations. The poor and the powerless of one generation tend to be the children of the poor and powerless of the previous generation and the parents of the poor and powerless of the next. Often, low social status is reified: the poor, for example, are often seen as inferior, weak, and lazy. Their children are assumed to be the same. When the economic facts of life—involving education, nutrition, and health—plus subcultural socialization are added to negative stereotypes, the perpetuation of low social status is likely.

Stratification systems operate like social institutions in that they tend to perpetuate the status quo. They support the survival of society. The advantage to society comes at the cost of individual disadvantage and dissatisfaction, however. There are even disadvantages to the society in the long run, since talented individuals may be effectively prevented from serving the society in positions of responsibility.

In spite of overall, general perpetuation of the status quo, most social stratification systems allow for a degree of movement. In most, it is possible for some individuals to rise or fall in social standing, a process called **social mobility.** I want to conclude this chapter by examining what sociologists have learned about mobility.

Social Mobility

"Social mobility" refers to individual and group movement from one social class or stratum to another. We're going to look at some aspects of social mobility, beginning with the category of *no* mobility, the category of caste.

Class versus Caste

Sociologists often distinguish between "class" and "caste" when they examine social stratification. A "caste" is a stratification category or group whose membership is determined on the basis of **ascribed statuses.** The traditional Indian **caste** system, which runs from the Brahmans at the top to the "untouchables" at the bottom, is a commonly mentioned example. A person is born into a specific niche in this rigidly stratified system, and there is virtually no hope of moving from that niche. People may move up or down within their caste, but there is no possibility of significant social mobility.

In America, various racial groups have suffered the disadvantages of at least a partial caste system. This was certainly the case for black slaves early in our history, and the castelike quality of being black survived the emancipation of the slaves, as Dollard (1937) pointed out in his classic discussion of the racial caste system in the United States.

Individual Mobility

Class systems—as opposed to caste systems—allow a degree of upward and downward movement, as we have already suggested in earlier sections of this chapter. Sociologists are interested in both upward and downward mobility, as measured either by a person's change of social status from the status of the family into which he or she was born (*inter*generational) or by changes of status during his or her own lifetime (*intra*generational).

Mobility can be measured in terms of any of the several dimensions of stratification: income, education, occupation, and so forth. The person who gets much more education than his or her parents, for example, would be considered upwardly mobile, while the child of a wealthy physician who becomes a laborer would be considered downwardly mobile.

Looked at from the point of view of class (as opposed to a continuum of socioeconomic status), social mobility is a matter of learning and accepting a new set of agreements as to what's true, good, and expected. When Professor Higgins tutored Eliza Doolittle (in George Bernard Shaw's *Pygmalion*), he was attempting to give her this kind of social mobility. Social mobility can often be a source of strain for the mobile person and for his or her family. Both the child "putting on airs" and the "black sheep" are a source of unhappiness for parents.

Societies differ in the degree to which they permit social mobility, even in the absence of a formal caste system; and sociologists often distinguish between relatively "open" and "closed" class systems. Most would regard the United States as having a relatively open class system, one that permits much social mobility, whereas the British system is more closed—although much mobility obviously occurs. In fact, the general American agreement on the value of achievement presupposes an open class system.

Still, the American class system is not as open as that general agreement would suggest. The children of poor parents do not stand the same chance of becoming wealthy as the children of rich parents stand of staying rich. The children—the sons at least—of physicians are still more likely than any other group to become physicians themselves.

Group Mobility

Often, an entire group of people within a society can be socially mobile. While, by definition, this means that the individual members of the group are mobile, there is often more at work than individual change. The emancipation of black slaves in America, for example, marked a degree of upward mobility for all blacks, even though it did not provide as much mobility as many had hoped. Women, to take another example, experienced a degree of group social mobility when, in 1920, they gained the right to vote.

Legislation is not a prerequisite for group mobility, as the history of America's many immigrant groups has shown. German, Irish, Italian, Jewish, Japanese, Chinese, and other immigrant groups began their lives in America at the bottom of the social structure. Most of these groups, as groups, have moved upward, often through national and ethnic self-help associations.

Perhaps the clearest example of this form of group mobility in America is the Chinese in Hawaii. Originally brought to Hawaii as day laborers for the large sugar and pineapple plantations, the Chinese steadily extricated themselves from the plantations to establish businesses and to invest in land. Today, the Chinese are the wealthiest racial group in Hawaii.

Upward economic mobility—for both groups and individuals—often involves what sociologists have called **deferred gratification.** Rather than spending the money available at a given time, some people save a part of it and invest it in the possibility of upward mobility. Such investments may be made in real property, in education, or in other things that hold the possibility of paying off in the long run. Studying for an exam instead of going to the movies is another example. Deferring gratification has been a common practice among the middle class in America, and it has also been the key element in the group mobility experienced by many immigrant groups. Thus were the Jews able to escape poverty in New York, while the Japanese and Chinese escaped the plantations of Hawaii where they began as indentured laborers.

There are many other sources and means of social mobility. Blau and Duncan (1967) have looked at some of the more generally important sources of mobility in America. Historically, they cite the westward expansion—with its vast opportunities for individual advancement—and the growth of technology, which freed people from manual jobs and created a demand for technicians and clerical workers. In more recent times, they find migration (sometimes called "geographical mobility") from farm to city an important source of social mobility.

Overall, Blau, Duncan, and others have stressed the importance of American values. In particular, our general agreements on achievement over ascription have been identified as important conditions for mobility. Social mobility is more difficult in societies sharing the agreement that who you *are* is more important than what you can *do*. Ultimately, the American social stratification system is a mixture of persistence and change. It is persistent enough to provide a measure of stability and structure for the society as a whole, yet it is open enough to provide opportunities for movement.

Summary

Social stratification is a matter of structured inequality in society. As we've seen, societies differentiate and rank people in a variety of ways, using different criteria for ranking and allowing differing degrees of flexibility for change.

Some degree of stratification has existed in all known societies throughout history. People have created degrees of inequality that go well beyond what Rousseau saw as "natural" dimensions of difference: age, health, strength, and wisdom. We create agreements as to the dimensions of difference that are to be considered in determining who is superior to whom.

The functionalist view sees stratification as an extension of the general value system of society. Talcott Parsons suggested that the ranking of people reflects the extent to which they approach those things most valued by the particular society. In societies where wealth is considered important, then, the wealthy will be accorded high status. In those where religious virtue is highly valued, that dimension will distinguish who ranks high and who low.

Kingsley Davis and Wilbert Moore, two other functionalists, suggest that stratification is inevitable in society, basing their view on three observations: (1) some positions seem more important for the survival of society than others, (2) some require rare skills and abilities, and (3) some positions entail duties that are unpleasant. Each of these situations, Davis and Moore suggest, will require that some social positions be rewarded more highly than others, thereby making stratification inevitable.

This point of view clashes directly with the conflict view of stratification. Most obviously, the suggestion that stratification is inevitable contradicts the Marxist belief in the eventual evolution of a "classless society." There is an even more fundamental difference between the functionalists and conflict theorists, however.

In the functionalist view of stratification, the ranking of individuals is along a continuum, ranging from low to high, with no significant breaks or groupings involved in it. From the conflict point of view, however, stratification is a matter of discrete social *classes*—categories of people sharing the same economic standing, similar life experiences, and common elements of lifestyle. From this point of view, stratification is a matter of competition between the social classes, each with its particular class interest. This view derives most importantly from the work of Karl Marx, though others such as Ralf Dahrendorf have made important contributions to our understanding of this aspect of social stratification.

An important aspect of the study of social stratification concerns the dimensions along which people are evaluated and ranked. In the traditional Marxist view, economics was the chief dimension, particularly the question of where people were located in terms of industrial production—as workers, as owners, and so on. In modern conflict theory, power has become as important as economic matters. Other theorists have pointed to other dimensions.

For Max Weber, stratification focused on three dimensions: the economic, the social, and the political. Like Marx, Weber used the term "class" in reference to economic stratification. Weber went beyond that, however, to separate politics from economics, referring to politics in terms of party. Finally, Weber spoke also of status in the sense of honor, prestige, and deference. Although Weber recognized that the three aspects of stratification often went hand in hand, he found it useful to distinguish among them analytically.

Other dimensions of stratification are family and kinship, age, sex, race, possessions, occupation, education, and religion, to name a few. In contemporary American society, it is generally felt that occupation, education, and money are the primary dimensions of social stratification, and the term "socioeconomic status" is used in reference to people's overall ranking on those dimensions.

For the most part, the main dimensions of stratification are correlated with each other. That is, those with prestigious occupations earn the most money and are highly educated. Those with little education, working in manual trades, earn little money. At the same time, the correlation is not perfect and some people experience what is called "status inconsistency." That is, they rank high on one dimension (say, education) and relatively low on others (say, money). An example would be the educated person who works in a poorly paying job—perhaps as a priest or minister.

When stratification is seen in terms of discrete social classes rather than as steps on a continuous social ladder, it makes sense to look for those things that members of a particular social class share in common. It makes sense to look at social classes as subcultures, characterized by particular political, religious, and other orientations. A number of social scientists have examined the nature of the social classes making up American society. W. Lloyd Warner, for example, focused on the small towns of America during the 1930s and 1940s, describing in great detail what characterized the lower class, the upper lower class, the lower middle class, and so forth.

Social stratification has real consequences for the people involved. As we saw, those ranked low suffer more problems of physical and mental illness; they are more likely to be wounded and killed in war; and they must, ironically, pay more money for poorer-quality goods. There are countless other differences between the classes.

We concluded the discussion of stratification with some observations about the functions that inequality serves for the society as a whole. For example, the presence of poor people ensures that there will always be someone to do the "dirty" work. It is important to realize that the examination of such functions of poverty in no way justifies its persistence. Indeed, if we do *not* pay attention to the functions poverty serves, we can never hope to overcome its injustices.

The latter part of the chapter was addressed to social mobility. We saw that societies vary in the degree to which people can move from one social standing to another. In a caste system, for example, people are inextricably locked into place from birth. Class systems, in contrast, allow for mobility, though some societies are more open than others. Deferred gratification is one method for achieving mobility—forgoing comforts now in favor of investing in greater achievements tomorrow. Thus, instead of spending your paycheck on a riotous night on the town, you might invest your pay in mutual funds. Or instead of going to the movies, you could stay home and study for your exam.

Social mobility occurs both for individuals—you may rise from a humble newspaper carrier to president of a major television network—and across generations within an ethnic or racial group. Many of the immigrant groups that came to the New World provide illustration of this process.

Important Terms

social stratification

strata

social class

socioeconomic status (SES)

ascribed status

achieved status

status inconsistency

social mobility

caste

deferred gratification

Suggested Readings

Baltzell, E. Digby
1958   *Philadelphia Gentlemen*. New York: Free Press.
Most sociological analyses of particular social classes have focused on those at the bottom of the heap, producing occasional charges of paternalism. Here is a rare examination of the other end of the stratification ladder: the rich and powerful. Baltzell examines the residential, religious, educational, occupational, family, and other aspects of upper-class status.

Bendix, Reinhard, and Seymour Martin Lipset, Eds.
1966   *Class, Status, and Power*. New York: Free Press.
This massive collection of articles and book excerpts covers virtually all aspects of the sociological inquiry into stratification. Included is Weber's differentiation of three aspects of stratification, the classic Davis-Moore statement of the functionalist view of stratification, and many other historical and modern analyses.

Coleman, Richard P., and Lee Rainwater
1978   *Social Standing in America*. New York: Basic Books.
Reviews findings of samples on social class in America.

Dahrendorf, Ralf
1959   *Class and Class Conflict in Industrial Society*. Stanford, Calif.: Stanford University Press.
Here's Dahrendorf's modern reformulation of Marx's view of the class struggle. This is an important work in the literature of conflict theory, providing a useful balance to the structural-functional view of stratification exemplified by the Davis-Moore article mentioned in the Bendix book, above. Dahrendorf's attempt to develop a formal theory of stratification and power is also instructive from the standpoint of sociological theory.

Gans, Herbert
1973   *More Equality*. New York: Pantheon.
Discusses causes of inequality in the United States, why it is perpetuated, and whether change is likely.

Hauser, Robert M., and David L. Featherman
1977   *The Process of Stratification: Trends and Analyses*. New York: Academic Press.
This is essentially a "state of the art" examination of the mathematical analysis of social stratification and mobility, especially the knotty problem of occupation. The mathematics goes far beyond an introductory level, yet it offers an excellent picture of the ways in which sociological topics can be pursued quantitatively. Both historical and cross-cultural data are presented.

Jencks, Christopher, *et al.*
1979   *Who Gets Ahead?: The Determinants of Economic Success in America*. New York: Basic Books.
Analyzes the role of family background, academic ability, personality and education in economic success of men in America.

Kreisberg, Louis
1979   *Social Inequality*. Englewood Cliffs, NJ: Prentice-Hall.
Discusses research on inequality and effects of stratification on individuals and group interactions in U.S. and other societies.

Marx, Karl, and Friedrich Engels
[1848]   *The Communist Manifesto*. New York: Appleton-
1955   Century-Crofts.
This is one of the most influential books of all time. It is a short, simple, and highly polemical tract that outlines Marx's view of history as a matter of class struggle in the face of economic oppression.

Matras, Judah
1975   *Social Inequality, Stratification, and Mobility*. Englewood Cliffs, NJ: Prentice-Hall.
Solid text which discusses the field of stratification, theories and research in the field.

Silk, Leonard, and Mark Silk
1980   *The American Establishment*. New York: Basic Books.
Here's a very readable analysis of America's "shakers and movers." The authors examine where the "establishment" attends college, worships, and works.

Treiman, Donald J.
1977   *Occupational Prestige in Comparative Perspective*. New York: Academic Press.
Compares studies of occupational prestige in different countries and attempts to interpret findings.

Tumin, Melvin, Ed.
1970   *Readings on Social Stratification*. Englewood Cliffs, N.J.: Prentice-Hall.
Here's an excellent collection of important writings on social stratification, compiled by one of the leading scholars in the field. Topics range from concepts and theories of stratification to empirical research methods and findings.

For the most part, the study of social stratification focuses on the inequalities among individuals, families, and subgroups within a society. At the same time, similar structures can be found among the societies that make up humankind on the planet. There are rich countries and poor ones, and many of the dynamics we observe within a given society can be seen among societies as well. I want to conclude this chapter with some observations on international stratification.

I'm sure you are already aware that some countries are wealthier than others, but you may not be aware of how great the differences are. Let's look at a few illustrations.

One measure of a nation's wealth is to be found in its *gross national product* (GNP)—the total value of the goods and services produced in the country during the year. Since this figure obviously reflects a country's population size, sociologists often examine the GNP per capita. In 1981, for example, the GNP per capita in the United States was $10,820. Canada's GNP per capita was similar: $9,650. The average GNP per capita for the entire world, however, was much lower: $2,340. Obviously, some nations must have still lower GNPs per capita. India's figure was $190, for example. In Bhutan, the GNP per capita was a mere $80 (Population Reference Bureau 1981).

Wealth and poverty are not randomly distributed around the world. Table 8–7 presents the GNP per capita of the several major regions of the world. Africa, Asia, and Latin America stand out as the most impoverished regions of the world.

While GNP per capita is a useful indicator of the quality of life in different countries, it can be misleading. Three oil-rich Middle Eastern countries have higher GNPs per capita than does the United States: Kuwait ($17,270), Qatar ($16,590), and the United Arab Emirates

Table 8–7

Per Capita GNP of the World's Regions, 1981

Region	GNP per capita
World	$2,340
Africa	620
Asia	800
North America	10,710
Latin America	1,580
Europe	6,820
U.S.S.R.	4,110
Oceania	7,080

Source: Population Reference Bureau, "1981 World Population Data Sheet" (Washington, D. C.: Population Reference Bureau).

Note: You should realize that while these figures and the others presented in this essay are the best, most recent estimates available, data collection quality varies widely around the world.

($15,590). In these latter countries, however, the vast oil wealth is concentrated in the hands of relatively few families, and the mass of the population in those countries is deeply impoverished. This can be seen when we consider other indicators of a nation's quality of life.

One of the key statistics used in determining the well-being of nations is the *infant mortality rate* (IMR): the number of babies who die during their first year of life, out of every thousand babies born. As a rough rule of thumb, IMRs of less than 50 represent a high quality of life; those above 50 indicate severe problems of malnutrition and poverty and a generally low quality of life. In 1981, the United States' IMR was 13, Canada's was 12. Some nations had even lower IMRs: Sweden's was the lowest in the world at 7 infant deaths per 1,000 births.

Other countries were not so fortunate. In the West African country of Guinea, for example, the 1981 IMR was 220: more than one in five babies died during their first year. The three richest nations—measured in per capita GNP—had relatively high IMRs, reflecting the maldistribution of wealth mentioned earlier: Kuwait (39), Qatar (138), and the United Arab Emirates (65). On the whole, however, the two measures generally paint the same picture of relative well-being on the planet, as a comparison between Tables 8–7 and 8–8 indicates.

A similar story is told by life expectancy at birth. In North America, a child born in 1981 could expect to live—on average—to age 74; in Europe, to 72. The average Asian baby could expect to live 60 years, the average African 49 years. In Ethiopia, with a per capita GNP of $130 and an IMR of 178, the average baby born in 1981 could expect to die at 39.

Figures such as these point to an enormous difference in the well-being of the world's rich and poor nations. Moreover, as I've indicated earlier, international wealth and poverty follow a fairly consistent geographical pattern. As the map in Figure 8-3 shows, the relatively wealthy

nations are located to the north, the poor ones to the south.

Whereas the years following World War II produced a division between the East (socialist countries) and the West (capitalist countries), today an equally potent division exists between the industrialized, economically developed North and the impoverished South. Sometimes this latter division is labeled the *developed countries* (DC) and *less developed countries* (LDC). In still another nomenclature, the capitalist countries of the West are referred to as the *First World*, the socialist countries of the East are the *Second World*, and the impoverished LDCs are referred to as the *Third World*. Indeed, the poorest of the poor are sometimes called the *Fourth World*.

Whatever terms we use, there is no denying the radical discrepancies in the relative well-being of the planet's nations. In recent years, this discrepancy has become the subject of a powerful international discussion: called the *North-South debate*. In 1974, more than 120 of the world's poorest countries, working through the United Nations, called for the establishment of a *New International Economic Order* (NIEO), which would restructure the economic relationships which link the world's nations. The proposition was discussed inconclusively by the leaders of many nations in Cancun, Mexico, in 1981.

David Morawetz (1977) describes the origins of NIEO as follows:

The "New International Economic Order" is a set of proposals created by the world's developing countries which call for basic structural changes in the global economy. The concept of the NIEO emerged in 1974 at the Sixth Special Session of the United Nations, when 77 third world nations (known as the "Group of 77") joined together to express their opposition to the workings of the

Table 8–8

Infant Mortality of the World's Regions, 1981

Region	IMR
World	97
Africa	142
Asia	102
North America	13
Latin America	75
Europe	17
U.S.S.R.	36
Oceania	51

Source: Population Reference Bureau, "1981 World Population Data Sheet" (Washington, D. C.: Population Reference Bureau).

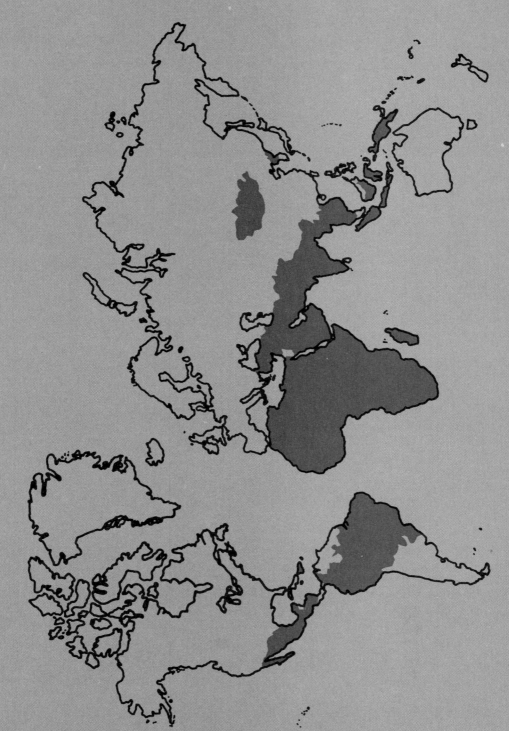

Figure 8–3 Nations for whom hunger is a major problem.

current international economic system as unfair to their interests.

By virtually any economic indicator, they argue, the gap in wealth between rich and poor nations is growing wider. The poor are being left behind. According to representatives of these poor countries, until basic structural change is made in the world's economy, the eradication of hunger and poverty will be impossible on an international scale. This is because the current system is so designed that the enormous wealth created in the world flows predominantly to the already rich nations. Foreign aid alone will not be enough, they argue—basic structural alterations are required.

Most simply put, the current world economic system operates as follows. The impoverished nations of the South produce the raw materials needed by industry and sell them—at a low price—to the industrialized nations of the North. The industrial products subsequently produced add to the wealth of the North. In a recent variation, the relatively cheap labor available in the South has been used for manufacturing, but the products still belong to companies of the North. In still another variation, countries of the South that are unable to feed their own people devote their prime agricultural lands to the growing of export crops such as coffee, sugar, and bananas for sale in the North. The upshot of this system is that the poor countries stay poor and the rich countries get richer and richer.

Julius Nyerere (1979), the president of Tanzania, described the NIEO as

a kind of "trade union of the poor." Seventy percent of the world's population—the Third World—commands together no more than 12 percent of the gross world product. Eighty percent of the world's trade and investment, 93 percent of its industry, and almost 100 percent of its research is controlled by the industrial rich.

A part of the South's demand for redress reflects a history of planetary colonialism. Many of the impoverished countries of the South were, in recent times, exploited colonies of the North. Many of India's current troubles are traced back to its decades as a British colony. Most African nations were previously European colonies. In precolonial times, many were wealthy, powerful nations in their own right. Egypt, after all, was once the most powerful civilization on earth. Today, Egypt has a per capita GNP of $460 and an infant mortality rate of 90; the average Egyptian born in 1981 could expect to live only 55 years.

While it is tempting to regard the poverty of other nations as "over there," it is increasingly being recognized as a problem for rich and poor alike. If nothing else, the poverty of the Third World represents a threat to world peace. Poor nations sometimes make war on their neighbors—the long-standing war between Ethiopia and Somalia over the Ogaden region is an example. Or, when poor nations threaten to withhold vital raw materials from the wealthy nations—as in the actions of the OPEC nations—the danger rises that the rich may take those resources by force. All of this, moreover, further complicates the East-West conflict, with the capitalist and socialist superpowers competing for resources and allies. Ultimately, the poverty of the Third World serves to threaten us all.

What can be done? Foreign aid is one mechanism often suggested. Following World War II, the American Marshall Plan was devised for the purpose of restoring Europe from the ravages of war. To accomplish that, the United States contributed 2.7 percent of its GNP to foreign assistance. In part, shipments of food stemmed the immediate threat of starvation. More important in the long run, the aid allowed European nations to rebuild factories, highways, schools, and other elements of their national infrastructures. As a result, they were able to become self-sufficient once more.

Since the Marshall Plan, foreign aid has become a well-established practice among nations. *Bilateral* aid is a contribution from one nation to another, and *multilateral* aid refers to contributions made to an international body—such as the World Bank or International Monetary Fund—for disbursement to poor nations. Although foreign aid is now firmly established on the international scene, levels of contribution are a faint shadow of the Marshall Plan.

In 1970, the United Nations recommended that the wealthy nations contribute 0.7 percent of their GNPs to foreign assistance. Very few nations have come close to that, however. In 1980, the bloc of Western industrialized nations contributed 0.37 percent of their GNPs; the United States was ranked 13th in this respect, contributing 0.27 percent. By contrast, the OPEC nations contributed 1.45 percent—mostly in aid to other Arab states.

Because the United States has the highest GNP in the world, our seemingly meager contribution nonetheless represented the largest *amount* of foreign aid given in 1980: $7.1 billion. This figure can be misleading, however. Most United States foreign assistance programs stipulate that much of the money be spent on American goods and services—about seventy percent of our foreign aid dollars are spent here in the United States. Moreover, most aid is in the form of low-interest loans, not gifts, and the repayment of those loans has become a major drain on many poor countries' already meager budgets.

The impact of foreign aid within recipient countries has been a hotly debated topic. Typically, bilateral aid is related to military considerations: it is given to nations whose strategic friendship is important to the giver. American aid to Israel is a good example. In some cases, this concern with national security has led the United States to pour aid into repressive military dictatorships, and critics ask how much this aid benefits the truly impoverished citizens. Often, the aid never reaches those in need but simply makes wealthy elites wealthier.

My purpose in pointing out these problems is not to argue against foreign assistance but merely to indicate how complicated the situation is. Clearly money is not enough. Also needed is a sociological understanding of international relations and of stratification systems within societies.

While you are certain to hear debates over inequality in the United States in the years to come, those debates are likely to be overshadowed by the gross inequalities that separate rich and poor nations.

PRACTICING SOCIOLOGY

In Chapter 7, we looked at voluntary associations. When a 1981 Roper Poll asked people, "Do you regularly do any type of volunteer work?" 25 percent said they did. The data presented below report the percentages doing volunteer work in various educational, income, and occupational subgroups.

	Percent who do volunteer work regularly
Education:	
Not high school graduates	12
High school graduates	21
Some college	30
College graduates	44
Family income:	
Less than $10,000	14
$10,000–$19,999	24
$20,000–$29,999	28
$30,000 and over	39
Occupation:	
Business and professional	37
White collar	27
Manual	20

Source: "Who Volunteers and How Much?" *Public Opinion,* February/March 1982, p. 22.

Write a paragraph in which you discuss the relationship between socioeconomic status and volunteer work. Suggest some possible reasons for that relationship.

9

Racial and Ethnic Relations

In Chapter 8, we looked at the structuring of inequality within society. This chapter and the following one pursue this theme of inequality by looking at the structuring of inequality in major social categories. In this chapter, we'll look at racial and ethnic inequality; in Chapter 10, we'll focus on age and sex.

Race is a much abused term. In popular usage, it often conjures up the image of "blood" and unchangeable "instincts." Very often it is the basis for ranking groups of people in terms of superiority and inferiority, as the Nazis did in defining the Aryan "super race" as superior to the Jews; and the essay that concluded Chapter 5 reported the long history of attempts to relate race and intelligence. Biologists and physical anthropologists offer no support for these popular notions.

> Anthropologists and geneticists speak of race to refer to a population sharing characteristics known to be inherited genetically. These specialists insist that the major biological types into which mankind is often divided—caucasoid, mongoloid, and negroid—are only convenient statistical categories and that no clear lines of demarcation can be drawn. Ironically, the actual, measurable hereditary differences among human beings are often of little consequence in the affairs of men. (Shibutani and Kwan 1965:39)

The agreements people share about "race," of course, are of far greater consequence. If people with quite different genetic makeups agree that they are of the same race or if people of similar genetic makeups agree that they are of different races, then "race" matters greatly. "Race," ironically, is more important in the sociological point of view than in the biological point of view.

This chapter refers to racial and "ethnic" relations, the latter referring to categorizations by national origin, religion, or a combination of the two. In popular usage, race and ethnicity are often confused, with references to the "Jewish race," the "French race," and so forth. In this chapter, we'll see how both of these categorization schemes are used in structuring relations among people.

In the course of the discussion, we'll refer to "minority groups," and you should understand how sociologists use that term. A **minority group** is not necessarily numerically small. Indeed, a minority group sometimes can be an overwhelming majority of the members of a society. Within the sociological point of view, the term "minority" is used to refer to those people who have a disproportionately small share of the power and "things" that are distributed in the society. They are a group pushed generally to the bottom of a society's stratification system.

Nearly 90 percent of the population of the Republic of South Africa, for example, are nonwhite; they are predominantly members of the black native Bantu tribes. The primary political power and wealth of the country, however, are concentrated in the hands of the numerically small white minority. The blacks and other nonwhites are prevented from participation in most sectors of the society and are relegated to third- or fourth-class citizenship, and thus are regarded as a "minority" from the sociological point of view.

The sociological notion of "minorities" in a society, then, is closely related to the concept of stratification that we discussed in the last chapter. People constitute a minority by virtue of social agreement, nothing more, although you need to remember that one group often imposes its agreements on another. Such agreements govern the behavior of majority and minority groups alike. In this chapter, we will see how members of minorities participate in the agreements that make them a minority, and we'll also see some of the ways in which they work to change such agreements. People tend to believe that the agreements that create minority groups represent an ultimate reality in the world. One of the first steps in changing those agreements is to draw attention to the fact that *agreements are only agreements*.

The chapter begins with a general discussion of **prejudice** and **discrimination**. In this, we'll look at the structure of the agreements that create minorities and see how they operate. We'll see the part that **stereotyping** plays in the definition of minorities and in the maintenance of agreements about who belongs in a minority group.

Much of the chapter is given to a look at the various racial and ethnic groups that make up the United States. In particular, we'll be concerned with the nature of minority group status—how it's defined and what difference it makes.

The chapter concludes with an examination of how minority-group members respond to the agreements that define them as minorities. Some, as we will see, simply accept the agreements passively. Others resist the agreements, and some change the agreements.

Prejudice

Strictly defined, "prejudice" is prejudgment. If you believe that tomorrow will be a rotten day, you have a prejudice. You have judged what kind of day tomorrow will be before it happens. In this sense, prejudices are nothing more than expectations you have about something; and they can be positive, negative, or neutral.

Some prejudices are a functional part of our lives. You can't take a bus without an expectation that it will arrive more or less as scheduled. When you walk across a busy intersection, you expect that cars will stop for the red light.

Sociologists are interested in all kinds of prejudices, but they are particularly interested in those that relate to social interactions. "Social interactions" refer to our expectations about other people—what they are like and how they will behave. Those expectations affect how *we* behave.

If you expect your instructor to give a very difficult examination, you are likely to study harder than if you expect an easy one. In writing this book, I have had countless expectations—prejudices—about you: your abilities, your interests, and what you know and don't know about sociology. Some of my prejudices were based on experiences with students and sociology instructors, some were based on the agreements as to what sociology is, and many were based on both.

Stereotyping and Prejudice

The term "prejudice," however, is normally used with a more limited meaning than the preceding comments suggest. Usually it refers to shared negative beliefs and feelings about all or most of the members of a particular group, especially a minority group. In this sense "prejudice" is an expectation you share about a *group* of people that forms the basis for your expectations about *individual* members of that group. Typically, these expectations are negative.

Sociologists use the term "stereotype" to refer to the pictures people share about a group, pictures that are the basis for prejudices. Stereotypes are reified agreements—beliefs—about the characteristics of a group. Stereotypes may or may not be based on actual experiences or observations. They are learned, often during early socialization.

In 1971, a sociological study of stereotyping was conducted among hundreds of second- and third-grade schoolchildren. Each child was asked to describe the "average American" using a five-point scale running between pairs of opposite adjectives. For example, they were asked to describe the "average American" as "very intelligent," "somewhat intelligent," "neither intelligent nor unintelligent," "somewhat unintelligent," or "very unintelligent." Twenty pairs of adjectives were used (Davis 1971).

Next, children were asked to describe the "average black American," using the same technique and the same sets of adjectives. On each of the twenty sets of adjectives, blacks were described in less favorable terms than the

"average American." Blacks were portrayed as less intelligent, less hardworking, less honest, and so forth.

What makes this study especially interesting is that it was conducted in Hawaii, where blacks constitute less than 1 percent of the population. A large proportion of blacks in Hawaii, moreover, are military personnel, and there were no black children in the classes sampled in the study. It seemed unlikely that the children could have had more than the most casual contacts with blacks. Although they might have picked up some stereotypes of blacks from old movies on television, that can't explain children saying that blacks "smelled bad" compared with the "average American."

Many minority group stereotypes are clearly a product of agreement rather than personal experience. Studies of anti-Semitism (anti-Jewish prejudice) consistently show higher levels of anti-Semitism in areas such as the South and Midwest that have fewer Jews than do other areas of the country. Anti-Semitism is also more prevalent in rural areas than in urban areas, although American Jews are heavily concentrated in cities.

Negative minority-group prejudices are dysfunctional and unjust in many ways. We should note two ways here. First, even when there is a kernel of truth in a stereotype, it is inappropriate and unjust to apply the stereotype of a group to all individual members of that group. During the mid-1960s, a Wayne, New Jersey, school-board election became the focus of a national controversy when an incumbent member of the board urged the community to vote against two Jewish candidates saying, "They're liberal like all Jews, and they'll spend all our money." Ironically, the man who said this professed to like the two Jewish candidates personally, and sociologists who interviewed him later concluded that he really did. He was puzzled and hurt to find himself labeled a bigot (Stark and Steinberg 1967). He believed—correctly—that American Jews *as a group* had a more liberal voting record than Protestants or Cath-

olics, so he felt justified in applying that characteristic to *all* Jews.

Second, minority-group stereotypes constitute a point of view through which people see
the world—and what they "see" is conditioned
by their point of view. If you believe that all
Italians are emotional and irrational, you are
likely to "see" only emotional and irrational
Italians. If you believe that all Germans are rude,
you will meet only rude Germans.

Reasons for Prejudice

People come to share negative agreements about
minority groups for many reasons. **Scapegoating**—identifying some other individual, group,
or category to take the blame for problems—is
one. Troubled by problems—personal, societal, or other—people search for causes. A man
who loses his job at a time of high unemployment may seek a "culprit" at work. Blacks,
women, or Chicanos may be seen as cutting
into the job market by working cheaply. The
Nazis blamed Germany's post-World War I economic woes on the Jews; American racists
blamed the black civil rights movement on
Communists. People unhappy about the general liberalization of sexual attitudes and practices in America may blame the loss of their jobs
on Communists, hippies, pornographers, or
homosexuals.

Competition is another common reason for
prejudice. When people feel they may suffer
some loss because of the rights of a minority
group, they often become prejudiced against
that group, seeking to limit the group's rights
and eliminate the competition. Competition can
center on jobs, houses, education, mates, or
any other scarce commodity. Competition from
immigrant groups, blacks, and women has
fueled prejudices against them.

Projection often lies at the heart of prejudice.
We may "see" in others those things we fear in
ourselves. Thus, people unsure about their own
intelligence willingly agree that the members

of some minority groups are less intelligent in
order to bolster their own standing. People
uncertain about their own honesty "see" dis-
honesty in others.

More generally, minority groups can represent a threat to the agreements we share because
they often share different sets of agreements
among themselves. Hindus are a threat to
Christians, homosexuals are a threat to heterosexuals, intellectuals are a threat to the uneducated. And when a minority group reifies *its*
agreements about what is true, the threat we
perceive is all the more pressing. The homosexual who sadly confesses to being "sick" is
less a threat to heterosexuals than one who
openly declares that homosexuality is right.

You may recognize the similarity of these
comments to the Chapter 4 discussion of *ethnocentrism* and the Chapter 6 discussion of *in-
groups* and *out-groups.* There is a common human
tendency to distrust, fear, and dislike people
unlike ourselves. This tendency varies from
weak to strong in different people; but, where
it is strong, it provides a fertile ground for prejudice.

In contrast to the factors supporting prejudice, education is the strongest factor working
against it. Research in prejudice has consistently shown that better-educated people are
less prejudiced against minority groups than
are less-educated people. Education generally
exposes agreements as only agreements and
works against their reification. In large part,
this happens because people are exposed to the
variety of agreements that others have created
in different times and places. They are also
exposed to information that contradicts negative stereotypes.

Discrimination

Like prejudice, the term "discrimination" has
two meanings. In one sense, all social behavior
is based on discrimination. We "discriminate"—that is, we distinguish—among the dif-

ferent statuses we interact with, and we form our behavior on that basis. The lieutenant discriminates between privates and generals in choosing an "appropriate" behavior. Ministers discriminate between bishops and parishioners in choosing "appropriate" behavior. The "appropriateness" of behavior is defined by the roles governing the interaction that takes place among occupants of different statuses.

People typically use the term "discrimination" in a more restricted sense, however. They use it to refer to the withholding of scarce, socially valued commodities—including respect, dignity, and opportunity to achieve—from the members of a minority group. This is the sense in which we will use the term in this chapter.

The Relationship between Discrimination and Prejudice

While prejudice and discrimination are obviously related to one another, the relationship is not as simple as you might imagine. Robert K. Merton (1976) argues that a person's conduct and beliefs can vary independently of each other. Merton classifies people in one of four different types, depending on the mix of their attitudes and conduct toward ethnic groups. These types he calls (1) the unprejudiced nondiscriminator, (2) the unprejudiced discriminator, (3) the prejudiced nondiscriminator, and (4) the prejudiced discriminator.

Unprejudiced nondiscriminators Merton labels "all-weather liberals" because they believe in the American creed of equal rights and practice it, regardless of circumstances. This group, Merton suggests, is capable of being at the forefront of civil rights battles, although they can suffer from talking only to themselves and believing that, since they personally measure up to the American creed, they need do nothing to end prejudice and discrimination.

The unprejudiced discriminators Merton labels "fair-weather liberals." This is the type

that, although not particularly prejudiced themselves, nevertheless discriminate against minorities because they profit from it or are scared to do otherwise. They are the "fair-weather liberals" because they treat different groups equally only when they lose nothing thereby. They believe in the American creed in principle; but, when it comes to practicing it, they discriminate because they're afraid that, for instance, white workers might be upset if a black were promoted on a construction crew.

Prejudiced nondiscriminators, or "fair-weather illiberals," are the mirror image of unprejudiced discriminators. This group is prejudiced; but, because conditions do not support it, they do not discriminate. They might rent to a black, Jewish, or Chinese person for financial reasons, because they are afraid of being prosecuted for a civil rights violation, or because they are afraid their friends might think they are bigots.

Finally, come the prejudiced discriminators, or "all-weather illiberals," who are both prejudiced and discriminatory, regardless of the circumstances. People of this type persist in believing, for instance, that blacks are inferior to whites and act accordingly, making no bones about what they are doing or why.

Distinguishing among these types, Merton believes, is important for assessing the likely impact of various policies aimed at eliminating prejudice and discrimination. For example, a policy of simply exhorting nonprejudiced discriminators to believe in the American creed wouldn't be successful because the problem for this type is not that they don't believe in the principle of equal rights but that conditions are not conducive enough to their practicing them. All-weather liberals should try to draw this group into their fold, Merton suggests, in order to provide a more supportive environment for nondiscriminatory practices; and, at the same time, they should work to change the environment so that there are fewer rewards for discrimination.

Forms of Discrimination

Discrimination may be based on official, legal agreements, or it may be based on unoffical agreements, such as tradition. Discrimination against American blacks in connection with voting illustrates these two types. Before 1870, when the Fifteenth Amendment to the U.S. Constitution was passed, blacks were prohibited by law from voting. Indeed, in the original Constitution, slaves and Indians each counted only three-fifths of a person in computing the populations of states for the purpose of determining the number of representatives to be elected to Congress. During the century following the passage of the Fifteenth Amendment, southern blacks were effectively prevented from voting through a variety of unofficial means. Discrimination against blacks' voting persisted even though the law had changed.

Whether sanctioned officially or unofficially, discrimination against minorities has taken many forms throughout history. Let's look at the most important of these.

In **annihilation,** the most severe form of discrimination, the majority tries to murder all the members of a minority group. The Nazi attempt to exterminate Jews, Gypsies, homosexuals, and "mental defectives" is a clear example of this pattern. Equally clear is the early American attempt to eradicate the Native American population of the country, based on an agreement that "the only good Indian is a dead Indian."

Expulsion is a pattern of discrimination in which the majority denies minority-group members their citizenship, their membership in the society. This pattern was followed when the United States government imprisoned Japanese Americans in detention camps during World War II. Sometimes, minority-group members have been forced to leave their country, as were millions of Germans living in eastern Europe at the end of World War II. Similarly, millions of Moslems were forced to leave India following the 1947 partitioning of Pakistan and India, and millions of Hindus were forced to leave what had become Pakistan.

Segregation is a pattern of discrimination in which minority-group members are separated from the rest of society, often geographically. The segregation of blacks in America is probably the most familiar example to you. Sociologists often refer to segregation as an institution in America because it is a relatively integrated and persistent set of beliefs, values, and norms separating blacks from whites in residences, schools, churches, and public services. Although officially outlawed, to some extent segregation still exists.

Many other groups have been segregated in America—some involuntarily, others by choice. Approximately three-fourths of the nation's Native American population live on or near federal reservations. Many large American cities have a Chinatown. Towns and cities of the American Southwest have Chicano barrios. Miami has Cuban sections. Other cities have Irish, German, Polish, Italian, Portuguese, and Puerto Rican neighborhoods. Some minority-group members willingly accept this segregation, wanting to live, learn, worship, and relax with others who share their subculture. Those who do not accept segregation willingly often work to change that agreement.

South Africa has an extreme case of segregation called apartheid. Besides strictly segregated living areas, the white majority, under former Prime Minister Hendrik Verwoerd, established and enforced an extensive system of political, social, and economic segregation as well. This system has begun falling apart in recent years, much to the consternation of some whites.

The tenuousness of continued apartheid in South Africa has produced somewhat bizarre proposals for solutions. In 1980, Dr. Chris Jooste, director of the South African Bureau for Racial Affairs, proposed that whites in South Africa create and withdraw into a separate ministate. Humphrey Tyler (1980) reports on Jooste's plan:

> He believes idealistic whites could be attracted to the project to build Orania from the ground up "with their own hands" instead of relying on blacks

to do heavy manual work, which is the present fashion.

"Everything will be done by whites," Dr. Jooste says enthusiastically. "The land will be bought privately with white money. White laborers will dig the trenches and make the roads and build the houses. And finally white servants will bring richer whites their coffee in bed."

Interestingly, Jooste insisted that his plan was not racist, since blacks would be allowed to visit for sporting and cultural events. His comments point to the ambiguity common in the language of prejudice and discrimination.

The denial of scarce goods is another common form of discrimination. One example of this pattern is the generally lower pay blacks receive even when they are doing the same job as whites. The denial of membership in exclusive social clubs is another example of the same pattern.

One of the most frustrating patterns of discrimination in America today is the denial of opportunity, and it is related to other forms of discrimination. Members of minority groups are often denied access to the jobs that would allow them to earn scarce goods and to fulfill their individual potentials. They may also be denied access to good education, critical to individual and group mobility.

Discrimination against minorities in America is a complex and often interrelated set of patterns. Because of the neighborhood-school system, segregated housing results in segregated education, which, in turn, results in minority-group members being denied the better-paying jobs that would allow them to move into better neighborhoods and gain better education for their children. The wheel of discrimination goes 'round and 'round.

Racism is a term used to refer to the interrelated combination of stereotypes, prejudice, and discrimination directed against a socially-defined racial group. Racism is fairly easily recognized in individuals, who express their bigotry in both words and deeds. More difficult to recognize, understand, and correct is the phenomenon of **institutional racism,** which is a function of the established structure of agreements of the society.

Institutional racism is seen in results, not intent. That black Americans suffer higher infant mortality, higher unemployment, and lower income than whites is evidence of institutional racism in America—even if it could be proven that not a single white person wanted it that way. The concept of institutional racism is important because it draws attention to practices that, while not intended to be racist, may have racist consequences. For example, until recently, law schools admitted only students who excelled on their law-school entrance exams. Because racial minorities typically receive inferior schooling and have many other disabilities to overcome, few could compete with white middle-class students on these supposedly "objective" tests. The admissions procedures of law schools, although not overtly racist, had racist consequences. All but a few minority applicants were excluded from the nation's law schools, and minority communities were deprived of badly needed legal representation.

The relative lack of minorities in the legal profession, moreover, made procedural reforms slow in coming. After all, institutions are inherently conservative, structured to persist rather than change. Only protests from minority communities in general and the dedication of Merton's "all-weather liberals" resulted in special minority-admissions programs.

With this background on prejudice and discrimination in general, let's now turn to an examination of some of America's minorities—particularly some of the racial, ethnic, and religious groups who have suffered from prejudice and discrimination.

Racial Minorities in America

Table 9–1 describes the "racial" composition of the United States population according to the 1980 census. This listing reflects an agreement

Table 9-1

The Racial Composition of the United States, 1980

Racial group	Number	Percentage
Total	226,504,718	100.0
White	188,340,790	83.2
Black	26,488,218	11.7
American Indian	1,361,869	0.6
Chinese	806,027	0.4
Filipino	774,640	0.3
Japanese	700,640	0.3
Asian Indian	361,544	0.2
Korean	354,529	0.2
Vietnamese	261,714	0.1
Hawaiian	167,253	0.1
Eskimo	42,149	*
Samoan	42,050	*
Guamanian	32,132	*
Aleut	14,177	*
Other	6,756,986	3.0

Source: U.S. Bureau of Census, "Race of the Population by States: 1980" (Washington, D.C.: Government Printing Office, PC80-S1-3, July 1981), pp. 6–7.

Note: *rounds to less than 0.1%.

about what a "race" is, and the data represent the ways in which people classified themselves in completing census forms.

In this section we'll examine some of the larger racial minorities shown in Table 9–1. We'll be primarily interested in assessing the amount of prejudice and discrimination directed against each.

Blacks

Brought from Africa to America as slaves, blacks were literally regarded as less than human. Thus A. Leon Higginbotham (1978:7) could introduce his probing inquiry into early American slave law by speaking of "the vacillation of the courts, the state legislatures, and even honest public servants in trying to decide whether blacks were people, and if so, whether they were a species apart from white humans, the difference justifying separate and different treatment." Blacks were finally declared to be human beings by an act of Congress in 1868, following ratification of the Fourteenth Amendment. Their struggle to get the majority to live up to its promise began then and still continues.

Writing as a Federal Appellate judge, often rumored a likely prospect for U.S. Attorney General or Supreme Court Justice, Higginbotham (1978:vii) recalled his college years:

In 1944, I was a 16-year-old freshman at Purdue University—one of twelve black civilian students. If we wanted to live in west Lafayette, Indiana, where the university was located, solely because of our color the twelve of us at Purdue were forced to live in a crowded private house rather than, as did most of our white classmates, in the university campus dormitories. We slept barracks-style in an unheated attic.

Finally, the winter grew so cold and the attic so unbearable that Higginbotham decided to act. "Perhaps all that was needed was for one of us to speak up," he reasoned. The next morning he made an appointment with the president of the university, explained the plight of the twelve black students, and asked that they be allowed to live in some section of the state-owned dormitories.

The president's answer was direct: "Higginbotham, the law doesn't require us to let colored students in the dorm, and you either accept things as they are or leave the University immediately" (1978:viii). Higginbotham was unwilling to accept things as they were: he transferred to Antioch, went on to Yale Law School, and set out on a career committed to gaining full citizenship for blacks. As we'll see throughout this chapter, the struggle for equality for minority groups requires the dedication of individuals who are willing to step forward and take

The struggle for equality has not been an easy one. Yet the courage of this woman in Birmingham in 1963 and of others like her served as a model and an inspiration in striving for the ideal of human dignity for blacks and whites both. The act of individual courage pictured here has made a difference in the course of American history.

a personal responsibility for bringing a society's practices into line with its stated values.

Black Americans clearly represent the nation's largest racial minority. Not surprisingly, more sociological research has been addressed to their situation than to that of any other group. Let's look separately at some of the indicators of antiblack prejudice and discrimination.

Antiblack Prejudice   In 1932, a team of Princeton researchers asked undergraduates to select from a list of eighty-four adjectives the five that best described each of several groups (Katz and Braly 1933). Eighty-four percent chose "superstitious" as one of the five adjectives best describing blacks, followed by "lazy" (75 percent), "happy-go-lucky" (38 percent), "ignorant" (38 percent), "musical" (26 percent),

"ostentatious" (26 percent), "very religious" (24 percent), and "stupid" (22 percent, in addition to the 38 percent for "ignorant").

In 1967, another team of researchers repeated the study among the Princeton undergraduates of that year (Karlins et al. 1969). "Superstitious" had declined to 13 percent, and the combination of "ignorant" and "stupid" accounted for only 15 percent of the choices. In 1967, the leading choices were: "musical" (47 percent), "happy-go-lucky" (27 percent), "lazy" (26 percent), "pleasure-loving" (26 percent), and "ostentatious" (25 percent).

These data illustrate the persistence of stereotypes in the face of contradictory evidence. In 1966, the Watts district of Los Angeles was rocked by racial riots and violence that captured headlines around the world. In 1967, there

Table 9-2

Whites' Attitudes toward Discrimination against Blacks, 1964

Percent who agreed that	North	South	Total
"An owner of property should not have to sell to Negroes if he doesn't want to."	89	96	91
"A restaurant owner should not have to serve Negroes if he doesn't want to."	47	82	56
"Before Negroes are given equal rights, they have to show that they deserve them."	58	74	62
"To be frank, I would not like my child to go to school with a lot of Negroes."	47	76	54

Source: Gertrude Jaeger Selznick and Stephen Steinberg, *The Tenacity of Prejudice,* Copyright ©1969 by Anti-Defamation League of B'nai B'rith. By permission of Harper & Row, Publishers, Inc.

were violent riots in Detroit, New York, Rochester, Birmingham, and elsewhere. In that same year, 27 percent of the Princeton undergraduates studied said that "happy-go-lucky" was one of the five adjectives best describing blacks.

These bizarre stereotypes fit nicely together with the attitudes of a majority of whites toward racial matters as shown in a national survey conducted by Gertrude Jaeger Selznick and Stephen Steinberg (1969). Some of those 1964 findings are presented in Table 9–2. Among other things, in 1964, 60 percent of the whites interviewed said they thought "there should be a law against marriages between Negroes and

whites." I have presented these data to show that antiblack prejudice in America is not merely ancient history.

Despite these findings, white attitudes toward blacks have become more egalitarian over time. For example, on the issue of segregated versus integrated schools, the percentage of whites saying that black and white children should attend the same school increased from 30 percent in 1956 to 88 percent in 1980 (*Public Opinion* 1981b:37).

Figure 9–1 summarizes some other changes in white attitudes toward blacks in America. As you can see, the old prejudices against blacks are steadily easing in America. Bear in mind, however, that those things whites are now more willing to grant to black Americans—the right to be president, to marry whom one wants to marry, and to live where one wants to live—are all rights supposedly guaranteed to all Americans. Realize also that the data describe *attitudes* expressed by survey respondents. As we've seen earlier, however, attitudes and actions do not necessarily go hand in hand.

Antiblack Discrimination   Despite the changes in white attitudes, blacks seem to have become more pessimistic in recent years about a rapid end to discrimination. Asked in 1968 what progress had been made in eliminating discrimination during the preceding ten to fifteen years, 65 percent said there had been a "lot of progress." Ten years later only 47 percent would give that answer (Ladd 1978:36).

When the question of progress was asked somewhat differently in 1981, the results seemed even more pessimistic. When asked "Compared to ten years ago, do you think blacks in America are a lot better off, a little better off, about the same, a little worse off, or a lot worse off?" only 18 percent of the black respondents answered "a lot better off." In fact, 17 percent said blacks were "worse off." When a sample of whites were asked the same question, 53 percent said blacks were "a lot better off" (Ladd 1981:32).

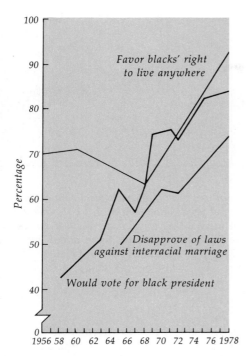

Figure 9–1 Changing attitudes toward black Americans. Source: Public Opinion (September/October: 1978):37. Reprinted by permission of the American Enterprise Institute.

Table 9-3

Trends in the Family Income of Whites and Blacks, 1950–1980

Year	MEDIAN INCOMES		Ratio of Black to White Incomes
	White	Black	
1950	$7,057	$3,828	0.54
1955	8,495	4,685	0.55
1960	9,716	5,379	0.55
1965	11,333	6,072	0.54
1970	13,000	7,978	0.61
1975	14,268	8,779	0.62
1980	21,904	12,674	0.58

Sources: U.S. Bureau of Census, "The Social and Economic Status of the Black Population in the United States: An Historical View, 1790–1978" (Washington, D.C.: Government Printing Office, Series P-23, No. 80, 1979), pp. 31, 196. U.S. Bureau of Census, "Money Income and Poverty Status of Families and Persons in the United States: 1980" (Washington, D.C.: Government Printing Office, Series P-60, No. 127, 1981), p. 2.

Has there been much progress toward ending discrimination against blacks in recent years? The answer depends on how much progress you think is "a lot." Table 9–3, for example, presents the ratio of black-to-white family income between 1950 and 1980. The chief observation to be made in Table 9–3 is that the relative incomes of black and white families have changed very little. Throughout the three-decade period—including the civil rights movement—black families earned less than two-thirds the income of white families.

In terms of employment, the continued willingness to discriminate against blacks is also mirrored in the actual status of blacks in American society. In November 1981, for example, the unemployment rate of blacks (15.5 percent) was more than double that of whites (7.4 per-

cent). Unemployment rates were much higher for persons from sixteen to nineteen years of age in general, but the situation was far worse for blacks (41.3 percent) than for whites (19.3 percent) (U.S. Bureau of Labor Statistics 1982:66). Nor is the black-white unemployment differential anything new, as Figure 9–2 demonstrates.

Even when blacks are employed in "good" jobs, they earn less money, on the average, than whites, which is a major factor in explaining why black-family income remains so much less than that of whites. Table 9-4 presents the average 1977 earnings of black and white men and women in various occupational categories. Notice, for example, that white, male professional and technical workers earned an average of $17,745, whereas their black co-workers earned $14,861. In every occupational category, black men earn less than whites. The pattern is not so clear among women. Another pattern is very clear, however; women earn less than their male counterparts without exception. We'll return to this pattern in Chapter 10.

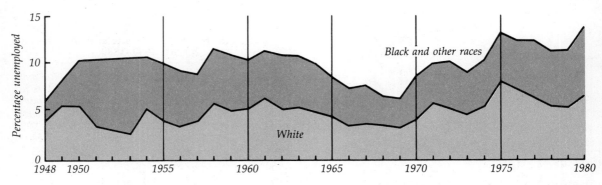

Figure 9–2 Unemployment rates for blacks and whites, 1948–1975. For most years, unemployment data are available only for "blacks and other races," not for blacks alone. The Census Bureau points out, however, that blacks make up 90 percent of the combined category and that the figures shown are close to what they would be for blacks alone. Source: U.S. Bureau of Census, The Social and Economic Status of the Black Population in the United States: An Historical View, 1790–1978, *Series P–23, No. 80, 1979, pp. 69, 209; U.S. Bureau of Labor Statistics,* Monthly Labor Review, *July 1981, p. 62.*

Of course, the occupational categories in Table 9–4 are pretty broad. It is possible, for example, that whites had higher status professions than the blacks, thus explaining the overall difference in income. This explanation, however, does not hold up when specific professions are examined. The 1970 census reported average incomes for specific occupations. Black, male accountants earned 79 percent as much as white, male accountants. Black, male architects earned 78 percent as much as white, male architects. Black, male engineers earned 79 percent as much as white, male engineers. Similar results are found in all other occupations (U.S. Bureau of Census 1975:361–362).

Differences in education and experience do not explain the racial differences in income. Table 9–5 presents the average 1977 incomes of male full-time wage and salary workers. Notice that blacks earn substantially less than whites even when they have the same education and experience.

Employment and income are only two among many instances of discrimination against blacks in America. What we have seen in those respects, however, illustrates the pattern that can also be found in relation to education, politics, housing, health care, criminal victimization, and many other areas of life.

Native Americans

Unlike blacks, Native Americans were not brought to the United States as slaves. They were here before there *was* a United States, and many have had good reason to wish there had never been a United States. From the beginning, the white colonists and settlers of the West robbed the Indians of their lands and carried out atrocities.

Today's Native Americans are perhaps the nation's most depressed minority. Their infant mortality rate far exceeds that of the rest of the nation. They suffer more than others from such diseases as tuberculosis, diabetes, and alcoholism. They are poorer than other Americans and more underemployed. In 1975, for example, those Indians living on reservations had an unemployment rate of 39.8 percent—many times higher than that of the rest of the nation (Sorkin 1978:5).

Table 9-4

Average Incomes in Various Occupational Categories by Sex and Race, 1977

| | Men | | Women | |
	White	Black	White	Black
Professional and technical workers	$17,745	$14,861	$11,947	$12,212
Managers and administrators (except farm)	19,138	15,024	10,150	12,225
Sales workers	16,049	—	6,814	—
Clerical workers	14,436	11,208	8,410	8,474
Craft and kindred workers	15,031	11,252	8,903	—
Operatives except transport	12,704	11,038	7,368	6,507
Transport equipment operators	13,689	10,154	—	—
Laborers, except farm	11,663	7,987	7,428	—
Service workers, except private household	10,966	8,072	6,248	6,096

Source: Anne McDougall Young, "Median Earnings in 1977 Reported for Year-Round Full-Time Workers," *Monthly Labor Review,* July 1979, p. 38.
Note: — not reported.

Ward Churchill and Norbert Hill, Jr., (1979:38) point out that the education status of Native Americans is substantially below that of the rest of the United States population. Worst of all are those Indians living on reservations:

a) More than fifty percent of all adults have less than an elementary education.
b) Less than twenty-five percent have graduated from high school.
c) Barely one percent have completed four years of college.
d) The percentage of graduate degrees among reservation Indians is so low as to be meaningless.
e) The median education of Native American reservation men is nine and four tenths years, while that of women is nine and seven tenths years.

Their financial status is no better. Churchill and Hill continue (1979:39):

3) Concerning rural/reservation Indians:
a) Sixty-four percent of all Native American adult males earn less than four thousand dollars while eighty-six percent of all adult Native females earn less than that figure.

b) Median family income for this half-million-person racial block of Americans is $4,469 annually.
4) Concerning the total Native population:
a) More than fifty percent of all Native American men earn less than four thousand dollars while more than eighty percent of all Indian females earn less than this amount.
b) Median family income for almost a million Native Americans is $5,832 annually.
c) Median income for all Native American males sixteen years of age or more is $3,509 annually, that of a Native female in the same group is $1,697.

An Indian scholar, Chris Cavender (1972), has suggested that the status of Indians in America is related to the negative stereotypes of them that have been maintained by school textbooks. (One such stereotype is disproved in the box "Native American Humor.") The image most Americans have shared regarding the way the "savages" dealt with white settlers, for instance, is summed up in the following description of a massacre.

They were scalped. Their brains were knocked out; the men used their knives, ripped open

Table 9-5

Average Incomes of White and Black Men with the Same Education and On-the-job Experience, 1977

Years of work experience	High School 1 to 4 years		College 1+ years	
	White	Black	White	Black
Less than 6	$4,702	$2,893	$7,065	$6,681
6 to 10	9,402	7,191	13,517	10,976
11 to 15	12,424	8,729	16,778	12,382
16 to 20	14,452	10,125	19,010	14,742
21 to 30	15,030	10,255	20,306	15,170
31 or more	14,386	10,509	18,575	14,547

Source: Daniel E. Taylor, "Education, On-the-job Training, and the Black-White Earnings Gap," *Monthly Labor Review,* April 1981, p. 29.

women, clubbed little children, knocked them in the head with their guns, beat their brains out, mutilated their bodies in every sense of the word. (Dulles 1959:41)

Outrageous? The passage I've just quoted is a description from a white witness of the way *white* soldiers dealt with the Cheyenne encampment at Sand Creek in 1864. Though Chief Black Kettle had been guaranteed safety for his people, the Colorado militia struck suddenly and killed 500 men, women, and children. A century later, the victims have been immortalized as brutal "savages."

Cultural differences and misunderstandings have produced other negative stereotypes of native Americans. Many tribes, such as the Apache, came to be regarded as "sneaky"— because they moved carefully across the countryside, covering their tracks. But they apparently were not trying to conceal their movements from others. Contemporary scholars suggest that the Apache regarded leaving their footprints everywhere as arrogant—an affront to nature (Lopez 1978:112).

Many tribes created instant kin relationships with strangers in order to converse, for there was no way except by kin relationship to address anyone but the enemy. It was for this reason,

not out of a sense of inferiority, that several tribes referred to the United States president as "the Great White Father." To call an outsider "father" and to refer to yourselves as "children" implied a social relationship in which there were mutual obligations. Part of the tragedy of white-Indian relations was the failure to understand this; when whites showed ignorance of what was expected of them, Indians felt insulted. Whites felt that Indians, in referring to themselves as "children," wished to be taken care of; and when they made efforts in this direction and were spurned, regarded Indians as haughty. As this misunderstanding escalated, the feeling of frustration generated in Indians was incalculable.

The problems created by centuries of misunderstandings between the original Americans and those who came later still linger on. Native Americans are not the only ones who have been misunderstood, however.

Asian Americans

Asian Americans began migrating to the United States in significant numbers in the latter part of the nineteenth century, when they served as

The original Americans have, in many ways, suffered most among America's minority groups. Though never slaves (like blacks), they often faced the threat of genocide on the American frontier.

imported labor in the development of the West Coast and Hawaii. According to the census, there were nearly three million Asian Americans in the United States in 1980. The oldest Asian migrants to the United States were Chinese and Japanese. Many Filipinos have been migrating here in recent decades; they have been joined by many Vietnamese, Cambodians, and Laotians since the wars in Indochina. In the remainder of this section, we'll focus on the American history of Chinese and Japanese Americans.

Early Chinese-American history was woven into the context of western expansion and the California gold rush. Chinese immigrants built railroads, highways, and buildings. They worked the mines. And, as Vander Zanden (1972:207) reports: "By virtue of the shortage of women in the frontier West, Chinese men were also hired to do work usually done by women, such

as cooking, washing, and gardening." This historical quirk was to lay the basis for much Chinese-American business enterprise later on.

Whenever the economy suffered, however, as in the business crash of 1876, Chinese Americans often bore the brunt of others' anger and frustration. Cheap Asian labor was often seen as the source of economic ills; and persecution, burning, and bloodshed often were the proposed antidotes.

Japanese Americans have had a similar history. Brought to Hawaii as plantation workers, many worked hard, saved their money, and slowly left the plantations to establish businesses and enter professions.

Japanese-American progress suffered a severe setback when Pearl Harbor was bombed in December 1941. Japanese aliens and citizens of Japanese ancestry alike were cast in the role of potential saboteurs. This informal agreement

Native American Humor

One common stereotype about Indians is that they are a sober and humorless lot. But according to Vine Deloria, Jr., author of *Custer Died for Your Sins*, "The Indian people are exactly opposite of the popular stereotype. I sometimes wonder how anything is accomplished by Indians because of the apparent overemphasis on humor within the Indian world." Here are some examples cited by Deloria.

Columbus Jokes

Rumor has it that Columbus began his journey with four ships. But one went over the edge so he arrived in the new world with only three.

It is said that when Columbus landed, one Indian turned to another and said, "Well, there goes the neighborhood." Another version has two Indians watching Columbus land and one saying to the other, "Maybe if we leave them alone, they will go away."

Custer Jokes

Indians say that Custer was well dressed for [Little Big Horn]. When the Sioux found his body after the battle, he had on an Arrow shirt.

Custer is said to have boasted that he could ride through the entire Sioux nation with his Seventh Cavalry and he was half right.

Custer's Last Words occupy a revered place in Indian humor. One source states that as he was falling mortally wounded he cried "Take no prisoners!"

Bureau of Indian Affairs

A story about the BIA [Bureau of Indian Affairs] concerns the Indian who wanted a new brain. He walked into the PHS [Public Health Service] clinic and asked for an operation that would allow him to exchange his brain for a better one.

The doctor took him into a room that contained many shelves upon which were rows of jars containing brains. Each jar had a price tag on it. A doctor's brain sold for ten dollars an ounce, a professor's brain sold for fifteen dollars an ounce. Similar brains from professional people ranged higher and higher until, at the very end of the back row of jars, there was a jar marked one thousand dollars an ounce.

The Indian asked why that type of brain was so expensive and wanted to know what kind of brain it was. The doctor said that the jar contained brains of the BIA, and added, "You know, it takes so many of them to make an ounce."

Civil Rights Movement

An Indian and a black man were in a bar one day talking about the problems of their respective groups. The black man reviewed all the progress his people had made over the past decade and tried to get the Indian inspired to start a similar movement of activism among the tribes.

Finally, the black man concluded, "Well, I guess you can't do much, there are so few of you."

"Yes," said the Indian, "and there won't be very many of you if they decide to play cowboys and blacks."

America the Beautiful

"Do you realize," [Clyde Warrior] said, "that when the United States was founded, it was only 5 percent urban and 95 percent rural and now it is 70 percent urban and 30 percent rural?"

His listeners nodded solemnly but didn't seem to understand what he was driving at.

"Don't you realize what this means?" he rapidly continued. "It means that we are pushing them into the cities. Soon we will have the country back again."

"I know," the Indian [said], "that . . . these cities must be rebuilt [and] the program would also mean a better life for my people. You see, after the cities are rebuilt and everyone is settled there, we are going to fence them off and run our buffalo all over the country again."

When questioned by an anthropologist on what the Indians called America before the white man came, an Indian said simply, *"Ours."*

Source: Excerpted with permission of Macmillan Publishing Co., Inc. from *Custer Died For Your Sins* by Vine Deloria, Jr. Copyright ©1969 by Vine Deloria, Jr.

Japanese Americans as a group have adapted successfully to the New World. During World War II, however, 110,000 like the members of this family—identified by the tags hanging from their lapels—were forcibly relocated to detention camps for the duration of the war.

was formalized on February 19, 1942, with the issuance of Executive Order No. 9066, authorizing the secretary of war to establish detention camps for persons of Japanese ancestry. Approximately 110,000 Japanese—two-thirds of them United States citizens—were taken from their homes and placed in ten "war relocation centers" in the West and Midwest (Masaoka 1972).

Homes and businesses were confiscated. More fortunate Japanese were able to get friends to occupy their homes and run their businesses during the period of relocation. Others were able to hire "managers" at very high salaries. In 1942, the Federal Reserve Board estimated that the evacuation cost the Japanese residents approximately 400 million dollars (Masaoka 1972).

Today, such excesses seem hard to comprehend; surely it couldn't happen today. Yet, it is sobering to know that the financial claims of many Japanese Americans still have not been settled, and the law permitting the camps remained on the books until recently. The whole episode should stand as a reminder of the vulnerability of our agreements on the civil liberties of all citizens.

National Minorities

Caucasians constitute the dominant majority in American life, but that group is far from homogeneous and contains within it several **ethnic minorities,** sometimes referred to as "white ethnics."

European Immigrants

Most Americans are descendents of immigrants to the New World, mostly from Europe. The breakdown by nationality of whites can be seen in Figure 9–3. The earliest immigrants came, of course, from the British Isles, and over a fourth of today's population are English, Scottish, or Welsh by national origin. As a group, they escaped persecution. The culture they brought with them to America, instead, formed the baseline of agreements that permitted the persecution of Native Americans and the subsequent waves of immigration from elsewhere.

From the early days of nationhood, English Americans feared the influence of other European immigrants. Benjamin Franklin expressed concern over the persistence of German culture and language in the New World (Gordon 1964). Thomas Jefferson was concerned for the survival of major American cultural agreements, suggesting the immigrants would

bring with them the principles of the governments they leave, imbibed in their early youth; or, if able to throw them off, it will be in exchange for an unbounded licentiousness, passing, as is usual, from one extreme to another. It would be a miracle were they to stop precisely at the point

Virtually all immigrants to America—including these nineteenth century Europeans—have faced resistance and discrimination from those already in residence.

of temperate liberty. These principles, with their language, they will transmit to their children. (quoted in Gordon 1964:91)

The mass immigration that Franklin, Jefferson, and others feared occurred around the middle of the nineteenth century when millions of German, Irish, and other European immigrants came to America seeking opportunity, often in flight from economic depression and political persecution in their native lands.

What many found in the New World was far different from what they had dreamed of. Their labor represented an economic threat to the jobs of many earlier immigrants and their descendants, and their native cultures seemed to differ sharply—as Jefferson had feared—with the mainstream agreements of the new nation. Prejudice, discrimination, even violent riots followed.

The Know-Nothing party of the 1850s was typical of the political-terrorist groups that formed to turn back the waves of foreign immigration. The name of the party was taken from the members' agreement that they would say they knew nothing if questioned by authorities (others felt the label was even more ironically appropriate than intended).

Overall, the European immigrants or their descendants eventually adapted to the ways of their new country, and now most discriminatory practices against them have disappeared. But many of the prejudices and stereotypes that marked their arrival in America still persist. In the 1967 study I mentioned earlier in this chapter, Princeton undergraduates said the Irish were best described as "quick-tempered" and "extremely nationalistic." Italians were seen as "passionate" and "pleasure-loving." Germans fared somewhat better, being described as primarily "industrious" and "scientifically minded" (Karlins et al. 1969). These stereotypes are probably a close reflection of the agreements shared by Americans generally, although we should add the Hollywood-perpetuated stereotype of Italians as gangsters.

On the whole, the relatively successful integration of European immigrants to America has created some problematic expectations about integration in general. In particular, it has created an impatience with the problems experienced by blacks, and it has been a problem for more recent immigrants from Latin America as well.

Spanish-Speaking Minorities

Recently, immigration of people from traditionally Spanish-speaking parts of the world has

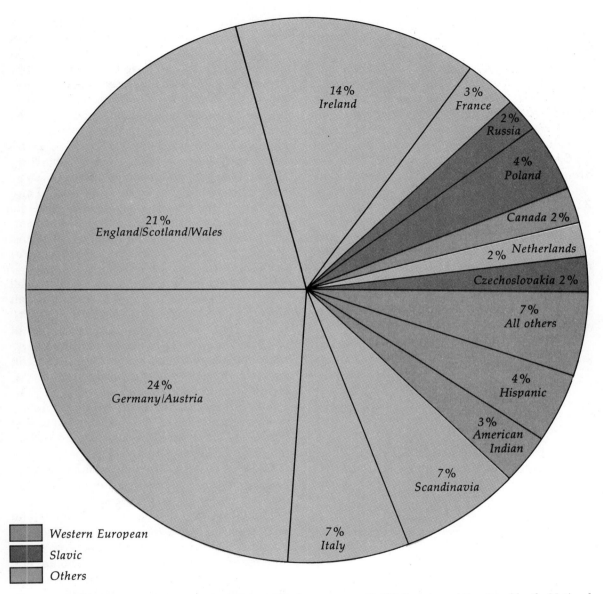

Figure 9–3 National origins of the white population. The data represent 10,652 Americans interviewed by the National Opinion Research Center (University of Chicago) between 1972 and 1978. Source: Public Opinion (November/December 1978):32. Reprinted by permission of the American Enterprise Institute.

increased. Few people have come from Spain itself; most have come from Mexico, Puerto Rico, and Cuba. As recent arrivals in the United States, they are currently very visible as a minority group facing much the same out-group treatment that earlier immigrants did. At present, these three major groups are concentrated in different areas of the United States: Chicanos (from Mexico) in southern California and the Southwest, Puerto Ricans in New York City, and Cubans in Miami.

Many Chicanos, the largest of the Spanish-speaking groups, have been visible as agricultural workers, but the great majority of all the Spanish-speaking minorities live in cities. In 1978, when two-thirds of all Americans lived in metropolitan areas, for example, the figure for Spanish-speaking people was 85.4 percent overall and even higher among the Puerto Ricans (95.2 percent) and Cubans (97.3 percent) (U.S. Bureau of Census 1979d:12).

Economically, Spanish-speaking Americans fall between other whites and black Americans. Table 9–6 represents Census Bureau statistics for 1978, showing the median family incomes for the several Spanish-speaking groups, in comparison with other whites and blacks. The table also shows the percentages in each group earning more than $15,000.

As Table 9–6 shows, the Cubans stand out among the Spanish-speaking minorities in

America. Most of them came to the United States shortly after Fidel Castro came to power in Cuba; many were educated professionals and business people (Rose and Rose 1972). At first, they settled in Miami with the expectation of returning to Cuba when Castro was ousted. As it became clear that Castro would remain in power, the Cuban refugees began to migrate to other large cities and to attempt to integrate themselves into American life, although there are almost half a million Cubans still in Miami. Many were educated urban people and adjusted rapidly; many opened small stores and made the same kind of adjustment as Europeans had earlier. They have met discrimination, but they have not had the same difficulties as Puerto Ricans or Mexican Americans.

Cuban refugees came dramatically to all Americans' attention again in April through September 1980, when a massive flight of 125,000 from Castro's regime came north in a fleet of small, private boats. In addition to those seeking to migrate for their own reasons, the Cuban government reportedly emptied jails and prisons to swell the numbers of refugees.

Like many European and Asian immigrant groups before them, the Spanish-speaking minorities have faced a language problem, though U.S. Department of Labor studies (1973:94) show that this problem is decreasing. Illiteracy in English still exists among older people, but almost all the young are literate. Educational levels are also being upgraded among Spanish-speaking Americans. In 1977, for example, the median years of school completed for Americans eighteen years old and older was 12.5, but for those of Spanish origin, it was only 11.0 years. Looking at specific age groups, however, we see changes taking place. Among people sixty-five years old, the comparison was 11.3 years to 6.9, whereas among twenty-five-year-olds, it was 12.9 (total) and 12.4 (Spanish origin) (U.S. Bureau of Census 1979d:19–28).

One focus of the language problem has been in regard to voting. The 1975 federal Voting Rights Act required that wherever language minorities composed at least 5 percent of the

Table 9-6

Annual Family Incomes in America, 1978

Type of family	Median income	Percent $15,000 or above
All American families	$16,009	54.1
Whites	16,740	56.9
Blacks	9,563	29.9
Spanish total	11,421	34.7
Mexican	11,742	34.9
Puerto Rican	7,972	24.4
Cuban	14,182	46.5
Central and South American	11,280	37.7
Other	12,855	39.4

Source: U.S. Bureau of Census, *Current Population Reports*, Series P-20, No. 339, 1979, p. 13; ibid., Series P-60, No. 336, 1979, p.58.

population, local officials must provide both bilingual ballots and special registration assistance. Its biggest impact was in California and the Southwest, where it has been hotly debated ever since.

One Spanish minority seems especially hard-pressed: unauthorized Mexican workers, entering the United States illegally to work for months, years, or even decades. Reynaldo Baca and Dexter Bryan (1982:2) describe the phenomenon of **binationalism:**

> Rather than give up ties to their home land, these *Mexicanos y Mexicanas* work in the United States and maintain residences in both countries. Maintaining a presence in their home towns in Zacatecas, Michoacan, Jalisco, and Oaxaca, they work for extended periods in the United States, often more than a decade. These workers recruit relatives from their *parentesco* (non-residential extended nuclear family) or compatriots from their *paistesco* (associates from their home region in Mexico) to take over U.S.-based jobs while they, the unauthorized workers, return to Mexico. Besides exchanging and sharing work and family roles, these workers finance others' migration and share living arrangements in the United States.

There are no reliable figures on how many unauthorized Mexican workers are currently in the United States, but unofficial estimates commonly number them in the millions. Because of their illegal alien status in the United States, such workers often find themselves at the mercy of unscrupulous employers. Often paid below the minimum wage, they have no recourse to government officials, nor are they entitled to welfare, unemployment insurance, and other "safety net" programs available to other poor people. Moreover, all these problems are further complicated by the language problems discussed above.

Religious Minorities

Among the ethnic minorities, sociologists include religious minorities, as we saw at the beginning of the chapter. In the United States,

Protestants constitute the dominant religious majority. Nonetheless, approximately one-fourth of the United States population are members of the Roman Catholic church, and approximately 3 percent are members of Jewish congregations. In this section, we will discuss these two religious minorities.

Jews

Jews have probably had as much experience with prejudice and discrimination as any other group of people in history. Migration to the United States offered little exception to that experience.

The Jews suffered the same prejudice and discrimination as the other European immigrants and for many of the same reasons. Their disagreement with the mainstream Christianity of the nation, however, always set them further apart than the others. The persistence of anti-Semitic stereotypes and prejudice in America is best seen in the findings of the 1964 national survey reported by Selznick and Steinberg (1969). Table 9–7 presents some of the agreements Americans share about Jews.

The 1964 survey results also point to a continued willingness among Americans to discriminate against Jews or at least to tolerate discrimination. Twenty percent of those polled said they would favor "a law to stop more Jews from immigrating to this country" (Selznick and Steinberg 1969:60–61). And another 25 percent said they didn't care one way or another. Thus, a bare majority said they would be opposed to such a law.

Apathy toward the discrimination others might wish to practice was a common pattern uncovered by the study. For example, the survey asked: "If a candidate for Congress should declare himself as being against Jews, would this influence you to vote for him or to vote against him?" A majority (58 percent) said they would vote against such a candidate, compared with only 5 percent who said they would vote for him. The sizable minority remaining, however, said the candidate's anti-Semitism wouldn't

Table 9-7

Potentially Negative Beliefs about Jews

Belief	Percent True	Percent False	Don't know	Belief	Percent True	Percent False	Don't know
Jews still think of themselves as God's chosen people.	59	17	24	International banking is pretty much controlled by Jews.	30	24	46
Jews always like to be at the head of things.	54	32	14	Jews are more loyal to Israel than to America.	30	47	23
Jews stick together too much.	52	38	10	Jews don't care what happens to anyone but their own kind.	26	62	12
Jewish employers go out of their way to hire other Jews.	49	32	19	Jews today are trying to push in where they are not wanted.	18	68	14
The movie and television industries are pretty much controlled by Jews.	47	21	32	Jews have too much power in the United States.	11	77	12
Jews are more willing than other people to use shady practices to get what they want.	42	46	12	Jews are always stirring up trouble with their ideas.	10	70	20

Source: Taken from Gertrude Jaeger Selznick and Stephen Steinberg, *The Tenacity of Prejudice.* Copyright ©1969 by Anti-Defamation League of B'nai B'rith. By permission of Harper & Row, Publishers, Inc.

influence them one way or the other. Many explained by saying they "vote on the basis of issues," evidently feeling that prejudice and discrimination are not political issues (Selznick and Steinberg 1969:54).

Roman Catholics

A good deal of the hostility and violence greeting the European migrants was directed specifically at Catholics. The Know-Nothing party of the 1850s, for instance, was formed largely in opposition to the immigration of Catholics. As I indicated earlier in the chapter, the Ku Klux Klan, formally committed to "maintain forever the God-given supremacy of the White Race" (Vander Zanden 1972:89), has traditionally taken violent exception to Catholics, along with Jews, Communists, and "foreigners."

America has countless other ethnic minorities, but it is impossible to discuss them all here.

This is unfortunate, because the agreements that keep minority groups in their disadvantaged status have always persisted most when ignored. Each of the racial and ethnic minority groups discussed so far has at one time or another been described as the "invisible Americans" or the "forgotten Americans." The first step in changing the agreements upon which minority-group status is based is awareness that the agreements are agreements only, nothing more.

Minority-Group Responses

Earlier in the chapter, I indicated that members of minority groups participate in the agreements defining their status as a minority. By this, I mean that minority-group members frame their behavior in terms of the agreements just as majority-group members do. Thus, the stereotype of Italians being involved in crime may lead one person to such a life, whereas another may react by becoming a police officer or public prosecutor. Both participate in the agreement to the extent that it determines their actions, even though one participates by denying its truth.

Submission

Some minority-group members simply accept that the agreements regarding their status represent "reality." Examples include the black who believes that blacks are "really" less intelligent and lazier than whites and the Italian who believes that Italians are more inclined to crime.

This response should not come as a surprise when you realize that minority-group members are—to some degree at least—socialized into the same set of agreements as members of the majority. Young blacks attend schools that offer an educational experience designed primarily by whites. Italian children watch movies and television shows that portray Italians as mobsters.

When minority-group members submit to such agreements, they perpetuate them. If blacks believe themselves to be less intelligent than whites, they lend support to the reification of the agreement for whites as well.

Protest and Resistance

Minority groups sometimes respond to the agreements making them a minority with resistance, even with violent aggression against the majority group. Race riots, economic boycotts, and symbolic protests are examples of such resistance.

Flagrant violations of the prevailing agreements can have two quite different consequences. First, such actions can draw attention to the existence of unjust agreements. By making members of the minority group more aware that the agreements are merely agreements, the potential for group solidarity and the creation of power is enhanced. Sometimes, the majority group can be frightened into modifying its agreements.

Resistance sometimes has a negative effect. It can solidify the prevailing agreements even further by bringing the majority group to their defense. Thus, race riots have often strengthened agreements that the minorities involved represented a threat to a "way of life."

Civil disobedience is a term closely associated with three men—Henry David Thoreau, Mahatma Gandhi, and Martin Luther King, Jr.—and it will be useful to distinguish it from the idea of resistance. "Civil disobedience" has come to mean the acknowledgment of an agreement's existence and the refusal to be governed by it. Thoreau, Gandhi, and King all shared the point of view that aggression against a distasteful agreement meant that the person resisting the agreement was being controlled by it as much as the one who accepted eagerly. Without violence and without withdrawing into their subcultures, each simply refused to be controlled by those agreements that he did not share.

Civil disobedience is a response to injustice that was powerfully effective in the Civil Rights movement of the 1950s and 1960s, as it was in India's rebellion against British colonialism.

Here's a clear and dramatic example that reshaped a nation. On December 1, 1955, Rosa Parks, a Montgomery seamstress, was riding the city bus home after a hard day's work. In Alabama at that time, there was an agreement that blacks sat in a special section in the back of the bus, and that's what Parks was doing. As the bus became more crowded and the "white" section was filled, the bus driver ordered Parks and three other blacks to give up their seats to whites just getting on the bus.

Rosa Parks chose not to be controlled by the agreements that December day, and in so doing she sparked a revolution in black-white relations in America: a revolution that is still continuing. Parks's refusal and her immediate arrest drew national attention to the situation prevailing in Alabama, showing other blacks that agreements were only agreements and that it was possible not to be run by them.

Montgomery blacks chose to dramatize their disagreement with a nonviolent boycott of the city bus system, forming car pools and walking to work. To everyone's surprise, the boycott was virtually total. Blacks had created their own agreement in the midst of a larger society. Very soon, the white power structure began *resisting* the black agreement, which made it more "real." Car-pool drivers were harassed and ticketed by police, and the Baptist minister Martin Luther King, Jr., and other boycott leaders were put in jail. Yet the nonviolent boycott continued. The white resistance drew international attention to the boycott and support for the blacks came from around the world.

The black leaders in Montgomery had at first envisioned a one-day, symbolic boycott. White resistance changed all that, and the black agreement took on the force of law in November 1956 when the U.S. Supreme Court ruled the segregation of buses was unconstitutional.

People like Thoreau, Gandhi, and King often seem a people apart, as though they are living in a reality different from the one the rest of us live in. In a sense they are, in that they create their own agreements and refuse to have their lives run by agreements they find unjust. Mocked, jailed, beaten, and finally assassi-

Prejudice and discrimination notwithstanding, something more innately human can and does burst through systems of agreed-on hatred.

nated, King chose to govern his own behavior by a set of agreements he felt were more proper for human relations. A minister, he spoke of the society those agreements represented as a "promised land."

Assimilation

Minority groups often become "assimilated" into the larger society, as has been the case with most European immigrants to the United States. Over time, the members of a minority group may come to share many of the predominant agreements of the larger society, becoming for the most part an indistinguishable part of it.

The process of **assimilation,** however, affects the larger society's agreements as well. The subcultural values of the groups being assimilated often become a part of the more general culture, and it is in this sense that America is often referred to as a "melting pot." Milton Gordon (1964:71), in a pioneering work, has suggested the process of assimilation involves the following steps:

1. Change of cultural patterns to those of host society.
2. Large-scale entrance into cliques, clubs, and institutions of host society, on primary-group level.
3. Large-scale intermarriage.
4. Development of sense of peoplehood based exclusively on host society.
5. Absence of prejudice.
6. Absence of discrimination.
7. Absence of value and power conflict.

If you've never given much thought to the Welsh, Danish, or English "problem in America," it's because those groups, among others, have pretty much blended into the mainstream culture of the United States.

Withdrawal

Very often minority groups respond to the prevailing agreements by withdrawing into their own subculture and developing more consciously their own subcultural agreements. The recent black emphasis on African culture and the theme "black is beautiful" and the growing attention American Indians have given their own cultural heritage are good examples of this response.

Minority groups, then, may acknowledge that their group agreements are different from those of the dominant majority while denying that they are inferior. Sometimes they simply acknowledge that different sets of cultural agreements are *only* different; sometimes they assert that their minority agreements are superior to those of the majority.

The general response may also take an extreme form, that of self-segregation, physical separation of the minority from the majority. Frequently in American history, for example, black militants have advocated the establishment of a separate black nation in America or the return of black Americans to Africa. American Indians have sometimes responded in a similar manner.

Multiethnic America: The Fragmented Mosaic

Having seen all the ways in which American society has failed in its democratic ideal, it will be useful to step back and take a somewhat broader view. For all our past and present problems, we also provide a relatively rare example in the world of a pluralistic society. **Pluralism** refers to the coexistence of differences in a society. In a pluralistic society, members of minority groups are able to maintain their subcultural sets of agreements without withdrawing from the larger society. This differs from the assimilation characteristic of the "melting pot," in which subcultural differences essentially vanish.

The state of Hawaii offers the clearest example of pluralism in the United States. In 1970, whites constituted 39 percent of the state's population; Japanese, 28 percent; Filipinos, 12 percent; Chinese, 7 percent; Hawaiians and part-Hawaiians, 9 percent. And Samoans, Puerto Ricans, blacks, and many other groups made up the remaining 5 percent (Gardner and Nordyke 1974).

In 1978, Hawaii's voters elected a man of Japanese ancestry as governor, and a half-Japanese woman as lieutenant governor. The state was represented in the U.S. Congress by a Hawaiian, two Japanese Americans, and a Caucasian. The state legislature and the various agencies of the state government were peopled by a variety of races and nationality groups. The mayors of the state's four counties included men of Filipino, Portugese, and Japanese ancestry, plus an Italian American from Hartford, Connecticut.

Despite instances of prejudice and discrimination, the many subcultures of Hawaii's people generally flourish. Individuals participate in a variety of subcultures other than their own in clothing styles, food, entertainment, and friends. The rate of intermarriage between racial and ethnic groups is high.

Life in a pluralistic society is not necessarily one of complete harmony and comfort. Many whites migrating to Hawaii are uncomfortable being in a "minority" group, and they are often quick to sense prejudice and discrimination directed against them as whites.

The maintenance of subcultural agreements—necessary in a pluralistic society—appears to require a certain degree of reification. To continue sharing in your own subculture's agreements, you must to some degree feel they have a *special* value, that they are in some ways "better" than the agreements of other subcultures. The Hawaiian experience, however, has shown that it is possible to maintain divergent sets of agreements side by side without violence or the subjugation of one group by another.

This chapter has focused on the savage side of racial and ethnic relations, because you need to be aware of our national and global problems. At the same time, I have wanted to leave you with the realization that racial and ethnic hatred is not inevitable. It's possible for even the bitterest of enemies to set aside their differences. Former Ku Klux Klansman C. P. Ellis, a labor organizer in Durham, North Carolina, offers a powerful example. Despite being an active participant and leader in the Klan during the 1960s, Ellis attended a community meeting to discuss school desegregation. By the end of the meeting, Ellis had been appointed co-chairperson of a committee to handle the problem; the other co-chairperson was Ann Adams, a black woman Ellis had previously hated and fought in community affairs. Their job was to bring blacks and whites together. It was not easy going: Adams was often rejected by blacks and Ellis by his fellow whites. Ellis later described his experience in an interview reported by John Turner (1981:63):

> One day, Ann and I went back to the school and we sat down. We began to talk and just reflect. Ann said: "My daughter came home cryin every day. She said her teacher was making fun of me in front of the other kids." I said: "Boy, the same thing happened to my kid. White liberal teacher was makin fun of Tim Ellis' father, the Klansman. In front of other peoples. He came home cryin." At this point (he pauses, swallows hard, stifles a sob) I begin to see, here we are, two people from the far ends of the fence, havin identical problems, except hers bein black and me bein white. From that moment on, I tell ya, that gal and I worked together good. I begin to love the girl, really. (He weeps.)
>
> The amazing thing about it, her and I, up to that point, has cussed each other, bawled each other, we hated each other. Up to that point, we didn't know each other. We didn't know we had things in common.

Summary

In this chapter, we looked at inequality as it is structured along racial and ethnic lines. "Race," we found, is a much-misused term, conjuring up images of blood and instincts, superiority and inferiority, and so forth. Though it is presumably a biological term, the biologists give it little credence, saying that it is of little use in understanding mankind.

"Race" has significant meaning as a sociological concept—a meaning attributed to it through agreement. To the extent that people believe that racial differences are important, they become important in terms of social interactions. As an extension of the same phenomenon, sociologists look also at "ethnic groups"— social categories based on national origins, religion, and similar characteristics. Categories such as these serve as the bases for the division of society into a "majority group" and several "minority groups," the latter distinguished not by their lack of numbers but by their disproportionate lack of power, scarce goods, and so forth.

"Prejudice" is a prejudging of individuals based on assumptions about the group or category to which they belong, plus any feelings (usually negative) associated with those prejudgments. The assumptions upon which prejudice depends grow out of "stereotypes"— generalized pictures about all members of the group or category in question. Thus, for example, the mainstream culture of the United States has contained a stereotype of black Americans as lazy and shiftless. Even without all whites believing this description to be true of all blacks, the stereotype has existed. Prejudice is the expectation that a particular black person will be lazy and shiftless by virtue of belonging to the category of black people.

"Discrimination" is the action component of prejudice; it refers to what people do based on the stereotypes they hold and the prejudice those stereotypes generate. Thus, if you hold a stereotype of blacks as lazy and shiftless, you will expect a particular black job applicant to be lazy and shiftless, and you will turn him or her down for the job. Stereotypes, prejudice, and discrimination form a system of "racism," which holds one race to be fundamentally superior to another, and people sometimes apply such systems to ethnic groups or, as we'll see in the next chapter, to division by gender and age.

There are many reasons for the existence and persistence of prejudice. One is "scapegoating": the blaming of some people for the problems we face in life. Thus, Nazis blamed the Jews for Germany's economic problems during the 1930s. Economic (and other) competition offers another explanation, as those threatened by the Irish immigrants of the 1840s quickly generated some very negative stereotypes about the Irish, which gave rise to both prejudice and discrimination.

Discrimination takes many forms, ranging from mild to extreme. "Annihilation" refers to the extermination or eradication of a social group or category, as Hitler intended for the Jews during World War II. It is also reflected in the slogan from the Old West: "The only good Indian is a dead Indian." "Expulsion" is a somewhat less severe form of discrimination—forcing people out of a society or imprisoning them within it, as in the case of the West Coast Japanese Americans during World War II. "Segregation" is less severe still: members of a minority group are permitted to live and operate within the society, but they are kept separate from the majority groups—as in housing, schooling, and so forth. This pattern has characterized the black American experience from the emancipation of the slaves until today.

"Institutional racism" is a particularly troublesome form of discrimination. Whereas individual racism is a function of the actions of specific, bigoted individuals, institutional racism is the result of a more basic social structure. The system can be so put together that members of a minority group suffer even though no individual has done anything bad to them. Examples from the present would be the shorter life expectancy of black Americans in comparison with whites or the high rate of alcoholism among Native Americans. The end problem cannot be traced to the actions of specific, bigoted individuals. It is a function of the system as a whole.

The primary racial minorities in the United States are blacks, Asian Americans, and Native Americans. Blacks were the only ones who began their American experience as slaves, and they have spent the past four hundred years attempting to escape that beginning. Though freed during the Civil War, blacks have gone through several forms of discrimination. Though blacks are today guaranteed equality by law and though most informal prejudices and discriminations are at an all-time low, blacks earn substantially lower salaries and wages, they have poorer health and shorter life expectancies and suffer a variety of other disadvantages—many of which are now difficult to trace to their roots and eliminate.

Native Americans have suffered also, though somewhat differently. Although never enslaved in great numbers, they were fair game for extermination early in our national history. Today, they suffer underemployment and lower wages when they do work; their rates of infant mortality are ten times as high as the national average, and the children who survive will receive less education (and of poorer quality) than others. It is now apparent that many of the difficulties experienced between the Indians and the white settlers stemmed from very different world views and forms of communication. Thus, for example, the Indian who felt it disrespectful to nature to leave footprints everywhere was regarded by whites as "sneaky" for wiping away his tracks.

Asian Americans have had still a different history in America. Brought to the growing nation as indentured laborers, they were never actually slaves and had a better chance for mobility than did blacks. Working together through strong family systems, both the Japanese and the Chinese were able to escape from the plantations and work camps to establish themselves as merchants and, later, as professionals. This is not to suggest that they suffered no prejudice or discrimination. Many were murdered because of their race; laws were often passed to discourage their advance to equality, and informal agreements worked even greater disadvantages. Most dramatically, during World War II, Japanese Americans were rounded up and taken to detention camps, to protect the nation against what was imagined to be their potential treason.

By comparison, the waves of European immigrants who have fleshed out the main substance of the American population have had an easier road to follow. Yet their history has hardly been a pleasant one. Jews and Catholics have suffered at the hands of the Protestant majority. Many died, millions suffered. In terms of national origins, we find the irony of one wave of immigrants establishing itself in the New World and then participating in discrimination against subsequent waves. Thus, for example, the Irish and Italians whose parents and grandparents suffered so much in years past now create problems for Chicanos and Puerto Ricans.

Minority groups respond to prejudice and discrimination in a variety of ways. Some submit, even joining in the agreements on negative stereotypes and behaving in accord with the majority's expectations. Others react in the opposite fashion—attacking the attacker, fighting fire with fire. Still others have succeeded in creating new systems of agreements. Often through civil disobedience, people like Martin Luther King, Jr., Mahatma Gandhi, and others have lived by their own standards rather than submitting to or resisting the standards of the majority.

"Assimilation" is the pattern in which members of a minority group are absorbed into the majority, taking on the agreements of the majority and becoming a part of it. In contrast, "withdrawal" is a pattern of extreme separation from the majority—a self-imposed form of expulsion.

Ultimately, America is all of these patterns. It is what sociologists call a "pluralistic society": one made up of several persistent subcultures. Though the subcultures do not always live in harmony, they do live side by side. And for all our problems in this regard, the United States still is one of the few pluralistic societies around.

Important Terms

race
minority group
prejudice
discrimination
stereotyping
scapegoating
annihilation
expulsion

segregation
racism
institutional racism
ethnic minority
binationalism
civil disobedience
assimilation
pluralism

Suggested Readings

Almquist, Elizabeth McTaggart
1979 *Minorities, Gender and Work.* Lexington, MA: Heath. Inventory of research on eight minority groups, including history, discrimination and assimilation. Minority women receive special attention.

Brown, Dee
1972 *Bury My Heart at Wounded Knee.* New York: Bantam. This is a moving account of history of Native Americans following the arrival of Columbus. It is an excellent and appropriate antidote to a long history of anti-Indian accounts of the American West and the "taming" of the frontier.

Feagin, Joe R.
1978 *Racial and Ethnic Relations.* Englewood Cliffs, NJ: Prentice-Hall.

Text covering concepts and major American racial-ethnic groups.

Glazer, Nathan, and Daniel Patrick Moynihan
1970 *Beyond the Melting Pot, Second Edition.* Cambridge, MA: MIT Press.
Describes how many ethnic groups have adapted to life in New York City—blacks, Puerto Ricans, Jews, Italians, and Irish.

Glock, Charles, and Ellen Siegelman, Eds.
1969 *Prejudice U.S.A.* New York: Praeger.
During the early 1960s, the Survey Research Center at Berkeley undertook a number of comprehensive studies of contemporary American prejudice. In 1968, the center sponsored a national conference in which leaders from the nation's major institutions were asked to respond

to the research findings. This book, drawn from the conference proceedings, offers both sociological and institutional views of prejudice in government, religion, education, the economy, and the mass media.

Gordon, Milton
1964 *Assimilation in American Life*. New York: Oxford University Press.
In this modern classic (sociology has a lot of "classics"), Gordon carefully examines the various ways in which different racial, religious, and national subcultures accommodate one another. Gordon discusses the assimilation of minority groups into the dominant Anglo culture, the proverbial "melting pot," and the issue of cultural pluralism. Throughout, he draws out the implications of such patterns for intergroup relations.

Higginbotham, A. Leon, Jr.
1978 *In the Matter of Color: Race and the American Legal Process. The Colonial Period*. New York: Oxford University Press.
In this first volume, of what is to be a multivolume study, an eminent jurist (U.S. Court of Appeals) traces the earliest origins of discrimination against blacks in American law. In particular, Judge Higginbotham lays out the structure and development of slave law in three southern and three northern states.

Rodgers-Rose, La Frances
1980 *The Black Woman*. Beverly Hills, CA: Sage Publications.
Papers on experiences of black American women, tied together by theoretical perspectives, examining what it means to be black in this country.

Rosaldo, Renato, and R. A. Calvert
1981 *Chicano: The Evolution of a People*, rev. ed. Huntington, N.Y.: Krieger.
This is a solid collection of readings on the growing Chicano population. The articles and book excerpts trace the Chicanos' past, their move to the United States, the prejudice and discrimination they have met, their present problems, and their attempts to organize themselves for an equal place in the United States society.

Rose, Arnold, and Caroline Rose, Eds.
1972 *Minority Problems*. New York: Harper & Row.
This collection of sociological and nonsociological pieces provides an omnibus view of America's many minority groups. It provides a wealth of historical and statistical data, analytical interpretations, and a human sense of the situations within which minority group members find themselves.

Rose, Peter I.
1974 *They and We: Racial and Ethnic Relations in the United States, Second Edition*. New York: Random House.
Basic discussion of processes of relationship between minority groups, especially conflict and accommodation in the United States.

In most of this chapter, we have looked at prejudice and discrimination and the ways in which minority-group members respond. What the minority groups do, however, cannot be fully understood without consideration of the actions and reactions of the majority groups as well.

In the area of race relations in the United States, we might first note that the white majority has legislated the legal changes that have followed, paralleled, and sometimes led changes in public opinion. The Congress that passed the Civil Rights Act of 1964 was virtually all white, for example. The actions of leaders have not necessarily been supported by the white majority, however.

Every advance by blacks and other minorities in America has been accompanied by a real or threatened "backlash." One form of this backlash has been right-wing political activity. In the 1968 and 1972 presidential elections, for instance, Alabama governor George Wallace drew the votes of many of those who resented blacks and were dissatisfied with changes in race relations. Periodic spurts in the popularity of the Ku Klux Klan and the American Nazi party are further examples of this response.

"White flight" has been another majority response. In recent decades masses of middle-class whites have moved from the central cities to the suburbs. As blacks and other minorities have moved into formerly all-white neighborhoods, the white residents have retreated into new all-white areas, thereby rapidly changing the racial composition of the nation's cities.

Most recently, white blacklash has taken the form of legal challenges to minority rights. Since the mid-1960s, *equal opportunity* and *affirmative action* legislation has made it unlawful for employers to discriminate against minority group members on the basis of race, ethnicity, religion, national origin, or gender, and—going beyond that—has required that employers ensure sufficient applications from minority group members. In some instances, quotas have been established to ensure representation of minorities in the various sectors of American life: in jobs, in schools, and so forth. Against a history of exclusion, affirmative action programs have offered not only equality but a degree of *compensation* as well.

A good example of the changing pattern occurred at the University of California School of Medicine at Davis. In each entering class of one hundred students, sixteen positions were held specifically for minority-group members. Thus, while academic ability would still be the yardstick for admission, minority group members were to compete separately, among themselves, for the sixteen special positions. This system (affirmative action) meant that a minority-group member might be admitted to medical school with lower test scores than those of a white candidate who was rejected.

But someone in the majority challenged the system. In 1973 a white applicant, Alan Bakke, applied for admission at Davis and was turned down. On the Medical College Admissions Test, Bakke scored in the 90th percentile—meaning that he did better than 90 percent of all those taking the test. That was not a high enough score, however, for admission within the *regular* positions. On the other hand, those students accepted for admission through the sixteen *special* positions averaged in the 35th percentile in 1973. Those accepted in 1974, when Bakke applied again, averaged in the 30th percentile (Bennett and Eastland 1978:33). Bakke protested, citing reverse discrimination, and in the process he lent his name (the "Bakke case") to one of the more controversial issues in majority-minority relations in recent years.

After a heated national debate, the U.S. Supreme Court decided by a 5 to 4 vote that Bakke had indeed been discriminated against and that he must be admitted by the Davis medical school. Did this mean that it was illegal to take race and ethnicity into account in such matters, even to compensate groups previously discriminated against? No, for the Court, basing its judgment heavily on the California rulings of World War II that justified detention of Japanese Americans (Glazer 1978:37), ruled in another 5-4 decision that *some* consideration could be given to race. This led David Riesman to conclude: "We're told that we can count race somewhat, but not too much." One of the main consequences of the ruling, he suggested, would be a period of "full employment for lawyers" (quoted in Bennett and Eastland 1978:30).

The most sobering barometer of prejudice and discrimination against blacks (and in general) can be found in the relative status of the Ku Klux Klan. Since its founding in 1865, the Klan has epitomized bigotry in America.

Though its origins have been romanticized in the 1915 film, *Birth of a Nation*, and in Klan literature as a valiant attempt to save the Southern, Christian way of life from the excesses of Reconstruction following the Civil War, John Turner (1981:8) reports a rather different beginning.

> It was the boredom of small-town life that led six young Confederate veterans to gather around a fireplace one December evening in 1865 and to form a social club. The place was Pulaski, Tenn., near the Alabama border.
>
> When they reassembled a week later, the six young men were full of ideas for their new society. It would be secret, to heighten the amusement of the thing, and the titles for the various offices were to have names as preposterous-sounding as possible, partly for the fun of it and partly to avoid

any military or political implications. Thus the head of the group was called the Grand Cyclops, his assistant was the Grand Magi; there was to be a Grand Turk to greet all candidates for admission, a Grand Scribe to act as secretary.

The greek word, *kuklos*, for "circle" or "cycle" was modified to form the club's name—Ku Klux Klan—and the initials KKK seemed to add to the mystery. Turner continues:

> Soon after the founders named the Klan, they decided to do a bit of showing off and so disguised themselves in sheets and galloped their horses through the quiet streets of little Pulaski. Their ride created such a stir that the men decided to adopt the sheets as the official regalia of the Ku Klux Klan, and they added to the effect by making grotesque masks and tall pointed hats.

From what we know sociologically about such groups, the Klan might well have lasted a few months or years and then quietly disappeared into history. Such was not to be the case, however.

> At some point in early 1866 the club, enlarged with new members from nearby towns, began to have a chilling effect on local blacks. The intimidating effect of the night rides was soon the centerpiece of the hooded order and bands of white-sheeted ghouls were paying late night visits to black homes, admonishing the terrified occupants to behave themselves and threatening more visits if they didn't. It didn't take long for the threats to be converted into action, violent action in many cases, against blacks who insisted on exercising their new rights and freedom. (Turner 1981:8)

The growing violence against blacks proved an additional spur for the passage of the federal Reconstruction Acts of 1867—aimed at insuring freedom and equality for the former slaves—

which, in turn, helped cast the die for the Klan's future. The federal legislation was passed in March; in April, a call went out to all the local Klans for a meeting to plan Southern resistance. The Klan's savagery escalated.

By the end of the decade, the Klan was a powerful force for terror throughout the Old South. Beatings, shootings, floggings, burnings, mutilations, and lynchings became commonplace. The burning cross was adopted as a perverse demonstration of the Klan's Christian commitment. In some communities, the mayor, police, and other public officials openly acknowledged membership in the Klan. In some, community officials expressed approval, and in the rest, the Klan was tolerated. At first, some white Southerners—ministers, newspaper editors, and others—spoke out against the Klan. Such voices were soon rare, however. Opposition to the Klan—whether from blacks or whites—became increasingly dangerous.

Throughout its history, the Klan's main target has been black Americans. Over time, however, many other groups have been the focus of threats, brutality, and death: Jews, Catholics, immigrants, Communists, liberals, and anyone else perceived as a threat to the pre-Civil War Southern way of life. The Klan's 1871 total membership was estimated at just over half a million. By 1920, it had declined to perhaps five thousand. The next few years, however, saw a massive immigration to the United States from Europe, bringing millions of people speaking foreign tongues and practicing foreign cultures, many of them Jews and Catholics. By 1925, Klan membership had swollen to an all-time high of 4 to 5 million. After a wave of violence, Klan membership once more receded (Turner 1981:23).

More recently, the Klan reappeared in resistance to the black civil rights movement of the 1950s and 1960s. Turner (1981:22–23) describes the quality of that resistance:

On March 25, 1964, in Lowndesboro, Ala., a white civil rights worker, Mrs. Viola Liuzzo, was shot and killed while driving between Montgomery and Selma. Four Klansmen were subsequently arrested. Coming just weeks after a Boston minister had been clubbed to death, the Liuzzo murder was the apex of the Klan's campaign of terror, a two-year spree of violence that resulted in almost 70 bombings in Georgia and Alabama, 30 black churches burned in Mississippi, the castration of a black man in Birmingham, 10 racial killings in Alabama, plus the notorious murders of three civil rights workers in Mississippi and the shotgun slaying of a black army colonel near Athens, Ga.

While the nation could regret though tolerate Klan violence against poor, Southern blacks, the national outrage grew every time a middle-class, Northern white was killed. Moreover the occasional arrest of Klan members for nonracial crimes such as bank robberies crystallized a picture of the Klan as unprincipled thugs. Once again, it went into decline.

There are two ways to regard terrorist organizations such as the KKK. First, and most obvious, they can be seen as a mobilization against the democratic and humane values of the mainstream society, just as organized crime represents a mobilization against the values of law and order. Second, and perhaps more important, groups like the Klan can be seen as a warning of more widespread discontent and prejudice in the society at large, just as a festering wound on the skin's surface warns of a larger, unseen infection below.

What are the indications of infection today? From a membership of 1,500 in 1974, the Klan had enlarged to an estimated ten to twelve thousand members by 1981, during a period of economic troubles at home and threats of war abroad (Turner 1981:23). The most recent decades, moreover, have seen the Klan expand beyond the Old South into the North and the West. In 1980, Tom Metzger, head of the Ku Klux Klan of California, won his district's Democratic nomination for Congress though he failed in November's general election. In the mid-1970s, many felt we were at last beginning to emerge from the long tunnel of racist bigotry. It now seems possible that the "light at the end of the tunnel" may turn out to be only another burning cross.

PRACTICING SOCIOLOGY

In 1835, the French aristocrat, Alexis de Tocqueville, wrote the following about relations between blacks and whites—with special attention to the new United States of America.

> I do not think that the white and black races will ever be brought anywhere to live on a footing of equality.
> . . . it is possible to foresee that the freer whites in America are, the more they will seek to isolate themselves.

De Tocqueville further observed that as slavery receded, racial discrimination became stronger. Free blacks were often severely restricted before the Civil War in the northern states which had abolished slavery.

Write a paragraph in which you discuss the ways in which de Tocqueville's observations help explain "white flight" to the suburbs.

Source: Alexis de Tocqueville, *Democracy in America*, quoted in Reid Luhman and Stuart Gilman, *Race and Ethnic Relations* (Belmont, Calif.: Wadsworth, 1980).

10

Inequalities of Age and Sex

The preceding two chapters have dealt with inequalities in society. First, we looked at stratification systems, which are by definition structures of inequality. Second, we learned that racial and ethnic relations are primarily relationships of inequality, even in societies—like our own—that are ideologically committed to equality.

Ultimately, the structuring of societies requires differentiation, which tends to produce inequalities. Different groups in society are not only treated differently; they are treated better or worse than other groups. In this chapter, we'll see that the same process occurs with regard to age and sex differences as occurs for education, occupation, or race.

As we examine the inequalities of age and sex, we'll see that many of the stereotypes associated with prejudice and discrimination against blacks in America—particularly the view that blacks are irresponsible and undependable, irrational and emotional—are also applied to other "minority" groups: the young, the elderly, and women. In delving into the inequalities of age and sex, however, we are also going to see a greater complexity than was true for race and ethnicity. Particularly in the case of age, the very young and the very old are both the targets of abuse, while also the recipients of special benefits. A similar schizophrenia exists for women: degrading discrimination on the one hand and the assertion that women are actually held in a "favored" position on the other.

There is one way in which age, as a basis for inequality, is unique. Whereas each of us is dealt a gender, a race, and an ethnicity that we must live with through all our days, we are likely to experience stages of inequality in regard to age. If we live a full life, we get to be discriminated against, then to discriminate against others, and then to be discriminated against once more. Let's see how this operates.

Inequalities of Age

Systems of age stratification are based originally on movement through the biological life cycle. We progress from a childhood of physical weakness and lack of self-sufficiency, through strength and sufficiency, into an old age of reduced strength and lessened self-sufficiency. Individual variations notwithstanding, all of us can anticipate this cycle, the only escape a premature death.

Other physiological processes occur during the life cycle. Newborn infants are not capable of sexual reproduction, for example, nor do they have the mental capacity (let alone the learned, intellectual skills and knowledge) for a variety of tasks. Manual dexterity comes and goes with age, as does general physical agility. Certain physiological differences do exist in relation to age.

We find, then, that all societies have some system of **age grading:** the association of certain roles with certain ages. Mating and parenting, for example, are universally delayed until the physiological ability arrives. No society sends its newborns off to war. Age grading is univer-

sal and inevitable. As we shall see, however, the social agreements with regard to age far exceed the physiological constraints of organisms at different ages and vary from society to society.

Atchley and Seltzer (1976:1) sum up the social aspects of age grading as follows:

> In *age grading* age is used as a criterion governing the individual's access to groups, roles, aspects of culture (including norms, attitudes, values, beliefs, and skills), and social situations. Age grading defines what individuals are allowed to do and to be. The system of age grading is loosely based on a set of beliefs about the significance of age for social functioning. Both children and old people are barred from various opportunities because it is *believed* that they are not fully capable. It can be easily demonstrated that such beliefs mask large individual differences and produce individual injustices. Yet the system persists because it is useful.

In the first half of this chapter, we'll look at some of these differences, focusing on the special issues and problems of particular age groups from children to the elderly.

Children as Humans

Through most of human history, preadolescent children have been regarded as property, although usually regarded as the most prized possessions. They *belonged* to their parents and clearly lived under their parents' domination. The Bible and other ancient sources report instances of parents selling or giving away children. Even in more recent times children have been used as a commodity. Though some of the things done to children today—which we'll examine—may seem horrible to us, they are a mild reflection of the past. Marian Eskin (1980:2) reports:

> In ancient Greece, a child was the absolute property of the father, and Greek law stated that prop-

"You sure Walter Cronkite got started this way?"

erty was divided among the male children. Thus, many fathers raised the first son and exposed subsequent sons and daughters to the elements.

Under ancient Roman law, the father had power of life and death (patria potestas) over his children and could kill, mutilate, sell or offer his children for sacrifice.

More recently, "injustices" against young children have provoked high emotion and outrage. Much of the labor radicalism of the late Industrial Revolution was a response to the exploitation of child labor. Before the child-labor laws of 1833 in Britain, children of eight or nine sometimes worked twelve to fourteen hours a day in the factories. These children were especially susceptible to injury, and often were maimed for life.

During the past century and a half, then, the governments of industrial nations have become increasingly involved in the protection of young children. Today, in America, laws exist that are designed to protect children from the dangers of alcohol and tobacco, from ignorance (through compulsory schooling), from lecherous adults (statutory rape laws), and a variety of other dangers. Such laws have been largely supported by parents who sought societal assistance in protecting their young from the dangers lurking in the world outside the home. As we'll see in the Application and Analysis section, however, children sometimes suffer at the hands of their own parents.

Let's now consider the age group that has passed through puberty—people who are variously called "adolescents," "youth," "young folks," "teenagers," and less flattering names.

Youth: A Social Invention

Until quite recently, "youth" did not exist as a social category. Babies grew into young children, passed through puberty, married early, produced children, and assumed most other adult work and responsibilities. We in modern industrial societies, however, have extended what was once a very brief interlude into a lengthy period of time, stretching from the early teens to the early twenties. This invention of youth has formed a genuine new constituency of society.

The expansion of childhood past puberty is itself a new social experiment only a few hundred years old and largely untried outside of industrial societies. It involves the postponement of marriage and career choices while maintaining the power of adult family members over the "adolescent," who typically remains at home and attends school. These "teenagers" are certainly different from their prepubescent and infant siblings: nonetheless, they remain under parental authority and direction.

Particularly since World War II in the industrial Western world, this postponement of adulthood has created a new form of social identity. The two characteristics that define "youthfulness" among postpubescent persons between their late teens and their early twenties are autonomy and affluence. Typically such persons live on their own (or at home, but with considerable privacy and freedom of movement), attend school, have not yet seriously committed themselves to a work career (and may not work at all), and are not married or parenting children. In unprecedented numbers, connected to the baby boom produced by the World War II rush to marriage, young individuals with money to spend and the opportunity to create a lifestyle and identity separate from their parents began to develop distinctive patterns of dress, dance, musical interest, and drug use—a new subculture. Many young people also developed more liberal sociopolitical attitudes than their parents held and a generalized belief that being young involves a special point of view or identity through which world events may be interpreted.

In the mid-1960s in the United States, the process of creating a youth subculture became entangled with racial turmoil, decaying urban life, overcrowded and unresponsive universities, and, most important, a very unpopular war. These events "radicalized" many young persons, pushing subculture into counterculture, in apposition to the majority culture. Young people moved from the civil rights movement to the black power movement, from the Peace Corps to the antiwar movement, from university reform to taking over or dropping out, and from beer and cigarettes to beer and cigarettes plus pot and psychedelics.

In the 1970s and 1980s, counterculture again became subculture. In the face of the United States military defeat in Vietnam and a decade of economic stagnation (in which the United States was "defeated" by Third World oil interests), young people have reacted by turning inward and recreating a depoliticized and more conservative new consensus.

The Adult Years

There is no precise age separating "youth" from "adult," of course, though eighteen or twenty-one are traditional ages for assumimg various political and social rights. More appropriately, however, the dividing line is a social one, mostly related to the assumption of social rather than legal statuses. Completing school, getting married, beginning your life's work—these are the main milestones in the transition from youth to adult in our society. Of course, people do not necessarily do these three things simultaneously, and those living in a mixed status often experience the ambiguity of whether or not they are "grown up."

Once young people have completed their exit from the youth subculture, they are likely to find that their long-awaited assumption of full status and relative privileges is not without its burdens and stresses. Perhaps the biggest issue to be handled in this age category is the economic support of others. No one expects young children to pay their own way; youth—though they may have part-time jobs—are seldom self-sufficient; and, as we'll see, the elderly also are often financially dependent. All these others depend on the adult group. Baby booms and increased life expectancy both increase the burden to be borne by this nondependent group.

Many adults clearly feel this financial burden on a personal level. It shows up in such problems as anxiety over occupational success. Some of the stress takes its toll on the individual, and some might spill over into family life, as we'll see later in the case of child abuse.

The adult years also involve child rearing, and the pressure to succeed as a parent can be as great as that in the marketplace. Furthermore, the strains of parental roles can sometimes aggravate existing marital problems. The child conceived as a way of "saving a marriage" is often the straw that breaks the marriage's back.

Wilbur Bradbury (1975:67) has called these the "years of choice." After many years of being dictated to by parents and before the narrowing of choice forced by old age, the adult years are the time when alternatives appear to be at their maximum—the time to choose a mate, an occupation, a place to live, and so forth. The other side of this coin, however, is that these years can be seen as the "years of last chance." Will you pick the right spouse, the right job? Were you right in choosing to take a job instead of continuing in school?

Not without reason, the study of adult stress in modern life has received much attention in recent years. Numerous stressful events are commonplace: divorce, the death of a family member, illness, financial troubles, sexual incompatibility, and all the worries of the workplace. Indeed, even "happy" events can be stressful: marriage, the birth of a child, and promotions at work.

Overall, the young adult period can be a mixed experience in modern society. The benefits of freedom are linked to responsibility, and the pressures to succeed in the use of freedom and the exercise of responsibility are sources of great stress and anxiety. Let's look at the final stage in the life cycle.

Table 10-1

The Percentages of Populations 65 and Older in the Major Regions of the World, 1981

Region	Percent
World	6
Africa	3
Asia	4
North America	11
Latin America	4
Europe	13
U.S.S.R.	9
Oceania	8

Source: Population Reference Bureau, "1981 World Population Data Sheet," Washington, D. C.

Issues of the Elderly

All people, of course, can expect to grow old and die. Culture does not affect whether that will happen, but differences in social agreements do affect how it happens.

The impact of culture begins with how many people in a society live to what we consider to be an old age. Average life expectancies vary widely from society to society, as we saw in Chapter 8, and so varying percentages of elderly people occur from society to society and even from region to region of the globe (see Table 10–1).

The number of older Americans has been growing dramatically throughout this century. At the turn of the century, there were about 3 million Americans 65 or older. By 1940, the number had tripled to 9 million. In 1980, there were 25.5 million aged 65 or over (U.S. Bureau of Census 1981a:9).

One reason for the dramatic growth in this age group is improved medical care and hygiene. But two sociohistorical factors are of greatest importance (Bouvier 1976).

First, a disproportionately large number of children were born during the latter part of the nineteenth century and the first part of the twentieth, and the surviving members of that "baby boom" are now sixty or older. Second, many Europeans who came as children to the New World around the turn of the century have swelled the ranks of the elderly.

Looking ahead, the relatively low birth rates experienced in the 1920s and 1930s and the drastic reduction in immigration during the same period will produce a much reduced growth rate for the number of elderly during the 1990s and the early twenty-first century. Figure 10–1 presents the Census Bureau's depiction of America's elderly population of the past and their projection into the future.

Despite their enlarged numbers, or perhaps because of it, older Americans often face a number of problems. Let's look briefly at three of them: poverty, isolation, and the feeling of uselessness.

Poverty   Elderly Americans, especially when they live within the constraints of "fixed incomes" despite runaway inflation, face extreme poverty. A sizable portion of the pet food sold in America is consumed by elderly people who cannot afford anything better.

While poverty remains a severe problem for many elderly, conditions have improved substantially in recent years according to the poverty index established by the Social Security Administration. This index establishes income levels for farm and nonfarm families; families below those levels are considered impoverished. The figures are revised each year, to take changes in the cost of living into account. In 1980, for example, the poverty cutoff point for a nonfarm family of four was $8,414. While such standards are obviously somewhat arbitrary, they do provide the basis for comparisons over time.

In 1959, 35.2 percent of all persons 65 and older were below the poverty line established for that year. By 1970, this figure had been reduced to 24.5 percent, and in 1980 only 15.7 percent of the nation's elderly were below the poverty line. Elderly blacks fared much more poorly than the national average however. In

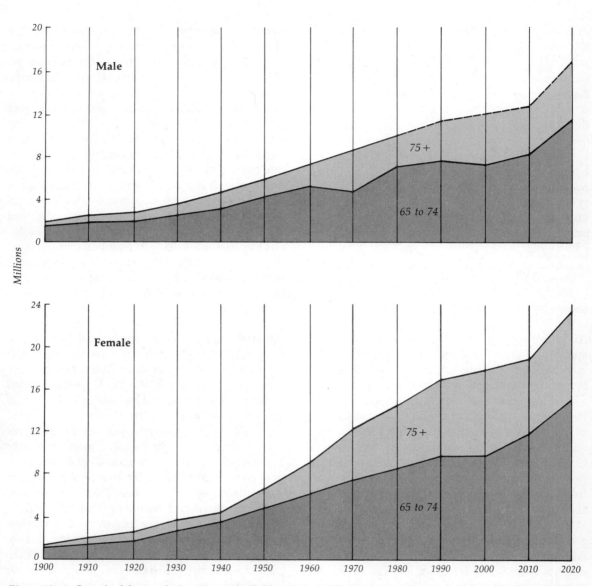

Figure 10–1 Growth of the population 65 years and older, 1900–2020. Source: Leon F. Bouvier, The Elderly Population: Its Relationship to Society, *The Center for Information on America, 1976, p. 3. Reprinted by permission.*

1959, nearly two-thirds were below the poverty line, and the percentage had only been reduced to 38.1 percent in 1980 (U.S. Bureau of Census 1981d:29).

James Schulz (1980:159) points out that women are particularly vulnerable to poverty in their old age—especially those who are separated, widowed, or divorced. Typically, these women have devoted their lives to the jobs of mother and homemaker. Upon the departure of their husbands, they have few opportunities to learn and begin new careers. All this is reflected in the Census Bureau data (1981d:33). In 1980, elderly women were nearly twice as likely to be below the poverty line as were elderly men: 19.0 versus 10.9 percent. Hardest hit in this regard were elderly black women: 42.6 percent were below the poverty line in 1980.

Despite these statistics, things have improved. However, the figures presented above deal only with money income. Not included are such programs as food stamps, Medicaid, and public housing. Eli Ginzberg (1982:53) assesses the impact of all such programs:

> When all income from all sources, including Social Security and means-tested programs [based on need], cash as well as in-kind, are taken into account, no more than 3 or 4 percent of the elderly fall below the poverty line. About a third of the elderly, however, are not much above that line. Of course, Social Security benefits were never meant to be the sole source of income for older people. Most aged families with a satisfactory standard of living receive less than half of their income from OASDI [Old Age Survivors and Disability Insurance] benefits; they rely also, in different proportions at different income levels, on continued earnings by family members, on savings and on private pensions.

Figure 10–2 shows how elderly Americans at different income levels put together the money to live.

The financial problems of the elderly are compounded by a number of factors. Old people in general have more medical problems than do the young, requiring greater financial expenditures in that regard. Poor health, moreover, makes it less likely they will be able to work. They may also need assistance with transportation, housework, personal care, and so forth.

One key difficulty that the elderly face in society is their lack of power. Workers can threaten to strike, and ethnic and racial minorities can threaten demonstrations with an overt or covert threat of violence, but what can the elderly do? For years, the elderly relied on the guilt of decision makers, their goodwill, or their realization that they will soon be old themselves. As we shall see shortly, however, the elderly have become increasingly militant and effective.

Isolation To an unprecedented extent in modern America, we have set older people aside from the mainstream of social life. Americans once grew old within the families they created and raised, but increasing numbers now live out their "sunset" years in communities bearing similar names, though most still live on their own (Atchley 1977:192).

Retirement communities have both positive and negative aspects. On the plus side of the ledger, those who need medical care and similar assistance usually find it near at hand. In addition, recreational and other activities especially appropriate for older people are provided, and the residents live with others having similar interests.

On the negative side, many people do not want to spend all their time with others just like themselves, especially when the sameness is organized around dependency and growing inability. Many would prefer to spend time with their own families, watching grandchildren grow up, children prosper, and so forth. Ultimately, many of the elderly feel that the move to a retirement community or nursing home is the preliminary step toward death.

The term **societal disengagement** refers to the steady decrease in the number of statuses occupied by the elderly as they grow old and a corresponding decline in social interactions. Atchley (1977:232) indicates that research into this aspect of aging shows a complex interweaving of desire for disengagement and an established social pattern in the society—whether desired or not. This personal withdrawal, combined with fewer demands on the elderly person from society and the family, leads to a feeling of uselessness.

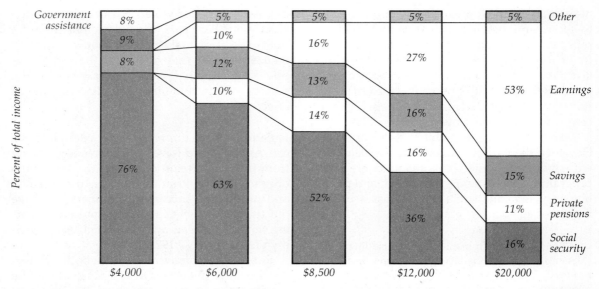

Figure 10–2 The components of different levels of income for elderly Americans, shown for five income levels in 1978. Government assistance for the $4,000 category is means-tested (based on need). Source: Eli Ginsberg, "The Social Security System," Scientific American, January 1982, p. 53.

Sense of Uselessness   Related to the problems of finance and isolation is the general sense of uselessness that can accompany aging. For those who have worked at careers, it is associated with retirement. For those who have organized their lives around child rearing, a sense of uselessness often arises when the children leave home.

Atchley (1977:153–55) describes several stages of retirement. Typically, there is a "honeymoon" period in which retirement is seen in exclusively positive terms: as a chance to relax and to do those things the retired person never had time for in earlier years. Atchley says that a disenchantment stage follows, in which the retiree realizes that his or her life must be reoriented around retirement. Disenchantment comes when the elderly person recognizes that financial and other limitations must be accommodated. A reorientation phase ("taking stock") and then a phase of stability follow, in which the retired person settles into the new patterns of life he or she has picked.

Atchley points to great variation in the passage through these stages. Some people skip stages, moving directly from the honeymoon stage into a reoriented and stable lifestyle. Others must suffer through a painful and lengthy period of disenchantment.

As with poverty and isolation, a root cause of the sense of uselessness many elderly people feel is the fact that our society does not provide enough jobs for them. Especially if they have been forced to retire from careers, are invalided, or if their children spurn any "interference" in child rearing and home management, the elderly can get the message loud and clear that their future existence will be tolerated but that it is unnecessary to others in society.

This predicament is, of course, somewhat ironic given the number of ways in which the society doesn't run smoothly and the number of jobs that aren't getting done. In recent years, there have been increased efforts to match those jobs with older people who are able to handle

Often old age means isolation and loneliness. Whereas some societies honor their elderly, our society tends to regard them as useless and a bother.

them (often without pay). Thus, for example, there are programs in which older people work as surrogate parents and grandparents for children who lack families of their own. Hundreds of thousands of older Americans are active in such organizations as the Retired Senior Volunteer Program (RSVP), the Service Corps of Retired Executives (SCORE), and the Foster Grandparent Program.

Politics and the Elderly   The vocalness of some groups of the elderly and the expectation that the proportion of Americans over 65 will climb

from 10 to perhaps 20 percent in the next few decades have led many commentators to speculate on the political influence of this age group. Let's look at the impact people over 65 now have on political life and then consider how this age group's political influence is likely to change in the future.

In terms of the less strenuous forms of political participation, at least, people over 65 in the United States are at least as active as the rest of the population. According to research cited by Atchley (1977), the elderly are more likely than younger people to follow news about political

Maggie Kuhn, leader of the Grey Panthers nationwide, represents one of the American minorities that has recently discovered the power that lies within organizations.

campaigns and public affairs; they are also more likely to identify with a political party and be active in its behalf. Americans in their fifties are the age group most likely to go to the polls, but the voter participation of those over sixty is virtually as high. Elderly people are often portrayed as highly conservative, but in recent years those passing middle age have tended to be more liberal than their forerunners, although still not as liberal as people in younger age groups.

The facts cited so far suggest that the elderly are likely to constitute a growing, active, and increasingly liberal element in society. But such a conclusion would be premature. First, these characteristics of people now over 65 may reflect something about them as a group that lived through a certain segment of history (a depression and two world wars) rather than something about normal maturational effects on behavior. Second, even if voting participation among the elderly remains high, their political power will not necessarily increase with their numbers: politicians are most responsive to interest groups that deliver votes as a bloc at election time, and the elderly do not often vote as a bloc.

Some sociologists argue that a subculture of the elderly *is* developing, which could mean increased bloc voting and thus more political power in the future. But other investigators have challenged this view. In an interview study of noninstitutionalized persons over age sixty in Madison, Wisconsin, Russell Ward (1977) found little evidence of aging group consciousness, for instance. And Simone de Beauvoir earlier (1972) suggested that the aged are unlikely to ever wield much power because they perform no critical economic function and they are dispersed throughout the general population. In addition, Atchley (1977) notes that the elderly are the age group least likely to abandon their traditional party affiliation for the sake of a special issue, that their voting power is fragmented among Democrats and Republicans, and—perhaps most importantly—that solidarity on the basis of old age has never proved as powerful as loyalties based on other political or economic interests.

In Atchley's view, the elderly haven't been particularly effective as a pressure group themselves; but, through organizations like the Gray Panthers, they have made enough noise and they constitute a sufficiently large portion of voters to interest groups like labor unions and political parties in pushing legislation advantageous to the elderly. More recent evidence of the growing power of the elderly is to be found in the early budget cutting of the Reagan administration. With virtually all nondefense programs—from school lunches to welfare to the arts—being cut, programs for the elderly survived relatively well.

Despite the progress that has been made, the problems of the elderly have hardly been resolved in general. Ultimately, all of us—regardless of age—will need to take on these problems together.

Sexual Inequalities

We turn our attention now to a "minority" group that numbers a slight majority of the American population: women. From the sociological point of view, women are clearly a minority group. Throughout our national history, women have been denied equal participation in countless sectors of society. Black Americans were denied the right to vote until 1870, but it took women another half-century to gain that right.

The status of women in America has, in large part, grown out of our agreements regarding the family, which we will discuss in Chapter 16. A persistent American agreement has been summarized in the cliche: "A woman's place is in the home." More specifically, the woman's "place" has been in the kitchen—with periodic trips to the children's rooms, the laundry room, and the master's bed. (Just for fun, see how well you do on the quiz in the box "A True-False Quiz on the Sexes.")

Many stereotypes have effectively kept the American woman in her "place." Women have frequently been told they were best equipped for raising children, although they have been depicted as emotional, flighty, weak, irrational, and impractical—characteristics certainly detrimental in those chosen to socialize society's new generations. Indeed, "paternalism" has been one of the patterns maintaining the second-class status of women in American society.

One powerful source of stereotypes has been found in preschool children's books. A study of Caldecott Medal-winning picture books between 1967 and 1971 (Weitzman et al. 1972) found that female characters—human and nonhuman—were greatly outnumbered by male characters. Richard Kolbe and Joseph LaVoie (1981:369) summarize the Weitzman findings:

They reported that few females were present in book titles, major roles, pictures, or stories—that is, most of the books concerned males. When present, female characters were inconspicuous or placed in insignificant roles consisting of activities directed toward serving and satisfying the needs of males.

In the 1967–1971 prizewinning books, there were eleven human male characters for every female. When nonhuman characters were analyzed, the ratio was 95 to 1, males over females. Even people tempted to joke about quota systems for picture-book characters cannot fail to see the discrimination present in data like these.

The situation has improved. When Kolbe and LaVoie (1981) examined the 1972–1979 Caldecott winners, they found radically different sex ratios in the characters. Males outnumbered females among human characters by only 1.8 to 1. Among nonhumans, the ratio was 2.66 to 1. Now preschoolers will know that females are important enough to appear in books. How the females appear, however, is still a problem.

Weitzman reported that traditional sex roles were portrayed in all eighteen of the 1967–1971 books; Kolbe and LaVoie found the same true in seventeen of the nineteen books in the 1972–1979 period. As one indicator, none of the books in either period portrayed a woman working outside the home (Kolbe and LaVoie 1981:371).

You should not think, however, that American men are a clique of evildoers who have simply bedazzled or subjugated women. What I've been describing represents generally shared agreements, and many women—past and present—have accepted those agreements, often willingly. Men and women alike have been socialized into a general acceptance of the roles appropriate to their own sex and the roles appropriate to the other one, as we saw in Chapter 5.

But in recent years both men and women have begun to recognize such agreements as agreements only. Progress toward equality seems slow and painful, but both men and women

A TRUE-FALSE QUIZ ON THE SEXES

Sometimes, in their reaction to discrimination against women, people suggest that there are few if any differences between the sexes. As the quiz below will show you, there are, in fact, numerous physiological differences.

How, based on the physiological differences described, do you account for the fact that American physicians are mostly men, while nurses are mostly women? That taxi drivers and barbers are mostly men? That secretaries and domestics are mostly women?

The answers to these questions lie, of course, outside the realm of biology. They are a function of the social agreements we create for the structuring and governance of social life.

On the average:	True	False	On the average:	True	False
1. Men's brains are heavier.	T		13. Girls are more likely to obey their parents.	T	
2. Men's hearts are heavier.	T←	F	14. Boys worry more about what their friends think.	T←	F
3. Men have more blood cells.	T←	F	15. Girls have less self-confidence.		F
4. Women's bodies contain more water.	T	F	16. Boys are more physically aggressive.	T	
5. Men's bodies contain more fat.		F	17. Girls are more sociable.	T→	F
6. Men breathe faster.		F	18. Boys are better at mathematics.	T	
7. Women live longer.	T→	F	19. Girls have greater verbal ability.	T	
8. Women use more energy to walk.	T		20. Baby girls smile more than baby boys.	T	
9. Men's muscles are heavier.	T				
10. Men's bones are heavier.		F			
11. Women are more inclined to be knock-kneed.	T←	F			
12. Women get drunk more quickly.	T				

1 T, 2 T, 3 T, 4 F, 5 F, 6 F, 7 T, 8 F, 9 T, 10 F, 11 T, 12 T, 13 T, 14 T, 15 F, 16 T, 17 F, 18 T, 19 T, 20 T.

Source: Human Behavior—Men and Women by Peter Swerdloff and the Editors of Time-Life Books, © Time Inc.

are working to change the agreements. We'll look primarily at the status of women in relation to occupational roles in American society. One main goal of the American women's movement has been equal opportunity in the economy.

Participation in the Labor Force

Women in America have never been kept totally at home. Some have always found employment in the labor force. During wars, in fact, women

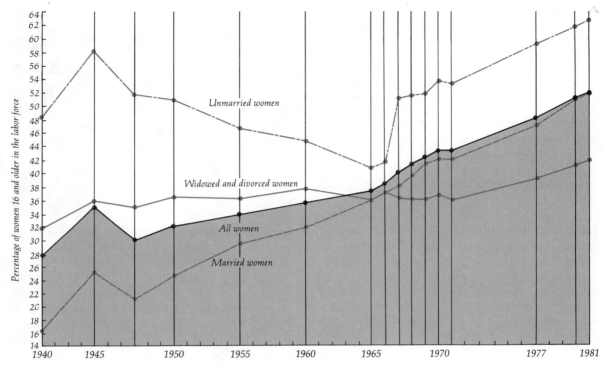

Figure 10–3 Women in the American labor force: 1940–1981. Source: U.S. Bureau of Census, Statistical Abstract of the United States, *1978, p. 404. U.S. Bureau of Labor Statistics, 1981a, "Half the Nation's Children Have Working Mothers," USDL 81–522, November 1981, p. 5.*

have been encouraged to take over vital production jobs and fill other positions outside the home.

In recent years, even in peacetime, more women than ever before have sought and found employment. Figure 10–3 shows the percentages of all women sixteen years of age and older who were in the civilian labor force during selected years between 1940 and 1981.

Several patterns in the figure are worth noting. First, we see a general increase in women in the labor force overall: from 27.4 percent in 1940 to 52.0 percent in 1981. Notice that the participation rates of unmarried, widowed, and divorced women—while fluctuating over the three decades—are about the same in 1981 as

they were in 1940. The participation of married women, however, has increased dramatically: from 16.7 to 51.7 percent.

This pattern suggests a growing feeling in America that a woman can hold a job and fill family roles at the same time. (It has always been agreed that men could do that.) Part of the evidence of the shift is seen in behavior. As of March 1981, more than half of the nation's children under eighteen had mothers in the labor force, according to the Labor Department (1981:1). This represented an increase of more than half a million working mothers from the year before, most of the increase accounted for by mothers of preschool-age children.

Another indication of the shifting patterns

regarding women working is seen in public-opinion-poll results. In 1938, the Gallup Poll asked a national sample of Americans, "Do you approve of a married woman earning money in business or industry if she has a husband capable of supporting her?" One person in five (21 percent) approved. Seven years later, after women had gone to work in full force to support the war effort, the percentage approval of working wives was still only 24 percent. By 1970, however, 60 percent approved, and this increased further, to 72 percent, by 1978 (*Public Opinion* 1980:33).

It is possible to overestimate the shift that has taken place, however. In 1978, 47 percent of American adults agreed that "While there are some exceptions, the statement that 'women's place is in the home' still makes sense." Only 30 percent disagreed, and 21 percent reported having no strong opinion. A majority, 57 percent, believed that "A woman with young children shouldn't work outside the home unless financially necessary." Another 20 percent said they partially believed that (*Public Opinion* 1978:33).

Occupation Types

Participation in the labor force is only part of the story, however. *How* women participate is another matter. The American occupational structure has always been quite closely related to sex. A number of agreements have defined those jobs more "appropriate" for men and those more "appropriate" for women.

As a general pattern, women have been nurses, not physicians; secretaries, not executives; teachers, not principals; flight attendants, not pilots; clerks, not managers; cooks, not chefs. As these examples illustrate, women have typically filled positions closely associated with, but of lower status than, those of men. Even when men and women served in exactly the same roles, they have often been labeled

On the whole, women occupy lower status occupations than men. Even when they do the same job as men, however, they often earn less money.

differently: a woman can be a poetess but not a poet, an actress but not an actor. Other occupational labels have seemed to exclude women altogether: fire*man*, police*man*, mail*man*, chair*man*.

The reification of the agreements linking sex to occupations has become especially evident as more and more people have started to violate them by "crossing over." Male nurses, female jockeys, male typists, and female police officers have seemed "unnatural" to many. When Burt Reynolds posed nude for a centerfold in *Cosmopolitan* magazine, many of those who for years had enjoyed *Playboy* and *Penthouse*, magazines that feature nude women, were horrified.

Many of the agreements Americans share with regard to sex-linked occupations are not shared elsewhere. In every known society, there has been a division of labor by sex, but the distinct productive roles filled by each sex have differed widely from culture to culture. According to a famous survey of over two hundred cultures conducted by anthropologist George Murdock (1935), tasks involving child care, food preparation, and clothing manufacture are usually performed by women, whereas tasks such as hunting, woodworking, and mining are generally performed by men in most cultures. But erecting houses, trading, clearing land for agriculture, herding, and building boats are done predominantly by women in some societies. In fact, except for metalworking, every economic activity done by men in one society is done by women in at least one other society.

Although men's work, whatever it might be, is valued more highly than women's in the world's cultures, the general social status of women, according to Jean Lipman-Blumen and Ann Tickameyer (1975), has tended to vary with their economic power and role in economic production. In Europe and America, for instance, industrialization often meant a decline in the respected work roles women performed, and consequently a decline in their status. In the preindustrial period, men were dependent on women for their skilled work in making clothing, foodstuffs, and other household goods; but with the advent of factory production this was no longer the case.

Reduction in the respected work roles of women has also occurred in cultures of the Third World because of Western industrialization, but in somewhat different ways, as Ester Boserup (1970) has pointed out in her analysis of the effects of industrial development on the productive roles of women. In many traditional tribes of Africa, for example, Boserup notes that women not only prepared the food but were also its primary producers; they were the culture's farmers. The men, on the other hand, spent their time hunting, making war, and clearing the land. Although women and men did not have equal status in these tribes, women were valued both as mothers and workers.

When the Europeans took power, they curtailed the war-making of the men; and, as the need for clearing the land and hunting diminished, the men were left with little to do. The Europeans capitalized on the situation and enticed or forced the men to produce cash crops for export, to build roads, or to work as miners.

Since the men received wages for their work, they gained economic power and status relative to women, who continued to produce without cash payment for the family and the village.

The distance in status and social power between men and women widened even more, according to Boserup, because of European prejudices about the place of women and the superiority of men, particularly in farming. The Europeans taught only the men how to use new farming technology and encouraged only their education. The Europeans also broke village land into private plots and recognized the land rights only of the men. Similarly, the Europeans initially encouraged the men, not the women, to work in modern industry and trade, further widening the status gap between men and women.

Women have not been uniformly denied occupational access in industrial societies however. Sullerot (1974) reports that 38 percent of the lawyers in the U.S.S.R. were women at a time when only 3 percent were women in America. Similarly, women constituted less than 1 percent of American engineers, but 37 percent of the engineers in the U.S.S.R. Women made up 6 percent of the medical profession in America, but an astounding 76 percent in the U.S.S.R. While these occupations have been opening up increasingly to American women, their proportions still lag well behind those of Soviet women.

Income

When women do work, they are often paid less than men, as Figure 10–4 shows. Between 1939 and 1980, women in the American labor force earned only a little over half as much as men. And although the average incomes of both men and women have increased (as has the cost of living) during the past two decades, women's *relative* income status has not improved. In 1939, the average full-time, year-round working

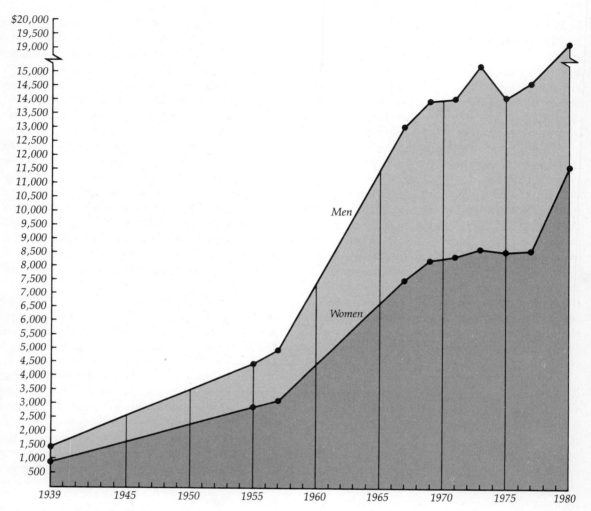

Figure 10–4 Median incomes of men and women working full-time, year-round: Selected years from 1939 to 1980. The percentages shown along the women's income line show the ratio of women's income to men's. Data for the years 1939, 1955, and 1957 include white workers only. Sources: U.S. Bureau of Census, Historical Statistics of the United States, *Washington, D.C., 1960, p. 168. U.S. Bureau of Census,* A Statistical Portrait of Women in the United States: 1978. *Washington, D.C., 1980 (P–23, No. 100), p. 73. U.S. Bureau of Census, "Money Income and Poverty Status of Families and Persons in the United States: 1980," Washington, D.C., 1981 (P–60, No. 127), pp. 19–20.*

woman earned 61 percent as much as the average man. In 1980, she still earned 61 percent as much.

Part of the explanation for the women's generally lower incomes lies in their general concentration in lower-paying occupations, as I mentioned earlier. Nurses earn less than physicians; secretaries earn less than executives. But this explanation is insufficient because women earn less money on the average, even when they are employed in the same occupations as men. Table 10–3 presents a more gen-

Table 10-3

Median Incomes of Men and Women in Specific Occupational Categories, 1977

Occupational category	Median income		Ratio of women's to men's earnings	Women as a percentage of the category
	Women	Men		
Whites				
Professional and technical workers	$11,947	$17,745	.67	35
Managers and administrators (nonfarm)	10,150	19,138	.53	19
Sales workers	6,814	16,049	.42	25
Clerical workers	8,410	14,436	.58	76
Craft and kindred workers	8,903	15,031	.59	4
Operatives, except transport	7,358	12,704	.58	35
Laborers, except farm	7,426	11,663	.64	8
Service workers except private household	6,248	10,955	.57	44
Blacks				
Professional and technical workers	$12,212	$14,861	.82	63
Managers and administrators (nonfarm)	12,225	15,024	.81	31
Sales workers	*	*	*	*
Clerical workers	8,474	11,208	.76	75
Craft and kindred workers	*	11,252	*	*
Operatives, except transport	6,507	11,038	.59	40
Laborers, except farm	*	7,987	*	*
Service workers except private household	6,095	8,072	.76	52

Note: *too few cases, not calculated.
Source: Anne McDougall Young, "Median Earnings in 1977 Reported for Year-Round Full-Time Workers," *Monthly Labor Review,* June 1979, p. 38.

eral comparison of the incomes earned by men and women in several occupational categories.

As the table indicates, women earn less than men—white and black both—in every occupational category. Nor does it matter if the comparison is made within a "man's occupation" or a "woman's occupation." For example, women only represent 4 percent of the crafts category among whites and only earn 59 percent as much money as men. Among clerical workers, however, white women are 76 percent of the category, yet they still earn only 58 percent as much as men.

Researchers at the University of Michigan (Levitin, Quinn, and Staines 1970) undertook a national survey on occupation and employment to examine in detail the charge that women are discriminated against in income. They began their analysis of the data by selecting half the men surveyed and by studying carefully the relative importance of different factors in determining their incomes. They considered the type of occupation, years of experience in it, education and special training completed, and many other relevant factors. They were able to construct out of those factors a complex equation that they felt would predict the income a given person might expect to receive.

When the researchers applied the equation to the qualifications of the men not used in the construction of the equation, their income estimates were off by only about $30 a year (thus reassuring them that they had discovered the determinants of different income levels). When the same equation was applied to the qualifications of the women surveyed, however, the researchers found that those women actually earned over $3,000.00 *a year less* than their qualifications predicted!

The Equal Rights Amendment

In response to the persistent deprivation of women in the economy and other sectors of society, a Twenty-seventh Amendment to the U.S. Constitution was proposed. This Equal Rights Amendment was passed by the United States House of Representatives in 1971 and by the United States Senate in 1972. To become law, the amendment required ratification by thirty-eight of the individual states. Within twenty minutes of the Senate action, Hawaii became the first state to ratify the ERA. As the 1979 deadline for ratification approached, however, only thirty-five states had acted favorably. On March 22, 1979, Congress extended the deadline for ratification by thirty-eight states until June 30, 1982.

The amendment reads:

> Equality of rights under the law shall not be denied or abridged by the United States or by any state on account of sex.

For the supporters of the amendment, nothing could have been clearer or more obvious than the legitimacy of the measure. Those opposed expressed a variety of concerns: some said they feared it would spell the end of the family, others said it would promote homosexuality, and so forth.

Though support rose and fell somewhat over the course of the ERA debate, the majority of the general public favored passage. In 1981, for example, 57 percent of a national sample of Americans favored passage, 33 percent opposed it, and 10 percent didn't express an opinion. The issue was largely a partisan one. Democrats among the sample were more likely (62 percent) than Republicans (48 percent) to support the amendment. The partisan factor was even clearer when pollsters surveyed the members of the Republican and Democratic National Committees: 92 percent of the Democratic National Committee favored passage of ERA, contrasted to 29 percent of the Republican National Committee (*Public Opinion* 1981a:29).

On June 30, 1982, the Equal Rights Amendment died. Two centuries after declaring that "all men are created equal," the United States left the status of women officially ambiguous. In July 1982, the Equal Rights Amendment was reintroduced in the United States Congress, and the struggle for passage resumed.

Liberating Both Men and Women

In the preceding sections, we have focused primarily on the economic inequalities separating men and women in America for two reasons: economic discrepancies are easily measured and the women's movement has often focused attention on economic issues. At the same time, our discussion is incomplete if we look only at economics.

Betty Friedan, often called the "mother" of the women's movement, has drawn attention to the economic focus of the movement in *The Second Stage* (1981). From the early 1970s on, the women's movement has largely focused on getting women into male-dominated profes-

The same agreements that have denied women access to the world of work . . .

. . . have denied men access to certain moving relationships.

sions. New magazines such as *Ms.* and *Working Woman* provided women with the information they needed to become business executives, for example, and the older women's magazines such as *Cosmopolitan* and *Vogue* did the same. This orientation was best illustrated in *Ms.*-founder Gloria Steinem's comment to students at Yale: "We have become the men we wanted to marry" (quoted in Lamb 1981:18).

Without denying that women should have access to male-dominated professions, Friedan feels that the "second stage" of the women's movement must involve changes in men as well. Men must be willing and able to participate more fully in family life, for example. During the first stage of the movement, this mostly took the form of husbands' concessions: agreeing to be responsible for a few family chores. ("OK, I'll clean the toilets and make Sunday breakfast.")

True equality will require a true partnership in the family, in work—in life.

In concluding this discussion of sexual inequality, it's worth observing that the same sets of agreements that have kept women in their "place" have also kept men in their "place." The man's "place" has generally seemed better than the woman's, but neither has been wholly satisfying. (The box entitled "Androgyny" describes one attempt to overthrow the traditional sex-role agreements.)

The same agreement that has labeled women "overemotional" has prevented men from learning to express *their* emotions. We have a comic expression that we "hate to see a grown man cry." In practice, "hating to see a grown man cry" is a serious agreement among Americans, even when men have good reasons to cry. The same agreement that labels women

ANDROGYNY

The term "androgynous" means the combining of male and female in one being. For years, this term was used primarily in reference to *herma-phrodites*, people who possessed both male and female genitals.

During the course of the movement for women's liberation, however, it has been more widely recognized that all individuals have feelings and emotions traditionally associated with one or the other gender. Sex-typing in society, however, has forced individuals to play down characteristics traditionally associated with the opposite sex. Thus, American boys are taught to give up sensitivity and compassion, for example, and girls are taught it's "unladylike" to be tough and aggressive.

The androgyny movement urges both men and women to develop and express their full range of feelings, emotions, and behavior. Here's an official statement from The Androgyny Center in San Diego:

Consciousness of our own androgyny can lead to a new sense of personal unity within the larger universe. It is no accident that men and women today are expressing previously undeveloped sides of their natures and taking roles generally assigned to the opposite sex. We no longer need to think of ourselves as exclusively feminine or exclusively masculine, but rather as whole beings in whom the opposite qualities are ever present.

There are many facets to the androgyny movement at this time. It touches family relations, dress styles, and occupations. For some, left/right brain psychology is the key; for others, the Eastern notions of *yin* and *yang;* for still others, homosexuality and bisexuality are central.

Across all these variations, however, the movement challenges the traditional notion that male and female are separate and distinct, as well as the notion that male is better.

Source: The Androgyny Newsletter, June/July 1980.

"weak" and "soft" requires that men of all ages maintain a strong and tough exterior, even when they don't feel strong and tough.

In reifying our agreements about the differences separating men and women, we have hindered our realization of ourselves as *people*. The liberation of women will inevitably liberate men in the bargain.

Summary

In this chapter, we have examined two forms of stratification in society: age and sex. Regarding age as the basis for minority-group status is unusual, because (1) most age groups can be seen as minority groups and (2) all of us pass through each of those stages. Thus, each of us will have the experience of minority-group membership—in several ways—yet we maintain the system of prejudices and discrimination.

"Age grading" is the process of associating specific jobs and statuses in a society with specific ages. Some degree of age grading seems inevitable and universal. For example, mating and parenting are restricted at least to the ages of biological potential. Wars are fought by the young, for the most part. Although some age grading makes sense, our agreements regarding the status and experiences of various age categories go well beyond what's essential.

Young children are a minority in many ways. For much of human history, they have been regarded primarily as the property of their parents. Despite a more "enlightened" view of children today, they have little power, and do not enjoy the political protections given adults. The plight of young children appears in the form of child abuse, since we have strong agreements granting authority over children to the parents who may originate the abuse. It is a dilemma as yet unresolved.

Adolescence or youth represents a special minority group created by social agreements. Throughout most of human history and in most less-developed societies today, people move more directly from childhood to adulthood. In industrial society, however, we have extended the period of dependence on parents beyond puberty, keeping young people in school longer. More recently we have provided them with some financial independence, so that we have seen the emergence of a youth subculture independent of but having influence on the mainstream culture.

Although young to middle-age adults represent the "majority" in a modern society, they also have pressing problems. In particular, stress and strain emerges from bearing the economic burden for dependent younger people and older people. The picking of the "right" career and the "right" marriage partner have become critical decisions, producing strain and uncertainty.

Finally, we looked at the problems of the elderly in modern society. Medical science has made it possible for us to live longer, but our agreements have not necessarily made the added years satisfying and nurturing. The ever-growing elderly population faces problems of poverty, isolation, and the sense of uselessness. In large part, these problems reflect the pattern of growing old outside the home of one's children. In contrast to earlier years in America and to contemporary arrangements in other societies, our old people are expected to live on their own—either with a spouse or, if widowed, alone—or in an institutional setting if required for medical or other reasons.

There is a somewhat different irony in regarding women as a minority group in America: they constitute more than half the population. This, however, merely illustrates the point that minority status is not a matter of number, but of access to power, scarce goods, and other sought-after things. In this light, women clearly have been and continue to be second-class citizens.

Traditionally, women have participated far less than men in the labor force, focusing their activities rather on family life. When they have participated in the labor force, they have generally held less prestigious positions than men—nurse rather than physician, teacher rather than principal, and so on—and even when they have held the same job as a man, they have received a substantially lower salary. On the average, women earn half as much as men in the labor force.

Equity for women has been a long time in coming and it is not here yet. We have seen some of the progress that has been made, some of the energy that has been put into the movement for liberation, and yet we have also seen the persistent frustrations faced by women. Their standing vis-à-vis men in the labor force has not improved. The Equal Rights Amendment—granting constitutional equality of men and women—did not become law and had to be reintroduced in Congress.

Ultimately, the liberation of women from their disadvantaged status will carry a liberation of men also. Indeed, a similar comment can be made of all our stratification systems, whether of race, religion, national origin, or age. To the extent that we limit one person's potential through the structures of society, we limit all. When one of us is forced to the back of the bus, all of us are sent there. Only a full understanding of how inequality is structured now, however, can offer the possibility of improving the quality of all our lives in the future.

Important Terms

age grading
societal disengagement

the Equal Rights Amendment
androgyny

Suggested Readings

Aries, Philippe
1965   *Centuries of Childhood*. New York: Vintage.
Discusses the evolution of "childhood" through time as an age category to Western civilization.

Atchley, Robert C.
1980   *The Social Forces in Later Life*. Belmont, Calif.: Wadsworth.
A solid textbook on social gerontology. Atchley examines all aspects of this biological/social process. He lays out in understandable fashion the biological foundations of aging, and he shows the variety of social agreements we have woven around that foundation.

Friedan, Betty
1974   *The Feminine Mystique, Second Edition*. New York: Norton.
The book that many claim started the current women's movement by drawing attention to the inequality of women.

Howe, Louise
1977   *Pink Collar Workers*. New York: Putnam.
Argues that despite changes in jobs, some work remains female-dominated with low wages and lack of security.

Kübler-Ross, Elizabeth
1969   *On Death and Dying*. New York: Macmillan.
Outlines her five famous "stages of dying," and discusses coping with dying for patients and relatives.

Mead, Margaret
1963   *Sex and Temperament in Three Primitive Societies*. New York: Morrow.
Anthropological view of three cultures and their different ways of carrying out gender roles.

Nielsen, Joyce McCarl
1978   *Sex in Society*. Belmont, Calif.: Wadsworth.
Subtitled "Perspectives on Stratification," this small book ranges very broadly across the structuring of inequality by sex both historically and cross-culturally. Nielsen begins with the anthropological data regarding the development of sex roles across time, then examines the various biological, psychological, and sociological explanations for sex roles, and concludes with some ideas about future developments.

Richardson, Laurel Walum
1981   *The Dynamics of Sex and Gender: A Sociological Perspective, Second Edition*. Boston: Houghton Mifflin.
Analysis of the role of women in society and its institutions with research studies on many aspects of women's lives.

Riley, Matilda
1979   *Aging From Birth to Death*. Boulder, CO: Westview Press.
Discusses the life cycle of aging process from a sociological perspective.

Rogers, Dorothy
1979   *The Adult Years: An Introduction to Aging*. Englewood Cliffs, NJ: Prentice-Hall.
Uses a developmental framework to discuss early, middle, and later adult years and aspects of life which are important at each.

Schulz, James H.
1980   *The Economics of Aging*. Belmont, Calif.: Wadsworth.
An excellent and easily readable sourcebook on what the title describes: the economic aspects of growing old. Schulz presents the empirical data on the financial status of the aging, and looks at pension programs, retirement systems, and other aspects of the nuts and bolts of the matter.

Sheehy, Gail
1976   *Passages: Predictable Crises of Adult Life*. New York: Dutton.
Covers the often neglected period in the age cycle of young adulthood to middle years.

Tavis, Carol, and Carole Offir
1977   *The Longest War: Sex Differences in Perspective*. New York: Harcourt Brace Jovanovich.
Theory and research in psychology and sociology on the status of women in society today.

Earlier in this chapter, I mentioned parental abuse of children in passing. In this essay, I want to examine the issue in greater detail.

While contemporary Americans have very strong feelings about the well-being of children, this concern has not always existed everywhere in the world. Marian Eskin (1980:2,3) offers these historical contrasts:

In China, Peru, Mexico, and India, children were cast into rivers in a ritualistic effort to insure a good harvest and good fortune. To ensure durability of buildings in India, China, Germany, and Canaan, children were buried alive under foundations of buildings and dikes. Greeks, Romans, Chinese, and Indians killed weak, deformed, retarded children and twins based on the superstitious notion that they were evil and carried bad luck and in belief of survival of the fittest. . . .

Mutilation of children was common in many cultures for religious, medical, cosmetic or economic reasons. Castration was an acceptable form of punishment and an economic necessity to increase the eunuch's appeal as beggar, freak performer, or royal aide. Foot-binding was common in China for cosmetic reasons, and in Africa, the bindings of lips, arms, and legs is currently fashionable. Cranial deformation was practiced in the Crimea, Greece, and among American Flathead Indians, and is still currently practiced by Solomon Islanders. Gouged eyes, deformed feet, and amputated or twisted limbs were inflicted so as to evoke pity on children, thereby making them good beggars.

Children had few if any rights in colonial America. The phrase "spare the rod and spoil the child" was a justification for stern punishments, including whipping and flogging. In colonial Massachusetts and Connecticut, disobeying one's parents was punishable by death. As Eskin (1980:4) elaborates:

The American colonist's child care practices were a reflection of the Elizabethan Poor Law of 1601 which recognized poverty as a sin; thus, poor children were either placed in institutions or sold as indentured servants. The colonists were also influenced by English common law which granted a father the absolute right to custody and control of the child; children were deemed part of the property of their father.

Obviously, American attitudes toward children have shifted substantially over the years. The parent who regards a child as property today is the exception, not the rule. Yet child abuse has not disappeared.

Beginning late in the nineteenth century, medical journals began reporting "bone diseases of unknown origin" (Eskin 1980:4)—mysterious multiple bone fractures in infants and young children. Not until the mid-twentieth century did the mystery begin to lift, with physicians increasingly suspecting—and saying publicly—that the fractures could be caused by parents mistreating their own children. Labeled "the battered child syndrome" by Dr. C. H. Kempe in 1962, it quickly became a national concern. As one response, individual states and then the United States Congress passed legislation requiring that medical personnel report possible child-abuse cases to authorities.

Today, it is still impossible to know with any certainty the incidence of child abuse. Recent estimates range from 40,000 to nearly 2 million cases per year (Eskin 1980:14). Mandatory reporting of suspected child abuse has resulted in more cases being reported; but, at the same time, the danger of prosecution surely has kept many parents from bringing their battered children in for treatment.

It is important that these large numbers not obscure the individual suffering that the numbers represent. Horton and Leslie (1978:192–193) provide graphic details.

> The torture visited upon the unfortunate children is almost unbelievable. Children brought to hospitals have cigarette burns on their bodies, burns from scalding water poured on their genitals, blackened eyes, broken bones, and skull fractures. In some cases the abuse is discovered only upon investigations into the death of the child.

The roots of child abuse are many. Craig Taylor (1971:212) points out that illegitimate children are more susceptible than the legitimate, though legitimacy is only partial protection. Fathers who doubt their children's paternity are more likely to abuse those children. So are mothers who feel they sacrificed careers for motherhood. Abuse is more common in lower-class homes, though it is a serious middle-class problem also. (The middle class is perhaps more adept at concealing its offenses.) Across all of these variations, however, child abuse appears to be the result of adult frustrations—at home or at work—that cannot be expressed within the situations generating them.

"Official" abuse of children is less openly brutal than physical torture in the home, yet it provokes emotion nonetheless. David Ferleger (1977:89), for example, describes three examples of parental use and abuse of mental hospitals for their children:

1. You are 14 years old and you don't like school. A juvenile court in suburban Philadelphia puts you on probation for truancy. When you cut school again, your parents sign you into a state mental hospital, where you refuse to help clean your ward. You are sent to a locked building for punishment.
2. Your Raggedy Ann doll goes everywhere with you. A retarded boy, 11, you speak fairly well and everyone expects you to stay in public school until you're 21. Your family wants to go on vacation for a week or two and they take you to an institution for the retarded to stay for a while. Ten months later you're still there.
3. Your mother signs you into a state mental hospital in Mississippi because she thinks you're acting unusually and might create a disturbance at home. You're 15. Once committed, you are drugged daily and spend most of your time on an adult ward, just sitting.

At present, such legal protections as the right to a hearing and the right to counsel are guaranteed to juvenile delinquents and to adult mental patients, but the courts have not yet extended them to juvenile mental patients. The latter are caught in a peculiar bind: they are too young to fight for their own rights, yet their parents—who would normally look out for their rights—are the adversaries.

In Chapter 11, we'll see that Americans have had ambivalent feelings about crime and its remedies. One view holds criminals as wrongdoers who should be punished, and the other holds them as maladjusted people who require therapeutic treatment. As Eskin points out, the same ambivalence exists toward child abusers, except the conditions of the crime are more difficult.

It is difficult to prove child abuse, since it typically occurs in private at home without impartial witnesses. Moreover, small infants cannot testify to what has happened to them, and children who are old enough to testify may be reluctant to speak against their own parents. To make matters worse, Eskin (1980:35) adds,

> the effects of the criminal court process often do more harm than good for the child since the court process may embitter the parents, causing them to resent their children even more and inflict fur-

ther abuse. If acquitted, parents may regard the court's decision as an approval of their parenting behavior. If convicted, a prison term or suspended sentence will seldom change their behavior.

The issue of children's rights is hardly settled, though its many aspects are coming under increasing public scrutiny. One promising sign is that the new public awareness of child abuse has generated such public-interest groups as the Youth Law Center in St. Louis and the Children's Defense Fund in Washington. Eskin lists twenty-two organizations devoted to the rights and protection of children. Ultimately, this problem will be solved only when we can get to the root causes and find remedies for them.

PRACTICING SOCIOLOGY

In this chapter, we've seen that American women are working outside the home (participating in the labor force) more than ever. The data presented below—taken from the Bureau of Labor Statistics—report participation in the labor force by women sixteen and older in various family situations: marital status plus whether they have children under eighteen years of age.

Look through the data in the table. Write a paragraph in which you discuss patterns or differences that particularly stand out. Suggest some reasons for the patterns and differences you noted.

Some of the women work full-time, some part-time. Discuss which types of women might fall into each category, and why.

	Percent in Labor Force Children under 18?	
	Yes	No
Never married	52.3	62.9
Married, husband present	55.7	46.3
Married, husband absent	61.7	59.9
Widowed	60.3	19.9
Divorced	78.1	72.4

Source: "Half of Nation's Children Have Working Mothers," U.S. Bureau of Labor Statistics, USDL 81–522, November 15, 1981.

11

Deviance
and Social
Control

In this chapter, we will address two major topics: **deviance** and **social control.** Most people believe that deviance simply involves perversity and immorality. The term "deviant" likely brings forth pictures of criminals, prostitutes, dope addicts, and the like. If you saw the movie *Dr. Strangelove*, you may recall that Keenan Wynn, as Colonel Bat Guano, leveled his submachine gun at Peter Sellers, playing the British naval officer Mandrake, and said, "I think you're a deviated prevert." That's the view of deviance that many people have.

"Deviance" is the violation of an established social agreement. Some examples of deviance are crime, mental illness, prostitution, and alcoholism. As you'll quickly see, the sociological view of deviance is quite different from conventional views generally held in society.

From the sociological point of view, all of us are deviants. However, even the most incorrigible criminal keeps *most* of society's agreements. Many sociologists have concluded that deviance is mostly a matter of what and who gets "labeled" as deviant.

That deviance might be just a matter of labeling does not diminish its importance in the study of society. Breaking the agreements—and reactions to those who break the agreements—has critical implications for the functioning and survival of society. Accordingly, sociologists have studied many different forms of deviance. We'll look at some forms of deviance and see how each fits—and conflicts—with established social agreements.

The chapter concludes with an examination of "social control": the enforcement of agreements. Social control is both a guard against and a reaction to deviance. Beginning with the socialization process as an example of social control, we'll zero in on those agents that have a special responsibility for enforcing the law: police, courts, and prisons. Finally, we'll see how social control itself creates problems.

 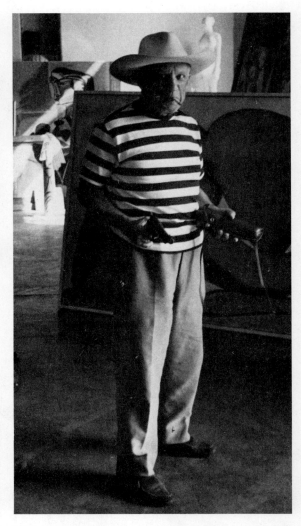

There are all sorts of deviants. Pablo Picasso, on the right, deviated as much from the "average" as the fellow on the left. Albert Einstein, Adolf Hitler, and Saint Francis of Assisi were all deviants.

What Is Deviance?

Deviance, I've said, is the breaking of agreements. In this section, I want to show exactly how complex this seemingly straightforward concept is. We'll find out that it matters greatly *who* breaks *what* agreements, to what *degree*, whether he or she gets *caught*, and how *other people* feel about it.

Who Is Deviant?

If you have ever driven too fast, lied, worn your hair "too long" or "too short," been late, or done something "surprising," you have been deviant. But you have plenty of company. We are all deviants, and we can't help being that way.

We've already seen that most societies have thousands of agreements relating to symbols, beliefs, values, and norms. Many of these agreements contradict one another, so it is simply impossible for you or any other person to avoid breaking some of the agreements every day. For example, you may know of a street nearby that has a posted speed limit of 25 miles per hour and an average actual speed of 35–40 miles per hour. You can't drive on that street without breaking one of those agreements. Moreover, there are sanctions in each case. Go too fast and you can get a ticket; drive 25 miles per hour and other drivers will shout angry things at you. Deviance is normal.

The expectations that we'll all deviate from prescribed norms at least somewhat is illustrated by our general reactions to people who "overconform," who follow all the agreements as closely as humanly possible. By driving strictly within posted speed limits, for example, "overconformers" aggravate other drivers who express their disapproval with blasting horns and shaking fists. When such people insist that others strictly adhere to the agreements, they are ridiculed, ostracized, and sometimes assaulted. Unquestionably, the person who managed to keep all his or her society's agreements would be regarded as the supreme deviant.

Like prejudice, deviance is normally viewed in a negative light. Strictly speaking, the negativity need not be. Albert Einstein was as much a deviant as Jack the Ripper, Mahatma Gandhi as much as Adolf Hitler. Sociologists, however, have tended to follow common usage in directing their attention to forms of deviance that are considered "bad" by general agreement within the society.

Divergence and Deviance

If we are all deviants, even in the "bad" sense of the term, we aren't all deviant to the same degree. Ordinarily the label "deviant" is reserved for those who do something that most of us don't do—or don't think we do. In this regard, J. L. Simmons (1969:44) has made a useful distinction between "divergence" and "deviance":

The rules are to be bent but not broken. The prevailing practices in a society are the divergences most common and most acceptable. Deviance is simply divergence that is much greater than the divergence of the majority, or at least the majority of the groups and classes of power.

Deviants, then, seem to be people who deviate *more* than the rest of us—people who go "too far." But how far is "too far"? People have different views on it. Even if we draw the line at "breaking the law"—even serious laws—the prevalence of deviance in America is astounding. Robert Merton, a prominent American sociologist, has summarized the results of a survey conducted during the 1940s, generally considered a "law-abiding" period:

A study of some 1,700 prevalently middle-class individuals found that "off the record crimes" were common among wholly "respectable" members of society. Ninety-nine percent of those questioned confessed to having committed one or more of 49 offenses under the penal law of the State of New York, each of these offenses being sufficiently serious to draw a maximum sentence of not less than one year. The mean number of offenses in adult years—this excludes all offenses committed before the age of sixteen—was 18 for men and 11 for women. Fully 64 [percent] of the men and 29 [percent] of the women acknowledged their guilt on one or more counts of felony which, under the laws of New York, is ground for depriving them of all rights of citizenship. (1957a:144)

For a more recent and perhaps more dramatic illustration of our "criminality," look at the percentages of self-reported crimes that Matthew Silberman found among a sample of undergraduates at a small private university, as reported in Table 11–1.

This table may help you realize the extent to which deviance—what virtually everyone would

Table 11-1

Percentages of College Students Admitting to Having Committed a Crime

Crime	% students admitting commission
Assault	8
Hard drugs	10
Petty theft	12
Vandalism	20
Shoplifting	30
Drunk and disorderly conduct	40
Premarital sex	54
Marijuana use	63
Drinking under age	95

Source: Matthew Silberman, "Toward a Theory of Criminal Deterrence," *American Sociological Review* 41 (June 1976), p. 446. Reprinted by permission.

agree is deviance—pervades our society. Deviants, however defined, are scarcely a "people apart" from you and me.

Although all of us are "deviants," there's another side to the coin. Simmons (1969:40) stated it very succinctly:

All deviants are conventional in the vast majority of their beliefs, attitudes, and activities. Even the most unconventional denizens of our society, for instance, prefer ground beef to rotted camel meat, speak a language which is unmistakably a mid-century American dialect of English, drive on the right-hand side of the road, and take aspirin for a headache. The vast bulk of a deviant's characteristics will be statistically common and morally accepted. Our upbringing in the same historical place and time gives us all—deviant and straight—a thousand common bonds.

Saint and sinner alike share countless agreements, and in most of our behavior we conform to those agreements. Otherwise, prostitutes would walk naked in the streets to advertise and murderers would murder everyone in sight.

Thieves wouldn't steal, by the same token, if they didn't share in a variety of agreements regarding the purpose and value of money. All in all, we deviants are a pretty conformist lot.

Sociological Perspectives on Deviance

Having looked at some of the complexities of defining deviance, let's look now at some of the different sociological points of view on deviance. I'll touch on these points of view briefly here and elaborate on them later in the chapter.

The **labeling** point of view on deviance suggests that people are deviants only or primarily because they are "labeled" as deviant. You are "mentally ill" if a psychologist or physician says you are. You are a "criminal" if a court says you are. In short, you become a deviant as a result of an *agreement* that you've broken the agreements. Two people might both break the same agreement, but perhaps only one is labeled a deviant. The soldier and the (privately) hired killer both kill people, but only the latter is labeled a deviant.

The labeling perspective reflects a more general interactionist point of view, focusing as it does on the process by which a person is labeled a deviant, responds to the labeling, is further judged on the basis of the response, and so forth. At the same time, however, the labeling perspective can be used profitably in conjunction with both conflict and functionalist points of view on deviance.

The conflict point of view suggests that deviance and social control are elements in the struggle between social classes or other groups in society. "Collective" deviance, such as riots, protest marches, and antitax movements, most clearly exemplifies this theory. Moreover, conflict theorists see social control through laws, police, courts, and jails as overt action by those with power to suppress those who lack power.

The functionalist point of view regards deviance as a threat to the stability and persistence of a society and its agreements. Functionalists may differ, however, on whether the threat is "good" or "bad." William Chambliss (1973:7) contrasts the conflict and functionalist approaches to deviance as follows:

> The functional and conflict perspectives emphasize very different things. The functionalist paradigm emphasizes the social psychological experiences of individuals (or groups), which lead some to accept and live by the customs of the society. The conflict perspective places primacy on the role of criminal law and asks how laws emerge and are enforced. Functionalists seek the explanation of crime in the behavior of those labeled criminal. Conflict theorists seek the explanation of crime in the institutions that define criminal acts and in the social relations created by a society's structure, especially its mode of production.

The functionalist and conflict points of view both grant that many agreements are being broken in any society at any one time. They differ on the kinds of agreement-breaking they label and treat as deviant. Sociologists taking the conflict point of view are interested in the breaking of agreements that protect the existing distribution of power in the society; sociologists taking the functionalist point of view look to the breaking of agreements that support major institutions. The threat to institutions may often be indirect. Prostitution and homosexuality, for example, may be seen to represent an indirect threat to the institution of the family—because they challenge its monopoly on sexuality.

Quite aside from these different points of view, most sociologists recognize that deviance per se has a function for society, and that it is a culturally relative concept. Most sociologists agree that deviance is functional because the identification and punishment of deviants draws the attention of others to the existence and "importance" of the agreements the deviants break. Making "an example" of deviants can keep others on the straight and narrow. The identification of deviants can strengthen the solidarity of the rest of society by creating an out-group that everyone else can feel superior to and united against.

Sociologists generally agree that all deviance is determined by the particular agreements established in a given society. Deviance is the breaking of a society's agreements, and thus one society's deviance can be another's conformity.

For example, although homosexuality is widely regarded as deviant in American society, it is *preferred* over heterosexuality among the Trans-Fly tribes of New Guinea (Kottak 1978:9). Eating beef is deviant behavior among Hindus, but vegetarianism is somewhat deviant in American society. Drinking alcohol is deviant among Hindus and Moslems, as is ordering a "Shirley Temple" at a fraternity bash.

By the time you complete this chapter, you should realize that there is no such thing as deviance without norms. It is not possible to break agreements unless there *are* agreements, and what constitutes deviance is totally a matter of agreements that have been established. Put more specifically, there can be no crime without laws, and what constitutes a crime is completely a matter of the laws in force in a society. In many societies around the world, for example, it is a crime to publicly criticize the government. In South Africa, it is a crime for blacks and whites to marry one another, as it once was in parts of the United States.

Forms of Deviance in America

Granting the arbitrary nature of deviance in any society, let's turn now to some of the things commonly regarded as deviance in contemporary American society, some illegal and some which merely violate nonlegal norms. In this section we'll examine various types of crime—including victimless crimes such as homosexuality, prostitution, drug use, alcoholism, and mental illness.

Table 11-2

Major American Crimes Known to Police: 1960–1980

| Crime category | Number of crimes | | | Rate per 100,000 inhabitants |
	1960	1970	1980	1980
Crime index total	2,019,000	5,582,000	13,295,500	5,899.8
Violent crimes	286,000	733,000	1,308,900	580.7
Murder	9,000	16,000	23,040	10.2
Forcible rape	17,000	38,000	82,090	36.4
Robbery	107,000	348,000	548,810	243.5
Aggravated assault	153,000	331,000	654,960	290.6
Property crimes	1,733,000	4,849,000	11,986,600	5,319.1
Burglary	900,000	2,177,000	3,759,200	1,668.2
Larceny, $50 & up	507,000	1,750,000	7,112,700	3,156.3
Auto theft	326,000	922,000	1,114,700	494.6

Source: Federal Bureau of Investigation, *Uniform Crime Reports for the United States,* 1975, p.59; 1980, p.38. (Because of rounding, offenses may not add to totals.)

Crime

Crime is a clear case of deviance; it represents the breaking of formal, legal agreements in a society. Wearing your hair too long or too short violates unstated, informal agreements, and its status as deviant behavior is, therefore, somewhat ambiguous. Breaking the law—stealing and killing—is not ambiguous in that regard.

Table 11–2 reports the numbers of crimes "known to police" in recent years. Among the points you might notice is that crimes against property greatly outnumber crimes against persons. In 1980, the ratio was about nine to one. In addition, the number of major crimes *known to police* is simply staggering. In 1980, over five major crimes were known to police for every 100 people in the United States population. (Figure 11–1 presents the magnitude of crime more graphically.) Third, over the twenty-year period shown in Table 11–2, the number of crimes increased more than six-fold. During the same period, the crime rate, a figure arrived at by dividing the number of crimes by the population size, more than quintupled.

There are some things you should be aware of about numbers of crimes and crime *rates*. First, crime, like other societywide phenomena, is strongly influenced by the age distribution of the population. The rapidly increasing number of crimes in the last twenty years partly reflects the "baby boom" following World War II. Crime rates are higher among young people in America than among older people, so the disproportionately large number of young Americans in recent years has resulted in higher nationwide crime rates.

Second, data on "crimes known to police" reflect enforcement policies. Whenever the police decide to "crack down" on drug use, for example, crime statistics will give the appearance of an increased crime rate for drug violations. DeFleur's (1975) analysis of drug arrests in Chicago between 1941 and 1970 graphically demonstrates the influence of enforcement policies on apparent crime rates. Those periods that seemed to show a radical increase in drug use (as reflected in arrests) coincided with—and appear to be explained by—"get tough" campaigns launched by public officials. The actual levels of drug use probably did not increase at all during those periods.

Third, official crime statistics also reflect reporting practices. The data reported here were compiled by the FBI from reports submitted by local police departments. Local procedures vary, however, and changes in those procedures (as well as those of the FBI itself) produce apparent changes in crime rates. The computerization of crime reporting, for example, often results in an apparent increase in crime rates.

Finally, more crimes are known to victims than are known to police. The discrepancy is caused by several factors. Crimes committed by family members or friends against one another often go unreported for obvious reasons. Similarly, in areas that support organized crime (ranging in type from neighborhood gangs to syndicates), victims and witnesses alike may keep quiet for fear of retribution. And many people believe that calling in the police won't bring anything but trouble. Rape victims, for

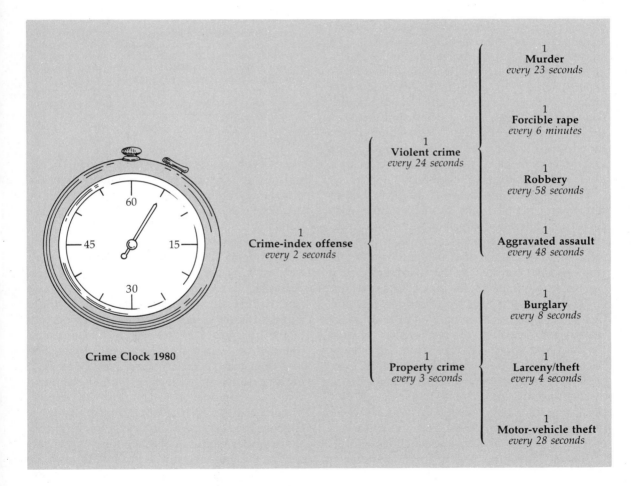

Crime Clock 1980

1
Crime-index offense
every 2 seconds

1
Violent crime
every 24 seconds

1
Murder
every 23 seconds

1
Forcible rape
every 6 minutes

1
Robbery
every 58 seconds

1
Aggravated assault
every 48 seconds

1
Property crime
every 3 seconds

1
Burglary
every 8 seconds

1
Larceny/theft
every 4 seconds

1
Motor-vehicle theft
every 28 seconds

Figure 11–1 This crime clock is prepared by the FBI to describe the volume of crime in the U.S. Some criminologists criticize the clock as being primarily a device to generate increased funding for law enforcement. Bear in mind that these crimes occur within a national population in excess of 200 million people. Source: Federal Bureau of Investigation, Crime in the United States, *1980, p. 6.*

example, often conceal the fact that they have been raped in order to avoid ugly publicity, painful questioning, and possible insinuations from police and others that they encouraged the assault.

It's impossible to know exactly how many crimes go unreported each year, but we can make some estimates. Besides the official FBI crime reports, the Law Enforcement Assistance Administration (LEAA) of the U.S. Justice Department has conducted a series of massive surveys that ask a national sample of people whether they have been the victims of crimes during the past twelve months. These "victimization surveys" offer a different window on crime in America, one that is even more alarming than that provided by the FBI's *Uniform Crime Reports*. Table 11–3 suggests that the number of major crimes committed in the United States is substantially higher than official crime statistics show, and the number may be even higher than the victimization surveys indicate. Again, rape victims may be as unwilling to talk to survey interviewers as they are to police.

You may find the data on property crimes unsettling, but you are probably more concerned about crimes directed against your person. Sociologists have discovered an interesting pattern in crimes of violence. I'm not sure you will take comfort in the discovery, but if you are going to be killed, raped, or assaulted, it will probably be done by a friend or relation. Of the 23,040 murders committed in 1980, police were able to determine the relationship between the murderer and the victim in just under two-thirds of them. Of those, the murders were committed by relatives in 25 percent of the cases, by friends and acquaintances in another 54 percent, and only one murder in five was committed by a stranger. One in eight murders was committed by the victim's spouse (FBI 1981:12).

A great deal of sociological attention has been paid to the characteristics of those arrested for committing crimes. The President's Commission on Law Enforcement reported that the largest number of crimes is committed by white

Table 11-3

Estimated Crime Rates as Reproted by Police and by Victims

Type of crime	Rates reported by police	Rates reported by victims
Rape	26.3	90
Robbery	218.2	670
Aggravated assault	227.4	670
Burglary	1,529.9	9,150
Larceny/theft	2,804.8	9,580
Motor-vehicle theft	469.4	1,940

Source: Federal Bureau of Investigatin, *Uniform Crime Reports for the United States,* October 18, 1978, p. 37 (for crimes reported to police); Law Enforcement Assistance Administration, *Criminal Victimization in the United States, 1975* (1977), p. 18 (for crimes reported by victims).

Note: Rate = Number of crimes per 100,000 population.

males over twenty-four years of age (1967:44). This group accounts for a large majority of the arrests for fraud, embezzlement, gambling, drunkenness, vagrancy, and crimes within the family.

Other crimes, however, are more typical among other social categories. Young people account for a large fraction of the burglaries, larcenies, and auto thefts committed. Of those arrested for such crimes in 1980, people under eighteen years of age accounted for 45 percent of the burglaries, 37 percent of the larcenies/thefts, and 45 percent of the auto thefts. Sixteen-year-olds alone accounted for 12 percent of the auto thefts, with fifteen- and seventeen-year-olds responsible for another 22 percent. Violent crimes, on the other hand, are more concentrated among a slightly older age group: those under eighteen account for only 19 percent of the violent crime arrests. Although the under-eighteen group accounted for 40 percent of the crimes against property in 1980, they accounted for only 19 percent of the violent crimes (FBI 1981:200).

Men are far more likely than women to be arrested for committing crimes. This, in fact, is the most salient characteristic distinguishing those arrested from the population at large. The sex difference has been decreasing in recent years, however, especially in larceny offenses.

Race is almost as important as sex in distinguishing persons arrested from the general public. Blacks commit fewer crimes than whites, but crime *rates* are considerably higher among blacks. Racial differences appear largely to reflect the differences in socioeconomic status and other social variables (President's Commission on Law Enforcement 1967:44). That is, poor people are more likely to commit robberies than are rich people, and blacks are, on the average, poorer than whites.

Juvenile Delinquency   Sociologists, like others in society, tend to treat crime by minors separately from crime by adults. This difference in treatment partly reflects the different patterns of crime for people of different ages, as indicated in the "portrait" presented above. In addition, many acts are considered criminal *only* when committed by young people. Adults committing the same act would not be considered deviant. Such "crimes" are referred to as *status crimes*, meaning that they are crimes only if committed by people occupying certain social statuses—such as being young. Thus, for example, no adult can be guilty of truancy. These status crimes add to the "criminal" *potential* of young people by giving them more regulations to follow and, hence, more to break. Few status crimes apply only to adults (statutory rape is one). In 1980, 10 percent of the under-eighteen arrests were runaways or curfew and loitering-law violators—not crimes for those eighteen and older (FBI 1981:200).

Juvenile status crimes highlight the fact that deviance is purely a matter of agreement within society. A given act by a given person is "criminal" only if we agree that it is. Thus, we have sometimes agreed that drinking alcohol is a deviant act for a person 17 years and 364 days old, but not a deviant act for a person 1 day older.

Of any form of crime, juvenile delinquency has probably received the most attention from sociologists and other crime watchers. Now let's turn to a form of crime that until recently has remained relatively unnoticed.

White-Collar Crime   In reading that virtually everyone has committed punishable crimes, it probably occurred to you that many of those "crimes" were the "little white lies" of lawbreaking: technically criminal, but pretty harmless on the whole. Anyone who has ever worked in an office, for example, has probably "stolen" pencils, paper clips, and the like. Even "nice people" like you and me do that.

In 1949, Edwin Sutherland published a book about the crimes "nice people" commit, and the title of his book has become the term associated with the crimes most typical of middle- and upper-class people: **white-collar crime** (Sutherland 1949). As Sutherland and later researchers have pointed out, white-collar crime extends well beyond paper clips and cannot be regarded as harmless.

Embezzlement is probably the most obvious and dramatic white-collar crime. In earlier years, this term conjured up images of the trusted bank clerk dipping his or her hand in the till and perhaps shocking the old hometown by running off to South America with a few thousand dollars. Donald Cressey captured this image when he titled his 1953 classic study of embezzlement *Other People's Money*. More in line with the current situation is the *Harvard Business Review's* 1975 "Embezzler's Guide to the Computer" (Allen 1975). In place of a few thousand dollars stuffed in a satchel, we have the two-*billion*-dollar Equity Funding Corporation fraud and similar capers involving the use of computers. With increasingly complex systems of electronic transfers of funds, sophisticated criminals have become increasingly clever in draining off some for themselves (Sykes 1978:105–106).

In April 1980, the Justice Department's Law Enforcement Assistance Administration published Jay Becker's *The Investigation of Computer Crime* as an operational guide for investigators. In it, Becker speaks of the reluctance of companies to report computer crimes, noting "the widely quoted statistic that only 15 percent of all computer crime is reported to law-enforcement authorities" (Becker 1980:5–6). Among the reasons for underreporting, computer crimes are embarrassing to the victim companies and could even threaten the confidence of customers and clients. In addition, there are serious doubts about the ability of law-enforcement officials to investigate and prosecute such complex cases. Becker suggests (1980:6) that such skepticism may be well-founded.

> Experts at the Federal Bureau of Investigation say only one of 22,000 computer criminals goes to jail. They estimate that only 1 percent of all computer crime is detected, only 14 percent of that is reported, and only 3 percent of those cases ever result in jail sentences.

Major white-collar crime is not limited to the business sector, however. Labor unions such as the Teamsters have spawned their own troubles in this respect, and government corruption has become so widespread that public regard for politics is at an all-time low. The 1972–1974 Watergate scandals of the Nixon administration only dramatized long-standing malpractices in American politics—wiretapping, bribery, slander, and other variations from textbook democracy.

Some other white-collar crimes, as identified by Sue Titus Reid (1982:233–34) are

Income-tax violations

Credit-card frauds

Bankruptcy frauds

Bank violations by bank officers

Securities frauds

Padding of payrolls

Food and drug violations

False weights and measures by retailers

Use of fictitious collateral

Physicians in collusion with pharmacists in the writing of unnecessary prescriptions

Immigration fraud

Housing-code violations by landlords

Commercial espionage

Deceptive advertising

Phony contests

Charity and religious frauds

Insurance frauds

Coupon-redemption frauds.

White-collar crime, then, is far more than the harmless filching of paper clips from the office. The United States Chamber of Commerce estimated in 1974 that the loss due to white-collar workers' thefts ran around 40 billion dollars per year (Sykes 1978:104).

All this notwithstanding, the more traditional American image of "crime" is inextricably linked to images of "the mob," "the Syndicate," "the Mafia," as well as the Al Capones and other figures of organized crime.

Organized Crime   Despite popular fascination with organized crime and the success of books and movies such as *The Godfather* and, in an earlier generation, *Little Caesar,* a debate continues over whether any single organization controls a substantial portion of the nation's crime. Although the existence of criminal gangs has long been evident, Estes Kefauver's Senate Crime Investigating Committee shocked many in 1951 by concluding that an organization called the "Mafia" did exist and that the group controlled traffic in illegal drugs, gambling, and prostitution across the nation. It was a national conspiracy, shrouded in secrecy, bound by a fierce loyalty among members, and frighteningly vengeful against any who broke its codes. The Mafia was described by the Senate committee as Sicilian in origin and generally of Italian ancestry in membership, creating a fair amount of anti-Italian hostility and negative stereotypes among the general public.

In the years following the publication of the Kefauver findings, some began to wonder if the reports of the crime conspiracies featuring the Mafia, the Cosa Nostra, and the Syndicate had perhaps been exaggerated. Was the publicity given organized crime merely a romantic successor to the dime novels about Jesse James, Billy the Kid, and other desperadoes of a century ago?

Donald Cressey, a prominent criminologist and sociologist, had such questions in mind when he was appointed a consultant to the President's Commission on Law Enforcement and Administration of Justice. After an intensive examination of the available evidence, however, Cressey concluded: "no rational man could read the evidence that I have read and still come to the conclusion that an organization variously called 'The Mafia,' 'Cosa Nostra,' and 'The Syndicate' does not exist" (Cressey 1969:x). He reported that it was apparently an alliance of two dozen quasi-families active in loansharking, narcotics, prostitution, extortion, and union and government corruption and deeply involved in legitimate business such as manufacturing, trucking, bars, hotels, and restaurants.

The controversy over the extent of organized crime will undoubtedly continue. Organized crime is, of course, difficult to study by conventional social-science techniques. Cressey has summed up the situation nicely in saying that we have learned about as much of the organization of organized crime (using bugs, wiretaps, and so on) as we could learn about the organization of the Standard Oil Company by interviewing gas-station attendants (1969:110).

One aspect of organized crime seems generally agreed on: the backbone of the industry is and has always been profits from goods and services that are desired by a large portion of the society though prohibited by law. Marshall Clinard and Richard Quinney (1967:224–25)

suggest that organized crime dates from the 1919 Volstead Act (Prohibition). While other scholars argue that organized crime had its roots in an earlier era, all agree that Prohibition gave the organized mobs a shot in the arm. When the sale of alcohol was later legalized again, Syndicate activity focused on such goods and services as drugs, gambling, and prostitution.

Of course, organized crime is not simply a provider of harmless goods and services. Sue Titus Reid (1982:235) points out:

> The basic difference between organized crime and white-collar crime comes not in the type of activities but rather in the methods for carrying out those activities. Violence will more often be found in organized crime, although it may also occur among white-collar criminals. The use of force and threat is also more common in organized crime.

Extortion, murder for hire, car theft, and the like are hardly practices to ignore. Still, it is unlikely that anything resembling a national crime syndicate could exist except for its involvement in what Edwin Schur has called "crimes without victims" (Schur 1965, Schur and Bedau 1974).

Crimes without Victims

If I stick a gun in your ribs and force you to give me all your money, everybody would probably agree that a crime had been committed. I would be the perpetrator and you the victim. The con man who bilks widows out of their life savings, we would surely agree, has committed a crime, as has the corporate executive who knowingly manufactures a product that contains severe health hazards for its consumers. Each of these actions is clearly a crime because someone gets hurt. Each has victims. Even crimes such as tax evasion and drunken driving can be seen to have victims or potential victims among the rest of us.

Some people, like these Skid Row residents, choose to drop out from mainstream society.

Quite different, however, are actions related to the host of "blue laws" that governed life in New England in its early years. Taking their name from the blue paper on which they were written in colonial New Haven, such laws were aimed at enforcing religious morality in secular life. They regulated leisure activities, travel, sports, dress, drinking, and just about anything else on the Sabbath. Today, few people see any "criminality" in dancing or in drinking beer while watching Sunday afternoon football on television. After all, nobody is getting hurt. The presence or absence of victims, however, does not determine whether behavior constitutes a crime. Let's look at some examples.

Homosexuality   Homosexuality is a good example of **crime without victims.** Murder and robbery have victims, but homosexuality is better described as an unconventional activity entered into voluntarily. The "unconventional" nature of homosexuality—as well as other intimate acts and even feelings of love—comes from its violation of the norm that sexual relations should be limited to persons of opposite sexes.

American norms pertaining to homosexuality are rather complex and largely unstated. For example, most young children engage in sexual experimentation with members of the same sex. Although this experimentation is typically discouraged by adults, the label of homosexuality is seldom attached to it. Moreover, Americans are more permissive with women in regard to same-sex affection than with men. Adult women may acceptably hug, kiss, and hold hands in public, but men may not do so as acceptably. It

European men can kiss each other on the mouth without fear of sanction, but this is only recently becoming acceptable among American men. American women, on the other hand, have had greater freedom in the matter of expressing affection openly.

is worth noting that many other contemporary societies—in Latin America and Europe, for example—do not make the same distinctions North Americans make about proper behavior for men and women.

The agreements relating to homosexuality in America are approximate at best. Fearing loss of jobs and legal and other sanctions, many homosexuals conceal their disagreement with prevailing sexual norms. Weinberg (1974) estimates suggest that perhaps 4 percent of the male population is exclusively homosexual.

The American agreements regarding homosexuality are clearly changing. Although homosexuality is still against the law in most states, it is legal among consenting adults in several states, including California and Illinois. At the same time, many homosexuals have "come out of the closet," publicly acknowledging their homosexuality. "Gay liberation" has joined the list of minority groups openly demanding equal treatment in American society.

Recent militancy and openness notwithstanding, gays do not enjoy overwhelming public support at this time. A survey by the National Opinion Research Center in 1977 found 78 percent saying "sexual relations between two *adults* of the *same* sex" was always or almost always wrong, a finding virtually identical to that of surveys done in 1973, 1974, and 1976. A 1977 survey by Lou Harris asked people whether admitted homosexuals should be permitted to hold various jobs. Nearly two-thirds (63 percent) would prohibit a gay from serving as a counselor in a camp for young people, 55 percent opposed gay teachers, and 42 percent opposed gay police officers. Twelve percent didn't think gays should work as clerks in stores, and 7 percent even felt gays shouldn't be allowed to work as artists (*Public Opinion* 1978a:38)!

Antigay prejudice is not equally distributed in America. Overall, only 43 percent of the respondents in a 1977 Gallup Poll felt "homosexual relations should be legal," but 57 percent of college graduates wanted to legalize homosexual relations, contrasted with 42 percent of those with high-school educations and 21 percent of those with only grade-school educations. Similarly, 29 percent of those fifty and older approved of gay relations, with approval increasing steadily as age decreased: 58 percent of those eighteen to twenty-four approved (*Public Opinion* 1978a:38). After examining patterns of prejudice against blacks, Jews, and women, the current situation faced by gays should be familiar to you.

Prostitution   Prostitution, another sexual crime without victims, represents an agreement between prostitute and client. It provides an excellent contrast to homosexuality. Although both men and women are involved in prostitution, women are the most likely to be identified with it and punished for it. In 1980, 67,920 people were arrested for "prostitution and commercialized vice." Over two-thirds of these were women; and many of the men arrested were procurers ("pimps") rather than clients (FBI 1981:195). Only recently have police begun arresting clients as well as prostitutes, spurred largely by charges that previous arrest patterns have constituted sex discrimination against women. (In 1971, three-fourths of those arrested were women.)

Prostitution, sometimes called the "oldest profession," is usually heterosexual in America. Although it supports the agreement on heterosexuality—too much, some would feel—it violates other agreements. First, it violates the prevailing agreement limiting sexual relations to the family, between married partners. In addition, it violates more informal agreements that sexual relations should be associated with feelings of love and lasting commitment. Anthropologists have pointed out that sexual experimentation before marriage (and other variations from the American agreement) is common in other cultures. Anthropologist Margaret Mead's classic book, *Coming of Age in Samoa*, is probably the most effective presentation of another culture's practices. Mead found that, in Samoa, early sexual experimentation was the rule rather than a violation of rules.

Prostitution's illegal status combined with its persistent popularity has created a secondary problem that clearly seems more serious than prostitution itself. Many independent entrepreneurs still exist, but a great many prostitutes are forced to ply their trade as employees of pimps, mobs, and syndicates. Where prostitution is well organized, the would-be self-employed prostitute risks severe punishment. And, because prostitution itself is illegal, she has no recourse to the police.

Finally, let's turn to another form of deviance that can be regarded as a crime without victims—one that can be performed all alone: drug use.

Drug Use   In 1980, Americans spent over 19 billion dollars on drugs. That same year, the nation's drug companies spent 430 million dollars on television advertising alone—more than was spent to advertise beer and wine (242 million dollars) or candy and soft drinks (281 million dollars) or products to get clothes whiter than white and to keep sinks spotless and shiny (306 million dollars). Only food (844 million dollars), toiletries (765 million dollars), and automotive products (520 million dollars) had higher television-advertising expenditures (U.S. Bureau of Census 1981i:100, 573).

We are clearly a drug-taking society. Some people suggest that we have a "drug problem." They usually are not referring to the misuse of over-the-counter drugs such as aspirin or even of prescribed drugs. Nor do people normally have alcohol or tobacco in mind. Instead, they are talking about deviant drug use, drug use (and abuse) that involves illegal substances such as heroin, cocaine, LSD, and marijuana.

For many people, the emotionally-charged term "drug addiction" primarily brings to mind heroin, an opium-derived depressant. Estimates are highly unreliable, but perhaps as many as 400,000 may be heroin addicts, people who are physiologically dependent on continued use (Weinberg 1974).

Cocaine is a stimulant, not a depressant like heroin. It is derived from the leaves of South American coca plants. Cocaine, which is typically ingested by sniffing, recently has become popular, especially among the middle and upper classes. In contrast to heroin, it is not known to be physically addictive.

During the 1960s, considerable national attention was focused on the use of LSD, a powerful manufactured hallucinogenic drug. Although LSD and the other hallucinogens such as peyote and mescaline are not known to produce physical addiction, some experts fear that heavy users can become psychologically dependent on these drugs and possibly suffer genetic damage. After reaching a peak in the mid-to-late 1960s, LSD use appears to have declined in America.

Easily the most talked about and most popular illegal substance in recent years has been

Table 11-4

Drug Use in America, 1979

	Percent of youths (12–17 years)		Percent of young adults (18–25 years)		Percent of adults (26 and older)	
	Ever used	Current user	Ever used	Current user	Ever used	Current user
Marijuana	30.9	16.7	68.2	35.4	19.6	6.0
Inhalants	9.8	2.0	16.5	1.2	3.9	.5
Hallucinogens	7.1	2.2	25.1	4.4	4.5	—
Cocaine	5.4	1.4	27.5	9.3	4.3	.9
Heroin	.5	—	3.5	—	1.0	—
Analgesics	3.2	.6	11.8	1.0	2.7	—
Stimulants	3.4	1.2	18.2	3.5	5.8	—
Sedatives	3.2	1.1	17.0	2.8	3.5	—
Tranquilizers	4.1	.6	15.8	2.1	3.1	—
Alcohol	70.3	37.2	95.3	75.9	91.5	61.3
Tobacco	54.1	12.1	82.8	42.6	83.0	36.9

Source: U.S. Bureau of Census, Statistical Abstract of the United States 1980 (Washington, D.C.: Government Printing Office, 1981), p. 129.

Note: — means less than 0.5 percent. Stimulants, sedatives, and tranquilizers are prescription drugs.

marijuana, derived from the female hemp plant. Used for years in black ghettos, this mild hallucinogen was "discovered" by college students in the 1960s and became part of the counterculture.

Table 11–4 reports U.S. Census data on the use of various substances—legal and illegal—by three age groups in 1979. The table confirms the popularity of marijuana, among illegal substances. Over two-thirds of the young adults (ages 18–25) report having tried marijuana at least once; over one-third say they are current users. Even among the older adults, one in five have tried marijuana.

Many of the substances we have mentioned have a similar potential side effect. In 1980, over half a million Americans were arrested for drug abuse violations. Opium and cocaine (and their derivatives) accounted for 68,100 arrests; 22,500 were arrested for synthetic or manufactured drugs; 84,700 for what the FBI labeled "dan-

gerous nonnarcotic drugs." Nearly half a million (405,600) were arrested for marijuana violations in 1980 (FBI 1981:191).

The status of marijuana in the United States highlights the role of agreements in society. Few experts would suggest that marijuana is more dangerous than alcohol or cigarettes, yet marijuana is illegal while alcohol and cigarettes are legal. Antimarijuana laws were established and enforced, however, by a segment of the society not personally interested in smoking it. Those laws initially violated the desires of ghetto blacks, who had little power to influence the law. The young people who popularized marijuana use during the 1960s were also relatively powerless to affect the laws. As they grew older and became a part of the mainstream political life of the society, however, the agreements began to shift.

With millions of Americans—many of them in the middle and upper classes—having used marijuana, there has been increased public support for its legalization or at least for a reduction in the penalties for its use and sale. After years of general public concern over the "killer weed" and "reefer madness," public opinion is now almost evenly divided on the issue. In a 1980 national survey, 57 percent said "smoking marijuana is morally wrong," while 43 percent said it was not a moral issue (*Public Opinion* 1981a:30).

All these factors have recently begun to find expression in the revision of antimarijuana laws. In some states and municipalities, the possession of marijuana is considered a "petty misdemeanor," and violations are handled much like parking and traffic violations.

This section concludes with an examination of two forms of deviance that are not generally regarded as criminal, though they are often "punished" by legal and social sanctions. Both alcoholism and "mental illness" bring up the same issues we have been discussing in connection with crimes without victims.

Alcoholism

For the most part, drinking alcoholic beverages is legal in America, and it is hardly considered deviant. If anything, total abstention from alcohol is the deviant pattern in terms of our informal agreements. In 1979, the per capita consumption of alcoholic beverages in America was 34 gallons of beer, 2.7 gallons of whiskey, and 2.75 gallons of wine. Compared with 1960, this represented a 44 percent increase for whiskey and a 96 percent increase for wine (U.S. Bureau of Census 1981i:795).

Drinking may be normative in America, but getting drunk is another matter. Drunkenness per se is not illegal, but state and municipal laws prohibit being drunk in a public place, being "drunk and disorderly," and "driving while intoxicated." The FBI estimates that 1,125,800 Americans were arrested for drunkenness in 1980 (FBI 1981:191).

Our informal agreements on drunkenness appear to discriminate by sex in a manner exactly opposite to our agreements relating to same-sex hugging and kissing. We are more permissive with men than with women. Americans are relatively tolerant of a "bunch of the boys whooping it up" as a sign of healthy camaraderie, and the man who refused to participate in such festivities would probably be regarded as deviant. Women gathering together to "tie one on," however, would be met with severe disapproval; they would probably be suspected of all kinds of other deviant behaviors, too.

Sociologists have given special attention to one class of drinkers. This class is composed of "alcoholics"—people who, by medical definition, are dependent on the consumption of alcohol. The Census Bureau has estimated (1979a:124) that there were more than five and a half million alcoholics in the United States in 1975, repesenting 7.3 percent of all males and 1.3 percent of all females.

Alcoholism illustrates an irony that is present in many forms of social deviance. As we've seen, Americans share a general agreement that the consumption of alcohol is expected. Drinking is the norm, and those who refuse to drink at all are regarded as deviant. Yet there's also an agreement that you shouldn't drink "too much." Abiding by the first norm sets up the risk of violating the second, and the "proper" middle ground—drinking the "right" amount— is not precisely defined.

Mental Illness

For many years, sociologists have been interested in the phenomenon of mental illness as a persistent and often tragic form of deviance. The term "mental illness" suggests a medical model of mental distress, a suggestion echoed in the slang expression "sick in the head." Much medical research, moreover, is devoted to the search for organic causes of mental illness, such

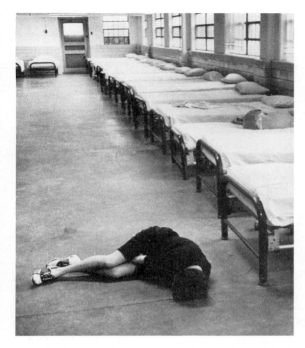

Mental illness is an especially problematic form of deviance. It is difficult to define and determine, and the "cure" is often more a punishment than the condition being treated.

as malfunctions within the nervous system or chemical imbalances in the brain.

But to many scientists today, "mental illness" is a meaningless term. Thomas Szasz (1961), for instance, has written persuasively about the "myth of mental illness." Szasz does not deny that people have the symptoms associated with the term "mental illness," nor that those symptoms can be dysfunctional for the individual, particularly in his or her interactions with others. Szasz objects, however, to the suggestion that something is wrong with the person that needs curing. The medical model overlooks, for example, the possibility that a person's interpersonal difficulties might be related to *situations*. Suppose the FBI and CIA really were tapping your telephone and following you around town. In the medical model,

you'd still be tabbed a "paranoid" and sent off for treatment.

In a related criticism of the conventional view of mental illness, Thomas Scheff (1966) has suggested that mental illness is primarily a matter of labeling: we are mentally ill if others agree that we are and especially if we ourselves join in that agreement. Scientists don't all agree with Szasz and Scheff, but no scientist suggests that the definition of mental illness is an easy one.

Like other forms of deviance, what we call "mental illness" is a matter of breaking agreements. People who are "too" excitedly outspoken in a group or who are "too" quiet and withdrawn may be suspected of harboring some mental "problem" or "disorder." The person who is easily angered or upset, the person who "flies off the handle" with little provocation, and the person who sobs uncontrollably over what seem like minor upsets are also likely to be regarded as abnormal or "just not right."

The more severe forms of what we call "mental illness" involve a person's "losing touch with reality." The paranoid who sees a secret conspiracy to "get" him or her is one familiar example. Or what about someone who is convinced that the world is flat and is trying to convince you of that belief? Anyone who believes that the world is flat is clearly "mentally ill," right? Seven or so centuries ago in Europe, however, anyone who believed the world was round was just as clearly "mentally ill." Both of these people break the prevailing agreements as to what's true. Today, Russians who suggest that the communist system in the Soviet Union ought to be revised or replaced are often judged "mentally ill," and they may find themselves incarcerated for life. Some in the United States feel that criticism of American society should result in a similar fate.

"Reality," after all, is a matter of agreement and "losing touch with reality" is nothing more than breaking agreements about reality. People who broke agreements about reality were once regarded as being possessed by devils and demons and therefore evil. We now regard them as sick and pitiable. Always, however, the notions of mental illness or insanity depend on the reification of agreements within the larger society. It is the process of reification that transforms "different" into "crazy." The purpose of these comments is not to persuade you that mental illness is a fiction; rather, I'd like you to see how complicated and often arbitrary the label is.

In studying mental illness—however it is defined—sociologists have traditionally examined its distribution throughout the population, noting the social characteristics most commonly associated with it. Hollingshead and Redlich (1958), in a classic study, examined rates of mental illness within different social-class groups. They found that the poor had more problems than others: they had poorer mental health, they were more likely to be diagnosed as ill and to be hospitalized, and—if later released—they were more likely to suffer relapses.

The ambiguities surrounding the notion of mental illness make it impossible to determine its extent. One study (Srole 1962) of nearly 1,700 residents of New York City reported that 80 percent of those studied had, at the time of the study, at least one psychiatric symptom. Nearly one-fourth of the sample was found to be "impaired because of psychiatric illness."

Earlier in this chapter, I stated that all of us are deviants. It seems likely that a case could be made for each of us in some way being "mentally ill." As a practical matter, however, only a small fraction of us are formally labeled in that fashion. At the end of 1977, there were 159,405 resident patients in the nation's state and county mental hospitals. Many more were being treated by outpatient clinics (U.S. Bureau of Census 1981i:117).

We've seen that many people are, one way or another, defined as deviant in American society. I have emphasized the extent to which deviance is a matter of labeling, and I'll return to that topic shortly. Whether deviance is a mat-

ter of labeling or not, however, it still is true that some people commit murder, some become addicted to heroin, and some do things that result in their being called "mentally ill"—while others do not. It makes sense, then, to ask what the causes of deviance are. Why do some people break social agreements that other people keep?

Causes of Deviance

Throughout much of human history, people have believed that deviance has a biological cause: some people were simply "born to be bad." This view gained academic support during the nineteenth century, especially in the writings of the Italian physician Cesare Lombroso (1911). Lombroso believed that it was possible to recognize "criminality" in people's faces, and he arranged to have the pictures of notorious criminals displayed in the corridor outside his office. They are said to have been a "criminal-looking" lot.

No reputable scholar now agrees with the **Lombrosian view,** and the ugly and the handsome alike are arrested for crimes every day. Indeed, biological explanations are in general disrepute, though the sociobiological approach, discussed in Chapter 1, may bring about some reconsideration.

Sociologists have given more credence to psychological explanations of deviance. The Freudian point of view, for example, suggests that all people have antisocial impulses that would result in deviant acts were it not for socialization. The development of the individual's superego, the internalization of social agreements, thus prevents deviance. Those who break the agreements, in Freud's point of view, were improperly socialized.

Unstable or broken families—where the parents are separated or divorced or where they fight a lot—are often seen as the source of improper or inadequate socialization. In this view, those deprived of normal family relations are more likely to become deviant than those who are not. Illustrating this point of view, a gang member in the musical *West Side Story* sings, "I'm depraved because I'm deprived."

Although sociologists have paid considerable attention to psychological factors in the study of deviance, they tend to concentrate more on the part played by social structure—with an ironic twist. As you will see shortly, there are two ways in which social structure seems to produce deviance: (1) when the agreements are poorly integrated, in conflict with each other, and/or breaking down and losing support, or (2) when they are operating effectively, shaping and controlling behavior. In other words, social structure can cause deviance when it doesn't work and when it does.

In this section, we'll look at the four major sociological theories about the causes of deviance. First we'll discuss the two theories that explain deviance in terms of the incompleteness of social agreements—Robert Merton's classic study of social disorganization and anomie and the theory of deviance based on the failure of social control. Then we'll look at two theories that relate deviance to the structure of social agreements itself—the theory of "differential association" and labeling theory. We'll conclude the section with a discussion of "conflict criminology."

Social Disorganization

Robert Merton and other sociologists have suggested that deviance results from **social disorganization.** In particular, Merton has focused attention on the disparity between social agreements relating to goals and means.

As we have seen in earlier chapters, every society has shared agreements about what is valued and desired. Wealth, for example, is an agreed-on goal for individuals in many societies. Societies also have established agreements on the acceptable means for achieving goals. In Merton's view, the problem of deviance arises

when individuals who internalize the agreements regarding goals lack the agreed-on means for achieving them. The person who accepts the desirability of a college diploma but lacks the scholarly abilities to achieve it has such a problem. This person might adopt other means—such as cheating on examinations—to achieve the desired goal. The potential discrepancy between goals and means led Merton to construct a typology (Table 11–5) of possible responses to both goals and means as a way to understand different kinds of deviance.

Merton (1957a) described four major types of deviance that result when goals are not integrated with means. "Innovation" is his term for the acceptance of agreed-on goals coupled with the rejection of agreed-on means (the means are often rejected because they are not available). Thus, the child of a poor ghetto family, who is unable to pursue the goal of wealth through conventional means may substitute other means such as stealing or cheating. "Ritualism" is Merton's term for the situation in which a person conforms to the agreed-on patterns of behavior but lacks a real commitment to the goals associated with that behavior. A clerk may continue going to work at an office, doing his or her job as prescribed, without any commitment to getting rich. "Retreatism" is a pattern of withdrawal from society. Heroin addiction is an extreme case of the rejection of both agreed-on goals and means. Finally, "rebellion" rejects both agreed-on goals and agreed-on means *and* replaces them with new goals and means. The person who rejects both the economic goals of capitalism and the accepted patterns of participation in it and who works for the establishment of a socialist economy is an example of a person in rebellion.

Merton's discussion of deviance as a function of the disparity between goals and available means corresponds to one of the most consistently discovered correlates of crime: social class. Whether measured by arrests or by self-reported crimes, the higher the class standing, the lower the crime rate (Braithwaite 1981). Those

Table 11-5

Merton's Typology of Deviance and Conformity

Term	Acceptance of agreed-on Goals	Means	Examples
Conformity	+	+	The nondeviant
Innovation	+	−	The thief, the "crooked" businessman
Ritualism	−	+	The lower middle-class office worker with little ambition
Retreatism	−	−	The tramp, the drug addict, the skid-row dropout
Rebellion	±	±	The political revolutionary

+ Accepts the agreement.
− Rejects the agreement.
± Replaces the agreement with another one.

Source: Reprinted with permission of Macmillan Publishing Co., Inc. from *Social Theory and Social Structure* by Robert Merton. Copyright 1957 by The Free Press, a Corporation, See especially pp. 139–57.

who lack the accepted means for achieving material success may be tempted to seek other means.

Many people who are motivated to engage in deviant behavior fail to do so, because social control mechanisms prevent them. When the social control mechanisms are weak, however, deviance may result.

Lack of Social Control

Psychologists have explained deviance largely as the failure of internal controls, but some sociologists have looked to the failure or lack of external controls. Travis Hirschi and Hanan Selvin (1967), for example, found this point of view useful in examining the frequently noted relationship between broken homes and delinquency. The lack of adult supervision, more typical in broken homes, affects the rate of juvenile delinquency. Children living in families with both a father and a mother are more likely to have after-school supervision than those living with only their mother, since she is likely to be out of the home working. In families where children *do* have adult supervision, broken homes produce no more delinquency than unbroken ones.

The importance of informal social-control mechanisms for deviant behavior is also illustrated in a study of marijuana use among students at the University of Hawaii (Takeuchi 1974). The study began with the observation that even though many people have tried to explain drug use among students, no one has ever thought to ask why students drink beer. Indeed, the student who steadfastly refused to drink beer would probably be regarded as deviant.

The study took the point of view that marijuana was like beer and that all college students would be motivated to try it because of its popularity and publicity. The study then asked why some students did *not* try it. Three different social constraints were found to explain nonuse. First, women were less likely than men to smoke marijuana because American society is generally less permissive about illegal behavior by women. Second, students living with their parents or in dormitories were less likely to smoke marijuana than those living in apartments, because the first two groups experienced greater social control from adult authorities. Finally, Asian-American students were less likely to smoke marijuana than others, perhaps because Asian-American subcultures in America have traditionally been more insistent about law-abiding behavior.

Together, these three social constraints offered better predictions of marijuana use or nonuse than did any of the study's measures of student attitudes or orientations. Among Asian-American women living at home, for example, only 10 percent had ever tried marijuana. At the other extreme, non-Asian men living in apartments, 77 percent had tried marijuana.

You should realize that the lack of social constraints did not *cause* students to smoke marijuana any more than the lack of adult supervision in the home caused the Hirschi-Selvin delinquents to be delinquent. Many people are motivated to be deviant, but only some of them are prevented from it by external social controls. Broken homes, then, don't cause delinquency, though they may fail to prevent it.

Now, our look at theories of deviances will take a strange turn. Having defined deviance as breaking agreements, we'll now see that deviance can result from *keeping* agreements.

Differential Association

The part played by subcultural agreements in creating individual deviance can be found in Edwin Sutherland's (1924) notion of **differential association.** Sutherland argued that the socialization process was essentially the same, regardless of whether the agreements being transmitted were conformist or deviant. The explanation for "deviance," in this view, was to be found in the social groups with whom one associated. A member of a juvenile gang learns and accepts the agreements of the gang, just as a Boy Scout learns and accepts the agreements of scouting and—by extension—the agreements of the larger society.

This point of view provides a basis for criticism of prisons and other penal institutions. Prisons are sometimes referred to as "schools for crime." Associating with no one but criminals can have the effect of further socializing people in criminal agreements. There is a wealth of anecdotal material describing people who were imprisoned for relatively minor offenses but who became dedicated and well-trained criminals during their stay in prison.

The importance of differential association has led some scholars to speak of a "subculture of violence." For example, Marvin Wolfgang and Franco Ferracuti (1967:158) argued:

> Our hypothesis is that this overt (and often illicit) expression of violence (of which homicide is only the most extreme) is part of a subcultural normative system, and that this system is reflected in the psychological traits of the subcultural participants.

This perspective is offered to explain the differing rates of violence in different social classes, ethnic groups, and regions of the country. The South, for example, is noted for more violence than other regions. While this view seems to align with casual observations of different groups, it has been criticized by several later researchers.

Judith Blau and Peter Blau (1982) analyzed rates of criminal violence in the 125 largest metropolitan areas of the United States. To begin, the researchers confirmed the higher rates of violence in the South, fitting common stereotypes of red-neck and good-ole-boy culture. Further analyses, however, show economic inequalities to be the real cause. When economics are taken account of, the greater violence of the South disappears.

The controversy over the "subculture of violence" perspective is likely to continue in the years to come. Here's another controversial view, one we've already mentioned.

The Labeling of Deviants

Although all of us are deviants in one way or another, only a few of us get labeled as such.

Some sociologists have pointed out that the process of labeling can itself be a cause of deviance. Let's look at how this might work.

Edwin Lemert (1951) has distinguished between **primary deviance** and **secondary deviance.** Primary deviance refers to deviant behavior that is generally tolerated by those around you (perhaps because it seems trivial) or deviant acts that you successfully conceal from others. In either event, nobody considers you a deviant nor do you consider yourself one. Although you may be able to continue your particular deviance with impunity forever, it can also provide a basis for your being labeled a deviant. Secondary deviance is that which occurs as a *consequence* of labeling.

Suppose, for example, that you are a young girl growing up in a small town with strict, traditional standards regarding sexual behavior. Premarital intercourse is prohibited in this town and almost nobody does it, especially young girls from respected families like yours. Suppose you did it anyway. That would be an example of primary deviance, and it might not amount to anything as long as nobody else knew about it. If word got around, however, you might find yourself branded as "loose," "easy," or worse. The boys might treat you as though you wanted to have sex with everyone, and the girls might avoid you—perhaps at their parents' urging— as immoral and a bad influence. Eventually, you might give in to the group's agreement and start behaving the way they all seemed to expect you to. Your sexual behavior at this point becomes an example of secondary deviance, illustrating the powerful effect of labeling in perpetuating standards and in structuring the experiences of individuals in society.

William Chambliss (1973) presents a graphic instance of the selective labeling of deviants in his study of two teenage gangs, the "Saints" and the "Roughnecks," which he observed over a two-year period.

The Saints were a group of eight upper-middle-class boys. School officials, teachers, townspeople, and police viewed them as fine,

upstanding youngsters, bound to do well in later life. But behind the backs of parental authorities they were a delinquent gang. Truancy was a daily occurrence for members of the group. One boy would ask to be excused from class. He would then go to the class of a fellow gang member and tell the teacher that his friend was needed at an activities meeting. The teacher would usually oblige, having defined the boys as good students and as honest and responsible. As a group, the boys were never caught in their subterfuge. When individual members were stopped, they would admit their error, apologize, and be forgiven.

Once the boys managed to escape school, they drove to a pool hall or a cafe outside town, where they'd horse around or harass the proprietor. On weekends, the boys would drive to a nearby city, get drunk, play "chicken," vandalize buildings, or uncover potholes and watch while motorists drove into them. The boys were never caught at any of their more serious activities; when they were stopped by the police, they were very polite and contrite, and were released.

In school, the students cheated heavily but were never caught. Since the teachers had decided these were good students, even when the boys didn't do well, they could expect to be given high grades.

The six Roughnecks were perceived quite differently by the community. They came from lower-class families, they didn't act as politely as the Saints did, and they didn't dress as well. Unlike the Saints, too, they were constantly in trouble with the police, who saw them as delinquents and picked them up frequently. Townspeople perceived them as drinkers, fighters, and petty thieves. They assumed that the Roughnecks were on their way to a lifetime of crime. Although the members of the group got passing marks in school, the teachers felt the boys would never "make something of themselves." Some told Chambliss that they were passing members of the gang only because they thought it would be worse for everyone if they didn't.

In terms of their actual delinquency, Chambliss judged the Saints and Roughnecks as about equal, although the Saints were able to indulge themselves more frequently because they had the cars and the money to do so. Community members viewed the two groups in radically different ways, Chambliss suggested, because the Roughnecks were more visible, expressed their attitudes toward those in authority more openly, and committed acts that people of higher classes thought particularly offensive. All these selective perceptions, Chambliss noted, are related to the different social-class origins of the boys.

As a labeling theorist might suspect, most members of the gangs grew to confirm the community's expectations of them. Almost all the Saints graduated from college and became managers or professionals. Of the Roughnecks, the two who had been star football players got scholarships to attend college and became high-school teachers. Two of the other boys were later convicted of murder, and a third became a small-time gambler.

In Chambliss's view, the labeling of deviants becomes a self-perpetuating process—unless the magic circle is broken, as, for instance, by the scholarships offered the two Roughnecks. The Roughnecks accepted the community's definition of themselves as delinquents and became increasingly alienated from the values of the community; the Saints, on the other hand, accepted the community's definition of themselves as basically good, ambitious boys who occasionally enjoyed a harmless prank, and they eventually became solid citizens.

While most research on labeling focuses on its impact on the later behavior of those labeled, labeling can have other impacts. Bruce Link (1982), for example, found that people who had completed psychiatric treatment could still suffer in terms of income and work status if they were labeled as psychiatric cases. The same, of course, is true of those labeled ex-convicts, regardless of their behavior.

Conflict Criminology

Notice how the labeling perspective differs from people's conventional views of crime and other deviance. Where the conventional view looks for the roots of crime in the maladjustment of those committing crimes, the labeling perspective puts the cause in the process by which people are labeled criminals. The labeling perspective is favored, though not exclusively, by conflict theorists.

Chambliss's analysis of the Saints and the Roughnecks illustrates the conflict approach. So does the work of Richard Quinney. For Quinney (1974:37–41), the analysis and understanding of crime should be reorganized around the role of the dominant classes in creating and enforcing the laws. In Quinney's analysis, they create the definitions of what is legal and illegal—and those behaviors that conflict with their special class interests are likely to be illegal.

Beyond their creation and enforcement of the official agreements that define specific instances of deviance, Quinney suggests that the dominant classes in society also establish a pervasive ideology regarding deviance. Crime becomes "morally wrong"; criminals become "evil," even when their behavior is only illegal by virtue of conflicting with the class interests of the dominant classes. If you have difficulty seeing this in your own society, consider those dictatorships in which any criticism of the government is regarded as treason.

While this view of crime and society has obvious value, it has been criticized as being oversimplified. The conflict view offers useful insights into the desperate acts of oppressed minorities—a portion of America's crimes—but it offers fewer insights into white-collar crimes such as price-fixing, deceptive advertising, and medical malpractice.

Individual and Society

Our discussion of deviance has come quite a distance from Bat Guano's "deviated prevert," but two issues traverse that distance. First, there is the issue of "right" and "wrong" that seems inevitably linked to deviance in our minds. One of the ways we've fixed our social agreements firmly in place is by reifying them—by believing them to represent something real and true. Thus, anyone who breaks those agreements seems evil.

By now, however, you should have seen that this view is an arguable one. One person's perverse violation of what's sacred can be another's act of conscience. During the Vietnam War, for example, many young men refused to be drafted into the army; some even fled the country. Some saw the refusal to make war as a supreme act of heroism; others saw it as treason and urged that the strongest sanctions be levied. The lesson of this chapter is that the refusal to be drafted and sent to war was definitely an example of deviance. Agreements were clearly broken, and yet from a sociological point of view the deviance was neither good nor bad. It was simply deviance.

Second, the causes of deviance are a topic of debate. As we've seen, various theorists have offered explanations that differ mainly in terms of who is responsible for deviance. Some argue that deviants themselves are responsible for their behavior and for the punishment they may suffer because of it. Others say that the very structure of society and the actions of those in power create deviance, and that deviants are themselves the victims. This disagreement has persisted throughout history, with occasional swings of the pendulum from one side to the other. It is a critical issue in the area of social control, especially with regard to the punishment or other treatment of deviants.

Social Control

If deviance is the breaking of agreements, "social control" is the enforcement of agreements. Every society has mechanisms for the enforcement of agreements. We have already discussed some important social-control mechanisms in the chapter on socialization. In addition, certain agencies in society have social control as their specific function. We're going to examine three of these—police, courts, and prisons.

Police

The most visible agents of social control in modern societies are police officers. Their job is to see that other members of society keep the agreements and that those who break the agreements are brought to the attention of the group for possible punishment. In recent years, the American police have been increasingly scrutinized by sociologists and the general public. Predominantly white and lower middle class, police are generally conservative politically and share the biases of their racial and socioeconomic classes. The abuse of power by police officers during the civil rights and peace movements of the 1950s and 1960s was widely reported, and many communities instituted civilian review boards to oversee police activities.

In *Police Riots,* Rodney Stark (1972) carefully examined several campus outbreaks of the 1960s. In many of those outbreaks, he found that relatively peaceful demonstrations had turned to violence when the police intervened. Sometimes the presence of large numbers of police sparked a reaction from campus demonstrators. Many times, unprovoked attacks by police led to counterattacks by demonstrators.

Much criticism of police is directed at their discretionary powers. The extent of lawbreaking in a society such as ours is too great to permit total enforcement. Police must choose the laws they will enforce and in what ways. The police could not apprehend every person exceeding the speed limits by one mile per hour, for example, so their efforts are limited to those speeding "too much." The officers on the beat decide what constitutes "too much," and evidence shows that they consider other factors besides the number of miles per hour a person is speeding. For instance, a sociology class at the University of California conducted a simple experiment. Twelve students with previously clean driving records put "Black Panther Party" bumper stickers on their cars. In two and one-half weeks, they had received thirty police citations at a cost of 1,000 dollars (Mitford 1973).

The most damning criticism lodged against police is that of corruption. When we give police special authority to employ force and violence, we expect them to keep the agreements of society even more faithfully than the rest of us do. A number of studies suggest they don't always do so.

Albert Reiss, Jr., (1971) and a team of researchers accompanied urban patrolmen on their rounds. They were astounded by the amount of crime practiced by the officers in their presence. Police rolled drunks, took objects from burglary scenes, accepted bribes, and assaulted numerous individuals without provocation. Overall, one officer in five was observed to commit a crime during the course of the study, and the researchers could only guess at the extent of such crime when the police were not accompanied by researchers.

When William Waegel (1981) spent nine months observing a city detective division, he was struck by the impact of organizational requirements on how the detectives did their jobs. Given forms to be completed and quotas for types and numbers of arrests, the officers tended to "see" the cases that came their way in those administrative categories.

For all their shortcomings, the police generally have the support of the public. Numerous public opinion polls indicate that most citizens believe (1) that the police are doing a satisfactory job or better and (2) that they are basically honest and fair. Paul Benson's (1981) analysis of public opinion data pointed to five qualities of those surveyed that were positively related to the belief that the police were doing a good job.

1. Being middle- or upper-class.
2. Being white.
3. Feeling a part of (not alienated from) the political process.
4. Believing the police were basically honest and fair.
5. Believing crime rates were not increasing.

People who did not have the qualities listed above—not surprisingly—were less likely to feel the police were doing a good job. It is precisely the nonwhites and the poor whom police are accused of not serving very well. Police are also accused of prejudice and discrimination primarily against nonwhites and the poor.

The police themselves, however, tend to feel they do not have the public's support. They tend to view police work as low in prestige and cite lack of community support as their most important problem (Sykes 1978:389–91). This perception of public feelings makes sense, of course, when you realize that the police spend a large part of their time among people who do not trust and support them. The police and impoverished minorities are trapped in a deadly cycle in which actions and feelings between groups reinforce one another (Figure 11–2).

Courts

The aspects of formal social control that begin with the police often—though not always—involve another social control agent: the courts. In theory, the police *allege* that individuals have broken society's agreements; the courts make the final decision and determine the sanctions warranted.

The current operation of the American judicial system has been greatly criticized. While the Constitution guarantees all citizens the right to a speedy trial, many spend long months in jail, awaiting trial. Justice is extremely expensive for those accused of crimes, well beyond the means of many. To create a degree of equity, legal repesentation is now guaranteed to all who are accused of crimes—through public defender offices, Legal Aid, and various other structures. Rather than solving the problem, however, some complain that victims must pay taxes to cover the costs of defending those who

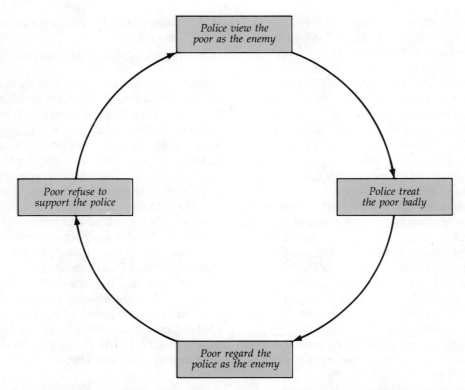

Figure 11–2 Police and the poor: a deadly cycle. (This cycle can be seen to start at any point. It can also be broken or reversed at any point.)

attacked them, while others complain the defense provided to the poor is often low in quality.

Only a fraction of those who commit serious crimes ever go to prison. To begin, we've already seen that many crimes are never reported to police. Many crimes that are reported are never solved. Law enforcement officials speak of "offenses cleared" as those cases in which an offender is identified, enough evidence is amassed to warrant a trial, and the suspect is taken into custody. Of the 13 million serious crimes recorded by the FBI in 1980, *only 19 percent were cleared*. Table 11–6 shows the percentage of crimes cleared by category. You'll notice there's a much greater likelihood of the police clearing crimes against persons than those against property.

Being arrested for a crime hardly means a person will end up in prison. In some cases, charges are never filed. In others, defense attorneys may *plea bargain* with prosecutors, reducing the charges to more minor offenses. Once brought to court, an accused's case may be dismissed by the judge if, for example, the judge feels a sufficient case for conviction is not being made. If the case is prosecuted to completion, the defendant may be found not guilty. If found guilty, the defendant's sentence may be suspended. All in all, it is not possible to calculate the percentage who go to prison among those who actually commit crimes that would warrant such punishment. We can estimate, however, that such a percentage is extremely small.

The apparent failure of the courts to punish

Table 11-6

Crimes Cleared in 1980

Crime	Percent cleared
Against persons	
Murder	72
Aggravated assault	59
Forcible rape	49
Robbery	24
Against property	
Burglary	14
Larceny/theft	18
Motor-vehicle theft	14

Source: Federal Bureau of Investigation, Crime in the United States (Washington, D.C.: Government Printing Office, 1980), p.181.

those who commit crimes has results in great public outcries. Most typical are demands for greater harshness. In 1972, the Gallup Poll found 74 percent of the public feeling that the courts did not deal harshly enough with criminals; by 1980, the percentage had risen to 86 percent. In 1972, 57 percent favored the death penalty for persons convicted of murder; in 1980, 74 percent supported it. These increases point to widespread public frustration with the court system (Public Opinion 1980b:37).

To complicate matters further, when the courts are tough, they are not necessarily fair. The people who are sentenced for crimes are not a cross section of America's criminals. They are disproportionately poor and nonwhite. Whites and the wealthy stand a better chance than poor nonwhites do of avoiding conviction and punishment if they are arrested.

Recent studies suggest, however, that outside the South, discrimination against blacks in the imposition of the death penalty has not been as great as earlier believed. Michael Radelet (1981) and Gary Kleck (1981), in analyses of capital crimes outside the South, find that blacks convicted of murder are somewhat less likely

to be sentenced to death and to be actually executed than are whites. The explanation for this pattern, however, is largely a function of the race of the victims. Those who kill whites are more likely to be executed than those who kill blacks—and most homicides occur within the same race rather than across racial lines. When cases involving white victims and those involving black victims are examined separately, however, black suspects are more likely than whites in both cases (1) to be found guilty, (2) to be sentenced to death, and (3) to be executed. This finding applies to "nonprimary" homicides— where the victim and murderer are not friends or relatives; when they are friends or relatives, the death penalty is seldom imposed (Radelet 1981:922).

As you can see, the court system operates in the midst of great controversy and has many problems. The same is true of the prison system.

Prisons

Near the bottom of the criminal-justice system lie the nation's several thousand prisons and jails. Exclusion from the normal activities of society is one possible punishment for the breaking of agreements.

Ever since prisons first gained popularity about 150 years ago, there have been continuing disagreements about their purpose. Four primary purposes that have been expressed are

1. Protection of society. Locking offenders away prevents them from committing crimes against the rest of society.

2. Punishment. Suffering is a morally just punishment for causing suffering to others.

3. Deterrence. The threat of imprisonment and the example made of offenders will deter others from committing crimes.

4. Rehabilitation. Offenders should be resocialized to permit their return to normal, productive social lives.

How successful are prisons in serving these four purposes? First, the prison system seems to serve partially the purpose of protecting society from criminal assault. Those in prison do not, in fact, commit many crimes against those on the outside *during their time in prison.* They *do* commit crimes against each other, however: homosexual assault, extortion, assault, and murder.

Second, prisons by and large seem to serve the purpose of punishment: loss of freedom and dignity, uncomfortable living conditions, and the punishment prisoners work on each other. Even the "best-adjusted" prisoners count the days until they get out.

Third, the deterrent purpose of prisons must play a part in keeping some individuals from committing crimes. Overall, however, the continual growth in crime rates nationally indicates that it is scarcely a *sufficient* deterrent to crime.

Finally, many sociologists and others have been particularly attentive to the rehabilitative purpose of prisons. Countless innovative programs have been instituted with a rehabilitative aim. This emphasis is reflected in the language we attach to prisons, calling them "correctional" institutions and (those for youth) "reform" schools.

How successful have prisons been at rehabilitation? Gene Kassebaum (1974:80-81) sets the stage for an evaluation:

> The highest priority concerns of 20th-century evaluation of correctional programs revolve around whether the recidivism rate goes down or up. Modern correctional philosophy implicit in the origins of the juvenile court and explicit in the new ideology of adult corrections is necessarily dependent on proof that its programs produce effects. It has nothing else to argue; without this evidence, or in the face of evidence to the contrary, modern juvenile and adult corrections is a pretense that falls short of justice and cure alike.

Recidivism refers to the return to prison by those previously imprisoned and released: the "repeat offenders." The success of prisons' rehabilitative function is measured by the extent to which ex-convicts stay out of prison after their release.

By the recidivism standard, the American corrections system is not very successful. The President's Commission on Law Enforcement (1967:259) reported that between one-third and two-thirds of those released from prison return and that an innovative program producing "a return rate of between one-seventh and one-eighth is remarkable." The general failure of the corrections systems to "correct" has led some critics to conclude that the only thing prisons are known to cure is heterosexuality.

Dysfunctions of Social Control

Throughout this section, I have pointed to various dysfunctions in systems of social control. Among other topics, we have looked at abuses of power by police and at the problems of prisons. In these final comments, I'd like to examine a dysfunction inherent in social control more generally.

Although deviance is generally regarded in a negative light, we have also noted that it is the only source of change in society. A society's agreements change only when individuals break agreements and substitute others in their place. Albert Einstein was a deviant who broke our agreements regarding the nature of reality. Martin Luther King, Jr., was a deviant who broke our agreements regarding black-white relations.

Social control, by definition, militates against social change—including changes that we might later agree are for the better. Social-control systems have the effect of reifying agreements, and social-control agents often behave as though all agreements are sacred.

This phenomenon is clearly illustrated by the following comment from Harry Anslinger of the Federal Bureau of Narcotics in response to a medical report suggesting that marijuana is harmless:

> Of course, the primary interest of the Bureau of Narcotics is the enforcement aspect. From this

point of view it is very unfortunate that Doctors Allentruck and Bowman should have stated so unqualifiably that the use of marijuana does not lead to physical and mental or moral deterioration. (quoted in Arnold 1967:127)

Enforcement of antimarijuana laws makes no sense if marijuana is harmless. From an enforcement point of view, it is reasoned, the harmlessness of marijuana would be "unfortunate." Social control represents a point of view that conflicts with others in society.

This further illustrates the dilemma that deviance presents to society. There can be no deviance without agreements to break; there can be no crime without laws. Still, we make agreements continually. Sometimes we do so out of a fear about the bad things others might do; sometimes we have agreements to ensure good things. In either case, we create deviance in the same pen stroke that creates the agreement. Having created the agreement and the resistance to it, however, we become locked in a seemingly endless struggle; for, once an agreement is made, it seems essential that it be enforced. Soon we have so reified the agreement that we can lose sight of the reason that produced it in the first place. We become "ritualists" in Merton's term, blindly carrying out the letter of the law even when it doesn't make sense to do so.

This dilemma will reappear throughout this book. We'll see that established social institutions can make life unsatisfying at the same time that they make it possible. And in the next chapter and others of this book, we'll see that struggle and change are an inextricable part of the social fabric.

Summary

"Deviance" is the breaking of agreements; "social control" is their enforcement. In this chapter, we have seen that each of these is more complicated than might first appear.

To begin, all of us are deviants to some degree, because all of us break some of the agreements making up the culture and social structure we live in. There are simply too many agreements for us not to break some; in addition, some of the agreements in force at any given time are contradictory, so we don't stand a chance of keeping them all. However, we've seen that most people keep the agreements most of the time— agreements on language, food preferences, clothing styles, the use of objects, and so on.

All of this notwithstanding, some forms of deviance are generally thought of as more serious than others—murder, burglary, rape, and treason are more serious than wearing your hair too long or your skirt too short. Crime is perhaps the clearest form of deviance: breaking those agreements that have been specified in the law, with formal sanctions specified as well. As we've seen, the number of crimes committed in the United States is simply staggering, with crimes against property outnumbering those against persons. Crime statistics are somewhat problematic, as we've seen, since many crimes are never reported to police, others go unsolved, and both the number of arrests and the reporting of them are susceptible to public policy, such as a crackdown on certain offenses.

There is a form of "crime" that raises hot controversy: so-called crimes without victims. Whereas murder has its murder victim, and the victims of burglary and robbery suffer losses, who suffers—it is argued—from homosexuality, prostitution, marijuana use, and other such behavior? Similarly, alcoholism and mental illness are other forms of deviance that—though not crimes per se—can subject people to governmental control, and yet the harm they bring to others is arguable. The issue here is the extent to which government should protect us from ourselves, and people disagree broadly on that.

Scholars have disagreed on the causes of deviance. The old, and now discredited, Lombrosian view suggested that deviance was a matter of genes, blood, and biology—that some people were just "born bad." Although that view may still have currency among the general public, few scholars seriously support it today. The Freudian view links deviance to faulty socialization. Although this perspective is useful to sociologists, three main sociological views see deviance as a matter of social structure and process.

Robert Merton and others have pointed to the ways in which social disorganization can generate deviance. To the extent that the norms and values of society are not well integrated, for example, or to the extent that social agreements are at variance with social conditions, we can expect people to stray from established agreements into what Merton called "innovation" and rebellion. And if social control is weak, the potential for deviance generated by malintegration is likely to become reality.

A rather different point of view holds that deviance can be a result of *keeping* rather than breaking agreements. Speaking of differential association as a source of deviance, Edwin Sutherland indicated that people who are socialized into subcultures of a society may—in keeping the agreements of the subculture—violate agreements of the larger, mainstream society.

Finally, the labeling perspective focuses on the extent to which deviance is a matter of identification. You are deviant to the extent that others label you as such. Whether you are labeled as a deviant, moreover, is more important than what you actually did or didn't do. "Primary deviance" refers to the deviant behavior that precedes any response from others—including all the trivial deviant acts you and I perform continually. "Secondary deviance" refers to deviant behavior that follows and reflects a person's being labeled as "deviant."

Social control is the enforcement of agreements, and it creates problems as well as solves them. The popular press has paid considerable attention to real and perceived misbehavior by the agents of social control—police, courts, and prisons. Ultimately, social control is a powerful force in the reification of society's agreements—creating all the problems that reification entails generally.

Important Terms

deviance
social control
labeling
status crime
white-collar crime
crime without
  victims

Lombrosian view
social
  disorganization
differential
  association
primary deviance
recidivism

Suggested Readings

Becker, Howard
  1963   *Outsiders: Studies in the Sociology of Deviance.* New York: Free Press.
  Here's an early statement of the labeling view of deviance by one of its main proponents. Writing prior to the general, informal acceptance of marijuana use, Becker devoted most of his attention to the subcultural aspects of that grass-roots movement and the nature of social control, zeroing in on what he calls the "moral entrepreneurs."

Goffman, Erving
  1961   *Asylums: Essays on the Social Situation of Mental Patients and Other Inmates.* Chicago: Aldine.
  No one has portrayed the life of inmates more vividly and perceptibly than Goffman. Focusing primarily on mental hospitals—with references to prisons, naval ships, monasteries, and other "total institutions"—Goffman examines both structural and interactionist aspects of life "on the inside." He brings his sociological insights together

in a discussion of the ways in which inmates "make out" by learning and playing the system.

Kassebaum, Gene
1974 *Delinquency and Social Policy.* Englewood Cliffs, N.J.: Prentice-Hall.
Kassebaum presents the many sides of juvenile delinquency as he summarizes the theories and research concerning the nature and causes of a persistent social problem. In part, however, the "problem" lies in the social-structural agreements that define deviance. A variety of "status crimes," for example, define certain behaviors as criminal for young people but legal for adults. Kassebaum examines the role of public policy in resolving delinquency as broadly understood.

Reid, Sue Titus
1982 *Crime and Criminology,* 3rd ed. New York: Holt, Rinehart and Winston.
Here's an excellent and up-to-date overview of the many faces of crime and punishment. Both legal and sociological points of view are presented.

Rubington, Earl, and Martin Weinberg, Eds.
1978 *Deviance: The Interactionist Perspective.* New York: Macmillan.
This is a comprehensive collection of the major sociological pieces in the area of deviance. Though stressing the interactionist perspective, the book offers variation in content and point of view.

Schafer, Stephen
1977 *Victimology: The Victim and His Criminal.* Reston, Va.: Reston.
Victimology is a relatively new focus of attention in sociology, and this readable little book will give you a good introduction to it. Beginning with a historical review of the ways victims have been viewed and treated, the book moves up to current trends.

Scheff, Thomas
1966 *Being Mentally Ill: A Sociological Theory.* Chicago: Aldine.
The ambiguities of defining and treating "mental illness" are examined in detail in this application of labeling theory. In a direct challenge to the "medical model," Scheff places this form of deviance within the context of social agreements, laying the basis for a more humane understanding and handling of emotional differences among people.

Siberman, Charles E.
1978 *Criminal Violence, Criminal Justice.* New York: Random House.
Readable discussion of research on America's crime problem and the criminal justice system.

Skogan, Wesley G., and Michael G. Maxfield
1981 *Coping with Crime: Individual and Neighborhood Reactions.* Beverly Hills, CA: Sage Publications.
Evaluates crime and reactions to crime in three large American cities, generalizing about problem. They find those most vulnerable to crime do least about it.

Straus, Murray, A., Richard J. Gelles, and Suzanne K. Steinmetz
1981 *Behind Closed Doors: Violence in the American Family.* Garden City, NY: Anchor Books.
Survey examining violence in American families and suggestions for reducing violence.

Violent Schools—Safe Schools: The Safe School Study Report to Congress.
1978 National Institute of Education, Washington, DC: U.S. Government Printing Office.
Looks at extent, seriousness, and location of school crime and ways schools and communities might prevent it.

One of the newest areas of research regarding the sociology of crime is called "victimology"— the study of crime's victims. The study of victims is important in many ways. We've already seen that studies of victimization may provide more accurate estimates of crime rates than police records do. Moreover, understanding the nature of some criminal acts requires knowledge of the victim as well as the criminal.

Some studies indicate that victims have an impact on the nature of social control. We've already seen that those who kill whites are punished more severely than those who kill blacks, and research also indicates that other variables can affect punishment. Gary LaFree (1981), for example, found that the likelihood of arrest and the seriousness of charges brought against suspects in sexual-assault cases were strongly affected by such things as the victim's relationship to the suspect, alleged misconduct, willingness to testify, and promptness of reporting. Douglas Smith and Christy Visher (1981) also found arrests less likely when victim and offender knew each other than when they did not. Police were also more likely to arrest the suspect when asked to do so by the victim than when the victim asked that the matter be handled informally. These findings point to the importance of understanding more about victims: who they are and how they behave.

What segments of the population are most likely to be the targets of crime? According to a 1973 U.S. Department of Justice victimization survey summarized by Joseph Sheley (1979:117–134), males are twice as likely to be the victims of violent crimes (except rape) than females and also more likely to be the victims of theft. Teenagers are much more vulnerable to crime than their older siblings, parents, or grandparents are.

The same survey shows that blacks are more likely to be the victims of physical assault than are whites, but that whites are somewhat more likely to be the victims of theft. The split by type of crime for race also holds for income groups: members of lower-income strata are more likely to be assaulted physically, but members of the higher-income strata are more likely to have property taken from them. Finally, statistics show that staying in the suburbs is safer than being in the city; and that within the city, the central district is the most dangerous place, at least in terms of physical assault.

These overall statistics notwithstanding, sociologists have shown special interest in particular types of victims. At the end of Chapter 10, we examined the special case of battered children. Now, let's look at two other special groups of victims: the elderly and women.

Although we have seen that the elderly are statistically less likely to be victimized, their vulnerability has made them a special concern for students of crime. In the poorer areas of large cities, impoverished elderly men and women are frequently mugged, beaten, and burglarized. Especially wrenching is the constant terror that marks the retirement years of many citizens. There is no more dramatic example of this terror than the case of Hans and Emma Kabel (as reported by Gross, 1976).

When Hans and Emma moved into New York City's Bronx borough, it was a happy place for them. Weekend trips into the country reminded them of their native Germany. They had good friends and a good life. Things began changing for the Kabels in the late 1930s when Hans's employer, a meat-processing company, moved its operations to Connecticut. Though Hans commuted four hours a day to his job, most of his coworkers moved from New York to be closer to work. That pattern continued until Hans retired from work in 1964.

Financially, the Kabels were reasonably well off. Besides social security, they had Hans's pension and around twenty thousand dollars in savings. In other respects, however, life was less rosy. The Kabels became increasingly isolated, having only a few close friends, and the growing problems of the city began closing in one them.

The South Bronx had become an urban jungle. Hostility and violence were everywhere. It was generally unsafe to be outside, and more and more Hans and Emma stayed locked in their apartment. When others encouraged them to move—they could afford it—they simply replied that they could not casually walk away from a home they had occupied for half a century.

Then, the violence all around them reached their home. Hans was mugged in the hallway of their apartment building. Even after the muggers took his money, they continued beating him, repeatedly smashing his head against the marble staircase. Friends said he never recovered mentally.

A year and a half later, thugs broke into the apartment and tortured the couple in an effort to find their money. When it became apparent that Hans was unable to communicate anything of value to them, the invaders tied and gagged and beat him.

They were more insistent in questioning Emma. After beating her severely in the face, one of the thugs began puncturing her arm with a roasting fork, leaving an orderly track of stab-marks up her arm until—as he neared her eyes—she gave in and told him where to find two hundred dollars in the apartment. The intruders stayed to terrorize the elderly couple for three-quarters of an hour.

Those two violent episodes marked the beginning of the end of the Kabels' residency in New York. Clearly they could no longer be safe even in their apartment. Emma began making plans to leave. Then, one day, she carefully cleaned and straightened the apartment,

wrote letters to relatives in California, and prepared detailed instructions for the Kabel's attorney. Their affairs thus set in order, Hans and Emma Kabel, seventy-eight and seventy-six years old, hanged themselves in the apartment they could not bear to leave in life. Emma's suicide note said simply "We don't want to live in fear anymore."

Cases like that of the Kabels have drawn both public and professional attention to the plight of crime's victims. From a sociological point of view, there are two avenues leading to the understanding and prevention of crime: learning why some people commit crimes and learning why some people become victims. Both kinds of knowledge offer ways of eliminating crime.

The experiences suffered by the Kabels required people willing to commit the crime and others who were vulnerable. Correcting all the factors that produce muggers would have prevented the attacks on the Kabels, of course. Another approach, however, would correct the conditions which made the Kabels vulnerable to attack: better police protection for the elderly, expansion of citizen groups such as the Guardian Angels, or similar actions.

Be clear that putting attention on the elderly as victims in no way suggests that they are to blame for the crimes they suffer. No one would say that the muggers should go free because the Kabels asked to be mugged by being vulnerable. Bear this in mind as we turn our attention to women as victims.

Two types of crimes committed against women have attracted special attention from sociologists: wife-beating and rape. Let's look at each.

Until fairly recently, wife-beating was considered a family matter, of no concern to police unless the beating created a public nuisance. This view was similar to early views of child abuse. Like children, wives were once regarded as a husband's property. Russell Dobash and R. Emerson Dobash (1981:564–565) describe the situation as follows:

> For centuries husbands have beaten their wives systematically and severely in order to dominate, punish and control them. . . . Husbands have used violence to coerce their wives into behaviors they may have been unwilling to undertake, to punish them for failing to live up to marital demands and expectations, and simply as a prerogative of the husband's superior position. Thus, men have used violence in their attempts to maintain control over their female possession, to retain personal authority, and to gain her personal service and domestic labor.

Not until the 1970s did battered wives receive serious support from outside their immediate families—in the form of shelters for wives and their young children. Battered wives could move out of their homes and live with other battered wives, safe from their abusive husbands. John Johnson (1981) reports that the first well-known shelter was Chiswick Women's Aid in London. Widespread television publicity and a popular book led to the establishment of the National Women's Aid Federation, which maintained 150 shelters throughout England by 1981.

The first American shelters were sponsored by alcoholic self-help groups, since a great deal of wife-abuse occurs under the influence of alcohol. During the 1970s, feminist organizations in America joined the shelter movement, and soon hundreds of refuges were available to abused wives.

Roger Petersen (1980) suggests there are two major explanations for wife abuse. Some argue that pervasive sexism in American society is the root cause, with the marriage contract being regarded as a "hitting license." Others argue that wife abuse is more a function of unem-

ployment, poverty, and the like; the stress associated with economic problems produces frustration, and that frustration results in violence.

If there is any truth to this explanation, we would expect to find wife abuse more common among people lower in economic status. In a partial test of this second explanation, Petersen examined the frequency of abuse among a sample of 602 married women in Maryland—categorized according to their husbands' occupations. His results are presented in Table 11–7.

In general, the table indicates that wife abuse *is* more common at the lower rungs of the social ladder than near the top. Petersen also examined employment stability, homeownership, and other relevant variables, with results pointing in the same direction. However, the frustration of economic problems is only a part of the story. As Petersen shows, wife abuse is a *learned* response to frustration: those who witness wife abuse as children are more likely to practice it as adults.

The other violent crime against women that has particularly interested sociologists is forcible rape. According to the FBI, 71 of every 100,000 American women were reported rape victims in 1980, totaling 82,088 cases. Half of these cases were cleared by an arrest or similar disposition. The FBI itself (1981:15) suggests *reported* rapes are only a part of the story:

> Even with the advent of rape crisis centers and an improved awareness by police dealing with rape victims, forcible rape, a violent crime against the person, is still recognized as one of the most underreported of all Index crimes. Victims' fear of their assailants and their embarrassment over the incidents are just two factors which can override their decisions to contact law enforcement.

As this comment suggests, part of the problem with rape has been the callous treatment

Table 11-7

Occupation and Wife Abuse

Husband's occupation	Percent abused	Number in category
Professional, technical	6	117
Management, administration	4	82
Sales, sales managers	3	41
Clerical	6	16
Craftsman	7	101
Semiskilled workers	15	27
Transport-equipment workers	18	22
Laborers	20	35
Service workers	19	16
Self-employed	16	32
Police, military	9	23

Source: Roger Petersen, "Social Class, Social Learning, and Wife Abuse," *Social Service Review,* September 1980, p. 398.

of victims. All too often, they have been accused—explicitly or implicitly—of asking for what they got. Sue Titus Reid (1982:313–314), for example, cites the not altogether atypical case of a Wisconsin judge who refused to jail a high school student for raping a fellow student at school: the judge informed women that they are indeed sex objects and that they tease men by the way they dress. Two things made the case unusual. First, the judge was unusually candid in expressing his views, saying what others think. Second, the judge was removed from the bench; most who share his views are still on the job. Women who report being raped can expect to be grilled by police and, often viciously, by the defendants' attorneys. Already humiliated by the offense itself, the victim may find herself portrayed publicly as a wanton woman who wanted to be raped and enjoyed it when it happened.

The role of victims in precipitating the crimes committed against them is another subject of interest to sociologists, largely spurred by two studies. The first study, conducted by Marvin Wolfgang (1957), suggested that in one homicide out of five, the victim had "precipitated" the final blow by striking first or initiating a quarrel. The second, more recent, was conducted by Menachem Amir (1971). In a study of violent rape in Philadelphia, he concluded that a number of rapes were "provoked" by the victim.

As you might imagine, Amir's conclusion has not gone unchallenged. Sheley notes that Amir based his conclusions on interviews with the offenders, who frequently claimed that their victims had secretly "wanted it." As proof they offered the fact that the women hadn't resisted or the opinion that their victims had led them on. What such rationales obscure, however, is that the women may not have resisted because they feared even greater harm and that, in many instances, claims of provocation were contradicted by the victim's bruises, cuts, and knife wounds.

As Joseph Sheley (1979:127-28) points out, even if victims do play a role in the crime, that in itself is no reason to "blame the victim."

To point to a victim's more than passive role in an offense neither suggests that the victim desired or caused it nor absolves the offender of guilt. Thus, while we may argue that the person who enters Central Park at night more actively facilitates a mugging than one who enters the park during the day, we do not argue that either wishes to be mugged. Nor is the mugger any less criminal at night than during the day.

Besides the problems described above, victims suffer in many other ways. By participating in the prosecution of the offenders, the victims may lose time from work and even their jobs. They may have to arrange and pay for child care, parking, and the numerous annoyances that accompany court appearances. In some cases, they may even face reprisals from those they testify against.

The rise in crime rates in recent years, along with increased attention to the rights of the accused has produced the beginnings of a backlash in America, concerned with "victim's rights." Some states have created *victim compensation programs* to pay back some of the losses they suffered. At this time, however, being the victim of a crime is a many-troubled thing.

PRACTICING SOCIOLOGY

The data presented below show the crime rates (crimes per 100,000 population) for towns and cities of different sizes. The fact that these are *rates* rather than total numbers of crimes permits comparisons.

In two or three paragraphs, discuss the relationship between population and crime. What are the patterns? Why do they exist? From the standpoint of a resident, what do these data say about your chance of being victimized if you live in a large city or a small town?

Population	Murder	Forcible rape	Robbery	Aggravated Assault	Breaking or entering	Burglary/larceny/theft	Motor-Vehicle theft
250,000 or more	24.4	75	800	515	2653	4250	1085
100,000 to 249,999	12.3	57	333	411	2475	4793	661
50,000 to 99,999	7.6	39	229	328	1980	3946	609
25,000 to 49,999	6.1	30	151	268	1689	3913	452
10,000 to 24,999	5.1	20	93	234	1344	3370	345
Fewer than 10,000	4.5	17	55	222	1131	3172	259

Source: U.S. Bureau of Census, *Statistical Abstract of the United States* (Washington, D.C.: Government Printing Office, 1981), p. 175.

12

Collective Behavior and Social Movements

Collective behavior is a term sociologists apply to relatively spontaneous and unstructured group action such as fads, panics, and political demonstrations. Collective behavior is distinguished from **institutionalized behavior,** which is by definition routinized and highly structured. If all the workers at a factory show up for work on time, that is an example of institutionalized behavior. If, on the other hand, they stay away from work on a wildcat strike or burn the factory to the ground, that is an example of collective behavior.

I'm not saying that collective behavior does not have organized aspects. Either the strike or the factory burning could have been planned in advance by some of the workers. To the extent that the group behavior lies outside institutionally established agreements and is somewhat spontaneous, however, sociologists are likely to regard it as collective behavior.

As we will see, collective behavior is a process in which some established agreements are broken and new ones created. These agreements are created through action rather than deliberation and negotiation. Think for a moment about some of the agreements we have regarding behavior in a theater. People are expected to sit quietly in their seats during the performance, and when they move up and down the aisles, they are expected to do so in an orderly fashion. Individuals are expected to respect the rights of others, and pushing and shoving are clear violations of those rights. When a fire breaks out in a theater, though, all those agreements disintegrate, and a new set of agreements is struck in the mad rush for exits.

Theater panics are only one type of collective behavior. Many different types have interested sociologists, and we'll look at some of the theoretical points of view that have been offered to explain collective behavior.

Social movements are similar to collective behavior because they are group actions that diverge from established agreements. Social movements often grow out of collective behavior, but they are more persistent and more organized. Over time, social movements may produce significant alterations in a society's agreements. The civil rights movement is an example.

Following the discussion of collective behavior, we'll look at some different kinds of social movements and at the elements that make them up. The chapter concludes with a case study.

Types of Collective Behavior

We'll examine two forms of collective behavior in this section. The first doesn't necessarily involve an assembled group. It is a *mass* phenomenon, exemplified by fads, fashions, and crazes, by rumors, and by public opinion.

The second form of collective behavior involves the actions of a group—a lynch mob, for example, gathered together and *acting as a group*. This type of collective behavior occurs in crowds, audiences, and mobs.

Fads, Fashions, and Crazes

Sociologists use the terms **fad,** "fashion," and "craze" to refer to widely shared points of view or practices that last for a limited time and concern matters generally agreed to be unimportant. Certain voguish phrases and manners of speech are examples: "blood," "dude," "do your own thing," "where it's at."

Dance crazes are another example of this form of collective behavior, ranging through the lindy, the Charleston, the jitterbug, marathon dancing, the tango, the mambo, the twist, the frug, the monkey, Kung Fu dancing, disco dancing, slam dancing, and other things that people do with their bodies to music.

Even a partial listing of the various crazes that have swept America during this century alone may cause you to wonder how we survive as a society: goldfish swallowing, telephone-booth crowding, miniature golf, can-asta, flagpole sitting, Monopoly, jogging, karate, barbecues, chain letters, grass, acid, pocket calculators, astrology, Mah-Jongg, massage, hula-hoops, drive-ins, topless dancers, and roller skating. The 1980s opened with home computers and video-game parlors, introducing such diversions as Space Invaders, Pac Man, and Defender.

The popularity of entertainers and other public figures is another example of fads and crazes. Different generations of Americans have become ecstatic and fainted over Rudy Vallee, Bing Crosby, Frank Sinatra, Eddie Fisher, Elvis Presley, the Beatles, Mick Jagger, John Denver, Ozzy Osbourne, and the Sex Pistols.

Clothing fashions and hairstyles go in and out of vogue. Women's hemlines and the length of men's hair have gone up and down for generations. Cardigans go in and out of fashion. So do cosmetics. Women curl their hair, then straighten it. Men grow beards, then shave them off.

Fads, crazes, and fashions are fun, and for many people, they break the monotony of drab existence. They provide a sense of excitement and identification with others, a sense of belonging.

Rumors

A second type of collective behavior involves **rumors**—unconfirmed stories that spread through groups or collectives. They are a type of collective behavior in themselves, and their communication can be an important spur to other types of collective behavior. In groups, the communication of rumors tends to be spontaneous, informal, and unpredictable. With the advent of the mass media, their dissemination can be more widespread and more calculated.

Tamotsu Shibutani has called rumors "improvised news," suggesting that they reflect a desire to understand ambiguous situations. Where "firm" information is both desired and unavailable, people create their own and pass

Joan Baez and Bob Dylan were among the most popular musicians of the 1960s, active in civil rights, peace, and environmental movements. Here they are in a 1976 appearance.

it around. Shibutani (1966:17) thus defines rumor as

> a recurrent form of *communication through which men caught together in an ambiguous situation attempt to construct a meaningful interpretation of it by pooling their intellectual resources*. . . . To act intelligently such persons seek news, and rumor is essentially a type of news. (emphasis in original)

In taking this view, Shibutani notes that the common view of rumors assumes them to be accurate. Indeed, much laboratory research on rumor transmission has focused on the manner in which stories get changed as they are passed from person to person.

Arthur Ponsonby (1930) has provided an excellent illustration of this process in analyzing the successive newspaper reports on the fall of Antwerp, Belgium, to the Germans in World War I. Notice how the initial report that churches in Germany heralded the victory by ringing their bells got continuously reinterpreted and revised—even in *Le Matin*, which reported the story twice.

> When the fall of Antwerp got known, the church bells were rung (*Kölnische Zeitung* [Germany]).

> According to the *Kölnische Zeitung*, the clergy of Antwerp were compelled to ring the church bells when the fortress was taken (*Le Matin* [France]).

> According to what *Le Matin* has heard from Cologne, the Belgian priests who refused to ring the church bells when Antwerp was taken have been driven away from their places (*Times* [England]).

> According to what the *Times* has heard from Cologne via Paris, the unfortunate Belgian priests who refused to ring the church bells when Antwerp was taken have been sentenced to hard labor (*Corriera della Sera* [Italy]).

> According to information to the *Corriera della Sera* from Cologne via London, it is confirmed that the barbaric conquerers of Antwerp punished the unfortunate Belgian priests for their heroic refusal to ring the church bells by hanging them as living clappers to the bells with their heads down (*Le Matin* [France]).

This transformation of presumably happy German priests into martyred Belgians illustrates the "distortion in serial transmission" that has been the focus of most scholarly studies of rumor.

Shibutani, however, points out that rumors need not be inaccurate. Barbara Suczek (1972), in her examination of the rumor of Beatle Paul McCartney's death, concludes that some rumors don't even change through communication: "Among its believers, the story was taught and learned, deviations from the theme were definitely discouraged, and the fundamental details were memorized like a litany" (p.71).

Public Opinion

A third type of collective behavior, one that has received increasing attention in modern mass democracies, is public opinion. **Public opinion,** as Hennessey (1975:5) defines the term, is *"the complex of preferences expressed by a significant number of persons on an issue of general importance."*

Put another way, "public opinion" refers to the attitudes and values generally shared by the members of a population. But unlike the persistent body of social agreements that this book has primarily focused on so far, the social agreements that make up public opinion are more transitory. Public opinion continually forms and reforms in regard to a variety of issues that gain and lose importance for members of a society over time.

Having seen what public opinion is, let's now look at the role it has come to play in our society, how it is formed, and how it is measured.

Role of Public Opinion In 1886, George Thompson addressed the implicit role of public opinion in the form of government envisioned by the United States Constitution, and he also noted the confusion that surrounds the concept.

> People may disagree about the facts; or agreeing about the facts, they may differ in their calculations; or agreeing in the calculation that a certain course will attain one object at the sacrifice of another, they may differ in their estimation of the relative worth of these objects. (1886:7)

Thompson went on to caution that "public opinion" and "the will of the nation," along with other such commonly used phrases, "are really nothing but metaphors, for thought and will are attributes of a single mind, and 'the public' or 'the nation' are aggregates of many kinds."

The Jeffersonian view of American democracy anticipated that citizens would have different points of view about the issues facing them as a society, but that the give-and-take of public debate (as occurred in the New England town meeting) would create a group course of action. This is the sense in which Blumer (1966:48) characterized public opinion as a "collective product," noting that "it is not a unanimous opinion with which everyone in the public agrees, nor is it necessarily the opinion of the majority." As Blumer indicated, it is often possible for a minority group to exercise an influence in the discussion of ideas that is greater than the group's weight in numbers.

The Jeffersonian view of public opinion as the product of rational debate has been increasingly criticized in the context of mass society. Their sheer mass prevents people from coming together to discuss, debate, and decide. Add to this the speed with which many societal decisions must be made and the complexity of many modern issues, and you have something quite different from what Jefferson had in mind when the Constitution was written two centuries ago. Nonetheless, public opinion is relevant to government.

Public officials who must seek reelection to office—plus those who serve at the will of those who must be reelected—have an interest in following (or appearing to follow) the public will. Many public officials, moreover, genuinely feel that they *should* reflect the feelings of those who elect them. By extension, people with a special point of view they wish to see enacted have a special, persuasive weapon if they can show that their point of view is supported by the general public.

During the Vietnam War, for example, many public officials began by supporting the war effort and later changed their minds. Public opinion on the wisdom of the war also changed over time, as Table 12–1 indicates. Some public officials were instrumental in changing public opinion, others changed their opinions on the war at the same time and for the same reasons

Table 12-1

Public Opinion on the Vietnam War

"Some people think we should not have become involved with our military forces in Southeast Asia, while others think we should have. What is your opinion?"

Date of answer	Should have	Should not have	No opinion
January 31, 1965	50%	28%	22%
May 16, 1965	52	26	22
November 21, 1965	64	21	15

"In view of the developments since we entered the fighting in Vietnam, do you think the United States made a mistake sending troops to fight in Vietnam?"

Date of answer	No mistake	Made mistake	No opinion
June 3, 1966	49%	36%	15%
September 30, 1966	49	35	16
February 26, 1967	52	32	16
May 14, 1967	50	37	13
July 30, 1967	48	41	11
October 25, 1967	44	46	10
January 3, 1968	46	45	9
March 10, 1968	41	49	10
May 1, 1968	40	48	12
March 23, 1969	39	52	9
June 28, 1970	36	56	8
June 6, 1971	28	61	11

Source: George Gallup, *The Gallup Poll*, vol. 3 (New York: Random House, 1972), pp. 1921, 1940, 1971, 2010, 2031, 2052, 2063, 2074, 2087, 2099, 2109, 2125, 2189, 2254, 2309.

as the general public, and other public officials undoubtedly changed their opinions to remain on the side of the majority.

Formation of Public Opinion   Although public opinion could conceivably be the mere summation of independently formed, individual opinions, this is hardly the case. Public opinion is the result of *social* processes, involving the influence of close friends, noted public figures, and the mass media.

Sociological research spanning several decades suggests that the impact of the mass media on public opinion is more complex than might appear. In particular, the research of Elihu Katz and Paul Lazarsfeld suggests that the mass media influence general public opinion in a "two-step flow of communication."

In *The People's Choice* (1944), Lazarsfeld and his colleagues developed a hypothesis that the mass media had their primary impact on the opinion leaders or the "influentials" of a community—respected business, governmental, and professional people—and that they, in turn, influenced the general public opinion. In this view, information and ideas flowed directly from the mass media to the community's influentials and then to the general public through networks of social interaction involving those influentials.

This hypothesis was tested by Katz and Lazarsfeld (1955) in a study of Decatur, Illinois, in the early 1950s. The results of the Decatur study, plus later studies by Irving Allen (1975) and others, confirm the "two-step flow" hypothesis. These findings bear an interesting relationship to the eighteenth-century idea of participatory, democratic public opinion. On the one hand, public opinion does indeed appear to grow out of interaction and discussion, as studies show the extent to which people report learning things about current events in discussions with friends. On the other hand, the special opinion-forming role played by the influentials contradicts the democratic aspect of the process. As Blumer pointed out, "public opinion" is not necessarily the opinion of the majority.

Measuring Public Opinion   The interest of politicians and others in knowing the views of the public on a given issue and in helping to form those views has led to the development of sophisticated polling techniques. Earlier in this century, political elections in the country were predicted in a number of ways. Movie theaters offered patrons a choice of popcorn bags printed with elephants (Republican) or donkeys (Democrats) in an effort to determine behavior at the polls, for example. The same symbols were printed on grain bags in agricultural areas as a means for predicting the farm vote.

Now, however, public-opinion measurement is usually undertaken through the use of the elaborate and carefully controlled survey-research methods discussed in Chapter 3. Political and public-opinion polls conducted by commercial organizations such as Gallup (Table 12-1), Harris, and Roper, plus those done by university researchers, give us our primary insight into public opinion.

To review the earlier discussion, effective public-opinion polling depends on selecting proper samples of respondents, asking proper questions, and interpreting the responses properly. (See Chapter 3 to learn what's "proper.") Of these three aspects, the formulation and asking of "proper" questions is perhaps the trickiest. Variations in the wording of questions or variations in the ways they are asked by interviewers—if interviewers are used—can significantly affect the answers obtained from respondents.

During the early years of World War II in Europe, for example, Hadley Cantril conducted two national surveys to determine how Americans felt about the likelihood of the United States getting involved in the conflict. The surveys were designed and conducted in such a manner that each should have given the same, accurate picture of public opinion at that time. In one survey, respondents were asked "Do you think that the United States will succeed in staying out of the war?" Most (55 percent of those with an opinion) said yes. In the other survey, a slightly different question was asked: "Do you think the United States will go into the war before it is over?" Most (59 percent of those with an opinion) said yes. What was public opinion then? Did people think we'd stay out of the war or get into it? There isn't an answer to these questions.

In an important sense, public-opinion polling *creates* public opinion: it doesn't exist until people are asked for their individual opinions, and the manner in which they are asked often shapes the manner in which they answer (see Babbie 1982, 1983).

Over the years, pollsters have grown increasingly aware that many people do not have an opinion on any given issue. They have also discovered that such people are reluctant to admit it, saving face instead by reporting some opinion. Studies that have asked for opinions on fictitious issues show this tendency most clearly. In a political poll in Honolulu, respon-

Rallies are usually a joyful form of collective behavior. These fans have gathered to meet television and movie actress Valerie Harper.

dents were given a list of public figures and asked several questions about each, beginning with whether they had ever heard of the person. Nine percent of the sample said they were familiar with a fictitious person (made up by the researchers). Of those, half reported seeing the person on television, and the same proportion had seen him in person.

Despite the difficulties involved in measuring public opinion, and several historical embarrassments notwithstanding, current activities by qualified and established pollsters provide a useful and often accurate insight into the public's thinking.

Public opinion, like fads, fashions, and the like, is an example of collective behavior in which the participants do not necessarily see each other. Many other forms depend on face-to-face interactions and what emerges from that social chemistry. Rallies are a good place to start with that type of collective behavior.

Rallies

People often engage in expressive group behavior, sometimes displaying a remarkable unanimity of response. College football rallies, religious revival meetings, political nominating conventions, rock concerts, protest marches, and holiday celebrations are all examples. Individuals invest a part of their emotional beings in the whole of the group and sometimes feel themselves to be almost inseparable parts of it. Swept up in the spirit of the moment, they can behave in ways they would otherwise avoid totally and do things that would be seen as inappropriate anywhere else.

Mass Hysteria and Panic

Neil Smelser (1962:84) defines a hysterical belief as:

> a belief empowering an ambiguous element in the environment with a generalized power to threaten or destroy. Examples of hysterical beliefs are premonitions of disaster and bogey rumors, both of which frequently build up as a prelude to panic.

On October 30, 1938, Orson Welles broadcast a radio dramatization of H. G. Wells's science-fiction classic, *The War of the Worlds*. The program used the format of "news reports" to describe a flying saucer invasion of Earth from Mars. Reporters "on the scene" told of mass destruction by Martian death rays. Before the program was over (when the "invaders" were done in by bacteria), thousands of Americans had fled their homes, and highways were jammed with frantic motorists attempting to flee the invaders. This is a perfect example of mass hysteria and panic.

When we want to describe some act as maliciously irresponsible, we often say "it was like yelling 'fire' in a crowded theater." Crowded theaters have often been the scenes of panic. Eddy Foy, an entertainer, described the pandemonium he witnessed at Chicago's Iroquois Theater in 1903.

> Somebody had of course yelled "Fire!"—there is almost always a fool of that species in an audience; and there are always hundreds of people who go crazy the moment they hear the word. . . .
> The horror in the auditorium was beyond all description. There were thirty exits, but few of them were marked with lights; some had heavy

portiers over the doors, and some of the doors were locked or fastened with levers which no one knew how to work. . . . The fire-escape ladders could not accommodate the crowd, and many fell or jumped to death on the pavement below. Some were not killed only because they landed on the cushion of bodies of those who had gone before. . . . In places on the stairways, particularly where a turn caused a jam, bodies were piled seven or eight feet deep. . . . The heel prints on the dead faces mutely testified to the cruel fact that human animals stricken by terror are as mad and ruthless as stampeding cattle. (Foy and Harlow 1928:96–97)*

The Iroquois Theater fire lasted from eight to ten minutes. In that time over 500 people died, and the final death toll from the panic was over 600.

In 1980, a rock concert by The Who in Cincinnati, Ohio, produced a tragic panic. Seats to the concert had been sold on a "general admission" basis, rather than "reserved-seat" basis. When the doors opened, there was a frenzied rush to get good seats: eleven fans were trampled to death.

The stock market has been a scene of panic when rumors of impending economic collapse send stockholders into a frantic flurry of selling. In the two months following the stock-market crash of October 29, 1929, a widely shared agreement held that prices would continue to go down. To avoid economic disaster, individuals unloaded their stock holdings—at low prices if necessary—which of course, drove prices down. Some 15 billion dollars (in 1929 dollars) were lost in the panic selling as tens of millions of stocks traded hands. To make matters more tragic, many of those who suffered financial ruin ended up taking their own lives as well.

---

*From the book *Clowning Through Life* by Eddie Foy and Alvin F. Harlow. Copyright, 1928, by E. P. Dutton and Co., Inc.; renewed © 1956 by Alvin F. Harlow, Reprinted by permission of the publisher, E. P. Dutton.

Mob Action

Panics represent a retreat from a real or imagined danger; mob action, in contrast, represents an attack. Typically, mob action grows out of an agreement that institutional agents are not doing their duty as they should. The mob then takes the matter into its own hands.

Mob actions almost always reflect more than the specific situation triggering them. The specific "evil" is usually the focus of a more general hostility and frustration among those joining the mob. Think, for instance, of the Boston Tea Party, when the destruction of British tea reflected a whole host of grievances with the British crown.

Once mob action begins, its target can widen broadly. An example is provided by the 1930 lynching in Leeville, Texas—just one of nearly 2,000 lynchings that have taken place in America in this century.

> When the mob discovered that their would-be victim was confined in the vault of the courthouse and was not readily accessible, they turned their fury on the courthouse itself, burning it recklessly and gleefuly. Then, having killed their now accessible victim, they took his body to the Negro section of town, mutilated and burned it, and wreaked havoc on the property of many innocent Negroes. (Turner and Killian 1957:133).

Riots

Riots are similar to mob actions in hostility and violence, but the targets tend to be more general. In race riots, all members of the hated race can become equal targets for violence; and once riots begin, violence for its own sake can become the norm. Race, religion, social class, ethnicity, and nationality have all provided the basis for riots. Often, several such bases are involved.

Midway through the Civil War, in 1863, the federal government enacted the nation's first draft law. It called for the conscription of young men into the Union army and allowed men to buy exemption from the draft for $300. The $300 exemption immediately outraged poor workers and labor organizations. The Civil War was already unpopular in the North, and the draft law was viewed as an attempt to force poor people to fight in it.

Ironically, blacks—the poorest of all—became the chief *target* of the riot. Most simply put, poor white workers felt they were being forced to fight for the liberation of blacks who would then flood an already-tight job market. This sentiment was strongest among the newly arrived Irish workers of New York City. The "New York draft riots" of July 1863 were probably the most severe riots in American history. An estimated 2,000 people were killed, and millions of dollars worth of property was damaged. One newspaper at the time called it "a perfect reign of terror" and expressed the belief that "not a single negro will remain within the metropolitan limits" (quoted in Lofton 1957:136).

Riots did not begin nor did they end in 1863, and you are probably already familiar with some of the more recent riots in America such as the "big-city" riots in New York, Detroit, Newark, Watts, and elsewhere during the late 1960s and the many campus disturbances of that same period.

Riots present a challenge that cannot be ignored to social-control agents such as the police. Local police have often, in the past, looked the other way when lynchings were taking place, but full-blown riots must be faced by institutionally constituted authorities. And, as noted in Chapter 11, the police themselves often become swept up in the hysteria of the moment, needlessly destroying, hurting, and killing.

Issues in the Study of Collective Behavior

As we've seen, the term "collective behavior" covers a wide variety of actions. Some, like fads, fashions, and crazes, are basically harmless (if you're not a goldfish) and simply fun. Others, like panics, riots, and mobs, are dangerous. To explain collective behavior, particularly that which takes place in crowds (rallies, panics, mob actions, and riots), sociologists have come up with a number of different theories. In this section, we'll look at the controversy surrounding the nature and behavior of crowds and then at an influential general theory of how collective behavior develops.

Behavior in Crowds

Historically, social investigators have been most impressed with the emotional force and unity of purpose often apparent in crowds. In the classical view, the crowd was an emotional, unreasoning force destructive of civilized life. This point of view, the dominant one in the study of crowds, is represented by Gustave le Bon, Sigmund Freud, and Herbert Blumer. We'll first look at some of their views and then at the theories of some of their critics, who see more rational processes at work in crowds.

Le Bon   The view of the crowd as irrational emerges most clearly in what is generally regarded as the first major work on collective behavior, Gustave Le Bon's *The Crowd* (1895). "The crowd is always intellectually inferior to the isolated individual," Le Bon (1895:33) wrote, and it is characterized by:

> impulsiveness, irritability, incapacity to reason, the absence of judgement and of the critical spirit, the exaggeration of the sentiments, and others besides—which are almost always observed in beings belonging to inferior forms of evolution—in women, savages, and children, for instance. (pp. 35–36)

Much of Le Bon's attention was directed at what he called the "law of mental unity of crowds." Individuals gave up their mental individualities to the "group mind," he said, forming a new entity akin to a biological organism. Under such conditions, the degree of emo-

tional contagion and suggestibility would be strong. If one person became angry, that anger could sweep across the others in the crowd. If one became violent, so did the others.

It seems fair to say that Le Bon reified the crowd. He often spoke of how the *crowd* thought, felt, and acted. The crowd was, for Le Bon, a hideous beast, threatening civilized society. More to the point, he had seen what crowds in the French Revolution had done to the old, aristocratic order, a set of agreements that he clearly shared.

Freud   Freud, who acknowledged his respect for Le Bon's ideas (Freud 1921) in his work on group psychology, also saw the crowd as an irrational force. But in contrast to Le Bon, Freud saw in this irrationality not a giving up of individuality so much as a regression of the individual to an infantile state. In crowds, individuals could experience dependence on a parentlike leader, identify with the leader, and take on the leader's characteristics, thoughts, and emotions as their own. As members of a crowd, moreover, individuals could experience the sense of omnipotence that infants appear to experience before they differentiate themselves from their environment.

Blumer   Building on the theories of Le Bon, Herbert Blumer, whose ideas on symbolic interactionism we discussed in Chapter 2, sought to describe the specific mechanisms through which contagion operates in crowds. Blumer defined his concept of "circular reaction" as "a type of interstimulation wherein the response of one individual reproduces the stimulation that has come from another individual and in being reflected back to this individual reinforces the stimulation" (Blumer 1939:170).

Blumer's examination of collective behavior reflected a more general interactionist point of view. Blumer thought the circular reaction of crowds was unlike the thoughtful reasoning that characterized other social interactions, and he likened it to the collective mindlessness of cattle.

Herbert Blumer
1900–
St. Louis, Missouri

Some Important Works

Symbolic Interactionism: Perspective and Method (Englewood Cliffs, N.J.: Prentice-Hall, 1969).
"Collective Behavior," in *Principles of Sociology,* ed. Alfred McClung Lee (New York: Barnes & Noble, 1946 [1939]).

Blumer is the foremost contemporary representative of the symbolic interactionist school of sociology that developed in the University of Chicago in the 1920s and 1930s. His main substantive contributions have been in the area of collective behavior, bringing an interactionist point of view to that subject.

Blumer's contributions to American sociology have gone far beyond his scholarship. He has served actively in editorial capacities; within professional associations (among other things, as president of the ASA); in helping create the great department of sociology at the University of California, Berkeley, during the 1950s and 1960s; and for hundreds (perhaps thousands) of contemporary sociologists, as a powerfully stimulating teacher.

One sees the process clearly amidst cattle in a state of alarm. The expression of fear through bellowing, breathing, and movements of the body, induces the same feeling in the case of cattle who, as they in turn express their alarm, intensify this emotional state in one another. It is through such a process of circular reaction that there arises among cattle a general condition of intense fear and excitement, as in the case of a stampede. (1939:170)

Pursuing this bovine metaphor, Blumer saw "milling" as a basic form of behavior in crowds: "individuals move around amongst one another in an aimless and random fashion, such as in the interweaving of cattle and sheep who are in a state of excitement" (1939:174). The circular reaction fostered by milling set the stage for the development of rapport among crowd members, collective excitement, social contagion, and, finally, spontaneous behavior.

For Blumer, collective behavior, with its circular reaction and contagion, was a source of more general social unrest, resulting in social movements and revolutions. Collective behavior forged individual "restlessness" into social unrest. Blumer saw social unrest, at the same time, as an "incipient preparation for new forms of collective behavior" (1939:173).

The Formation of Crowds

One way in which sociologists have attempted to study crowd behavior is by creating incidents outside the laboratory and seeing how people in the neighborhood respond to them. In one such investigation, Stanley Milgram, Leonard Bickman, and Lawrence Berkowitz (1969) tried to determine whether the size of a crowd influences the decision of newcomers to join the group or pass by.

Milgram and his colleagues constructed the following situation. In 1968, on a busy street in New York City, they marked off a fifty-foot segment of sidewalk. At the beginning of each of thirty trials, one or more of their confederates would enter the segment, stop and stare at a particular sixth-floor window for one minute, and then move on. A few barely visible figures could be seen talking near the window, but otherwise there was nothing noteworthy about the view.

The researchers found that when only one confederate stopped and gazed at the window, 4 percent of passersby stopped to look up. As more confederates were sent in on each trial, the percentage of bystanders they attracted increased. On trials when fifteen confederates stopped to look (the maximum number used), up to 40 percent of the passersby were enticed enough by the scene to stop and look for themselves.

Some passersby, while not actually stopping, nevertheless looked up at the window as they walked by. For this group, one confederate standing and gazing at the upper-story window was enough to cause 42 percent of the passersby to glance upward. As the number of confederates in the crowd increased to fifteen, the percentage of passersby who looked rose to 86.

Emergent Norms

Earlier, I characterized collective behavior—unlike institutionalized behavior—as a process in which people create their own agreements. This creation of agreement is the focus of another point of view taken by scholars studying collective behavior. In contrast to the "contagion" theories of Le Bon and Blumer, other scholars, such as Ralph Turner and Lewis Killian (1972), have approached collective behavior as the creation of **emergent norms.**

Turner and Killian suggest that what we call "collective behavior" occurs in situations where conditions and expectations are ambiguous. In the case of a theater fire, for example, people may not know the extent of the danger, and most of us have not had many prior experiences with such situations. The collective behavior that emerges, then, represents the process of arriving at some solution to the unfamiliar situation. The chaos that often accompanies collective behavior is caused by people not knowing what's expected of them, in a context of unfamiliar circumstances.

The view of collective behavior as a form of coping with life's situations also anticipates another view. In more recent analyses, scholars have come to see increasing signs of rationality in collective behavior. The stereotype of such behavior as emotional and irrational is not a sufficient picture of the phenomenon.

Reason in Crowds

Whereas the earlier view of crowd behavior saw mostly emotional unpredictability, Richard Berk's (1974) analysis of an antiwar demonstration portrays crowd behavior as far more calculating, all the more so because he recognizes that crowds are composed of individuals. In that context, he observes:

> In summary, each individual in the crowd is faced with a series of decisions. Options for actions are noted, the likelihood for various events assessed, preferences are constructed and eventually the "best" outcome selected. In a group context, all these processes depend on others in the crowd. Hence, one can view milling before concerted action as a period in which these assessments are made. . . . Crowds will continue to mill until mutually satisfactory solutions occur and are widely known.*

Berk's suggestion that crowd behavior can be examined as a rational, decision-making process has opened up a new line of inquiry. As only one example, Norris Johnson and William Feinberg (1977) have offered an elaborate, mathematical model of crowd behavior, considering such factors as suggestibility, the actions of speakers, and so forth. Like Berk, they too have been interested in the part played by "milling

---

*Richard Berk, "A Gaming Approach to Crowd Behavior," *American Sociological Review* 39:3 (June 1974):364. Reprinted by permission.

about," as individuals float from one small group to another, seeking the ideas of others and finding people with whom they agree. It seems likely that future studies of collective behavior will look more to the rationality of crowds than to their irrationality.

The Structural Sources of Collective Behavior

The structuralist point of view on collective behavior has been most thoroughly stated by Neil Smelser, a student of Talcott Parsons, in the classic *Theory of Collective Behavior* (1962). Smelser's examination of collective behavior is patterned after the economic **value-added model.** In the economic version, new "value" is added at each stage in the processing of a resource as it becomes a usable commodity. As iron ore successively becomes steel, parts of a machine, and finally the assembled machine, it becomes gradually more valuable. In a similar fashion, Smelser (1962) traces the "production" of collective behavior from start to finish. Let's look at each stage in Smelser's model.

1. *Structural conduciveness.* To begin, in Smelser's view, collective behavior cannot occur unless certain structural conditions permit it. Using an economic example, he notes that a financial panic cannot occur under conditions in which property can be passed only from father to eldest son at the father's death. By the same token, a race riot cannot develop without races, nor a confrontation with police without both police and confronters.

2. *Structural strain.* Next, collective behavior requires some degree of "disagreement," as we have used the term in this book. It requires conflicting points of view. They may occur in disagreeing groups, such as racial, ethnic, or religious groups. There may also be a disagreement between ideas—between the general value placed on economic success and beliefs about the future of the economy, for example.

3. *Growth and spread of a generalized belief.* Members of a group must create and share their own agreements, such as the belief that Martians are invading Earth or that blacks are invading Cicero, Illinois. Such agreements can take the form of hysterical beliefs about present or future events, hostile beliefs about outgroups, and the like.

4. *Precipitating factors.* Against the backdrop of general unrest, something must occur that brings matters to a head. In a situation of general concern over the possibility of residential integration, a black family's moving into a white neighborhood may be sufficient. At a time of general economic concern and uncertainty, the meeting of high-level economic officials may be the precipitating factor for a financial panic.

5. *Mobilization of participants for action.* Collective behavior needs a triggering event. Sometimes it takes the form of a fistfight in an assembled crowd. A financial panic may be triggered by the sale of a large block of stocks. Stark (1972) has suggested that the arrival of police at a demonstration can trigger a riot. At the Iroquois Theater it was someone screaming "Fire!"

Finally, Smelser (1962:17) discusses the effects of social-control agents on collective behavior. "Stated in the simplest way, the study of social control is the study of those counter-determinants which prevent, interrupt, deflect, or inhibit the accumulation of the determinants just reviewed."

In applying his value-added model to the control of hostile outbursts such as a riot, Smelser (1962:267) summarizes the following principles for maintaining order and preventing violent collective behavior:

1. Prevent communication in general so that beliefs cannot be disseminated.
2. Prevent interaction between leaders and followers so that mobilization is difficult.
3. Refrain from taking a conditional attitude toward violence by bluffing or vacillating in the use of the ultimate weapons of force.
4. Refrain from entering the issues and controversies that move the crowd; remain impartial, unyielding, and fixed on the principle of maintaining law and order.

Smelser's is a comprehensive and carefully thought-out model of collective behavior and social movements, intended to be general enough to include all instances of the phenomenon. As we move on now to an examination of social movements per se, we'll see that other scholars have taken exception to Smelser's model.

Types of Social Movements

In addressing **social movements,** sociologists have sought first to define the phenomenon and to create typologies of movements. They have not always agreed, but the ways in which different sociologists have defined and typed movements is a useful introduction.

Blumer defines social movements as "collective enterprises to establish a new order of life" (1939:199). He goes on to say that social movements "have their inception in a condition of unrest, and derive their motive power on one hand from dissatisfaction with the current form of life, and on the other hand, from wishes and hopes for a new scheme or system of living" (1939:199).

Along the same lines, William Cameron says, "A social movement occurs when a fairly large number of people band together in order to alter or supplant some portion of the existing culture or social order" (1966:7). A social movement, then, is an attempt to alter a society's agreements. Collective behavior such as riots may have the consequence of changing agreements, but changing agreements is the *overt* purpose of social movements.

All sociologists agree that there are different types of social movements, but they disagree on what the types are. Blumer (1939), for example, refers to "general" social movements, such as the peace movement and the labor movement, as distinct from "specific" ones for reform and revolution. He also distinguishes "expressive" movements (for example, religious, fashion) from "revivalist" and "nationalistic" movements.

Cameron (1966) speaks of four major types: "reactionary," "conservative," "revisionary," and "revolutionary." Smelser (1962) distinguishes "norm-oriented" from "value-oriented" movements. Louis Wirth (1957) has suggested four types among minority groups: "pluralistic," "assimilationist," "secessionist," and "militant." Other sociologists, as you might imagine, have suggested other classification schemes. In this section, we'll examine some of the major types of social movements that we have mentioned.

Expressive Movements

As the name suggests, **expressive movements** have the primary purpose of allowing the expression of feelings. Religious revivals such as those led by Dwight Moody, Billy Sunday, and—more recently—Billy Graham are good examples of expressive social movements. They draw on an individual's inner feelings and provide a vehicle for their expression. The encounter-group movement is a secular example.

Such movements focus directly on a changing individual, but they typically have social goals as well. To those participating in them, they offer a set of beliefs, values, and norms different from the agreements prevailing in the general society. Understandably, participants in such movements are likely to hope that the whole society will come to accept the new set of agreements. In some cases—as in Billy Sunday's support of Prohibition—expressive movements seek a more direct influence on society.

Reactionary Movements

Some social movements represent a reaction to real or perceived shifts in society's agreements. The aim of these **reactionary movements** is to replace the new agreements with old ones. Religious revivals—as the term "revival" suggests—sometimes have this flavor. So do a variety of cultural and political "nativistic" movements. These movements are characterized by efforts of the original residents of an area to restore patterns threatened or destroyed by newcomers.

During the early 1870s in California and during the 1890s elsewhere, Native Americans formed a movement popularly called the "Ghost Dance," which foretold a time when all American Indians would be reunited and their past glory restored. The whites who stole away their lands would be no more, and they would live happily without death, disease, or misery (Mooney 1939). The more recent militancy of Native Americans and the rebirth of aboriginal Indian culture is a nonmystical nativistic movement, at least in part.

As indicated in Chapter 9, every major wave of immigration to America has been met with nativistic resistance from earlier immigrants. Longing for "the good old days" and urging the restoration of old values, groups such as the American Protective Association, the Ku Klux Klan, and the John Birch Society are examples of reactionary, nativistic social movements.

Conservative Movements

Conservative movements are similar to reactionary ones, except that they seek to maintain the agreements that they regard as being *in danger* of change. The distinction between the two types, then, depends on whether you think the old agreements have already changed or not.

During the late 1960s and early 1970s, the loosely organized movement in support of American involvement in Vietnam could be considered an example of a conservative social movement. The antiwar movement was correctly seen as a challenge to the influence of the military and the role of military solutions in American foreign policy. More recently, movements in opposition to the Equal Rights Amendment and gay liberation and in favor of stockpiling nuclear armaments offer examples of conservative social movements.

Reformist Movements

Crossing the line between stability and change, we find a wide variety of social movements dedicated overtly to the change of society's agreements. Such movements typically have specific and limited goals, as distinct from revolutionary movements, which we'll discuss shortly. Opponents of **reformist movements** may damn them as revolutionary whether they are or not.

The tremendous variety in reformist movements is perhaps illustrated by the following goals: prohibition of alcoholic beverages, legalization of marijuana, declaring war on Cuba, withdrawing from the war in Vietnam, promoting birth control, giving women the vote, and ending the death penalty.

Revolutionary Movements

The border line between reformist and **revolutionary movements** is as fuzzy as the one separating reactionary and conservative movements. In general, however, while reformist movements seek to improve on existing social structures bv changing some specific agreements, revolutionary movements have a broader goal: to supplant all or most of the structure with something new. The fight for American independence, then, was revolutionary in the sociological point of view as well as in our everyday language.

Some social movements are both reformist and revolutionary, depending on one's perspective and on future events. An example of such an ambiguous movement is the mass labor strikes that immediately followed World War I in the United States. In 1919 alone, there were major strikes involving hundreds of thousands of workers in shipbuilding, railroads, coal, steel, and textiles.

The strikes of 1919, according to labor historian Jeremy Brecher (1972), were brought on by the rising cost of living and by the new sense of power workers had gained during the war when they realized how crucial they had become to the functioning of the economy. Even during the war, the number of strikes grew dramatically. With the end of the war, workers wanted to cash in on the promises made to them in the previous years. Their employers, however, wanted to recoup the wage gains workers had been able to make during the war years and tried to whip up antilabor sentiment by raising the specter of another Russian Revolution, which had occurred only two years before.

One of the most important confrontations between workers and owners took place in Seattle, Washington, where 35,000 shipyard workers struck for higher wages in January 1919. When it became clear that the shipyard owners, with the aid of the government, were determined to break the strike rather than negotiate, organized workers in industries throughout the city planned a general strike. A General Strike Committee was formed to run the strike, drawing representatives from all the participating locals.

Until mid-February, when the strike was called off, the General Strike Committee was, in effect, a parallel government for the city of Seattle. Under the committee's auspices, work-

ers coordinated the continuation of basic services for the duration of the strike. They set up a milk distribution system and a meal service for the strikers. So much effective power had flowed from the traditional institutions of control to the strike committee that one reporter quoted by Brecher wrote: "Before the committee, which would seem to have been in well-nigh continuous session day and night, appeared a long succession of businessmen, city officials, and the Mayor himself, not to threaten or bully, but to discuss the situation and ask the approval of the committee for this or that step."

Was the Seattle general strike a reformist or a revolutionary action? Contemporaries had different views on the matter. The participants themselves weren't sure. It had begun as a simple demand for higher wages, but it had grown far beyond that. As an editorial in the labor-oriented *Union Record* said: "We are undertaking the most tremendous move ever made by LABOR in this country, a move which will lead— NO ONE KNOWS WHERE!" From the point of view of government officials, capitalists, and a large segment of the middle class, the general strike was seen as a step toward revolution, aimed at the replacement of the capitalist system. This fear led officials to call in federal troops and deliver an ultimatum to the strikers. The strikers, aware that they would be completely outnumbered and outgunned, and facing strong opposition from the national headquarters of the AFL affiliates, capitulated.

Although there were no general strikes like Seattle's, the other strikes of the year tended to involve reformist demands—usually, higher wages or union recognition—but were also inspired by more radical sentiments. This example illustrates the point that there is no clean dividing line separating the different types of social movements. Nonetheless, the conceptual distinctions made in this section can provide insight into the different ways people attempt to make an impact on the established agreements of society.

Elements in the Study of Social Movements

Merely cataloguing social movements according to "type" doesn't tell us very much about the ways societies operate, although examining their similarities and differences is a first step toward understanding. Sociologists have devoted most of their attention to an analytical dissection of the several aspects of social movements. In this section, we'll review some of the things sociologists have looked at and what they've seen.

Conditions

The expression "an idea whose time has come" probably describes *all* social movements to an extent. No social force can become a movement unless it appears among people who are somewhat receptive to it. The agreements it proposes to protect or change must seem in need of being protected or changed.

When Marx and Engels began the *Communist Manifesto* with the cry, "Workers of the world, unite! You have nothing to lose but your chains," they touched a well of preexisting frustration and misery throughout the Europe of the Industrial Revolution. The same pronouncement today at a labor union's national convention, however, would probably produce little more than yawns or embarrassment.

There have been supporters of sexual equality throughout our nation's history. The centennial celebration of 1876 was "marred" by the opposition of feminist activists who loudly protested a century of sexual discrimination. Yet the women's movement in America continued to ebb and flow, requiring a century and a half of nationhood before women were allowed to vote. It has taken another fifty years to reach only the eve of full equality.

Similarly, there have been opponents of nuclear power ever since its inception, but only recently has this newest social movement gathered momentum. The same can be said about popular opposition to the nuclear arms race; I have examined both of these issues at the conclusion of this chapter.

The Role of Discontent

For the most part, social movements feed on feelings of discontent: fear, frustration, anger. Few grow purely from feelings of love, joy, or hope. Even expressive religious movements or utopian movements such as recent communalism represent a disillusionment with the way things are in the general society. The current environmental movement, for example, comes less from a love of nature than from a fear of its destruction. Social movements provide an outlet for such feelings and a vehicle for changing conditions that cause them.

Sociologists have found "discontent" to be a complex phenomenon. Relative deprivation, for example, appears to be a more powerful source of social movements than objective deprivation, as students of revolutions have discovered.

James Davies (1962) has suggested a model of the conditions under which revolutions are the most likely to occur. "Revolutions are most likely to occur," he argues, "when a prolonged period of objective economic and social development is followed by a short period of sharp reversal" (1962:6). Davies's model is represented graphically in Figure 12–1.

In Davies's view, then, economic deprivation per se does not produce revolutions; rather the cause is the discrepancy between what is wanted and what is gotten. People will tolerate *some* "gap," be willing to live with somewhat less than they want. As conditions improve, however, their desires expand accordingly, and they continue expanding even when objective circumstances become less favorable. Ironically, people who have lived quietly in abject poverty may revolt after a period of substantial improvement, a situation often referred to as "the revolution of rising expectations."

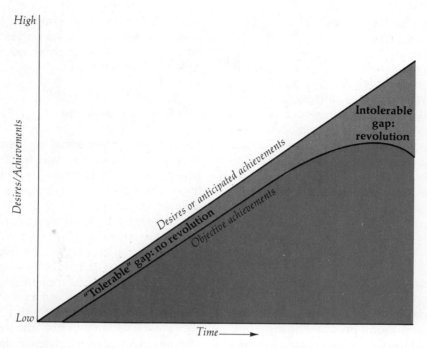

Figure 12–1 A model of revolutionary conditions. Source: Adapted from James Davies, "A Theory of Revolution," American Sociological Review 27 *(February 1962):6. Reprinted by permission.*

What we have just said about economic conditions holds for freedom as well. Revolutions usually do not occur because people have little or no freedom; they are more likely when freedoms are reduced. The Berkeley free-speech movement of 1964, for example, occurred when students were told they could *no longer* sell political materials on campus after years of a gradual liberalization of such activities. Earlier generations of students never would have considered protesting such a lack of freedom.

It was in this context of reducing freedoms already held, that Smelser warned against vacillation by social-control agents in preventing or quelling hostile outbursts such as riots. Remaining firm and unswerving throughout a confrontation was less likely to produce violence than was a tightening up of controls after allowing more freedom.

Breakdown versus Solidarity

Although Smelser's analysis makes sense and has enjoyed popularity in sociology, it has come under criticism in recent years. One of the more powerful critiques has come from Charles Tilly and his associates (1975).

Tilly traces Smelser's view of collective behavior and social movements back to Durkheim's depiction of society in terms of a collective morality that keeps individuals in check. In times of social upheaval, disruption, and great social change, according to Durkheim's view, people become detached from the tradition and from the power of normal social constraints. As social control weakens, deviance—including protest and rebellion—can be expected.

Tilly suggests that this view of rebellion implicitly (and sometimes explicitly) assumes that the rebels are drawn from the misfits of society and that rebellion in this context must be seen as fundamentally wrong. Tilly labels this view of rebellion the "breakdown" theory.

The main alternative to breakdown theories of rebellion, Tilly suggests, is a variety of *solidarity* theories. From this contrasting viewpoint, rebellion can be seen as something positively and intentionally created rather than something that stumbled out of chaos. The Marxist perspective offers one example of the solidarity theory—the working class unites to overthrow the capitalists in the simplest version of this view. In his examination of the period 1830–1930 in Europe, Tilly finds more support for the solidarity view than for the breakdown view of collective behavior and, especially, of violence. Violence does not grow so much out of times of chaos as it grows out of the normal functioning of society.

To bring the issue up to date, Tilly cites two different explanations for the 1960s rioting in the Watts district of Los Angeles. The contrast is an interesting one since both explanations come from official, government-sponsored studies.

> "When the rioting came to Los Angeles," the [Governor's Commission] commissioners concluded, "it was not a race riot in the usual sense. What happened was an explosion—a formless, quite senseless, all but hopeless violent protest—engaged in by a few but bringing great distress to all." Pure breakdown theory.
>
> Three years and many ghetto conflicts later, a president's commission on civil disorders (the "Kerner Commission") edged away from the simplest version of breakdown theory. It still described the "basic causes" of the 1967 conflicts as (1) pervasive discrimination and segregation; (2) black migration and white exodus; (3) black ghettos; (4) frustrated hopes; (5) legitimation of violence and erosion of respect for authority; (6) powerlessness; (7) incitement and encouragement of violence by extremists; (8) bad police-civilian relations in the ghetto. These were, to the commissioners' minds, the prime components of

> an "explosive mixture" which led to a "chain reaction of racial violence." (Tilly et al. 1975:292)

We'll be returning to this and related differences in the implicit views people have in regard to disruption and conflict in society. For now, let's turn to the issue of success and failure. Like all other aspects of collective behavior and social movements, it is more complex than might be imagined.

The Role of Success or Failure

It seems logical to predict that social movements will flourish and grow when they are successful and wither away when they fail. This prediction is not necessarily accurate, however. Movements may lose support as they begin to achieve their objectives, thereby reducing the discontent that was their source, and fall short of full success.

More interesting are those movements that suffer clear and undeniable setbacks, such as happens with prophecy-based religious movements. What happens when the prophecies fail to come true?

During the first half of the nineteenth century, an American preacher, William Miller, announced that he had calculated from biblical sources the time of Christ's Second Coming and the attendant ending of the world. The result of his preaching was the Millerite movement—people began giving up their worldly goods to prepare for the millennium. When the world failed to end on the day prophesied, Miller recomputed doomsday, and his followers began preparing anew, urging their friends and relations to join them. Although the world still refused to end, the movement became organized in 1863 as the Seventh Day Adventist church.

Leon Festinger and his colleagues (1956) discovered a similar phenomenon when they set out to study a small group in the Midwest who had been warned of doomsday by visitors on flying saucers. Only a chosen few were to be rescued from the doomed planet, and members of the group feverishly attempted to get friends and relations to join with them. When the rescue saucer failed to appear on schedule, a new time of departure was set, and the members worked all the harder to get others to join them.

Festinger, a psychologist, saw the renewed proselytization as a way of resolving "cognitive dissonance," the conflict between beliefs and experiences. "If more and more people can be persuaded that the system of belief is correct, then clearly it must, after all, be correct" (1956:28). Lofland (1966) reached the same conclusion in his study of a Korean-based "doomsday cult," later to become famous as the Unification Church of the Reverend Sun Myung Moon.

Sometimes when people fail, they try harder, become desperate, and seek to gain broader agreement that what they are doing is right. Sometimes when they succeed, they become complacent and lose their dedication to the cause. The role of success is not as straightforward as might be imagined.

Louis Zurcher (1981:437) describes some of the "personal and organizational dilemmas" common to movements aimed at social change:

> process paradoxically becoming opposed to impact;
> enthusiasts seeming inevitably to become bureaucrats;
> elitist leadership proving to be more "efficient" than the fullness of participatory democracy;
> intervention efforts originating "within the system" juxtaposed with efforts originating "outside the system";
> the difficulty of discerning when a call for participation in a program of social change actually is part of a program to resist that change;
> the challenge of salutary compromise between the needs of individuals and the needs of organizations or programs;
> the sometimes enormous gap between program purpose and program implementation;

the competing advantages and disadvantages of single-issue as compared to multiple-issue attempts at social change.

Some of Zurcher's points may remind you of the Chapter 7 discussion of the dilemma of success in voluntary associations, when we looked, for example, at the growth of The Holiday Project.

Ideology

In a sense, social movements grow out of inarticulate agreements: the dissatisfactions, fears, and frustrations that many individuals share. Individuals feel the pressure of population growth, and Zero Population Growth emerges. Individuals feel that a war is unjust, and an antiwar movement emerges. Social movements, then, are vehicles for articulating and integrating such feelings.

An ideology is a relatively coherent and integrated set of agreements describing a group's point of view, and ideologies have several functions for social movements. First, they reinforce the feelings of initial participants and place those feelings within a more coherent point of view. Individuals frustrated by unemployment and inflation, for example, get validation for their feelings—learning that others share them—and they discover who is "to blame" for the unsatisfactory situation. Second, the ideologies point toward actions that might remedy the dissatisfactions. They specify the changes that must be made and suggest the means for making them. Third, an important function of ideology is education. Ideologies can be written down, published, and circulated, thereby bringing attention to problems. The women's liberation movement, for example, has frequently focused around "consciousness-raising" groups. Women who have reified the agreements making them inferior are brought together and exposed to the movement's point of view, its ideology.

One way of looking at the role of ideology

Concerns over the dangers of nuclear power plants have prompted both collective behavior and social movements during the 1970s and 1980s. This woman at Three Mile Island exemplifies the concern that we might be passing nuclear problems on to future generations.

in a social movement is that it represents the imposition of agreements on a group. Suppose you and I want to stop the cutting of trees in a public park, for example. We would probably seek to generate public opinion in support of our position. We'd talk to people and write letters to the editor, telling people how important it was to save the trees and seeking to establish as widespread an agreement as possible.

The problem with this imposition model is that the agreement is created as a layer over a preexisting lack of care or concern. Although the newly created agreement can be effective sometimes—it may in fact save the trees for a time—the agreement depends always on the initiative and the continued activities of the opinion leaders. In other words, you and I would have to keep revitalizing the movement for it to last. If we lost interest in saving the trees, so would some of those we had brought over to the cause. What if Ralph Nader were to announce that he was tired of fighting for safer cars, that he was buying a new Burpo hardtop and moving to the suburbs? Some people would abandon their zeal for auto safety.

Participation

Much of the sociological attention devoted to social movements has been focused on learning what types of people participate in social movements and why some of them become leaders.

Leadership   Regardless of the degree of discontent among people, social movements do not occur without leaders, people who are willing and able to direct the energies of others. They focus discontent and point to actions to remedy it. Some leaders volunteer, others (like Martin Luther King, Jr.) are drafted, and others have to compete for the position.

The leaders of social movements differ so greatly in background and temperament that they can't be generally characterized. Adolf Hitler was an aspiring artist when he began the Nazi movement in Germany. Paul Ehrlich was a Stanford biologist when he began the organization called Zero Population Growth as a way of focusing concern on the problem of overpopulation. Mahatma Gandhi was a contemplative lawyer before becoming a revered religious and political leader.

Smelser (1962) notes that social movements require two types of leaders at different points in their histories. The agitator is important in getting the movement going; but, as the movement develops and expands, more bureaucratic skills are needed. Offices must be opened, clerks hired and supervised, mail answered, membership lists maintained, and so forth.

This aspect of social movements can present a double bind. Without organization, a social movement may die. Yet, an organization that is too "slick" elicits skepticism. Thus, John McCarthy and Mayer Zald (1973) write sometimes cynically of popular entertainers who lend their leadership to movements among the poor, leading McCarthy and Zald to suspect their motives. In general, they suggest, there is always enough discontent in society to prompt a protest—thus the actual appearance of protest is often more the result of leadership than conditions of deprivation.

Frances Piven and Richard Cloward (1977) take a very different view of the relative importance of leaders and conditions, however. In their analysis of protest among the poor, they acknowledge that a latent reservoir of discontent and suffering usually exists; yet the actual outbreak of protest depends on "momentous changes in the institutional order." Protest is not and essentially cannot be created by leaders, they insist (1977:36). Indeed, Piven and Cloward paint a picture of organizers continually fighting against the ebbing of protesters' commitment and the cooptation engaged in by the targets of protest.

Leadership of a social movement requires the establishment of authority through noninstitutionalized means. Who gets to be president of the United States is not very problematic because we have established means for selecting the president. There are no agreed-on means for selecting the leader of a movement to abolish the income tax or stop a war, however. As a result, **charisma,** which we will discuss in Chapter 13, plays an important part in the selection of leaders.

General Membership   Just as leaders of social movements can't be generally characterized, neither can regular participants. For one thing, different social movements appeal to the feelings and interests of different groups. The women's movement obviously has a special appeal for women, the black-power movement a special appeal for blacks, and the poverty-rights movement a special appeal for poor people.

People join social movements for a variety of self-interests. Politicians may join in search of voters. Business people may join in search of business. People may feel they will gain prestige by becoming identified with certain movements. And most find the fellowship of primary-group relations in working with others on a cause.

Some students of social movements have suggested that certain types of people are *generally* more likely to join movements. Eric Hoffer (1958) called these people "true believers," and he noted, for example, that Hitler drew many of his Nazi recruits from Communist groups, even though the two movements were ideologically opposed.

Most social movements have their beginnings among friends and relations, and they grow initially through communication with such networks. This is not surprising since people tend to associate with others who share the same points of view (see Lofland and Stark 1965).

The growth and spread of a social movement beyond kinship and friendship networks is a function of its appeal, of course, but also is governed by the movement's attitude toward membership. Some secret societies, for example, are exclusive and restrict membership. Others are merely receptive to new members, and still others actively seek members through proselytization. The last of these is no doubt the most common.

Finally, something should be said about the difference between support, participation, and membership. Some people may be in sympathy with the goals and purposes of a social movement without actually *doing* anything on its behalf. Others may participate in movement activities, such as attending public meetings and marches or writing letters to public officials. Still others may become formal members in organizations associated with the movement.

Organization

If social movements are to succeed in changing the agreements of a society, their activities must be organized and coordinated. Money must be raised, letters typed, and members informed. In the most other-worldly religious revival, for example, someone must collect contributions and someone must count the money and decide how it should be invested. The endless lists of bureaucratic, organizational tasks is often disillusioning to the idealistic supporter. Margaret Sanger, the founder of the birth-control movement in America, said of her earliest support-

ers: "When they remained they found work, work, work, and little recognition, reward, or gratitude. Those who desired honor or recompense, or who measured their interest by this yardstick, are no longer here" (1938:354–55).

The fact that organizational necessities can create serious role strains for those involved bears repeating. Organizational necessities can threaten the goals of the movement, as in the case of the idealistic, populist political candidate who feels obliged to make somewhat shady deals in order to win the still-higher office that will put him or her in a position to "really" change things. Such a person may become so socialized into the wheeling and dealing as to lose sight of the lofty ideals that started the movement in the first place (see Selznick 1952).

You may have noticed a parallel between this latest discussion of the problems created in the organization and bureaucratization of social movements, on the one hand, and the general problems associated with institutionalization of a social movement. All these discussions point to a persistent social dilemma, as we saw in the Chapter 7 discussion of The Holiday Project, for example.

We have seen that individuals' desires and aspirations can often best be achieved through some form of organized group life. Yet, organized group life has "system needs" of its own, and those latter needs often conflict directly with the initial desires and aspirations of the individuals involved. This dilemma was caricatured years ago in a satirical advertisement placed in a college newspaper: "There will be an organizational meeting of the American Anarchist Association next Tuesday night."

We've now examined those aspects of social movements that are of special interest to sociologists, and you've seen what social movements look like from the sociological point of view. I'd like to conclude this chapter with a short case study of a social movement that emerged in Honolulu. It illustrates a number of the points that have been made in the chapter and, more importantly, the application of sociological training to bringing about a change in social agreements.

The account is personal. My wife, Sheila, and I organized the group discussed in the report, and I served as president of it. Throughout the organization of the group and the direction of its activities, I knew that my sociological background was invaluable even though I did not set out to use specific sociological principles. I think you'll see that as the story unfolds.

A Case Study: Saving Wawamalu

In June 1971, a major Honolulu land developer, in collaboration with the city planning department, held a public information meeting to announce plans for the development of a major resort and residential complex near the popular surfing area of Sandy Beach. The purpose of the meeting was to inform nearby residents of the development plans and to indicate that the planning department was considering whether to recommend approval of the plans.

The meeting ended in an uproar with a loud protest against the proposed development. Foremost among the protesters were members of a group made up of surfers and environmentalists, but they were joined by older residents, including a state representative.

Residents left the meeting feeling that they had clearly demonstrated their opposition to the proper authorities and that the project would be scrapped. In December 1971, a rumor began circulating that the planning department was on the verge of recommending approval of the project. My wife, Sheila, and I met with a small group of residents to discuss the possibility of stopping the project.

We decided to call another public meeting, this one sponsored and run by the residents themselves. A school cafeteria was rented and announcements of the meeting were hastily printed and circulated. The city planning director was invited to attend, but declined the invitation, saying he would prefer to receive written questions from residents and promising to answer any that were received.

The public meeting was held within a week of the decision to act. Approximately 150 residents turned out to learn about the proposed development and to voice their opinions. The main purpose of the meeting was to find out what residents wanted to know. Ninety-seven questions were recorded and sent to the planning department. The questions ranged from such matters as planned public facilities (schools, parks, health care, and so forth) to issues of traffic congestion, mass transportation, sewage disposal, and tidal-wave protection.

People attending the public meeting were urged to write directly to the planning director and other public officials asking that the project not be approved until the many questions raised had been answered. Many did so, and the planning department delayed action on the project for a month while it prepared a thirty-page response to the questions.

During that time, the organization—by then named the Save Wawamalu Association (Wawamalu was the traditional Hawaiian name of the beach)—was busy conducting research on its own. A public health graduate student began conducting water-quality tests near the outfall of the existing sewage-treatment plant and analyzing statistics from the department of health. Sheila and I designed, organized, and supervised a public-opinion poll of residents to learn their sentiments toward the proposed development. Two women drove the whole length of the highway that connected the community to downtown, counting the number of driveways feeding into it. This information was combined with official traffic studies to estimate the added traffic congestion that would be produced by the development.

By the time the planning department had completed its response to the original ninety-seven questions, we had many additional questions, supported this time by empirical studies. The planning department went back to work, and we began preparing a fact sheet describing the probable impact of the development.

By February 1972, the planning department still had not made a recommendation, much to the consternation of the developer. As the state legislature opened its annual session, we arranged with our local legislators to have a resolution introduced that would declare the area in question a state park. At the legislative hearings on the resolution, the Save Wawamalu Association and some fifteen other organizations (representing a broad political spectrum) presented carefully coordinated testimony in opposition to the development and in support of the park. Only the developer and the land-owner testified against the resolution.

As an intergovernmental courtesy, the city planning department deferred its recommendation until the state legislature handled the park resolution. The decision was, thereby, effectively delayed until around May, when the legislature would recess.

During this time, another important event occurred. The city councilman representing the area in question resigned to accept a judicial appointment, and a special, no-primary election was called for June. A variety of candidates began announcing for the post.

By this time socialized into the norms of American politics, the original small group of residents gathered in a dimly lit, smoke-filled bar to discuss whether to run a candidate for the council on a platform of opposition to the development. The decision was yes, and a candidate was picked. I was chosen campaign manager.

As the campaign become more intense, it became clear that the proposed development at Wawamalu was to be the key issue, but in a peculiar fashion: all seven candidates were against it and debating who opposed it the most! Finally, the planning department announced an official public hearing—scheduled to occur one week before the city-council election.

The Save Wawamalu Association immediately began organizing testimony for the public hearing, as we had done for the legislative session; 7,000 leaflets were printed to inform residents of the meeting. With the prospect of seven city council candidates all testifying against the development, however, the developer withdrew his request and asked that the meeting be canceled. The reason given for this surprise move was that the developer wished to make slight modifications to his request. A revised request was to be submitted within a few weeks.

By this time, however, campaigns for the regular 1972 election were beginning, with United States representatives, a mayor, and state legislators to be elected. We immediately prepared and mailed a questionnaire to all political candidates asking for their position on the proposed development. All were against it.

The next three years were a standoff, and the developer never did submit the "revised proposal." In 1975, with little or no fanfare, the state began the incremental purchase of Wawamalu for a park.

In our struggle to save Wawamalu, we were all novices. None of us had ever organized a social movement before, so we learned as we went along. People who had never been involved in politics found themselves testifying before the legislature on technical matters quite new to them. Ultimately, though, it was possible to change a set of agreements that had seemed immutable.

Summary

I began this chapter by distinguishing collective behavior from institutionalized behavior: the former is more spontaneous and disorganized, less governed by preestablished agreements. Agreements are created in collective behavior as participants share in beliefs, feelings, and actions.

Social movements represent a more persistent and ultimately more organized form of noninstitutionalized behavior. They aim at changing social agreements. Social movements often develop out of collective behavior.

Sociologists have distinguished many forms of collective behavior. Some require the presence of a crowd; others occur across a society. Fashions, fads, and crazes are examples of collective behavior that do not require the assembly of a group of people. They typically last for a short time and deal with some trivial aspect of life. Mass hysteria and panic are other forms of collective behavior. Panics may occur in an assembled crowd—as in a crowded theater— or can occur across a society—as in the mass selling of stocks. Terrorist mobs represent an attack against a perceived threat, whereas panic is a retreat. Riots are generally more haphazard in their selection of targets for aggression, though terrorist-mob actions can result in riots.

After examining different forms of collective behavior, we turned to some of the scientific points of view that have been used to understand it. Le Bon was chiefly concerned with the irrationality and impulsiveness of crowds, and he saw them as a threat to "civilized" social life. Collective behavior fit neatly into Freud's general psychoanalytical theory. Freud regarded it as an attempt to return to infancy, and he felt crowd members regarded their leaders as parent figures.

Blumer, an interactionist, has been particularly interested in the contagious nature of emotions in crowds, suggesting "circular reaction" as the way in which the emotions expressed by one person were reflected back by another, thereby reinforcing that emotion in the first person. Blumer likened collective behavior to the herd behavior of cattle.

Although there has been a tendency in the past to see collective behavior—especially crowd behavior—as fundamentally irrational and emotional, the newer approaches to the phenomenon are quite different. Some, such as Turner and Killian, have examined collective behavior as a way of coping with ambiguity and have spoken of "emergent norms" as the outcome of the process. Others, such as Richard

Berk, have drawn attention to the rational aspects of crowd behavior and of those individuals who make up crowds.

Many scholars have focused their attention on the processes through which collective behavior evolves. Smelser has presented a structural point of view, outlining the stages in the development of collective behavior through the use of a "value-added" model. The several stages are structural conduciveness, structural strain, the growth and spread of a generalized belief, precipitating factors, the mobilization of participants for action, and the operation of social control.

Next, we turned to social movements, looking first at some of the different types sociologists have studied. Expressive movements, such as religious revivals, have the primary purpose of letting individuals vent their feelings, though such movements typically have social goals as well.

Reactionary social movements, such as nativistic movements, represent a concern for perceived changes in society's agreements and a longing for a return to the "good old days." Conservative social movements are based on the belief that social agreements *may* change, and they seek to maintain the status quo.

Reformist social movements seek relatively specific and limited changes to social agreements without overturning basic structures. Revolutionary movements are more radical and ambitious in their objectives—seeking a major restructuring of society.

When sociologists study social movements, a number of things interest them. First, they often examine the conditions that give rise to movements. In the case of revolutions, we noted that they most frequently occur as a result of relative deprivation and rising expectations, quite aside from the objective conditions.

Sociologists have been particularly interested in the characteristics of leaders of social movements, though they differ so greatly as to preclude general characterization. Different types of leaders are needed at different times in the history of a movement. The fiery and emotional agitator may be needed to get it started, with more bureaucratic leadership required later on.

Ideology serves several functions for social movements. It makes the feelings of individuals more coherent and validates the feelings. It also makes education of the general public possible.

Different social movements appeal primarily to different types of people, sometimes, but not always, because of their relevance to special group interests. People participate in social movements for a variety of reasons, and the organizational needs of movements may require them to do things they feel are unrelated to the movement's goals. Movements must become organized (with a corresponding division of labor) if they are to be successful.

Important Terms

collective behavior
institutionalized behavior
social movements
fad
rumors
public opinion
riots
emergent norms

value-added model
expressive movements
reactionary movements
conservative movements
reformist movements
revolutionary movements
charisma

Suggested Readings

Cameron, William
1966 *Modern Social Movements*. New York: Random House.
In this excellent little book, Cameron has reviewed the major sociological points of view on social movements, providing a useful introduction to the topic. He discusses typologies of social movements and examines leadership, followership, and the development of movements over time. All this is fleshed out with numerous illustrations.

Erikson, Kai
1966 *Wayward Puritans*. New York: Wiley.
Documents way early Americans viewed and dealt with evil.

Lofland, John, and Rodney Stark
1965 "On Becoming a World-Saver: A Theory of Conversion to a Deviant Perspective." *American Sociological Review* 30:862–75.
This article is interesting from two perspectives. First, it offers an inside view of a religious movement, based in Korea and active in America, that the authors have disguised as the "divine precepts" movement of "Mr. Chang." Second, their participant-observation of the movement's growth in California provides the basis for the development of a theory of religious conversion.

Pacelli, Pamela, and David Dolittle
1982 "The Cry for Peace." *New Age*, June 1982, pp. 34–45.
This article contains an excellent history of the global peace movement of the 1980s. It begins with the European protests late in the 1970s and progresses into the American response. The authors provide rich materials for the study of social movements.

Piven, Frances Fox, and Richard A. Cloward
1977 *Poor People's Movements: Why They Succeed, How They Fail*. New York: Pantheon.
As the title suggests, this book examines the nature of political protest among the poor. To do that job adequately, the authors must look to the nature of protest in general and—even more broadly—to the organization and operation of power in society.

Rosnow, Ralph L. and Gary A. Fine
1976   *Rumor and Gossip: The Social Psychology of Hearsay.* New York: Elsevier.
Reviews topics of gossip and rumor and their role in collective behavior and group life.

Smelser, Neil
1962   *Theory of Collective Behavior.* New York: Free Press. Utilizing the "value-added" model developed in economics, Smelser traces the development of the many forms of collective behavior and social movements. Since Smelser takes a structural-functional view, this book provides about the best analysis of structural strain available.

Stark, Rodney
1972   *Police Riots.* Belmont, Calif.: Wadsworth. While the police are a formally established agency of social control, Stark's chronicling of student-police clashes during the 1960s shows that social control agents are themselves subject to collective behavior. In addition, the book contains valuable insights for social policy regarding protest. A wealth of examples point to the likely possibility that riots are generated by the application of excessive force.

Tilly, Charles, Louise Tilly, and Richard Tilly
1975   *The Rebellious Century.* Cambridge: Harvard University Press.
Here's an excellent examination of political/social rebellion in France, Germany, and Italy between 1830 and 1930 (the "century" referred to) specifically, and other times and places more generally. The book draws lessons from a violent past to clarify a sometimes violent present. In addition, it is an excellent discussion of the various analyses of rebellion.

Touraine, Alain
1981   *The Voice and the Eye: An Analysis of Social Movements.* (Translated by Alan Duff.) New York: Cambridge University Press.
Reports on several movements now underway with sophisticated theoretical sociological interpretation.

Wood, James L., and Maurice Jackson
1982   *Social Movements: Development, Participation, and Dynamics.* Belmont, CA: Wadsworth.
An up-to-date examination of theories of social movements and concrete examples. Part 3 of the book examines movements among the New Left, Vietnam veterans, Chicanos, environmentalists, Moonies, and others.

Zald, Mayer N., and John D. McCarthy, eds.
1979   *The Dynamics of Social Movements: Resource Mobilization, Social Control, and Tactics.* Cambridge, MA: Winthrop Publishers.
Contains essays on the nature of social movements, with theoretical and historical information.

One of the most compelling social movements of the early 1980s has been the international protest against the nuclear-arms race. Let's look at the movement in the terms of earlier discussions of social movements.

As you'll recall, social movements grow out of environmental conditions. In this case, the condition was the persistent and worsening threat of thermonuclear holocaust. The drama opened with America's Manhattan Project during World War II and the first chapter concluded late in the summer of 1945 in Japan. On August 6, 1945, a B-29 Superfortress bomber, *Enola Gay*, dropped a 20-kiloton uranium-based bomb nicknamed "Little Boy" on Hiroshima, Japan—a city of 300,000 population. Within an hour, 100,000 were dead. Another 100,000 were to die more slowly from the burns and radiation sickness caused by the bomb. Three days later, a second bomb, nicknamed "Fat Man," was dropped on Nagasaki, killing another 36,000 people. The age of nuclear weapons had arrived.

In August 1945, the United States had a monopoly on nuclear weapons, but this was not to last. The Soviet Union developed atomic weapons in 1949, and the nuclear-arms race was on. On February 2, 1954, the United States exploded a hydrogen bomb, representing an "improvement" on the original, uranium-based weapons. Since then, more and more powerful weapons and delivery systems have been developed. Although other nations have developed nuclear weapons—Great Britain (1952), France (1960), China (1964), India (1974), and others—the competition between the United States and U.S.S.R. has been of greatest concern to people of various nationalities and ideologies around the world.

During the "Cold War" of the 1950s, the threat of nuclear war was a major concern to many people. At first, Americans and Russians were the most fearful, since their countries would be the battleground for a nuclear war. The allies of both sides realized, however, that they might be dragged into and destroyed by an American-Soviet shootout. In fact, there was the possibility that the superpowers might try to fight their battles away from either's home.

In the 1960s and 1970s fears of nuclear war receded. Except for the Cuban Missile Crisis, the superpowers seemed inclined to coexist. At the same time, the stakes involved in a nuclear exchange became far higher. Now the danger was that a major nuclear exchange between Russia and America would almost literally destroy the possibility of life on the planet.

Over the years, ever more powerful weapons had been developed in ever greater numbers. David Lancashire (1981:37) summarized the situation that existed in the early 1980s:

> A UN report on doomsday machines estimates that more than 40,000 nuclear bombs and warheads now lurk in the world's arsenals, each of them surpassing Fat Man and Little Boy in technology or destructive power.
>
> "The total strength of present nuclear arsenals may be equivalent to about one million Hiroshima bombs," says the report issued by UN Secretary General Kurt Waldheim. "This is equivalent to more than three tons (of TNT) for every man woman and child on Earth."

But here's an even bigger danger. Six hundred million years ago, the formation of the ozone layer in Earth's upper atmosphere made life on the land surface of the planet (as opposed to the ocean) possible, by filtering out hazardous rays from the sun. In recent years, scientists have raised concerns about the effects of technology on the ozone layer: ranging from aerosol cans to supersonic jetliners. Those threats to the ozone layer pale in comparison with the potential damage that would be done by a nuclear exchange. Jonathon Schell (1982:81) reports on a 1975 study by the National Academy of Sciences which found that:

> the explosion of ten thousand megatons of nuclear weapons would . . . reduce the ozone layer in the Northern Hemisphere, where the report assumes that the explosions would occur, by anything from thirty to seventy per cent, and that it would reduce it in the Southern Hemisphere by anything from twenty to forty per cent.

Congressman Ron Dellums of California (1982) spelled out the practical implications for his constituents this way:

> Because the protection afforded by this atmospheric layer against the sun's ultra-violet radiation would no longer be effective, blindness in all species would result. The planet's ecology would suffer catastrophic damage without parallel in recorded history. It is doubtful that life as we know it would continue. In summary, nuclear war would inflict suffering of such dimensions that the survivors would truly envy the dead.

These circumstances surrounded the rise of the antinuclear movement of the early 1980s. As we've seen throughout the chapter, however, circumstances alone are not enough. Protest doesn't arise automatically.

Resistance to the threat of nuclear war has existed from the very beginning of the nuclear age. The prestigious *Bulletin of the Atomic Scientists*, for example, was founded in 1945, the same year the first atom bomb was exploded. The *Bulletin* publishes articles on the current state of the arms race and is best known for its "Bulletin Clock"—a symbolic representation of how close the world is to nuclear doomsday. Over the years, the minute hand has been moved closer to or farther from midnight, based on world events that pushed us either toward or away from war. As of April 1982, the clock stood at four minutes to midnight.

The late 1950s and early 1960s saw "Ban the Bomb" protest marches and demonstrations, most notably in Great Britain. While demonstrations also occurred in the United States, antinuclear protest was dismissed by many Americans as "communist-inspired."

American public opinion has not been very supportive of disarmament during the years since World War II. In March 1946, for example, the Gallup poll asked Americans whether they agreed with the following: "It has been suggested that Russia, Britain, and the United States get together and do away with armaments and military training." Sixty-two percent said they disagreed with the suggestion (Gallup 1972:566). Eight months later, Americans were asked whether they thought "the United States should stop making atom bombs and destroy all those we now have." Seventy-two percent said "no" (Gallup 1972:613).

In 1950, Gallup presented the American people with two views toward the prospects of developing a hydrogen bomb:

> There is a possibility that a new bomb may be made that might be up to a thousand times more powerful than the atom bomb. Some people say the United States should try to make such a bomb because other countries may make it and use it against us. Other people say we should not take the responsibility of making a bomb that could kill so many people at one time. With which point of view do you, yourself, agree?

Three-fourths said we should build the bomb (Gallup 1972:888).

This pronuclear sentiment was not limited to defense, moreover. In 1949, 70 percent were opposed to the United States taking a pledge not to be the first to use the atom bomb in warfare (Gallup 1972:839). In 1955, 55 percent said we should use atom bombs if the United States got into a war with China (Gallup 1972:1322).

A similar picture appears over the years with regard to nuclear-weapons testing. In 1958, Gallup asked national samples of Britons and Americans if they favored a two-to-three-year ban on testing—provided the Russians also agreed. Half the Americans and three-fourths of the British agreed (Gallup 1972:1541). As it turned out, testing was halted. Three years later, in 1961, Gallup asked Americans how they felt about it:

> Since November, 1958, the United States and Russia have been trying to reach a permanent agreement on the control and inspection of nuclear bomb tests. During this period each country voluntarily agreed not to conduct any tests, but no permanent agreement has been reached. Do you think the United States should resume tests at this time, or not?

Fifty-five percent said we should resume testing, 26 percent were opposed, and 19 percent had no opinion (Gallup 1972:1726).

For Americans, the late 1960s and early 1970s were a time of concern over the war in Vietnam. While that long-running and costly war raised some fears of war with Russia, the conclusion of the war in 1972 ushered in a period of general relaxation in Cold War tensions. For the most part, Americans were content to ignore the continued nuclear threat. All that changed dramatically in the early 1980s, however.

In June 1981, 100,000 protesters marched in Hamburg to protest nuclear weapons. It was the largest demonstration in postwar German history. Large demonstrations also occurred in Britain, Scandinavia, Holland, and elsewhere in Europe. This time, the protest caught on fully in the United States. Massive demonstrations occurred in large cities, small demonstrations in small ones. Soon, the primary form of the American protest was a proposal for the United States and the Soviet Union to "freeze" the fur-

ther development, production, and deployment of nuclear weapons. The proposal was introduced by a disarmament researcher, Randall Forsberg, to a 1980 meeting of thirty peace groups. It was not surprising that the idea found favor among people already working against the nuclear-arms race. The spread of the proposal was surprising, however.

In March 1981, eighteen Vermont town meetings voted to approve the freeze proposal. In 1982, another 161 joined the ranks. David Alpern (1982:22) reports that many of the towns approving the freeze had voted for Reagan in 1980; this was no far-left subversive movement. "After endorsing the freeze in West Windsor, citizens rose and sang 'God Bless America.'" Alpern continues:

> Success in Vermont—and earlier in eight Massachusetts election districts—caught the media's attention and stimulated freeze proponents elsewhere in the country. So far, nuclear-freeze resolutions have been passed by 309 New England town meetings, 33 city councils from coast to coast, ten county councils, and one or both houses in eleven state legislatures. Organizing efforts are underway in 43 states.

Perhaps the most activity was witnessed in California. There an effort was launched on December 1, 1981, to place the freeze proposal on the November 1982 ballot. State law required that 346,000 signatures be collected from registered voters for the measure to appear on the ballot. By the time the April 22 deadline for filing arrived, 700,000 signatures had been collected. A survey of Californians in late March 1982 found 64 percent in favor of the freeze (Field 1982:8). A *Newsweek* poll found that 68 percent of the American adults who had heard of the freeze were in favor of it.

What can acount for the meteoric rise of the nuclear-freeze movement? While the movement is too new for there to be a body of careful sociological research and analysis—it's still in progress as this is being written—the discussions of social movements earlier in this chapter suggest some of the places sociologists will look for the answers.

Changing conditions offer part of the explanation. After years of apparent easing in the Cold War, several events threatened to heat it up. First, the United States Senate failed to ratify the SALT-II agreements negotiated by the Carter administration and the Soviet Union—designed to limit strategic weapons. The immediate trigger for protests in Europe can be traced to American plans for rearming Europe with nuclear weapons in 1979.

Then the election of Ronald Reagan and his adminstration's generally hawkish stance on international relations seemed to increase the likelihood of war. The Soviet invasion of Afghanistan, the threat of an invasion of Poland, fighting in El Salvador, the confrontation between England and Argentina over the Falkland/Malvinas Islands, and the Israeli invasion of Lebanon all provided other possibilities of World War III. Added to these international tensions, worsening American economic conditions—which required domestic-assistance programs—called into question increased military spending proposed by the Reagan administration.

Precipitous conditions are not enough for a social movement, however. Someone must take action. In this case, several individuals and groups had powerful impacts. We have already seen some of these: Randall Forsberg's proposal of a nuclear freeze was obviously critical, for example.

During the 1960s, a Boston-based organization called Physicians for Social Responsibility (PSR) had publicized the medical damage that would be done by a nuclear blast in the Boston area. In 1979, PSR became active again. Under PSR urging, Harvard and Tufts Medical Schools sponsored a two-day symposium on "The Medical Consequences of Nuclear Weapons and Nuclear War" in February 1980. Beginning with United States government estimates that about 20 megatons (the equivalent of 20 million tons of TNT) would explode over Boston in a nuclear exchange with the Soviet Union, the physicians estimated that 2.1 of the 2.9 million residents of the Greater Boston area would die, and another half million would be maimed or disabled (Leonard 1980).

Subsequently, several physicians and medical clinics refused to cooperate with the government in developing plans for medical treatment in the event of nuclear war. They reasoned that the devastation would be so catastrophic that recovery plans would be a farce. Howard Hiatt, dean of the Harvard School of Public Health carried the message directly to President Reagan. Reminding the president of the blood transfusions he had received after the 1981 assassination attempt against him, Hiatt pointed out that the hospital wouldn't have been able to handle another five such patients. "I told him there would be 800,000 people in shock from burns and radiation if a 1-megaton bomb exploded over Washington" (Quoted in Alpern 1982:22).

Other officials raised similar protests. Officials in Marin County (California) and Boulder, Colorado, for example, refused to develop evacuation plans in the event of nuclear attack. Normal commuter traffic was almost unmanageable; an evacuation would be impossible. It is important to realize that all these events were the results of individuals taking action. There were many others.

Harold Willens, a Southern California businessman, is generally regarded as primarily responsible for the California ballot initiative.

Investing his own money and gaining the moral and financial support of others, he mounted the campaign that was to garner 700,000 signatures. Ian Thiermann, another Californian businessman, attended a San Francisco conference on the medical consequences of a nuclear exchange in 1980. He was so moved that he sold his home and dedicated the next five years of his life to ending the threat of nuclear war. He and his son produced a film, *The Last Epidemic*, which graphically portrayed the message of the conference. That film mobilized hundreds more to join in the movement.

The Nuclear Freeze movement clearly created its success out of an already existing sentiment among millions of Americans. It would not have been possible to persuade 700,000 Californians tht something needed to be done to avert thermonuclear holocaust. That feeling already existed. What was needed, however, was individuals willing to take a stand, thus providing an opportunity for others to act.

PRACTICING SOCIOLOGY

Early in 1980, the main riot story in America took place in Miami, in the predominantly black Liberty City area. Although the first reports from Miami suggested that the roots of the riot lay in the massive influx of some 100,000 exiles from Castro's Cuba, Robert Press (1980) disagreed, citing a multilayered set of structural causes. Nearest the surface was the acquittal of four white policemen by an all-white jury. The policemen had been charged with beating a black insurance salesman to death. That triggering event occurred in a context of already-bad relations between police and blacks. Even deeper down, Press found:

a year-after-year intolerably high rate of unemployment among young blacks; frequent lack of good maintenance by owners of low-income rental apartments; a serious lack of job training programs; inadequate measures by police to curb crime in the black communities; slow city and federal response to planned housing improvement projects in the black communities.

Write several paragraphs describing this riot in terms of the stages in the development of collective behavior suggested by Smelser.

Source: Robert Press, "Miami Riots: Don't Blame the Cubans," *Christian Science Monitor,* June 10, 1980.

Part Four

Institutions and Institutional Problems

Institutions are sets of agreements that govern broad areas of life, such as politics, economics, education, religion, and family. Each institution deals with a set of problems for the survival of society and specifies the ways in which those problems will be handled.

As we'll see, the various problems of system survival can be solved effectively through numerous forms. Institutions specify, defend, and enforce particular forms—capitalism as opposed to socialism, for example.

Politics and Economics   Political institutions deal with the distribution and operation of power and authority in society. Economic institutions deal with the production, distribution, and consumption of scarce goods and services.

In addition to examining the many political and economic systems that people have devised, we're also going to see that no system has proven totally satisfying to everyone, and institutional change is continuous.

Educational Institutions   Educational institutions have a primary function of socialization: teaching the society's culture to individuals and perpetuating that culture across generations.

You'll see that educational institutions take a variety of forms in different societies. For the most part, however, we'll examine both the strengths and weaknesses of education in America.

Religious Institutions   Religious institutions deal in matters of ultimate meaning. What is the meaning of life? Why is there suffering and death? How should people treat each other? Different religions have provided a great variety of answers to questions such as these.

We'll examine the major religions of the world. We'll see that the United States has great religious diversity, and we'll look at current trends.

Family as Institution   The family is often called the fundamental institution. Originally, families were the seat of government, economics, education, and religion. While many of these functions have been taken over by separate institutions, the family still serves essential functions for the survival of society and of individuals.

You're going to see that the American monogamous, nuclear family is only one of the family forms present in the world. Moreover, American family forms have been changing.

Rural and Urban Society   The operation of institutions can be seen in the examination of whole societies.

We'll look at the nature of rural society and then examine the rise of great cities. Much of the chapter deals with the nature and problems of urban living, and we'll focus on the experience of "community."

13

Politics and Economics

The notion of "power" has been implicit throughout many earlier discussions in this book. We've seen how institutionalized agreements control our thinking, feeling, and behaving, and we've seen how those agreements put some people in positions to control others. In a sociological context, "power" is ability to have your desires carried out, with other people helping carry them out whether they want to or not. In this chapter, as we consider political and economic institutions, we will deal with power directly—the question of whose agreements are dominant in society.

Bertrand Russell (1872–1970), the noted English mathematician and philosopher, likened power to energy, saying that power was the primary concept of the social sciences, just as energy was the primary concept of physics. He also said (Russell 1938:11):

> Like energy, power has many forms, such as wealth, armaments, civil authority, influence on opinion. No one of these can be regarded as subordinate to any other, and there is no one form from which the others are derivatives. . . . The laws of social dynamics are laws which can only be stated in terms of power, not in terms of this or that form of power.

I'm sure you've had the experience of making people do what you wanted, and you've undoubtedly had the experience of doing what others wanted. You may have resented or regretted "going along" with another's wishes, but doing so is part of social life.

All of us have also had the experiences of "wanting" and of "having." In part, the desire to possess things is related to the comfort and pleasure they offer. You enjoy having the money for a movie because the movie is enjoyable. At the same time, as Russell noted, possessions are a form of power; they can be used to get others to do what we want them to.

It is probably safe to say that all people have a "natural" desire for power and possessions, although the degree of desire varies. Unfettered, however, the individual pursuit of these desires would result in what Thomas Hobbes, a seventeenth-century English philosopher, called a "war of all against all." For society to survive, established agreements are necessary to regulate individual desires for power and possessions.

I am going to discuss political and economic institutions separately in this chapter, referring back and forth from one to the other as appropriate. We'll look at some special issues regarding American political and economic institutions. We'll close with an examination of people's experiences of these institutions and their attempts to find functional alternatives.

Throughout, we are going to see the great role institutions play in how we experience power and possessions. This was the point of departure C. Wright Mills took in his classic analysis, *The Power Elite* (1956:10–11)*:

> If we took the one hundred most powerful men in America, the one hundred wealthiest, and the one hundred most celebrated away from the institutional positions they now occupy, away from their resources of men and women and money, away from the media of mass communication that are now focused upon them—they would be powerless and poor and uncelebrated. For power is not of a man. Wealth does not center in the person of the wealthy. Celebrity is not inherent in any personality. To be celebrated, to be wealthy, to have power requires access to major institutions, for the institutional positions men occupy determine in large part their chances to have and to hold these valued experiences.

How do the institutions that provide—and deny—wealth, power, and fame operate? Let's begin by examining political institutions.

Political Institutions and Their Functions

Political institutions are sets of established agreements that specify who may exercise con-

---

*Reprinted by permission.

trol over whom in what ways and under what conditions. Governments are the clearest examples of political institutions, though other examples include political parties, big business, bar associations, and other sectors of society that possess and exercise political power.

Sometimes the power you see exercised around you seems "right," and other times "wrong." It might seem right and proper for your professor to "force" you to write a term paper for a course. It would seem altogether wrong and improper for one of your classmates to force you to write a term paper for him or her (under the threat of a beating, for example).

The primary function of political institutions is the creation and perpetuation of agreements regarding the "proper," "appropriate," or "just" exercise of power, what sociologists refer to as "legitimate power" or "authority."

Power, Legitimacy, and Authority

As I've just indicated, power is essentially the ability to have people do what you want them to do, even if they don't want to. Clearly, this occurs in different ways. A bully exercises power over smaller children in a school, but most agree that such a situation is somehow inappropriate or unjust. On the other hand, a supervisor exercises power over a worker by assigning him or her a task to perform, and that's usually regarded as appropriate.

When a particular exercise of power is generally agreed to be appropriate, we say that it is "legitimate" or that it has **legitimacy**. More simply, we speak of legitimate power as **authority**, in the sense of saying that the president has the authority to veto a bill, for example, or that a police officer has the authority to question, detain, or arrest people under certain conditions.

Political institutions, then, provide the systems of agreements against which to determine the legitimacy of a particular exercise of power. Political institutions specify who has what authority, over whom, and under what conditions.

Earlier I quoted Rousseau as saying that nothing but agreements serve as the "basis for all legitimate authority among men." Authority reflects an agreement as to who may "legitimately" exercise power over whom. For example, most societies have an agreement that parents can legitimately exercise certain powers over their children.

Typically, the main agreements of political institutions are carried in the form of a **political ideology:** a largely reified set of beliefs, values, and norms regarding the exercise of power. The principles and policies governing who does what to whom, then, become far more than a convenient or useless way of running things. They become "right," "just," "God's will."

This is the process by which the particular political forms adopted by the United States become "American*ism*," "the American way," or similar representations of our agreements as bigger than life. Political systems take on the emotional power of religious ones. And by the same token, competing political ideologies are cast in demonic garb. Communism thus becomes much more than a political-economic model; for those committed to "American*ism*" it is Satan come to earth.

Sometimes, then, political authority becomes reified within a political ideology. This says nothing, however, about where the legitimacy of power as authority comes from. As we'll see, it has a number of sources.

In his classic analysis, *The Theory of Social and Economic Organization* (1925b), Max Weber delineated three major types of authority: **charismatic, traditional**, and **rational-bureaucratic authority.**

Charismatic Authority   *Charisma* is a personal quality that sets some people apart. A Greek word, it literally means "divine gift," and charismatic people—especially in the past—have been regarded as somehow divine.

The earliest form of authority, in Weber's view, grew out of special personal qualities. Some individuals in a group simply stood out because of extraordinary strength, beauty, agility, wit, intelligence, communication skills, or the like. Such persons were granted the right to lead purely on the basis of their special qualities. If you think back to your high-school peer group, you'll probably be able to identify certain individuals who always seemed to take the lead in deciding what the group should do. People just seemed to agree with what those individuals suggested. That's because they had some degree of charisma.

Traditional Authority   In the course of time, Weber said, charismatic authority gave way to "traditional" authority. Rather than depending on special personal qualities in individuals, authority became associated with certain statuses based, for example, on age or kinship. In some societies, the elders were the seat of authority, and the right to lead was passed from one group of elders to their successors. In others, authority was passed down through the generations of a particular family.

Weber spoke of the **routinization** of authority. Although charismatic authority appeared in an unpredictable way, the transmission of traditional authority was regular and routine. The justification for traditional authority was similar to the justification for customs and traditions more generally. Things were done in a particular way because they had *always* been done that way. The elders had authority because they had always had authority.

Rational-Bureaucratic Authority   Weber was particularly interested in bureaucratic authority. Bureaucracy made authority rational, because it flowed not from charisma or tradition, but from logical, rational, and explicit agreements relevant to achieving the goals of an organization. Authority was vested in officials for the purpose of supporting them in serving the interests of the group. Supervisors assign tasks to workers, then, on the assumption that the tasks serve the purposes of the organization.

It is possible to wield political power without seeking or holding political office. Walter Cronkite . . .

Whether political authority is studied in terms of the struggle to get it or in terms of how it operates at any one time, it is important to note that its legitimation often links political institutions to other ones. For example, religious institutions may legitimate the political authority of a king through the notion of the "divine right of kings." Sometimes educational institutions also get involved. When the Congress was considering the impeachment of President Richard Nixon, for example, constitutional scholars at prestigious law schools were asked to comment on the constitutional provisions for impeachment.

Codification of Norms

Political institutions are also the focus for the creation of laws, an explicit and formal specification of what is expected and what is prohibited in society. Congresses and parliaments pass laws. Courts often clarify or legitimate those

. . . and Martin Luther King, Jr., illustrate the power of charismatic authority.

laws. Monarchs pass edicts, and presidents issue executive orders.

The creation of laws represents a codification and specification of norms. Some laws merely formalize agreed-on customs, and others impose norms not previously agreed on. The historic court decision in *Brown* v. *The Board of Education* in 1954, for example, clarified the implications of the American value of equality while contradicting local agreements on the norm of racial segregation in schools. The failure of local school districts to immediately comply with

the Court's decision points to the power of traditional norms. Simply passing a law does not guarantee changes in behavior.

The survival of society depends on people's generally keeping the agreements of the group, and the codification of norms as laws makes that more likely. Laws also specify the sanctions associated with the breaking of them, which adds incentive to keeping them.

The codification of norms as laws presents a danger that we'll look at later in this chapter. Formally stating norms as laws can lead to their reification and internalization. Charles Andrain suggests that this happened to some American legal documents early in our national history.

> Soon after the Constitution was accepted by each state, it began to assume sacred qualities. In some people's minds, the Constitution formed the equivalent of the ancient Hebrew covenant or even the whole Bible itself. Veneration of the impersonal law replaced reverence for the personal monarch. Thus legal norms took on sacred value. (1974:79)

You can probably observe the internalization of laws in your own experience. There's an agreement in cities that you must put money in parking meters if you are going to park your car on the street. Fines are specified for breaking that agreement. It's a pretty straightforward, contractual matter. If you've received a parking ticket for breaking the agreement, though, you may have felt just a little bit "bad," as if you'd been slightly immoral or evil. If you don't feel that way about parking tickets, how about tax evasion or treason? If you feel that selling military secrets to a foreign power violates something more than a businesslike agreement individuals have with the group, then you've internalized the norms involved.

Social Control

Political institutions not only create laws but enforce them as well, as we've already seen in Chapter 11. Police, military, courts, and bureaucracies have the job of seeing that codified agreements are kept. This function is aptly summarized in the phrase "maintaining law and order."

The potential that social control has for the internalization of agreements should be obvious. When political leaders speak of creating "respect for the law," what they have in mind is usually more than a recognition of the need for agreements in a society. Rather, what they mean is

that laws should be imbued with a sanctity of their own and become "Law." In America in recent years, however, increasing numbers of citizens have begun questioning this aspect of our "lawful" society, as we'll see later in the chapter.

Group Identity and Solidarity

Another function political institutions serve, especially among modern societies, is to focus group identity and solidarity. The identity of "being an American," for example, is virtually impossible to separate from the idea of the United States as a political unit. This by no means implies that you must agree with the policies of a particular administration. It does not even mean that you support our present form of government. It's just that "being an American" refers to membership in a particular political unit, one distinguished from France, China, and Chile.

Andrain (1974:53) cites the "creation of a common identity" as the first basic problem of political institutions, and he mentions four possible sources of identity: primordial, sacred, personal, and civil. Some preliterate societies trace their lineage back to a common primordial ancestor. They share a group identity because they are relatives. Shared religious values would be a sacred source, and Andrain says that the personal feelings people have about a charismatic leader can also create a group identity. Finally, the source of group identity that Andrain labels "civil" is similar to Weber's rational-bureaucratic structure of authority, a more formal, corporate statement of groupness as found in the constitutional definition of who is and is not an American citizen.

The formation of a common political identity is never a simple and conflict-free process. As Seymour Martin Lipset has noted in *The First New Nation* (1963), early American politics was filled with conflicts and disagreements over the form the new government in America should take. Nevertheless, a national identity was created. The difficulty of that accomplishment was not unique: "For countries, like people, are not handed identities at birth, but acquire them through the arduous process of 'growing up,' a process which is a notoriously painful affair" (Lipset 1963:16).

The major functions of political institutions, then, are (1) the legitimation of power in the form of authority; (2) the codification of norms as laws; (3) social control; and (4) the creation of group identity and solidarity. As you will have anticipated, many different social structures can satisfy these functions. Let's look at some of them.

Varieties of Political Structures

Andrain (1974) has suggested three major types of political institutions that people have created to serve the functions we have been discussing: traditional autocratic, totalitarian, and democratic.

Traditional Autocracy

Strictly speaking, **autocracy** is a form of government in which all power is vested in one person, the autocrat. Monarchs and dictators are examples of autocrats, and many governments over the course of history have been autocratic. The pharaohs of ancient Egypt are one illustration; the reigns of Francisco Franco in Spain and Haile Selassie in Ethiopia are more contemporary examples.

The traditional autocrat's political authority is legitimated by tradition (leadership may be inherited, for example), by the autocrat's charismatic qualities, or by coercion. Typically, all three are involved.

The autocrat is never the only powerful person in an autocratic society. The nobility (often landowners), the military, and the clergy pos-

sess a degree of power; and the autocrat is partly a mediator among these elite groups. They, in turn, generally support and further legitimate the autocrat's authority.

In this form of government, the autocrat is the chief source of laws and the chief agent of social control. The power to make and enforce laws, understandably, is typically exercised to maintain the status quo rather than to develop new social and economic programs. Group identity and solidarity are primarily a matter of tradition.

Traditional autocracies have successfully served the functions of political institutions for millennia. Totalitarian regimes, by contrast, are generally considered to be a phenomenon confined to our own century, often based on the coups d'etat of military juntas.

Totalitarianism

The "total" in "totalitarian" has two meanings, both of which apply in the form of government called **totalitarianism.** On the one hand, "total" means that all members of the society are to be brought under a single set of agreements; totalitarian political institutions have no place in them for dissent. And on the other hand, the word means that all aspects of social life are to be covered by the agreements shared by all members. In this sense, every thought and action in a totalitarian society is "political."

The sets of agreements that apply to all members of society in all aspects of life in a totalitarian society are thoroughly reified in the form of a **political ideology,** as discussed earlier in the chapter. The shared beliefs, values, and norms are seen as ultimately true and proper, sometimes even mystically so.

In contrast to traditional autocracies, which function to maintain the status quo, totalitarian regimes more typically represent a "rebirth" of national identity and purpose. Hitler's "superrace" and what was to be a "1,000-year Reich" were prototypes of this aspect of totalitarianism. Often a charismatic leader will come to symbolize both the group and the ideology. The society is united under a single banner, and the union is further substantiated by the identification of out-groups perceived as a threat to survival. German Jews, for example, were portrayed as particularly dangerous people, not "really" Germans.

The legitimacy of the totalitarian regime can rest on several bases. Frenzied popular support of an ideology that takes on sacred, quasi-religious qualities is one base. The personal appeal of a charismatic leader is another; and, as we've just said, the perceived threat of out-groups further supports the regime. The long-term survival of totalitarianism, however, also requires political organization.

Political parties are unusual in traditional autocracies, but they are essential to totalitarianism. A totalitarian regime rests ultimately on a tightly organized party that enjoys a political monopoly. Usually only a small precentage of the population actually belongs to the party, and the party itself is usually run by a small elite. It is the party, however, that strengthens the regime's coercive ability and permits the control of other institutions in the society. In the "model" totalitarian society, the party is the vehicle for embedding the political ideology in the family, the schools, the churches, and the economy. This has the dual effect of adding immediate legitimacy to the totalitarian regime and of socializing people into agreement with the ideology.

Eric Hoffer (1958) added the term "true believer" to our popular language as a result of his examination of the great similarities among totalitarian regimes based on very different ideologies. The pattern of social organization and of individual commitment to ideology and to party was the same under Stalinist Communism and Nazi anti-Communism. Hitler is reputed to have instructed party organizers to seek converts among the young Communists, realizing that Communist zealots could be Fascist zealots with little modification. The term "true believer" has come to mean anyone who is totally and uncritically committed to any ideology, whether of the Right or the Left, whether political or religious.

Like traditional autocracies, then, totalitarian regimes serve the major functions of political institutions. They create legitimate authority; they create laws and enforce them; and, in contrast to traditional autocracies, which enjoy a preestablished group identity, they create a renewed sense of group identity and solidarity.

Democracy

Finally, I want to say a few words about **democracy** as a political form contrasting with autocracy and totalitarianism. Democracy is based on the notion of self-governance. The key principle of self-governance is that those subject to the laws should also be the source of them. This general principle allows considerable room for variation, however. In a mass democracy, everyone participates directly in all decisions. This is possible in small groups, and in a modified sense it characterized the New England town meetings of the past. For the most part, however, democratic societies operate on the basis of representative democracy. In a representative democracy, people are self-governing, once removed—that is, citizens elect others who will represent them in the actual decision making of government. The American Congress, the British Parliament, and the Communist Party Central Committee of the People's Republic of China are all based on the model of representative democracy.

Kenneth Bollen and Burke Grandjean (1981:652) suggest that democracy has two dimensions—popular sovereignty and political liberty:

[Popular sovereignty] concerns the extent to which the elites of a country are accountable to the nonelites. Popular sovereignty implies free elections, as wide a franchise as possible, equal weighting of votes, and fair electoral processes. The second dimension, political liberties, concerns institutions through which nonelites can influence the decisions of elites, including free speech, a free press, and freedom of opposition.

While the two dimensions are separate from each other in theory, Bollen and Grandjean's analysis of 113 nations indicates that the two are not separate in practice: popular sovereignty and political liberty go hand in hand.

I'm not saying that democracy always works as planned. In theory, in a democracy the people temporarily relinquish their power through the election of leaders, reclaiming and then reassigning it periodically. In Lincoln's well-known phrase, democracies are designed as governments "of the people, by the people, and for the people."

In the sections to follow, we will discuss American politics, as an example of democracy, in both its realization of the ideal and its falling short.

Government in America

In the examination of American democracy, we'll focus on the concentration of political power. Although the fundamental principle of government holds us all equal, it turns out—in George Orwell's phrase—that some of us are "more equal than others." This condition has arisen in several ways in American government.

We'll begin this section with a quick look at the balance of powers established in law and the centralization of government that has developed. In that connection, we'll see that those in power tend to perpetuate their rule. Then we'll move to the issue of *who* actually has the power in America, and we'll conclude with a look at the part "average" citizens play in government through their voting behavior.

Centralization and Perpetuation

The United States Constitution created a system of "checks and balances" aimed at preventing any person or group from achieving unchecked power. It established a tripartite governmental structure: executive, legislative, and judicial. Although the executive branch—headed by the president—offered the greatest potential for one individual to exercise power, the presidency was held in check in numerous ways by the other two branches of government.

Over the course of our national history, however, the executive branch has grown steadily stronger, in comparison with the other branches, and people have sometimes spoken of an "imperial presidency." The president of the United States of America, for example, is the commander-in-chief of all the armed forces, nearly a million in peacetime, and the head manager for millions in the civil service.

The growing centralization of power in the presidency is accompanied by the trend toward concentration of power in the federal government rather than in the states and municipalities. Though beginning with a relatively loose federation of autonomous states, we have moved increasingly in the direction of a single, all-powerful federal state.

Concerns over the concentration of power in the federal government have been voiced frequently—especially by conservatives. Early in the 1960s, just after President Kennedy had won a head-on confrontation with the steel industry, conservatives suggested the following observation about the presidency:

With Roosevelt, we saw that the presidency could be a lifetime job.

With Truman, we saw that anyone could be president.

With Eisenhower, we saw that maybe we don't need a president.

With Kennedy, we've seen that we might be better off without a president.

A cornerstone of Ronald Reagan's successful campaign for the presidency in 1980 was his promise to reduce the cost, size, and power of the federal government. In fact, the size of the federal civilian work force had been declining relative to the rest of the economy during the previous six administrations—conservative and liberal alike—spanning three decades. In 1952, the year President Eisenhower took office, federal civilian employees made up 4.8 percent of the nation's nonagricultural payroll employees (excluding the self-employed). In 1960, when President Kennedy replaced Eisenhower, federal employees were 4.2 percent. In 1963, the year of Kennedy's assassination, the percent remained at 4.2. By the end of the Johnson administration, in 1968, 4.0 percent were federal employees. In 1974, the year of Nixon's resignation from the presidency, federal employees were 3.5 percent of the total. At the end of the Ford administration in 1976, the figure was 3.4 percent, and it decreased further to 3.2 percent during the Carter years, ending in 1980 (U.S. Bureau of Labor Statistics 1981c:85).

In an interesting contrast, state and local governments were steadily growing during that same period. In 1952, they were 8.6 percent of the nonagricultural payroll; in 1980, they were 14.7 percent. Overall, in 1980, two of every eleven nonagricultural, civilian payroll employees in America worked for the government (U.S. Bureau of Labor Statistics 1981c:85).

Numbers of employees at different levels of government, however, do not necessarily reflect the distribution of power, and the debate continues over the degree of power that is and ought to be concentrated in Washington.

Sociologists have observed another tendency in democracies that conflicts with democratic theory—one perhaps more sinister than centralization. Robert Michels called this process the **iron law of oligarchy**. Writing in 1911, Michels argued that large-scale organizations necessarily gave birth to ruling cliques (oligarchies) that would do everything possible to perpetuate their own rule over the organizations. Michels was led to this conclusion by the observation that large-scale organizations could not be administered by a mass democracy; they required the work of bureaucracies, as we've already discussed in Chapter 7. Inevitably, then, power is wielded by a few rather than by the many, and those who wield the power today will naturally wish to continue doing so tomorrow. Thus, any officeholder, according to Michels, will spend much of his or her time and energy consolidating political strength, creating bastions of loyal supporters, and so forth.

Thus, we have seen that democracy means one thing in theory, but in practice it is subject to countervailing forces, pushing it in less democratic directions. Let's turn now to an examination of some of the ways American democracy has turned out. Granting that some of us seem to have become "more equal" than others—who is in charge?

The Power Elite or Veto Groups?

In Dwight Eisenhower's "Farewell to the Nation" speech, given as he retired from the presidency in 1961, he surprised many by warning against the danger of too great a cooperation between the military and industry.

> In the councils of government, we must guard against the acquisition of unwarranted influence, whether sought or unsought, by the military industrial complex. The potential for the disastrous rise of misplaced power exists and will persist.

The military leader who led the United States and its allies through World War II had, ironically, coined a phrase that has become symbolic of the concern of some sociologists and others about the power of war-related industries in America. Three years before, C. Wright Mills had warned against the establishment of a "permanent war economy" in his ominously titled work *The Causes of World War Three* (Mills 1958). Mills contended that American industry had become so dependent on the production of war materials that the nation's economy required the continued threat of war to survive. Within this context, Mills was particularly bothered by the extent to which retired military officers entered executive positions in industry and the extent to which industrial leaders held reserve commissions in the military.

Analysts have debated the issue of the military-industrial complex. Some, such as economist John Galbraith (1969), suggest it is more coincidental than conspiratorial. Others, such as political scientists Dye and Zeigler (1975), argue that the notion of a "war economy" has been exaggerated. No one, however, suggests that the military-industrial complex is insignificant as a source of power in American politics.

Mills's warning against the dangers of a permanent war economy is in line with his more general analysis of power in America. In 1956, he published *The Power Elite*, in which he argued that the nation was run by a **power elite** consisting of the "higher circles" of business, government, and the military.

> They rule the big corporations. They run the machinery of the state and claim its prerogatives. They direct the military establishment. They occupy the strategic command posts of the social structure, in which are now centered the effective means of the power and the wealth and the celebrity which they enjoy. . . .
>
> The people of the higher circles may also be conceived as members of a top social stratum, as a set of groups whose members know one another, see one another socially and at business, and so, in making decisions, take one another into account. (Mills 1956:4, 11)*

---

*Reprinted by permission.

C. Wright Mills
1916–1962
Waco, Texas

Some Important Works

The Power Elite (New York: Oxford University Press, 1956).

The Sociological Imagination (New York: Oxford University Press, 1959).

The Causes of World War Three (New York: Simon & Schuster, 1958).

C. Wright Mills's chosen role in both American society and American sociology was that of radical critic. In American society, he saw and warned against the "power elite" of military, industrial, and governmental leaders whom he saw controlling the fate of the nation and the world.

Within his profession, Mills was particularly critical of "established" sociology, seeing many of his colleagues as either conscious or unconscious supporters of the social status quo. In contrast to Weber's "value-free sociology," Mills clearly felt that sociological knowledge should be put into use to create better social forms. Indeed, he felt scholars had an obligation to use their scholarship in that fashion.

In particular, Mills was concerned over the political power that money could buy. As we'll discuss in the second half of this chapter, the social-structural link between political and economic institutions is fundamental.

Several sociologists have questioned the validity of Mills's assertions regarding the power elite. Talcott Parsons (1957), for example, argued that wealth and power had become largely separated through the development of modern corporations. Those who owned the corporations no longer controlled them. Parsons also criticized Mills for failing to acknowledge the power of the legal and other professions in America.

Another view on the nature of power in America is found in David Riesman's *The Lonely Crowd* (1953). Riesman and his colleagues thought national "power" was a function of veto groups that had the capacity to prevent the exercise of power by others. Whereas Mills saw a danger that a small elite could enforce its agreements on others and therefore direct the nation's destiny, Riesman and his colleagues saw the inability of any group to lead as the problem: "Where the issue involves the country as a whole, no individual or group leadership is likely to be very effective, because the entrenched veto groups cannot be budged" (Riesman et al. 1953:257).

William Kornhauser (1966) suggested that the views of Mills and Riesman on the nature of exercise of power in the United States could be fruitfully compared along five dimensions: (1) how power is distributed, (2) how this distribution has changed over time, (3) how power is exercised today, (4) what its bases are, and (5) what the consequences are of its present distribution.

In the first regard, as we've seen, Mills saw power concentrated in a "power elite," while Riesman emphasized the role of several "veto groups." With regard to changes in the distribution of power, Kornhauser noted that Mills and Riesman had similar analyses of the American past, but differed radically in their view of current trends. For Mills, the trend since World War II had been toward increasing centralization of power, whereas Riesman believed the trend had been toward increasing dispersal of power.

Regarding the exercise of power, Mills believed that the power elite dominated all major political affairs, while Riesman argued that different groups held sway on different issues. With regard to the bases of political power, Mills concentrated on the similarity of interests among the leaders of different groups, whereas Riesman emphasized the ways in which the interests of these groups conflicted.

Concerning the consequences of their views of power for American society, Mills argued that political decisions clearly favored the interests of the dominant group. Riesman, on the other hand, argued that the decisions of political life, if not always in the best interests of society, at least did not consistently favor one particular group. Riesman and Mills agreed, Kornhauser noted, that one consequence of the present structure of power was increasing noninvolvement and apathy among the public. From Mills's point of view, the rise of a power elite meant the erosion of democracy, while for Riesman, the existence of so many powerful veto groups, each concentrating on its own particular interests, meant an erosion of national leadership.

In Kornhauser's own view, Mills underestimated the constraints on the elite's exercise of power, and Riesman was unwarranted in his assumption that power among various groups was more or less equally distributed. Finally, Kornhauser suggested that both their analyses lack any positive image of power, an image of how power could be distributed so that the political system would be responsive to the needs of the people and at the same time provide direction to political affairs.

Power in the Community

The debate over the existence of a power elite has had a local as well as a national focus in sociology. In studies of middle-American towns such as Muncie, Indiana (Lynd 1929, 1937), and Morris, Illinois (Warner et al. 1949, Hollingshead 1949) in the decades following 1920, researchers repeatedly discovered the presence and significance of **community elites.** In each town, either one family or a few families seemed to run everything. They owned the most important local industries. They either held political office locally or controlled those who did. Directly or indirectly, they had an influence on the day-to-day lives of everyone else.

More recent studies of other American towns and cities suggest that the monolithic power structures of a few decades ago are less typical. Robert Dahl's study of New Haven, Connecticut (1961), Aaron Wildavsky's study of Oberlin, Ohio (1964), and Edward Banfield's examination of decision making in Chicago (1961) have pointed to **pluralistic power** structures. Each of the communities studied had several *pockets* of power that competed and cooperated in the struggle for community control.

The Creation of Power

Both the pluralist and elite theorists suggest that there is a fixed amount of power to be distributed. This view of political power has been challenged by a number of sociologists. In his critique of the concept of the "power elite," Talcott Parsons (1957), for instance, criticized Mills for assuming an unchanging, or "zero-sum," notion of power. Parsons argued that power is continually *created* in society, through the formation of voluntary associations, for instance.

More recently, William Gamson and other "resource management" theorists have challenged the pluralistic view of American politics on similar grounds. These theorists focus on the role played in the creation of power by the mobilization of resources and the generation of groups that did not exist before the mobilization effort.

To discover the process whereby resources are created and managed in American politics, Gamson (1975), for instance, undertook a study of fifty-three "challenging groups" formed

between 1800 and 1945. To qualify as a challenging group, the organization had to seek the mobilization of a new constituency and had to be challenging someone outside its own constituency. Gamson's sample of challenging groups was roughly equally divided among occupational groups (such as the American Association of University Professors and the United Brotherhood of Carpenters and Joiners of America), social-reform groups (such as the American Birth Control League and the American Anti-Slavery Society), and left- and right-wing political groups.

A central focus of Gamson's analysis was the success or failure of the challenging groups. Gamson measured success in terms of "acceptance" (consultations, negotiations, formal recognition, and so on) and/or achieving new advantages for its constituency. In examining why some groups were successful while others were not, Gamson considered three variables: strategy, violence, and "combat readiness." To begin, he found the most successful groups to be those pursuing a single issue (as opposed to multiple-issue groups) and those who avoided radical attacks on the legitimacy of authority of those they challenged. Two-thirds of these groups gained advantages and over half gained acceptance.

Gamson also found that violence and other direct measures (such as strikes and boycotts) were related to success. Two-thirds of those using such methods gained new advantages, and 71 percent won acceptance. This finding contrasts with more traditional, pluralistic theories that generally regard violence as counterproductive—closing more doors than it opens.

Finally, as you would expect, Gamson found that groups were more successful if they were able to keep internal disputes to a minimum. In this context, Gamson found that both centralization and bureaucratic organization promoted maximum "combat readiness" and made the groups more successful in getting both acceptance and new advantages.

Sociologists and other social scientists, then,

have looked at power in American democracy in a variety of ways. But since democracy is based ultimately on the agreements made by the public in the voting booth, we will now move further in that direction, looking first at the part played by political parties, then at voting behavior.

Political Parties

The Constitution makes no mention of political parties, yet the Democratic and Republican parties exercise more political power in America than any other groups outside the government. The two major parties first competed with one another in 1856; and, since then, no other party has elected a president of the United States, though "third parties" have tried. Individuals who run for political office as "independents" are at a serious disadvantage in comparison with candidates who enjoy major-party backing. Why is this so?

Political parties in America are a form of voluntary association, as discussed in Chapter 7. Like other associations, they derive their power from organization and knowledge, which, in turn, can create money and produce people at the polls. Suppose for a moment that you decided to run for an office such as mayor. You'd probably want to tell the public about the way you stood on the issues and what you'd do as mayor. One way to do so would be to mail a statement to all the voters. For that you'd need a list of the voters' names and addresses; you'd need money to print the statement and to buy envelopes and stamps; and somebody would have to stuff the envelopes and type the names and addresses on them. Would it be more effective if people went door to door, discussing your candidacy with voters? If you decided today to run for mayor, between now and election day you would face an unending string of unexpected problems, decisions to be made, and lessons to be learned. The special strength of established political parties is that they have

Though they are not mentioned in the Constitution, America's political parties are a major focus of political power. It is virtually impossible to win national office without the endorsement of one of the two major parties.

faced those decisions and problems before and have learned many of those lessons. They have already organized to deal with electoral policies. Political "machines" at the local level tend to be extremely well organized.

Formal membership in our major political parties—actually joining a party organization and participating in caucuses—has always accounted for only a small fraction of the American voters. Yet, in those states that do not have primary elections, the members of the parties are the ones who choose the candidates for office. More generally, the role of parties in a democracy can be stated this way: the people

Table 13-1

Republican and Democratic Contrasts

	Republicans		Democrats	
	RNC	Public	DNC	Public
Increase government spending on defense	89%	60%	22%	48%
Decrease government spending on food stamps	71	63	14	40
Decrease government spending on jobs programs and CETA	66	41	17	33
Favor ERA	29	46	92	62
Agree there's too much government regulation of business	98	72	35	59
Should allow abortions with doctor's consent	52	55	80	64

Source: Martin Plissner and Warren Mitofsky, "Political Elites," *Public Opinion*, October/November 1981, p. 49

get to choose, but the parties decide what the choices are.

People on the right or left extremes of the political spectrum often complain that the two major American political parties do not really differ from one another, but this is not altogether true. Overall, Democrats tend more to the liberal end of the spectrum, Republicans to the conservative end. This is true of both the party "inner circles" and of the more loosely identified general public.

Evidence of the differences separating Democrats and Republicans can be found in the results of surveys conducted by CBS News and the *New York Times*. In one survey, members of the Democratic and Republican National Committees (DNC and RNC)—the ruling bodies of the parties—were asked their opinions on various national issues. In the other survey, members of the general public were asked the same questions. Martin Plissner and Warren Mitofsky (1981:49) summarized some of the responses, as shown in Table 13-1.

We can draw several conclusions from Table 13-1. First, there are consistent differences in the opinions of Democrats and Republicans, even among the general public. Second, party leaders' opinions are farther to the extremes than are those of the rank and file of their respective parties: Republican leaders are more conservative than Republicans in the general public and Democratic leaders are more liberal than rank-and-file Democrats. Let's turn now to a closer look at the rank and file.

The Individual in American Politics

The subject of choosing in American politics has been a main focus of attention for sociologists. Who votes for whom—and why? Here's a summary of some sociological studies.

Voting Behavior

In 1940, Paul Lazarsfeld and two colleagues undertook a study of voting in Erie County, Ohio. *The People's Choice* (1944), which reports their research, has become a classic account of why people vote the way they do. Foremost, the study pointed to the influence of "background factors" on voting choices: religion, social class, place of residence (rural or urban), and so forth. Upper-class, rural, Protestants were primarily Republicans, and working-class,

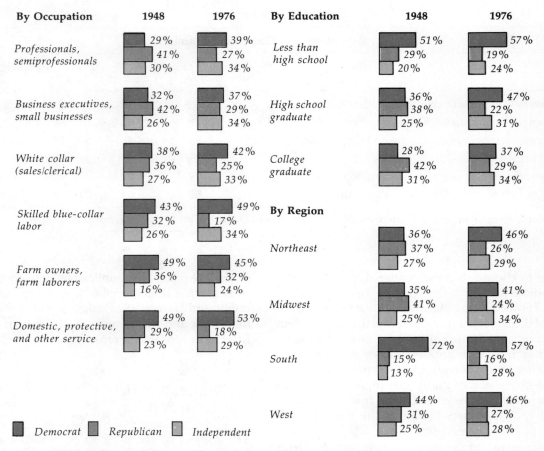

By Occupation	1948	1976
Professionals, semiprofessionals	29% / 41% / 30%	39% / 27% / 34%
Business executives, small businesses	32% / 42% / 26%	37% / 29% / 34%
White collar (sales/clerical)	38% / 36% / 27%	42% / 25% / 33%
Skilled blue-collar labor	43% / 32% / 26%	49% / 17% / 34%
Farm owners, farm laborers	49% / 36% / 16%	45% / 32% / 24%
Domestic, protective, and other service	49% / 29% / 23%	53% / 18% / 29%

By Education	1948	1976
Less than high school	51% / 29% / 20%	57% / 19% / 24%
High school graduate	36% / 38% / 25%	47% / 22% / 31%
College graduate	28% / 42% / 31%	37% / 29% / 34%

By Region	1948	1976
Northeast	36% / 37% / 27%	46% / 26% / 29%
Midwest	35% / 41% / 25%	41% / 24% / 34%
South	72% / 15% / 13%	57% / 16% / 28%
West	44% / 31% / 25%	46% / 27% / 28%

■ Democrat   ■ Republican   ▢ Independent

Figure 13–1 Shifting Political Allegiances. The graphs represent responses to the question, "In politics: as of today, do you consider yourself a Republican, Democrat, or Independent?" Source: Public Opinion (September/October 1978):29. Reprinted by permission of the American Enterprise Institute.

urban, Catholics were overwhelmingly Democrats.

More recent surveys of party identification and voting point to some shifts in these patterns, as indicated in Figure 13–1. As you study the several graphs, you'll note a general decline in Republican Party identification. In early 1981, a Gallup Poll found 43 percent identifying themselves as Democrats, 25 percent as Republicans, and 33 percent as Independents (*Public Opinion* 1981c:29).

Although the pattern of background factors has changed somewhat, another finding by

Lazarsfeld (1944) still seems to hold: the effect of background factors on voting behavior is cumulative. Voters whose social characteristics all suggest a Republican vote, for example, vote Republican, overwhelmingly. Voters with "mixed" characteristics—for instance, upper-class Catholics living in the country—are likely to switch their preferences back and forth during the campaign and, on election day, are the most likely not to vote at all.

Later studies (Berelson et al. 1954, Campbell et al. 1954, and others) have generally confirmed the original Lazarsfeld findings, pointing

Paul Lazarsfeld
1901–1976
Vienna, Austria

Some Important Works

The People's Choice, with Bernard Berelson and Hazel Goudet (New York: Columbia University Press, 1944).

The Language of Social Research, ed., with Morris Rosenberg (New York: Free Press, 1955).

Lazarsfeld will be regarded as one of the founders of empirical research in modern sociology. Trained in the European tradition of scholarship, he came to the United States in 1933 on a research fellowship. His subsequent research career seemed organized around a pattern that might be summarized as follows: (1) he would take interest in a topic of real, social concern; (2) he would create ways of looking at the topic logically and empirically, bringing the two together in the form of data analysis; and (3) he would leave a new methodological technique as the residue of his analysis. Among his chief substantive interests were voting behavior, the mass media, and public opinion.

Perhaps Lazarsfeld's most enduring methodological contribution will be the *elaboration model:* understanding the relationship between two variables by statistically holding a third constant. While most clearly illustrated in data analyses using simple percentage tables, the elaboration model—often called "the Lazarsfeld method"—is also the basis for other, more complex statistical techniques.

to the conclusion that there are two major types of voters in America. One type is made up of people whose social statuses indicate a particular affiliation. These people are concerned about politics and active in political affairs, and they consistently vote according to their social statuses and their party. The other type of voter—voters with "mixed" characteristics—holds the power to swing elections one way or the other. Such voters do not always vote for the same party's candidates. They are the least interested in politics and the least likely to vote. More recent research on voting and political attitudes suggests that the second type of voter is becoming more common.

Political Alienation and Apathy

The 1960s and 1970s were widely regarded as a period of political alienation and disenchantment in America. The excessive use of force by police, instances of political corruption, and other perversities of power mentioned elsewhere in this book appear to have fueled an increasing skepticism about politics and authority in modern America. Although studies of disenchantment have focused primarily on young people, Table 13–2 suggests that they weren't the only ones affected. Comparing national surveys of voters between 1966 and 1977, we see increases in the number of people who feel alienated and powerless in a variety of ways.

In a more detailed study, Jennings and Niemi (1975) reported growing political alienation between 1965 and 1973 among both young people and people of their parents' generation. Both groups were more likely to feel that government wasted money, that government officials were both crooked and inept, and that government was controlled by a few big interests. In 1965, for example, 12 percent of the young people studied said that government was run by a

Table 13-2

Growing Political Alienation in America

Statement	1966	1968	1971	Percent who agree 1972	1973	1974	1976	1977
"Rich get richer and poor get poorer."	45	54	62	68	76	77	76	77
"What you think doesn't count much anymore."	37	42	44	53	61	54	62	61
"People running the country don't really care what happens to you."	26	36	41	50	55	48	59	60
"You feel left out of things around you."	9	12	20	25	29	32	40	35

Source: *Public Opinion* (May/June 1978):23. Reprinted by permission of the American Enterprise Institute.

few big interests; in 1973, 57 percent felt that way. Among the parental generation, the percentage increased from 23 to 53 percent.

The symbolic peak of political disenchantment was reached with the Watergate break-in of 1972, followed by the unfolding tale of political wrongdoing by members of the Nixon administration, and culminating with the president's resignation from office. How did the American electorate respond? From mid-May to early August, 1973, the national television networks broadcast live 235 hours of the hearings held by the Senate committee on Watergate. The hearings drew smaller audiences than the daytime soap operas they replaced, and there was a hue and cry around the country for the return of regular programming (Dye and Zeigler 1975). Revelations of antidemocratic actions by the FBI, the CIA, and other governmental agencies have not (as of this writing) outraged the public generally.

Political apathy also is apparent in surveys of views on human rights. Every year or so a high-school or college class draws national attention by conducting a survey in which members of the general public are asked to support or oppose political positions taken directly from the Bill of Rights. Almost invariably, the Bill of Rights loses. In 1963, researcher Fred Greenstein reported that fewer than one-fourth of the adults studied could correctly cite *any* of the bill's provisions, and Herbert McClosky and his colleagues (1960) have shown that the nation's political leaders are far more supportive of our basic civil liberties than is the public at large.

Political alienation and apathy in America are evidenced in action as well as in attitudes. In recent decades, only half to two-thirds of the nation's eligible voters have actually voted during presidential election years. In fact, the percentage voting declined from 69.3 percent in 1964 to 59.2 percent in 1980 (U.S. Bureau of Census 1982a:2).

Figures are even more dramatic for "off-year" elections—years when there is no presidential race, though the entire U.S. House of Representatives, one-third of the U.S. Senate, plus countless local and state offices are contested. In these elections, 55.4 percent voted in 1966, compared with 45.9 percent in 1978 (U.S. Bureau of Census 1978b:2).

Not only are the percentages low in absolute terms, but they have been generally decreasing in recent years. Even more troublesome to some observers is the dismal voting turnout among the nation's recently enfranchised eighteen-to-twenty-year-old voters. In the 1980 general election, only 35.7 percent voted (U.S. Bureau of Census 1982a:13).

To find out more about nonvoting patterns, the Census Bureau conducted a massive, national survey about two weeks after the 1980 general election. Here are some highlights of what they discovered (U.S. Bureau of Census 1982a:1).

Voter participation rates are higher among Whites (61 percent) than among Blacks (51 percent) or persons of Spanish origin (30 percent). The very low voter participation rate for the Hispanic population is due principally to the large proportion of this population who reported that they were not citizens (32 percent) and therefore were not eligible to vote.

Voter participation was found to be relatively higher among white-collar (71 percent) than blue-collar (48 percent) workers, among college graduates (80 percent) than high school graduates (59 percent), and among homeowners (68 percent) than among renters (45 percent).

Of the 37.2 million people reporting that they had not registered to vote, 47 percent said that they had not done so because they did not prefer any of the likely candidates or that they were not interested in the election. The same reasons were given by 27 percent of the 12.0 million people who registered to vote but did not go to the polls. In all, lack of interest in either the candidates or the election accounted for approximately 21 million people not voting in the November 1980 election.

Political Alienation and the Tax Revolt

In 1978, a dramatic, apparent exception to the general pattern of political apathy in America surfaced in California and elsewhere. Calfornia voted 2 to 1 in favor of Proposition 13, which placed a constitutional limit on the rate of prop-

Table 13-3

California Voters' Suggestions for Proposition 13 Spending Cuts

"Now that Proposition 13 has passed, are you willing to see [service] cut back a lot or only a little or not all?"

Service	% of voters who want service cut a lot
Fire protection	1%
Police services	3
Garbage collection	5
Schools	6
Street repairs and improvements	7
Public transportation	9
Library hours	13
Park maintenance	16
Welfare and social services	43

Source: Everett Carll Ladd, Jr., "The Polls: Taxing and Spending," *Public Opinion Quarterly*, Spring 1979, p. 131.

erty taxes that local governments could levy and slashed existing tax rates as well.

It is clear that voters were demanding cuts in government spending. Where they wanted those cuts made was not altogether clear, however. In June 1978, CBS News and the *New York Times* conducted a survey of California voters to find out. Table 13–3 indicates those areas in which the respondents said "a lot" of funding should be cut.

Clearly, almost half the California voters indicated a disenchantment with the welfare system, feeling that large cuts could and should be made there. All the cuts required by Proposition 13 could not be taken from that single source, however, but voters did not indicate a willingness to see cuts in other areas. Only 16 percent were willing to see park maintenance reduced a lot. Only 5 percent were willing to have garbage collection reduced in order to save tax expenditures.

Clearly, the 1978 tax revolt did not represent a return to popular participation in government. It was an act of defiance grown out of frustration. It was a dramatization of the feeling of citizens "versus" government, rather than citizens taking charge of or becoming government.

The Jeffersonian vision of self-governing citizens meeting together, discussing differing points of view, and forging a united, national agreement has proved more visionary than real. While it is an easy matter to blame the current state of affairs on an ignorant and irresponsible public on the one hand, or on an unscrupulous and conniving elite on the other, what is needed is to view the current state of American political life in terms of basic institutional processes.

Political Alternatives

The disenchantment with political institutions we've been observing has parallels in other institutions, as we'll see in our examinations of the economy, education, religion, and the family. Political experiences need to be structured through agreements if society is to survive, yet the structuring of those experiences makes them less satisfying to individuals. Moreover, the continual changing of *political* forms throughout history has not remedied the basic problem. The political form alienating many Americans today began as an alternative to the unsatisfying colonial government that preceded national independence. The colonial government, however, arose as an alternative to the European politics that the colonists fled in coming to the New World.

The 1960s and early 1970s have been popularly characterized by the phrase "politics of protest." These years have been represented in part by an attempt to find political satisfaction outside the institutionalized structure of electoral politics. Direct protest and mass demonstrations—sometimes civil, sometimes violent—were fairly common, and many observers felt American political institutions would be permanently altered. Despite specific legislation and modifications in national policies coming about in connection with protests by minorities and antiwar demonstrators, however, the chief results may have been to make the existing agreements among the elites and general public alike appear even more granitelike in their reification (see Dye and Zeigler 1975).

At the same time, we have seen in earlier discussions—voluntary associations in Chapter 7 and social movements in Chapter 12—that citizen participation in government and other aspects of society can make a difference. Numerous reforms have come about through individuals getting together to work in concert. There is disagreement, however, as to whether reform is the way to go.

Some argue that revolution is the only solution to dissatisfaction with political systems, but it is precisely in the case of revolution that the general problems of institutionalization are most clearly seen. The revolutionary, having successfully overturned the established political agreements, must immediately—and often autocratically—establish new political agreements. The cycle begins all over again. Without some structuring of individual political experiences, a nation cannot survive. The Maoist attempt to maintain a "continuing revolution" in China appears to be a recognition of this problem, but it does not yet appear a solution to it. Regardless of ideology or philosophy, whether democratic or dictatorial, institutionalized political agreements become reified and dissatisfying. The solution needs to be found in an understanding of the nature of social agreements themselves.

Summary: Political Institutions

Political institutions are organized around the exercise of power in society. More specifically, they define the legitimate use of power, which is authority. Weber discussed three major types of authority: charismatic, traditional, and rational-bureaucratic. Despite a trend toward the last of these, even the most modern societies have elements of all three types of authority.

Other functions of political institutions include the codification of norms as laws, the enforcement of norms through social control, and the creation and maintenance of group identity and solidarity. In all these regards, political institutions function to support the survival of group life in societies.

Varied political forms appear to serve the necessary functions. In traditional-autocratic systems, all power and authority are theoretically vested in a single leader, although in practice the control may be less direct. Totalitarian systems operate by exercising control over all aspects of life for all members of society. Where traditional-autocratic systems tend to support a continuation of the status quo, totalitarian governments are more likely to work toward the "rebirth" of the nation, organized around an ideology. In contrast to totalitarian and traditional-autocratic systems, democracy grows out of the participation of a broad base of society's members in politics and government. In a mass democracy, people participate directly in government; in representative democracy they elect officials.

In a democracy, political power is clearly created by the joining together of people in a common agreement. In America, there are several focuses of such power. Among them, of course, are political parties. In general, voters choose their leaders, but the parties decide who the voters will choose from. C. Wright Mills and others have written about the importance of a power elite—leaders of government, business, and the military—in running the nation. He has been criticized for taking a "zero-sum" view of power and for underestimating the power of professional interest groups. David Riesman suggests that American politics are controlled more by veto groups that have the power to prevent certain actions than by groups that direct the actions to be taken.

A number of sociological studies have examined the place of community elites in American political life. Some studies have suggested that towns are essentially run by a single family or a few families, while other, more recent, studies suggest a greater pluralism of community power.

The main way that individuals participate in American democracy is through voting. Research suggests that there are two types of voters in America. One type consists of people who vote consistently in terms of their social statuses. For example, the poor would vote Democratic and the rich, Republican. Nothing is likely to sway these people from their voting pattern if several of their statuses suggest it. These people are also likely to be interested and active in politics. The other type of voter consists of those whose statuses do not suggest a clear voting pattern. Such people are less interested in politics; they vacillate in their voting behavior; and they are the most apathetic and the least likely to vote at all. Often, the apathetic voters hold the balance of power in American elections.

There is evidence that American voters—both young and old—have become more and more alienated and apathetic about our political institutions. They are less and less likely to think that public officials care what they think and more likely to think they have no say in government. The percentage of voters turning out for elections has been decreasing. Disenchantment with current political forms has led some people to seek functional alternatives such as mass protest. Although it is too early to tell for sure, it appears that these new political forms will be no more satisfying than the ones they oppose. Some writers have suggested that the political protest of the 1960s and 1970s may even have furthered the reification of established political agreements among the general public.

Economic Institutions and Their Functions

The stuff of political institutions is control over people. Economic institutions deal with control over the scarce things that people want. Capitalism and socialism, industrialization, corporations, and the labor movement are some examples of economic institutions. Very often political and economic control go hand in hand. If you had control of all the world's crude oil reserves, for example, you'd be in a good position to get people to do what you wanted them to.

The desire for *things* is a powerful motivator in human affairs. It makes some people work hard, and it sometimes makes people lie, cheat, and kill. Clearly, the unfettered seeking after desired things would make social life chaotic and unstable. Economic institutions act to control potential chaos. They are made up of agreements that order acquisition.

The primary function of economic institutions involves two sorts of transformations. First, a society's economy is designed to bring about a transformation of the environment to satisfy individual and social needs. It does this through a system of production, distribution, and consumption of scarce goods and services. Second, a society's economy transforms individuals by organizing them into social statuses. As we saw in Chapter 8, the structure and operation of the economy is, in most societies, a keystone of social stratification in general. Let's now look at each of these functions in more detail.

Production

Economic production, most generally viewed, is a matter of transformation. Things people do not need or cannot use are transformed through production into those things they *do* need, in a form they can use. As we noted in Chapter 2, Talcott Parsons has used the term "adaptation" in connection with the functions of economic institutions. They adapt a society's environment to its needs.

Economic institutions transform many "things." Economists have generally focused their attention on three: land, capital, and labor. These are the three great resources that are transformed by economic institutions into the goods and services that people need and want.

Land   Different societies have had different agreements about land. Some have revered it, feeling obliged to bring themselves into harmony with it. Others have exploited it. Different agreements have also arisen regarding the ownership of land. In many preliterate societies, the notion of private ownership of land was unthinkable; it was simply there for all to use. When these societies—such as the American Indians and the native Hawaiians—have been intruded upon by societies favoring private ownership, the result has been disastrous for them. "Titles" to land have been given freely or sold cheaply, because the "privacy" of private ownership was a concept too foreign to be comprehended.

Capital   Capital might be regarded as the tool by which land is transformed into commodities through economic production. Although we tend to think of capital as "money," this is too narrow a view in the economic context. The farmer's plow is an example of capital, as is the hunter's spear. The factory capable of turning cotton into clothing is also capital. In modern societies, we have come to regard capital as primarily financial. It is a commodity with which to buy the plows, spears, and factories that can transform the land.

Labor   "Labor" is the abstract noun referring to the workers who operate the tools that transform the land. Plows are useless without people to direct them, spears are useless without people to aim and throw them, and factories are useless without people to operate them. Economic institutions transform people into labor. They organize people for the production of goods and services. We'll examine this aspect of economic institutions in some detail when we discuss the organization of occupations.

Distribution

Economic institutions are systems through which the fruits of production are distributed within a society. Stores are an obvious example of organizations serving this function, but so are trucking companies, airlines, and shipping companies. Payroll offices, banks, and loan companies are involved in the distribution of money, which makes the distribution of goods and services easier.

In preliterate societies, distribution occurs through a system of barter. Goods and services are exchanged directly, without the intermediary role money plays in more modern societies. Barter is not limited to preliterate societies, though. Children exchange baseball cards from packs of bubble gum. American farmers exchange many things among themselves. A bushel of fresh corn may be exchanged for the use of a tractor or a bull. People exchange favors.

Consumption

Consumption is the final stage in the operation of economic institutions; it gives production and distribution their purpose. Consumption patterns and preferences can explain much about the character of production and distribution in a society. They are a matter of agreements, and these differ from society to society. Symbols, beliefs, values, and norms shape the ways in which people consume as well as *what* they consume.

Table 13–4 reports some of the things consumed by the average American in 1980.

Personal-expenditure patterns are only one view of consumption in American society. In addition to our consumption as individuals, we

Table 13-4

Selected American Consumption Patterns, 1980

Item	Per capita consumption	
Meat	180.1	pounds
Fish	12.7	pounds
Eggs	272	
Chicken and turkey	60.5	pounds
Dairy products	345.2	pounds
Fats and oils	55.9	pounds
Fruits and vegetables	646.3	pounds
Grains	201.2	pounds
Coffee	10.4	pounds
Tea	0.8	pounds
Soft drinks	37.8	gallons
Cocoa beans	3.2	pounds
Cigarettes	195	packs
Cigars	25	
Beer	34	gallons (1979)
Wine (1979)	2.75	gallons
Liquor (1979)	2.70	gallons
Petroleum energy	154	million British thermal units
Natural gas	92	million British thermal units
Coal	71	million British thermal units
Books	7.1	(1979)
Newspapers	99.4	
Shoes	1.4	pairs
Firearms	0.28	

Source: U.S. Bureau of Census, *Statistical Abstract of the United States*. (Washington, D.C.: Government Printing Office, 1981), p. 126, 568, 579, 795, 796, 798, 803.

consume *as a society*. In 1981, for example, Americans paid 284 billion dollars in individual income taxes to the federal government. When this is added to other sources of federal revenues and loans, we spent nearly *two-thirds of a trillion dollars* as a nation, not counting state, county, and local government expenditures (U.S. Bureau of Census 1981i:247, 248). Table 13–5

Table 13-5

American Federal Government Expenditures, 1981

Item	Billions of dollars	Percent
National defense	162.1	24.7
Income security	229.7	35.1
Health	66.7	10.2
Veterans benefits and services	22.4	3.4
Education, training, employment	30.6	4.7
Commerce and housing credit	3.2	0.5
Transportation	24.0	3.7
Natural resources and environment	13.7	2.1
Energy	9.3	1.4
Community, regional development	10.3	1.6
Agriculture	1.2	0.2
Interest	77.3	11.8
Revenue sharing	6.8	1.0
International affairs	11.3	1.7
General science, space, technology	6.2	0.9
General government	5.1	0.8
Administration of justice	4.7	0.7
Undistributed offsetting receipts	−29.3	−4.5
	$655.3	100.0%

Source: U.S. Bureau of Census, *Statistical Abstract of the United States* (Washington, D.C.: Government Printing Office 1981), p. 248.

Note: Social services included under "Education, training, employment." "Revenue sharing" includes general-purpose fiscal assistance.

describes our consumption pattern as a society in 1981. We can make inferences about values and priorities from this pattern, too.

Transformation and Individuals

Aside from transforming the physical environment into things that are distributed to people for their consumption, economic institutions effect another transformation. They transform people by structuring them into social statuses. People become consumers, workers, supervisors, and so forth. The transformation of people into statuses has an organizational function. It coordinates individual activities in the cooperative production, distribution, and consumption of goods and services. The transformation is also relevant from the individual's point of view. In many societies, "what you do" is the most important element in "who you are."

The transformation of people into economic statuses has, of course, been influenced by the division of labor in modern societies. The occupational statuses that constitute a significant part of many people's personal identities have grown increasingly specialized.

That the transformation of individuals (like the transformation of the physical environment) is a mixed blessing we'll see in more detail later in the chapter. At this point, however, let's look at some of the different forms economic agreements have taken in support of the social functions we've just examined.

Varieties of Economic Institutions

Throughout most of human history, our ancestors handled economic functions through hunting and gathering. Then about 9,000 years ago, a major economic development occurred: people began planting and harvesting crops rather than simply gathering what they found in their wandering. The development of agriculture meant that societies could form and settle down in particular areas and that more people could live together.

Our economic institutions have gone through a long history of development since the establishment of agriculture. For the purposes of this discussion, however, I want to pick up the story with the set of developments we have come to call the Industrial Revolution.

Capitalist Industrialization

The detailed occupational specialization that characterizes modern economics had its beginning in the mechanized, mass production of the first factories late in the eighteenth century. The Industrial Revolution grew out of a number of technological innovations within the British textile industry. The first of these, spinning and weaving machines, simply increased the productivity of individual workers; later innovations harnessed steam power and outstripped the productivity of individuals altogether.

The rise of mechanized factories radically restructured the economic agreements. First, economic production became far more specialized than it had been in the craft guilds. Where an individual once did everything from the spinning of yarn to the weaving and dyeing of cloth, a factory worker might have a single task of loading spools of yarn on a machine.

Second, and equally important, the worker no longer owned the result of his or her labors. The factories required capital for buildings, machinery, and raw materials. Individual weavers lacked such funds, and a new class of capitalists invested in the factories and employed workers for wages.

With the rise of industrial **capitalism,** economic power shifted from feudal lords to capitalistic entrepreneurs and merchants. The greater profits provided by factories generated new capital for investment in expansion and even greater economic power.

Capitalism is an economic system based on an agreement regarding private property. In practice, that agreement relates especially to *big* property: factories, machines, mines, and large sums of money. It is agreed that individuals may properly exercise control over such property.

The United States economy, of course, operates under the capitalist model and has done so—with minor, local exceptions—throughout its history. And while numerous individuals and groups have argued for a move to socialism, the mass of public opinion still supports the capitalist model. In 1977, for example, a national sample of Americans was asked whether the private control of business had been a factor in America's greatness: 67 percent said it was a "major" factor; another 23 percent said it was a "minor" factor. When a 1976 sample was asked whether "The country would be better off if big business were taken over by the government as in certain European countries," three-fourths disagreed (Lipset 1980:32, 33).

Following the Great Depression of the early 1930s, there was some support for government ownership of business, but even then it was a minority view. A 1936 Gallup poll, for example, found 29 percent in favor of the government ownership of railroads, and 38 percent favored a takeover of the banks. (During the Depression, many banks had been unable to return customers' deposits.) By 1974, 24 percent favored government ownership of railroads, but only 12 percent felt the banks should be taken over. Three years later, amidst popular unhappiness with and suspicions about the large oil companies, 23 percent of Americans favored government ownership, 62 percent said it would be a mistake, and 14 percent had no opinion (Lipset 1980:35).

This does not mean Americans favor unbridled capitalism, however. In 1946, following World War II, 61 percent of a national sample said "companies should be allowed to make all they can," 31 percent said "the government should limit profits," and the remainder had no opinion. By 1979, these percentages had been reversed: 34 percent now favored unlimited profits, while 60 percent favored limitations, with 6 percent unsure. That same year, a majority—54 percent—agreed that "big business is a threat because it has become more active politically." Only 14 percent disagreed, with a substantial 30 percent having no opinion (Lipset 1980:33, 36).

In summary, Americans maintain a basic commitment to the capitalist model but feel it needs to be somewhat controlled by government regulation. As we'll see shortly, socialist economies have been similarly tempered by capitalist tendencies.

Socialism

In the mid-nineteenth century, Karl Marx spoke and wrote against what he regarded as the inhumanity of capitalism. He objected to the dismal working conditions existing in factories and the low pay workers received, and he criticized the dissociation of specialized workers from the creative act. Primarily, however, he rejected the agreement regarding private ownership of the means of production, because of the excessive inequality and oppression it tended to produce.

The set of agreements put forward by Marx and others placed ownership of the means of production with the society at large. Factories, raw materials, and industrial products, Marx said, should belong to everyone. In this socialist scheme, political institutions would be wedded to economic ones in the production, distribution, and consumption of scarce goods and services.

In the socialist economic institutions that have appeared in the world since Marx's time, workers are typically employees of the state. They receive wages in return for their work, and they use those wages to purchase the things they need from the state. In socialist agreements, economic institutions are centrally planned and operated since ownership of all enterprises rests with the same entity, the government. **Socialism** does not usually abolish private property, altogether, however, because people's attachment to immediate possessions is usually pretty strong.

Marx looked beyond socialism in his writings to a system of **communism** that would totally abolish private ownership. In communism, all would share in the production of the society's goods, and all would enjoy them afterward. Marx summarized these sentiments in his dictum: "From each according to his abilities, to each according to his needs."

No major society today operates under this particular model, though many—most notably the Soviet Union and China—operate under the socialist model. Just as Americans have tempered their commitment to capitalism, there is also evidence of a tempering of the socialist model. Although China has organized its agriculture around large communes, Dinah Lee (1981:18) reports a mixed policy in that regard:

> The encouragement of private plots for peasants has been going on for many years, but since mid-April Chinese peasants have been permitted to double the amount of land for private use in the community from 7 to 15 percent. Some family members may now be excused from collective farming to work for themselves.

While a part of the private farming in China is a way for farm families to feed themselves better, Lee reported in 1981 that there were approximately 2,200 "free markets" in which the farmers offered their produce for sale—and profit. This capitalistic development has been viewed with mixed feelings, as Lee (1981:18) continues:

> A backlash of discrimination against the private entrepreneurs has already begun, and it remains to be seen how well the government can keep peace between those with a fixed income and those

with growing profits. On the other hand, the private sector has proved too popular with some farmers and workers who report sick and are then discovered working their private plot or business on "commune time."

Capitalism or Socialism?

The lesson to be learned from the above discussions is that both capitalism and socialism have had mixed success in the world. Where either model has been officially adopted, tendencies toward the other have been common. Most of the world's nations operate with "mixed economies."

Recall Lipset's comment—discussed earlier in Chapter 4—about the strains between achievement and equality in America. This strain would appear to be much more universal, and it relates to the current examination of economic systems. Simply put, capitalism emphasizes the value of achievement, socialism the value of equality.

Motivating individual workers is a basic problem faced by socialist economies. When they recognize that working harder and more effectively will not earn them additional, material rewards, many workers in a socialist situation slack off. The solution to this problem typically takes such forms as ideological indoctrination and threats of punishment. Neither works perfectly, and punishment produces dissatisfaction and can even prompt greater resistance to the system.

Capitalism faces a different set of problems. While the "profit motive" offers a fundamental incentive to hard work and productivity, it is a system that ultimately destroys itself. We have popular expressions in America that "Success breeds success" and "It takes money to make money." As some individuals and groups are more successful than others, the unequal distribution of rewards undercuts the equality of opportunity. As "the rich get richer and the poor get poorer" under a pure model of capitalism, hard work and "pluck" no longer result automatically in rewards for someone who starts out poor. As "profit" disappears from the "profit motive," so does the motivation.

It is no surprise that both capitalist and socialist governments around the world have been forced to tinker with their economic agreements. The complexities of economic systems are not limited to national societies, however. International affairs complicate the economies of individual nations and create a complex "world economic system."

Immanuel Wallerstein (1974, 1979) has argued that the most appropriate level of economic analysis is global rather than national. This is so, he suggests, because capitalism operates on a global basis—with a global division of labor—and the result is that the world economic system is fundamentally capitalist: organized around profits. In part, the players in this international system are large capitalist corporations (which we'll examine shortly). Ironically, however, socialist nations must operate as capitalist entities in the world system.

The Soviet Union, for example, is a petroleum exporter. There are no private oil companies in the U.S.S.R., of course. The oil belongs to the state. In the world system, however, the U.S.S.R. must negotiate and market its oil the same way America's privately owned oil companies do. In this sense, the Soviet Union is as capitalist as ARCO or Standard Oil.

Susan Eckstein (1981:193) describes the impact of the world economic system on the domestic economy in socialist Cuba:

Wallerstein's world economy perspective illuminates the kinds of tensions and constraints faced by a country embarked on a socialist transformation. Cuba's development prospects continue to be shaped by global capitalist dynamics, its position within and relationship to the world economy, and domestic political pressures, some of which oppose rapid social transformations and an emphasis on maximum export profits.

Despite nationalization of most of the economy and propagation of socialist principles, the Castro government continues to be concerned with profits from trade, and the economy has been restructured on several occasions with this end in view. Because of the small size of Cuba's economy and its limited resource base, the island's capacity to expand production hinges, in part, on its capacity to generate export earnings with which to acquire needed development inputs. Sugar is the main product that Cuba can produce with a comparative advantage. Despite integration into the Soviet bloc, the Cuban economy continues to expand and contract with world sugar prices.

We'll return to the world economic system later in this chapter and in later chapters. At this point, however, we're going to focus specifically on the United States.

American Economic Structures

The most striking characteristic of the American economy is its size. Our GNP (gross national product)—the total value of the goods and services we produce as a nation—was around two and two-thirds trillion dollars in 1980. This was more than the combined total for the entire Third World, with its 3.4 billion people (Population Reference Bureau 1982). With about 5 percent of the world's population, it is estimated that the United States accounts for around 40 percent of the resources consumed in the world annually.

In this section, we're going to look at three aspects of the "bigness" of the American economy: "big business," "big labor," and "big government."

Big Business

How big is American business? In 1977, 2,205 corporations in America had assets greater than 250 million dollars, over half of them in finance, insurance, and real estate. In 1980, the 200 largest American industrial corporations had assets totalling nearly a trillion dollars (U.S. Bureau of Census 1981i: 543, 544).

The immensity of American business is something that Karl Marx might have predicted as an extension of what he observed a century ago in Europe. Some twists in our capitalist agreements, however, Marx could not have foreseen. Most notably, the advent of the large corporation has deeded ownership of the means of production to the hands of the many rather than the few. In 1980, for example, American Telephone and Telegraph, the nation's largest company, was owned by nearly three million stockholders. General Motors had over a million "owners" (Moskowitz et al. 1980:276, 420). Not all those owners participated significantly in the running of their companies, however. The greater part of the stock in each corporation is controlled by a relatively small number of stockholders.

Public ownership of business has represented a transfer of power within the economy, as A.A. Berle (1958) and others have pointed out. Today, the managers of business, corporate presidents and boards of directors, wield the power. Corporate power is concentrated, moreover, through the phenomenon of "interlocking directorates." Certain individuals seem to turn up on the boards of directors of corporation after corporation.

One function of interlocking directorates is to link corporations with one another. With Director X serving on the boards of Corporations A and B, a channel is opened for collaboration between the two companies. And if Director Y serves on the boards of Corporations B and C, Directors X and Y together provide a channel linking Corporations A and C. In a complex analysis of the cobweb of interlocking directorates of major American corporations, Beth Mintz and Michael Schwartz (1981:856) found that General Motors' directors served on the boards of twenty-nine other corporations. Those twenty-nine corporations were directly linked to another hundred more corporations.

Figure 13–2 presents General Motors' ties to other corporations.

Mintz and Schwartz (1981:865–66) conclude their analysis as follows:

> The evidence presented here suggests that the large American corporation is not an autonomous unit, that interorganizational alliances are not characterized by industry coalitions, and that discrete financial groups are not the typical unit of corporate organization. We have found that the interlock network is dominated by a handful of major New York banks and insurance companies.

The interlocking of American corporations has taken a new turn in recent years with the development of what is popularly called the **conglomerate:** the giant corporation that diversifies its activities by participating in several different sectors of the economy. Conglomerates are based on the principle that diversification provides greater economic stability as the fortunes of specific industries rise and fall. They have provoked considerable controversy.

The **multinational corporation** is the latest development in the evolution of economic organization. We've been looking at economic organizations in terms of the functions they serve within a society, but the multinationals, as the name suggests, reach across societies. They may have raw materials acquired from one nation processed in other nations (where labor costs are low) and sell the finished products in still other nations (where consumer demand and wealth are high). You've probably done business with a multinational corporation yourself, perhaps buying a souvenir ashtray proclaiming the wonders of New York City and bearing the inscription "made in Taiwan." You can look forward to doing business with more in the future.

The rise of multinational corporations is significant in a number of ways. The obvious economic implications were just mentioned. The political implications may not be as obvious. Primarily, it comes down to a question of who will watch over the activities of such corporations, who will protect the public against possible excesses? In the case of American corporations, for example, extensive federal laws specify what corporations may or may not do. Antitrust laws are designed to encourage competition and to protect consumers from price-gouging. In addition to the laws, we have agencies responsible for enforcement and sanctions prescribed for violations. But what constraints will hold the multinationals in check? That's a question yet to be answered.

Much of the current concern over the power of multinationals today relates to their impact on Third World countries. In some instances the multinationals exploit the raw materials of poor countries in a manner reminiscent of colonialism. Often multinationals can determine a nation's economic patterns. In numerous countries, American multinationals have established export agriculture—bananas, coffee, and sugar, for example—as primary industries, making less land available for agriculture which would feed the members of that country. By the same token, multinationals can have a significant impact in determining the job opportunities available to people in poor countries.

Finally, the multinational corporations have been charged with unethical, even inhumane, dealings with Third World consumers. The most publicized controversy in recent years has centered on the marketing of infant formula in the Third World by the gigantic Swiss food conglomerate, Nestlé. Critics charged that Nestlé provided infant formula free to new mothers in hospitals. Use of the formula instead of mother's milk caused the mothers' breasts to dry up, thereby forcing them to continue using the formula—paying for it once they left the hospital. Being poor, however, they tended to "stretch" the formula with too much water. To make matters worse, the water available in many poor countries is contaminated. The result was increased infant disease and death. The worldwide criticism produced a massive consumer boycott of Nestlé products and a United Nations condemnation.

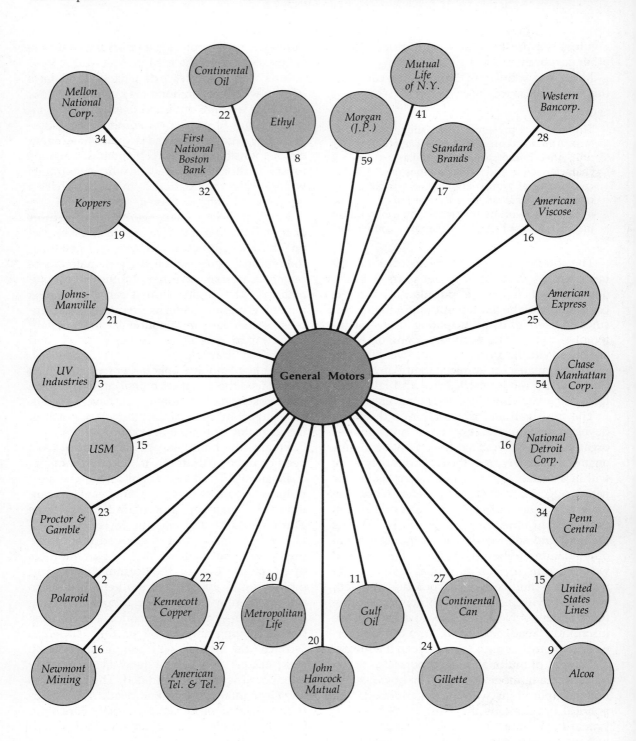

The North-South debate, discussed in Chapter 8, involves more than relations between rich and poor nations. We can expect increased attention to the role of multinationals' relations with the countries of the South.

Big Labor

If business in America is *big*, so is labor. It would be impossible to understand the American economy or that of many other industrialized nations without an examination of the part played by unions.

Unions serve to put the force of numbers behind workers' point of view in framing the agreements that define industrial relations. For example, if one worker in a factory is unwilling to accept the working conditions, duties, pay, and fringe benefits there, he or she can be replaced with little or no disruption to the factory's production. If *all* the workers in the factory unite, however, the matter is quite different. For this reason, "solidarity" has been the rallying cry of the union movement throughout its history.

The earliest American unions were formed of skilled craft workers, such as carpenters and teamsters. Beginning in the 1930s, however, increasing numbers of assembly-line workers began organizing. The threat their organized power represented to management produced extreme and often violent resistance. Union organizers were fired and sometimes jailed. Union meetings were broken up and workers locked out of their jobs. Strikes were broken by the army, and people were killed in the process.

From the Roosevelt administration onward, unionization has become increasingly legitimized within American economic agreements. Federal laws now prescribe the manner in which

Multinational corporations often spread cultural components from society to society. Now you can get a Big Mac anywhere from Topeka to Tokyo.

employees of an organization can elect a union to represent them and the manner in which employers must deal with unions in collective bargaining.

The present political strength of labor unions in America is more than a matter of individual workers joining unions; unions have themselves organized into larger bodies. The American Federation of Labor (AFL) was organized in the late nineteenth century as a vehicle for coordinating existing craft unions. In 1935, following a dispute over the inclusion of unions being organized in the mass-production industries such as steel and automobile manufacture, a number of unions bolted the AFL to form the Congress of Industrial Organizations (CIO). Both organizations continued to grow until they merged into the AFL-CIO in 1954. By 1978, the AFL-CIO was composed of 137 unions repre-

Figure 13–2 General Motors' interlocking directorates. The numbers next to firm names represent the total number of corporations to which the organization is intertied. Source: Beth Mintz and Michael Schwartz "Interlocking Directorates and Interest Group Formation," American Sociological Review, vol. 46, December 1981, p. 857.

senting a total of more than 17 million members. This figure accounts for over 75 percent of the union members in America and one-sixth of the total civilian labor force (U.S. Bureau of Census 1981i:379, 412). In recent years, the organization of farm workers and government and other clerical workers has represented an important new direction in the union movement.

Big Government

To round out our overview of the American economic system, we turn to big government. The various levels of American government are involved in the economy in a number of ways. In 1981, over 16 million Americans—about one worker in six—were employed by federal, state, or local governments (U.S. Bureau of Census 1981i:394). The federal government alone owned one-third of the nation's land in 1979 and nearly half a million buildings (U.S. Bureau of Census 1981i:225, 226). With some justification, the federal government is sometimes called the largest "business" in the world.

A variety of government regulatory agencies exercise considerable control over the operation of private businesses. Radio and television stations, for example, are licensed, reviewed, and relicensed by the Federal Communications Commission, and that agency specifies certain rules about the nature of broadcasting. Other government agencies tell savings and loan institutions how much interest to pay on deposits, specify the quality of materials to be used in building construction, test and license professionals, and so forth. In all these and other ways, the federal government is in a position to have an enormous impact on what would otherwise be "natural business cycles."

The Experience of Economic Structures

The "big news" of the American economy is its own bigness, reflecting big business, big labor, and big government. But where are the individual people in the economy? And what experiences do individuals have within such economic structures? We'll begin to find out by examining occupation as a source of social identity and by looking at some of the interactions that occupations provide. Then we'll turn to the question of the "morality" of work for work's sake, and finally, we'll examine the experience of individuals at the consumption ends of the economic process.

Occupation as Identity: Satisfaction and Alienation

When you meet a stranger at a party, one of the first questions you'll be asked—particularly if you're a man—is "What do you do?" As you may have discovered, saying you're a student is not an entirely satisfactory answer. Being a student means that you don't "do" anything yet, and you may be asked a slightly sophisticated version of "What do you want to be when you grow up?" Occupation has come to be a central source of identity in modern industrial societies, much as kinship was in more traditional societies.

The link between occupation and social identity did not begin with modern industrialism, however. The cabinetmaker, cobbler, or other artisan of an earlier day derived his or her identity from work. Much has been written about the extent to which such people identified with the *products* of their crafts, enjoying the satisfaction of personal creativity. While such satisfactions have sometimes been overromanticized, Marx was surely correct in noting that division of labor in industry was significant in this respect. As a member of an assembly-line team, the worker could no longer regard the product of industry as a personal creation, and Marx spoke of "alienated labor."

In a modern factory hundreds or thousands of assembly-line workers repeat the same specific operation countlessly. The output of one worker becomes the input for another's specific

Occupations can imprison human beings behind their social masks . . .

. . . and occupations can be a focus for creativity and a source of satisfaction.

operation. Their specific tasks typically involve the use of equally specialized equipment, and the objects of production may flow endlessly from one worker to another on conveyor belts.

The differentiated functions of the assembly line can be reasonably easily coordinated, but the further differentiation of staff positions is often the source of conflict within organizations. The corporation treasurer, with his or her point of view, may object to the equipment purchases the line personnel, with their point of view, want; and the sales staff, with their point of view, may urge modifications to the product that will be difficult to accomplish on the assembly line.

Different roles in a modern factory are interdependent. Every specific role is based on numerous agreements as to the roles others in the organization are to play. If assemblers were

to stop assembling, if salespersons were to stop selling, if shipping clerks were to stop shipping, all the efforts of the rest of the organization would be useless.

Although it is tempting to speak casually and simplistically about "alienation" in the modern world of work, Robert Blauner (1964), in his study of workers in different types of industry, has shown the matter to be more complex than might be imagined. To begin, Blauner showed that alienation has dimensions: *powerlessness* (the worker's lack of control over production), *meaninglessness* (reflecting the worker's contributing only a part of the production process), *isolation* (when the worker does not work as part of an integrated social unit), and *self-estrangement* (when the job is merely a way of earning a living rather than a form of self-expression and fulfillment).

Taking these dimensions into account, Blauner found that different types of industry produced different levels of alienation, not that dissatisfaction arose uniformly from all modern work. Auto workers on an assembly line were found to be highly alienated, as you'd imagine from a reflection on the several dimensions just mentioned. The textile workers that Blauner studied were less alienated than the auto workers, which he explained in terms of the small-town, southern setting of the textile plant: the workers enjoyed an integrated social life not found among the urban auto workers.

Among printers and among workers in an automated chemical plant, Blauner found far less dissatisfaction and this seemed to reflect differences in the several dimensions of alienation. Both the printers and the chemical workers operated as members of a team, had far more control over their work pace than did the auto or textile workers, and were, in general, more in charge of their own work. Blauner's findings about the chemical workers are particularly interesting since more and more work in the future will probably be similar to theirs.

The Future of Alienation and Work

In the most developed nations today, automation is creating a transformation in work, producing what is often called the **postindustrial society,** where the economic focus has shifted from the manufacture of goods to the provision of services. There are two main factors to consider. First, the production industries have fewer jobs and those that remain are less boring and routine, since computers and other advanced machines do the boring work. So, the new jobs in the production industries are those of machine watchers, testers, and handlers.

The other trend lies outside production altogether, as the developed nations have generated more and more of their new jobs in the "service industries." Fewer and fewer people work in manufacturing facilities, while more and more are clerks, tellers, waiters, barbers, physicians, teachers, salespeople, and other occupations organized around serving people rather than making things.

The growth of service occupations is typical throughout the industrialized world. Figure 13–3 shows—for the United States and seven other nations—the percentages of national labor forces employed in industry, agriculture, and service. Most notable in each of the seven countries is (1) the decline of agricultural employment and (2) the increase in service occupations.

In the years to come, more and more of us will earn our livings by providing services to each other. And it is worth noting that the occupations likely to grow the most have, in the past, been relatively more satisfying to workers. Overall, moreover, public-opinion polls report high levels of job satisfaction. When the National Opinion Research Center asked a national sample "on the whole, how satisfied are you with the work you do—would you say you are very satisfied, moderately satisfied, a little dissatisfied, or very dissatisfied?" the largest number, 45 percent, said "very satisfied" and another 34 percent said "moderately satisfied." When asked "if you were to get enough money to live as comfortably as you would like for the rest of your life, would you continue to work or would you stop working?" two-thirds said they would continue working (de Boer 1978:419, 421).

The "Morality" of Work

In part, the significance of occupation as a source of social identity in the West is linked to the "morality" of work embodied in the "Protestant

Figure 13–3 Employment by economic sector in seven countries, 1960–1978. Source: U.S. Bureau of Census, Social Indicators III, Washington, D.C., Government Printing Office, 1980, p. 347.

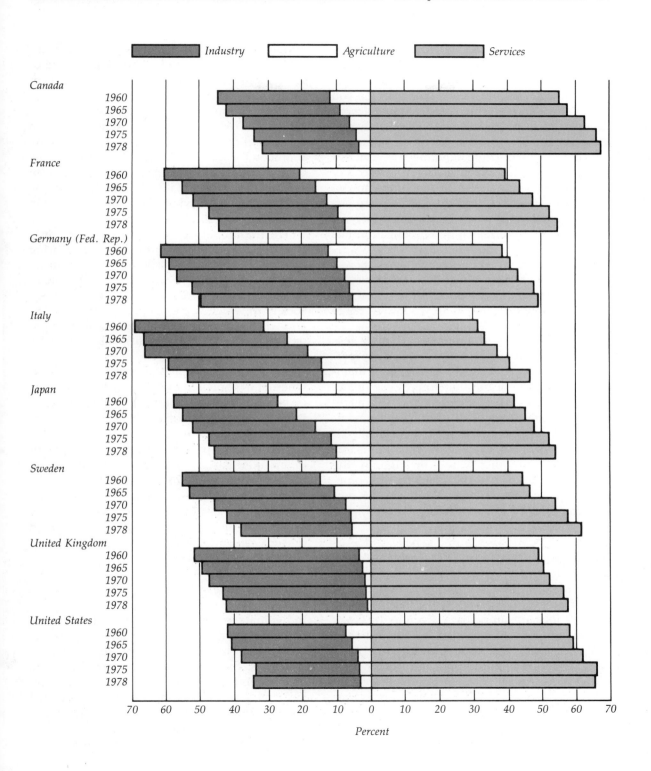

ethic," as we'll discuss in Chapter 15. In early Calvinism, for example, one's economic vocation was seen as a stewardship under God. If you worked hard and well at whatever job you had, your actions glorified God. Sloth and sloppiness were a shame and a sin. The strictly religious roots of this point of view have withered, but there is still a strong agreement in America and elsewhere that working at a job—especially for men—is a moral and proper thing to do. Playboys, jet-setters, and the idle rich are targets of scorn, even when they are envied.

The view of work as a moral obligation has been considerably modified, at least in its specific application. When the average workday was reduced from twelve to eight hours, some saw the hand of the devil at work. More recent talk of a thirty-hour or twenty-hour work week raises the same specter for some.

Unemployment is a similar, though less happy, problem. In mid-1981, with a 7.6 percent unemployment rate, over 8 million members of the American labor force were out of work (U.S. Bureau of Labor Statistics 1981b:60). Added to the financial difficulties that unemployment obviously causes is the social stigma of being worthless, even "immoral." Nor is this problem evenly distributed throughout the population. Young blacks, aged sixteen to nineteen, had an unemployment rate of 33.6 percent in mid-1981 (U.S. Bureau of Labor Statistics 1981b:62).

Calvin Coolidge is reputed to have said, during his administration: "The reason we have such high unemployment rates is because there aren't enough jobs." Despite the logic of this view, a widespread suspicion remains that those without jobs are simply lazy. Even in the Great Depression, in which as many as one-fourth of the labor force were unemployed, Americans were unhappy about supporting people who didn't work. In a 1935 Gallup poll, 60 percent of those interviewed felt too much money was being spent on relief programs; 9 percent felt it was too little. In a 1938 Gallup poll, one person in five favored a proposal to deny the vote to

people on relief, and the next year 78 percent said they would favor a law prohibiting "reliefers" from making political contributions (Gallup 1972).

The continuing controversy over welfare programs reflects the persistent American agreement that work is moral and not working is immoral. Popular myths, unsupported by the data, picture "welfare mothers" getting rich from an unending string of illegitimate children, the typical recipient driving to the welfare office in a Cadillac, and similar horrors.

The traditional view of work as a moral duty is complicated by the practice of retiring employees early. The continued growth of automation further aggravates the problem. Some observers urge that we begin planning a society in which some people will never work and will be supported by government throughout their lives, but the traditional view so far appears firmly entrenched.

In a 1978 Roper poll, Americans were asked whether "People should place more emphasis on working hard and doing a good job than on what gives them personal satisfaction and pleasure." Sixty-one percent agreed, 23 percent disagreed, and 15 percent had mixed feelings or no opinion. Possibly attitudes are changing on this, however. While 76 percent of those 60 and older agreed with the statement, this percentage decreased steadily with decreasing age: only 49 percent of the 18-to-29 age group agreed (*Public Opinion* 1979a:25).

The Individual as Consumer

Individuals experience economic institutions both as producers and as consumers of what is produced. The more complex the economic structures, the more interdependent people are on one another in both these regards. The mere fact that you are reading this book—which I wrote, Wadsworth published, your instructor assigned, and you bought—illustrates the web of interdependencies in which you operate as a consumer. None of us is self-sufficient; we all depend on each other.

An industrial economy based on mass production has special implications for your experience as a consumer. Most apparent, your choices of what you will consume depend very largely on what manufacturers believe—on the advice of their marketing consultants—the greatest number of people will desire. Unless your tastes agree with those of the majority, you may be out of luck. At the same time, you have an opportunity to consume things that would be unavailable without mass production.

In a capitalist economy such as ours, decisions on what will be produced for consumption flow from the profit motive. Goods and services will be made available only if their producers can turn a profit in the process. The question of what you "really want" or how satisfied you are with what you get is irrelevant except as those considerations are translated into profits. This is not necessarily "bad"; it's just the agreement our economic institutions are based on. And like the other types of economic institutions we've examined in this chapter, it supports the survival of group life.

There's another way in which you are a consumer in the economy. Earlier in this discussion, I said that the function of economic institutions was the transformation of the environment. When you purchase a new car or a new stereo, you are experiencing some of the results of that transformation. The depletion of natural resources and various forms of pollution are other results of the transformation that you experience. Until recently people were not particularly conscious of or concerned about this latter aspect of the transformation. Today, however, all of us are being forced to confront it.

The experience of economic institutions has both satisfying and unsatisfying aspects for individuals. And, as we would expect, people's dissatisfactions have produced attempts to create alternative agreements and forms. Let's look at some of those.

Some Economic Alternatives

Dissatisfaction with the environmental damage done by modern industrialism has produced an active social movement in recent years. Recycling industries have slowly begun developing as a means of stopping the depletion of natural resources, and the search is on for new energy sources, as we'll see in Chapter 18.

Many environmentalists argue, however, that the necessary solutions to current problems must be more radical than recycling and new energy sources. Economic growth, they say, simply cannot continue, regardless of the technology it employs. Instead, it will be necessary to restructure societies around stabilized economies and populations. More pessimistic observers say flatly that American economic standards will, in fact, have to be lowered.

Consumer dissatisfaction with the current production and distribution of goods has taken a number of forms. Outrage over price increases has frequently resulted in consumer boycotts. Consumer cooperatives are another response, with individuals joining together in associations to purchase food wholesale, often sharing both the financial savings and the work of distribution. In 1979, 485 such co-ops did 185 million dollars worth of business. As a partial alternative to commercial banks, 43 million people belonged to credit unions that handled 52.2 billion dollars in transactions (U.S. Bureau of Census 1981i:554). Yet another alternative to the mass-production economy has been the renewed production of handcrafted articles.

Concern with rising inflation has been one of the most noted forms of consumer dissatisfaction in recent years. A key indicator of inflation is the Consumer Price Index (CPI), calculated and published by the federal government as an indication of the cost of living. The year 1967 is the base for this index. The cost of living in later years is presented as a percentage of 1967 costs. For example, the CPI for 1968 was 104.2, meaning that the cost of living was 4.2

Beginning in the 1970s, recycling became a popular solution to the problem of resource depletion, as it had been during World War II. At the present time, however, only a tiny fraction of our waste is recycled.

percent higher in 1968 than in 1967. The CPI was 116.3 in 1970, 161.2 in 1975, and 247.0 in 1980. In other words, it cost you about two and a half times as much to live as well in 1980 as it would have cost in 1967 (U.S. Bureau of Labor Statistics 1981c:77).

How have Americans coped with inflation? David Caplovitz (1978) asked people what effects the recession that began around 1975, with its accompanying high rate of inflation, had had on them. Over half of the respondents—59 percent—were financially worse off (23 percent said "a lot worse off") than a few years before, due to inflation. Hardest hit were the poor, those with unskilled or semiskilled jobs, the less educated, and the nonwhite. How, Caplovitz wanted to know, did they handle the problem?

The most popular way to cope with inflation was to curtail expenditures, especially by shifting from more expensive to less expensive foods. Over a third of the families also tried to raise their incomes by working more overtime or, less frequently, by sending an additional family member into the workforce or by moonlighting. Poor and low-income families, however, were much less successful at this strategy; many of them are unable to work even when they want to. Two of the strategies used more often by the have-nots were greater self-reliance and bargain hunting. These might be considered the poor man's strategies for coping with inflation. (Caplovitz 1978:52)

Another solution to inflation and to economic problems in general is *barter*. Essentially barter is the trading of goods or services for goods or services without money changing hands, sometimes referred to as the "underground economy." Suppose I decide to chuck textbook writing to become a banjo player. If you'd decided to give up the banjo to become a writer, we might do a deal. I'd give you my typewriter and typing paper in exchange for your banjo and Pete Seeger song books. The only problem lies in our finding each other.

During the 1970s and 1980s, barter became so popular that a number of "barter clubs" were organized to put traders in touch with each other. The clubs, publishing newsletters, served as a disinterested third party to the exchange. Soon, there was an interested fourth party, as Mickey Friedman (1982:1) reports.

> Carl Larsen, speaking for the local office of the IRS says, "Our view is that whatever changes hands is taxable and should be assessed at fair market value. Fair market value is the price which would be paid by a willing buyer to a willing seller for the commodity on the open market."
>
> In fact, Larsen says, the government is not particularly interested in low-level informal exchanges: "If a lady bakes a pie and exchanges it with her neighbor for a coffee cake, no. But if hundreds of pies and cakes are involved, we would be."

Dissatisfaction with the capitalistic aspect of the American economy has produced many movements advocating the establishment of a socialist agreement. Some advocates have favored the evolution of socialism in America; others have urged revolution. Both groups have clearly felt that a socialist structure would remedy the problems presented by capitalism. Lurking behind the suggested change in economic form, however, is the question of what problems the new agreements would present for individuals.

Summary: Economic Institutions

The primary function of economic institutions is the transformation of the environment in support of the production, distribution, and consumption of goods and services. A variety of economic systems and organizations accomplish that function. Every kind of system—from hunting and gathering to capitalist, multinational conglomerates—seems to work in its own fashion.

The different economic agreements that we've examined all have the effect of structuring individual experiences. Capitalism structures economic experiences one way, socialism another. Overall, economic institutions affect individuals in two ways. Through occupations, they structure participation in the production of goods and services. The role of consumer represents another set of experiences.

In examining economic structures, we have paid special attention to the extent to which individual identity and experience of life is mediated through the world of work. Who we are is largely a matter of what we *do*, and there is a continuing agreement among Americans and others that work is "good." This creates a special problem for those unable to get work when jobs are scarce. Not only do the unemployed suffer financially, but also they must bear a moral burden. They are likely to question their worth as humans.

Important Terms

legitimacy
authority
political ideology
charismatic authority
traditional authority
rational-bureaucratic
   authority
routinization
autocracy
totalitarianism
democracy
iron law of oligarchy

power elite
community elite
pluralistic power
capitalism
socialism
communism
conglomerate
multinational
   corporation
automation
postindustrial society

Suggested Readings

Abramson, Paul R.
   1977   *The Political Socialization of Black Americans.* New
         York: Free Press.
   Explores political socialization of Black Americans and
   the results of this process.

Boles, Janet K.
   1979   *The Politics of the Equal Rights Amendment: Conflict
         and the Decision Process.* New York: Longman Press.
   Analyzes the process through which the ERA has proceeded and the blocks to passage. Good overview of ERA
   history.

Dye, Thomas R.
   1976   *Who's Running America?* Englewood Cliffs, N.J.:
         Prentice-Hall.
   Here's a readable and fascinating accounting of institutional power in America. It is in a sense an updating of
   Mills's *The Power Elite,* naming names and—especially
   useful—tracing the web of interlocking directorates.

Lindblom, Charles
   1977   *Politics and Markets: The World's Political-Economic
         Systems.* New York: Basic Books.
   Current major world economic systems are described
   and analyzed.

Lipset, Seymour Martin
   1963   *The First New Nation.* New York: Basic Books.
   In an era of national liberation and nation-building around
   the globe, Lipset suggests that the prototypical "new
   nation" was the United States. In this historical analysis,
   he examines the creation of national identity and political
   legitimacy, focusing on American values, economic matters, and the role of political parties.

Marchetti, Victor, and John D. Marks
   1975   *The CIA and the Cult of Intelligence.* New York: Dell.
   Describes how the intelligence system works and gives
   detailed analysis of the process.

Mills, C. Wright
   1956   *The Power Elite.* New York: Oxford University Press.
   A controversial modern classic, Mills's thesis that American society is ruled by a small, powerful elite formed of
   business, military, and governmental leaders offers a
   graphic picture of the interrelationships among social
   institutions. Mills's portrayal of power in America offers
   a useful framework for understanding more recent events
   such as the Nixon administration scandals and the bribery of foreign officials by multinational corporations.

Orum, Anthony M.
   1978   *Introduction to Political Sociology: The Social Anatomy
         of the Body Politic.* Englewood Cliffs, N.J.: Prentice-
         Hall.
   Text discussing basics of political sociology—theories,
   power structures, socialization, participation.

Portes, Alejandro, and John Walton
   1981   *Labor, Class, and the International System.* New York:
         Academic Press.
   Argues that the world is a system of global interdependence and looks at political-economic systems in this light.
   Suggests new forms of inequality are arising from economic structures.

Smelser, Neil

1963   *The Sociology of Economic Life.* Englewood Cliffs, N.J.: Prentice-Hall.

In this small book, Smelser has provided the most thoroughgoing sociological view of economics since Weber's *Theory of Social and Economic Organization.* Smelser examines the economy as an institutional social system in its own right and as a subsystem within the larger society. Special attention is given to the interrelationship between the economy and other social institutions.

Stouffer, Samuel

1966   *Communism, Conformity, and Civil Liberties.* New York: Wiley.

I can think of no more worthy introduction to how sociologists go about studying political attitudes than the work of Sam Stouffer, patron saint of empirical researchers. In this classic study, Stouffer examines political tolerance and intolerance during the (Joe) McCarthy era of the early 1950s. Basing his analyses on massive surveys of political leaders and the general public, Stouffer provides still-valuable insights into the fate of democracy in America.

Terkel, Studs

1974   *Working.* New York: Random House.

Reviews findings from discussions with workers across the United States. Interesting and sociologically important work.

In this chapter, we discussed labor unions in America, but it should be noted that unions are not limited to either the United States or even to capitalistic systems. Nowhere has this been more evident in the 1980s than in Poland.

Much of the postwar political history of Poland has centered on the most basic of issues: food. In a socialist society, the Polish government has had direct control over the kind, amount, and price of food available to the Polish people. In 1956, riots over food shortages forced the Stalinist administration out of office and saw the formation of unions and worker councils. The new national leadership soon came to see the labor unions as a threat to their centralized power. By 1958, the unions had been emasculated and served as little more than channels for the promulgation of party policies.

For many years, government subsidies kept food prices constant, despite rising production costs. When the government attempted to raise prices in 1970, a violent worker riot broke out. Another administration was driven from office, and the incoming Gierek regime promised meaningful reforms.

In 1976, the Gierek administration attempted to deal with the problem of food prices. The announcement of price hikes brought workers into the streets again. And again, the government capitulated. The economic problem—although ignored—did not go away. Four years of recession forced Gierek once again to face the issue of food prices.

On July 1, 1980, the Gierek administration announced an increase in meat prices. The protests that followed were not to be quelled this time by price rollbacks. By mid-August, workers of all kinds were on strike: bus drivers, garbage collectors, aircraft and textile manufacturers, railway workers—more than 150 industrial and service units in all.

Besides demanding lower meat prices, some workers—led by the Lublin railway workers—demanded the right to nominate their own candidates for worker-council elections, scheduled for August 19. As the elections neared, 16,000 workers at the Lenin Shipyard at Gdansk walked off their jobs. The government still would not yield; and, by August 24, 150,000 workers were on strike across the nation. By now, a new name had come to international attention: Leszek (Lech) Walesa, chairman of the Inter-Factory Strike Committee.

By the end of August, the government had offered substantial economic concessions and was willing to pay workers for the time spent on strike, to release jailed activists, and grant other political concessions. In return, the government demanded that the unions accept the "leading role" of the communist party in Poland and promise not to join with any international union movement. The workers refused. The government gave in.

On August 31, Walesa signed a set of agreements with representatives of the Gierek administration. The government agreed to the establishment of a nationwide union, called *Solidarnosc*, or *Solidarity*. During the next year, Solidarity was to serve as the primary voice of Polish workers. On September 5, 1981, 892 elected representatives met in Solidarity's first constituent congress, elected officers, and enacted policies on behalf of their 9.5 million members. Walesa was elected chairman by an overwhelming margin.

Clearly, Solidarity and the worker protest had come to represent much more than a conflict between workers and their government over meat prices. For some workers, the issue had become one of national identity and pride. Poland had been carved up by Russia, Prussia, and Austria in 1772, 1793, and 1795. Following the last of these partitions, Poland disappeared as a nation until after World War I. After twenty years of restored nationhood, Poland again disappeared under Hitler's boot in 1939. Though the country was officially recreated at the close of World War II, the Polish people had no misconceptions about Soviet control over their succession of governments. Now, it seemed to many that a genuinely independent Poland might be rising out of the worker strike.

The Polish strike was a real problem for the Soviet Union. More than anything else, communism has been presented to the world as the ideology and salvation of workers. After all, Marx and Engels had begun their *Communist Manifesto* with the words, "Workers of the world. Unite!" The uniting of Polish workers, however, was a direct challenge to a communist regime supported by the Soviet Union. Soviet leaders also feared that a successful worker strike in Poland might be repeated in other Eastern European satellites or even in Russia itself.

There were ironies, if not problems, on this side of the Atlantic as well. Ronald Reagan—no friend of wildcat strikes by labor unions in America—supported the strike with enthusiasm. In the midst of his presidential campaign, he appeared on the same platform with Lech Walesa and identified the Polish protest with the "American model" of labor unions. (Reagan was to be less supportive of labor union strikes when American air controllers went on strike after he became president.)

Edward Gierek, who had come to office through a worker protest, left under the same conditions. Stanislaw Kania—the head of state security—assumed the post of communist party leader. Step by step, the new administration began dismembering the gains presumably won by the workers. On the evening of December 12, 1981—with Russian troops massed threateningly on the Polish border—the government imposed martial law. Soon, Walesa and thou-

sands of other Solidarity leaders were in jail, where they remain as this is written. Clearly, we have not seen the final chapter in the history of Polish unions.

So far, we have looked at the union movement in Poland primarily from an historical point of view. But we can also examine the attitude of Poles toward their political and economic situation. During November and December 1981, the magazine *Paris Match* sponsored a public opinion poll among a national sample of Polish citizens. Let's look at some of the results of that poll, as published in *World Opinion Update* (1982:4–6). Such data are valuable in describing the social climate within which the workers defied the government and went on strike.

To begin, we might ask how the general public felt about Solidarity and other groups involved in the difficulties. Respondents to the poll were asked "In your opinion, who is the best representative of Poland and the Polish people at the present time?" Here are the answers given:

Solidarity	45%
The church	43
The government	7
The army	4
The communist party	1

This obvious support for the protest and lack of support for the government and the communist party was equally evident in responses to another question: "In your opinion, who is responsible for the very serious economic crisis Poland is undergoing today?"

The government	38%
The communist party	35
Russia	16
Solidarity	2
The western bloc	1
Undecided	8

Respondents were also asked if there is a "privileged class or group" in contemporary Poland—and if so, who they are. As you might expect from the above data, 56 percent identified communist party members as the privileged group. Another 21 percent identified the government; 19 percent said either the police or the army.

You'll recall that people on both sides of the worker protest were concerned about what it might mean for relationships with the Soviet Union. Other responses to the poll indicated a good deal of popular dissatisfaction with Poland's big brother. For example, 54 percent said that Poland was "not at all independent," while most of the remainder—41 percent—said the country was only partially independent. A resounding 85 percent said they thought Soviet-Polish relations were more profitable to Russia than to Poland. Over half—52 percent—said they felt Soviet influence on their daily lives and most of the rest—41 percent—felt some influence.

It was, you'll recall, a continuing question of whether Russia would send troops to Poland to quell the workers. Most Poles, in November-December 1981, doubted that Russia would intervene: only 32 percent thought it would happen. But what if Russia *did* intervene? Sixty percent of the respondents said they thought the Polish army would fight on the side of the Polish people, and three-fourths of the respondents said they themselves would resist. The youngest respondents were the firmest in their resolution to fight back. Eighty-five percent of the eighteen-to-twenty-five age group said they'd resist the Russians.

Public-opinion-poll data such as these can add to our understanding of social movements like the Solidarity workers protest in Poland. Moreover, the Polish events expand our understanding of political and economic institutions in society more generally.

PRACTICING SOCIOLOGY

The following is taken from a newspaper article:

WASHINGTON—Heavy military spending has a negative effect on black employment, and for every $1 billion rise in the Pentagon budget, 1300 jobs are lost for blacks, according to a study made public yesterday.

Employment Research Associates of Lansing, Mich., a group opposed to military spending said of its research, "During the period 1970–1978 when the annual average of military spending was $85 billion, it cost the jobs of 109,000 black Americans each year. This means that every time the Pentagon's budget goes up $1 billion, 1300 jobs disappear for black Americans.

In reaching the figure of 109,000 jobs lost, the study applied its analysis to figures from the Labor Department's Bureau of Labor Statistics that breaks down black and white employment in different job categories on a state-by-state basis.

Discuss the following:

1. Why might military spending cost black jobs?

2. What does this study indicate about the relationship between political and economic institutions?

3. Since the Employment Research Associates' antimilitary views might influence their analyses, how could you be sure that their conclusions are valid?

Source: "How Military Budget Hurts Blacks' Jobs," *San Francisco Chronicle*, September 11, 1981, p. 7.

14

Educational Institutions

As an institution, education has the function of maintaining and passing from generation to generation the body of agreements that make up the culture of a society—all the beliefs about the way things are, the values, norms, and all the rest of it. As we shall see shortly, education also has the task of generating new knowledge, a function that can be a source of trouble both within education itself and in its relationship with religion and other institutions.

You've undoubtedly had experiences of insight, discovery, and sudden rational understanding of things more than once in your life. If that weren't the case, you wouldn't be reading this book right now. At the same time, these personal flashes of insight, discovery, and understanding can present a problem for society.

Without agreements on the way things are, we can't live together. Educational institutions transmit the group's agreements about reality. Schools, in this sense, are inherently conservative: they perpetuate the status quo and channel "dangerous" ideas—the flash of insight, the "disassembly of the clock"—arising from direct cognitive experiences. As we shall see, however, educational institutions contain *within* them a direct threat to their conservative orientation.

Functions of Education

In this section, I want to delineate the different functions educational institutions serve. Then we'll look at some of the different forms that serve those functions. We'll conclude with a look at American education and at some specific issues regarding the experiences of individuals within educational institutions

General Socialization

The primary function of education is, as already noted, the transmission of agreed-on symbols, beliefs, values, and norms to new generations of a society, essentially a "standardization" function. This function has two facets. First, the society itself is perpetuated through a continuity in its agreements, and interpersonal harmony is enhanced. Second, individuals, as they learn to operate within society, gain a sense of who they *are* as seen through the point of view of the generalized other (see Chapter 2). We'll return to this latter point in the section on the experience of education.

Special Skills

Particularly in modern societies, educational institutions have the function of training individuals in the special skills required for the operation of a complex and specialized social structure. Not everyone needs to learn the skills of an auto mechanic or a brain surgeon; but some people must in order to keep the economy operating, and schools teach them.

Social Mobility

In many societies, education serves the function of social mobility for individuals and subgroups within society. "Getting a good education" is a way of improving your position in society. Many ethnic subgroups in America such as the Jews and the Japanese have achieved rapid social and economic mobility by stressing education among their young. This, of course, is the great American dream, and it sometimes comes true.

At the same time, educational institutions can also function to "keep people in their place," to maintain those agreements and institutions that keep one group dominant over others. Unfortunately, this function of educational institutions can be a subtle and largely unrecognized one, making it all the more difficult to correct. That's why I want to be sure you come away from this chapter seeing both sides of the matter.

Custody of the Young

Educational institutions often serve a function that is easily overlooked, a custodial function. Schools can serve as an alternative to the family in caring for and supervising children. This function is represented by the term *in loco parentis,* "in the place of parent." Schools are often granted legal and quasi-legal rights to act as parents in dealing with students.

The custodial function of schools is also relevant from the economic point of view. Especially in the case of mandatory schooling, education keeps young people out of the job market. Even when it is not strictly mandatory, schooling can serve this same function because so many jobs now require a high-school diploma or a college degree for entry.

Creation of Knowledge

As I've indicated, through the transmission of agreed-on knowledge and skills, educational institutions tend to perpetuate agreements. But there is another side to education: educational institutions are a chief source of *new* knowledge; and, by its nature, new knowledge often contradicts old knowledge, thereby threatening established agreements.

Theologians of medieval Europe, for instance, were comfortable with the notion that God had arranged the stars and planets around the human race on earth, and a carefully elaborated system of Ptolemaic astronomy made it possible to predict heavenly movement. Then Copernicus upset that comfortable knowledge of how things were by suggesting that the earth moved around the sun, which, in turn, moved around in the universe.

More recently, the physicist Albert Einstein upset our most fundamental, comfortable views on space, time, energy, and matter. Everyone "knew" that an hour was the same period of time under all conditions, yet Einstein offered a new scientific view that time ran more "slowly" at very high velocities. Everyone "knew" that matter and energy were inherently distinct from one another, yet Einstein offered theoretical proof that one could be converted to the other—later given dramatic demonstration in the atomic bomb.

Workers within educational institutions often challenge agreements not only about the physical universe but also about the organization of social life as well. American colleges and universities were generally aligned with the views and goals of government and economics in the 1950s, but the following decade was quite different. The most radical critiques of our foreign and domestic policies came from college campuses. They were the source of major opposition to the war in Vietnam, just as they have figured importantly in the reorientation of attitudes toward race relations, women's rights, poverty, and the environment. Even in matters of "taste," educational institutions have assaulted accepted standards of what is "good" in music, painting, and literature.

Variations in Education

Although most educational institutions perform all the various functions just described, the forms these institutions take vary too widely to be covered here. We can, however, look at some of the major dimensions along which variations in educational institutions occur.

Content

Educational content includes both ideas and skills, and each of these varies in different institutions. Some schools have as their purpose the transmission of religious ideas; others focus on science, literature, philosophy, and the like; still others focus on teaching more "practical" skills like nursing and computer programming.

Literacy is a fundamental goal of educational systems in modern societies, but its achievement varies greatly from country to country, as reported in the box entitled "World Literacy Rates, 1982." Even these figures can be misleading, however, as we'll see in the discussion of **functional illiteracy** later in this chapter.

In addition to these cognitive orientations, education can involve more affective, or "feeling," matters. Recently in American education, for example, there has been a growing emphasis on self-actualization, interpersonal relations, and similar concerns.

Americans continue to be ambivalent about the proper balance to be struck between the "3 Rs" and other educational possibilities. In a 1981 Roper poll, for example, 98 percent of the respondents favored "more stress in schools on teaching basic skills to children." At the same time, shown in a Gallup poll, 48 percent of the public favored sex education in elementary school and 76 percent favored it in high school (*Public Opinion* 1981d:24, 25).

Different social circumstances, of course, call for different educational contents. In preliterate tribes around the world, children learn hunting and gathering skills and the other necessities of life in an apprenticeship under their parents and other adults in the tribe. The spread of colonialism, along with social and economic development generally, however, has resulted in more and more participation in the model of education most familiar to you and me. This has not always been appropriate, however.

Bowden Quinn (1982:12) describes the dysfunctions of the educational systems planted in Africa by British colonialism.

The educational systems that African countries inherited from their colonial rulers emphasize academic subjects. They produce graduates trained for white-collar jobs rather than for farming.

School-leavers are reluctant to return to farming, after having imbibed the belief that physical work is degrading. They form a swelling group of urban unemployed, becoming a drain on the economy and a source of political instability.

World Literacy Rates, 1982

One measure of the extent of education in a country is its **literacy rate**—the percent of adults who can read and write. So important is literacy considered, in fact, that it constitutes one-third of the *Physical Quality of Life Index (PQLI)* commonly used as a summary measure of how different countries are doing. (The other two indicators are infant mortality rate and average life expectancy.)

As of 1982, fifteen nations of the world reported 100 percent literacy—everyone above the age shown (usually 15) could read and write. Another nine countries report being within 2 percent of that goal. At the other end of the spectrum, only a small percentage of the populations of some countries were literate. The table reports the seven countries in which one-fifth or fewer could read and write.

Country	Percent literate	Above the age of	Country	Percent literate	Above the age of
Denmark	100.0	15	Austria	98.0	15
Finland	100.0	15	Cuba	98.0	15
France	100.0	7	Portugal	98.0	15
Germany, East	100.0	15	China	95.0	15
Ireland	100.0	15	Mexico	86.7	15
Japan	100.0	15	Costa Rica	84.7	15
Luxembourg	100.0	15	Brazil	83.0	15
Netherlands	100.0	15	Indonesia	64.0	15
New Zealand	100.0	15	El Salvador	49.0	15
Norway	100.0	15	Egypt	45.7	10
Romania	100.0	8	Bolivia	39.8	15
Soviet Union	100.0	15	India	34.2	15
Sweden	100.0	*	Pakistan	26.7	10
United Kingdom	100.0	15	Ivory Coast	20.0	15
United States	100.0	15	Malawi	16.5	15
Czechoslovakia	99.5	15	Afghanistan	16.2	15
Germany, West	99.0	15	Nepal	12.5	15
Australia	98.5	15	Cameroon	12.0	*
Colombia	98.5	15	Mozambique	7.0	*
Western Samoa	98.3	10	Mali	2.2	*
Hungary	98.2	15			

* = not reported

Source: Reprinted with permission from the 1982 *Britannica Book of the Year,* copyright 1982 by Encyclopedia Brittanica, Inc. Chicago, Ill., p. 336.

To counteract this problem, Zimbabwe established a system of "education with production." Students in the Chindunduma primary school, for example, worked with their teachers in constructing the school buildings. They also grew food to feed themselves, with enough left over to sell, raising thousands of dollars for the school. Chindunduma was one

The physical forms of education vary greatly around the world as illustrated by these classrooms in the Sudan and the Soviet Union.

of several schools created in this model. Quinn continues:

> The schools, located in rural areas, combine farms and workshops with classrooms and dormitories. Students learn farming and building skills, the basic requirements for rural life, in addition to studying the normal academic subjects. Ultimately, if all goes according to plan, the schools will provide students with at least one other marketable skill.

Paulo Freire, a Brazilian educator, offers another example of how content can be tailored to students' needs. Freire was born and raised in northeast Brazil, an area of crushing poverty. Though his family was middle class at the time of Freire's birth, the Great Depression of 1929 reached even this out-of-the-way corner of Brazil, and his family fell into the poverty suffered by most people in the region. Richard Shaull (1968:10) wrote of Freire's childhood:

> This had a profound influence on his life as he came to know the gnawing pangs of hunger and fell behind in school because of the listlessness it produced; it also led him to make a vow, at age eleven, to dedicate this life to the struggle against hunger, so that other children would not have to know the agony he was then experiencing.

Ultimately, Freire was able to complete his education, earning a doctorate and becoming a professor at the local university. He then undertook the task of teaching illiterate adults to read and write, for he had seen personally how poverty, illiteracy, and oppression went hand in hand. The content of Freire's instruction—the vehicle for teaching reading and writing—was a critical examination of society, addressing the poverty, oppression, and paternalism his students knew firsthand. As they learned to read and write, Freire's adult students recognized their abilities to engage in meaningful dialogue and they came to regard themselves as "subjects" in life, rather than merely as "objects."

This educational system was widely adopted and used in literacy campaigns throughout the region. In 1964, a military junta came to power in Brazil, and Freire was jailed. The educating of impoverished illiterates was clearly perceived as a threat to the status quo. After seventy days in jail, Freire was released with the suggestion that he leave Brazil. He went to neighboring Chile, where he taught for five years. In the years since then, he has taught illiterates and, more importantly, has taught his system of teaching illiterates in many countries.

Control

Since education is so largely a matter of socialization to established agreements—whether scientific knowledge, political values, or the skills of a craft—it is important to recognize the variations in who decides which agreements are to be taught and learned.

In the United States, educational institutions, particularly at the primary and secondary levels, have largely been controlled by government. Modern socialist states provide an even clearer illustration of this pattern. The linkage of educational and political institutions is particularly important from the standpoint of social control, where it represents a linking of internal and external controls, respectively.

Sometimes religious institutions have run educational institutions. Many of the earliest universities were organized by churches, and American parochial schools are a modern illustration of this practice. Church-related schools vary greatly in the degree to which they focus on religious education and secular education.

In the United States and elsewhere, some education is conducted by private, strictly educational, organizations. Private secondary schools such as Exeter and private colleges and universities such as Harvard are instances. Although such schools are not under the direct control of either government or religion, they are still integrated into the rest of society and relate in many ways to other institutions.

Traditionally in America, public education has been a locally controlled enterprise, and Americans seem to still want it that way. In 1981, Gallup asked "In your opinion, who should have the greatest influence in deciding what is taught in the public schools here—the federal government, the state government, or the local school board?" Seventy-four percent chose local control, 16 percent chose the state, and only 10 percent chose federal control. In fact, 49 percent of the public in 1981 felt there was no need for a U.S. Department of Education (*Public Opinion* 1981d:26).

Physical Forms

I would guess that when you see the word "school," you automatically visualize students sitting in rows of chairs in a room, being confronted by a teacher. This picture is only natural, since it probably represents the main form your own education has taken. I'm sure you realize that it is only one form among many. A "school" is any place where learning occurs.

An exciting modern innovation in the physical form of education involves the use of mass media. Children and adults alike are learning many subjects by means of newspapers, radio, and television. Probably the best-known illustration of this innovation in America is television's "Sesame Street." Taking much of their format from the advertising, soap operas, game shows, and dramas of commercial television, the producers of "Sesame Street" have sought to "market" education among young children.

A two-year examination by the Educational Testing Service, moreover, suggests they have been successful in teaching conventional academic skills such as reading and arithmetic (Ball and Bogatz 1970, 1971).

Teaching versus Learning

Finally, educational institutions vary in the mode of learning they stress. Increasingly, American educators have distinguished between "teaching" students and "letting them learn." This dimension runs from rote memorization at the one extreme to some form of Socratic dialogue* at the other.

The difference is important in the interplay between personal experience and institutionalization. The rote learning of the 3 Rs that characterized the one-room school in colonial America is an extreme illustration of institutionalized education. "Knowledge," in that instance, is firmly agreed on, and the function of schools is merely to transmit the agreements from one generation to the next. By contrast, many innovations in modern education involve *leading* students to *learn* and *discover* things for themselves. The purpose of Socratic questioning is to open the way for the personal discovery and understanding of ideas and of the nature of physical reality. The fundamental dilemma of this latter orientation, as we'll see shortly, is that it does not necessarily support the agreements that, in turn, support the continuation of group life.

American Education

Now that we have considered a few of the ways in which educational institutions vary, let's look at how mass education has developed in America and how it is related to the current social inequality.

The Development of Mass Education

In many and perhaps in most societies, formal education has been reserved for a few. In ancient Athens it was available to young, free *men* (not to women and slaves). A number of societies have limited education to the children of the wealthy or to the nobility.

Although education in the American colonies largely reflected European heritage, the birth of independence and the commitment to political democracy had an impact on education that is still felt today. The early national leaders, believing that an effective democracy required an educated populace, laid the groundwork for broad public access to education. Beginning shortly after independence, public land was granted and taxes appropriated for the purpose of establishing free, public schools.

In the middle of the nineteenth century, schooling in America began to be made mandatory. Massachusetts was the first state to require school attendance, in 1852, and by 1918 all states required it. Today, most states require children to attend school between the ages of eight and sixteen, and individual states have broader age ranges.

Because of compulsory attendance laws, almost all Americans complete at least eight years of elementary school. Many receive much more, as Table 14–1 indicates.

Increasing participation in education has extended well beyond the traditional four years of college. Graduate programs have expanded greatly. In 1980 alone, 55,815 persons received doctorate degrees from American universities. The largest single field was medicine, with 14,902 degrees granted; next was education, with 7,978. And 584 people received Ph.D.'s in sociology (U.S. Bureau of Census 1981i:166–167).

Mass participation in education in America

---

*A method of teaching used by Socrates in ancient Greece. The method involves the teacher's asking a series of easily answered questions, which inevitably lead students to a logical conclusion that the teacher foresees.

Table 14-1

Percent of High-school and College Graduates among Americans Twenty-five Years and Older, 1940–1980

Year	Percent high-school graduates	Percent college graduates
1940	24.5	4.6
1950	34.3	6.2
1960	41.1	7.7
1970	55.2	11.0
1980	68.6	17.0

Source: U.S. Bureau of Census, *Statistical Abstract of the United States* (Washington, D.C.: Government Printing Office, 1981), p. 141.

is undeniable. But is this mass participation used to create the educated public the founding fathers envisioned? Has equality for all been achieved through mass education?

Education and Equality of Access

College in America was originally the domain of rich, white men, and they have predominated there throughout our national history. Each of these three variables has grown less important in recent years. Among high school graduates aged eighteen to twenty-four, 33.5 percent of the men were enrolled in college, as compared with 30.3 percent of the women. Among whites of both sexes, 32.0 percent were enrolled, compared with 27.8 of the blacks (U.S. Bureau of Census 1981i:158).

When the Census Bureau interviewed high-school seniors in October 1979, 51.8 percent of the whites and 47.3 percent of the blacks said they planned to attend college. Women were more likely (54.6 percent) than men (48.1 percent) to plan college, diverging from past patterns.

The strongest impacts on college plans were family income and parents' education. Students in families with incomes of $10,000 or less were the least likely (33.6 percent) to plan college; those with family incomes of $25,000 and over were the most likely (67.3 percent). Where the heads of households had not graduated from high school, only 35.8 percent of the seniors planned college; compared with 74.8 percent of those where the household head had completed some college (U.S. Bureau of Census 1982a:25).

Black Americans, along with other racial and ethnic minorities, have received a lower quality of education—on the broad average—than have the white majority. Regardless of race or ethnicity, poor people have received poorer quality education than have the rich. The institution of the "neighborhood school" has been the primary cause of this discrepancy.

Americans have generally preferred to have their children attend school as close to home as possible. Given social-class variations from neighborhood to neighborhood, however, this preference has resulted in some schools being attended predominantly by the children of poor people and other schools being attended predominantly by the children of rich people. Since the rich have more political power, it is not surprising that disproportionately more funds have been spent on schools in rich areas than on those in poor areas. And since the funding and control of schools has been a predominantly local matter, the dispossessed have found it difficult to correct the situation by a direct appeal to the federal government.

Where social class and race have pretty much coincided, racially segregated schools have resulted. Before 1954, many schools in the South and border states were officially segregated on the basis of race. In 1954, in the landmark *Brown v. Board of Education of Topeka* decision, the U.S. Supreme Court ruled racial segregation of schools unconstitutional. Ten years later, the Civil Rights Act of 1964 specified the details of integration in law. Even so, the generally lower economic status of blacks, coupled with neighborhood schools, has maintained a degree of *de facto* segregation: that is, schools have often remained segregated in fact if not in law.

Throughout the 1960s, a series of **compensatory education** measures were instituted to make up for the inequalities of birth through special programs and courses. Perhaps the best known, *Operation Head Start* was instituted in 1964 to provide preschool children from poor families with special summer-school training to prepare them for elementary school. Although Head Start seemed to achieve its immediate objective, later studies showed the effects wore off by the time children reached second or third grade. The legacy of poverty had taken over (Coleman and Cressey, 1980:110).

A 1966 report by sociologist James Coleman had a powerful impact on this issue of whether American schoolchildren from different social-class backgrounds received the same quality of education. His massive study, sponsored by the federal government, of more than half a million students in four thousand schools produced a number of surprises. First, he found that by the mid-1960s, there were only slight differences in the quality of predominantly white and predominantly black schools, measured in terms of physical facilities, teachers, curriculum, and similar indicators. Next, Coleman discovered that such differences as did exist in schools had virtually no effect on the performance of students on standard achievement tests. Nonetheless, students from middle-class families did better on the tests than did those from lower-class families.

Coleman indicated that the differences in academic performance of students from different social-class backgrounds represented the effects of their class cultures. One thing seemed to overcome that disadvantage of poor children, however. When lower-class children were in classes with middle-class children, they did better than when all their classmates were also from lower-class families. Middle-class students, incidentally, did no worse in mixed classes than in purely middle-class ones.

The analysis offered by Christopher Jencks and his colleagues (1973) seven years after the Coleman report further demolished the view that our educational system could be counted on to remedy ills generated elsewhere in the social system. No amount of funding pumped into innovative programs, the researchers found, made a dent in the structure of inequality that the children grow up in and live with long after school is completed.

It seemed, from the data and interpretations of the Coleman report, that racial and social-class integration of the schools was the way to resolve the persistent legacy of inequality. The most volatile means devised for achieving that end was the *busing* of students from one school district to another, overturning the traditional pattern of neighborhood schools. Begun in the early 1970s in response to court orders for more rapid desegregation, it has been opposed by the majority of whites and even by about half the blacks (Coleman and Cressey 1980:97). In Boston and elsewhere, antibusing feelings have prompted violence; and, as of this writing, the long-term future of busing is unclear at best.

The demand for equal access to quality education has not been limited to primary and secondary schools. Blacks and other minorities have had to struggle for equal access to the nation's colleges and universities as well, and the struggle has not been easy. In 1962, for example, James Meredith became the first black admitted to the University of Mississippi. Though Meredith had a federal court order guaranteeing his right to attend, the matter was not that simple. Wallechinsky and Wallace (1975:246–247) recall the events surrounding Meredith's entrance to Ole Miss:

> Before his admission, Governor Barnett of Mississippi declared that State schools were not answerable to the Federal Government and that public officials would be willing to go to jail for the cause of segregation. He ordered the arrest of

Federal officials who tried to enforce the court order. The State legislature appointed Barnett special registrar to deny Meredith admission. Four times Meredith failed to register, blocked twice by Governor Barnett personally, the 3rd time by the lieutenant governor and 20 State troopers, the 4th by a crowd of 2,500 whites. He succeeded the 5th time, escorted by several hundred U.S. marshals. This provoked a riot of 2,500 white students—leaving 2 dead and 375 injured, including 166 marshals—which was finally quelled by 3,000 Federal troops and National Guard.

With the issue of black-white school integration possibly moving toward resolution after being fought and debated since the 1954 Brown decision, a new issue of equal access faces many areas of the United States. The 4 to 6 million undocumented Mexican immigrants to the United States force school officials to face serious questions.

Despite the opinion of some experts that such immigrants pay more in property and income taxes than they receive in social services, other people object to the children of noncitizens "draining" their local schools and teaching staffs. Paul Van Slambrouck (1980) quotes Chad Richardson, director of the Institute of Borderlands Studies at Pan American University in Edinburg, Texas, as follows: "Raising these children as illiterates becomes a tremendous drain on society in future years." Richardson feels that granting these immigrants the right to education is in the best interests of the United States in the long term.

In summary, mass education has been an American ideal and goal throughout most of our history. In terms of sheer participation, we have been enormously successful. The idea of equal access to education, however, has been far more difficult to achieve. There's a parallel here to the American experience in other institutions. In the economy, for example, we have achieved a very high standard of living *on the average*, but we have not achieved equal access to that high standard.

The Experience of Schooling

You'll recall that our discussion of education began with our taking note of the exciting personal experiences of insight, discovery, and understanding. In the succeeding pages, we've looked at some of the ways in which those experiences become structured in educational institutions. In this section, I want to examine some of the ways in which individuals experience those structures.

Creating Identities

One function of educational institutions that we discussed earlier is the creation of social identities. In a society such as the United States, you cannot escape the fact that your social identity is a function of the educational system. You are required to attend school for a number of years, and you must emerge from that as a bright, average, or poor student. You can't escape one of those identifications. In this society, moreover, you must have educational certification to get most jobs.

The bestowal of educationally based social identities, however, has been considerably criticized in recent years. Consider the matter of school **tracking systems.** As individual schools have become larger and more complex, grouping students according to similar levels of ability seemed a good idea to many educators. Poorer students are presumably taught at their own level and not forced to compete with better students. More qualified students should be able to realize their full potentials, without being held back by slower classmates. That is the theory.

In practice, however, the tracking system appears to have worked against the interests of students identified as slow. Contrary to expectations, the Coleman report, for instance, found that slow students performed better in mixed classes than in remedial ones.

Educational institutions tell us what and who we are, and they tell us where and how we fit into the rest of society. Full self-expression is not an inevitable outcome, as this photo illustrates.

This situation is further complicated by the fact that IQ tests are often the basis for the assignment of students to tracks in school. As we saw in Chapter 5, many educators feel that conventional IQ tests are a poor measure of intelligence. Among other things, they are challenged as too "culture-bound"—putting at a disadvantage all but the white middle and upper classes. In a study of systems for tracking the "mentally retarded," however, Richard Berk, William Bridges, and Anthony Shih (1981) found IQ tests having greater weight in student placement than any of the other evidence available to school officials, including factors felt to predict school performance better than IQ.

The basis for student tracking is very important because, once identified as a poor student, you are virtually trapped. It is unlikely that your teacher will ever see improvement in your performance and suggest reclassifying you. Perhaps the most frightening evidence of this pattern has been provided by an experiment conducted by Robert Rosenthal and Lenore Jacobson (1968).

Rosenthal and Jacobson administered what they called a "Harvard Test of Inflected Acquisition" to students in a West Coast school. The researchers than met with the school's teachers to discuss the results of the test. They identified certain students as very likely to exhibit a sudden spurt in academic abilities during the coming year, based on the results of the innovative predictive test. As measured by later IQ tests, the identified students far exceeded their classmates during the following year, just as the researchers had predicted to the teachers. The significant thing about this experiment is that the Harvard test was a hoax! The researchers had identified the potential "spurters" *arbitrarily* from among both good and poor students. What they told the teachers did not really reflect students' test scores at all. The progress made by "spurters" was simply a result of the teachers expecting the improvement and paying more attention to those students, encouraging them, rewarding them for achievements.

Recall that social identities are a matter of agreement. Once an agreement about your academic abilities has been established, it is difficult to change. The structure of educational institutions seems to support the persistence of those agreements, and the individuals involved tend to incorporate those agreements in their self-images and behavior.

Bureaucratized Learning

Schools are social organizations, and they have the same survival needs as other organizations. When schools are very large, they tend to be bureaucratically structured. A bureaucracy is the most efficient structure for processing students. Many students and others have objected, however, that "processing" is not education, and they particularly object when bureaucratic efficiency seems to take precedence over what might be the thrill of learning.

You have probably had times when the organizational requirements and procedures of your school have seemed to interfere directly with the kind of educational experience you thought school was all about. You may have been prevented from enrolling in a class that perfectly suited your intellectual curiosity perhaps because you couldn't fulfill the prerequisites or because the class was cancelled when too few students

Some people complain that modern education has become an assembly line, with little or no allowance for students' individuality. At the same time, the administration of educational institutions has become increasingly bureaucratized.

registered for it. Or perhaps you succeeded in enrolling, only to discover that a thousand classmates had done the same. Instead of the excitement of personal inquiry, you found yourself listening to lectures that permitted no participation on your part. Even if you maintained your enthusiasm for the topic, your hardy enthusiasm for expressing yourself may have suffered a head-on collision with a multiple-choice examination that had no questions relating to the thrill of personal insight, discovery, and understanding.

It's a simple matter to see the problem inherent in such situations, but it is more difficult to find solutions. The organization of mass education seems inherently incompatible with the personal quest for educational experience.

A Report Card for American Education

Let's close this section with a look at how Americans rate their public-school system. There are two sources of evidence to be considered: educational experts and the general public. Both groups are generally negative in their assessments.

In 1981, respected educator and writer Jacques Barzun characterized American education as a "wasteland" (1981:34):

> The once proud and efficient public school system of the United States—especially its unique free high school for all—has turned into a wasteland where violence and vice share the time with ignorance and idleness, besides serving as battleground for vested interests, social, political, and economic.
>
> The new product of that debased system, the functional illiterate, is numbered in millions, while various forms of deceit have become accepted as inevitable—"social promotion" or passing incompetents to the next grade to save face; "graduating" from "high school" with eighth-grade reading ability; "equivalence of credits" or photography as good as physics; "certificates of achievement" for those who fail the "minimum competency" test; and most lately, "bilingual education," by which the rudiments are supposedly taught in over ninety languages other than English.

Barzun is not alone in his assessment. Jerome Bruner is a prominent psychologist who has long been concerned with American education. Interviewed in 1982, Bruner expressed despair:

> During the 1970s Americans responded to the perpetuation of class and caste by prescribing fair

Table 14-2

The Public Rates Public Schools, 1981

Classification	Percentage giving the following grades, of those giving grades				
	A	B	C	D	Fail
Public schools in this community	10	30	38	14	8
Principals and administrators in local public schools	12	31	33	14	10
Teachers in public schools in this community	13	33	36	11	7

Source: *Public Opinion,* October/November 1981, p. 21.

educational practices. We were in great part successful, but we almost killed ourselves with the prescription. In our effort to provide equal education, we so lowered standards that we're now facing a serious decline in educational quality. (Bruner 1982:58)

These comments on the declining quality of public education in America are echoed by a great many other experts, and they are also found among the general public. In May 1981, the Gallup poll asked a national sample of adults to grade the public schools. Table 14–2 presents some of their answers.

Overall, the public grades the local public schools somewhere between a C and C+. Between 1973 and 1981, the percentage of the public expressing "a great deal" or "quite a lot" of confidence in the public schools (as opposed to "some" or "very little") declined from 60 percent to 40 percent (*Public Opinion* 1981d:23).

The C rating of the public schools shows up again when people are asked how well they think public high schools prepare students for jobs or college. Table 14–3 presents the public feelings on that.

Table 14-3

Public Perceptions of High-School Preparation

Preparation	Percentage giving the following grades, of those giving grades				
	A	B	C	D	Fail
For jobs	7	24	34	21	14
For college	10	31	34	15	10

Source: Public Opinion, October/November 1981, p.23.

The box entitled "Public Attitudes About Public Education" presents additional data regarding the public's perceptions of their school system. Clearly, a part of the current public concern relates to the issue of "functional illiteracy," discussed in detail in the Application and Analysis section at the conclusion of this chapter. For now, let's look at some of the things people have done to remedy their dissatisfactions with educational institutions.

Functional Alternatives

When individuals are dissatisfied with an institution—as many are with the experience of learning in America—they often attempt to remedy that dissatisfaction by substituting new forms and functional alternatives. Let's look at some of those alternatives.

Student Rights, Powers, and Protest

Not surprisingly, much of the dissatisfaction with educational institutions and attempts to modify them have come from students. I want to begin this section with a look at some examples of student protest. Let's recognize, however, that student disenchantment is not something new. Horton and Leslie (1974:316–17) bring us nicely up to date on the matter:

To cite only a few instances, students at Plato's Academy rioted through Athens in 387 B.C., thirteenth-century Paris students rioted over wine prices, with many casualties; fourteenth-century Oxford students had a three-day battle with townspeople, with over 58 fatalities; Harvard in 1655 felt necessary to forbid students to "weare Long haire, Locks or foretops;" Princeton has no complete records on student behavior because students twice burned down Nassau Hall which housed the archives.

The specific issues students of today complain about vary, of course, as do the forms in which they manifest those complaints. Some student complaints relate directly to curricular matters: the courses and majors available, the requirements for graduation, and so on. Other complaints have to do with noncurricular matters: faculty hiring and firing, codes of student conduct and discipline, athletics, food, or housing. Both types of complaint have to do with the quality of student life, as do academically relevant issues such as the military draft or community politics.

The 1960s were a turbulent time for American colleges and universities. With the beginning of the Berkeley "free-speech movement" in the fall of 1964, campuses across the nation were rocked with protest, violence, and death. In large part, the protest movement was organized around major social issues, such as civil rights and the war in Vietnam. Running through these specific issues, however, were two broader questions. What rights do students have while attending school? What role should they play in the governance of educational institutions?

The conflicts over the first question highlighted the second question. Could and should students be full participants in the governing of the college—in the establishment of agreements on its operation and purpose—or were they merely clients? Should students have a say in what courses were taught, what faculty were hired, tenured, and promoted? Was "student discipline" a matter to be handled by administrators or by fellow students?

Public Attitudes about Public Education

Clearly the American public has formed a collective opinion that the public schools have a number of problems. When the Gallup poll asked parents to identify the *biggest problems* the public schools in their community faced, most—23 percent—said the "lack of discipline." The next most common response was "use of drugs" (15 percent). Fourteen percent cited "poor curriculum and poor standards," and 11 percent said it was "difficulty getting good teachers." While 12 percent said the school's biggest problem was "lack of proper financial support," two-thirds said they would vote *against* a tax increase to support the schools.

What do parents want from their public schools? As we've already seen, an enormous 98 percent said the schools should put more stress on basic skills. Asked to specify, their list began with mathematics, English, history, American government, and science. But this is not all that parents expect from their schools. Here are some of the things parents felt the schools did not pay enough attention to:

What schools don't pay enough attention to	Percent of sample agreeing
Developing students' moral and ethical character	62
Teaching students how to think	59
Preparing students who do not go to college for a job or career after graduation	56
Preparing students to become informed citizens prepared to vote at 18	55
Preparing students for college	43
Developing students' appreciation of art, music, and other cultural pursuits	37

Source: Public Opinion, October/November 1981, p. 25.

Questions such as these often were focused on extremely specific points. Ethnic and racial minorities called for courses dealing with the history of their groups—plus qualified faculty to teach those courses. Marxist students called for better courses in Marxist philosophy. Women called for courses dealing with the role of women in American society. Some asked for modified admissions policies that would allow the entry of more disadvantaged students.

The implicit assumption of all such demands was that changes in the form of the institution would alleviate dissatisfactions. Overall, colleges and universities responded to the demands in part but never in full. The quieting of the nation's campuses seems less a consequence of satisfaction with the new arrangements than of a renewed interest in other matters, such as training for jobs in a tightened economy.

Free Schools

The free-school movement is another alternative to established educational forms. Allen Graubard (1973:153–154) has described the fundamental premises on which such schools are founded:

The basic theoretical concept is, naturally, freedom. The literature of radical school reform associated with the free schools vehemently opposes the compulsory and authoritarian aspects of traditional public and private schools. This literature attacks the emotional and intellectual effects of conventional pedagogy and projects a radical theory . . . that children are naturally curious and motivated to learn by their own interests and desires. The most important condition for nurturing this natural interest is freedom supported by adults who enrich the environment and offer help.

Graubard noted that the number of free schools in the country grew from twenty-five to around six hundred in the space of five years, with two hundred being added in a single year. Clearly, such schools are an attempt to recapture the *experience* of education that many feel is lost in the structuring of conventional schools. Whether they will be able to satisfy organizational needs such as financing and acceptance within the larger society without losing the experience they are intended to foster remains to be seen.

Other Reactions to Declining Quality

Public disenchantment over the quality of education offered in the nation's public schools has generated numerous other proposed solutions. Some proposals have represented a retreat from the public schools, others a taking charge.

Voucher systems have often been proposed as a solution to the problems of the public schools. Though the systems vary, the idea is essentially this: the government would allot a certain amount of money for each child's education, and parents could determine how they wanted to spend it. They could send their child to the public schools and pay nothing (other than taxes), or they could credit the allotment toward private-school tuition and make up the difference themselves.

The main objection to voucher systems is that only the rich would be able to exercise any choice in their children's schooling, and the allotments used to subsidize private-school education would reduce the funds available to support the public schools, thereby lowering their quality even further. Ultimately, the poor would suffer more than they already do. Public opinion on voucher systems has been divided for years. In 1981, for example, a Gallup poll found

43 percent in favor, 41 percent opposed, and 16 percent undecided. Virtually the same responses were discovered a decade earlier (*Public Opinion* 1981d:26).

The concern that students are not learning enough in school—expressed above by Barzun and Bruner—has resulted in **competency testing** programs: students do not graduate from high school, for example, unless they pass a standardized test. When a national sample was asked about this in a 1980 poll, 79 percent were in favor. In the same poll, 90 percent favored the requirement that teachers pass standardized tests before being allowed to teach courses in high school (*Public Opinion* 1981d:24). We'll return to the concern that lies behind these attitudes in the essay that concludes this chapter.

As an extension of competency testing, some school districts have turned over the task of education to private contractors, utilizing *performance contracts*. In this system, the contractor agrees to provide instruction to students that results in their achieving some minimum score on standard tests such as the Scholastic Aptitude Test. Unless the contractors produce the specified test scores, they don't get paid.

Summary

The major functions of educational institutions include general socialization, teaching special skills, providing means for social mobility for individuals and groups, and serving as custodians. Educational institutions also serve the function of *creating* new knowledge and agreements about reality—especially through science.

A wide variety of institutional forms accomplish these functions. Some of the dimensions of variations include the content of instruction, who controls the institution and the agreements transmitted, and the physical forms and facilities within which education takes place. There is also variation in the relative emphasis placed on "teaching" versus "learning."

The goal of equal, mass education in America reflects a political value and has resulted in a large degree of participation in educational institutions by the members of society. The goal of *equal* access has not been achieved. This is currently most notable in relation to college attendance: women, blacks, and the poor are underrepresented, though less so today.

American education has been on the receiving end of much criticism, from both the experts and the general public. Many argue that the quality of instruction has declined severely in recent decades, and there is controversy over what should be taught in our public schools.

The structuring of educational experiences within our schools, colleges, and universities has been a source of dissatisfaction of those within the institution as well. Many people complain that organizational needs and other aspects of institutionalization have taken the natural thrill out of learning. Innovations and functional alternatives to conventional forms have appeared as a result.

Important Terms

literacy rate
compensatory education
tracking systems

voucher system
competency testing
functional illiteracy

Suggested Readings

Ballantine, Jeanne
1983 *The Sociology of Education: A Systematic Approach.* Englewood Cliffs, N.J.: Prentice-Hall.
Comprehensive analysis of issues and problems facing education from a sociological perspective.

Carnegie Council on Policy Studies in Higher Education
1980 *3000 Futures: The Next Twenty Years for Higher Education.* San Francisco: Jossey-Bass.
Analysis of the future of higher education based on projections of population and economics.

Freire, Paulo
1968 *Pedagogy of the Oppressed,* trans. by Myra Bergman Ramos. New York: Seabury Press.
While somewhat difficult in style, this is a very important book. It presents a radical approach to instruction among impoverished illiterates.

Illich, Ivan
1972 *Deschooling Society.* New York: Harper & Row.
Presents controversial idea of doing away with schools and having alternative learning styles.

Jencks, Christopher, et al.
1973 *Inequality: A Reassessment of the Effect of Family and Schooling in America.* New York: Harper & Row, Colophon Books.
This controversial book calls into question the implicit American faith in the power of education. Much of what we expect schools to accomplish, the authors suggest, needs to be addressed in the family instead. Special attention is given to economic concerns such as employment and poverty.

Lortie, Daniel C.
1975 *Schoolteacher: A Sociological Study.* Chicago: University of Chicago Press.
Study of what a teacher in the classroom must deal with, and how teachers cope with the job.

Parelius, Ann Parker, and Robert J. Parelius
1978 *The Sociology of Education.* Englewood Cliffs, N.J.: Prentice-Hall.
This is a comprehensive survey of the sociology of education. The various theoretical perspectives and a summary of research findings are presented, along with a discussion of how modern education has been shaped by industrialization, bureaucratization, and the rise of the professional.

Silberman, Charles
1971 *Crisis in the Classroom.* New York: Vintage.
Describes what goes on in American classrooms, reforms, and teaching.

Earlier in this chapter, I reported that the United States is considered to have 100 percent literacy in those above fifteen years old, meaning that everyone can read and write.

In recent years, however, there have been many indications that this statistic is misleading. The Census Bureau defines an illiterate as a person fourteen or older who has not completed at least the fifth grade. However, at the same time that duration of education has been increasing, average scholastic achievements have been *declining*. This trend has appeared in various places, most visibly in the average scores earned by students taking the College Entrance Examination Board's Scholastic Aptitude Tests (SAT). In the twelve years from 1963 to 1975, the average math scores were down 30 points while verbal scores plummeted 44 points. Students appear to be spending more time learning less.

There is general agreement that this decline in SAT scores is not a result of the test becoming more difficult; in fact, a sample of students who took both the 1963 and 1973 tests tended to score better on the later one. And it is clear that money spent on education was not the cause, since per pupil expenditures by schools rose during the period scores fell. So what does account for the decline?

Some commentators have argued that greater access to college has caused the scores to drop because now more poor people, who traditionally have not done as well on the tests, are taking them. While that may account for a part of the trend, all socioeconomic groups seem to be doing more poorly, so further explanations are needed. Other reasons offered are increased television viewing (taking time away from studies), the political turmoil of the 1960s (distracting students), less parental involvement in educating children due to increased divorce, working mothers, and so on. There is no short-age of possible explanations for the decline in SAT scores, but there is little agreement as to which is the more important.

The slide in test scores is significant beyond the educational fates of the individual students involved: it reflects also on the general educational level of the country as a whole. This is an issue of relevance in any nation, ours included.

In 1870, the Bureau of the Census reported that 20 percent of American adults were illiterate. A century later, it was being argued that 20 percent were still **functionally illiterate:** unable to read, write, and figure sufficiently well for normal functioning in contemporary society. Although the official level of illiteracy in the United States was around 1 percent, a study by the Office of Education in 1975 reported that 20 percent of American adults between eighteen and sixty-five could not read the daily newspaper. The following examples from the National Education Association (reported in McVeigh 1978:30) illustrate the problem:

58 percent could not read a simple paragraph explaining the law and tell why it would be illegal to be held in jail for two weeks without being charged with a crime.

30 percent could not select an airline flight at the right time to make a meeting in a distant city.

26 percent could not determine the best unit price for three different sizes of cereal boxes.

20 percent could not correctly explain "equal-opportunity employer."

13 percent could not properly address an envelope for mailing.

Stanley Wellborn (1982:12) summarizes the situation this way:

Today, a staggering 23 million Americans—one in five adults—lack the reading and writing abilities they need to handle the minimal demands of daily living. An additional 30 million are only marginally capable of productive work. Thirteen percent of high school students graduate with the reading and writing skills of sixth graders.

The Adult Performance Level Project analyzed the 1980 census and conducted surveys of its own to determine the numbers of American adults who were unable to perform rudimentary intellectual tasks required in the day-to-day coping with life's situations. Here are its estimates of the number of people unable to handle certain activities (reported in Wellborn 1982).

Activity	Number of people unable to do
Computation	52.1 million
Managing a family budget	46.5 million
Solving problems	44.3 million
Awareness of government, legal rights	40.8 million
Knowing how to use community resources	35.8 million
Reading	34.3 million
Getting, keeping a satisfactory job	30.2 million
Writing	26.0 million

In 1977 and 1978, the Gallup poll conducted surveys of teenagers (13–18 years old) to find out what they had learned. As Table 14–4 indicates, there were a few holes in their education.

The costs of illiteracy are many. Stanley Wellborn (1982:12) reports some estimates of the financial costs:

Table 14-4

What Do Teenagers Know?

Question asked	Percent correct
In what year did the United States declare its independence?	67
In what year did Columbus discover America?	51
What document guarantees the right of a free press in this country?	41
In what war was the issue of states' rights a major issue?	33
Please identify the nation with which each of these individuals is associated:	
Adolf Hitler	79
Napoleon Bonaparte	52
Winston Churchill	50
Indira Gandhi	31
Which of the arts is this person associated with:	
Pablo Picasso	60
Robert Frost	48
Johann Strauss	42
Helen Hayes	38
Rudolph Nureyev	22
James Michener	15
Alexander Calder	6

Source: *Public Opinion,* August/September 1979, p. 39.

One estimate places the yearly cost in welfare programs and unemployment compensation due to illiteracy at $6 billion. According to Literacy Volunteers of America, a private nonprofit literacy program based in Syracuse, N.Y., an additional $237 billion a year in unrealized earnings is forfeited by people who lack basic learning. Local school officials fear that the problem could worsen in the wake of Reagan administration proposals to curtail federal aid to schools and to cut adult-education funds sharply.

Illiteracy is also correlated with crime, producing both financial and nonfinancial costs. Businesses suffer from employee illiteracy, and some have been forced to create their own remedial education programs. Employees have been killed in accidents because they couldn't read warning signs.

A 1981 study of 106,000 school children (nine, thirteen, and seventeen years old) by the National Assessment of Educational Progress project pointed to another problem. Students who struggled to understand written materials tended to rely on their first impressions of what they read, and they were "genuinely puzzled" by requests that they explain or defend the points of view expressed. In the researchers' assessment, critical thinking is a victim of illiteracy (Wellborn 1982:13). All of this, of course, raises concerns as to the quality of the American electorate in evaluating leaders, programs, and policies.

Illiteracy in modern society also carries a cost in human dignity. Wellborn (1982:12–13) quotes a young job-seeker in Detroit: "I would call companies and ask if the applicants had to fill out forms. If it was required, I would pass up the opportunity. About the only thing I was sure I could spell right was my name." And to the extent that illiteracy is concentrated among the poor and minorities, they are doubly disadvantaged.

Many causes have been suggested for functional illiteracy. Demographic changes account for some of the problem, with the arrival of non-English-speaking immigrants. Television is also cited often as a culprit in the matter. Increasingly, people turn to television for information and entertainment, spending less and less time reading.

As we've seen, the public schools have been singled out for blame by many, and no indictment is more damning than that directed against illiterate teachers. There are countless, depressing anecdotes about English teachers who can't spell or punctuate, math teachers who can't calculate. But the problem extends well beyond a few individual cases, as Charles Hardy (1982) reports:

> In 1978, in suburban San Diego, Lemon Grove Elementary District applicants for teaching and aide positions took a locally prepared grammar, spelling and mathematics test. The reading and writing test was one that eighth graders should have been able to pass; the math portion was designed for seventh graders. A score of 80 was needed to pass. Thirty-five percent of the teachers failed one or more of the tests.

> In the mammoth Los Angeles Unified School District, similar tests were administered three years in a row and each year at least 13 percent of the people with teaching credentials looking for jobs failed.

Many explanations are offered for the incompetence found among America's teachers. Some criticize the college programs that train our teachers—too little education is required for certification. This is complicated by the fact that education majors are drawn disproportionately from among those with low scholastic scores. This pattern, in turn, obviously reflects the low salaries paid to teachers generally. Many bright students who would be excellent teachers choose careers in better paying, though academically more demanding, fields.

Clearly the problem of functional illiteracy is a complex one, and the solutions required are likely to be equally complex. Ultimately, changes are required in many of society's institutions.

PRACTICING SOCIOLOGY

In his introduction to Paulo Freire's *Pedagogy of the Oppressed*, Richard Shaull says the following:

> There is no such thing as a *neutral* educational process. Education either functions as an instrument which is used to facilitate the integration of the younger generation into the logic of the present system and bring about conformity to it, *or* it becomes "the practice of freedom," the means by which men and women deal critically and creatively with reality and discover how to participate in the transformation of their world. The development of an educational methodology that facilitates this process will inevitably lead to tension and conflict within our society.

What interrelationships among economic, political, and educational institutions are indicated by Shaull's comments? Give examples from American society to illustrate his point—*or* give examples to contradict his point.

How might comments made today differ from those made on the same subject in 1970?

Source: Richard Shaull, "Foreword," in Paulo Freire, *Pedagogy of the Oppressed* (New York: Seabury, 1970), pp. 9–15.

15

Religious Institutions

You've probably had the experience of gazing at all the distant stars and planets on a quiet night, wondering how it all began and what it means. Probably you didn't plan the experience; it just happened. Most people have experiences like that now and then.

I'm sure you've also had experiences of intuition, insight, and discovery. You may have "known" that something was going to happen without being able to explain why or to justify your expectation. Or perhaps you've had the experience of grappling with a problem—trying to figure out how something worked or trying to understand a subject you were studying in school—and had what some people call an "aha!" experience: the sudden feeling of clarity in which you broke through to an *understanding* of something. The history of science is filled with such experiences, and they are common outside science as well.

Early in the fifteenth century, a young French peasant girl of thirteen began hearing "voices." In 1428, her voices told her that she must take up arms and deliver her native France from the English. Putting on armor, she led the French army into battle and became a popular folk hero. Her popularity was her undoing, however, because the rulers of France came to regard her as a threat to their religious and political power. Through intrigue and treachery, they had her delivered over to the English, who tried her for "heresy." The charges lodged against her involved her voices and visions; in addition, her wearing of men's clothes figured importantly in the trial. In 1431, the trial was concluded, and the young girl was burned at the stake. The story of Joan of Arc illustrates the danger of direct, personal experiences when seen in the light of organized group life.

Here's the problem. Each of us has direct, personal experiences of knowing and understanding the way things are. Yet we can't live together in societies without some agreements on the nature of reality. Religious and educational institutions embody our general agreements about the way things are, as well as the values and norms that follow from that shared view. Such agreements, however, limit our personal experiences; and they are a potential source of dissatisfaction.

In this chapter, we're going to look more closely at the functions served by religious institutions, and we'll see some of the different agreements that appear to serve those functions. Then we'll examine the ways in which institutional structures affect our experiences of social life and how we respond to those experiences.

The Functions of Religious Institutions

The great theologian Paul Tillich (1952) said that religion was addressed to our ultimate concerns, to the fundamental problems of meaning. Religion grows out of the feelings of awe we sometimes have when we survey the enormity of the universe, the power of natural forces, or the persistent mystery of life itself. It is similarly a response to questions about human purpose, suffering, and death. Individual religious experiences offer personal answers to such "why" questions, and organized religious institutions provide agreed-on answers for members of a group to share.

Religion, from a sociological point of view, is an institution—comprising symbols, beliefs, values, and norms—that addresses these ultimate problems of meaning, especially in relation to a supernatural or transcendent order, though sociologists disagree among themselves as to whether a belief in a supernatural order is a necessary component of religion. If the supernatural is required, then some religions like Zen Buddhism become problematic. If it is not required, however, then philosophies and ideologies—like communism, for example—might appropriately be considered religions.

The function of religion, like other institutions, is to support the survival of group life. It does this primarily by (1) providing a set of

agreements about the world and (2) encouraging a sense of group solidarity. Clearly, we cannot continue living and interacting together without some fundamental agreements on the nature of reality and our place within it. If I felt that life would go on forever and you felt the world would end next week, think how unlikely our cooperation on a long-range project would be. Religion is an important source of agreements on such things.

While religion provides a shared view of reality, it also gives people a sense of belonging. Religions define who we are and they offer people a shared identity as believers. The ancient Hebrew idea of "the chosen people" is an excellent example. Religion can bind people together in another way as well. In the face of grief and anguish, people need the support and the nurture of others. Religion provides patterned ritual activity in the context of group support to channel deeply felt emotion and to reintegrate the person under stress with the group.

Let's look more closely now at some of the ways religious institutions serve their functions. I want to begin with a consideration of religious beliefs, values, and norms.

Beliefs

Much of what we "know" about the nature of reality can be seen as a result of direct experiences that people have. You "know" about the force of gravity long before people can tell you about it. People also "know," in the same fashion, the changing of the seasons, the regularity of the sun's rising, and countless other things. The reasons *why* such things are this way are more elusive.

In the Western world, we tend to look for explanations of reality in science, which, as you'll recall from Chapter 3, is based on empirical observations and measurements of the "natural" world around us and the logical-rational understanding of what we observe. Throughout human history, however, people have also sought explanations of the natural world in a supernatural realm—that is, in a realm where the laws of nature no longer apply.

The supernatural realm is what individuals say they experience directly. Joan of Arc said that her instructions to deliver France from the English came from that realm. Religious institutions explain our earthly existence as part of a much larger reality. Through them, we agree on the nature of that larger reality and its implications for our more immediate reality. How do these religious explanations arise?

Many of the world's religions are so old that we can only speculate about the origins of the **beliefs** associated with them. Historical records of newer religions, however, suggest the following pattern. An individual—such as Gautama Buddha, Jesus, or Joseph Smith (of Mormonism)—has a personal experience that creates a point of view that seems to solve the problems of meaning we have been discussing.

Imagine for a moment that you had a sudden experience of total clarity on *everything*. Imagine suddenly seeing the world around you without the constraint of any particular point of view, knowing with utter certainty all the hows and whats and whys. The reports of such experiences frequently incorporate the idea of "waking up," as in the following account of the Buddha's early preaching:

> "Are you a god?" they asked. "No." "An angel?" "No." "A saint?" "No." "Then what are you?"
> Buddha answered, "I am awake." His answer became his title, for this is what Buddha means. In the Sanskrit root *budh* denotes both to wake up and to know. Buddha, then, means the "Enlightened One" or the "Awakened One." While the rest of the world was wrapped in the womb of sleep, dreaming a dream known as the waking life of mortal men, one man roused himself. Buddhism begins with a man who shook off the daze, the doze, the dream-like enchoateness of ordinary awareness. It begins with the man who woke up. (Smith 1958:90)

Most formal religions appear to have begun with individuals' having experiences as dramatic and powerful as Buddha's. As they have attempted to share their experience with others, however, the experience became transformed into concepts and points of view. Once that happens, people then agree on the points of view. They create beliefs about the way things are in lieu of personally having the kinds of experiences that the beliefs grew out of. In this fashion are religious points of view institutionalized. Beliefs become reified and sanctified; sometimes sanctions are created to enforce conformity to them.

Most contemporary Christians believe in a God who created the universe and, some believe, guides the events that occur in our day-to-day existence. For most of them, however, this belief is not a result of their own direct experience but a matter of agreement, based on religious socialization stemming ultimately from the personal experience that Jesus had and from his preaching "about" that experience.

Max Weber (1922) has pointed out that persons having such profound experiences have communicated their experiences differently. He distinguished between **emissary** and **exemplary prophets.** An emissary prophet has felt obliged to instruct others in how to behave in this life; an exemplary prophet has merely demonstrated "proper" behavior in his or her own life. Muhammad was an "emissary" prophet, Buddha an "exemplary" one. Both types of religious leaders illustrate the transformation of experiences into beliefs.

The experiences that people such as Buddha and Jesus had may not have been exactly the same, although of course we cannot know that. It is clear, however, that the transformation of those experiences has produced quite different beliefs. Beliefs about the existence of supernatural beings, for example, vary widely; consider the monotheistic Jehovah of the Jews, the Christian Trinity, the many gods of the ancient Greeks and of Hindus, and the all-pervasive "godness" of Buddhism, animism, and other religious forms.

Similarly, beliefs about life after death vary markedly from one religion to the next. There appear to be three basic religious views of life

Some religious expressions are openly experiential and emotional . . .

after death: (1) a belief in a just afterlife, as exemplified in Christianity's construction of heaven and hell; (2) a belief in cyclical and deserved rebirth, as exemplified by the reincarnation ideas found in Hinduism; and (3) a belief in imminent or interior transcendence—that is, death and injustice are seen as illusions (all that dies or suffers is ego, and ego is an illusion), and/or eternal life and perfect justice are available to everyone inside themselves because everyone is already infinite, eternal, and complete. Taoism and Buddhism are famous for this kind of view, although such "mystical strands" exist within all the major world religions.

Religious beliefs, then, are agreements on answers to the basic problems of meaning that people confront in life. These beliefs may explain such mundane matters as why it rains, why crops fail, or why commuter traffic is so heavy.

. . . while others are more quiet and reserved.

And they may describe a life after death, cycles of reincarnation, or great legions of heavenly deities.

Values

Religious beliefs have a societal value in their own right because they create agreements on the nature of reality. This is only a part of the story, however. Religions also prescribe the ways things "ought to be." Religious **values** are agreements about what's good and preferred, based on the agreements about the way things are.

For Christians, the belief that all are the children of God leads logically to the valuation of peace over war. For Buddhists and Taoists, the belief in the "oneness" of all things leads to the value of "flowing" with events rather than

The Second Coming of Christ?

The Second Coming of the Christ is a doctrine that has been with the Christian churches since their beginning. Essentially, the doctrine holds that the long-awaited Christ of the Hebrews appeared in the form of Jesus of Nazareth, was reviled and rejected by the people of that time, and would return at a later date. The Biblical description of the prophesied return is contained in the Book of Revelations.

During the past two thousand years, the imminent return of the Christ has been announced numerous times. In 1839, an American farmer and Baptist preacher, William Miller, announced that he had calculated, from Scriptures, the date of Christ's reappearance: between March 21, 1843, and March 21, 1844. Miller's prophesy attracted thousands of followers. When the prophesied time came and went without Christ's appearance, Miller's followers established themselves as what was to become the Seventh Day Adventists.

The Jews still await the coming of a Messiah, just as Christians await the return of their Messiah. Buddhists await the coming of another Buddha, the Lord Maitreya; Hindus await the appearance of Krishna; and Muslims await the Imam Mahdi. Common to all these expectations is a time when earthly affairs will be taken over by a god-force in human form.

The most recent prophesy of the Messiah's coming appeared in the writings and lectures of a Scottish writer, Benjamin Creme. In early 1959, Creme began receiving telepathic messages from Lord Maitreya who told Creme to prepare people for the Christ's return, an event predicated on the following conditions:

That a measure of peace should be restored in the world;

That the principle of Sharing should be in process of controlling economic affairs;

That the energy of goodwill should be manifesting, and leading to the implementation of right human relationships;

That the political and religious organisations throughout the world should be releasing their followers from authoritarian supervision over their beliefs and thinking.

(Creme 1980:32)

Under those conditions, the Christ would appear and begin the restructuring of world affairs. In preparation for the Christ's coming, a vanguard of "World Masters" had been sent in 1976 to begin work in five cities: New York, London, Geneva, Darjeeling, and Tokyo.

With preparations having been made, Creme reported, Maitreya the Christ took human form and reentered the world on July 19, 1977, and began participating in human affairs in a modern country. Finally, on May 14, 1982, Creme held a press conference in Los Angeles to announce that Maitreya had been working among the Pakistani community in London and would reveal himself shortly.

Source: Benjamin Creme, *The Reappearance of the Christ and the Masters of Wisdom* (London: The Tara Press, 1980).

---

resisting them. In the words of Lao-tzu (c. 604–531 B.C.), the founder of Taoism:

Those who flow as life flows know
They need no other force:
They feel no wear, they feel no tear,
They need no mending, no repair.*

---

*From *The Way and its Power,* tr. Arthur Waley. Reprinted by permission of George Allen & Unwin Ltd. and Barnes & Noble, 1965:206.

In religions with a Hebraic root, humans are separated from nature via a "special creation" belief and are expected to use nature for specifically human purposes. Humans are also granted "natural rights"—special privileges denied the rest of nature.

Then God said, "Let us make man in our image and likeness to rule the fish in the sea, the birds in heaven, the cattle, all wild animals on earth and all reptiles that crawl upon the earth." (Genesis 1 : 26)

Some religions place primacy on the value of inner peace, others on pleasure. In some traditions, the highest value is placed on conquering challenges and facing tests: in others, the emphasis is on knowing and understanding, and in yet others on doing and obeying. Later in this chapter, we'll see how religious and secular values interact in the political arena.

Norms

The survival of society depends, ultimately, on how people behave toward one another. **Norms,** you will recall, are agreements about what behavior is expected, and religious institutions provide a wide variety of such expectations.

To begin, most religions prescribe many strictly *religious* norms: rituals and other practices that are expected of those sharing the beliefs and values of the religion. Thus, Catholics are expected to attend church and partake of Communion. Jews are expected to attend synagogue and to carry out a variety of religious rituals within the family. Shintoists make pilgrimages to sacred temples and maintain family altars. Moslems bow toward Mecca five times daily. Buddhists meditate; others pray.

Of greater interest to sociologists are religious norms that prescribe expectations regarding *secular* behavior. Most religions, for instance, have prohibitions against murder, stealing, and adultery. Since the time of Marx and Weber, sociologists have disagreed on how to view this aspect of religion.

For the German sociologist Karl Marx, religion was a tool of the powerful in maintaining their dominance over the powerless. "Religion is the sigh of the oppressed creature," Marx wrote in a famous passage, "the sentiment of a heartless world, and the soul of soulless conditions. It is the opium of the people" (Bottomore and Rubel 1956:27).

In his research in the sociology of religion, Max Weber examined the extent to which religious institutions were themselves the *source* of social behavior rather than mere reflections of economic conditions. Where Marx said religion grew out of economics, Weber said it was also possible for economics to derive from religion. His most noted statement of this side of the issue is found in *The Protestant Ethic and the Spirit of Capitalism* (1905). In it, Weber examined the early history of the Protestant churches. Here's some of what he found.

John Calvin (1509–1564) was an important figure, along with Martin Luther (1483–1546), in the Protestant reformation of Christianity. Calvin's predestinarian point of view said that the ultimate salvation or damnation of every individual had already been decided by God. Calvin also suggested that God communicated his decisions to people by making them either successful or unsuccessful during their earthly existence.

Ironically, this point of view led Calvin's followers to *seek* proof of their coming salvation by working hard, saving their money, and generally striving for economic success. In Weber's analysis, Calvinism provided an important stimulus for the development of capitalism. Rather than "wasting" their money on worldly comforts, the Calvinists reinvested it in economic enterprises, thus providing the *capital* necessary for the development of capita*lism.*

The Protestant ethic of which Weber and others wrote has had numerous implications both for society and for its sociological students. On the one hand, quite aside from capitalism per se, the Protestant ethic has spawned a value of "rugged individualism" that still shapes personalities, influences relationships, and—as we'll see in Chapter 18—affects the way we treat our environment.

In the world of scholarship, the relationship between capitalism and Protestantism fueled a fundamental philosophical debate that remains uncompleted. For Weber, as we've just seen, religious ideas could be the source of economic change. Recalling earlier discussions of Marx, however, it becomes apparent that this contradicts the Marxist view that economics determines everything else—including religion. All of this illustrates the part played by religious norms within religion and within society at large.

Group Solidarity

Religion, as we noted above, can also support the survival of society by binding believers together with a sense of unity, belonging, and identity. Cooley's "we feeling," described in Chapter 6, can be generated by membership in a religious body.

Eviatar Zerubavel (1982) suggests that Easter was created as a holiday separate from the Jewish Passover to establish the early Christians as a separate body. This modification to the religious calendar created a group identity for Christians and strengthened their group solidarity.

One of the most important studies of this aspect of religiosity involved a French sociologist and the preliterate Australian aborigines, although they never met each other. The sociologist was Emile Durkheim, who relied totally on the ethnographic reports of anthropologists to piece together a powerful understanding of the function of religion among preliterate people—and by extension for us all.

The religion that Durkheim (1915) found most elementary among the aborigines was **totemism.** In totemism, it is agreed that some animal, plant, or inanimate object possesses special powers. The members of the group sharing such an agreement see themselves as having a kinship relationship to that "totem." The totem has special symbolic meaning for the group. They take its name as their own. Thus, in worshipping the totem, they worship themselves.

Durkheim saw religion—among the aborigines and in modern society—as the basis for a "moral community." Members of the community are held together by shared beliefs, values, and norms pertaining to whatever is defined as "sacred."

The creation of group solidarity can be seen in countless examples. Certainly the "civil religion" that is discussed elsewhere in this chapter has provided a solidarity and continuity for the United States. Or consider the part played by Judaism in Israel. Islam provides an equally powerful illustration.

Muhammad was the founder of Islam. Aside from this, he is remembered for uniting the Arabs, no simple task. Huston Smith (1958:202) describes it:

> Life under the conditions of the desert had never been serene. The Bedouin felt almost no obligation to anyone outside his tribe. Scarcity of material goods and a fighting mood chronically inflamed by the blazing sun had made brigandage a regional institution and the proof of virility. In the sixth century A.D. political deadlock and the collapse of the magistrate in the leading city of Mecca made this generally chaotic situation worse. Drunken orgies often ending in brawls and bloodshed were commonplace.*

Muhammad united the Arabs by creating a shared religious identity. During his final pilgrimage to Mecca, he enjoined his followers: "Know ye that every Muslim is a brother to every other Muslim, and that ye are now one brotherhood" (Smith 1958:223). Here's how Kenneth Cragg (1975:1) characterizes the result, in contemporary Islam, this way:

> For Islam, by its own showing, is a unity in which culture, society, and the political realm, no less than devotion and cultic forms, partake. It is, for Muslims, a western and deplorable notion to think of religion as separable from the totality of human context. All must be claimed for the sacred loyalty.

Clearly, this view differs drastically from mainstream American religion. Yet, as we'll see shortly, religion serves a solidarity function in America as well.

---

*Reprinted by permission.

Religion often conflicts with other institutions. These members of an Amish family are seen entering the United States Supreme Court to defend their refusal to pay unemployment taxes on their employees.

Religion and Other Institutions

The chief function of religion, then, is to provide agreed-on answers to the problems of meaning and to spell out the implications of those answers for human social behavior. Religion also serves another important function, as our discussion of Weber and group solidarity suggests. It supports the persistence of other social institutions. Because the problems they address are so basic, religious points of view are relevant to almost all aspects of life. Economic and political systems are frequently given religious justification. Religious support for the family in America is evident. Slavery, in the early history of America, enjoyed religious support, and many believed blacks to be a lost tribe of Israel that God had made servants for all time.

Institutions often enhance social integration through mutual support and reinforcement, but they are often a source of conflict as well. Religious differences within a society can turn citizen against citizen and interfere with orderly affairs in the schools, the economy, and government. Religious intermarriage can be a source of family conflict. Moreover, religious points of view can conflict directly with those of other institutions, as we'll see later in the chapter.

Varieties of Religious Institutions

In the preceding discussions, I have mentioned several different religions. In this section, I want to deal more directly with religious variations. We'll look at some of the world's different major religions, noting their basic characteristics and the extent to which they share agreements.

Although sociologists have sometimes examined preliterate religions, they have more typically directed their attention to the larger, formally established religions of the world. Statistics on religious affiliations are difficult to compile, but it is estimated that over half the world's total population is either Christian, Muslim, Hindu, or Buddhist (*Encyclopedia Britannica* 1982:605).

Table 15–1 presents the estimated religious population of the world as of 1981. Notice that Christianity as a whole is the largest religion, with about a billion adherents. Islam, Roman Catholicism, and Hinduism each have around half a billion adherents.

Some religions—like Christianity, Islam, and Buddhism—have spread from society to society; others have primarily remained near their birthplaces: Shintoism in Japan, Hinduism in India, and Confucianism in China. Reasons for this difference are many, including the extent to which the points of view embodied in the religion reflect the specific agreements of the particular culture in which the religion first appeared. In addition, while some religious leaders have openly stressed the importance of spreading the faith, others have not (Babbie 1966).

Spreading the faith accounts for the far-flung outposts of given religions circling the globe. It also helps account for the religious mosaic found in many societies. Although some societies exhibit virtual unanimity in religion, many others include a variety of religious forms. The United States is a good example of religious diversity.

Religions in America

Perhaps the most striking thing about religion in America is its perceived importance. Table 15–2 compares the United States with several other Western countries, showing the percentages of people saying (1) their religious beliefs are "very important" to them, (2) they believe in God or a universal spirit, and (3) they believe there is life after death. As you can see, Americans are out in front on all three measures.

American Religious Affiliations

While religion is generally important to Americans, there are numerous differences in the patterns of religious faith. To begin, Americans belong to many different denominations.

Figure 15–1 presents the current relative popularity of different religious denominations in America. As you'd expect from Table 15–2, virtually all Americans identify with some religious group: two-thirds are Protestants, one-fourth Catholics, and 2 percent are Jews. Baptists are the largest Protestant denomination, although they, and most other Protestant denominations, are further subdivided. The

Table 15-1

Estimated Populations of the "Great Religions," 1981 (representing 58 percent of world's population)

Religion	Number of adherents
Total Christian	997,783,140
Roman Catholic	580,061,800
Eastern Orthodox	74,174,600
Protestant	343,546,740
Jewish	14,684,520
Muslim	592,157,900
Zoroastrian	276,050
Shinto	58,154,200
Taoist	30,286,000
Confucian	154,080,100
Buddhist	256,387,200
Hindu	481,241,300

Source: Reprinted with permission from the 1982 *Britannica Book of the Year*, copyright 1982 by Encyclopedia Britannica, Inc., Chicago, Ill., p. 605.

"Lutherans," for example, include members of the American Lutheran Church, the Lutheran Church in America, Missouri Synod Lutherans, and others.

Religious affiliations in America are more than a matter of labeling. They are associated with numerous other social differences. For example, the members of different religious denominations vary substantially in terms of social and political conservatism/liberalism. Table 15–3 presents attitudes toward three issues, arranged by religious affiliation. Members of various religions were asked whether they agreed with the following three statements:

Premarital sex: Premarital sex is always or almost always wrong.

Abortion: A woman should be able to obtain an abortion if she is married and doesn't want children.

Tolerance: A person who is against churches and religion should be allowed to speak.

Table 15-2

An International Religious Comparison

Country	Religious beliefs very important	Percent who said: Believe in God	Believe in life after death
United States	58	94	71
Canada	36	89	54
Italy	36	88	46
Belgium/Luxembourg	26	78	48
Australia	25	80	48
United Kingdom	23	76	43
France	22	72	39
West Germany	17	72	33
Scandinavia	17	65	35

Source: Public Opinion, March/May 1979, pp. 38–39.

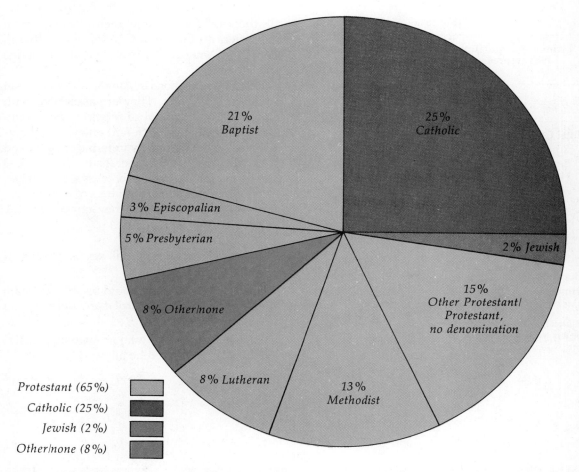

Figure 15-1 Religious affiliation in America. Source: Public Opinion *(November/December 1978):33. Reprinted by permission of the American Enterprise Institute.*

The data presented in Table 15–3 show some fairly consistent patterns. First, there is a wide range in the attitudes of American Protestants, and the ranking of denominations—from conservative to liberal—is quite consistent across the three items. Second, with the exception of abortion, American Catholics' attitudes fall in about the middle of the Protestant range, while American Jews are more liberal than any of the other affiliations.

There is more here than meets the eye, however. Those Protestant denominations that show the greatest social and political conservatism (such as Baptists) are also the most religiously conservative. They are the most likely to believe in Jesus's divinity, in the literal truth of the Bible, in life after death, and to believe Satan really exists and acts in the world (Glock and Stark 1966).

American religious groups differ in other ways as well—in social status, for example. Here is an occupational profile of the religious affilia-

Table 15-3

Religion and Social/Political Issues

Religious affiliation	Said premarital sex is wrong	Percent who: Said abortion is all right	Supported tolerance
Baptist	61	36	50
Methodist	51	50	60
Lutheran	45	47	65
Presbyterian	37	62	73
Episcopalian	31	69	86
Catholic	43	35	70
Jewish	20	83	83

Source: Public Opinion, April/May 1981, pp. 26–27.

tions shown above. To simplify the comparisons, I've presented only the percentages of each group who are professionals or managers and manual workers. To remove the effects of race, these data represent only whites.

	Professional/ manager	Manual workers
Baptist	24	54
Methodist	36	41
Lutheran	29	47
Presbyterian	45	30
Episcopalian	55	23
Catholic	29	47
Jewish	53	12

Denominational differences are important in understanding religion in America, and we'll return to this issue from time to time in the chapter. Still, there is another view which sheds light on other aspects of American religiosity.

American "Civil Religion"

Denomination differences notwithstanding, American religious orientation does not nec-

essarily reflect a commitment to the specific doctrines of particular religions. Robert Bellah (1967, 1975) has written of a **civil religion** in America, noting the contrast between our formal separation of church and state and the persistent presence of religious sentiments and symbols in government and other aspects of "secular" life.

Central to the American civil religion is the belief held by the first Puritan settlers that they were God's people chosen to bring civilization to the wilderness, to erect a new Jerusalem for all the world to see. George Washington echoed this charge in his inaugural address: "The preservation of the sacred fire of liberty and the destiny of the republican model of government are . . . entrusted to the hands of the American people."

This theme is repeated on our coins as "In God We Trust," and above the pyramid on the great seal of the United States, where it says in Latin "God has favored our undertaking." Throughout our history, the God of American civil religion has been called upon both to legitimize the actions taken by government and to provide some moral and humanitarian direction for them.

Russell Richey and Donald Jones (1974) report that scholars have used the term "civil religion" with many different meanings. Richey and Jones label one of these as *folk religion:* informally arising from day-to-day experiences in which American values are legitimized and group solidarity achieved. *Religious nationalism* refers to a more explicit, even idolatrous glorification of the nation. *Democratic faith,* for Richey and Jones, represents the replacement of formal religions with an Americanized, humanistic creed: liberty, equality, and justice. Other scholars identify American civil religion specifically with the predominance of Protestantism; Richey and Jones call this *protestant civic piety.* The final form of civil religion distinguished by Richey and Jones is *transcendent universal religion of the nation.* This religious view assumes a set of ideals and values by which American society is judged and through which our history can be understood.

Gail Gehrig (1981) provides an excellent review of these various uses of the term "civil religion" by sociologists and religionists. Moreover, she suggests, these several distinctions are primarily theoretical, with little empirical research addressed to how the different forms are manifested in practice.

Religious institutions in America, including civil religion, serve to structure human experiences—those experiences relating to the fundamental problems of meaning. Let's take a closer look at some of the different forms these structures take.

The Structures of Religious Experience

Sociologists have looked at the structuring of religious experience from a number of different points of view. I want to consider some of those in this section. First, we'll look at the variety of organizational structures that people have created around their religions. Next we'll examine the different kinds of religious experiences that are possible within religious institutions. Then I want to say something about the structuring

of religious deviance. Finally, we'll look at religious tolerance and prejudice, concluding with the links between religion and politics.

Religious Organizations

Sociologists classify religious bodies according to their type of organization and size.

Cults   In the sociological point of view, **a cult** is a small religious group typically organized around the powerful personality of a single **charismatic** leader or a particular religious practice. Most of the world's great religions began as cults, centering on such figures as Jesus, Buddha, and Muhammad. At the present time, there are a number of tiny cults in the United States; some have gained national attention for practices such as "speaking in tongues," handling poisonous snakes, faith healing, and communication with the dead.

In 1979, a broad interest in cults was sparked dramatically by a series of bizarre events in Guyana. Attention centered on a tiny, little-known Christian communal cult: The People's Temple.

Founded and led by the charismatic Reverend Jim Jones, the group had fled the United States to establish an agricultural community on 27,000 acres of land many miles from the influences of modern society. When rumors reached the United States that some cult members were being held faithful against their desires, a delegation headed by Congressman Leo Ryan of California flew south to investigate.

Suddenly, like a nightmare, news reports arrived saying that Ryan and others in his party had been slain in a sudden attack. Then even stranger news arrived: the cult's members—913 of them—had ritually committed suicide rather than face the sanctions they felt must surely follow. Thus, suddenly, a cult simply died.

In an examination of 501 contemporary cults in America, Stark et al. (1979) found several geographical patterns. Cults formed before 1930 were primarily established in the East, but the predominance of cult-formation has moved westward since then. At present, one-third of the nation's cults are headquartered in California. There were other patterns (1979:358):

Theosophy and Spiritualism are prominent among the cults of Arizona and Florida, probably as a result of the large retirement populations in those states. Flying saucer cults predominate in Oregon. New York is high in Asian faiths, as is Colorado.

Sect A **sect** is similar to a cult, but it is typically larger, more firmly established, and more persistent. Most sects begin when members break away from a larger, more established religious body. Sects are characterized by personal religious fervor and religious experiences such as talking with God and seeing religious visions. Within American Christianity, sects tend to be fundamentalist and orthodox. They interpret the Bible literally, and they reify the traditional Christian beliefs. The Jehovah's Witnesses are a contemporary American example of a sect, as are the Amish.

Churches Sociologists distinguish churches from sects. A **church,** such as the Episcopal or Methodist, is even more firmly established and persistent than a sect. It is also usually larger. The primary differences between churches and sects, however, are similar to those between secondary and primary relations and between gesellschaft and gemeinschaft (see Chapter 6 if you want to review this discussion).

Membership in a church is a more casual matter generally than membership in a sect. Church membership is typically inherited, but sect membership is often a matter of personal conversion. On the average, sect members participate in their religion more regularly and more fervently than do members of churches.

Religion tends to be a more central part of the lives of sect members than of church members. Church members are less orthodox in their acceptance of religious beliefs. On the whole, the beliefs, values, and norms of churches are more likely to be in agreement with those of the larger society than are those of sects. Finally, churches tend to be more bureaucratically organized and operated than sects.

From Sect to Church A topic that has long fascinated sociologists has been the evolution of sects into churches (see, for example, Troeltsch 1931, Wilson 1959, Niebuhr 1960, Yinger 1963, Glock 1964). Very often a sect begins with the disaffection of some group—typically the poor—within an established church. The members of the sect establish a separate religious life. As the sect becomes more established, as its members become economically more prosperous, and as the children of members inherit membership instead of being converted, the sect begins to take on many of the characteristics of a church. It becomes less fundamentalist, and its beliefs, values,and norms gradually approach those of the larger society. Eventually it becomes, in the sociological point of view, a "church," which may then be the source of subsequent sects.

Ecclesia Some established churches enjoy the status of being "state religions," or **ecclesia.** They have a virtual monopoly on the religious life of a society's members. The Anglican church in England and the Roman Catholic church in Spain are examples of this. In 1979, Americans became suddenly aware of the centrality of Islam in Iran, through the actions of the Ayatollah Ruhollah Khomeini. While other religious bodies may be tolerated in theory or in fact, or both, the ecclesia is officially recognized for its central place in national life.

Dimensions of Religiosity

I've said repeatedly that religious institutions structure human experience. Now I'd like to look at some of the different religious experiences arising out of those structures. Sociologists usually look at the issue in terms of **religiosity,** or "religiousness," referring essentially to the ways people participate in religious institutions.

In America, the most obvious way of measuring religiosity is by church attendance. Thus, for example, a 1981 Gallup poll asked respondents: "Did you, yourself, happen to attend church or synagogue in the last seven days?" Forty-three percent said "yes" (Benson 1981:580). Similar results were produced by a 1978 National Opinion Research Center survey which asked people how often they attended religious services (*Public Opinion* 1979b:34):

Frequency of attendance at religious services	Percent of sample
Several times a week	8
Every week	20
Nearly every week	7
2–3 times a month	9
About once a month	7
Several times a year	11
Less than once a year	9
Never	16

Although church attendance is a simple and obvious indicator, religiosity can also be measured along a number of different dimensions. Glock and Stark (1965) have suggested five major dimensions:

1. *Ritual:* Participating in the religious events and practices prescribed by one's religion—for example, attending church, praying, taking Communion.

2. *Belief:* Accepting one's religion's agreements about how things are—for example, believing in the existence of God(s), believing in reincarnation, believing in the divinity of Jesus.

3. *Cognitive:* Simply knowing about one's religion, its history, beliefs, and practices.

4. *Experiential:* Having religious experiences, such as communication with supernatural beings, and having visions and seizures.

5. *Consequential:* Living one's secular life in accord with the teachings of one's religion.

Stark and Glock (1968) have undertaken extensive studies of the levels of these different dimensions of religiosity among the various religious groups in America. Some of their findings regarding personal religious experience are of particular interest in the context of this chapter. These are presented in Table 15–4.

The Stark-Glock findings came as a surprise to many observers of American religion, as it had been previously assumed that only a minority of Americans had had direct, mystical religious experiences. Yet such experiences were relatively common among their sample of church members in the San Francisco Bay area.

The election of Jimmy Carter, a "born-again Christian," as president in 1976 brought the matter of direct religious experiences to public attention. Soon, it was clear that his religious status was hardly rare in America. When a 1980 Gallup Poll asked a national sample of Americans, "Would you say that you have been "born again," or have had a "born again" experience—that is, a turning point in your life when you committed yourself to Christ?" 38 percent said "yes." Forty-five percent said they had "encouraged someone to believe in or accept Jesus Christ as savior," and 41 percent said they believed "The Bible is the actual word of God and it should be taken literally, word for word" (*Public Opinion* 1981e:22). The box entitled "Born-Again Fundamentalism" looks into this religious orientation in more depth.

In earlier discussions in this chapter, I mentioned that direct, personal experiences can threaten the survival of group life. Does the high frequency of personal religious experience

Table 15-4

Religious Experience in America, 1963
(San Francisco Bay Area Church Members)

Types of religious experiences of church members	Percent	
	Protestants	Catholics
"A feeling that you were somehow in the presence of God"		
Yes, I'm sure I have	45	43
Yes, I think that I have	28	23
"A sense of being saved in Christ"		
Yes, I'm sure I have	37	26
Yes, I think that I have	23	22
"A feeling of being punished by God for something you had done"		
Yes, I'm sure I have	16	23
Yes, I think that I have	25	30
"A feeling of being tempted by the Devil"		
Yes, I'm sure I have	32	36
Yes, I think I have	20	26

Source: Rodney Stark and Charles Glock, *American Piety: The Nature of Religious Commitment* (Berkeley, Calif.: University of California Press, 1968), pp. 131, 133, 137.

in America threaten the survival of the religious agreements that support the persistence of society?

According to Stark and Glock (1968:214), religious experiences of the sort described in Table 15–4 are most typical among people with denominations marked by a high level of orthodox religious *belief* and among those most likely to think that their particular religion is the "only true faith"—in other words, people who have most thoroughly reified and internalized the agreements of their religious experiences. Their

experiences, moreover, are in accord with the established agreements, so that the personal experiences *support* rather than threaten the group.

The fact is that the institutions of society—including religion—are structured for survival. If they weren't, they wouldn't survive. A part of that survival structuring involves socialization; another part involves social control in the face of deviance. Let's look briefly at what happens when people break the agreements of religious institutions.

The Structuring of Deviance

I began this chapter with a brief account of Joan of Arc's violation of the fifteenth-century religious agreements in France. What happened to her is not unique in the history of religious deviance. The Spanish Inquisition of the Middle Ages provides equally brutal examples. Countless religious wars throughout history also point to one solution to the problem of religious deviance: those who disagree are killed or tortured into agreement.

There are milder solutions as well. In societies in which a particular church holds absolute religious power, persons deviating from its agreements can be denied the benefits of the secular society—employment and marriage, for example. Religious social control can operate even more subtly than that. In his discussion of the civil religion, Bellah (1967) noted how careful all presidents are to cast their vote for God. It is unlikely that an avowed atheist will be elected president of the United States anytime soon.

Sometimes religious institutions have disagreements within their inner circles—among the clergy, for example. Phillip Hammond and Robert Mitchell (1965) have looked at some of the ways churches have dealt with the problem of radicalism. They noted that during the Renaissance and Reformation, monasteries were

Born-Again Fundamentalism

By and large, the religious history of this century has been one of religions becoming more tolerant by admitting the possibility of more than one road to the "Truth." Within the Roman Catholic church, for example, the Vatican Councils called by Pope John XXIII were heralded as one sign among many that the world's religions might make peace with one another and encourage the same among governments. Starting in the late 1970s, however, many observers have begun speaking of a resurgence of more dogmatic and chauvinistic religious views.

Martin Marty (1980:606–607) speaks of a "resurgent fundamentalism" around the world, one of the more dramatic episodes being the overthrow of the Shah of Iran "by the uncompromising Ayatollah Ruhollah Khomeini, [whose followers] rallied around the symbols of a hardline Sh'ite version of Islam, one that did not even recognize other Islamic sects as being faithful to the Muslim tradition."

Marty found other examples of fundamentalism all around the globe, however: the traditionalist Hindus of India, Soka Gakkai in Japan, the Gush Emunim of Israel, Archbishop Marcel Lefebvre of the Roman Catholic hierarchy, and many others. And ironically, the American presidents required to deal with this resurgence of fundamentalism around the world were, first, born-again Baptist Jimmy Carter, and then Ronald Reagan, a man whose election was vocally supported by many nationally known fundamentalist ministers.

The fundamentalist revival Marty speaks of has appeared in America as well. *The Economist* of London (April 5, 1980) describes it this way:

The U. S. revival is a grassroots affair that political scientists would call a "revolution from below." It has used to segregate radical priests from the rest of society. Based on the results of a 1963 survey of some 5,000 ministers in parishes and assigned to college campuses, they suggest that the campus ministry serves a similar function in American Protestantism today.

Religious Tolerance and Prejudice

As all American schoolchildren are taught, many of the early colonists came to the New World from Europe to escape religious persecution. Different religious groups soon concentrated in different regions of the country: the Congregationalists in New England, the Quakers in Pennsylvania, and so forth.

Robin Williams (1959:320) has suggested that the religious tolerance that developed in America arose more from the fact of diversity than from an ideological commitment to tolerance for its own sake. He gives the following reasons for the great degree of religious freedom and toleration in America:

1. There was a fragmented diversity of groups.
2. None was powerful enough to seize political dominance.
3. There had been no established church in America before settlement.
4. Most of the colonists were indifferent to organized religion.
5. Tolerance was encouraged by the generally shared Protestant view that each person had direct access to God.
6. The economic need for new immigrants reduced the significance of their religious affiliations.

Wherever there is religious diversity, however, religious prejudice and persecution are possible. The history of the United States can

ignored the old, familiar churches and sprouted large numbers of varied, often exotic, new ones.

Strict churches grow while permissive churches contract. The people turning to these new forms of Protestant Christianity seek enduring standards by which to conduct their lives, finding there a satisfaction no longer available in much of the contemporary world. More than nine out of ten Americans say they believe in God; seven out of ten say they believe in an afterlife. One-third describe themselves as born-again Christians, and more than 40 per cent attend a church or synagogue each week.

Marty (1980:607) also comments on the political aspect of the revival in America:

In the political realm it has shown up in a new lobby called Christian Voice. This organization intends to rally support through the "electronic church"—evangelistic television—and work for the passage of laws it favors and the selection of fundamentalist candidates for public office.

A 1980 Gallup poll identified 19 percent of the population as "evangelical": those who (1) reported being "born again," (2) said they had "encouraged someone to believe in and accept Jesus Christ as savior," and (3) believed "The Bible is the actual word of God and it should be taken literally, word for word." Evangelicals were more likely to live in the South (54 percent) than was true for the general public (31 percent). Also, 62 percent of the Evangelicals were women, compared with 52 percent of the general population.

We'll have more to say about this evangelical religion in the Application and Analysis section of the chapter.

Sources: Martin Marty, "Resurgent Fundamentalism," in 1980 *Britannica Book of the Year,* Chicago: Encyclopedia Britannica. *Public Opinion,* April/May 1981, p. 23.

be read as one of religious persecution. The nation began as a refuge from religious persecutions in Europe. Upon arriving in the New World, however, the settlers set about converting the "heathen" Indians. And they were no better in dealing with heretics in their own midst.

As noted earlier, the United States is a predominantly Protestant nation. The various waves of immigrants in the nineteenth and twentieth centuries have not fit that mold, however. Jewish refugees from European persecutions have found themselves persecuted in their new home as well. A similar experience has awaited the substantial numbers of Roman Catholic immigrants—Irish, Italians, and Germans in the nineteenth century and Hispanic immigrants in this century.

Sects and cults have not fared very well either. Mormons were persecuted and killed as that religion was being established in the nine-

teenth century. Their religious norm of polygamy was prohibited by secular law. Fundamentalist communal groups such as the Amish and the Shakers have been ridiculed, and the Quakers have been despised for their conscientious objection to war. The public attention given to the wave of new religions arising in America during the 1960s and 1970s often seem to be "guilty until proven innocent."

In recent years, a great deal of media attention has been devoted to the "deprogramming" of young people who have converted to membership in the Unification Church ("Moonies"), the International Society for Krishna Consciousness ("Hare Krishnas"), and other groups. Typically, parents of converts have hired people to kidnap their children and hold them in captivity for a period of intensive unindoctrination—until they give up their new beliefs and return to their parents' faith. As this is being written, the practice is still open for debate, with charges of "brainwashing" being hurled at both sides in the controversy.

Barbara Hargrove (1980:20) explains the fervent opposition to the new religions in terms of an "evil eye" theory similar to primitive notions of demons and evil spirits: "There is in this 'evil eye' theory no more place for rational decision making or personal freedom of choice than could be found in the old theories of witchcraft, sorcery, and possession."

The sorrow of some parents whose children have made radical religious shifts is both profound and genuine. The demonic nature of the competing religion is always clear to those engaged in the battle, and religious wars are always the bloodiest.

I've focused on religious intolerance in the United States because it is more familiar to you, and because we have an official policy of religious tolerance. I do not mean to suggest that Americans are unique in having punished religious diversity. Indeed, I would not be allowed to publish such outrageous "heresies" in many nations of the world. Nor is religious persecution the perversity of religions alone. Communist Bloc nations—in their zeal to free people from the "yoke" of religion—have been no more tolerant than those they perceive as the enemy. Not only is religious practice a risky business in the Soviet Union, but the government places obstacles in the way of those who wish to emigrate out of Russia in order to practice their religion. Elsewhere, religion divides nations. In Canada, the conflict between French- and English-speaking people in Quebec is also a conflict between Catholics and Protestants, a conflict that has been even bloodier in Northern Ireland. In India, Hindus and Muslims struggle for domination, with bloodshed not an uncommon result.

Religious differences also create divisions between nations. Many Americans regard the decades-old struggle between the United States and the Soviet Union as a struggle between Christianity and Communism. The conflict between Iran and the United States has ele-

ments of an Islamic Holy War, as do the more general strains between the OPEC nations and the West. And nowhere is the intensity of religious conflict more obvious than in the struggle between Israel and her Arab neighbors.

Religion and Politics

The separation of church and state in America has been a national issue since the founding of the republic two centuries ago. In recent years, the issue has come to center stage in relation to tax support for parochial schools, prayers in schools, and in regard to the religious affiliations of political candidates. In truth, religion and politics have never really separated—as we saw in the discussion of civil religion—though we have kept them farther apart than have other countries.

In part, the controversy over the "proper" relationship between religion and politics involves disagreements over the dividing line between politics and morality. While religions actively involve themselves in moral issues, many of those issues are governed by law.

For example, religion has figured importantly in public discussions about abortion, with Catholics and fundamentalists arguing for the sanctity of all human life, though it has not been a significant force in the debate over capital punishment. Anita Bryant's Florida campaign against gay rights was firmly rooted in fundamentalist Christianity.

Organizations such as *The Christian Voice* and the Rev. Jerry Falwell's *Moral Majority* were particularly active during the 1980 political campaigns, urging voters to support right-wing positions on such issues as abortion (anti), busing (anti), capital punishment (pro), military (pro), and so forth. At a rally in Sacramento, California, Falwell told a gathering of 1,500 that God was opposed to the Equal Rights Amendment (*San Francisco Chronicle* October 30, 1980).

The involvement of religion in politics actually points to a more general issue: to what extent

Jerry Falwell's Moral Majority was regarded by many as a potent political force in the 1980 elections. Subsequent sociological analyses have questioned how much support Falwell really has.

should religion involve itself with worldly things? The authority of religious leaders to prescribe behavior has been a continuing issue within the Roman Catholic church, where the Vatican's pronouncements have become increasingly questioned over the past few years. Thus, for example, Andrew Greeley (reported in Grant 1980) reports that "only a third of U. S. Catholics, and only a fifth of those under 30, believed in 1974 that the pope is infallible when speaking on matters of faith and morals," and that in spite of papal prohibition, only about 4 percent of active Catholics in the United States oppose birth control.

American public opinion is mixed on the participation of churches and clergy in politics, as indicated by the results of an NBC News/Associated Press poll in 1980. Asked "Do you think the churches and members of the clergy should be involved in politics, like backing a candidate for public office," 69 percent said "no." At the same time, 63 percent said the churches and clergy should "express their views on day-to-day social questions." Perhaps the key in all this is the *impact* of religious lobbying in politics. When asked "If you were asked by a member of the clergy, such as a minister or a priest, to vote for a specific candidate in an election, would that make you more likely to vote for that candidate," only 3 percent said it would. Eight percent said they would be *less* likely, and 88 percent said the clerical endorsement would make no difference (*Public Opinion* 1981f:21).

Functional Alternatives to Religious Institutions

Religious critics of the modern church often complain that the church gets in the way of the individual's relationship with his or her God. As with other institutions, there have been many diverse attempts to develop substitutes for unsatisfying religious institutions. Christianity grew out of dissatisfaction with Judaism, and Islam grew out of dissatisfaction with Christianity. Protestantism grew out of dissatisfaction with Catholicism, and the subsequent fragmenting of Protestantism points to the continuing process of disaffection.

New Religious Expressions

Recent American interest in the religions of the East marks a further continuation of the search for more satisfying religious forms. Many have characterized the drug subculture of the 1960s as another example of the same thing, best typified, perhaps by Timothy Leary's "League of Spiritual Discovery" (LSD).

The counterculture movement of the 1960s and 1970s, represented in part by "encounter," "self-actualization," transcendental meditation, yoga, and the martial arts, seems to address the ultimate concerns that Tillich said formed the prime focus of religion.

It is too early to say what will become of these attempts, but we can recall some lessons from the past and from other institutions. To the extent that personal experience becomes replaced by belief through reification and internalization, it seems likely that the new forms will prove as unsatisfying as those they replaced.

Religious sects, you'll recall, are characterized by a greater fervor of personal experience. People do and feel things in newly formed sects that would shock and embarrass the average Episcopalian. When it comes time to socialize a new generation into the sect, however, the fervor of personal experience is reduced. Those born into the sect usually come to *believe* what their converted parents have experienced. The sect thus becomes institutionalized as a church. Within a few generations, it is likely to produce sects of its own, and the process continues.

Secularization

Another response to unsatisfying religious options is to reject religion altogether. At a broad societal level, this has been the official response of many Marxist governments. This substitution of secular for religious orientations—**secularization**—has been the response of numerous individuals in America.

In the broadest, sociological view, secularization is a common result of modernization—seen repeatedly as traditional, agrarian societies begin to adopt Western science, technology, and urban life patterns. It is less clear whether that relationship holds once a society becomes thoroughly modernized, as in the case of the United States. The recent popularity of fundamentalism, discussed earlier, gives us reason to suspect that the relationship between modernization and secularization is not a continuous one.

Robert Wuthnow (1976:852) has summarized some of the mixed evidence regarding religious trends between the late 1960s and early 1970s. Contributions to churches and the awarding of religious degrees both increased. New church construction, church attendance, and the publication of religious books (as a percentage of all books published) decreased. Church membership (just under two-thirds of the population) stayed about constant.

For Wuthnow (1976:854) and others, much of the apparent decline of religion in America has centered on young people, especially those active in the counterculture movement of the 1960s: "Part of the counterculture was aimed specifically at finding alternatives to established religion, whether in Marxism, mysticism, or other philosophies . . ." Wuthnow continues:

> But perhaps more importantly, many of the more specific characteristics of the counterculture were activities to which established religion, either explicitly or implicitly, had long been opposed . . . political radicalism . . . civil rights militancy . . . anti-war activism . . . civil libertarianism . . . homosexuality . . . drug use . . . alternative life styles.

Andrew Greeley (1979), a sociologist and Roman Catholic priest, suggests that while Wuthnow's assessment may apply to American Protestants, it does not hold for Catholics. For Greeley (1979:255), the key is to be found in the *family*. "Marriage and religion seem linked inseparably," he says. More specifically, Greeley (1979:261) feels the Church's position on sexuality is central to disaffection among Catholics.

> As far as I'm concerned, the touchstone is sexuality. As is undoubtedly clear by now, I am con-

vinced that any religious effort which does not seriously address the problems and the opportunities for religion in the current ambiguities of human sexuality is going to be a wasted effort.

While Greeley suggests that the established churches are in decline because they have not kept up with the times, Rodney Stark and William Sims Bainbridge (1981) offer a radically different assessment. The churches have lost their flocks precisely because they have tried to stay modern, creating a religious vacuum. This can be seen, Stark and Bainbridge suggest (1981:372), in the popularity of cults.

> We argue that cults find room to grow only as the conventional faiths have created vacuums. We have emphasized how secularization has produced these vacuums in the modern era as the most prominent denominations have offered an increasingly vague and inactive conception of the supernatural. But . . . [c]enturies ago cult movements such as Christianity, Judaism, Islam, and Buddhism originated and rose to power because of the grave weaknesses in the dominant religions of their time. And back then, many sophisticated observers also warned that religion was doomed, and gave little or contemptuous notice to the first stirrings of the religions of the future. Many religions did perish. But religion went on. If we are to learn from history, perhaps we should not merely note the falling membership statistics of liberal Protestantism but also note that the Mormons continue to double each decade.

Summary

We've seen thus far in the chapter that religious institutions center on the ultimate concerns that people have regarding the nature of reality and its meaning. Although people sometimes have direct, personal experiences of reality and its meaning, the purpose of religion is to structure those experiences so as to support the survival of group life.

Religions serve their function through systems of beliefs, values, norms, rituals, and the experience of community. Religions appear to rise out of the personal experiences of a founder, and they become institutionalized through the creation of beliefs reflecting the founder's experiences and agreed to by others. Religious beliefs are statements about the nature or meaning of reality, and they provide a basis for values (statements of what "ought to be") and norms (expectations about behavior).

Religious institutions also provide a source of group solidarity, based on feelings of belonging and identity. This especially supports the survival of a society in which a single, established religion is shared by all.

As we saw in the case of other institutions, a variety of religious forms can serve these functions. Religions with one god, three, or many all seem to provide support for the unity and persistence of societies. Ritually devouring a totem seems to work as well for the Australian aborigines as the Eucharist does for Christians. Both rituals create a sense of moral community.

In all societies, religious institutions are relevant to other institutions and aspects of social life. Weber pointed to the implications of religious beliefs for the economy, for example.

The relatively high degree of religious tolerance in America has resulted in a great variation in religions. Religions include those transplanted from Europe and elsewhere and the many new ones born here. In addition, Bellah suggested that Americans of all faiths share in a "civil religion" that supports the generally moral concerns that characterize our national posture on issues.

Cults, sects, churches, and ecclesia are some of the different structural forms that religions take in America and elsewhere. In general, cults and sects are characterized by a greater experiential fervor, and their members are typically converts from other religions. The behavior of church members is more conservative. The membership of churches, as opposed to sects, tends to come through inheritance rather than conversion. Successful sects have a general tendency to become established as churches as the children of members become socialized into membership.

The structuring of religious experience can also be seen in terms of the dimensions of religiosity. Glock and Stark have suggested five key dimensions: ritual, belief, cognitive, experiential, and consequential. We saw that a rather large percentage of Americans—particularly church members—report having had religious experiences: feeling they were in the presence of God, being saved in Christ, being punished, or being tempted by the Devil. Such personal experiences, while they might represent a threat to the established institution, occur most typically among those who have most thoroughly reified and internalized the agreements of the institution itself. Thus, their experiences support rather than threaten the institution.

Religions deal with religious deviance in a number of ways. Historically and, less frequently now, one solution has been death or torture to force agreement. When a religion is powerful enough, it can also punish religious deviance through secular sanctions. Churches have handled radical clergy through devices such as monasteries and the campus ministry.

Dissatisfaction with established religious institutions is evident in the continuing attempts to find functional alternatives. Today's established religions began as alternatives to unsatisfying predecessors. There is no evidence that the process is ending, and many of today's alternatives will be tomorrow's reasons for further change.

Important Terms

belief
emissary prophet
exemplary prophet
value
norm
totemism
civil religion

cult
charismatic
sect
church
ecclesia
religiosity
secularization

Suggested Readings

Durkheim, Emile
    1961   *The Elementary Forms of Religious Life*. New York: Collier.
    Classic work on religious belief and religious ritual as they interrelate with the integration of society.

Glock, Charles Y., Ed.
    1973   *Religion in Sociological Perspective*. Belmont, Calif.: Wadsworth.
    Much of the contemporary empirical research in the sociology of religion has been generated within the Research Program in Religion and Society at the Survey Research Center at the University of California (Berkeley) under the direction of Charles Glock. In this book, Glock has brought together a representative selection of the studies conducted in that program, providing an excellent introduction to current sociological research on religion.

McGuire, Meredith B.
    1981   *Religion: The Social Context*. Belmont, Calif.: Wadsworth.
    Here's an excellent introduction to the sociology of religion. Special attention is given to the impact of social change and secularization on religious institutions.

Richardson, James T., et al.
    1979   *Organized Miracles: A Study of a Contemporary Youth,*

Communal, Fundamentalist Organization. New Brunswick, N.J.: Transaction Books.
Describes the process of the "Jesus Movement" becoming established and institutionalized.

Scherer, Ross P., ed.
1980   *American Denominational Organization: A Sociological View.* Pasadena, Calif.: William Carey Library.

Shupe, Anson D., and David G. Bromley
1980   *The New Vigilantes: Deprogrammers, Anti-Cultists, and the new Religions.* Beverly Hills, Calif.: Sage Publishers.
Looks at reasons for, success, and impact of anti-cult movement and new religious groups in the U.S.

Smith, Huston
1958   *The Religion of Man.* New York: Harper & Row.
This is an excellent introduction to the world's great religions: Hinduism, Buddhism, Confucianism, Taoism, Islam, Judaism, and Christianity. Smith describes the founders, history, and main teachings of each. Excellent bibliographies guide you toward deeper study.

Weber, Max
[1922] *The Sociology of Religion.* Trans. Ephraim Fischoff.
1963   Boston: Beacon Press.
This is the classic work by one of the most important sociologists of religion. While the book is replete with historical and crosscultural examples, Weber's main concern is the analytical understanding of different religious structures and orientations. A particular interest in this book, as in Weber's other studies, is the relationship of religions to other social institutions, especially economic ones.

The first regularly scheduled radio broadcast began in 1920 at Pittsburgh's KDKA. Two months later, the station was regularly broadcasting religious services to its listeners. Over the next six decades, the marriage between religion and the electronic communications media was to flourish.

During the 1920s and 1930s, radio made its place in American homes, and with it came a variety of radio preachers, gospel singers, and other religious programming. Today, religious broadcasting still fills the airwaves. In part, the success of religion on the radio results from federal regulations, which require stations to dedicate some portion of their air time to religious, educational, or other public-service broadcasting. In part, then, religion has had a free ride on commercial broadcasting.

With the advent of television in the 1940s, both broadcasting and religion took on a new dimension of communication. Early television viewers came to form personal relationships with such superstars as Milton Berle, Howdy Doody, and a Catholic bishop, Fulton Sheen. Bringing televised religion into hundreds of thousands of American households, Bishop Sheen opened the door for what has come to be known by such terms as the "cathode church," the "video vicarage," or, more popularly, the "electronic church."

While Bishop Sheen was a reflection of mainstream religion in America, those who have followed in his footsteps differ significantly. For the most part, the electronic church today represents a fundamentalist evangelical challenge to the mainstream churches. And it is quick to criticize those churches for straying from the "true faith." Jeffrey Hadden and Charles Swann (1981:57) point to another strain:

> The mainliners' programs that were aired on gratis time were pushed off the air as a direct result

of the evangelicals' coming along and offering to pay for that time. One can much more easily appreciate the deep anger of mainline Protestant and Catholic broadcasters when one has examined the simultaneous growth curve of paid religious television and the sharply declining curve of sustaining-time audiences.

Sunday morning, long a "give-away" time slot for broadcasters, has become a lucrative source of income. At the same time, religious broadcasting itself has become big business. Full-blown broadcasting organizations such as the Christian Broadcasting Network and the Trinity Broadcasting Network produce professional quality programming, replacing the solitary preacher delivering a conventional Sunday sermon.

The electronic church of today reflects the medium that transmits it. Entertainment, dramatic timing and camera angles, and all the other devices that have made television so popular are now employed to get the religious message across. Sometimes big names from politics and the entertainment industry liven the show, but the real stars are the TV preachers, or "televangelists" themselves: Oral Roberts, Rex Humbard, Jimmy Swaggart, and the current superstar Jerry Falwell.

During the late 1970s and early 1980s, Jerry Falwell's Moral Majority seemed like the hottest thing in televised religion. Daniel Yankelovich (1981b:6) summarizes Falwell's message to America:

> Briefly, it opposes abortion, busing, the Equal Rights Amendment, homosexuality, pornography, premarital sex, easy divorce; and it supports prayer in the schools, community censorship of textbooks, capital punishment, military superiority over the Soviet Union, a strong and traditional family. All of these varied positions express the core of the Moral Majority's conservatism—

an explicit rejection of what it calls "secular humanism," the tradition of modernism that promotes the individual, pluralism, tolerance, and skepticism toward the authority of government and other institutions.

Falwell and the Moral Majority first came to the attention of many Americans during the 1980 political campaigns. The Moral Majority proved a potent political force for conservatism in many local elections, and some felt Falwell's televangelism contributed importantly to the national conservative sweep, including Reagan's election as president. Unchurched liberals who had discounted the Moral Majority as irrelevant reconsidered.

How many Americans actually support Jerry Falwell and the Moral Majority? As Yankelovich (1981b:5) reports, that all depends on how you define "support." Published estimates vary from 400,000 to 67 million.

One key indicator of support for the televangelists is the audience they command on television. Hadden and Swann consulted Arbitron, a TV rating service, and Table 15–5 reports what they learned. Of the top ten shows, Hadden and Swann identify two as "mainline": "Davey and Goliath" is a Lutheran children's show, and "Insight" is a Catholic drama. Surprisingly, perhaps, Jerry Falwell's "Old-Time Gospel Hour" was rated sixth in terms of viewing audience.

Another surprise is forthcoming when audience trends are examined. Working again with Arbitron data, Hadden and Swann (1981:55) report that the combined audiences of the electronic church doubled between 1970 and 1975—from 9,803,000 to 20,806,000—and then flattened out during the next five years. There was, in fact, a nine percent decline in viewers between 1978 and 1980, although a short-term shift of

Table 15-5

Audiences of the Top Ten Religious Television Shows

Rank	Show	Preacher	Audience Size
1	"Oral Roberts and You"	Oral Roberts	2,719,250
2	"Rex Humbard"	Rex Humbard	2,409,960
3	"Hour of Power"	Robert Schuller	2,069,210
4	"Jimmy Swaggart, Evangelist"	Jimmy Swaggart	1,986,000
5	"Day of Discovery"	Richard De Hann Paul Van Gorder	1,519,400
6	"The Old-Time Gospel Hour"	Jerry Falwell	1,455,720
7	"Gospel Singing Jubilee"		939,200
8	"Davey and Goliath"		672,000
9	"The PTL Club"	Jim Bakker	668,170
10	"Insight"		497,920

Source: Jeffrey K. Hadden and Charles E. Swann, *Prime Time Preachers: The Rising Power of Televangelism* (New York: Addison-Wesley, 1981), p. 51.

that magnitude can't be taken as proof of a long-term trend.

The people involved in producing the religious programs argue that measurements such as these miss a substantial audience who receive the shows on cable. Whatever the actual figures, there is no doubt that the Moral Majority represents a substantial minority of the population. Ultimately, the question is not one of numbers at all, but as Yankelovich (1981b:5) notes: "What we really want to know is whether the Moral Majority is a passing fad or will take hold in the mainstream of American life."

No one can predict the answer to Yankelovich's question with certainty. One approach to answering the question lies in an examination of who supports the electronic church today. Hadden and Swann (1981:62) point out that the audiences are disproportionately female and old, corresponding to what we have seen earlier regarding fundamentalism in general. This also fits with findings that young people are the most disaffected with religion. What this discovery doesn't tell us is whether the resurgence of American fundamentalism will fade away as its current supporters die off, or if they will simply be replaced by a new generation of elderly.

Perhaps Robert Bellah (1978:321) best touched the source of contemporary fundamentalism when he reminded us that

> there are large sectors of our population for whom our problems are so great and so confusing that they do not wish to hear about them. They are attracted by a conservative evangelical preaching that makes little attempt to analyze the world except as the arena of conflict between God and Satan.

PRACTICING SOCIOLOGY

The Reverend J. Bryan Hehir, director of the Office of Foreign Affairs for the U.S. Catholic Conference, wrote the following regarding the role of the Roman Catholic Church in Latin America.

The meetings of Latin American bishops at Medellin, Colombia, in 1968 and at Puebla, Mexico, in 1979 symbolize the developments of the last decade. These conferences and the activities they generated transformed the church's posture. Once a socially conservative force, the church became a leading voice for reform. The Medellin conference set the direction of the church for the decade when it described Latin America as beset by "internal and external colonialism." The theology of liberation that has developed in Latin America since the Vatican II seeks to mobilize the Christian community to address the reality described by Medellin.

How might Latin American governments react to the shift in Church policy from conservative to reformist? What other consequences might there be in Latin American countries? Discuss possible changes in the relationship between the Church and parts of other social institutions, especially government, business, and education.

Source: J. Bryan Hehir, "A View from the Church," *Foreign Policy*, Summer 1981, pp. 83–88.

16

Family as Institution

We continue our analysis of social institutions with the oldest and most fundamental—the family. We start examining the functions performed by families around the world, noting differences that separate one culture from another. Then we'll focus on changes taking place in the American family. We'll look at changing attitudes toward the roles played by men and women and toward having children. We'll look at living together and at divorce.

This chapter concludes with an examination of the dissatisfaction many people have expressed about the contemporary American family and the alternatives that have been tried in its place.

The Universality of the Family

I said above that the family is the most fundamental of social institutions. You'll see that for yourself if you just take a minute to reflect on your own experiences. If you had a relatively conventional childhood, then the first eighteen or so years of your life were inseparable from your experience of family. If you had the misfortune of growing up without a family, you probably are even *more* sensitive to the importance of having a family.

In sociological terms, **family** has two meanings. As a social organization, family is the basic unit of kinship, or relatedness through blood, marriage, or adoption. The family consists of spouses, their children, and—as we'll see shortly—possibly other kinfolks. As an institution, family is that set of agreements describing preferred kinship structures and relationships. Thus, family as an institution is the set of rules determining the composition and operation of families as organizations.

As we will see in this chapter, family is virtually universal in human experience. Almost every society known has a set of agreements and social organizations that are recognizable as forms of the family. In those rare societies where the existence of the family is debatable, we shall see that other arrangements have been made to handle the functions served by the family. It is those functions, indeed, that make the family—or a substitute for it—essential to all societies. The family serves important functions for children, for adults, and for the society as a whole. Let's look at those functions now.

Functions of the Family

Every institution is a reconciliation of certain group needs with certain individual experiences. The group need most relevant to the family as an institution is the need for new group members. You simply cannot have a group without people, and as long as individuals die, new ones will have to be generated to take their place. The group need for new members extends beyond mere biological reproduction, however, because reproduction without child rearing does not ensure the survival of the group. Consider the following aspects of the problem:

1. Babies and young children require nurturance—food, warmth, and protection.
2. From the beginning, children must be socialized into meeting their own needs, into becoming more self-sufficient.
3. Children must also be socialized into patterns of interaction within the group.
4. Children need emotional support and guidance in the formation of self-image and self-confidence.

These needs for individual and group survival, largely performed by the family, are one of the reasons why the family is often called the "fundamental unit of social organization." The first human social "group" was probably some kind of family, made up of at least a mother and a child and perhaps a father. Recall the discussion in Chapter 2 of George Herbert Mead and his theory of the need for cooperation. This discussion points to the importance of enlarging the family group beyond the mother and child. If human beings were fundamentally ill equipped to survive in the presence of stronger and faster enemies, consider the predicament of a mother saddled with a dependent baby. This prehistoric problem has modern parallels that we'll see later.

No one can say how or why families developed beyond the simple mother-child dyad. If an answer to this question is ever found, it will probably involve some of the functions that families serve for their adult members. For one thing, couples living together on a regular basis can satisfy each other sexually. Families, then, have individuals express their sexuality in ways appropriate to the survival of society.

Families are also a source of emotional support for adults, potentially able to provide love, comfort and security. Adult family members, moreover, can protect each other in the face of illness and injury. As one indication of the importance of this function, Norval Glenn and Charles Weaver (1981) found that marital and family happiness were stronger predictors of people's overall happiness than were satisfaction with work, health, financial situation, community, friendships, or other nonworking activities. Similarly, a 1978 national poll asked people which was the most important to them: "a happy family life, a fulfilling career, the opportunity to develop as an individual, making a lot of money." Three-fourths picked a happy family life (*Public Opinion* 1980d:22).

Although the growth of social organization involved the joining together—voluntarily or by force—of families in cooperative mutual support, the earliest human families were undoubtedly self-sufficient. We can see self-sufficiency in families in today's preliterate societies and in families from earlier, more developed societies. Indeed, many types of families have performed *all* the functions required for the survival of group life, including political and economic ones (discussed in Chapter 13). Winch (1971:31) has described the traditional

The Origin of the Family

While no one can say for sure how the family began as an institution, this has not stopped scholars from speculating about the matter. Marie Withers Osmond (1980) offers an excellent summary of some recent theories advanced.

First, E. K. Gough suggests that the young child's dependence on its mother resulted in her dependence on the child's father. Here's how Osmond (1980:1003) summarizes Gough's views:

Gough (1971, 1975) traced the origins of the family to the earliest division of labor between the sexes. According to Gough's logic, a stable alliance between mother and child was necessitated by the human child's long period of dependency. This, in turn, made the mother dependent on others for protection and subsistence functions. Because of convenience or efficiency, in maximizing survival, the biological father adopted the protection-subsistence-production roles.

I suspect this explanation comes pretty close to what most people think of if they ever think about how the family began. Other scholars—E. Morgan, N. Tanner, and A. Zihlman—offer a very different explanation. Osmond (1980:1004) summarizes:

Our *homo habilis* ancestors emerged in the 10–12 million year Pliocene era, in which social-fathers were conspicuously absent. The mother-child with, perhaps, her brothers, sisters, and prepubertal sons formed the original "family" which preceded the "nuclear" (mother-father-child) family by millions of years. The older children stayed with the mother because of her food-gathering abilities and because food-sharing was customary only between mother and young. In essence, reproduction was quite separate from the family unit which was primarily economic.

In still another view, J. Goody's (1971, 1973, 1976) research suggests that the family originated through a pattern of male dominance in which wives were regarded as property and used for slave labor. Ultimately, each of these patterns probably occurred in various times and places, but it is unlikely that we will ever identify the "first" family.

Source: Marie Withers Osmond, "Cross-Societal Family Research: A Macrosociological Overview of the Seventies," *Journal of Marriage and the Family*, November 1980, pp. 995–1016. Other citations can be found in the bibliography at the end of the book.

peasant family of China, for example, as "a family of great functionality," saying: "For perhaps twenty centuries there existed among the peasants of China a familial form that was just about as completely functional as is theoretically possible." In addition to the functions I've mentioned, the Chinese family carried responsibility in religious, education, political, and economic matters.

The modern family is very different from the Chinese peasant one. Its development is often seen as a process in which functions have been transferred from the family to other institutions. This has occurred gradually, over the course of thousands of years of social evolu-tion, and the sources of the shift have been many. As populations grew, for example, it was necessary for some form of leadership to emerge, beyond the family. With economic complexity and specialization, it was no longer possible for the economic processes of production, distribution, and consumption to occur through the family alone. Thus, over time, many of the family's original functions—religious, educational, political, and economic—have been shifted to separate institutions bearing the names we associate with those functions.

The family has survived as a social institution despite this shifting of functions. In a variety of forms, it continues to serve the needs of

The universality of the family stems largely from the bonds that link mother and child.

The extended family—comprised of three or more generations—is the norm in many societies. In the U.S., it is less common but not unheard of.

society *and* individuals with regard to reproduction, sexuality, and physical and emotional nurturance. Once we see the variety of workable agreements that can satisfy the needs for reproduction, sexuality, and nurturance, we'll have a better perspective for assessing the American case.

Dimensions of Variation

In this section, we'll look briefly at two general areas of variation in family forms. We'll begin with some organizational and structural variations, summarized in Table 16–1. Then we'll look at variations in sex roles defining interactions within families.

Organizational Differences

Family Composition For most Americans, the word "family" refers to a wife, a husband, and

their children, a type of family called (technically) the **nuclear family.** Although the nuclear family is the norm in American society, it is only one type of family among many. An **extended family**—like the traditional Chinese peasant family mentioned earlier—includes more than two generations. It is composed, for example, of a husband-wife couple, their children, and their children's children.

Carol Stack (1974:31) has suggested that versions of the extended family are especially common and functional for America's poor. In three years of participant observation among black families in the poorest district of a midwestern

Table 16-1

Family Variations

Dimension	Form	Meaning
Composition (spouses)	Monogamy	One husband, one wife
	Polygyny	One husband, more than one wife
	Polyandry	One wife, more than one husband
Composition (generations)	Nuclear	No more than two generations
	Extended	More than two generations
Lineage	Matrilineal	Descent traced through females
	Patrilineal	Descent traced through males
	Bilateral	Descent traced through both males and females
Residence	Patrilocal	Couple lives with man's parents
	Matrilocal	Couple lives with woman's parents
	Neolocal	Couple establishes a new residence
Power	Matriarchal	Women predominate in family
	Patriarchal	Men predominate in family
	Egalitarian	Men and women share power in family

city of about 50,000, Stack found individuals frequently moving from one household to another.

> A resident in The Flats who eats in one household may sleep in another, and contribute resources to yet another. He may consider himself a member of all three households.

Although I've spoken of a husband-wife couple, the couple is not the only type of sexual union that exists in families. In **monogamy,** the couple involves one husband and one wife. **Polygamy** is an agreement permitting more than one spouse. A man can have more than one wife (called "polygyny") or a woman can have more than one husband (called "polyandry").

The agreement on monogamy has been reified in America, so the idea of polygamy may seem strange to you. As children and young adults, we are brought up believing and feeling that one husband and one wife is the "proper" basis for a family. Note, however, that most societies in the world have at least permitted polygamy, and some have held it as the ideal,

although none seems to have required it. In 1970, in the west African nation of Togo, 36 percent of the married men had more than one wife (Welch and Glick 1981:192). In American society, the original Mormons provide an example of polygamy. Insistence on monogamy has been most typical of modern, developed countries, and the Mormons were forced to give up the practice.

Lineage   The notion of lineage or "descent" is also somewhat foreign to Americans. If I asked you to sketch out your "family tree," you'd probably begin with your mother and father, add their mothers and fathers, and the tree would branch out across successive generations. Our society has a general agreement on **bilateral descent:** we trace our ancestry back through both males and females. Other societies—the Dobu islanders, for example—have a **matrilineal** society. They trace ancestry only through females. Still others—such as the ancient, traditional Jews and Japanese—are **patrilineal.** They trace their descent through males.

Some patrilineal elements exist in American agreements. The clearest example has to do with our use of family names. Traditionally, women have taken their husbands' family names upon marriage. Children take their fathers' family names also. Recently, however, many American women, seeing this patrilineal agreement as evidence of sexual inequality, have objected to it and have retained their maiden names after marriage.

Location   The question of where a newly formed family should live is also a matter of differing agreements. In America, the predominant agreement reflects a **neolocal** pattern for the residence of nuclear families: they are expected to set up housekeeping on their own at a location of their own choosing.

Among the **patrilocal** Baganda of central Africa, however, the new family establishes its residence with the husband's family. The traditional Japanese (and others) share a similar agreement.

The **matrilocal** Hopi Indians see things just the opposite, as indicated in the following description of the events following a Hopi wedding:

> The bride dresses in her new clothes and returns home, where she is received by her mother and her female relatives. She is accompanied on the journey by her husband's relatives, who make a final exchange of gifts with her mother's household. During the evening the groom appears at his mother-in-law's home and spends the night. The next day he fetches wood for her and from then on is a permanent resident in her house—unless a divorce sends him packing. (Queen et al. 1974:54)

The description of marital patterns among the Hopi points to something you probably already knew: picking a mate is something that should be taken seriously. And as we see next, the rules and methods of mate selection vary greatly from society to society.

Mate Selection

All societies have rules regarding who may or may not mate with whom. At the most general level, anthropologists have found two patterns based on *kinship groups:* those people regarded as related to one another. The pattern of **endogamy** requires that you marry someone *within* your kinship group. Definitions of the group, of course, vary: you might be expected to marry someone within your tribe or your clan, for example. **Exogamy** is a pattern requiring marriage *outside* your kinship group; thus you are prohibited from marrying relatives.

There are elements of both endogamy and exogamy in most societies, however, though they may not occur to you immediately. First, all societies are exogamous in prohibiting marriage between people *too closely related.* Indeed, Freud wrote of the **incest taboo** as perhaps the most fundamental agreement in social organization. Children and parents are prohibited from having sexual intercourse with one another, as are brothers and sisters.

There are some rare exceptions to the prohibition against incest. It was permitted, for example, among the royalty of ancient Incan, Egyptian, and Hawaiian societies.

While it has been generally assumed that the frequency of incest in America is extremely low, there are growing indications that violation of this prohibition may be fairly common, though it is difficult to obtain reliable data on the subject. The rough estimates, however, are astounding. Benjamin DeMott (1980:12) says:

> The original Kinsey sample suggested that 1 out of 16 women had experienced an incestuous relationship. In a study published last year, Robert L. Geiser, chief psychologist at the Nazareth Child Care Center in Boston, dismissed an estimate of 40,000 cases a year as too low, accepting as possible both an annual incidence rate six times higher and a claim that 10 percent of our population may have known such a relationship.

Moreover, the incest taboo has been overtly challenged by what DeMott calls "the pro-incest lobby" (1980:11–16). Incest has been presented, sometimes favorably, on television and in movies and books, giving rise to the term "positive incest." DeMott (1980:12) reports:

> Some of the new permissivists seem actually to have succeeded in presenting themselves as defenders of the family—persons with remedies for the divorce rate, runaway children, teenage pregnancy, drunkenness, and the like. Their argument begins by stressing that safeguards against inbreeding are no longer needed, but moves quickly to the assertion that incest fear has a chilling effect on the expression of loving feeling within the home and that many domestic problems are attributable to this very inhibition.

As Liz Einstein (1980:2) points out, this taboo can create special problems for a stepfather and stepdaughter: "Sexy adolescent stepdaughters create tension for the most guarded of stepfathers. Because they are not his biological daughters, the 'incest taboo' is lowered. To compensate for sexual feelings toward their stepdaughters or to avoid having their wives misinterpret them, stepfathers often withdraw affection from their stepdaughters, making them feel rejected."

In any event, the incest taboo represents a common pattern of exogamy across cultures, requiring that people marry those removed from their immediate circle.

There is at the same time, a strong pattern of endogamy that has been amply documented among Americans and occurs in other societies as well. Sociologists use the term **homogamy** in reference to the pattern of marrying people who are very similar to you in a variety of ways. Mary Reilly (1976:2) summarizes some of the things sociologists have discovered in this regard:

> It appears that "like marries like" is more accurate than "opposites attract." Vast amounts of data indicate that generally people marry within their social class to those with a similar educational background and from the same ethnic group, race, and religion. Sociologist William Goode notes: "It is not surprising, then, that in the United States about half of all marriages occur between people who live no more than one mile from one another. . . ."

The observations of homogamy in mate selection point once more to the power of informal agreements in social life. Though no law requires it, people tend to marry others of about the same age in American society, though we'll look at the finer tuning of this agreement a little later. Consider, also, the extent to which people choose mates of about the same body type and other physical characteristics as themselves.

The above references to "choosing" a mate set the stage for the last comments I want to make regarding mate selection. Societies differ in their agreements as to *who* makes the selection. In particular, two general patterns stand out. In our society, and in some others, it is assumed that the individual is responsible for choosing his or her own mate— with no end of assistance and advice from friends and relatives, of course. And, in particular, it is expected that the choices will hinge heavily on feelings of love. The person who openly marries for money or other social advantage in America is a subject of scorn.

Other societies, however, are more pragmatic in this regard. Marriage is seen as an alliance—one that should accomplish more than sexual union. Marriage among national leaders can bind nations to one another, and much of European history is the history of such alliances. Marriages can further commercial development, with great business empires resulting. At a more mundane level, marriages might be created for the purpose of ensuring security, nurturance, hot meals, and other domestic niceties. In all these latter respects, the young prospective couple have been generally regarded as incapable of creating the best

Children learn their sex roles primarily from their parents. This has the effect . . .

possible deal, whether a national alliance, a business merger, or simply a stable home. In those cases, then, marriages have been arranged by the parents of the bride and groom. You may recall the popular Broadway musical *Fiddler on the Roof.* A main theme of the show concerned the activities of a professional matchmaker among Russian Jews.

In traditional India, marriage by arrangement of the elders was almost universal. According to M. S. Gore (1965), Indian marriages have traditionally revolved around three basic rules: (1) marriage should occur if possible before the girl reaches puberty, (2) the prospective partners should both be of the same caste, and (3) the marriage should be arranged by the elders, with the prospective pair having no say in the matter. Although laws passed in recent decades no longer require that marriage occur within the same caste and now prohibit marriage before the age of fifteen for girls and eighteen for boys, marriage within caste is still the norm and the age prohibitions are frequently ignored. Boys, however, increasingly are asked for their consent to the partner chosen for them.

Bernard Murstein (1980:778) suggests there is a worldwide shift away from arranged marriages, more in the direction of the American pattern.

The world as a whole, seems to be moving towards the idea of free choice in marriage, sometimes referred to as "love" marriages, although this is more a euphemism than an accurate appraisal, since love, especially romantic love, is not invar-

. . . of perpetuating sex-stereotyping of particular jobs, such as police officer and homemaker.

iably the goal of marriage. Data from Africa, India, Israel, and Malaya indicate some concomitants of freedom of choice: later age at marriage, higher educational levels, high socioeconomic status or promise of such status, and urban living.

Murstein indicates that freedom of choice is also increasingly common in communist countries. In China, couples are encouraged to select partners on the basis of political compatibility. "The Soviet Union has a similar ideology, but accepts individual love more readily . . ." (Murstein 1980:779).

Granting differences in how mates are selected, let's turn now to what can be expected once a family has been formed. In particular, we're going to look at the differences in sex roles in families around the world.

Sex Roles in Families

Who was the "boss" in your family when you were growing up—your mother or your father? The sex of the person who holds the power in the family is another way in which families differ, and different societies have different general agreements on this.

Had you grown up in a traditional Japanese family, you would have had no trouble in answering the question, for the traditional Japanese are **patriarchal.** They have an agreement on the dominance of males. Your mother would have had little or no say in whether your father should establish a business or in whether you should go to college. Your father would have made those decisions, and he would have been strongly influenced in making them by his father.

In **matriarchal** societies, women are dominant. E. Franklin Frazier (1939:125), among others, said that the matriarchal pattern was common among the black American families immediately following Emancipation.

> These women had doubtless been schooled in self-reliance and self-sufficiency during slavery. As a rule, the Negro woman as wife or mother was the mistress of her cabin, and, save for the interference of master or overseer, her wishes in regard to mating and family matters were paramount. Neither economic necessity nor tradition had instilled in her the spirit of insubordination to masculine authority. Emancipation only tended to confirm in many cases the spirit of self-sufficiency which slavery had taught.

Earlier in this book, we examined the controversy over whether the contemporary black family is matriarchal—noting that blacks were no more matriarchal than whites. Gerald Leslie (1982:50) goes so far as to suggest that matriarchy is only a logical possibility, not a reality.

> Except in the comic strips, however, and in B-grade Hollywood movies, true matriarchies are never found. The fabled Amazon women are just that—a fable. Even in societies organized about women, in societies which follow matrilineal descent, inheritance, and residence, power tends to be held by males in the female lineage.

Whether any matriarchies exist anywhere, it is clear that they are far outnumbered by patriarchal and **egalitarian** patterns. An increasing body of sociological research, moreover, questions how typical the egalitarian family is in America. Mirra Komarovsky (1962), for example, concluded that the lower-status–blue-collar families in America are relatively patriarchal, while families of higher status are more likely to be egalitarian. A study of families in Detroit (Blood and Wolfe 1960), on the other hand, suggested that neither race nor social class is as important as urban-suburban differences, finding that urban families are the more egalitarian.

The question of who has power within the family should be placed in the context of what men and women *do* in families: what their roles are. It has long been recognized that a given society has agreements about the tasks men and women in families are to perform. It has also been recognized that those specific tasks vary somewhat depending on the society's level of development. As a very broad generalization, men hunt and fish in preliterate societies; women gather fruit, nuts, and berries and raise the children. In industrial societies, on the other hand, a general pattern is that men work in the economy to earn support for the family while the women run the internal affairs of the family, though this pattern has changed dramatically since World War II.

Talcott Parsons and Robert Bales (1955:151) have suggested a general pattern in the roles assigned to men and women in families, a pattern that crosscuts cultures and time. Using terms taken from Parsons' theoretical discussions of the social system, they concluded that men were generally responsible for the **instrumental functions** of the family (relating the family to the outside world), while women were generally responsible for the **expressive functions** (concerned with affection and emotional support within the family).

This view corresponds generally to the experiences of people brought up in developed, Western societies, but recent investigations of preliterate societies suggest that the generalization may not be as general as it appeared. A study of over eight hundred societies characterized by subsistence economies (Aronoff and Crano 1975) found that women played appreciable roles in satisfying the instrumental functions that Parsons and Bales assigned to men. Overall, Aronoff and Crano estimated that women produced 44 percent of the food consumed in the societies studied, an instrumental activity.

We have seen that a variety of family structures have been created to fulfill the functions the family serves for the survival of group life.

None is necessarily more effective than another, and very different forms appear to accomplish the social task. Now I want to take a closer look at the changing structure of the family in America.

Issues Facing the American Family

Probably no other sociological topic is more the subject of popular media discussion than the changes that have occurred and are occurring in the American family. Some writers herald the changes they observe as progressive, but others see the same changes as threatening to the society at large; some speak of the "demise" of the family.

To discuss changes in the American family, we need to see where we've been—what we're changing from. Fifty years ago, the typical middle-class American family was an "extended nuclear" arrangement. There were many children (four or more) at home, and some grandparents, uncles, and aunts were nearby or at home, sharing in domestic tasks. The family and its ancestors lived in a small town or city (and usually in the same neighborhood) for several generations. Most neighbors and friends, as well as relatives, were the same from childhood on.

An adult male—the father of the juveniles in the family—was the sole economic provider, while the mother produced infants, raised the children, prepared food, and maintained the household. The family was part of a religious structure, formally enrolled and participating as part of a church—usually mainline Protestant. Church involvement typically extended back through generations, like everything else.

Today the typical middle-class family is an unextended and isolated nuclear one. There are few children in the family, being raised by few adults. The family lives in a suburb of a big city, in a residential neighborhood that probably did not exist when the family was formed. Our family knows its neighbors in isolation of any generational ties.

The adult male may be the primary breadwinner, but he is probably not the sole one in the family. In 1940, only 14.7 percent of the married women with husbands present worked. By 1980, 50.2 percent of women in this category worked (U.S. Bureau of Census 1981i:388). Although the family remains a unit for economic consumption, its role as an economic production unit lies as a dim memory of the family farm and frontier cottage industry.

Who Marries in America

Despite the changes we've just catalogued and others we'll look at shortly, marriage seems likely to remain an established pattern in American life. In a 1974 national poll (see Reilly 1976:2), 96 percent of the women and 92 percent of the men said they would prefer being married to being single. And around three-fourths of Americans over eighteen years old *are* married. Moreover, the annual marriage rate (number of people marrying per 1,000 population) has varied remarkably little over time. Except for upward spurts following World Wars I and II and dips during the Great Depression and during the 1960s, the marriage rate has varied little during this century. It was 10.3 per thousand in 1910 and 10.9 in 1980 (U.S. Bureau of Census 1981i:58).

The age at which people get married has fluctuated. In 1890, the average age at first marriage for men was 26.1 and 22.0 for women. Age at first marriage grew younger and younger for both men and women until 1956: 22.5 for men and 20.1 for women. Since 1956, men and women have been marrying later. In 1980, the average man married for the first time at 24.6, the average woman at 22.1, as indicated in Table 16–2.

Not everyone marries, however, even if they want to; and the reasons are subtler than you might imagine. Recall, for example, that women

Table 16-2

Median Age at First Marriage, 1890 to 1980

Year	Men	Women
1890	26.1	22.0
1900	25.9	21.9
1910	25.1	21.6
1920	24.6	21.2
1930	24.3	21.3
1940	24.3	21.5
1950	22.8	20.3
1956	22.3	20.1
1960	22.8	20.3
1970	22.5	20.6
1980	24.6	22.1

Source: U.S. Bureau of Census, *Marital Status and Living Arrangements: March 1980* (Washington, D.C.: Government Printing Office, 1981), Series P-20, No. 365, p. 7.

Table 16-3

Percent of Persons Aged 35 to 44 Who Are Single, by Income and Sex

Income	Men	Women
No income	72.3	15.6
$1–$9,999	39.1	17.3
$10,000–$19,999	18.3	18.3
$20,000 or more	7.4	17.2

Source: U.S. Bureau of Census, *Money Income and Poverty Status of Families and Persons in the United States: 1980* (Washington, D.C.: Government Printing Office, 1981), Series P-60, No. 127, p. 21.

tend, on the average, to marry men slightly older than themselves. (This pattern is reflected in state marriage laws that typically permit women to marry at a younger age than men.) Think about a woman at the upper end of the age range. If she wants a husband older than herself, then the older she gets, the fewer prospects she will find—not only because the age range of eligible men is reduced, but also because men tend to die sooner than women. Ultimately, then, older women are at a special disadvantage if they wish to marry. The matter is even more complicated, however.

Jessie Bernard (1972) has spoken of a "marriage gradient" for education and income similar to the pattern just discussed in relation to age. Overall, she argues, women tend to marry men with slightly more education and with more income than themselves. This would place a special disadvantage in finding partners on (1) rich and well-educated women and (2) poor and less-educated men.

Census data on the distribution of unmarried people seem to confirm Bernard's theory.

Table 16–3 shows the percentages of single men and women at different income levels. As we see, men with low incomes are far more likely to be single than are women. As income increases, however, women are more likely to be single than are men. It looks, then, as though the tongue-in-cheek advice to "marry a rich woman" is frequently superseded by the agreement that husbands should be wealthier than their wives.

Let's move on from the question of who marries to four areas of change that have been the focus of controversy during recent decades in America. We'll look first at some changes in the roles played by men and women in families. Next, we'll examine changing childbearing patterns and also the increase in unmarried couples living together. Finally, we'll look at the increasing divorce rate and some of its causes and consequences.

Sex-Role Equality in the Family

Earlier in this chapter I discussed the different roles men and women play in the American family. Although we noted considerable variation, we saw that the predominant American agreement regarding roles gives the husband primary responsibility for supporting the family financially and the wife primary responsibility for managing the internal affairs of the family.

Criticisms of this agreement are not hard to find. In a radical critique, David Cooper (1974) has called the American nuclear family a "fur-lined bear trap," a seductive and subtle mainstay of the capitalist society. The family, in Cooper's view, provides a firsthand experience of authoritarian social organization, thereby conditioning people to accept the same orientation in their economic institutions.

Other, less radical observers have noted that the American woman has generally gotten a bad deal from her particular status in connection with the family. For generations, young American girls have been taught that they could best realize their human worth as wives and mothers. Those who have sought careers outside the family have had to fight agreements to the contrary.

While there is nothing fundamentally wrong with this division of labor per se, two additional factors have made it problematic. First, the homemaker role has generally been treated as less important than the breadwinner role; thus the traditional division of labor has also suggested women were inferior to men. Second, the firm establishment of the traditional division of labor has limited choices for both men and women. Even if the homemaker roles were fully rewarded, some women would still not want to do it, just as some men would prefer not to be breadwinners. Given the downgrading of the homemaker role, however, the lack of choice has seemed more troublesome for women than for men.

Both men and women have internalized the view of women as wed to the family and domestic chores, and it is hard to exaggerate the extent to which we have done this. None of us is exempt, as Sandra Bem and Daryl Bem (1971:259) report:

Consider, for example, the 1968 student rebellion at Columbia University. Students from the radical left took over some administration buildings in the name of equalitarian principles which they accused the university of flouting. They were the most militant spokesmen one could hope to find in the cause of equalitarian ideas. But no sooner had they occupied the buildings than the male militants blandly turned to their sisters-in-arms and assigned them the task of preparing the food, while they—the menfolk—would presumably plan further strategy.

Even in those presumably equalitarian "dual-profession" families in which both husband and wife pursue careers, Margaret Poloma and T. Neal Garland (1972) found a fundamental belief that the husband was ultimately responsible for the family's financial support while the wife was ultimately responsible for the internal affairs of the family. In case of conflict or crisis, the families Poloma and Garland studied would resort to the traditional sex roles. This, the researchers suggest, is the basis for women's disadvantage in the professional world.

We wish to argue that underlying the discriminatory evidence uncovered by researchers is an institution of our society that most are very reluctant to attack—the institution of our family system. It is the family that stands in the way of a woman's career advancement and is perhaps a major reason for employers discriminating against women. (1972:201–2)

Whether married women work is importantly affected by their husbands' attitudes in that regard. Yet when wives *do* work, their husband's attitudes are likely to come into line. This is particularly the case when family finances are substantially improved by the two incomes and when the wives continue to be responsible for household chores. As Glenna Spitze and Linda Waite (1981:123) point out: "Husbands seem to have little to lose and much to gain through their wives' employment. Bringing their wives' employment into line with their own preferences could be costly, but a change in attitudes is cheap."

I do not wish to suggest that there is anything wrong with women's occupying the family roles traditionally associated with their sex. Indeed, as is often reported, many women—perhaps a majority—prefer the traditional family role to an occupational role in society. The point is that institutional agreements become reified and internalized in such a way as to interfere with the desires and aspirations of individuals. The established agreements that make social life possible can also make it dissatisfying.

There is special irony in the reified view that in America families are for women. Against the backdrop of considerable folklore about marriage being a trap laid by women for unsuspecting men, Jessie Bernard (1972) has compiled a body of rather curious data. In terms of health, happiness, and a host of other variables, married men fare better than single men, while married women fare *worse* than single ones. If anyone benefits from marriage, it is likely to be men.

To find out how couples regarded the *equity* of their respective roles in the family, Robert Schafer and Patricia Keith (1981) asked 336 Iowa couples to examine five family roles: cooking, housekeeping, provider, companion, and parent. For each job, husbands and wives were asked whether they felt they should increase or decrease their own efforts in order "to make the marriage relationship more fair for both of you," and they were asked the same questions regarding the need for their spouses to increase or decrease their efforts. Those who answered "present effort is fair" to both questions, then, perceived "equity" in the division of labor in their families. Others judged the situation as being unfairly favorable to themselves or unfairly favorable to their spouses.

What do you suppose their overall answers were? The majority of both men and women said they felt the division of labor was fair on each of the tasks. For men, most of the remainder felt the inequity was in their favor. Women were more evenly divided as to the direction of the inequities that existed. When the researchers examined attitudes at different points in the family life cycle, they found increasing feelings of equity over time. You may be surprised by the overall level of satisfaction expressed by these husbands and wives, but you should remember that the survey was conducted in Iowa, a relatively traditional area of the country. Different results might be found in, say, New York or California.

The growing concern over rights and responsibilities in marriage has produced another innovation. In all societies, marriages are by contractual arrangement, either formal or informal. They represent a set of agreements binding on the marital partners and perhaps on others as well. In the United States, the nature of the agreements has typically been specified by law and by religious traditions.

Many couples getting married today are changing this situation. They are tailoring the agreements of marriage to their own liking. In place of the traditional vows to "love, honor, and obey," many modern marriage contracts specify the details of rights and responsibilities of both husband and wife. An excerpt from one such contract illustrates this practice.

THE PARTIES AGREE to share equally in the performance of all household tasks, taking into consideration individual schedules and preferences. Periodic allocation of household tasks will be made, in which the time involved in the performance of each party's task is equal. (reprinted in Ritzer 1974:302)

The idea of writing such a marriage contract seems bizarre to many Americans. But is it so strange? As Susan Edmiston writes, "Sitting down and writing out a contract may seem a cold and formal way of working out an intimate relationship, but often it is the only way of coping with the ghosts of 2,000 years of tradition lurking in our definitions of marriage" (1973:133).

Marriage is a contractual structuring of certain human experiences so as to support the survival of society. Traditional marriage contracts represent *tested* ways in which such experiences can be structured in the interests of group survival. The innovations of couples writing their own marriage contracts, however, is further evidence that the established institution has not always been satisfying to the individuals involved.

Having Children

The traditional American family was composed of a husband, a wife, and children—usually several of them. Several shifts have taken place with regard to the children in American families in recent years. Couples are delaying the birth of their first child, they are having fewer children, and more couples than ever are remaining childless altogether. Finally, in a different development, increasing numbers of single Americans are choosing to raise children in one-parent families. Let's look at each of these trends.

During 1960–1964, the average American newly married couple had their first child fourteen months after getting married. In 1975–1978, the average length of time was twenty-four months. The delay of childbearing can also be seen in the percentage of ever-married women aged twenty to twenty-four who have not had a child: 24 percent in 1960, 43 percent in 1977 (Wilkie 1981:583–584).

Jane Riblett Wilkie (1981) suggests a number of reasons for the trend toward delayed childbearing. In part, it results from the fact that Americans are waiting longer to get married. The availability of effective birth-control measures has made childbearing a matter of choice rather than chance. Increased female participation in education and employment are other reasons.

As Margaret Mooney Marini (1981) has pointed out, both delayed marriage and delayed parenthood result in smaller families. At the same time, attitudes toward family size have been changing substantially in America. A 1936 Gallup poll, for example, found only 29 percent of the American public saying that the ideal number of children in a family was two. In 1978, 53 percent said two (*Public Opinion* 1980c:31).

All these factors have resulted in smaller and smaller families. It is estimated that each woman in America would have to bear, on average, 2.1 children to stabilize the nation's population (excluding immigration)—taking account of the fact that some of those children will die before they have children of their own. In 1980, American women had an average of 1.9 children each, below replacement level.

A part of this low rate of childbearing is the pattern of intentional childlessness. As we'll see in Chapter 18, this goes against some firmly established agreements in American life that a woman is not "complete" until she becomes a mother and that men are not "real" men until they've fathered children. Yet, these agreements are changing.

In a different variation, increasing numbers of families are headed by single parents—created either by divorce, death, or by simple choice. Celebrities such as Vanessa Redgrave and Mia Farrow have dramatized this latter pattern—somewhat legitimating what was traditionally a source of shame for young women. But women are not the only ones carrying the whole job of parenthood. Increasingly, men are showing up at single-parent meetings, and judges no longer automatically assign custody of minor children to the mother in the case of divorce. This issue has been recently dramatized in the very popular film, *Kramer vs. Kramer.*

Here's who American children were living with in 1980:

Living with both parents	74 percent
Living with mother only	19 percent
Living with father only	3 percent
Living with neither parent	4 percent

This amounts to twelve million children living in single-parent families (U.S. Bureau of Census, 1981e:27).

Table 16-4

Unmarried Couples, by Age, 1980

Age	Men	Women
Under 25	24.5%	38.2%
25 to 34	40.8	36.2
35 to 44	13.6	8.0
45 to 64	14.7	11.8
65 and over	6.3	5.9

Source: U.S. Bureau of the Census, *Marital Living Arrangements: March 1980* (Washington, D.C.: Government Printing Office, 1981), p. 5.

Although single-parent families are more acceptable today, Sara McLanahan et al. (1981) report that these parents and their children experience more psychological distress—anxiety and depression—than does the average parent. Support networks—friends and relatives—are especially important for successful adjustment.

"Living Together"

Another recent pattern, much touted in the mass media, is the increased number of people living together as a family or quasi-family without actually being married. Although it is difficult to know exactly how many people have chosen this way of life, as of 1980, the Census Bureau (1981e:5) estimated there were 1,560,000 unmarried couples living together in the United States, triple the 1970 number.

Living together is not limited exclusively to the young. As Table 16–4 shows, 6.3 percent of the men and 5.9 percent of the women were over sixty-five years of age.

Many people living together in nonmarriage families regard the arrangement as a possible prelude to marriage itself. The purpose of such "trial marriages" is to give the couple an opportunity to learn whether they are compatible enough to enter into a more binding relation-

ship. The pattern parallels a suggestion made by Margaret Mead in 1966 when she proposed a two-stage marriage. In stage 1, a couple lives together as husband and wife but avoids having children. If they find living together satisfactory, they can move on to stage 2 and childbearing. Mead's proposal is clearly being tested although it never received serious legislative consideration. In part, the proposal and practice of trial marriage reflects a growing recognition of the difficulties of parenthood.

Divorce

The clearest evidence of dissatisfaction in marriage is divorce. In the United States, divorce is a legal and—especially for Roman Catholics—a religious matter. The legal aspect is a function of state laws, so the agreements on divorce have differed greatly around the country. In recent years, however, divorce laws have been generally liberalized. Many states have instituted a "no-fault" form of divorce in which married couples—especially if they are childless—can dissolve their marriages by mutual consent.

Our national divorce rate is evidence of one of the most radical changes in the American family during this century. In 1980, there were 2,413,000 marriages in the United States and 1,182,000 divorces or approximately half as many divorces as marriages. Contrast these figures with 1 divorce for every 11.4 marriages in 1910 (U.S. Bureau of Census 1981i:58). Figure 16–1 shows the long-term pattern of marriage, divorce, and remarriage.

You should realize that the above data do not mean that half of all marriages result in divorce. The number of divorces in 1980 were drawn from among all the marriages of previous years. Another way of looking at divorce is to compare the number of married and divorced people in the population at a given time. In 1970, for example, there were 47 divorced people for every

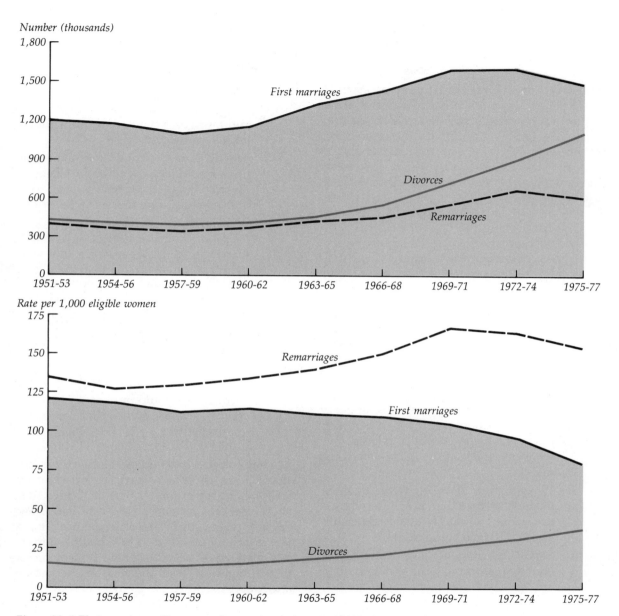

Figure 16–1 First marriages, divorces, and remarriages of women: 1950–1977, numbers and rates. Source: U.S. Bureau of Census, Social Indicators III, *Washington, D.C., Government Printing Office, 1980, p. 28.*

1,000 who were married. In 1975, there were 69 divorced people, and in 1980, there were 100—1 divorced person for every ten married people (U.S. Bureau of Census 1981i:15).

Why do people get divorced? To find the answers, we can't just accept what the contending parties told the judge. Looking at long-term trends, we find a dramatic reduction in adultery and desertion as the "official" reasons for divorces over the past century and an equally dramatic increase in mental and physical cruelty. Does that mean that there is less adultery and desertion and more cruelty among married couples? No. It points rather to a shift in what the courts have been willing to accept as adequate and proper grounds for the dissolution of marriage (Reilly 1976:5). And the advent of "no-fault" divorce laws, of course, doesn't mean the contending parties had no grievances against each other.

The divorce laws, however, act only as a gateway controlling the flow of divorces. The laws do not cause the divorces. In a recent review of the research literature on the causes of divorce, Sharon Price-Bonham and Jack Balswick (1980) reported the following findings:

1. *Income:* Couples with low income are more likely to divorce than those with high incomes. It is not clear whether low incomes cause divorce or whether it works the other way around.

2. *Race:* While blacks overall have a higher divorce rate than whites, this appears to be a function of income. When they have the same incomes, blacks and whites have essentially the same divorce rates.

3. *Working wives:* Working wives are more likely to divorce than are those who do not work, although this relationship appears to be a complex one.

4. *Education:* In general, those with less education are more likely to divorce than are those with more education, but this, too, is not altogether consistent. Factors such as age at marriage, race, and religion, for example, complicate the relationship.

5. *Age at first marriage:* The younger people are when they first marry, the more likely they are to get divorced. In part, however, this reflects the fact that lower-class people tend to marry younger than do upper-class people.

6. *Religion:* Catholics are less likely to divorce than are Protestants, and "mixed marriages" (across Protestant, Catholic, and Jewish lines) are more likely to end in divorce than are those within a particular religion.

7. *Parents' divorce:* Children from broken homes seem somewhat more likely to divorce than are those who grew up with both parents, but the evidence is not consistent.

8. *Premarital pregnancy:* Consistently, marriages that begin with the wife pregnant result in divorce more frequently than those in which the wife is not pregnant.

9. *Previous divorces:* Those people previously divorced are more likely to do it again than are those who have not previously been divorced.

10. *Loss of love:* Not surprisingly, the loss of love, friendship, and empathy for a spouse increases the likelihood of divorce.

Demographic changes have also affected the prevalence of divorce. Longer life expectancies have meant, for example, that marriages that might have been terminated by early death now may last long enough to result in divorce. Those people getting divorced in 1979 had been married an average of 6.8 years, while those divorced in 1950 had only been married an average of 5.8 years (U.S. Bureau of Census 1981i:80).

Sociologists have also studied the *consequences* of divorce for those involved. Morris Rosenberg (1965), for instance, in a study of self-image among adolescents, found that self-esteem was lower among those whose families were disrupted by divorce, and self-esteem was lowest in those cases where the mother and children were relatively young at the time of divorce. This makes sense, of course, in terms of the function that families serve for the development of self-identity, as you'll recall from Chapter 5. Rosenberg also found that children whose mothers remarried exhibited higher self-esteem than those whose mothers did not remarry.

Before automatically condemning divorce among couples with children because of its negative consequences for the children, consider the alternative: growing up in an unhappy, loveless marriage. Children run the risk of suffering whenever the parents are unable to make a happy marriage, and there is no general rule about whether "suffering through" an unhappy marriage or divorce is the better solution.

Divorce also disrupts the family's economic support function. This is particularly evident in the case of the divorced mothers of dependent children. Besides the fact that women earn less money than men, the presence of a dependent child limits the kind of work a woman can do or adds the financial burden of baby-sitters and day-care centers.

In this context, recent changes in alimony laws and practices are worth noting. Much has been written in the past about alimony as a penalty levied on ex-husbands, often seen as punishment of the "guilty" party. With the advent of no-fault divorce, however, the question of guilt has fallen away, and alimony has followed it to some extent.

Today ex-wives are getting less support and for shorter periods of time. They are expected to become self-sufficient—especially if no children are involved—rather quickly. Against a history of often repressive alimony laws, this shift can be seen as a progressive trend. Yet, like most pendulum swings, it is also an over-correction in some ways. Roger Williams (1977a:76) describes an example of the new inequities:

More common than the poor woman who becomes poorer [through divorce] has been the middle-to-high-income woman who suffers a sudden, precipitous drop in living standard. . . . There are formerly well-to-do wives working as salesladies in the chic shops where they used to buy their clothes. "After all," says an attorney who has represented such women, "an eye for fashion is about the only marketable skill they have." There are other women who worked to pay their husband's way through college or professional school and now that they're getting divorced, are having a difficult time getting the husbands to do the same for them.

Men adjust to divorce somewhat differently. They tend to devote increased time to their work, though studies indicate that divorced men are less successful occupationally than those who stay married (Price-Bonham and Balswick 1980:964).

Here are some of the things that have been found to make adjustment to divorce harder: not wanting the divorce, economic problems, children (especially young ones), and the lack of support from family and friends (Price-Bonham and Balswick 1980:964).

The debate over divorce as ultimately a healthy or an unhealthy sign for a society will not be quicky resolved. In years past, there was little debate: divorce represented a failure and was a disgrace for the persons involved, extending even to their parents and other relatives. Public acceptance of divorce has certainly liberalized over the years, however. In a 1979 NBC/Associated Press national survey, 87 percent of the respondents said they thought it all right for a couple who couldn't get along to get divorced if there were no children involved. Almost as many—72 percent—said it was all right even if there were children.

Yet even when it's the best thing that can happen for the parties involved, divorce represents the failure to establish a lasting family. And often, it is much more than that, a source of dissatisfaction, sometimes deep bitterness. Whenever the attempt at family life fails to satisfy fully, people may ponder substitutes for it altogether.

The Future of the Family

For all its problems, no one seriously predicts the disappearance of the family in America. I'm not saying it won't experience more changes, of course. As we've seen thus far in Part Four, changes in one institution ripple across other institutions as well. Women's increased participation in the labor force, inflation, and changing divorce laws are but a few of the changes we have seen reflected in family life.

When all is said and done, the family remains a fundamental institution. It was the first institution; and, if life on the planet were to be virtually destroyed by nuclear holocaust, the family would undoubtedly be the first institution to reappear.

At the same time, the form of the family in America is likely to continue changing. And those changes are going to produce controversy and be resistant as in the past. There are Americans who firmly believe that unmarried couples living together are immoral, that a woman's place is in the home, and that childless families are defective. They will attempt to enforce their views on the rest of society.

Summary

This chapter began with an examination of the basic functions served by the family as an institution. Its primary contribution to the survival of group life is in replacing group members. As we saw, this is more than a matter of sexual reproduction; it involves physical and emotional nurturance as well. Families also serve the sexual and nurturant needs of adult members. Various families in history have served many additional functions, but in modern societies most of those have been transferred to other institutions; yet the family remains essentially universal in the experience of humankind's social existence.

A variety of institutional forms appear to satisfy the functions of the family. There have been varied agreements pertaining to family composition, descent, residence, and sex roles. Different agreements work, too, as we saw in looking at the changing character of the American family.

Mate selection, we found, is governed by various agreements. In some societies, an endogamous norm requires marrying within one's kinship group, whereas in others an exogamous pattern requires marriage outside the group. In all societies, an incest taboo prohibits sexual relations among immediate family members. At the same time, we found a pattern of homogamy in mate selection, meaning that people tend to select mates similar to themselves in a variety of ways.

In the past, sexuality has largely been limited to married couples. This agreement has changed radically in American society. Both premarital and extramarital sexual activity have increased. More directly relevant to the family itself, however, is the increased popularity of trial marriages. It is possible to form and operate a family without the marriage ritual. Also, single-parent families are more common and more accepted.

No less significant is the trend toward greater sexual equality within marriage. At the same time that women have demanded equality with men in the economy and other institutions, women have increasingly rejected their traditional role within the family. One result is the framing of egalitarian marriage contracts.

The rapidly increasing divorce rate in America points to another significant change in agreements pertaining to the family. Divorce has implications both for individuals and for the functions of the family.

The family offers a prototype for the analysis of social institutions. As a means for structuring the individual's drives and experiences so as to support the survival of the group, the family exemplifies the purpose and process of all institutions. It also exemplifies the general tendency for institutions to produce dissatisfaction.

Important Terms

family
nuclear family
extended family
monogamy
polygamy
bilateral descent
matrilineal descent
patrilineal descent
neolocal
patrilocal

matrilocal
endogamy
exogamy
incest taboo
homogamy
patriarchal
matriarachal
egalitarian
instrumental functions
expressive functions

Suggested Readings

Bernard, Jessie
1972   *The Future of Marriage*. New York: Bantam.
At a time when many people are speculating about the future of the conventional norms of marriage and the family, Bernard has brought together a mass of empirical research data to provide a factual basis for such discussions. She then proceeds to draw out the implications of those data in a way that seves both those who may be contemplating marriage as well as those who are interested in studying it from a sociological point of view.

Gross, Beatrice, and Gross, Ronald, eds.
1977   *The Children's Rights Movement*. New York: Anchor Books.
Reviews the issues surrounding demand for children's rights including subjugation to parents, school and community.

Kurian, George, ed.
1979   *Cross-cultural Perspectives of Mate Selection and Marriage*. Westport, CT: Greenwood Press.
Cross-cultural comparisons of mate-selection, pre-marital sex and marriage in a number of countries. Reviews traditional patterns and change in mate selection and marriage.

Lamanna, Mary Ann, and Agnes Riedmann
1981   *Marriages and Families: Making Choices throughout the Life Cycle*. Belmont, Calif.: Wadsworth.
This is a comprehensive introduction to the sociology of the family. It is organized around the life-cycle process, so you can observe the impact of the family over the course of your life.

Queen, Stuart, Robert Habenstein, and John Adams
1974   *The Family in Various Cultures*. Philadelphia: Lippincott.
As the title suggests, this book presents an excellent cross-cultural picture of the variety of family agreements that people have created around the world and over time. This is a valuable book for sociology students, since the family is a commonly reified institution, and a healthy dose of cross-cultural disagreements enhances the kind of personal detachment that is needed in understanding the nature and functioning of social agreements.

Rappoport, Rhona, and Rappoport, Robert
1976   *Dual-career Families Re-examined*. New York: Harper & Row.
Reports on husband and wives who both work, the problems, responses, and benefits of such relationships.

Scanzoni, Letha, and John Scanzoni
1976   *Men, Women, and Change*. New York: McGraw-Hill.
Here's an up-to-date look at the nature of sex roles in the family and other institutions. With an emphasis on *human* relationships, the authors examine the life history of a family: premarital relationships, the decision to marry, the process of being married, having children, and long-term marital relations. Like the Bernard book mentioned above, this one is useful from both personal and professional points of view.

Skolnick, Arlene
1978   *The Intimate Environment: Exploring Marriage and the Family*, 2nd ed. Boston: Little, Brown.

Earlier in this chapter we noted that a key function of families is to provide sexual security for adults. As an institution, the family offers a vehicle for satisfying the sexual urges of individuals in a way that (1) holds sexual competition in check and (2) turns sexual urges to a social purpose of replacement. In principle, this aspect of the family seems to represent a typical institutional trade-off. In exchange for sexual security, individuals accept sexual restrictions and limitations. For example, husbands and wives can be assured of having each other, but they cannot have anyone else.

A simplistic view of American sexual history would suggest that men and women have accepted the institutional trade-off until very recently. A closer look, however, contradicts this view. At least since the beginning of this century, American men and women in surprisingly large numbers have sought sexual satisfaction outside of marriage. Let's look at some of the research that's been done on American sexuality.

At the opening of this century, Henry Havelock Ellis created a national uproar through his studies of human sexuality—ordinary and extraordinary. Though Ellis produced no statistics on the incidence of various sexual behaviors, his seven volumes of case studies—derived from medical journals, correspondence, and other sources—depicted the varieties of sexual expression among early twentieth-century Americans and debunked many post-Victorian sexual myths. Masturbation, he found, was common—among both boys and girls—and nobody seemed to have gone blind from it. In general, he found women to be sexual creatures, in stark contrast to the Victorian image. Impotence and frigidity were more psychological than physiological, he discovered, a point made about most sexual disorders in general more than a half-century later by William Masters and Virginia Johnson in their well-researched book, *Human Sexual Response* (1966).

During the late 1920s, Dr. G. V. Hamilton provided some quantitative data in support of Ellis's findings. A New York psychiatrist, Hamilton surveyed 200 married men and women among his patients, most of them young to middle-aged, educated whites in New York. Among the admittedly unrepresentative sample, 97 percent of the men and 75 percent of the women reported having masturbated. A majority, moreover, appear to have continued after marriage. Twenty-nine percent of the men and 24 percent of the women reported having had extramarital sex (Easton 1975:977–989).

At about the same time that Hamilton was studying his marital patients, Dr. Katherine Davis was undertaking a national survey of 2,200 married and unmarried women. Again, the respondents were predominantly young, educated, and white. By today's standards, Davis's respondents seem conservative regarding premarital sex, though they evidenced no double standard. Twenty-one percent said a young man might be justified in having sex before marriage, and 19 percent said that for women. Was extramarital sex ever justified? A similar pattern emerged: 24 percent said yes for men, 21 percent for women.

With regard to family planning, the women's responses seem surprisingly liberal, however, even granting the cosmopolitan nature of the sample. Ninety percent favored contraception in principle, and nearly three-fourths of the married women reported practicing it. Sixty-three percent favored making birth-control information available to unmarried people, and a surprising 72 percent approved of abortion.

Davis's data on masturbation accorded with the findings of both Ellis and Hamilton: 65 percent of the unmarried and 40 percent of the married women said they masturbated. One-fourth of the single women reported that they had had an overt homosexual experience (Easton 1975:978–79). By the late 1920s, then, the evidence was mounting that the theoretical stereotype of American sexuality was not altogether reflected in behavior.

In 1948, Americans publicly began to lose their sexual innocence, with the publication of Dr. Alfred Kinsey's research on the sexual behavior of American males, based on some 5,300 interviews. Like the sex studies before it, the Kinsey report (Kinsey 1948) provided sometimes shocking data on sexual behavior. Male masturbation was again found to be virtually universal. Substantial percentages reported premarital and extramarital sex. In purely descriptive data, Kinsey broke new ground by reporting on homosexuality (one-third of males had some homosexual leanings, and perhaps 13 percent were predominantly homosexual) and sexual relations with animals (8 percent of all the respondents, with much higher percentages among farm boys).

Kinsey also broke new ground with his analytical findings—in particular examining the relationship between sexual behavior and social class. The differences separating upper- and lower-class men were many. For example, nudity, petting, and masturbation were far more acceptable among the upper-class respondents than among the lower-class ones, whereas lower-class respondents were more likely than their wealthier counterparts to patronize prostitutes and to have premarital sexual relations. Among those who went to college, for example, some 7 percent reported having premarital intercourse, compared with 84 percent of those who went as far as high school only and 98 percent of those who did not go beyond grade school.

Kinsey also shed light on the functions of marriage in providing a sexual outlet for the partners. Overall, he estimated, marriage provided perhaps 85 percent of the married male's sexual outlet, with the remaining 15 percent coming from masturbation, nocturnal emissions, extramarital affairs, animals, and the like. Even this was affected by social class, however, with upper-strata men receiving a lower proportion of their expression from their marriages. Finally, Kinsey estimated that about half of the married men had extramarital sex at least once during their marriages (Easton 1975:980-83).

Five years later, Kinsey fired his second broadside—this time on female sexuality (Kinsey 1953). Like Davis's study, the Kinsey report flew in the face of the hard-dying, Victorian view of nonsexual womanhood. Kinsey's interviews with nearly 6,000 women indicated that two-thirds had experienced orgasm before marriage. One-sixth of those had done so through sexual intercourse. Two-thirds of his respondents reported having masturbated and further reported reaching orgasm 95 percent of the time. Within marriage the success rate of intercourse was about three-fourths.

One-fourth of Kinsey's female respondents reported extramarital intercourse. Twenty-eight percent had had homosexual experiences by the time they were forty-five, and Kinsey's data suggested that such experiences were more common among upper-class women.

Overall, the second Kinsey report described the human female as eminently sexual. From childhood through old age, females had sexual urges that they expressed and satisfied in various ways. By the time they were thirty-five, 90 percent had achieved orgasm and 98 percent had experienced sexual arousal. "Frigidity," then, was rare, and Kinsey suggested that much of it was a consequence of male inability. Like its predecessor, the second Kinsey report was condemned by the pillars of society—and it was a popular success (Easton 1975:983-86).

Where do we stand today? A representative sample of American adults in 1973–1974 pointed to further liberalization of sexual behavior. As an indication, three-fourths of the single women in the sample had had intercourse before their twenty-fifth birthday, and half of those who married before twenty-five had had premarital sex. Anal and oral sex appear to have become much more popular than in the past, sex with animals has decreased, and masturbation appears to have retained its timeless popularity (Easton 1975:989-91).

The 1973–1974 survey also examined "mate swapping" and found it more talk than action. Though the press has titillated its consumers with tales of swinging couples joining together for small-scale dalliances or full-blown orgies, only about 2 percent of the married respondents reported ever participating in mate swapping. And though 13 percent of the married men and 2 percent of the married women reported having engaged in "multiple-partner" sex, most of those occasions seem to have occurred before marriage, and most of the participants seem to have tried it only once (Easton 1975:989-91).

In a survey of University of Wisconsin students and college-age nonstudents living in Madison, Wisconsin, J. D. DeLamater and P. MacCorquodale (1979) asked respondents whether they had ever engaged in various premarital sexual behaviors and the age at which they had their first experience. Table 16–5 presents their findings.

Several factors affect the likelihood of people engaging in premarital sex. Past experience, of course, provides encouragement for current activity. People are more likely to engage in various premarital sexual activities if their friends report doing so. Also, the length and quality of a relationship both increase the likelihood of sexual activity. Finally, for young people, their parents' attitudes also have an impact (Clayton and Bokemeier 1980).

Attitudes about premarital sexual behavior seem to have been shifting along with shifts in the behavior itself. In 1939, for example, the great majority of both men and women characterized premarital sex as either "wicked" or "unfortunate." More recent surveys by Gallup and by the National Opinion Research Center indicate a growing acceptance of this increasingly popular practice. In three recent years, the percentages saying that premarital sex was *not wrong* were: 23 percent in 1969, 51 percent in 1972, and 59 percent in 1978 (*Public Opinion* 1978b:36).

Attitudes toward extramarital sex are generally more conservative, however. In 1973, 85 percent of a national sample of Americans said extramarital sex was always or almost always wrong. In 1980, the figure was 87 percent (*Public Opinion* 1980b:38). In a survey of students at a New England college, David Weis and Michael Slosnerick (1981) found only 15 percent who characterized extramarital sex as acceptable in a set of hypothetical examples.

In summary, during the course of the century, there has clearly been a steady liberalization of both attitudes and behavior in our sexuality. In the process of that trend, however, behavior seems to have led attitudes. Americans by and large have been likely to engage in premarital sex, for example, and then to approve of it. The same has been true of extramarital sex, homosexuality, masturbation, and so forth. And as the earliest studies showed, Americans were never as prudish in their sexual behavior as people have generally thought.

Table 16-5

Premarital Sexual Experiences of College-Age Men and Women, and Age of First Experience

Activity	Men				Women			
	Student		Nonstudent		Student		Nonstudent	
	%	Age	%	Age	%	Age	%	Age
Necking	97	14.2	98	13.9	99	14.8	99	14.9
French kissing	93	15.3	95	15.1	95	15.8	95	16.0
Breast fondling	92	15.8	92	15.5	93	16.6	93	16.6
Male/female genitals	86	16.6	87	16.3	82	17.2	86	17.5
Female/male genitals	82	16.6	84	16.7	78	17.4	81	17.8
Genital apposition	77	17.1	81	16.8	72	17.6	78	17.9
Intercourse	75	17.5	79	17.2	60	17.9	72	18.3
Male oral/female genitals	60	18.2	68	17.7	59	18.1	67	18.6
Female oral/male genitals	61	18.1	70	17.8	54	18.1	63	18.8

Source: J. D. DeLamater and P. MacCorquodale, *Premarital Sexuality: Attitudes, Relationships, Behavior* (Madison: University of Wisconsin Press, 1979), p. 59.

PRACTICING SOCIOLOGY

As we've seen in this chapter, the single-parent family has become increasingly common and accepted in American society. As a part of the phenomena, Georgia Dullea speaks of a new breed of "supermother":

> seemingly self-sufficient women in their 30s who are choosing to combine careers with child rearing in a home where there is no father and no serious talk of marriage. . . .
>
> Whatever the psychology underlying a woman's decision to rear a child alone, it is far easier to do so today because of certain social changes: more working women financially able to support a child; more support systems for the single-parent family; more parents divorcing so that a child growing up without a father at home does not feel so out of place at school.

What are some other social changes that have made it easier for a single parent to raise children today? What obstacles still remain in terms of the other institutions of society?

Source: Georgia Dullea, "Why They Want to Raise Their Children Alone," *San Francisco Chronicle*, December 18, 1981, p. 55.

17

Rural and Urban Society

In the latter part of the twentieth century, to talk about "society" is to talk about urban society, about city life. Certainly in the United States, most people have a direct, personal experience of city living, and there is hardly anyone who has not experienced it at least vicariously, through the mass media. Three out of every four Americans now live in urban areas. And we are hardly the most urbanized country on the planet. (See Tables 17–1 and 17–2.)

Because of the general urbanism of contemporary human existence, much of what I've said in previous chapters has related to urban society. In this chapter, I want to focus directly on this aspect of modern life, which has become the fabric of living rather than an object within it. We're going to look at how cities arose and how they grew. Then we'll compare the nature of rural and urban life, including an examination of what many call the "crisis of the cities."

Throughout this discussion, I'll be explaining the concepts and tools that sociologists have developed for the analysis of rural and urban society. As we'll see, the development of urban society and the development of urban sociology have gone hand in hand.

The Development of Cities

A city is a large aggregation of people in a densely populated area, but "how many people" and "how densely populated" are matters of arbitrary definition. For its bookkeeping, the United States census defines a city as an incorporated area with 2,500 or more residents. As sociologists use the term, however, no population size can define a city. A "city" is a form of social organization, the existence of which is related to population size and density but is not synonymous with them. Sociologists speak of **urbanism** as the experience of city life and **urbanization** as the process by which increased proportions of a population live in cities.

Table 17-1

World's Most Populous Urban Areas

Rank	Metropolitan area City and country	Population	Year
1	Tokyo, Japan	28,637,000	1980 estimate
2	**New York City, U.S.**	16,120,000	1980 census
3	Osaka, Japan	15,527,000	1980 estimate
4	Mexico City, Mexico	14,750,200	1979 estimate
5	São Paulo, Brazil	12,708,600	1980 census
6	London, U.K.	12,074,600	1981 census
7	Cairo, Egypt	12,000,000	1980 estimate
8	Rhine-Ruhr, West Germany	11,777,800	1980 estimate
9	**Los Angeles, U.S.**	11,496,200	1980 census
10	Shanghai, China	11,320,000	1980 estimate
11	Buenos Aires, Argentina	10,796,000	1980 estimate
12	Calcutta, India	9,165,700	1981 census
13	Rio de Janeiro, Brazil	9,153,500	1980 census
14	Paris, France	8,765,500	1980 estimate
15	Beijing, China	8,706,000	1980 estimate
16	Seoul, South Korea	8,367,000	1980 census
17	Bombay, India	8,202,800	1981 census
18	Moscow, U.S.S.R.	8,015,000	1981 estimate
19	**Chicago, U.S.**	7,868,200	1980 census
20	Nagoya, Japan	7,461,000	1980 estimate
21	Tianjin, China	7,390,000	1980 estimate
22	Jakarta, Indonesia	6,556,000	1981 estimate
23	Chongqing, China	6,000,000	1978 estimate
24	Manila, Philippines	5,900,600	1979 estimate
25	**Philadelphia, U.S.**	5,548,800	1980 census

Source: Reprinted with permission from the 1982 *Britannica Book of the Year*, copyright 1982 by Encyclopedia Britannica, Inc., Chicago, Ill., p. 360.

What a city *is* can best be seen in comparison with what noncities—towns and villages—are. Most simply put, a city is organized as a *gesellschaft*; it does not have the *gemeinschaft* character of towns and villages (as discussed in Chapter 6). Most urban interactions are secondary rather than primary. City dwellers depend on countless people whom they don't know by name and may never see face to face, whereas small-town residents are all likely to know one another.

The Preindustrial City

Gideon Sjoberg (1965:27), a leading historian on the preindustrial city, gives this picture of the origin of cities:

As far as is known, the world's first cities took shape around 3500 B.C. in the Fertile Crescent, the eastern segment of which includes Mesopotamia: the valleys of the Tigris and the Euphrates. Not only were the soil and water supply there

Table 17-2

Worldwide Urbanization, Selected Countries

Country	Percent of population living in urban areas
Burundi	2
Rwanda	4
Nepal	5
Upper Volta	8
Mozambique	8
North Yemen	10
Bangladesh	10
Ethiopia	14
Democratic Kampuchea	14
Chad	18
Vietnam	19
Iraq	72
United States	74
Venezuela	76
United Kingdom	77
Japan	76
France	78
Argentina	82
Sweden	83
Australia	86
Netherlands	88
Israel	89
Hong Kong	90
Belgium	95
Macao	98
Singapore	100
World	37

Source: Population Reference Bureau, "1982 World Population Data Sheet," Washington, D.C.

Note: Individual countries have determined which areas are *urban*. Estimates refer to some point in 1970s.

the cities they've visited. Yet, cities have always been more than just crossroads of life on the move. They have been the anchoring points of civilization, the seats of commerce—first agricultural, then industrial. They have been the centers of learning, government, religion, and culture.

Cities have not always been supportive of change, however. Kingsley Davis (1955:430) suggests that the very earliest cities probably had a "stultifying effect on cultural progress," attributing that to "the unproductive insulation and excessive power of the urban elite." Davis continues: "There is no doubt that the religio-magical traditionalism of the early cities was profound."

It is useful to grasp how tenuously the earliest cities clung to existence. Even with the potential and much-discussed bankruptcy of several modern American cities, we still tend to regard cities as firmly established, invincible, and perpetual. In fact, the earliest "cities" hardly cast that sort of shadow. To begin, the first cities were relatively small: Davis estimates the legendary city of Ur probably had a population of around 5,000. This was so because of the inefficiency of agriculture. Davis estimates (1955:432) that in the ancient cities of Egypt and Mesopotamia, fifty to ninety farmers were required to support one person living in a city. When you add the difficulty of transportation, it was necessary for all the people supporting cities to live nearby, and the ancient cities were ringed by farms and by various craftspeople.

Davis describes some of the innovations that allowed urban development to break out of the barriers to expansion:

If urbanization was to escape its early limitations, it had to do so in a new region, a region more open to innovation and new conceptions. As it turned out, the region that saw a later and greater urban development was farther north, the Greco-Roman world of Europe, flourishing approximately during the period from 600 B.C. to 400 A.D. Iron tools and weapons, alphabetic writing,

suitable; the region was a crossroads that facilitated repeated contacts among peoples of divergent cultures for thousands of years.

Cities have served as crossroads for people from diverse backgrounds ever since. Traders, nomads, and soldiers have all left a mark on

The city, as a social innovation, has arisen independently all around the world. Examples range from Machu Picchu, Peru, part of the preindustrial Incan civilization high in the Andes . . .

improved sailboats, cheap coinage, more democratic institutions, systematic colonization—all tended to increase production, stimulate trade, and expand the effective political unit. Towns and cities became more numerous, the degree of urbanization greater. A few cities reached a substantial size. Athens, at its peak in the fifth century B.C., achieved a population of between 120,000 and 180,000. Syracuse and Carthage were perhaps larger.*

In terms of sheer size during the preindustrial period, Greek cities and then Rome were

the clear leaders, and Rome was the leader of the two. The Roman city was a part of the Roman imperial system of conquest and tribute. With massive support pouring in from all over the known world, Rome and Constantinople were able to sustain populations of several hundred thousands. Yet, as Davis points out, they were not able to survive:

They were not able to resist conquest by far less urbanized outsiders. The eclipse of cities in Europe was striking. Commerce declined to the barest minimum; each locale became isolated and virtually self-sufficient; the social system congealed into a hereditary system. When finally towns and cities began to revive, they were small, as the following estimates suggest: Florence (1338), 90,000; Venice (1422), 190,000; Antwerp (sixteenth cen-

*Kingsley Davis, "Origin and Growth of Urbanization in the World," *American Journal of Sociology* 60 (1955):432. Copyright ©1955 by the University of Chicago. Reprinted by permission.

. . . to Daly City, California.

tury), 200,000; London (1377), 30,000; Nuremberg (1450), 20,165; Frankfurt (1440), 8,719.*

The Industrial Revolution

The development of what we have come to know as cities depended in part on *changes* and improvements. Agriculture became more efficient, so fewer farmers were needed to support each city dweller. Transportation improved, so the farms could be farther from town, and cities were better able to serve as crossroads for com-

*Kingsley Davis, "Origin and Growth of Urbanization in the World," *American Journal of Sociology* 60 (1955):433. Copyright ©1955 by the University of Chicago. Reprinted by permission.

merce. Defense systems improved. All these things supported the development of cities as a persistent form of social life. But more was needed; it took a *transformation* for cities to appear and take hold as we now know them.

The Industrial Revolution was the transformation responsible for the establishment of permanent cities in the modern sense. It is not possible to specify a date for the first shot fired in this revolution, but it was largely a creature of the eighteenth century, especially in England. Throughout the century, manufacturing was coming of age. Increasingly, groups of workers were gathered together to produce goods in large number and in a systematic fashion. In the imagery of H. G. Wells's classic *Outline of History* (1920:685):

Hitherto, throughout the whole course of history from the beginnings of civilization, manufactures, building, and industries generally had been in the hands of craftsmen and small masters who worked in their own houses. They had been organized in guilds, and were mostly their own employers. They formed an essential and permanent middle class. There were capitalists among them, who let out looms and the like, supplied material, and took the finished product, but they were not big capitalists. There had been no rich manufacturers. The rich men of the world before this time had been great landowners or money-lenders and money manipulators or merchants. But in the eighteenth century, workers in certain industries began to be collected together into factories in order to produce things in larger quantities through a systematic division of labour, and the employer, as distinguished from the master worker, began to be a person of importance.

The Industrial Revolution had two main foundations. One was mechanical. A still-continuing string of inventions, largely involving energy, made it possible. First, water power was captured to drive the machines in the cotton and other factories. Watt's invention of the steam engine in 1765 was a giant step forward; the adaptation of coal as the fuel for steam engines was another step. Even today, we find ourselves in the midst of the never-ending energy dilemma created by the Industrial Revolution. We have totally adjusted our social existence to the harnessing of petroleum-based energy sources in the environment, and we have locked ourselves to the twin problems of resource and result: getting enough of the energy raw material (such as oil) and what to do with the by-products of its use (such as pollution).

Invention, however, has been only one of the foundations of the Industrial Revolution. The other, as we saw earlier, was social. The Industrial Revolution both sparked and required a revolution in social organization. It required innovations in the structuring of face-to-face interactions in production, a topic discussed at length in Chapter 13 in connection with the world of work. And, as the quotation from H.

G. Wells indicated, it both sparked and required a broader-scale, societywide revolution in property and power.

The Postindustrial City

The city of the Industrial Revolution was a different creature from those that preceded it. It was not the end of the line, however. The modern city of today is not simply a more industrialized version of cities of the nineteenth century, any more than they were simply larger towns than those before. Another transformation is under way, and we are living in the midst of it. Those of us living in, say, American cities of today stand with one foot in industry and one in what has been called the **postindustrial society.**

In Chapter 13, we saw that employment has shifted significantly from manufacturing to service industries. The modern city dweller is far less likely to be a factory worker than to be a secretary, salesperson, or professional. For the most part, this occupational switch has grown out of the logistical needs of cities and their hundreds of thousands or millions of residents. It is too early to judge the long-term implications of this transformation—much less predict what will follow.

To see the urban process in more concrete detail, as well as the sociological perspectives that have been brought to bear on it, we turn now to the American experience of cities.

The American Experience

Beginning with toehold settlements in Jamestown and Plymouth, the New World colonies had developed five cities by the time of independence: Boston, Newport, New York, Philadelphia, and Charleston. As Kramer and Holborn (1970:37) point out, many of the leaders of the agitation resulting in the War of Independence were from those cities, even though the great majority of early Americans lived in the country.

Following the war, the cities grew to meet the needs of nationhood. From the start, however, American urban development differed from that of Europe. Whereas France had Paris and England had London, no single American city became the clear center of all activity. Philadelphia was the center of banking and government for a time, while New York was the center of commerce.

By the second half of the twentieth century, the concentration of population in cities had given rise to a new creature in the northeastern United States and in other places around the world. *"Bosnywash"* was the name given to the 600-mile urban strip grown out of Boston, Hartford, New York, Newark, Trenton, Philadelphia, Baltimore, and Washington —and now stretching all the way from southern Maine through central Virginia. French geographer Jean Gottman revived the name of an ancient Greek city, **megalopolis** (meaning "the great city") to describe the new urban animal.

Elsewhere in the United States, megalopolises are forming around Chicago, across the Florida peninsula, between Seattle and Portland, and from San Diego to San Francisco (see Figure 17–1). Quite aside from sheer size and greater complexity, these supercities create new problems of governance, especially when they cross state boundaries.

Since it is possible to oversimplify the emergence of megalopolises, a word of caution is in order. First, you should realize that none of the megalopolises mentioned has actually become a single city. All comprise politically independent municipalities. Second, even *Bosnywash* contains rural pockets: farms, woods, and trees. In other words, the term "megalopolis" still describes a potential more than a reality. Its potential, however, is significant enough to demand our serious attention. To simply allow megalopolises to happen by chance and without forethought—the pattern until now—is to court disaster.

The description of American urbanization presented so far is itself something of an oversimplification. The steady growth in size and numbers of cities is only a part of the story, and recent decades have drawn our attention to other—somewhat countervailing—trends. First, there have always been residential settlements on the peripheries of cities—now popularly referred to as "suburbs," a term having no precise, agreed-upon meaning.

Berry and Kasarda (1977) present data to indicate that the growth of American suburbs has exceeded that of cities at least since the 1920s, but popular as well as sociological attention didn't focus directly on them until after World War II. In part, the heavy demand for housing at the close of the war led to the development of large housing projects, referred to as "Levittowns," named after the first such community, built in 1947 on the edge of New York City, just thirty miles from Times Square. It was a mass-produced, assembly-line community.

At mid-century, the growth of urbanization was a constant feature in American life. In 1950, for example, 36 percent of the population lived in rural areas (towns of less than 2,500). By 1960, this was reduced to 30.1 percent; by 1970, it was 26.5 percent. Beginning in the 1970s, a more radical countertrend has appeared: migration from metropolitan to nonmetropolitan areas, from the city to the country. Between 1970 and 1973, metropolitan counties grew 2.9 percent, while nonmetropolitan counties grew 4.2 percent—the first time in the century that rural America has grown more than the cities (Beale, 1975:197). By the end of the decade, 26.3 percent of the population lived in rural communities (U.S. Bureau of Census 1981i:25).

Rural America

As urban as we've become, it's easy to forget how much the United States was an agrarian society in the past. As Richard Bushman (1981:238) points out, there were only twenty-

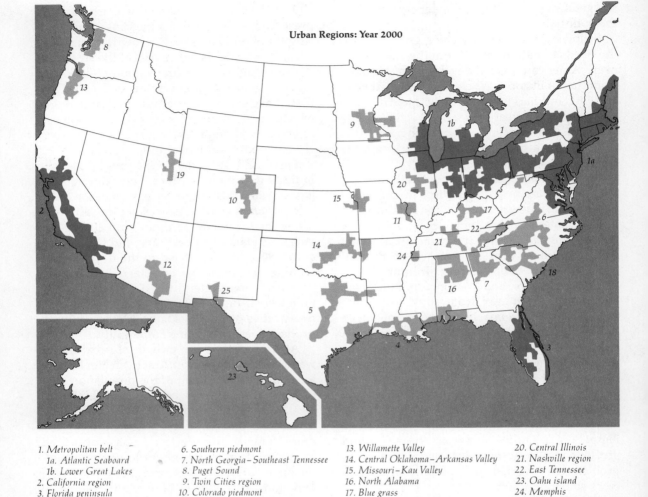

Figure 17–1 Anticipated American megalopolises in the year 2000 (based on two-child family projection). Source: Presidential Commission on Population Growth and the American Future, 1972.

four places in the country with more than 2,500 population at the time of the first national census in 1790. According to the 1790 census, 5 percent of the nation's population lived in those urban centers (U.S. Bureau of Census, 1960:9). As we've seen earlier, just under three-fourths of the nation lives in urban areas today.

The transition from country to city occurred in two ways. For some people, it was simply a matter of watching their hometown grow large. For others, it involved picking up stakes and moving to the city. In both cases, the transition required substantial shifts in social and psychological patterns. Bushman (1981:238) suggests that the most significant feature was separation from the land:

> The most elemental change, affecting all who left the farm, shopkeepers and transportation workers as well as factory hands, was separation from the land. For the traditional peasant, land was a source of nearly every human need—nourishment, warmth, clothing. Landowners derived income from their property during illness and old age. Land was both subsistence and security. Planning for a season, a life, or coming generations turned on the acquisition and use of land. The industrial work discipline may have disrupted familiar work rhythms, but separation from the soil jeopardized survival itself.

In a study of life on the American farm between 1920 and 1955, Joann Vanek (1980) reviewed a number of independent studies to construct a composite picture. The workweek was six days long, with Sunday off except for essential chores. Both husband and wife worked about eleven hours a day on a variety of tasks. For most farmers, the amount of work did not vary much with the season. While there was no field work to be done during the winter, that was a time when the livestock required more attention, making up the difference. Vanek (1980:425) was particularly interested in the division of labor between men and women:

> Although the length of the workday was identical for husbands and wives on the farm, there was a sharp division of tasks. Housekeeping and family care were women's work. Farmers spent only about two hours a week in domestic tasks, and this was mainly in carrying wood and pumping water. . . . Child care was rarely shared. Only one-fourth of the fathers with children under six years of age spent any time caring for children; the average amount of time was two and one-half hours a week.

Overall, then, the farm wife was responsible for the home and family, while the husband was responsible for the farm. At the same time, Vanek (1980: 425) found wives spent about ten hours a week on farm work. Rather than simply assisting their husbands, however, they tended to have specific jobs they were responsible for. Here's a partial listing of who did what on the typical farm:

Women
  Garden work
  Caring for poultry
  Washing the milking equipment
  Selling eggs, butter, and garden produce

Men
  Field work
  Caring for livestock
  Cleaning the barn and chicken coop

Both
  Milking

Vanek finds some support for the popular image of the farm family "gathered around the hearth in the evening popping corn and telling stories." At least, family members spent a lot of time together: working in the fields and in the barn, eating their meals together and spending a little time afterward to talk, and gathering in the evening to listen to the radio, play phonograph records, or play musical instruments together.

In 1920, when the Census Bureau first began identifying the farm population separately from the rest of rural America, 30 percent of the nation lived on farms. Sixty years later, in 1980, only 2.7 percent of the population lived on farms. Just over 6 million Americans made their homes on farms, defined technically as "all persons living in rural territory or places which had, or normally had, sales of agricultural products of $1,000 or more during the reporting year" (U.S. Bureau of Census 1981g:1).

The exodus from farms has been especially dramatic for blacks. Figure 17–2 presents the declining farm population, separately for blacks and whites. In 1920, nearly half the blacks in America lived on farms—mostly in the South. By 1980, less than 1 percent remained.

The family forms the focus of the traditional farm. Recent years have seen a shift from the family farm to large-scale agribusiness, with the family replaced by a corporation.

Although the numbers of Hispanics in the farm population has increased in recent years, they are—as a group—underrepresented on farms. In 1980, Hispanics were 5.9 percent of the total United States population but only 1.9 percent of the farm population (U.S. Bureau of Census 1981g:2).

Of course, a significant sector of the Hispanic population is very heavily involved in agriculture—pointing to an important shift in American agriculture and rural life. While our traditional image of country life involves family farms and sleepy villages, much of modern American agriculture goes by the name **agribusiness.** Extremely large farms—thousands of acres—are tilled and harvested by hired hands and expensive, heavy equipment. The box enti-

tled, "Cow No. 598" describes the agribusiness version of a livestock farm.

Agribusiness producers are only a part of the picture. Where the traditional farmer took a portion of the farm's produce to market, much agricultural marketing today is carried on by giant organizations. Minnesota's Cargill company, for example, is the largest privately owned company (not corporation) in America; in fact, its sales rank eighteenth among *all* American firms. Cargill is also the largest agribusiness company in the world (Moskowitz et al. 1980:86–87):

Through their hands go as much as a quarter of the corn and wheat exported from the United States, making Cargill the biggest single contrib-

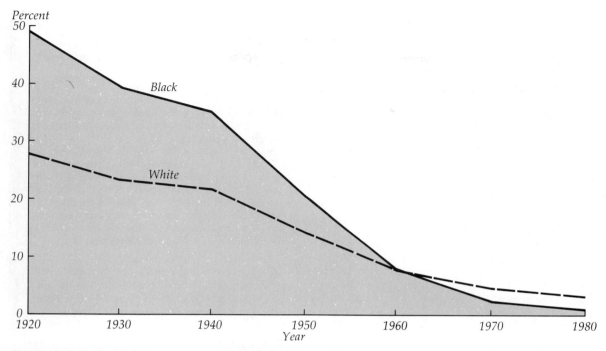

Figure 17–2 Declining farm population, by race. Percent of population living on farms, 1920 to 1980. Source: U.S. Bureau of Census, Farm Population of the United States: 1980, *Washington, D.C.: Government Printing Office, 1981, Series P–20, No. 365. Graph taken from cover.*

utor to the plus side of the U.S. balance of trade ledger. Cargill operates on an enormous scale. They have access to $1 billion of prime-rate credit to finance grain purchases. Their 140 foreign subsidiaries and affiliates run plants and offices in 38 countries. They own and lease 5,000 rail cars, 500 river barges, and 14 ocean-going ships. Each of their 345 storage elevators can hold enough grain to make six loaves of bread for every person in the United States; together they hold a total of 300 million bushels of grain.

These and related changes in agriculture and rural life have generated considerable controversy. As we'll see in Chapter 18, America has become more productive at the same time that the number of people engaged in agriculture has declined radically. The nature of that productivity has raised both nutritional and environmental debates. Much of the controversy, however, has centered on changes in the qual-

ity of life as we have shifted from a rural to an urban society. Let's turn now to the study of urban life.

Urban Ecology, Urban Crisis

This section starts with a discussion of the "Chicago school"—a term used in reference to a university (the University of Chicago), an era (the 1920s and 1930s), and a group of scholars (to be introduced shortly). As we'll see, the Chicago school represented an influential approach to the sociological study of urban life, and its influence is still present, though sociologists since then have taken other approaches to the subject. Once we've examined the various sociological perspectives on urban society, we'll turn our attention to the problems of cit-

Cow No. 598

On the traditional farm, the small herd of cows was milked by hand every morning and then put out to pasture for the day. Early in the evening, the young people from the family—typically the boys—would be sent out to find and bring in the herd. Once they were brought into the barn, each cow with its own stall, the evening milking would be done. Some grain would be given to the cows as a supplement to their grazing.

At the proper time of the year, the farmer would have each of the cows bred, either using his own bull or hiring one. When the calves arrived, they would nurse from their mothers for awhile and then be weaned. The farmer would have to decide—based on family financial needs as much as anything—whether to raise a calf to maturity or sell it.

By contrast, hear how Milton Moskowitz et al. (1980:97) describe the modern dairy "farm."

Calf No. 598 first opened her wide brown eyes on a spring afternoon in 1974. She had a brief glimpse of her mother, No. 411. It was her first and last contact with the big black-and-white spotted Holstein. Her sire, the champion bull named Dauntless, No. 598 would never meet. No matter; her mother had never met Dauntless either. He was selected for her by a computer crammed with data on dairy cow genetics. Conception was by artificial insemination.

The new calf was taken to a calf pen and spent her first few weeks of life in a tiny enclosure—one of many, arranged in row after row. Her mom (No. 411) went back to work immediately.

No. 598 grew fast and progressed to a bigger calf pen, then to a corral. Like her mother, she never roamed green pastures in search of tender grass and clover. Her feed, laboratory-tested, came to her in the troughs of a feeding corral. . . .

Twice each 24 hours No. 598 trotted from corral to milking barn, so cluttered with gleaming metal machinery and plastic tubing that there was barely room for the cows and the laborers who, working at frenzied speed, washed udders, attached and detached milking suction cups, regulated machinery, and dispensed feed via devices calibrated to give each cow the optimal ration for her maximum output.

On the traditional farm, a cow that continued producing milk year after year was prized indeed. By the end of her time, she had become a real member of the family. Not so for No. 598.

When the computer at last showed No. 598's yearly milk output dropping, she was culled from the herd. She could still be giving enough to satisfy the dairyman of two decades ago but no matter, the inexorable logic of cost-profit ratios dictated No. 598's end. Although cows can live into their twenties, No. 598 was only six years old when she made her final contribution to the nation's food supply, as dairy beef.

Source: Milton Moskowitz, Michael Katz, and Robert Levering, eds., *Everybody's Business: An Almanac* (San Francisco: Harper and Row, 1980) p. 97.

ies—seeing, in the process, that urban life has both pluses and minuses, with the two often wed to one another.

Human Ecology

Albert Hunter (1980) accounts for the rise of the "Chicago School" of sociology using two factors. First was the incredible growth of Chicago itself. Incorporated as a city in 1837 with a population of 10,000, Chicago had grown to 1,000,000 by the Columbian Exposition of 1893. Then came the founding of the "instant university" in 1892. Created as a graduate research institution, the University's founders immediately set about raiding the nation's better universities, luring a prestigious faculty to the new industrial center of the Midwest. Among these, sociologist Robert Park urged his students to regard the "City as a Laboratory." And so they did.

Aside from their influence on the study of urban social interaction, the sociologists of the Chicago school fostered an interest in looking at **human ecology,** looking at the city as an ecological unit, with interrelated parts. As Robert Park said in his 1926 presidential address before the American Sociological Society:

> Ecology, in so far as it seeks to describe the actual distribution of plants and animals over the earth's surface, is in some very real senses a geographical science. Human ecology, as the sociologists would like to use the term, is, however, not identical with geography, nor even with human geography. It is not man, but the community; not man's relation to the earth which he inhabits, but his relations to other men, that concern us most.

Sociologists needed, Park continued, to examine the structure, the growth, and the changes in modern American urban centers. He saw the modern city as being organized around the marketplace. This characteristic largely determined the distribution of businesses, residences, and interactions.

To develop a portrait of the city as an ecological unit, members of the Chicago school wove together the findings from their on-location examinations of the different faces of the city: ghettos, boardinghouses, red-light districts, and so forth. Out of this process came one of the best-known products of the Chicago school—Burgess's concentric zone theory of urban expansion as it applied to Chicago (see Figure 17–3).

For Burgess, Chicago's commercial Loop served as the hub for several concentrically arranged social bands. Nearest the central business district (zone 1) was the deteriorating residential area (zone 2) containing the city's slums. Social class increased the farther one moved from the hub: the working class lived in zone 3, the middle class in zone 4, and the urban fringe of the commuters in zone 5, where the suburbs were located. Burgess cautioned that

Robert Park
1864–1944
Harveyville, Pennsylvania

Some Important Works
Introduction to the Science of Sociology, with Ernest Burgess (Chicago: University of Chicago Press, 1921).
Collected Papers of Robert Ezra Park, ed. Everett Hughes, 3 vols. (Glencoe, Ill.: Free Press, 1950–1955).

Sociology was essentially a second career for Park; journalism was the first, although Park himself did not necessarily distinguish the two. He saw sociology as the reporting of "big news," and he was most interested by those issues that also figured importantly in the real world.

One of Park's chief interests was race relations, and he served for a time as an assistant to Booker T. Washington, learning about the situation of blacks in America and traveling with Washington through Europe. Following a full academic career at the University of Chicago, Park returned once more to the on-site study of race relations, traveling around the world in the pursuit.

Another major theme running through Park's work was the "city," a vehicle he used to uncover various aspects of human nature. Park is probably best remembered for his work, with colleague Ernest Burgess, in the development of "human ecology," the analysis of the sociogeographical organization of cities. He was the chief creator of this aspect of the "Chicago school."

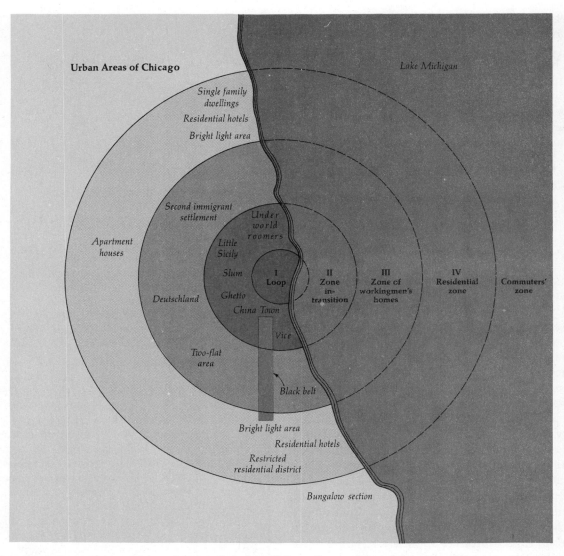

Figure 17–3 Burgess's concentric zone point of view on Chicago. Source: Adapted from Ernest Burgess, "The Growth of the City," in The City, *ed. Robert Park, Ernest Burgess, and R. D. McKenzie. Copyright © 1925 by the University of Chicago Press. Reprinted by permission.*

the city's social structure was not so neatly layered as the concentric circles might suggest, but the model was reasonably accurate. The growth of Chicago, moreover, had proceeded from the center outward. Over the years, the residential area nearest the center, zone 2, had become the home of the city's poorest residents, with the wealthier people moving away from the center.

Burgess further cautioned that the concentric zone model might not fit all cities, and a number of sociologists developed other models.

**Three Generalizations of the
Internal Structure of Cities
District**

1. *Central business district*
2. *Wholesale light manufacturing*
3. *Low-class residential*
4. *Medium-class residential*
5. *High-class residential*
6. *Heavy manufacturing*
7. *Outlying business district*
8. *Residential suburb*
9. *Industrial suburb*
10. *Commuters' zone*

Concentric Zone Theory

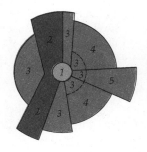

Sector Theory

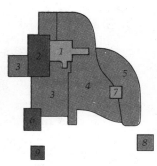

Multiple Nuclei

Figure 17–4 Three city models. Source: Reprinted from "The Nature of Cities," by Chauncy D. Harris and Edward L. Ullman in volume 242 of the Annals of the American Academy of Political and Social Science. *Copyright © 1945 by the American Academy of Political and Social Science. Reprinted by permission.*

Harris and Ullman (1945) summarized three models, including the concentric zone model. Those three models are presented in Figure 17–4.

Some cities are structured much as Burgess suggested Chicago is. Others, as indicated in the sector-theory diagram, are organized more as spokes radiating from a central hub than as concentric bands around it. Still others, as illustrated in the multiple-nuclei diagram, are organized around several more complex structures.

As these diagrams indicate, no single pattern describes the organization of urban areas. You'll recall from the discussion of institutions that a variety of forms serve the functions required for group survival. Similarly, a variety of layouts work for cities.

The geographical layout of cities and the sociophysical interactions of different areas are only a part of the picture, however. Let's move on to other aspects of cities as ecosystems.

Resources and the City

The size and density of cities, we have seen, affects the nature of social interaction. These factors also pose problems and yield advantages in terms of access to and control over the physical and cultural resources that influence the nature of life in cities.

The most obvious resource problem cities have faced involves their dependence on the countryside for foodstuffs and raw materials. In recent years, in the United States at least, this problem has been overshadowed by environmental concerns. These latter concerns involve what Abel Wolman (1965) has called the "metabolism" of cities, comparable to the metabolism of living organisms—the intake and assimilation of food, the processing of wastes, and so forth. He sees three major metabolic problems—providing adequate supplies of fresh water, disposing of sewage, and controlling air pollution—that many large cities are unable to handle.

It is ironic, Wolman points out, that modern men and women, demonstrating such technological and managerial power in other realms, have been having such trouble making cities work. Glenn Hilst (1970:98) suggests that part of the problem lies in the resilience of the ecosystem:

The atmosphere can and does readily dilute waste gases to one-millionth their initial concentrations (say, from a chimney) in just a few minutes; a free-flowing stream can dilute liquid wastes, too, in relatively short distances. Similarly, solid materials which are "degradable," that is, decompose in the presence of water, sunlight, and occasionally, biological actions, can be disposed of in several ways. When underused, these resources can be easily taken for granted.

People living in the country don't worry about burning leaves or trash. Certainly no one worries about chimney smoke—the smoke curling out of a farmhouse chimney on a winter day is a source of nostalgia rather than of environmental concern. Yet, the mass created by the human concentration in cities presses the ecosystem's capacity to the limit—and beyond. During "smog alerts" in Los Angeles, schoolchildren are told to rest quietly at their desks instead of taking recess. Garbage piles up in mountains on city streets whenever there is a strike of sanitation workers, creating both aesthetic and health problems.

The sheer mass of cities turns annoyances into crises. In a small town, residents can and do join together to solve problems. People can work out ways of moving about when they number in the hundreds or even thousands, but when millions attempt to go to work or to go home from work, it's not the sort of thing that can be played by ear. Schooling, feeding, or providing leisure for millions creates problems of scale. The same holds true for the provision of health care, library books, dog licenses—anything that it takes for people to live together. Those things that can be jerry-rigged when a few are involved can become disasters when there are millions.

Of course, the sheer mass of cities can be a source of convenience and enrichment as well as of potential problems. The concentration of population means that inhabitants are likely to have access to diverse products and special services—varied cuisines, music concerts, sporting events, museums, plays, movies, and newspapers—that are financially impossible for a small town to sustain. By the same token, health care for the elderly, schooling for children, and other social services can be problematic in rural areas with people spread out thinly across the countryside.

Urban life, then, is not a simple plus or minus. Table 17–3 summarizes some of the pros and cons of city life and country life. It describes the relative "quality of life" that each has to offer and illustrates the trade-offs people must make in deciding which best matches their own preferences. As you look over the list, remember that the notion of "choosing" where to live is a relatively new one in human history. For thousands of years, most people have simply lived where they were born, without even being aware that there *were* other places they might live.

Also notice in the lists of advantages and disadvantages of city life that some of the "good" and "bad" aspects of the city are inseparably paired. The much-discussed anonymity of urban society, for example, has advantages. Small, rural societies in which everybody knows everybody else make social mobility and personal growth difficult. If you were a big-city fire fighter, on the other hand, it would be easier for you to organize your fellow workers to strike for better wages. But you would also be more likely to suffer through a police or garbage workers' strike. City life can also free you from the stagnation of small-town traditions, but continuing social change can produce a sense of anomie. We'll return to the pros and cons of city life in the concluding essay of this chapter.

Financing the City

The fact that city life has both advantages and disadvantages is a major reason for the growth of that ecological hybrid, the suburb. By living in small towns and villages on the fringes of large metropolitan centers, people have attempted to enjoy the best of both worlds. Thus, the resident of, say, Tenafly, New Jersey, can live in a relatively large house with a large lawn and friendly neighbors, yet be within driving dis-

Table 17-3

The Relative Pros and Cons of City Life

Advantages of city	Disadvantages of city
1. Sense of being where the "action" is	1. Higher crime rates
2. Greater variety of people to interact with	2. Higher rates of mental illness
3. Freedom to rise above family origins	3. More pollution
4. Variety of occupational choices	4. More crowding
5. More extensive cultural and entertainment options	5. More impersonal, anonymous interactions
6. Better medical facilities	6. Less access to top leaders
7. Closer to government agencies	7. Social problems more difficult to remedy
8. Easier mobilization of people for social action and social change	8. Harder to reach agreement among populace
9. Quicker access to technological advances	9. More competition for jobs
10. More innovation; tradition less restricting	10. Less that you can depend on (because of more social change)

tance of the commercial and cultural life of New York City. This development has serious costs, however.

The flight of wealthier residents to the suburbs has undercut the tax base of the cities. Suburban residents do not pay property taxes within the city, but they use the city's facilities: its parks, streets, libraries, museums, and so forth. With the flight to the suburbs, there is no less need for police, sanitation workers, and the others that keep a large city functioning. There are simply fewer people to pay for those facilities and services. Thus, in 1975, the city of New York requested federal assistance in the amount of one *billion* dollars to help it survive as a municipality, and other big cities teeter on the brink of bankruptcy.

Roger Starr, one-time administrator of New York City's Housing and Development Administration, suggests that the financial plight of cities can be seen more clearly by recognizing that any city is in fact two: the "economic city" and the "political city."

The Economic City produces wealth, some of which is turned over as taxes and fees to the Political City by the vendors of goods and services.

The Economic City also employs people. It spreads wealth, though unevenly, among its residents. . . . The Political City provides services that people want or require, but for which they are unable or unwilling to pay directly—criminal justice, elementary education, fire protection, for example—or for which it is simply impractical to collect fees, like the use of public streets. (1976:33, 99)

The fundamental problem lies in the imbalance between the economic and political cities, and Starr points to three possible solutions: (1) a program of economic development might increase the revenues of the economic city; (2) a cutback in services could bring the political city into line with the revenues of the economic city; or (3) the political city could be supported by outsiders—either the state or the federal government.

As you will imagine, there are differences of opinion as to which of these solutions is the most promising, and the debate will undoubtedly continue for some time. I trust you will have seen how complicated the issues have become. For now, let's shift gears a bit and take a look into the future to see what may be in store for cities.

Urban renewal has had a mixed record: sometimes regenerating parts of a city and making them more livable; sometimes destroying neighborhoods altogether.

The Future of the American City

In this chapter, I have described a rather dismal pattern of the American city's recent past. After a lengthy history of getting bigger and bigger, as well as better and better, the quality of our cities had begun to slide ever more rapidly downhill during the past two decades or so. It began with the departure of affluent city residents from the inner city to the suburbs, thereby reducing the tax base for the maintenance of city services. The decline of services produced further departures—by those who could afford to leave and, by the same token, those who could best afford to pay the taxes necessary for maintaining services.

Inner City Renewal

In this light, the most recent prognosis for the cities of the 1980s may come as a surprise. Numerous urban observers now predict a return of upper-middle-class residents into the inner city and a corresponding regeneration of residential areas. Townhouses are being restored and new ones built. Slums, with crime-ridden streets and dilapidated houses, are converted into cultural centers, such as Detroit's new Renaissance Center (at a cost estimated at $337 million). For a more detailed look at this new phase of urban renewal, see the box "New Directions in Urban Design."

This luxurious **urban renewal** is not welcomed by all, however, since its likely effect on

New Directions in Urban Design

One urban specialist who shares the view that prospects for the regeneration of the American city are good is the architecture critic Wolf Von Eckardt. In his view, the "urban crisis" of today represents a turning point in Americans' attitudes toward their cities. After a long period of fearing the city for what it would do to "natural" values and a shorter but more recent period of neglecting the city and escaping to the suburbs, Von Eckardt believes that Americans are now finally adapting themselves to their cities and realizing what vital places they can be.

An important dimension of the "urban renaissance" that Von Eckardt believes is taking place is a new sense of building design and space utilization. The renovations of downtown areas in such cities as Chicago, Kansas City, San Francisco, and Detroit are designed to encourage urban life.

There is something distinctly, inherently urban about festive pedestrian malls and plazas, reclaimed rowhouses and waterfront markets, professionally staffed theatres and concert halls, outdoor cafes and enclosed shopping arcades. Suburban surrogates, while often commendable, somehow lack the vitality and diversity that is derived from the city's critical mass of talent and activities.

Von Eckardt contrasts the city planning currently being done with that of past decades, when architects and city planners were more under the influence of the architect Le Corbusier's urban philosophy. In his city designs, Le Corbusier tried to maintain urban density and at the same time create a sense of more space by planning developments that consisted of high-rises separated by parks and wide-open spaces which were woven together by superhighways. The trouble with this sort of planning, Von Eckardt points out, is that frequently "parks became parking lots" and few provisions were made to encourage social life and variety of experience.

From the evidence of urban renewal today, and the predictions some architects have made, it appears that cities of the future won't consume much more geographical area than they do today, but better use will be made of what already exists. Emphasis will be on renovating existing structures rather than destroying them and replacing them with antiseptic skyscrapers. According to a number of architects, building design and space utilization in the future will also reflect greater consciousness of the environment and the need to make more efficient use of resources, particularly energy. Opportunities for the use of natural light will be more frequently seized, for example, and buildings will likely be designed to make use of shade and wind currents to cut down on air conditioning. More emphasis is also likely to be placed on the use of public transportation systems.

Sources: Wolf Von Eckardt, "Cities: The Age of Recovery," *Mainliner Magazine* (March 1979): 83–97; "Future Talk: Thirteen Visions of Tomorrow's Cities," *Mainliner Magazine* (March 1979): 111–17.

the current, impoverished city residents is either negative, or, at best, uncertain. Where will the displaced move, for example? Will they have any access to the new facilities? These are some of the questions asked by critics. While the proponents respond with references to the revitalization of the city, the creation of jobs, and the restoration of public safety, the critics point to past "urban renewal" failures.

Consider what sometimes happens with urban renewal programs. The construction of a new freeway, for example, can cut neighborhoods in half, disrupting and redirecting patterns of interaction. Families who were once close friends may find they must travel miles to the nearest freeway interchange and an equal distance back to see each other. The friendships may not survive the trip. Urban renewal projects can involve the "improvement" of living conditions, as slum areas are torn down and replaced by modern apartment buildings. Frequently, however, the new residences are inappropriate to the needs, desires, and financial abilities of the former residents. Where people once interacted regularly on doorsteps and in the street, these patterns are often no longer possible (Greer 1966).

Aside from the urban renewal designed to lure members of the upper middle class back to the inner city, there are some hopeful signs of urban regeneration that appear more directly beneficial to present inner-city residents. A growing corps of "urban pioneers" have taken on the task of urban self-renewal through the investment of "sweat equity." In some areas, low-income city residents, such as New York's Danny Soto Diaz and the People's Development Corporation (PDC), are attempting to transform urban desolation into something habitable and even uplifting by renovating tenements, building parks, establishing food cooperatives, and even constructing "solar greenhouses" (Williams 1977b).

Soto described his vision for PDC in stark contrast to what his group seeks to replace:

> All around this area you see people sleeping in doorways, drinking all day, cleaning a car for three dollars when they can get it. Their fathers taught 'em nothing, and they don't know nothing. We want to change all that. We want to create a village of ten thousand people surviving on their own, with their own firemen, police patrols, schools—people for maybe forty blocks living good, the way everybody else lives good in this country. (quoted in Williams 1977b:9)

Obviously, the final chapter has not been written on urban renewal. Despite previously negative connotations, some recent attempts at urban renewal actually seem to have "renewed" rather than wreaked havoc. At the same time, the whole idea of urban renewal will forever be complicated by the simple fact that different people have different notions about what con-

stitutes a high or low quality of life. This factor, however, is hardly unique to urban renewal. It forms an undercurrent for all things social. Were it not so, there'd be no sociology.

Urban Changes in the 1980s

John Kasarda and Robert Lineberry (1980) suggest that three major developments in urban dynamics have established the agenda for urban sociology in the 1980s: "(1) a deepening dependence in an era of resource constraints, (2) demographic shifts, and (3) the demise of the policy 'fix.'" Let's look briefly at each.

Dependency Whereas the Chicago school produced a focus on the city as an ecological unit, Kasarda and Lineberry suggest the modern city is largely determined by dependency on outside units—foreign oil, for example. We have already seen examples of urban financial problems that tie cities to other governmental units, such as the federal government.

Demographic Shifts Much of the early history of cities was a history of rapid growth: foreign immigration and migration from rural America. As we saw early in this chapter, however, metropolitan growth has slowed dramatically, even halted in many cases. At the same time, we have seen a regional shift of population into the "Sunbelt" stretching across the southern portion of the United States. The "deindustrialization" of cities—with a shift from manufacturing to service firms—is another factor. Kasarda and Lineberry also mention the "gentrification process," the restoration of center cities mentioned above, though they hold as an open question whether this process will continue. Finally, the authors suggest that the rise of a black middle class and the increased participation of women in the labor force are also likely to affect the future of cities and require study.

Demise of the Policy "Fix"   From the time of the New Deal, it has been assumed that public policy changes were sufficient to alter the course of urban development. Recent years, however, have seen a weakening of this option. In part, this reflects a growing public disenchantment with local government, resulting on occasion in tax revolts.

We'll return to the problems of cities in the concluding essay of this chapter. In all this, recall that urbanization is a long-running and powerful trend worldwide. According to the Population Reference Bureau (1982), 41 percent of the world's population now live in urban areas—that's nearly 2 billion people—and both the number and percentage is increasing all the time.

Summary

The story of modern social life is the story of cities. At the present, three-fourths of the American population lives in cities, and the rest of the world is moving in that direction. Cities began as simply large towns, but they became much more than that. The first cities were largely crossroads on great trade routes in the Middle East, and commerce figured importantly in them. All the same, the level of agricultural efficiency was not high enough to support all those who produced no food. Thus, the legendary cities of Egypt and Mesopotamia were probably not very large. Moreover, they were frequently overrun by invaders from the surrounding countryside or nearby nations.

The city established itself as independent and permanent only with the advent of the Industrial Revolution. On the one hand, the city became the center of manufacturing—with coal- and steam-powered factories. At the same time, cities became special social systems, requiring innovative structuring of social relations in support of the economic changes. After centuries of greater and greater industrialization, we've now seen a shift toward service activities in today's cities, which are sometimes described as "postindustrial."

In part, the history of American urbanization seems rather straightforward and simple. Beginning with a handful of cities, the nation has both increased the number of cities and has seen each grow greatly in size. At present, we seem on the eve of the "megalopolis"—the giant supracity of urban sprawl linking several cities into a new urban creature. *"Bosnywash"* is a name coined to refer to the urban ribbon stretching down the East Coast of the United States—linking Boston, New York, and Washington.

At the same time, there have been interesting countervailing trends in urbanization. First, there have always been suburban developments on the peripheries of cities, and these have grown in popularity (and population) in recent years. Most recently, we have actually seen an unprecedented population growth in the rural areas of the nation, growing faster than either urban or suburban areas.

The "Chicago school" refers to a group of sociologists at the University of Chicago during the 1920s and 1930s. One of their chief substantive interests was the "human ecology" of the city—the manner in which human social activities were distributed around the geographical area available to the city. Park and Burgess described one model of urban development as a concentric-circle model, in which various activities were concentrated in circular bands emanating from the city center. Other cities were found to be organized in a sector form: particular activities were concentrated in pie-shaped wedges that expanded outward as the cities grew. Finally, some cities were seen to be organized around different centers of activity, called the "multiple-nuclei model."

Cities have posed an especially heavy burden on the environment, a burden now making itself unavoidably evident. Air and water pollution are vivid examples, though they hardly exhaust the list. The sheer mass of cities gives their environmental problems a complexity and difficulty previously unknown. Whereas small towns with few residents can create intuitive, makeshift solutions to problems that arise, this is not possible when millions of people are involved.

The problems facing modern cities are manifold, leading people to the expression "urban crisis." Pollution, crowding, crime, and decaying physical facilities are a few of the problems most often mentioned. At the same time, each of the problems of city life is matched with an advantage. The pairing of pros and cons is perhaps inevitable in some sense. You can't have the experience of being where the action is, for example, without life being hectic. You can't have a wide variety of goods and services to choose from without the potential for "dog-eat-dog" competition. Urban life comes as a package—containing good and bad, depending on your point of view—and people must choose whether the relative balance is what they want or not.

The most recent forecasts for the future of the city suggest that increasing numbers will be choosing the city and attempting to create the balance of good and bad they do want. Whereas in the past urban renewal has often meant tearing down slums to build new slums, there have been recent signs of urban renewal associated with a return of middle- and upper-class residents to the center city. It is now predicted that the 1980s will see a rebirth of the American center city, and by the time you are reading this, you should have a clearer picture of how that turned out.

Important Terms

urbanism
urbanization
postindustrial society
megalopolis
agribusiness

human ecology
urban renewal
gemeinschaft
gesellschaft
primary group

Suggested Readings

Abrahamson, Mark
  1980 *Urban Sociology,* 2nd ed. Englewood Cliffs, N.J.: Prentice-Hall.
  Text covering major aspects of urban areas including structure, growth, and problems. Integrates ecological and other approaches.

Editors of *Scientific American*
  1965 *Cities.* New York: Knopf.
  This is a milestone collection of articles on urbanization by the leading scholars in the field. Kingsley Davis and Gideon Sjoberg present the long-term historical view of cities, a number of case studies are presented, and particular attention is paid to the problems of modern cities.

Fischer, Claude S.
  1976 *The Urban Experience.* New York: Harcourt Brace Jovanovich.

Discusses social and psychological factors and results of urban life.

Garrlan, Joel
  1981 *The Nine Nations of North America.* Boston: Houghton-Mifflin.
  Provocative, journalistic account re-defining the political maps of North America into economic, social, and cultural patterns.

Goolrick, William, et. al., Eds.
  1976 *The Community.* New York: Time-Life.
  The editors of Time-Life Books have created an eminently readable and informative overview of communities, both rural and urban. Beginning with the roots of community life, they move on to modern urban forms: both the problems and the promise. Cross-cultural materials show the varieties of community forms, and excellent graphics give you a nearly personal experience of community life around the world.

Greer, Scott
  1966   *Urban Renewal and American Cities.* Indianapolis, Ind.: Bobbs-Merrill.
  The renewal of the nation's decaying cities has seemed like a good idea in general, but it has often produced disasters in practice. Established social networks are destroyed as freeways cut through neighborhoods. Poor people are evicted from substandard homes and are unable to afford the modern housing built in their place. Greer offers data and a sociological point of view on understanding the problem.

Jacobs, Jane
  1961   *The Death and Life of Great American Cities.* New York: Random House.
  Reviews success of urban renewal projects in American cities and makes suggestions for urban planning.

Wellman, Barry
  1979   "The Community Question: The Intimate Networks of East Yorkers," *American Journal of Sociology,* Vol. 84:1201–31.
  Wellman presents an excellent analysis of varied points of view on "community." At the same time, his empirical analyses describe the nature of community networks in modern urban life.

Williams, Roger
  1977   "The New Urban Pioneers: Homesteading in the Slums." *Saturday Review* (July 23, 1977):9–16.
  Here's an interesting look at the new face of urban renewal, which some feel represents the future of American cities. Williams presents a concrete picture of the renewal in action, so that you can have a real sense of what it is about.

July 13, 1977. At around 9:30 P.M., New York City—the largest city in America throughout most of our national history, the fourth largest city in the world, Gotham, the Big Apple—seemed to die. The city went blind as electric power failed, and this home of millions fell into sudden darkness. People were stranded in subways and in elevators. Traffic degenerated into greater chaos than normal. Crowds at restaurants, sports events, and theaters sat suddenly in darkness. Airline pilots landing at New York saw the city disappear before their eyes.

For many New Yorkers, the 1977 blackout looked like a replay of the 1965 electrical failure throughout the Northeast. They recalled stories of heroism and general good-naturedness as total strangers helped each other, as pedestrians took on the task of directing snarled traffic. A year after the 1965 blackout, demographers were to debate whether the increased birth rate nine months after November was the result of random fluctuations or random flirtations.

In retrospect, the 1965 blackout was a rather fond memory for most New Yorkers. But the 1977 replay was not to be fondly remembered. Despite examples of mutual assistance and neighborliness, the main statistics concerned the damage done by arson (some 900 fires), looting, fighting, and the number of people arrested (some 3,700 to 3,800). And the repercussions were to continue on and on.

For most observers, the problems created in the 1977 blackout seemed somehow more "normal" than did the happy experience of 1965. It was as though 1965 was the tooth fairy, and 1977 was the dentist—less pleasing but more "realistic." After all, it is widely agreed that cities around the world are in big trouble, tinderboxes on the verge of ignition. Observers speak of the "urban crisis," and commentators vie with one another in forecasting the death date of the big city.

Earlier in this chapter—indeed throughout the book—we have seen the problems facing modern cities. Many people question whether our largest cities are really manageable at all. We have seen how problems of finance complicate matters, and the new wave of problems facing cities in 1980s and beyond compound those complications.

As a backdrop to all those problems is a long-standing issue usually summarized in the term *community*. Specifically, people often speak of the "loss of community." For many people, large cities do not promote the sense of "belonging" or the sense of civic ownership and responsibility that characterized small towns and villages. This was the concern voiced in Toennies's distinction between **gemeinschaft** (community) and **gesellschaft** (society).

To review, members of a gemeinschaft tended to know and care about each other, and people experienced and acted on a personal responsibility for the well-being of the whole. By contrast, members of the gesellschaft were strangers to one another—thrown together in the same place by chance and each operating on the basis of a narrow self-interest. People living in cities were not necessarily less compassionate or humane than country folk, but they did not live in circumstances which prompted such feelings among those living near each other.

For years, the concern about "loss of community" was essentially regarded as old-fashioned, conservative. The city represented the next step in evolutionary progress. This view was reflected in Durkheim's reaction to Toennies, as we saw in Chapter 6. Taking the long view, there is much truth in that characterization of cities. Urban areas have been the scene of more than technological advances: they have fostered intellectual advances, liberation, tolerance. Still, it is argued increasingly, something has been lost.

Barry Wellman (1979) suggests there are three major points of view on the subject today: community lost, saved, or liberated. The *community-lost view* "holds many urban phenomena to be concrete and concentrated manifestations of industrial bureaucratic societies. It contends that the division of labor in these societies has attenuated communal solidarities" (Wellman 1979:1204). In this view, the tightly knit primary groups of old have been replaced by impersonal and contractual secondary relationships.

The *community-saved view* essentially contradicts this, pointing to the persistence of primary-group relationships—especially evident among the poor and ethnic minorities—in even the largest cities. The gemeinschaft quality that once characterized whole towns and villages now lives in neighborhoods or sections of the city.

Finally, the *community-liberated view* suggests that people still create and enjoy primary-group relationships, but these are based on work and friendship and are not geographically concentrated as in earlier times. Thus, you may feel closely and intimately connected to "your group," but the members of that group may live all over town. In essence, the sense of belonging persists, but the form has changed. In place of neighborhoods, gemeinschaft now takes the form of *networks*—the linking of individuals on the basis of interest rather than geography. The "liberated" quality suggests that primary-group ties are now a matter of choice, not chance.

Wellman's own research in East York (Toronto) most closely supports the community-liberated point of view (1979:1217):

> In support of the Liberated argument, we find that the great majority of East Yorkers (81%) report that help in emergency situations is available to them from somewhere in their intimate network. A smaller majority (60%) report help to be avail-

able through their intimate network in dealing with everyday matters; such routine help is often available as part of less intensive relationships (e.g., with acquaintances, neighbors, co-workers), and there is less use of intimate relations for it.

In contrast to the view that close friends should live close together, Wellman finds that even among a person's most intimate friends, those living far away are as likely to help as those living closer.

The issue of community has not been resolved, either sociologically or popularly. The different attractions inherent in large, metropolitan cities versus small, intimate communities form one of the persistent dilemmas facing modern people. Implicitly, each of us grapples with the issue of what would constitute the ideal community. By way of a summary, Roland Warren (1970) suggests there are nine major dimensions to the issue.

Primary-group relationships, as we've seen, mark one of the more immediate differences in these two social forms. In small, intimate communities, everyone knows everyone—not superficially but in depth. In the city, as Warren recalls (1970:113), urban sociologists sometimes found that "neighbor did not know neighbor, where one was truly anonymous, . . . there was the greatest freedom from the prying eyes of neighbors . . ." As in all the dimensions of the issue, we'll see there are tradeoffs.

Local-community autonomy is another dimension. On the one hand, there are arguments for placing local problems and their solutions in the hands of local people, rather than in the hands of the federal government, national associations, national corporations, and other outside agencies. Yet, each of these outside entities is also a source of support and assistance to local communities. This is particularly true in relation to another dimension: *viability*, the ability to survive. Sometimes, local communities seem unable to confront their problems effectively. As Warren points out, the desires for local autonomy and local viability seem to conflict with one another.

The dimension of local community autonomy is complicated by the question of *neighborhood control*. Whereas some argue for the sovereignty of the local town, village, or city, others would place sovereignty even closer to home. If a community should have the right to structure and operate its schools uncontrolled by outside entities, shouldn't such authority actually reside with the neighborhood residents whose children will attend that particular school? Historically, this system has resulted in racially and economically segregated schools of vastly different quality.

Power distribution is a frequently discussed dimension of the community issue. Study after study has documented that local power tends to be concentrated in relatively few hands. Ironically, this is most typical of communities with little outside interference. Local autonomy appears to work directly against an even distribution of power at the local level.

Participation is a goal people commonly cite in relation to the ideal community: everyone taking a full part in community affairs. Yet, Warren notes (1970:115) "there is often widespread apathy, and many citizens do not participate, even where the opportunity is there for them." He goes on to note that the affairs of any community are too varied and numerous for everyone to participate in everything. What, he asks, would be the ideal distribution and limitation of participation?

As theoretically popular as participation is *commitment*. It seems as though the truly good community would be one in which all the citizens identify themselves with the community and its interests. But this, too, turns out to be a two-edged sword. What of all those people whose commitment is to a larger entity: to the nation or to the world?

Heterogeneity represents a somewhat different dimension of the issue. Warren notes that city planners have generally supported the idea that communities should be composed of diverse populations, homogeneous ghettos. Yet "many of these same city planners show through their behavior that they themselves prefer to live in communities which are segregated, in the sense of being economically, racially, and ethnically homogeneous" (Warren 1970:117). Nor are city planners alone in this. For all our theoretical commitment to heterogeneity, minority and majority groups alike evidence a tendency to separatism.

Finally, Warren discusses the question of *conflict:* specifically, how much conflict can be tolerated in the ideal community? Where the answer might once have been "none," many now realize that conflict is a source of change. Harmony and consensus typically support the status quo, the concentration of power, and a variety of injustices. But how much conflict is right?

These, then, are the dimensions of the issue that we must confront and master in creating the ideal community. We need to realize that each dimension represents a two-edged sword, and the several dimensions conflict with each other. In confronting this challenge, we would do well to bear in mind a passage Warren quotes (1970:112) from Josiah Royce:

I believe in the beloved community and in the spirit which makes it beloved, and in the communion of all who are, in will and in deed, its members. I see no such community as yet, but nonetheless my rule of life is: Act so as to hasten its coming.

PRACTICING SOCIOLOGY

Pierre Simonitsch writes in Germany's *Frankfurter Rundschau* about the problems of urbanization in poor nations including the miserable condition of poor squatters who own no land. He also describes a possible solution.

Urban blight is a fact of life in the Third World. Cities grow beyond their means to accommodate burgeoning populations living in metal, cardboard, or tin shanties. When these urban sores fester, bulldozers level the shanties and displace the occupants, who struggle to a new location and build another shanty town. . . .

Hyderabad is India's fifth most populous city. Its industry, trade, and government have drawn increasing numbers of people, causing unemployment and overcrowding. In 1971 some 270,000 of Hyderabad's 1.6 million people lived in slums; today that figure has doubled.

But in recent years 13,000 Hyderabad families have been legally "settled" where they have lived for decades, their slum ownership confirmed with receipt of a *patta,* or plot of land measuring about 16 square yards. This ownership has awakened their desire to improve living conditions. Crude cooperative systems have been arranged to supply water and dispose of garbage and sewage. Jobs are usually found in neighboring parts of the city.

Why do you suppose the ownership of land— even 16 square yards—has such an impact on these poor people? What problems does this program in Hyderabad face? Would similar programs succeed in other poor Third World nations? Why or why not?

Source: Pierre Simonitsch, "Hyderabad's Model 'Slum,'" *Frankfurter Rundschau*, reprinted in *World Press Review*, August 1980, p. 58.

Part Five

Global Issues

Despite the inherent conservatism of social institutions, societies are undergoing continuous change. Some change is intended, other change is not.

In Part Five, we are going to conclude our examination of the world's societies by looking at the major types and sources of social change.

Population and Environment   In the long view of human history, no development is more significant than population growth and its impact on the physical environment. Today's world population rests at about 4.5 billion people and is currently doubling every forty-one years.

In this chapter, we'll look at the history and nature of population growth. We'll also examine the impact of that growth in the form of pollution and the depletion of environmental resources, plus social impacts such as crowding, war, and hunger. We'll also cosider the prospects for stemming population growth in the future.

Technology   Technology represents a fundamental human activity: developing techniques for dealing with the world. The harnessing of fire and the invention of the wheel are examples of technology, as are the inventions of computers, bombs, and medical vaccines.

We'll begin this chapter with an examination of the basic nature of technology and science. We'll review the impact of technology in many areas of social life, focusing specifically on communication and medicine.

Social Change   Some social change appears to proceed steadily in a particular direction: from simple to complex social structures, for example. Other change occurs in jumps and spurts. In still other cases, social change appears more cyclical—with people recycling through the same series of patterns endlessly.

This chapter begins by examining the many sources of social change and then the models of change sociologists have developed. We conclude with an examination of the modernization process that is radically transforming societies around the world.

18

Population
and
Environment

Early in this book, I described a "society" as a social system with people living in it. One characteristic of present-day society clearly is *lots* of people. This characteristic of present-day society highlights a fundamental aspect of society in general. Societies are made up of individual human beings, each following his or her individual course, and all that individual behavior adds up to what's going on in the society at large. Throughout the book, we've seen the countless ways in which social structures influence the actions of individuals, but you've probably also had a sense that society is the uncontrollable sum of what individuals do. One person throws a candy wrapper on the ground, others do too, and eventually an enormous amount of litter has accumulated. The unplanned, incidental, aggregated result of individual actions often appears as a frightening surprise.

The creation of human populations is something like the creation of litter. Becoming a parent seems like a very personal thing. Nonetheless, when individuals—moved by all sorts of personal, individual reasons—have babies, all those babies form what is probably the most significant group product in social affairs—population. Sociologists study this aspect of group life, too.

Demography is the scientific study of population. Demography is often regarded as a subfield of sociology and taught within sociology departments. At the same time, demography has become sufficiently specialized and developed to be seen as a separate discipline.

Demography is addressed to: (1) measuring the size and composition of human societies, (2) understanding the factors involved in determining population size and composition, and (3) understanding their consequences. In the first half of this chapter, we are going to examine some of the concepts and theories that have been developed in demography, and we'll also look at what demographers have discovered in their empirical studies of population. We want to see what demographers can tell us about the pressing world problems of population explosion and overpopulation.

The impact of humans, especially in our ever-greater numbers, on the planet's ecosystem—the system made up of ourselves and our environment—is the topic for the second half of the chapter. In particular, we'll look at the social agreements that have resulted in the depletion of various resources and the creation of noxious pollutants.

By the time this chapter is completed, you should have a clearer picture of how human beings—as sociobiological creatures—fit into the larger ecosystem. Let's begin, then, with an overview of population size, composition, and growth in the world and, more specifically, in the United States, in order to see the dimensions of the population problem.

A "Head-Counting" Overview

One of the oldest methods of empirical social research is the **census**: the enumeration (counting) of populations. Records show that this practice existed at least as long ago as the ancient Egyptian civilizations. In part, the ancient Egyptian rulers counted the members of their societies to tax them. Later, the Romans conducted censuses throughout their far-flung empire for the same purpose, and the Bible tells us that Jesus was born in Bethlehem because Joseph and Mary were required to journey there—Joseph's ancestral home—to be counted.

Since the time of the pharaohs, methods of census taking have been developed to considerably greater scientific precision. Not all contemporary societies have developed scientific enumeration procedures, however, so it is difficult to determine the actual population of the world at any given time. All we can do is *estimate* it.

World Population

The Population Reference Bureau (1982) has estimated that the 1982 population of the entire world was about 4,585,000,000—*four and a half billion* people. This means that in the world today there are roughly 1,500 people for every letter in this book. Placed head to toe, they would reach from earth to the moon about eleven times. If, on your birthday, you decide to have a party for everyone else with the same birthday, you'll need over 10 million party hats and you'll have to rent Tokyo, Paris, or New York City for the party. (If your birthday is February 29, however, you can get by with Boston or Pittsburgh.)

Table 18–1 presents the estimated population for different areas of the world in 1950 and 1982. Several things are deducible from the data. First, over half the world's population lives in Asia, with the percentage increasing slightly between 1950 and 1982. Second, the population growth of different parts of the world varied a great deal during the 1950–1982 period, ranging from 133 percent in Latin America and 129 percent in Africa to 24 percent for Europe. This difference is also illustrated by a comparison between Latin America and North America. In 1950, the population of Latin America was 2 percent less than the population of its northern neighbors; in 1982, its population was 48 percent larger than that of North America. Finally the data show that in general the underdeveloped continents of the world have experienced a much greater rate of population growth than have the more developed continents.

To round out the picture of current world population, Table 18–2 presents the populations of the world's largest nations, showing all those with 50 million or more people. Taken together, these seventeen nations account for over 70 percent of the world's population. Indeed, more than one-fifth of the world's population lives in China alone.

If current population estimates lack total accuracy, estimates of earlier years and centuries are even more approximate. Nevertheless,

Table 18-1

World Population Estimates, 1950 and 1982

| Area | Population | | 1950–1982 growth |
	1950	1982	
World	2,486,000,000	4,585,000,000	84%
Africa	217,000,000	498,000,000	129
North America	166,000,000	256,000,000	54
Latin America	162,000,000	378,000,000	133
Asia	1,355,000,000	2,671,000,000	97
Europe	392,000,000	488,000,000	24
Oceania	12,600,000	24,000,000	90
U.S.S.R.	180,000,000	270,000,000	50

Source: United Nations, *Demographic Yearbook* (New York: United Nations, 1973), p. 81. Population Reference Bureau, "1982 World Population Data Sheet," Washington D.C.

scholars have found it useful to make such estimates, especially in trying to understand the dynamics of population growth and overpopulation. One of the most frequently cited estimates was developed by A. M. Carr-Saunders in 1936. According to his calculations, between the years 1650 and 1900, the total world population increased from 545 million to about 1.6 billion.

Other estimates (Durand 1968) suggest there were 5 million people on earth in 800 B.C. and perhaps 300 million at the time of Christ. Figure 18–1 provides a graphic illustration of world population growth from 8000 B.C. through projections for the year A.D. 2000. The precise population figures for any given year are irrelevant in comparison with the general story that the graph tells.

Throughout most of human history, world population hardly increased at all. The number of people was governed by the same natural checks and balances that keep other species from overflowing the earth. Only during the past three or four hundred years has the rate of population growth increased dramatically, largely as a consequence of developments in medical science and health care, plus other technolog-

ical developments (in food production, for instance). In the section that follows, we'll look at some consequences of population growth.

In making sense of these recent population changes, demographers use the concept of **doubling time,** the length of time it takes a population to double in size. Thus, it took several hundreds of thousands of years for a human population of one-quarter billion to develop in the world, a figure achieved by about the time of Christ. It took 1,650 years for the figure to double again. The next doubling took about 200 years: a population of 1 billion around 1850. The second billion was achieved about 80 years later, in 1930; and the fourth billion was achieved 45 years later, in 1975. The Population Reference Bureau (1982) has estimated that our current doubling time is 40 years.

Until recently, most demographers believed that population growth would continue unabated into the foreseeable future, producing a world population of 8 billion by the year 2010. Now, however, the rate of growth appears to be slowing—even in the developing countries. As 1978 drew to a close, the United Nations was predicting a population of 6.3 billion in the year 2000, the World Bank was predicting 6.0 billion,

Table 18-2

Population Estimates for the World's Largest Nations, 1982

Nation	Population	Percent of the world's population
China	1,000,000,000	22
India	713,800,000	16
U.S.S.R.	270,000,000	6
United States	232,000,000	5
Indonesia	151,300,000	3
Brazil	127,700,000	3
Japan	118,600,000	3
Bangladesh	93,300,000	2
Pakistan	93,000,000	2
Nigeria	82,300,000	2
Mexico	71,300,000	2
West Germany	61,700,000	1
Italy	57,400,000	1
Vietnam	56,600,000	1
United Kingdom	56,100,000	1
France	54,200,000	1
Philippines	51,600,000	1

Note: Most recent estimates as of 1982, through not necessarily measured in 1982.

Source: Population Reference Bureau, "1982 World Population Data Sheet," Washington, D.C.

Table 18-3

The Changing "Doubling Time" of the U.S. Population

Year	Population	Doubling time (years)
1790	4 million	
1814	8 million	24
1838	16 million	24
1861	32 million	23
1891	64 million	30
1936	128 million	45
1992	256 million	56

and two University of Chicago demographers, Amy Ong Tsui and Donald Bogue, had predicted "only" 5.8 billion (Strout 1978).

United States Population

As in the world as a whole, the population of the United States has risen dramatically over the past few centuries. In 1790, the new United States had a population of just under 4 million. The 1982 population was estimated at around 232 million, or about fifty-eight times what it had been 191 years earlier (U.S. Bureau of Census 1975; Population Reference Bureau 1982). Figure 18-2 shows the American census counts from 1790 to 1980 and Census Bureau population projections through the year 2000.

Early in our national history, the United States had a shorter doubling time than the world as a whole. It has become longer than the world average during this century, as the figures in Table 18-3 indicate.

This is not an indication that population growth has become insignificant in the United States. During the five years from 1970 to 1975, we *added* double the 1790 population. And as we'll see later in the chapter, American population growth has an environmental significance far beyond sheer numbers of people.

Now let's look at some of the causes and components of population growth in more detail.

The Components of Demographic Change

The size of a society's population changes as a function of three factors: births **(fertility)**, deaths **(mortality)**, and **migration.** In this section, we'll look at how each of these factors individually and in combination contributes to population

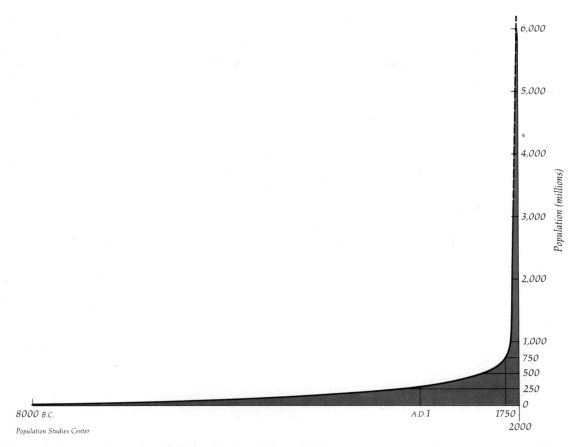

6,000
5,000
4,000
3,000
2,000
1,000
750
500
250
0

Population (millions)

8000 B.C.   A.D.1   1750
                                                                                    2000

Population Studies Center

Figure 18–1 Long-term world population growth. Source: Redrawn from John Durand, "The Modern Expansion of World Population," Proceedings of the American Philosophical Society, June 1967, as reprinted in Charles Nam, ed., Population and Society (New York: Houghton Mifflin, 1968), p. 111.

growth. We'll also examine some broad historical patterns in birth and death rates and what demographers have theorized about these patterns.

Birth Rates

The simplest measure of births in a society is called the **crude birth rate:** the number of births divided by the size of the population. Typically, the number of births during a given year is divided by the total population at the beginning of that year. This rate is most often expressed as the number of births per 1,000 population. In 1982, for example, the United States crude birth rate was 16 per 1,000. By contrast, Nigeria's 1982 rate was 50, and West Germany's was 10 (Population Reference Bureau 1982).

While the crude birth rate figures directly in the year-to-year change in population, a fuller understanding of population change involves the concepts of **fecundity** and **fertility.** "Fecundity" refers to the biological ability of women within a particular age range to bear children. Societies with more women in the

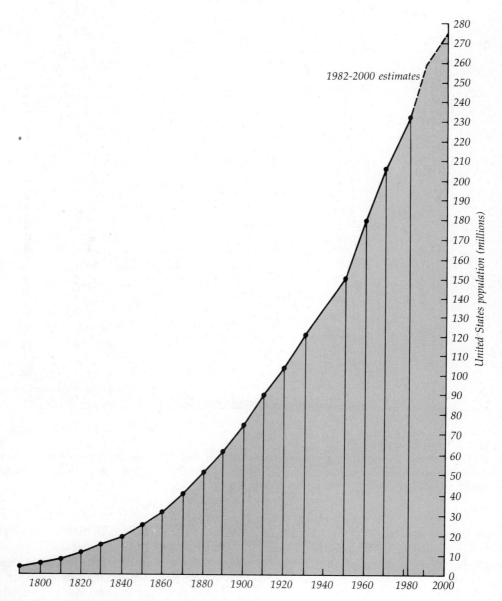

Figure 18–2 Population growth in the United States, 1790–2000. Source: Data taken from U.S. Bureau of Census, Statistical Abstract of the United States, 1975, pp. 6–7; Population Reference Bureau, "1982 World Population Data Sheet."

childbearing years have a greater potential for births than do those with fewer such women, regardless of the total population sizes.

Fertility is the actual bearing of children. So, the "fertility rate" used by demographers is the number of births divided by the number of women in their childbearing years. Although women vary in the number of their childbearing years, a specific period, usually from ages fifteen to forty-nine, is used for the calculation.

Education is importantly related to fertility. In 1979, American women eighteen to thirty-four years of age with less than a high school education had had an average of 1.7 children; high school graduates had had 1.2; those with one to three years of college averaged 0.8 children; and college graduates averaged 0.7 children. A similar pattern was found when women were asked how many children they expected to have during their lifetime (U.S. Bureau of Census 1980a:11).

Table 18–4 shows that educational level is also related to fertility rate in several less industrialized countries of the world, as reflected in the findings of the Population Reference Bureau's World Fertility Survey (Lightbourne and Singh 1982). As the table shows, the more education a woman has, in general, the fewer children she bears.

Similarly, family income relates to family size. As Table 18–5 shows, American families with the highest incomes generally have the smallest families. Again, this same general relationship holds when we compare the average incomes in various countries with the average family size.

A society's birth rate has numerous ramifications for the quality of life of all living in it. If the birth rate exceeds the death rate, the population will grow larger and larger, with the birth rate functioning like compound interest.

A society's fertility rate for a given year is thus the number of babies born per 1,000 women between the ages of fifteen and forty-nine.

Demographers distinguish between fecundity and fertility since most women do not bear all the children they would be biologically capable of bearing. The difference between the two is to be found within the realm of social factors. As a result, demographers have been especially interested in learning which agreements encourage many children and which encourage few. Let's turn now to some of the factors that have been found to matter in that respect.

Death Rates

When asked "What's the death rate in these parts?" a Vermont farmer is reported to have replied, "One apiece." Undaunted by this native wit, demographers pay as much attention to death rates as to birth rates in order to learn about population change. The **crude death rate,** as you might imagine, is the number of deaths in a year per 1,000 population. The United States crude death rate in 1982 was 9 per 1,000. In Africa, by contrast, the average death rate in 1982 was 17 (Population Reference Bureau 1982).

Since everyone is biologically capable of dying in any given year, it makes no sense to limit the calculations to a particular sex or age range as is done with fertility rates. Even so, demographers often compute **infant mortality rates:** the number of children per 1,000 who die during

Table 18-4

Relationship between Education and Fertility Rates in Developing Countries

(Average number of children ever born per ever-married woman aged 30–34 at time of interview)

| | Education level | | |
Country	None	Primary	Secondary and higher
Africa			
Kenya	5.6	5.7	5.0
Lesotho	4.2	4.0	2.9
Senegal	5.4	5.1	3.1
North Sudan	4.9	5.8	3.9
Asia and Pacific			
Bangladesh	5.7	5.7	4.9
Fiji	4.8	4.2	3.1
Indonesia	3.9	4.3	3.6
Republic of Korea	4.1	3.6	2.7
Malaysia	4.7	4.4	2.6
Nepal	4.1	3.5	3.5
Pakistan	5.0	5.2	3.9
Philippines	4.5	4.7	3.5
Sri Lanka	4.7	4.3	3.0
Thailand	4.8	3.9	2.2
Latin America and Caribbean			
Colombia	5.9	4.6	3.1
Costa Rica	5.1	4.3	2.6
Dominican Republic	5.4	5.0	2.5
Guyana	5.5	5.1	3.6
Haiti	3.6	3.4	2.5
Mexico	6.0	5.1	2.9
Panama	5.1	4.7	3.0
Paraguay	5.1	4.3	2.2
Peru	5.4	4.9	3.1
Venezuela	5.8	4.5	2.5
Middle East			
Jordan	6.4	5.3	3.4
Syria	5.6	5.2	4.1
Turkey	4.3	2.9	1.7

Source: Robert Lightbourne, Jr. and Susheela Singh, *The World Fertility Survey: Charting Global Childbearing* (Washington, D.C.: Population Reference Bureau, 1982), p. 22.

Table 18-5

Income and Fertility of American Women

Family income	*Average number of children to date* *Age of wives*		
	18–24	*25–29*	*30–34*
Wife in labor force			
Under $3,000	*	*	*
$3,000–$4,999	0.9	*	*
$5,000–$7,499	0.8	1.6	*
$7,500–$9,999	0.9	1.3	2.4
$10,000–$14,999	0.6	1.3	2.0
$15,000–$24,999	0.5	1.1	1.9
$25,000 and over	0.3	0.8	1.4
Wife not in labor force			
Under $3,000	*	*	*
$3,000–$4,999	1.3	*	*
$5,000–$7,499	1.2	2.4	3.0
$7,500–$9,999	1.3	2.0	2.7
$10,000–$14,999	1.3	1.9	2.5
$15,000–$24,999	1.3	1.8	2.3
$25,000 and over	*	1.6	2.2

Note: * = not reported

Source: U.S. Bureau of Census, *Fertility of American Women: June 1979* (Washington, D.C.: Government Printing Office, 1980), p. 15.

their first year of life; if 10,000 children were born in a given year and 500 died before reaching one year of age, the infant mortality rate would be 50. The infant mortality rate is important for many reasons. For example, those who die in infancy cannot have children of their own and thus will not add to population growth.

Infant mortality rates are also closely related to birth rates. In general, the higher the infant mortality rate, the higher the birth rate is likely to be. Throughout much of human history, most children have not survived infancy, and societies have survived only because they had very high birth rates. By way of illustration, Ralph Thomlinson dedicated his *Demographic Problems* (1967) to Wolfgang Amadeus Mozart, saying:

One of seven children, five of whom died
   within six months of birth;
Father of six children, only one of whom
   lived six months;
Himself a survivor of scarlet fever,
   smallpox and lesser diseases,
Only to die at the age of thirty-five
   years and ten months
From a cause not diagnosable by the
   medical knowledge of his time;
Thus making his life demographically
   typical of most of man's history.

This historically typical pattern is still maintained in many nonindustrialized countries. Table 18–6 presents some illustrative birth and infant mortality rates.

Table 18-6

Selected Birth and Infant Mortality Rates and Life Expectancy, 1982

Country	Crude birth rates	Infant mortality rates	Life expectancy at birth
High rates			
Afghanistan	48	205	40
Niger	50	143	42
Somalia	46	147	42
Low rates			
Japan	14	7.4	76
Sweden	12	6.7	75
United States	16	11.8	74

Source: Population Reference Bureau, "1982 World Population Data Sheet," Washington, D.C.

Another way of looking at the differences we've been discussing is in terms of "life expectancy." In demography, this term refers to the average number of years that babies born at a given time and in a given society can be expected to live, if current mortality patterns continue throughout their lives. Since women generally tend to live longer than men, life expectancies are usually calculated separately by sex. And as you would imagine, there are great variations from society to society in this respect, as in other respects. In addition to rates of infant mortality, then, Table 18–6 also presents some contrasting life expectancies.

Natural Increase

Although everyone who is born must die, the disparity between the rates at which they do so is what causes the overall increase in world population. Most simply put, there are more births than deaths each year. In 1982, the average annual crude birth rate for the world was 29; the corresponding death rate was 11. As a result, the world's population increases nearly 2 percent per year (Population Reference Bureau 1982).

The excess of births over deaths—**natural increase**—is a worldwide pattern, although an uneven one. Societies have survived by matching death rates with higher birth rates. When the death rate is high, the birth rate tends to be higher still. When the death rate drops, the birth rate often begins to fall, too. But many societies have experienced a lag between the decrease in the death rate and the subsequent decrease in the birth rate. Latin America offers a clear illustration of this situation.

Until recent decades, most of Latin America has been characterized by the high birth and death rates that still characterize much of Africa. The vast improvement in public health and other medical conditions, however, has drastically reduced the death rate in Latin America, bringing it slightly below that of North America in 1982. Birth rates, however, have stayed at the same high levels that were needed to offset the earlier death rates. With an annual death rate of 8 in 1982, Latin America had a birth rate of 32. This is in contrast to a death rate of 9 and a birth rate of 16 for North America (Population Reference Bureau 1982).

Figure 18–3 shows birth and death rates of several societies over time. Notice the lag between decreasing death and birth rates; notice,

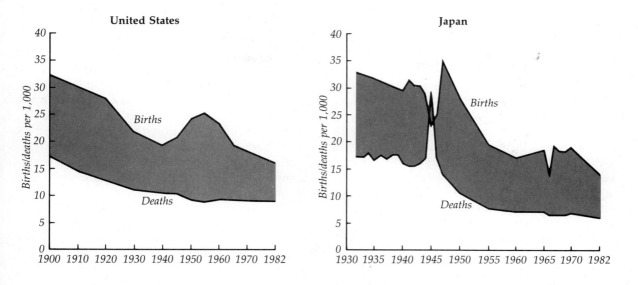

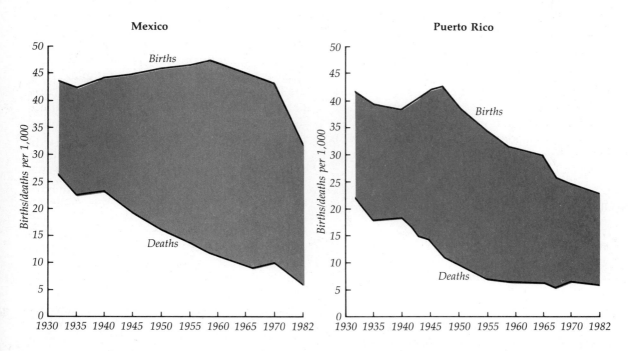

Figure 18–3 Changing birth and death rates for the United States, Mexico, Puerto Rico, and Japan. (The shaded area on each graph represents the natural increase, the difference between birth rate and death rate.) Sources: U.S. Bureau of Census, Historical Statistics of the United States: Colonial Times to 1957, *1960, pp. 23, 27; U.S. Bureau of Census,* Statistical Abstract of the United States, *1973, p. 52; others: United Nations,* Demographic Yearbook, *1948, pp. 260–65, 312–17; ibid., 1960, pp. 476–83, 598–605; ibid., 1973, pp. 225–30, 279–85; Population Reference Bureau, "1982 World Population Data Sheet," Washington, D.C.*

too, how birth rates are almost always higher than death rates.

The United States and Japan illustrate the pattern in which birth and death rates generally decrease together, although the American "baby boom" of the 1950s and the war-related fluctuations in Japan vary from the general pattern. Puerto Rico illustrates the lag between decreasing death and birth rates: about ten years' time separates the start of a steady decline in the death rate and the steady decline in the birth rate. Mexico, on the other hand, illustrates the case in which the death rate declines significantly while the birth rate has declined much more slowly. Finally, notice that even when both rates decrease, the birth rate remains higher than the death rate. That persistent disparity is why populations continue to grow even though birth rates decrease.

Demographic Transition Theory

Patterns of birth and death rates such as those we've just seen have led many demographers to distinguish them in the form of typologies. The United Nations' population division (1956), for example, has proposed a fivefold classification:

Type	Birth rate	Death rate
I	High	High
II	High	Declining
III	High	Low
IV	Declining	Low
V	Low	Low

Societies around the world have been seen to move through these several stages in a process that demographers have described as the **theory of demographic transition.** Figure 18–4 graphically portrays the process that the theory refers to. The main steps in the process are as follows. A society begins with high birth and death rates—producing a slow rate of population growth—and a low level of economic development. Then comes industrialization, usually introduced by some other, more industrialized society. With industrialization comes modern medical practices, better sanitation systems, and other innovations that dramatically lower the death rate in the society. This reduced death rate—along with a still-high birth rate—produces rapid growth in overall population size, and rapid urbanization. Eventually, as the society becomes more industrialized and urbanized, the birth rate declines and the rate of population growth slows.

This then is a simplified picture of the process described by the theory of demographic transition, in which nonindustrialized, sparsely populated societies are transformed into large, industrial ones. The actual processes are, of course, somewhat more complex than this simplified picture suggests, and they vary from society to society.

Declining death rates have a rather complicated effect on birth rates, relating to changes in life expectancies. In 1982, for example, Ethiopia had a life expectancy of 40 years, as compared with 74 in the United States. In part these figures reflect grossly different rates of infant mortality: 147 per 1,000 in Ethiopia and 11.8 in the United States. But they also reflect a difference in the average longevity of those who survive infancy (Population Reference Bureau 1982).

Since women's ability to bear children extends, on the average, to their mid- to late forties, low life expectancies have a limiting effect on birth rates. As death rates go down and people—especially women—live longer, more babies will be born unless people change their patterns of reproduction.

As death rates are further reduced and life expectancies further extended, however, the effect on birth *rates* is reversed. More and more people living beyond their childbearing years does not increase the number of babies born, but it does increase the total population, thereby decreasing at least the crude birth rate. For example, if 400,000 babies are born in a society with a population of 10 million, that society will have a crude birth rate (40 per 1,000) twice as

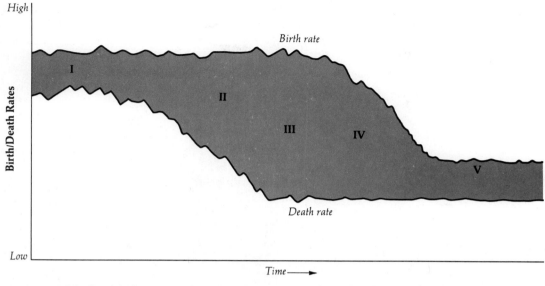

I: *High birth and death rates*
II: *High birth rate, declining death rate*
III: *High birth rate, low death rate*

IV: *Low death rate, declining birth rate*
V: *Low birth and death rates*

Figure 18–4 The theory of demographic transition.

high as the society of 20 million that produces the same number of babies.

The decrease in death rates, then, eventually creates at least the appearance of declining fertility. Because the appearance may not reflect the reality, demographers pay more attention to age-specific fertility rates. This is only the beginning of the attempt to understand the structure and process of a given population.

Age-Sex Profiles

Once the birth and death rates for a society are known, the potential for population growth can be assessed from the society's **age-sex composition.** The potential for growth is greater if a large proportion of the women are in their childbearing years. Depending on the agreements governing mating, the sex ratio of the group is also important. In a monogamous society like the United States, for example, an equal balance of men and women creates an

optimum condition for growth: there is a potential father for every potential mother.

The importance of age and sex distributions for population growth has led demographers to develop the age-sex pyramid, a graphic description of the proportional composition of the population by age and sex. Two age-sex pyramids are superimposed over one another in Figure 18–5.

The shaded pyramid describes the population of the United States as of April 1, 1970; the pyramid outlined in bold lines is the United States age profile ten years later. These two profiles tell a story about recent trends in American society. The most striking difference can be seen in terms of young children: they represented a much larger proportion of the population in 1970 than in 1980. Also, senior citizens, especially women, were a larger proportion of the 1980 population than they were in 1970.

An even more striking comparison is presented in Figure 18–6, which shows the 1970

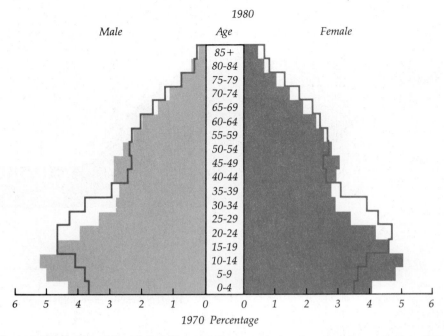

Figure 18–5 Percent distribution of the United States resident population, by age and sex: April 1, 1970, and April 1, 1980. Source: U.S. Bureau of Census, Population Profile of the United States: 1980, *Washington, D.C., 1980, p.4. Shaded areas represent 1970 figures; colored lines represent 1980 figures.*

age-sex profiles of Ghana and Sweden. These two countries illustrate the extremes in population distributions. In Ghana, 42 percent of the population was under 15 years of age in 1970, and only 3 percent was 65 and over, whereas in Sweden, the percentages were 21 and 13, respectively. It should be apparent to you how these profiles account for the grossly different birth rates in the two countries. With a large proportion of its population in the child-bearing years, Ghana will have a higher birth rate than will Sweden.

Migration

We've seen that population size increases because of births, that it decreases because of deaths, and that the excess of births over deaths is called the "natural increase." Natural increase is the chief source of population growth in virtually all nations of the world, but it is not the only one. Populations also grow and decline because of **migration:** people moving in and out. The difference between in-migration and out-migration is referred to as the "net migration."

The reasons for migration are many. Demographers often speak of "push" and "pull" factors. People can be "pushed" out of an area because of unsatisfactory conditions there. Wars, unemployment, persecution, famine, blight, and pollution are only a few of the reasons why people may choose to pack up and leave the place where they are living. Correspondingly, people may be "pulled" to areas because of good economic opportunities, good climate, congenial political and social conditions, and a countless variety of other reasons. Very often, migration reflects both push and pull factors, as in the migration of many people from Ireland to the United States in the 1840s. Ireland was suffering a devastating potato famine, while the

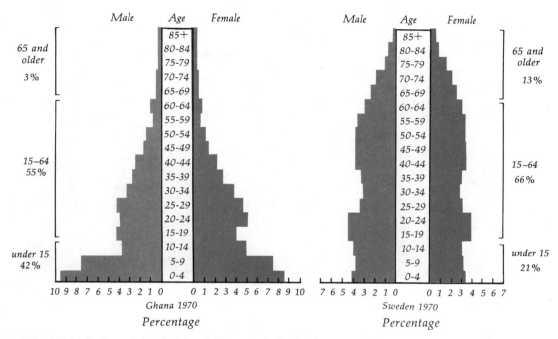

Figure 18–6 Distribution of populations of Ghana and Sweden by age and sex, 1970. Source: Everett S. Lee, The United States among the Nations, *The Center for Information on America, 1971, p. 7. Reprinted by permission.*

United States was regarded as the land of golden opportunity. American population growth during the nineteenth century was largely a function of European migration to the New World.

Aside from the direct and immediate consequences of migration on population growth, there may also be indirect and long-term consequences depending on the *kind* of people migrating. As a general rule, young immigrants, because of their potential for childbearing, will affect population growth more than old ones will. Thus, for example, the large migration of retired people to Florida creates less long-term population growth there than the migration of young people to California does there.

The sex of migrants is also an important consideration in determining the impact of migration on population growth. Unless there is a reasonably even sex ratio, having a large proportion of a population in the childbearing years

has little consequence for population growth. But men and women do not always migrate in equal numbers. Look at the example of Hawaii.

Late in the nineteenth century, large numbers of young Japanese and Chinese men were brought to Hawaii to work on the large agricultural plantations. This event is reflected in the first age-sex pyramid (*a*) of Figure 18–7. In 1900, nearly one-third of the total population was composed of young men between twenty and thirty-five years of age. Many of them eventually decided to remain in Hawaii beyond the period of their labor contracts; brides were imported from Asia; and by 1920, as we see, the sex ratio had nearly evened out (*b*). During the military buildup before World War II, however, the number of young men in Hawaii was again out of proportion (*c*), and the continued military presence in 1970 (d) provides for the same pecularity.

Population growth, in summary, is the result

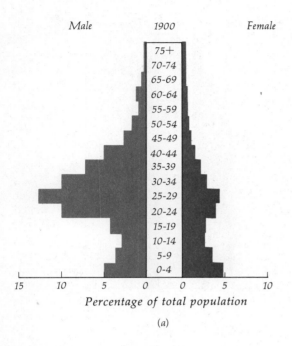

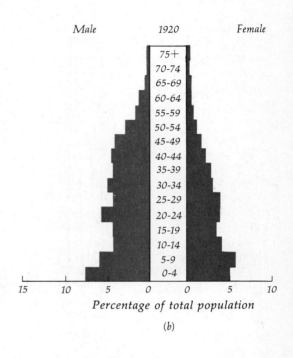

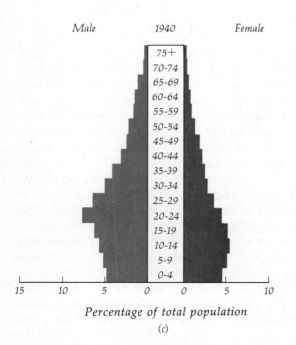

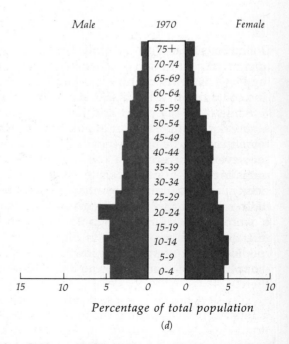

Figure 18–7 Age-sex profiles in Hawaii. Source: Adapted from Robert Gardner and Eleanor Nordyke, The Demographic Situation in Hawaii *(Honolulu: East-West Population Institute, 1974), pp. 14–19.*

of an often intricate and complex interaction among births, deaths, and migration. For many years nations regarded growth as good and encouraged their citizens to be fruitful and multiply. Why is population growth now regarded as bad?

The Problem of Overpopulation

People have for a long time thought that "bigger is better," and public officials have pointed to population growth with pride. Yet now many people regard population growth as the world's most pressing problem. Why? To set the stage for this discussion, you might want to review Figure 18–1, which shows the long-term pattern of world population growth. That the world population might double every 41 years at its present rate of growth is a staggering thought: today's 4.5 billion becomes 9 billion, which becomes 18 billion—in less than a century.

The human species has been on this earth for more than a million years. Yet Ansley Coale (cited in Nam 1968:63) has calculated that if we were to continue increasing at our present rate for another 6,500 years, people would be piling on top of each other around the entire globe and the mass of bodies would be expanding into outer space at a rate faster than the speed of light.

We know that this dramatic extrapolation won't come true. The reasons why it won't, however, point to the reasons why even lower rates of population growth are a problem. Let's look at some of them; and in the process, we'll add some clarity to the loosely used term "overpopulation." Though lacking any scientific definition, it refers generally to "too much" population—for the space available, for the food supply, for the available resources in general.

Crowding

The most obvious problem population growth creates is overcrowding. Studies of the ways animals behave in crowded conditions provide a useful backdrop for the examination of human crowding. Studies of rats, elephants, deer, monkeys, and other animals show that crowding produces a variety of problems, among them aggression, infertility, high mortality rates, and erratic behavior. Many of the animal responses to crowding, as you may have noted, have the effect of reducing population size.

Studies of the effects of human crowding are more complicated. The behavior of small groups crowded together under experimental conditions may not reflect the effects of crowding in natural social settings, such as crowded apartment buildings. On the other hand, studies of natural crowding—numbers of people per acre or people per room—are complicated by differences in social class and cultural patterns. Thus, when studies show that crime rates are higher in densely populated areas of a city than in more sparsely populated areas, part of the answer may lie in the generally lower social status of people in the more crowded areas.

Having recognized the research complexities of this issue, some of the findings are of interest. For example, Schmitt, Zane, and Nishi (1978) examined the correlations between census-tract density and various social problems in Honolulu for the 1973–1975 period. The researchers measured density in three different ways: (1) the number of residents per acre, (2) the number of people working in the census tract per acre, and (3)—given the importance of tourism in Hawaii—the number of hotel units per acre.

The social problems they examined were (1) infant-death rate, (2) illegitimate-birth rate, (3) welfare-case rate, and (4) psychiatric-case rate. Psychiatric problems and illegitimacy were found to be related fairly strongly to each measure of density, and all the social problems were found to be related when all three density measures were taken into account.

What makes this study of particular interest is that Schmitt (1966) had undertaken a similar analysis for the period 1948–1952. In the earlier study, he found the same relationships between density and social problems—except that the links were *much stronger in the earlier study.* This observation led the researchers to conclude that the relationship between crowding and social problems is more complex than previously imagined, a conclusion roundly supported by Fischer and his associates (1974) in an excellent review of studies on crowding.

War

Overpopulation has often been cited as a factor in creating international hostilities. German aggression in World War II, for example, was often justified by the need for *lebensraum*—"living space." As a nation begins to outgrow its space, it may look elsewhere, across its borders.

This problem is complicated by another factor. National policies of population growth are often justified as a means of developing military potential—for defense, of course. Small nations sometimes fear that their size makes them weak in relation to larger neighbors. Israel is an excellent example; with a population of under 4 million, it is surrounded by far more populous Arab neighbors. Egypt alone, for example, has a population ten times that of Israel.

Sometimes this fear will lead a small nation to seek growth, eventually running out of space and needing to look around for *lebensraum.* Notice how this parallels the nuclear-arms race, as nations compete with one another for the security of military superiority, increasing the danger of war in the same process. So it is with the "population bomb" as well.

Hunger

A third reason why continued population growth is viewed with alarm is that, many believe, it may mean mass starvation. The argument that a growing population will inevitably lead to mass starvation was made most forcefully by an English parson and economist, Thomas Robert Malthus.

In 1798, Malthus published *An Essay on the Principle of Population.* Malthus's primary thesis

Hunger strikes children the hardest. Victim of a severe drought throughout the Sahel region of Africa and a persistent war in the Ogaden region of Ethiopia, this Somalian refugee mother feels helpless as her baby wastes away day-by-day.

was that while food production increases *arithmetically,* population growth is *geometrical.* These two types of mathematical progressions are illustrated below:

Arithmetic (food)	Geometric (people)
1	1
2	2
3	4
4	8
5	16
6	32
.	.
.	.
.	.

Malthus recognized that the discrepancy between population and food could not continue growing indefinitely: starvation would prevent unlimited population growth if nothing else did. Since Malthus believed that people were so sexually driven that they could not control their fertility, however, he concluded that there would always be great masses of people on the brink of starvation. Mass poverty would always exist.

At present, it is generally estimated that between 15 and 20 million people die each year from starvation and malnutrition. Three-fourths of them are children, averaging out to some twenty-one children dying every minute of every hour of every day, day after day. That most of these deaths occur in countries with high birth rates would seem to confirm what Malthus had concluded about the relationship between population and hunger.

Upon closer analysis, however, the relationship between population and starvation is more complex than Malthus suggested. We'll return to this issue in the Application and Analysis essay at the end of this chapter.

Stemming Population Growth

If the world's population is to cease growing, the global birth rate must equal the global death rate. Beginning where we are today, then, either the birth rate will have to be reduced or the death rate increased. No one seriously suggests raising the death rate to halt population growth, so we will devote this section to a discussion of lowering birth rates.

Zero Population Growth

The term **zero population growth** (ZPG) has become a popular one in recent years, largely because of the efforts of the American organization of that name. The ZPG concept is simple

in theory, but more complicated in actual application to human populations.

Basically "ZPG" refers to the condition in which a population merely produces its number generation after generation. Given the dyadic way we produce, this equation is often stated in terms of each couple's producing two and only two children. To put this notion in perspective, Figure 18–8 shows the population sizes resulting from patterns in which couples produce two, three, and four children each.

As indicated in Figure 18–8, the pattern in which each couple produces only two children leads to a stable population over the generations. Each person in one generation is replaced by one person in the next. The patterns in which each couple produces more than enough children for simple replacement, of course, result in population growth over the generations. Most dramatic is the case of four children per couple, since this results in a doubling of the population each generation.

The enormous implications of geometrical progressions such as these are sometimes difficult to understand. Consider the pattern of four children per couple for a moment. In this pattern each person in a given generation is replaced by two in the next. Beginning with a single couple in the first generation, there would be four people in the second generation. Our hypothetical population would reach a million in the twentieth generation. The thirty-first generation would equal just about half our current world population of 4.5 billion. How many more generations would it take to reach 4.5 billion? Just one more: the thirty-second generation.

The patterns illustrated in Figure 18–8 are somewhat simplified. In practice, of course, not every person produces offspring. Some children still die in infancy in every society and some adults never bear or father children. Because of these facts, it is estimated that a society like the United States could stabilize its population over the generations if each couple produced an average of approximately 2.11 children. Interestingly, the United States has actually

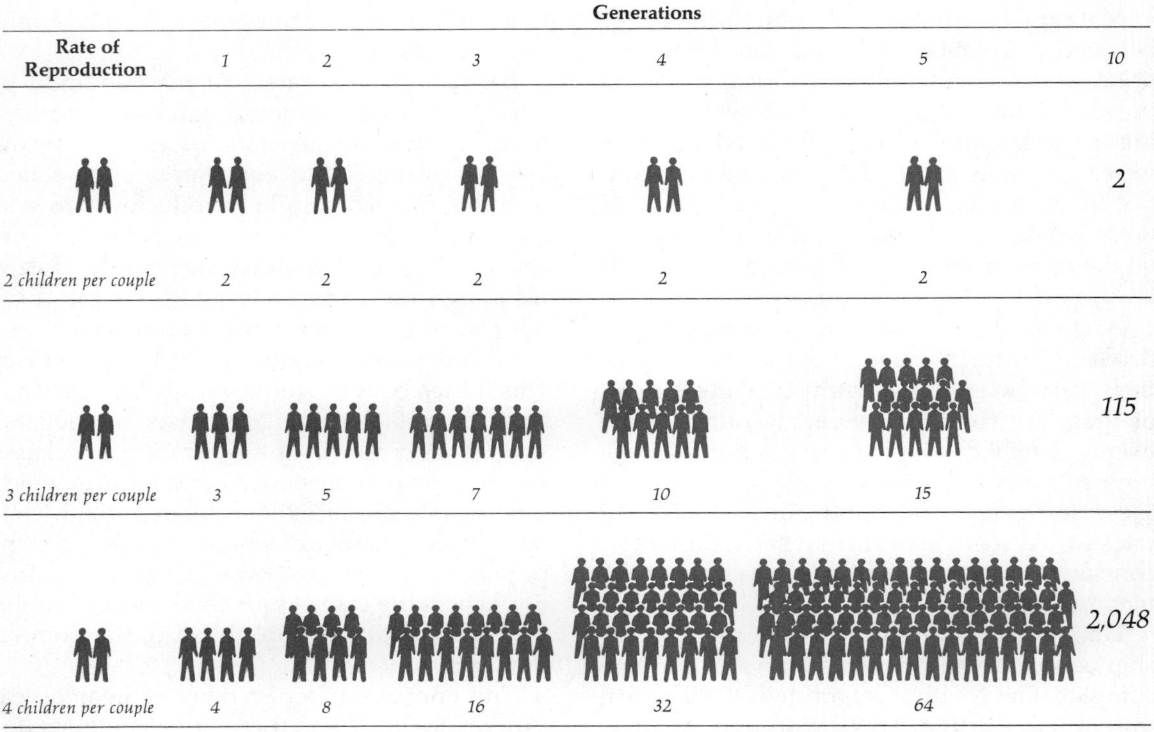

| | Generations | | | | | |
Rate of Reproduction	1	2	3	4	5	10

| 2 children per couple | 2 | 2 | 2 | 2 | 2 | 2 |

| 3 children per couple | 3 | 5 | 7 | 10 | 15 | 115 |

| 4 children per couple | 4 | 8 | 16 | 32 | 64 | 2,048 |

Figure 18–8 Populations resulting from different reproductive patterns. (The figures shown are rounded, although exact figures were carried forward in computing subsequent generations.)

reduced its reproduction below this level. Given the proportion of the United States population in or approaching childbearing years, however, it will take us about fifty years at current birth rates to reach a point where our total population stops growing. For an indication of what society would be like after the achievement of ZPG, see the box "Life after ZPG."

The United States is hardly typical, however. Recall that *worldwide* birth and death rates at the present time are such that global population will double every forty-one years. This is not very different from the most extreme pattern shown in Figure 18–8. And since the less developed countries of the world have larger proportions of their populations in the child-bearing years, it would take them even longer

than the United States to reach a point of population stability.

Childbearing Agreements

Sociobiologists are particularly interested in the levels and changes in birth rates because these reflect social agreements. Whereas death rates are largely—though not exclusively—a function of medical knowledge and practices, birth rates depend more directly on social norms.

People have three general kinds of agreements regarding childbearing:

1.   An agreement to bear whatever number of children result from sexual behavior

Table 18-7

The Dollar Cost of Raising a Child from Birth to Age 18 around the United States in 1978

Item	North Central	Northeast	South	West
Food at home	12,936	14,780	13,156	13,841
Food away from home	1,382	1,526	1,598	1,780
Clothing	4,826	5,044	5,098	4,904
Housing	17,718	18,944	19,254	19,356
Medical care	2,952	2,952	3,267	3,600
Education	840	1,044	1,260	1,044
Transportation	8,440	7,848	9,034	9,334
All other	6,578	6,750	7,622	7,750
Total	$55,672	$58,888	$60,298	$61,609

Note: Figures are for families of no more than two children, operating on "moderate" budgets.

Source: Reprinted from Carolyn Edwards, "User's Guide to USDA Estimates of the Cost of Raising a Child," *Family Economics Review,* Summer 1979, pp. 9–12.

2. An agreement that *more* children is better
3. An agreement that *fewer* children is better

The first of these agreements undoubtedly characterized most of human history. People engaged in sexual relations without even realizing that it was related to reproduction, and they took what they got. The race survived because the numbers of children produced in that fashion more or less matched the relatively high death rates.

The second kind of agreement—that having lots of children is good—has appeared many times in human history. Early American settlers needed many children to assist them in settling the wilderness. Small, weak nations and minority groups within a given nation have sometimes seen population growth as a means to political power. And numerous religious groups have taught that bearing many children glorified their god, adding ever larger generations of believers.

The third agreement—fewer children is better—has been increasing in popularity in the United States and in other developed countries. The source of popularity is at two levels. First, increasing numbers of people recognize the dangers of overpopulation both in societies and around the globe. Second, people recognize that small families have economic and other advantages at the individual family level. It has been estimated, for example, that raising a child from birth through independence can cost the average American tens of thousands of dollars, as Table 18–7 indicates. Many young couples are coming to recognize and reject the loss of freedom that children impose upon parents.

Average family size in America has been getting smaller for some time. Attitudinal surveys have shown a fairly steady decrease in the number of children *desired* by American couples as well, as you'll recall from data presented in Chapter 16 on the family.

People's *desires* regarding family size are important, of course, because, unlike the situation for most of the time our species has been around, we now have a reasonable choice in the matter. Even after our ancestors became

Life after ZPG

Twenty-six countries, including the United States, are now at or nearing ZPG (zero population growth). What will be the consequences of a stationary population for these countries? A demographer, Lincoln Day, has made the following projections, based on the assumption of a stationary age-sex structure.

In a ZPG society, the population would likely be older. Median age would be thirty-seven years in the United States when a stable population is reached, as compared to twenty-nine, which it was in 1975. Since the population would be older, death would be a relatively more frequent occurrence compared to today. A more equal sex ratio would also be likely. This, combined with the likelihood of stable age groups, would mean that no individual would be forced to remain unmarried simply because there weren't enough eligible partners.

Because the population would be somewhat older, an increased demand for health care might be expected. Day points out, however, that such an expectation may not be justified because there are so many other health-related factors involved: the extent of air pollution, amount of exercise, level of diet, degree of financial security, and sense of social worthiness gained from remaining active in society all influence the extent of health care needed by the elderly. If conditions conducive to fitness improve, it is conceivable that proportionately less money and effort will be needed to care for the elderly; if these conditions deteriorate, then society may have to expend proportionately more money and effort than currently.

What is true for health care is also true for most other aspects of social life, in Day's view. Demographics establishes the limits of social life, but doesn't determine variations within those limits. In general, cultural and social variations are more important in determining the shape of future social life, he believes, than the achievement of a stable population alone. With this caution in mind, let's look at some other areas.

---

conscious of the link between reproduction and intercourse, there wasn't much they could do to separate the two, and there may not have been as much pressure in that direction as recently. Having a choice, however, doesn't necessarily mean that people exercise it.

Parallel to the childbearing attitudes of individuals, national governments also have "attitudes"—in the form of population policies. Marden Parker et al. (1982:63) identify four national policies:

1. *Pronatalist:* This policy favors population growth. Argentina is an example.

2. *Developmentalist:* Here, population size is to be determined by economic development. The country has no explicit population policy aside from this. Most of the Third World fits this pattern.

3. *Family planning:* The government makes birth control methods available and encourages couples to use them. India has fit this pattern in recent years.

4. *Population planning:* Here, the government establishes a national policy of slowing or halting population growth and takes steps to penalize couples who have too many children. China is the best example of this though Indira Gandhi's first regime in India attempted it unsuccessfully.

For many years, China's official population policy was pronatalist. A massive population was seen as the best protection against threats from the Soviet Union and other neighbors, and government officials bragged that even a nuclear holocaust would leave more Chinese than any

In terms of economic conditions, because of the increased age of the general population, skill and work discipline might be more prevalent in a ZPG society, but, for the same reason, the flexibility necessary to adapt to a changing economy might decline. There might be a relative decline in the demand for goods by younger society members (new cars, stereos, and the like) in a ZPG society, but again, other changes, such as higher wages for young workers, could be a much more important factor in altering economic demand. With a slightly older population, there probably would be an increased demand for living quarters that would allow easier accessibility to shops, medical facilities, and cultural life. There probably would also be increased demand for Social Security programs, and perhaps more mandatory pension plans would be instituted. At the same time, the proportion of people of working age is expected to increase, so that the cost of increased social programs would be spread over more persons.

There might be less opportunity for occupational advancement with a stationary and slightly older population because positions would be occupied longer by individuals. Day suggests that, other factors being equal, there might be greater competitiveness for these relatively fewer positions, but eventually there might be a decline in personal ambitiousness and lessened status anxiety and feelings of failure.

The most certain consequence of ZPG would be a lowering, on average, of fertility, and therefore, on average, women would spend fewer years rearing children. This might further induce women to look for more roles outside the home and encourage men to look at them as more than wives and mothers.

Source: Lincoln H. Day, "What Will a ZPG Society Be Like?" *Population Bulletin* 33, no. 3 (Population Reference Bureau, Inc., Washington, D.C., 1978).

---

one other nationality. Eventually, the government came to recognize the economic drain of population growth. The Hong Kong newsmagazine *Asiaweek* (1981:58) describes the current policy in the Peoples' Republic:

Every worker in 1979 supported .93 unproductive people—infants, students, invalids, aged parents. By the year 2000 the worker will have to foot the bill for only .39 persons, allowing him to enjoy more of the fruits of his labor.

If zero population growth is to be achieved by 2000—and all national efforts are being directed toward that end—the new policy must be stringently enforced. For the moment Chinese parents can get away with having two children. In Peking and Canton those who refuse to abort a third pregnancy must pay a fine of 10 percent of their combined income from the fourth month of the pregnancy until the child's fourteenth birthday.

Compulsory abortions are expected to be introduced soon for second pregnancies, but authorities stress that contraception or sterilization is preferable.

Birth Control

Contemporary methods of birth control are many and varied: birth control pills, condoms, diaphragms, intrauterine devices, foams, jellies, and sterilization. Some people attempt to control conception through practices including celibacy, withdrawal before ejaculation, the "rhythm method" (limiting intercourse to infertile periods of a woman's menstrual cycle), astrology, breast-feeding, and a variety of douches.

Knowledge of birth-control methods is largely a function of educational level—both within

Table 18-8

Methods of Contraception Currently Used: Developing and Developed Countries

(Percentage distribution, by method, of contraceptive use at time of survey—of those using some method)

	Pill	IUD	Diaphragm, foam	Douche	Condom	Rhythm	Withdrawal	Abstinence	Female sterilization	Male sterilization	Other methods	Injectables	Percent using inefficient methods
Developing countries													
Kenya	30	10	0	0	2	16	2	16	13	1	1	8	35
Nepal	16	2	0	0	9	0	0	2	3	67	0	0	2
Philippines	13	7	0	0	10	24	26	5	13	2	0	0	55
Sri Lanka	5	15	0	0	7	25	5	11	29	2	0	1	41
Mexico	36	19	5	1	3	10	12	0	9	1	1	6	24
Turkey	16	8	1	11	8	3	44	0	1	0	7	1	65
Developed countries													
Finland	14	36	1	—	40	1	3	—	5	1	—	—	4
Italy	18	3	3	—	17	11	46	—	1	—	1	—	58
United States	34	9	10	—	11	5	3	—	12	13	2	—	10
Yugoslavia	9	3	6	—	4	8	65	—	—	—	5	—	78

Note: Inefficient methods include douche, rhythm, withdrawal, abstinence, and "other methods."—means no information available.

Source: Robert Lightbourne, Jr., and Susheela Singh, *The World Fertility Survey: Charting Global Childbearing* (Washington, D.C.: Population Reference Bureau, 1982), pp. 34–35.

The world's most populous nation, the Peoples' Republic of China has now instituted rigorous population control measures, strongly urging couples to have no more than one or two children.

societies and across them. David Heer (1966) has concluded that the general relationship between economic development and reduced birth rates probably reflects an increased flow of communication concerning birth control. Many nations of the world have not experienced the economic development Heer spoke of.

Today, birth control knowledge varies widely across the Third World. The World Fertility Survey found that 100 percent of those interviewed in Fiji, Costa Rica, and the Dominican Republic were aware of one or more effective methods of birth control. By contrast, this was true for only 20 percent of those interviewed in Senegal and only 22 percent of those in Nepal (Lightbourne and Singh 1982:31).

The *practice* of birth control varies greatly as well. Lightbourne and Singh (1982:32–33) report that 3 percent of the procreative population uses birth control in Nepal, compared with 95 percent in Czechoslovakia. In the United States, it was 77 percent. Table 18–8 reports the forms of birth control being used in different countries, according to the World Fertility Survey.

The increased acceptance and practice of birth control in America has many sources. The women's movement, for example, has won some acceptance for the position that women have functions other than bearing and caring for children. Increased availability of occupational careers for women has had a similar, related effect. This latter factor has become increasingly important as young couples have sought

A preindustrial view of the world held that human beings should live in harmony with the rest of nature; this view has seen a rebirth in connection with modern ecology movements.

to achieve and maintain reasonably high standards of living during times of economic inflation. The birth of a new child both adds family costs and takes away the wife/mother's income.

Contraception is only one form of birth control. Norms that delay marriage and cohabitation until later in life also reduce birth rates. Abortion is another alternative to contraception, albeit a hotly controversial one.

People are attempting in some localities and in several different ways to take control of their own reproductive capacity. I don't want to create the impression that individual practice of birth control around the world reflects a general concern for overpopulation, however. After all, *one* baby more or less does not make or break a population explosion, and while some people report that overpopulation figured in

their decision to limit their families, most birth control activities reflect individual, personal objectives. Leon and Steinhoff (1975), for example, report that the most common reason for seeking an abortion under Hawaii's liberalized abortion law was that the prospective mother was unmarried. Following that, the most common reasons given were: (1) financial, (2) interference with the woman's education, (3) inability to "cope with a child at this time," (4) having enough children already, and (5) the prospective mother's feeling that she was too young.

To recap briefly, we humans have just completed two or three centuries of incredible population growth, with all the problems accompanying it. As little as five years ago, the prospects for slowing down the growth short of disaster were dim. In the past year or two,

A different view has held that human beings could subjugate nature without fear of reprisal.

however, there have been signs of slowed growth. It is still too early to know what the signs represent, but we haven't even had signs until now.

Environment

In the remainder of the chapter, I want to focus on a related matter: the physical environment of earth. Obviously, population growth has a direct impact on the environment because it increases the number of people sharing limited resources. So, as we'll see, do our agreements regarding what use we should make of our environment.

Florence Kluckhohn and Fred Strodtbeck (1961:13) have described three views of the interaction between people and environment that are especially relevant to our discussions. They are (1) human subjugation by nature, (2) human harmony with nature, and (3) human mastery over nature.

We'll look at each of these points of view and the agreements different societies have created around them. Then we'll look more specifically at the environmental consequences of our present way of life.

Three Views of Nature

In this section we'll examine each of the attitudes identified by Kluckhohn and Strodtbeck. We'll also explore the modern ecosystem point of view, noting the relationship between that and the three different points of view that different societies have agreed on.

Subjugation by Nature As nearly as we can tell, our earliest ancestors regarded themselves as being at the mercy of the environment. Their existence on earth seemed dependent on the whims of climate, weather, vegetation, and hungry animals. Lightning burned the forests around them, droughts drove them from place to place, predators drove them into hiding, and ice ages forced them to relocate permanently.

The earliest men and women probably differed little from other animals in being ruled by the forces around them. By virtue of their greater brain capacity, however, people were able to reflect on their condition, as the other animals could not.

Much of our speculation about their reflections comes from what anthropologists and others have learned about contemporary preliterate societies. Much of the religion of these societies, for example, is devoted to the "propitiation" of nature, to gaining the good graces of all-powerful natural and supernatural forces. The Tsembaga of New Guinea, for example, thank their ancestors for assistance in war and seek continued support. Rappaport (1969:191) describes the ritual in which they plant the *rumbin* plant and say, in essence:

> We thank you for helping us in the fight and permitting us to remain on our territory. We place our souls in this *rumbin* as we plant it in our ground. We ask you to care for this *rumbin*. We will kill pigs for you now, but they are few. In the future, when we have many pigs, we shall again give you pork and uproot the *rumbin* and stage *a kaiko* (pig festival). But until there are sufficient pigs to repay you the *rumbin* will remain in the ground.

From this point of view, human survival occurs at the pleasure of forces in the environment that people cannot control, although a variety of religious practices are aimed at seeking the favor of these forces. Realize that there is considerable empirical evidence to support this point of view in the experiences of people who share it. Fear and discomfort, starvation, and violent death provide ample evidence for people to conclude that men and women are mere pawns in a cosmic chess game.

Harmony and Nature Another point of view shared by many people around the world and through history suggests that human beings are equal partners with other animate and inanimate forms in nature. Rather than controlling or being controlled by the environment, people exist in harmony with it.

Many Eastern religions, such as Buddhism and Hinduism, share a view that all elements in the environment are sacred. Members of the Jain sect of Asia, for example, are especially careful not to tread on insects and worms; and they cover their mouths with cloth to avoid inadvertently swallowing and killing tiny flying insects.

This point of view has been presented to a Western audience recently in the form of several popular books. Among them are the "Don Juan" books of Carlos Castaneda (1969, 1971, 1972, 1974) and Robert Pirsig's *Zen and the Art of Motorcycle Maintenance* (1975).

It is important to distinguish stated agreements from practices in this regard, however, as Paul Ehrlich and Anne Ehrlich (1972:352) have cautioned:

> While Chinese religions, for example, stressed the view that man was a part of nature (rather than lord of it) and should live in harmony with it, the Chinese did not always live by this belief. . . . By the twentieth century, China's once plentiful forests had been nearly destroyed to build cities and clear the land for agriculture. . . . Ironically, the present government, which explicitly rejects the traditional religions, has attempted to restore the forests on a large scale.*

---

*From *Population, Resources, Environment: Issues in Human Ecology,* 2nd ed., by Paul R. Ehrlich and Anne H. Ehrlich, copyright 1972 by W. H. Freeman and Company. Reprinted by permission.

Mastery over Nature   You are no doubt most familiar with the last of the three points of view described by Kluckhohn and Strodtbeck: human mastery over nature. This is the point of view that best characterizes the developed nations of the world. By adapting nature to suit human whims and desires, people have produced great industrial engines, brought manifold increases in the productivity of the soil, cured disease, tamed wild animals and raging rivers, and placed men on the moon.

This point of view finds considerable support in the Judeo-Christian tradition. In the Book of Genesis, human beings are given dominion over the other creatures of the earth. Ehrlich and Ehrlich (1972) argue that Christianity—in comparison with other religions—has created a mood of indifference to other elements in the environment, permitting them to be manipulated in the service of human beings. It should be noted, however, that this view has not been uniformly accepted by Christians and Jews. Essene Jews, Christian Transcendentalists, and Quakers have tended more toward harmony with nature. And, of course, there have been numerous individuals who varied from the norm: St. Francis of Assisi comes first to mind.

We'll turn our attention shortly to some of the consequences of our civilization's having acted out the mastery-over-nature point of view—through technology, in particular. Before doing that, however, we should look at what point of view workers in the modern ecological sciences take regarding the place of human beings in their environment.

The Ecosystem Point of View

Ironically perhaps, modern ecologists take an environmental point of view strikingly similar to that of the Eastern mystics: humans exist in harmony with the rest of the environment. It's not so much that we *should* but that we have no choice in the matter.

To understand the ecological point of view, it is necessary to recall the notion of **homeosta-** sis from the discussion of social systems theory in Chapter 2. The Greek term *stasis* means literally "a standing," as in a stoppage in the flow of blood from a body. "Homeostasis," then, essentially means "staying the same," and what the term suggests is very similar to the notion of social stability discussed earlier in this book.

Our physical environment, including us, is a system: an ecosystem. Like a social system, the ecosystem is made up of interrelated components. Each component affects and is affected by all the other components of the system. The rain accelerates the growth of grass, which cows eat, thereby providing milk, and so forth. If people transform the fields of grass into subdivisions and parking lots, there is less grass for the cows to eat, so there may be less milk, and the rain runs off the concrete, causing floods. Everything is related to everything else, and someone has said that the first law of ecology is that you can't do just one thing. Anything you do has many, many effects.

In a system where everything is related to everything else, two kinds of things can happen. The components of the system can balance and counterbalance each other, creating homeostasis over time, or a series of events can create continuing and often accelerated change in the state of the system. Some examples will illustrate these two different possibilities.

Imagine water leaking through a tiny hole in a dam. The water trickling out erodes the edges of the hole, making it larger. As the hole enlarges, more water pours out faster, causing more erosion. This chain of events is creating a continuing and accelerating change in a system. By contrast, consider this example of homeostasis in a system. Some forms of automobile antifreeze contain tiny magnetic pellets. Whenever the antifreeze begins leaking through a hole in the radiator, the magnetic pellets stick to the edges of the hole, eventually clogging it up and stopping the leak.

In the case of our physical environment, homeostasis means the survival of the ecosystem, the continuing possibility of life on earth, including us. Ecosystem survival is not intrinsically "good," but virtually everybody on earth *agrees* that it's good. Let's turn now to a consideration of how technology has affected the chances for homeostasis.

Stresses on the Environment

Like all living things, human beings modify the physical environment by taking things away from it and adding things to it. These two human activities are referred to by the terms "resource depletion" and "pollution." Human beings are not alone in depleting the world's resources and in polluting. Other animals do it too—but we are special.

When wild goats deplete their food resources through overgrazing, for example, the situation is remedied by natural checks and balances. Many of the goats starve to death, and their population is reduced to the point at which grass, trees, and shrubs can recover. Our technological ingenuity, however, has allowed us to devise stopgap measures to put off nature's reckoning. In the process, we have created forms and levels of pollution well beyond the abilities of other animals.

Resource depletion and pollution have serious implications for the ecosystem. Of what relevance is sociology? What can the understanding of social agreements contribute to the solution of environmental problems? Let's see.

Resource Depletion

"In April, 1968, a group of thirty individuals from ten countries—scientists, educators, economists, humanists, industrialists, and national and international civil servants—gathered in the Accademia dei Lincei in Rome . . . to discuss a subject of staggering scope—the present and future predicament of man" (Donella Meadows et al. 1972:9). Eventually calling itself "The Club of Rome," this group commissioned a series of research projects aimed at determining the long-term effects of human consumption of global resources and the production of pollution.

In 1972, a major report on the research was published, and *The Limits to Growth* by Donella Meadows and her colleagues at M.I.T. became one of the most important and most controversial books of the generation. Using advanced computer-simulation techniques, the researchers constructed computer-program models that explored the implications of factors and relationship governing past and present behavior. Population growth, resource use, and pollution were among the factors considered. The programs resulted in forecasts, some of which were extremely dismal. They indicated that past patterns simply could not continue without totally exhausting certain resources.

The research findings were perhaps most shocking in regard to "nonrenewable natural resources": the fuels and minerals that require millions of years for natural production. Table 18–9 shows some of the researchers' forecasts (Dennis Meadows et al. 1978). Estimates of how long various resources will last depend on two important variables. First, do we currently know the volume of resources available to us, or can we expect to discover more in the future? Second, will levels of production (consumption of the raw materials) continue at current levels, or will production rates continue to grow in the future as they have been growing in the past? Table 18–9 considers each of these possibilities.

Resources like coal, petroleum, and iron are called "nonrenewable" because of the millions of years it takes nature to produce them. Other resources, such as lumber, food crops, and water are regarded as "renewable" because of the *relative* speed with which they are produced. Even with renewable resources, consumption often matches and temporarily exceeds production. Fresh water is in short supply in many places, and the world's forests, especially in the tropics, are being depleted.

Table 18-9

Estimates of the Future of the World's Natural Resources

Resource	Current consumption		Years to deplete resource assuming	Increased consumption	
	Low estimate	High estimate	Low estimate	Low estimate	High estimate
Aluminum	110	340	33	49
Chromium	730	1,300	115	137
Coal	3,100	5,100	118	132
Cobalt	190	420	90	132
Copper	52	160	27	46
Gold	7	25	6	17
Iron	840	—	154	—
Lead	38	490	28	119
Manganese	710	1,200	106	123
Mercury	25	84	19	44
Molybdenum	390	1,400	65	92
Natural gas	30	300	19	58
Nickel	130	350	50	75
Petroleum	38	110	23	43
Platinum	100	140	41	49
Silver	18	32	15	23
Tin	88	160	62	92
Tungsten	39	—	27	—
Zinc	280	930	76	115

Notes: Consumption based on estimates by the U.S. Bureau of Mines.
Low estimate assumes currently known resources; i.e., no new discoveries.
High estimate includes new resource discoveries as estimated by the U.S. Geological Survey and others.

Source: Adapted from Dennis Meadows et al., *Dynamics of Growth in a Finite World* (Cambridge, Mass.: Wright-Allen, 1978), pp. 372–73.

Alarm has also spread among the world's scientists who fear that deforestation could both alter the world's climate and result in the loss of countless wildlife species. Also lost could be future life forms, as the tropical forests are considered the last of earth's genetic "hothouses." (Sullivan 1978:3)

Who is responsible for the depletion of tropical forests? Is it the large, multinational conglomerates, the logging industry? Are the tropical forests being sacrificed for urban development in the wealthy nations of the world?

In this case, the problem seems more directly linked to the survival needs of the rural poor.

Bit by bit, they are destroying the developing countries' forests in a relentless quest for enough food and fuel to survive. More than 90 percent of wood used in developing countries is thought to go for fuel, not housing or paper. (Sullivan 1978:3)

The box entitled "The Search for Energy and the Fate of Forests" discusses this problem from a long historical perspective.

The Search for Energy and the Fate of Forests

The fate of wood on the planet is part of a complex, historical process. Jeremy Rifkin and Ted Howard (1980) argue persuasively that human history is intimately tied to our use of different energy sources, and wood illustrates perfectly the interaction between humans and the environment.

Wood was the main energy source in Europe before the Industrial Revolution. Originally, Europe was covered by a dense forest; and, over time, small clearings were opened up to support human settlements. Given the heavy, sticky soil of Western Europe, plowing for cultivation was particularly difficult. This difficulty, however, led people to create technological solutions. During the sixth century, Rifkin and Howard report, Slavic peasants had begun using a heavier "cross plow"—with wheels and two blades. The new plow had many consequences.

The new cross plow changed the entire organization of agricultural life. Because it was so heavy, the cross plow required a team of eight oxen to move it. Since no single peasant family owned that many oxen, teams had to be used cooperatively. Equally important, with the new cross plow it was no longer practical to fence off land into private strips. The big heavy plow performed best in long open fields. For both these reasons, communal farming became the pattern on most feudal estates in Northern Europe. (Rifkin and Howard 1980:69)

The increased effectiveness of the new agricultural technology made it feasible to clear ever-larger fields for cultivation, and population pressure made it necessary. To support the need for more food, farmers had to make further adjustments. Traditionally, they had left half their land fallow at any time, so it could recover its nutritive powers. Now, they began leaving only a third of the land fallow. This put more land under production at any given time, producing an initial increase in food.

To plow the larger fields, horses were increasingly used in place of oxen. The horses worked faster than the oxen, but they required oats, where the oxen had gotten by on hay alone. Some of the increased cropland, then, had to be

---

Simply taking life forms away from the ecosystem without being responsible for their replacement can result in severe problems. Asked to give an example of this, food authority Lester Brown (1978) cited the case of anchovy fishing off the coast of Peru during the 1960s and 1970s. During the late 1960s the Peruvian harvest of anchovies accounted for almost one-fifth of the world's annual supply. It was estimated, moreover, that the "maximum sustainable yield" was just under 10 million tons a year: that amount could be harvested each year, with the anchovies still replacing their numbers. The fishermen got greedy, however and the 1970 harvest reached a peak of 13 million tons. Figure 18–9 shows what happened (Brown 1978:200).

Pollution

Earth's ecosystem is for all practical purposes a "closed system." This means that nothing is permanently taken away from it. When iron ore is taken out of the ground and processed into steel, it remains in the ecosystem, but in a transformed state. The transformations we work, which we have termed generally "pollution," have an impact on other aspects of the environment. Let's look at some of those.

Air Pollution The massive atmosphere surrounding the planet has been visibly and invisibly changed in many significant ways by our activities. The clouds of smog hovering over most modern cities, often extending out to sea

turned to the growth of oats. On balance, none-theless, food surpluses were common during the ninth through twelfth centuries—resulting in a rapid growth in population.

By about the fourteenth century, however, the consequences of these several changes began to be felt. The lands under cultivation had become more and more exhausted by overuse. This had been solved by clearing more and more forests to enlarge the fields, but now the forests had become so scarce that the shortage of wood was a real problem. The main source of energy and of building material was nearing exhaustion.

The answer to the wood crisis was coal. But it was not just a simple matter of replacing one energy base with another. The cultures of Europe had been thoroughly integrated into a wood-based existence. The change-over necessitated the radical uprooting of an entire way of life. The way people made a living, the way people got around, the way people dressed, the way people behaved, the way governments governed—all of this was turned inside out, then upside down. (Rifkin and Howard 1980:72)

One of the important characteristics of coal, however, was that it was more difficult to get than wood. Put in system terms, the new energy source required a greater input of energy to obtain it. Rifkin and Howard point out that the modern steam engine was developed for the purpose of ventilating the coal mines and pumping water out of them. The difficulty of transporting coal created another problem. The roads of the time simply could not support the heavy loads. As a result, railroads were developed—again requir-ing massive amounts of energy for their con-struction and operation.

Rifkin and Howard point out that every new energy source—from coal to oil to atomic fis-sion—has required ever-greater expenditures of energy to get it. We are, they warn, headed down a one-way street. Nor is solar energy wholly divorced from this process. Although solar energy is essentially inexhaustible, the energy and resources that will be required to capture it are tremendous. The depletion of resources, then, is a critical and complex consequence of human/environmental interactions.

Source: Jeremy Rifkin (with Ted Howard), *Entropy*, New York: Viking, 1980.

or merging with the smog of other cities, are the most visible evidence of our impact. This painful fact of modern life has drawn our atten-tion to the problem of air pollution, but it has also deceived us. What you see is not all you get, and it may not even be the most dangerous part.

Table 18–10 offers a partial description of the air we breathe in the United States. The table shows the amount of pollutants pumped into the air in 1970 and in 1976. Notice three things in this table: (1) the sheer volume of the pol-lutants, *over one hundred million tons* of carbon monoxide in 1970, for example, (2) the gener-ally lower levels of pollution in 1976 as com-pared with 1970, and (3) the amount of pollu-tion judged uncontrollable in 1976—that is, the amount produced by natural ecosystem processes. Comparing columns 2 and 3 indi-cates how much of the pollution is produced by our technological civilization.

Air pollution of this magnitude affects hearts, lungs, and eyes. It kills crops that might have been consumed and poisons those that are. All this seems trivial in comparison with what air pollution may be doing to the atmosphere itself and the gaseous layers beyond it: reducing the radiant energy reaching earth from the sun while allowing more deadly radiation to pass through, changing the earth's climate.

The United States has no corner on the mar-ket for air pollution. It follows industrialization and civilization around the world. Here's how Lloyd Timberlake (1982:56), writing in the *New*

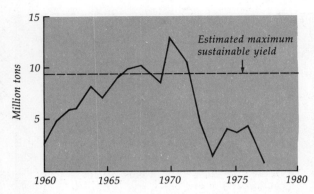

Figure 18–9 Peruvian anchovy catch, 1960–1977. Source: Lester Brown interviewed in "The Plowboy Interview," The Mother Earth News (March/April 1978):17--23. Reprinted by permission.

Table 18-10

Estimated Air-Pollution Emissions, 1970 and 1976

	Millions of tons		
	1970	1976	Uncontrollable (1976)
Carbon monoxide	110.0	96.1	6.3
Sulfur oxides	32.1	29.6	.1
Hydrocarbons	32.7	30.7	6.1
Particulates	24.9	14.8	1.0
Nitrogen oxides	22.5	25.3	.3

Source: U.S. Bureau of Census, *Social Indicators III*, Washington, D.C.: Government Printing Office, 1980, p. 152.

Scientist of London, describes the situation in Poland:

> In Poland's Katowice region, the nation's industrial heartland, the sulphuric and nitric acids that fall with each rain have so corroded the railway tracks that trains are restricted to 25 miles an hour. Environmental hazards annually kill and cripple many of the people of Katowice and destroy their homes and farms. . . .
>
> The industrial dust falling on Cracow is nine times the acceptable national limit. Water trucks race around the central square and marketplace throughout the day spraying streets in an effort to keep the dust down. Farmers have had to give up growing sugarbeets because the leaves, used as fodder, poisoned livestock. The traditional growing of green vegetables and berries has also been abandoned.

Water Pollution   Water is as essential to sustained life on earth as is air, and various of our activities are converting this source of life into a deadly poison. Sewage disposal in waterways adds disease-causing and death-dealing bacteria and viruses. Industrial wastes contaminate water with no-less-deadly inorganic materials such as lead, mercury, and sulfuric acid. Agricultural pesticides and herbicides also end up in the rivers, streams, and springs that supply us with drinking water.

Only a portion of these poisons reach people directly through their drinking water. Others are introduced into the complex food chain that eventually reaches dinner tables. Poisons in the water are ingested in algae, for example, which are in turn eaten by small fish which are then eaten by bigger fish, the last of these being caught and eaten by people. Not only are the poisons transmitted from step to step in the food chain, but many of them become more concentrated at each step.

The complexity of relationships in the ecosystem often causes a delay between pollution and the appearance of its consequences. Researchers have only recently discovered mercury concentrations in some Antarctic animals. These are believed to have resulted from the gold-mining practices of the California gold rush of 1849! Recent discoveries on the lasting effects of DDT in the ecosystem are probably only the tip of a noxious iceberg that will surface in years to come. By the time we begin noticing the effects of the deterioration of the ozone layer surrounding the earth's atmosphere, there will probably be no way to remedy it.

Like air pollution, water pollution is also a worldwide problem, more serious in many of the world's developing countries than in the United States. Here's how Vithal Nadkarni (1981:55) described the situation in the *Illustrated Weekly* of Bombay:

> The world's water crisis is far more serious than the oil crisis. Half the world's population has no potable water. More than thirty countries will face a severe shortage in the next twenty years. As populations grow and water becomes scarcer, one cannot rule out the possibility of countries going to war for it.

This gloomy description is echoed by Anil Agarwal (1980:34–35) in London's *Earthscan*. Agarwal links the water problem to population, on the one hand, and disease on the other.

> During the 1960s and 1970s there was some increase in the proportion of people served by water supply and sanitation facilities. But this increase has been much slower than the increase in population. As a result, the total number of people in the Third World without water supply or excreta disposal facilities has been increasing. . . .
> WHO [World Health Organization of the UN] estimates that 80 per cent of all sickness in the world is attributable to inadequate water or sanitation. This includes the effects of drinking contaminated water, of water as a breeding ground for disease, and of disease caused by lack of washing.

Nuclear Wastes   The search for new energy sources has produced a new and terrifying pollutant for the world to deal with. Once thought to be a salvation for the modern world, nuclear energy has come under a variety of attacks in recent years. Some people have feared the danger of accidents, a fear that was greatly heightened by the crisis of Three Mile Island. Others have questioned the simple economics of nuclear power. Probably the biggest problem of all concerns the disposal of radioactive wastes, some

of which remain lethal for tens or hundreds of thousands of years. Catherine Theil Quigg (1982:8) gives an indication of the magnitude of the problem:

> While three of the nation's six commercial nuclear dumps have been closed because of environmental pollution and the three remaining ones are drastically curtailing their intake, the wastes are piling up at university laboratories, hospitals, and factories at an ever-increasing rate. A large nuclear power plant generates about 1000 cubic meters of low-level radioactive waste each year—enough to cover a football field to a depth of one foot. There are 71 operating nuclear reactors with 90 new plants under construction.

Public Opinion and the Environment

These are but a tiny fraction of the number of examples that might be discussed in relation to pollution around the world today. Long ignored, these problems were addressed with some degree of urgency as a consequence of a wave of environmental activism during the 1970s. The American public became more aware of the problems, and a good deal of state and federal legislation was passed for the purpose of reducing pollution. And, as we saw in the case of air pollution earlier, some progress was made. Has this progress lulled Americans away from their commitment to environmental protection?

At first glance, public-opinion-poll data suggest that Americans are still firmly committed to environmental quality. In a 1981 poll, Americans rated their nation's air quality as follows:

Excellent	4%
Good	29
Fair	46
Poor	20

Asked to compare current air quality with that of five years ago, only 17 percent felt it had

The search for new energy sources has led in many directions. In Three Mile Island, shown here, it took the form of nuclear power generators.

improved. Forty-four percent felt it was about the same, and 39 percent felt things had gotten worse (*Public Opinion* 1982b:33).

With the Reagan administration threatening to ease up on environmental protections, only 30 percent of the public supported that policy; 50 percent were opposed, and 20 percent had mixed feelings. In answer to another question, 40 percent felt current air pollution standards were "about right," and another 42 percent said they were not tough enough. Only 19 percent subscribed to the view that existing standards were "overly protective" (*Public Opinion* 1982b:32).

At the same time, however, public concerns over the environment do not stack up very well in comparison with other social problems. In January 1982, the Roper Organization asked people to pick two or three things—from a list—that they were the most concerned about. Economic concerns proved to be the most troubling: inflation and high prices (53 percent), recession and unemployment (34 percent). Crime and lawlessness was picked by 37 percent; "the way the courts are run" by 25 percent. International relations were a concern for many: our relations with foreign countries (21 percent) and getting into another war (16 percent). Seventeen percent of the public were concerned about drug abuse, and twelve percent picked "the way young people think and act." At the bottom of the list—tied with alcoholism—seven percent of the public picked "pollution of air and water" (*Public Opinion* 1982b:33).

This section began with a question about the extent that our technological developments had affected the natural balance in the ecosystem. I trust that even the brief overview presented in the past few pages will have pointed to the vastness of the impact we have had on our planet. We are truly capable of making earth uninhabitable. The next question, then, is where do we look for the knowledge to prevent that destruction?

Sociology and the Environment

What has all this to do with sociology? Don't the problems discussed above all fall within the realm of other scientists? Aren't they problems to be worked out by physicists, chemists, and biologists? No.

The point of view that saw human beings as masters over nature has produced a myth that technology has created environmental problems and will be sufficient to save us from those problems. Most physicists, chemists, and biologists do not agree with the myth. For example, Garrett Hardin (1968:1243), an eminent biologist, has defined the technical solution as: "one that requires change only in the techniques of the natural sciences, demanding little or nothing in the way of change in human values or ideas of morality." Hardin is clear that such technical solutions are insufficient, no matter how tempting it is to think that they will work.

As we have seen throughout this chapter, our behavior as human beings, including our use of technology in our relationship to the ecosystem, is part of our values and ideas of moral-

ity. Those values and ideas, in turn, are a function of social agreements. Although technological advances—such as the Meadows' computer-simulation techniques—will assist in solving the problems of pollution and resource depletion, they clearly will not be enough (any more than the development of effective birth control techniques has been enough to halt population growth). The ultimate solution to environmental problems—like the problems of war, prejudice, and crime—rests with human behavior and the agreements that shape it. If sociologists are not able to understand the operation of those agreements, nobody will.

Sociologists will have to take the lead in the restructuring of human beliefs, values, and norms and in the creation of institutions that support the ecosysem rather than undermine it. As Ehrlich and Ehrlich (1972:347–48) indicate:

> Our problems cannot be solved by destroying our existing institutions, however; we do not have the time or the wisdom to dismantle them and put them back together again in better ways. But these institutions must be successfully altered—and soon—or they and we will not survive. Whether significant changes in attitudes and institutions can occur fast enough to affect mankind's destiny is an open question.*

In the same vein, Lewis Lapham (1977:58) has interpreted the "energy crisis" we face as follows:

> If it were a question of moving oil and gas from one place to another, or finding new fuels or designing new machinery, then in a nation as inventive as the United States I would expect the problem could be solved without much difficulty. But the crisis unfortunately has little to do with

---

*From *Population, Resources, Environment: Issues in Human Ecology,* 2nd ed., by Paul R. Ehrlich and Anne H. Ehrlich, copyright 1972 by W. H. Freeman and Company. Reprinted by permission.

technology, or even with raw materials. It is a political crisis, and, like most things political, resolves itself into quarrels about who has the right to do what to whom, at what price and in whose interest, under what definition of government and according to which interpretation of the democratic idea.

As I've already indicated in the case of world hunger, the problems we face on this planet today are less technological than social. We possess the technology to end hunger, to stem population growth, to drastically reduce pollution, and so forth. What remains to be done is to restructure the social agreements that generate the behavior patterns that keep us from using the technological solutions available to us.

Summary

Demography is the scientific study of population and is often considered a subfield of sociology. Demographers examine population size, composition, change, and the factors involved in each of those.

The current population of the world is approximately 4.5 billion and growing at about 1.7 percent a year. At the current growth rate, the world's population will double about every forty-one years.

Rapid population growth is relatively recent. It got its first significant boost with the invention of agriculture and exploded following the Industrial Revolution and the important advances made in the fight against disease. Only in recent years have we seen some evidence of a worldwide slowdown in population growth.

The United States census, first conducted in 1790, offers a good illustration of the current methods employed in learning how many people live in a society as well as the characteristics of those people.

Esssentially, three factors determine changes in the size of a society's population: births, deaths, and migration.

Birth and death rates differ greatly among the various societies in the world today, and these patterns change over time in a given society. The "demographic transition theory" suggests that many societies move through stages as they industrialize.

Overpopulation in the world is a problem that must be solved or it will solve itself. Most simply put, world population would stop increasing if every person alive were replaced by only one person in the next generation: if birth and death rates were equal. As a rough rule of thumb, this would occur if every couple were to limit themselves to no more than two children. Given the current age structure of the world's population, even this practice would produce population growth for the next half century or so, but the population would then stabilize. The situation in which population does not grow from one year to the next is called "zero population growth."

High birth rates and resistance to birth control are largely functions of implicit or explicit agreements regarding childbearing. Those societies that have an implicit agreement to take what they get will experience rapid population growth when death rates decline. Those sharing agreements in favor of large families will show the same pattern.

Our examination of environmental concerns began with a discussion of three different points of view that people have had regarding the relationship between human beings and the physical environment: (1) subjugation by nature, (2) harmony with nature, and (3) mastery over nature. Following that discussion, we examined the modern, ecosystem view suggested by ecological scientists, a view strikingly similar to that of many ancient Eastern religions. We are a part of nature and must exist in harmony with it and its other components. Some of the consequences of technology in the ecosystem are clear today; others are only becoming clear. Many of the earth's life-support elements—air, water, soil—have been severely damaged by the fruits of technological "progress" and urbanization.

Radical changes are needed in social agreements if basic biological processes are to continue.

Technology alone will not provide sufficient solutions to the various problems that make ecology such a dismal field of study. Many ecosystemic problems arise directly out of agreed-on patterns of social behavior. Other agreements prevent us from taking advantage of technological solutions. There is every reason to conclude that sociology will play an increasingly important part in the solution to environmental problems.

Important Terms

demography
census
doubling time
fertility
mortality
migration
crude birth rate
fecundity
crude death rate

infant mortality rate
natural increase
theory of demographic transition
age-sex composition
zero population growth
homeostasis

Suggested Readings

Brown, David L., and John M. Wardwell, eds.
1980 *New Directions in Urban-Rural Migration: The Population Turnaround in Rural America*. New York: Academic Press.
Discusses trends in population migrations, including United States and other Western industrial nations.

Brown, Lester R.
1978 The Twenty-Ninth Day. New York: Norton.
Analysis of population trends in the 1970s—growth of population, food production, ecological balance.

Carlson, John E., Marie L. Lassey, and William R. Lassey
1981 *Rural Society and Environment in America*. New York: McGraw-Hill.
Text in rural sociology, its sociological foundations and interpretations. Primary production, development are major discussions, taken from an ecological perspective.

DeBell, Garrett, Ed.
1970 *The Environmental Handbook*. New York: Ballantine.
As environmental consciousness has increased in America and elsewhere, many people have expressed frustration over the complexity of the problems involved. Ecosystems are complicated and not fully understood by anyone. This book, prepared in connection with the April 22, 1970, national teach-in on the environment, provides some practical guides. The several articles describe various aspects of our environmental problems and suggest how *you* can work on solving those problems—both in your day-to-day behavior and in an attempt to bring about social change.

Erhard, Werner
1977 "The End of Starvation: Creating an Idea Whose Time Has Come." San Francisco: The Hunger Project, transcript of speech.
This is an edited transcript of a presentation given in eleven cities during the fall of 1977, and it lays out the abstract principles of the Hunger Project, an organization aimed at the elimination of world hunger by 1997. In it, Erhard describes the principles that keep starvation persisting in the world as well as the principles for eliminating it.

Heer, David
1975 *Society and Population*, 2nd ed. Englewood Cliffs, N.J.: Prentice-Hall.
General discussion of field of population, its composition, and impact of change on people and societies.

Lappé, Frances Moore, and Joseph Collins
1977   *Food First: Beyond the Myth of Scarcity.* Boston: Houghton Mifflin.
This book presents and examines the empirical facts of food production, food requirements, and why millions starve each year in the face of plenty. The authors demonstrate beyond doubt that scarcity is *not* the explanation for starvation, and they suggest political and economic reforms that should alleviate the problem that exists.

Meadows, Donella, et al.
1972   *The Limits to Growth.* New York: Universe.
Like Ehrlich's *Population Bomb*, this is one of the most powerful influences in the growing environmental concern of the present day. Utilizing computer-simulation techniques, the researchers have traced out the likely implications of recent patterns of population growth, resource utilization, and pollution. Their main conclusion is contained in the title. We can't continue into the future without radically modifying some past patterns of behavior.

Vayda, Andrew, Ed.
1969   *Environment and Cultural Behavior.* Garden City, N.Y.: Natural History Press.
This collection of ethnographic reports gives an excellent picture of cross-cultural variations in human responses to the natural environment. You'll see many of the ways preliterate societies have created social patterns that permit them to live in harmony with the rest of the ecosystem.

Weeks, John R.
1981   *Population: An Introduction to Concepts and Issues.* Belmont, Calif.: Wadsworth.
Here's an excellent introduction to the field of demography. Weeks presents both the basic scientific concepts and also the practical implications.

Westoff, Charles, and Norman B. Ryder
1977   *The Contraceptive Revolution.* Princeton, N.J.: Princeton University Press.
Discusses the increased usage of sterilization as a method of contraception.

In earlier comments on the problems of over-population, I indicated that some 15 to 20 million people die *each year* as a consequence of hunger in the world. Since it's hard to visualize 15 to 20 million people dying in a year, let me put it on a different scale: 41,000 people die every day, on the average, as a consequence of hunger. That amounts to 28 people a minute, and 21 of them are children.

Clearly, hunger and population size are related to each other. Given some fixed amount of food (or any other commodity), the more people there are to share it, the less will be each person's share. Not without reason, therefore, many people have urged the reduction of population growth as a way of easing the problem of hunger in the world. In this essay, I want to look more deeply into the matter, seeing some of the complexity of the relationship between population and hunger—and seeing the relevance of sociology to all that.

Five Types of Hunger

To begin, let's look more closely at what's meant when we say that people die as a consequence of hunger. There are five major types of hunger relevant to this discussion.

Famine First, and best known, many people die each year as a result of *famine*, which can result from droughts, floods, crop diseases, wars, and other natural and unnatural disasters. Famines are recorded in the Bible and other ancient writings. Some recent famines occurred in Biafra (late 1960s), Bangladesh (early 1970s), the Sahel of Africa (mid-1970s), and Kampuchea (Cambodia) in the late 1970s. The term *starvation* is generally reserved for deaths due to the severe deprivation of food under such circumstances.

There are three things you should know about famines. First, nations such as the United States have been able to survive floods, droughts, and the like without suffering famine because of grain reserves and similar protections. Famines are primarily a problem for societies that have relatively little food even in good times. Second, the existence of famine in a country doesn't mean there is no food available in that country. However, masses of people have no way of buying the food they need, and there are inadequate provisions for giving it to them free. It is not unusual for a country experiencing a famine to continue exporting food to other countries. Third, famine and starvation account for only about 10 percent of the deaths due to hunger in the world. Most of those who die of hunger do so quietly and undramatically. They never appear on television.

Chronic Undernutrition When people regularly receive too few calories and/or too little protein, their bodies weaken or—in the case of children—never fully develop. While such people seldom die as a *direct* result of hunger, they die from problems that would be minor and temporary for healthy people: measles, diarrhea, respiratory infections, and the like. It has been estimated that as many as three-fourths of the deaths among children one-to-four-years old in Latin America result from chronic undernutrition.

Malnutrition Many people's diets regularly lack certain essential vitamins or minerals. Death can result in much the same way as for chronic undernutrition. In addition, people can be severely and permanently injured. The lack of vitamin A, for example, is estimated to cause blindness in 200,000 children a year.

Malabsorptive Hunger   Many people around the world actually eat enough of the right foods, but they suffer (and die from) hunger anyway. This occurs because parasites in their bodies consume the nutrients before those nutrients can be absorbed by their bodies. As much as 20 percent of the food eaten can be lost this way.

Seasonal Undernutrition   Finally, many hunger-related deaths occur on a seasonal basis, just before the harvest. You might think of this as a mini-famine, except it occurs year after year in many countries. In one Ugandan tribe, for example, the term for the month of May is translated: "The month when children wait for food."

Ninety percent of the deaths due to hunger on this planet do *not* result from unusual events: they are "normal." They occur year in and year out, regardless of whether crops are good or bad. It is this *persistence* of hunger that we are going to focus on in the remainder of this essay. Taking a sociological approach to the problem, let's begin with the reasons people tend to give for the persistence of hunger on the planet.

Explanation: "Hunger Is Inevitable"

When you ask people why hunger persists, the answer most give is that—"like death and taxes"—hunger is inevitable. There has always been hunger and there always will be. Actually, this is probably not true. For most of the time humans have been on this planet, hunger was not a major problem. For hundreds of thousands of years, our ancestors lived in small hunting and gathering bands of forty to fifty people. It probably took about twenty hours a week to get enough food to live. Massive hunger seems to have become common only after people began forming large civilizations—around nine or ten thousand years ago.

More to the point, however, sociologists are not inclined to accept the explanation of "inevitability" since it doesn't explain anything. It doesn't explain why hunger is inevitable. When you ask people to give reasons, here's how they usually elaborate.

Explanation: "There Isn't Enough Food"

The main reason given for the "inevitability" of world hunger is *scarcity*, pretty much following the Malthusian argument discussed earlier in the chapter. There are too many people on the planet, so there isn't enough food to go around. The main problem with this explanation, however, is that it's not accurate either. As Frances Moore Lappé and Joseph Collins (1977:13) report:

> The world is producing each day two pounds of grain, or more than 3,000 calories, for every man, woman, and child on earth, and 3,000 calories is about what the average American consumes. And this estimate is minimal. It does not include the many other staples such as beans, potatoes, cassava, range-fed meat, much less fresh fruits and vegetables.

And beyond that, in the United States, we are still paying farmers *not to grow crops,* so the potential for food production is far greater than current levels. Indeed, the potential for food production is staggering.

Explanation:
"The Problem Is too Complex To Be Solved"

When people recognize that enough food is currently produced to feed everyone, they often point to the complexity of the problem. For instance, if we were to eliminate hunger in the world, there would be an additional 15 to 20 million people around each year, and the hunger problem would be even greater next year or next generation.

We've already seen one response to this question—food production could be increased. More important, the discussion of the *theory of demographic transition* earlier in this chapter showed that reducing death rates—through the elimination of hunger, for example—has been followed by reduced birth rates in countries around the world. When people think that the children they have might live, they are more willing to reduce the number they have. In this sense, hunger is as much a cause of overpopulation as overpopulation is a cause of hunger.

A number of other factors are offered as proof that the hunger problem is too complicated to be solved. Problems of food storage, for example, account for considerable waste. Government corruption and economic-system complexities are also mentioned. When all is said and done, however, two things argue against explanations that the world hunger problem is too complicated to solve.

First, thirty-two countries that had a hunger problem have eliminated it since World War II. They used a variety of means, including land reforms, better fertilizers, and better strains of grain. South Korea solved its problem by emphasizing agricultural development, Hong Kong did it by emphasizing trade, finance, and tourism (earning money to buy food). Taiwan solved the hunger problem through family farms, China did so through collectivized agriculture. Hunger has been ended under a variety of political systems: communist (Russia), liberal democratic (Costa Rica), right-wing (Chile). These facts suggest that no nation with a hunger problem would be unable to solve it through one or a combination of the methods already proven in the field.

Second, many experts confirm that it is not a lack of food or a lack of agricultural or economic solutions that causes hunger to persist. For instance, after a two-year study involving some 1,500 individual researchers and organizations, the prestigious National Academy of Sciences (1977) reported that it would be possible to eliminate the worst aspects of world hunger by the end of this century *if we had the political will to do it.* Essentially the same conclusion was offered by the Brandt Commission (1980), the Presidential Commission on World Hunger (1980), and others.

These conclusions place the elimination of world hunger squarely in the lap of the social scientists. The nutritionists have shown what the human body needs to survive and be healthy. The agronomists have demonstrated that we are now producing more than enough food for everyone on the planet. Thirty-two nations have shown us that it can be done. If the continued failure to solve the problem of world hunger comes down to a lack of collective will, then sociology is the only place to seek an answer. The problem now lies in the social agreement we have created as a framework for social life.

The main force maintaining the persistence of world hunger is *the belief that it is inevitable.* Here's how it works. Once we have *decided* that there will always be starving people on the planet, we only do things we "know" won't really make a difference. Surprise! They don't make a difference, and hunger persists. The persistence of hunger reinforces our view that it's inevitable.

If ending hunger still seems impossible to you, it might be useful to review some of the other things people "knew" were impossible—and note when the impossible became reality.

"Impossibilities"	Achieved
Ending slavery	late 1800s
Humans flying	1903
Running a four-minute mile	1954
Flying to the moon	1969
Eradicating smallpox	1977

Of course ending hunger will not be easy. There is much to be done, and sociologists will be central to the work. Some of the topics to be researched and mastered are the social psychology of hunger's "inevitability," the acceptance and use of birth-control methods, the economics of zero population growth, the international economic order, political corruption, the acceptance and use of new agricultural techniques, to name just a few. There is much to do, but world experts generally agree that hunger could be ended this century. If so, it will be possible to realize the vision expressed by the Spanish poet, Federico García Lorca:

The day that hunger is eradicated from the earth, there will be the greatest spiritual explosion the world has ever known. Humanity cannot imagine the joy that will burst into the world on the day of that great revolution.

PRACTICING SOCIOLOGY

Shown at right are crude birth and death rates per 1000 population for the United States from 1910 to 1980.

Examine the rates. Describe their changes over time. Which changed more regularly, and why? Which changed less regularly, and why?

Calculate the rate of natural increase for each year by subtracting the death rate from the birth rate. Describe the trends in rate of natural increase.

By 1910, the United States had already experienced part of the demographic transition. Describe the patterns of birth and death rates in terms of stage of the demographic transition for 1910, 1940, and 1980.

Year	Birth rate	Death rate
1910	30.1	14.7
1920	27.7	13.0
1930	21.3	11.3
1940	19.4	10.8
1950	24.1	9.6
1960	23.7	9.5
1970	18.4	9.5
1980	16.2	8.9

Source: U.S. Bureau of Census, *Statistical Abstract of the United States* (Washington, D.C.: Government Printing Office, 1981), p. 58.

19

Technology

Perhaps no aspect of modern life has so capti-
vated people's imaginations as have the changes
wrought by science and technology. Ours is often
called a "technological" society, and every year
new developments in data processing, transportation, communications, energy, and medicine transform our lives. Some people glory in
these fruits of modern science and technology,
seeing in them the potential fulfillment of age-
old dreams and an end to drudgery, epidemic
disease, and starvation. Others believe these
developments will bring on our collective doom
through genetic mutation, nuclear holocaust,
mind control, or spreading pollution. Some fear
that we'll be superseded by clones, robots, and
computers; some worry more generally that our
capacity for invention is far outstripping our
capacity to control these creations or to adapt
to the many social changes their use brings.

In this chapter, I want to examine some of
these issues by looking at the impact of technology on society. We'll begin with an examination of technology as a social institution. As
we'll see in the first part of this chapter, technology has to do with the transformation of the
physical environment. Throughout history,
humans have accomplished that transformation in a variety of ways; in the past two or three
centuries, however, it has become impossible
to separate technology from one special
approach to the transformation: science. Thus,
we'll turn next to science as an institution, looking at the agreements and social organizations
that make it a persistent feature in all modern
societies.

Then, we'll focus in more detail on some of
the important applications of modern science—in communication and in medicine. We'll
conclude with an examination of the "computer
revolution."

What Is Technology?

No one has written more insightfully on the
fundamental underpinnings of technological

society than has the French scholar Jacques Ellul. In *The Technological Society* (1964), he points to "technique" as the organizing principle. Robert Merton's introduction paraphrases Ellul's use of the term this way:

> Technique refers to any complex of standardized means for achieving a predetermined result. Thus, it converts spontaneous and unreflective behavior into behavior that is deliberate and rationalized. The Technical Man is fascinated by results, by the immediate consequences of setting standardized devices into motion. (Ellul 1964:iv)

In Ellul's view, technique has been a part of human social life from the beginning, as people have continually developed *methods* for dealing with their environment. Rather than merely handling situations that arise *as they arise*, Ellul suggests, we tend to create systems for handling such situations in general.

Consider your "study habits," for example. Have you worked out a system for studying? Do you have a special time or place for studying, a method of note taking, a special review technique? If you do, your study habits are an example of what Ellul is talking about. He says the creation of techniques is a fundamental human response. "Technical activity is the most primitive activity of man. There is the technique of hunting, of fishing, of food gathering; and later of weapons, clothing, and building" (Ellul 1964:23). Thus, for Ellul, the development of magic, no less than the development of agriculture, was an example of the urge to develop techniques.

What we refer to as **technology**, then, is that part of a culture consisting of the techniques we have developed for dealing with the environment, plus any tools we've created for that purpose. Our knowledge about metallurgy, for example—plus Bessemer converters and smelting plants—is a part of modern technology, but no more so than are overhead projectors and "teaching techniques."

Whereas people tend to see technology as a subset of science—as the *application* of sci-

ence—Ellul reverses the order. Science, as we'll see later in this chapter, is merely the latest form of technique in human affairs, the most powerful form developed to date.

Since Jacques Ellul's views on technology may be unfamiliar to you, I have elaborated on them further in the accompanying box, "Ellul's View of Technology." Ellul offers only one view of the subject, however, and we're going to look at some other views now.

Views of Technology

Bernard Gendron (1977) suggests three major viewpoints that people have taken in examining technology in human social life: the utopian view, the dystopian view, and the socialist view.

The "utopian view" links all social progress to technology. Indeed, utopians believe that technological growth, if unimpeded by any major disaster, will in the long run bring about the demise of every major social evil. They believe that it will eliminate scarcity and disease, significantly improve communications and education, and undermine the environmental conditions that reinforce aggression, prejudice, sectarianism, nationalism, oppression, and exploitation. Utopians construe the major world problems as "technical" rather than as "political" or "ideological."

At the opposite pole of opinion is what Gendron calls the "dystopian view." Rather than seeing technology as the salvation for humans in their various miseries, the dystopians regard it as the *source* of trouble. According to them, while technology creates affluence and increases our collective power over nature, it undermines freedom and democracy; it stimulates the growth of bureaucracy and the use of techniques of mass manipulation; it cuts humans off from nature, their bodies, and their fellow humans; it makes work more tedious, unchallenging, and psychologically unhealthy; and it increases the dangers of annihilatory war and ecological catastrophe (Gendron 1977:3).

Jacques Ellul says that the creation of techniques is a fundamental human tendency. This tendency can be seen in the creation of complex planning/budgeting systems by modern financial analysts and in the creation of fire by the Stone Age Tasaday tribe of the Philippines.

Perhaps the most dramatic episode of resistance to technological change involved the Luddites in early nineteenth-century England. "Luddites" is the name given to British artisans in the woolen and clothing trades who wrecked industrial machinery, following the example of a semimythical figure of the eighteenth century, Ned Ludd.

Ellul's View of Technology

Jacques Ellul suggests that the drive to develop techniques for handling various aspects of our environment is a fundamental human response. It is one that can cause problems when it becomes the foundation of social organization and social interaction. Following are several of the dangerous tendencies that Ellul observes in modern, technological societies.

Automatism of Technical Choice

Not only do we generally choose technological solutions to problems—choosing systems, tools, routinized methods, in favor of less technological ones—but we automatically employ technology as the means to choosing the best alternative. Thus, for example, we may assess different solutions to a problem on the basis of a "cost-benefit analysis"—asking for the relevant ratios of what we put into the solution in comparison to what we get out of it—and automatically pick the one that "scores highest" on the test. This is not to say that a "cost-benefit analysis" of alternatives is bad or even inappropriate. Yet to the extent that we are unconscious of what we are doing, Ellul is led to conclude that "The human being is no longer in any sense the agent of choice" (1964:80).

Self-augmentation

So committed to technology in our approach to life, we have developed numerous techniques for the development of techniques. Thus, technology appears to have become self-generating, automatically improving itself. Although people are not as blindly faithful to such "improvement" as they were in the years since Ellul wrote, the self-augmenting aspect of technology is still very much a part of modern life.

Monism

The fundamental, single-minded principle of technology is "efficient ordering," and all the apparently separate elements of technology are united. "Production becomes more and more complex. The combination of machines within the same enterprise is a notable characteristic of the ninteenth century. It is impossible, in effect, to have an isolated machine" (Ellul 1964:112).

Luddite activity began in earnest in March 1811, when a group of workers in the stocking trade, having been dispersed by the military for protesting unemployment and low prices for their work, destroyed sixty stocking frames in Nottingham. For almost a year thereafter, bands of workers made nightly raids on other stocking frames in the region. From Nottingham, machine breaking spread to other parts of England and included the destruction of not just machinery but also occasionally entire factories. Since then, the term "Luddite" has been used—usually disparagingly—in reference to people who are adamantly opposed to new technology (Hobsbawm 1967, Thompson 1963).

Finally, Gendron describes the "socialist view." In this view, technology in itself is neither good nor bad, but is usable for either good or evil depending on the dominant political/economic system. According to socialists, social progress is dependent on economic and political revolutions, which are partially dependent on technological revolutions. If these political and economic revolutions do not take place, then all the scientific and technological development in the world will fail to stimulate even a modicum of social progress (1977:4).

Noting both the pros and cons, Daniel Boorstin (1978) has labeled the United States "The Republic of Technology," suggesting our tech-

Technical Universalism

Technology transcends the cultural differences that distinguish nations from one another. Ultimately, American, French, and Hindu textiles will not differ from one another. Technology has its own characteristics, and they overshadow cultural differences. In this sense, Ellul differs with Marxist critics of modern industrialism. Capitalism, Ellul argues, is less a culprit in the world's woes than are the technological systems that capitalists have mastered (or been mastered by). Socialist technology is no more righteous or humane than capitalist technology in Ellul's judgment.

The Autonomy of Technique

Finally, as an extension of the foregoing characteristics, technology has become an autonomous force in the world. It forms, Ellul argues, a universal language: Moslem or Jew, capitalist or communist, liberal or conservative—all can grasp and understand the norms of efficiency and order. Technology is beyond politics, economics, and morality. Ellul (1964:142) says it ultimately challenges and destroys all that we have considered sacred:

Technique worships nothing, respects nothing. It has a single role: to strip off externals, to bring everything to light, and by rational use to transform everything into means. More than science, which limits itself to explaining "how," technique desacralizes because it demonstrates (by evidence and not by reason, through use and not through books) that mystery does not exist. Science brings to the light of day everything man had believed sacred. Technique takes possession of it and enslaves it.*

Thus, Ellul is not especially romantic about technology, though he sees it as a necessary feature of any social life that is anything like what we are familiar with. He urges, therefore, that we understand the nature of technology and master it to whatever extent possible, rather than be mastered by it.

---

*Jacques Ellul, *The Technological Society* (New York: Knopf, 1964). This and all other quotations from this source are reprinted by permission.

nological orientation is fundamental to our approach to the world. Boorstin (1978:4) sees two especially potent forces in the technological approach: *obsolescence* and *convergence*.

For most of human history, the norm had been continuity. Change was news. Daily lives were governed by tradition. The most valued works were the oldest. The great works of architecture were monuments that survived from the past. Great literature never went out of date.

Today, we are ever searching for the *new*. New products make old ones obsolete or "secondhand," not antiques. Today's newspaper makes yesterday's virtually useless. Obsolescence—the process of becoming out-of-date—is a common fact of life today.

While technology can drive people apart, it also brings about a special kind of convergence in Boorstin's view (1978:5): "Technology is convergence, the tendency for everything to become more like everything else." During World War I, Boorstin points out, American schools stopped teaching German; Beethoven and Wagner lost public favor in this country. Yet American scientists were busily studying German technology, demonstrating a commonality of interests among scientists of nations at odds with one another.

These ghostly combines demonstrate our planet's great abundance. Yet some 15 to 20 million people die as a consequence of hunger each year, regardless of whether the harvests are good or bad.

The Social Impact of Technology

Differences in opinion over the net good or evil inherent in technology aside, no one will disagree about its impact. Let's look briefly at some of the areas in which technology has radically transformed social life. In this section, we'll look at food production, industry, and transportation. In later sections of the chapter, we'll look more fully at science, communications, medicine, and computers.

Food Production

As nearly as we can tell from the archaeological record, humankind began as foragers, hunting and gathering what we could to eat. Early tech-

nological developments that supported those activities—spears, arrows, clubs, axes, and tools for digging—probably were what enabled the species to survive.

Around ten thousand years ago, our ancestors began cultivating the soil in the Mesopotamian basin. Discovering soil cultivation was surely one of the most significant technological developments in human history. The necessity for migration was reduced, and people stuck around to harvest the crops they planted. Cultivation, moreover, increased the amount of food produced in a given area over what could be found growing wild. Thus, people were able to maintain themselves and live together in somewhat larger groups.

We know little about the history of agricultural specialization, but by the time of the first written records, many members of society were freed from the need to engage in food production. (Somebody wrote those records, for example.)

Later agricultural development has been largely in the direction of greater intensity. A smaller and smaller proportion of a population has become able to produce sufficient food for the remaining members. Nowhere has this tendency been illustrated more dramatically than in the United States, where the absolute *number* of farm workers decreased by 47 percent between 1960 and 1979. During that same period, farm output in America *increased* by 45 percent, even discounting the effects of inflation (U.S. Bureau of Census 1981i:670,680).

The increased productivity of American farmers, of course, is based on countless technological developments. A variety of planting, harvesting, and processing machines have played a major role. Chemical fertilizers have increased the productivity of the soil, just as chemical pesticides have decreased crop losses resulting from insects and worms.

Several social impacts have been felt as a result of technological developments in food production. The relative abundance of food—most evident in the United States, but true everywhere when a very long historical perspective is taken—has made possible lower death rates and increased population. Technological developments have also freed many men and women for nonagricultural functions. Less than 4 percent of the American work force is currently engaged in agriculture, for instance, although a variety of social organizations and interactions have grown up around the distribution of food (think of workers employed in grocery stores, supermarkets, and restaurants, for example).

Not so obvious, perhaps, as the fact that food production has become an activity that few of us engage in, is the fact that food has become *power* in human social relations. Those who control food have political leverage over those who do not. The exercise of such power may be seen in international grain shipments or—at the domestic level—in food stamp programs.

These are but a few of the ways in which technological developments relating to food have reshaped social structure and interaction. Future developments, involving the increased production of totally artificial foods, for example, or the development of new food sources in the ocean, will have further effects on the way we run our day-to-day lives.

Industry

Industrial development has had enormous social consequences, as we've seen in previous chapters. Technological developments in industry, as discussed in Chapter 13, for instance, moved the locus of work out of the family and into the factory. Except for the early years of the Industrial Revolution, this relocation of work removed children from the labor force and removed men from the family for much of the day. In more recent years, it has increasingly removed women from the home as well, with the result that family life is being restructured.

The development of interchangeable parts paved the way for industrial mass production based on assembly lines. It would be impossible to overstate the importance of these developments in regard to, among other things, the differentiation of function, the relation of the worker to the product, and social stratification. All aspects of mass industry, in fact, have influenced stratification and political power.

More recently, automation is further restructuring social relations, and, as we discussed in Chapter 13, is certain to prove one of the most significant developments in industry in the years to come.

Transportation

On or about April 1, 4837 B.C., Mary Gar was coming over the crest of a hill in the forest on her way home. Because she stepped on a fallen log, she inadvertently began a revolution in transportation. Her weight on the log dislodged it, and it began rolling down the hill. Mary, arms flailing in the air, managed to stay atop the rolling log, like a prehistoric lumberjack, as it rumbled down the hill, crushing saplings and bushes in its path. Lying dazed in a heap at the bottom of the hill, Mary realized that she had cut twenty-three seconds from her normal commute time and decided to capitalize on it. She borrowed a chain saw from a neighbor, lopped four cross sections off the log, and invented the little red wagon. (Well it probably happened *something* like that.)

Technological developments in transportation have revolutionized social relations in countless ways. The automobile is perhaps the most obvious example in developed nations. Many regard the automobile as a necessity rather than a luxury, especially given the extent to which interactions are organized around it. As serious efforts are being made to create more reliance on public mass transit, we are learning of more and more functions cars have for us. Cars give us status. We eat meals and watch movies in them. They give us freedom, opportunities to escape parents and crowded cities. Cars made suburbs possible. People get engaged in cars, and some start families there. Imagine robbing a bank and then jumping aboard a bus for your getaway.

In 1980, there were 159,029,000 registered motor vehicles in the United States, or one for every 1.4 men, women, and children in the nation. There were approximately the same number of registered motor vehicles as there were licensed drivers. Moreover, Americans owned nearly forty percent of the motor vehicles in the entire world in 1979 (U.S. Bureau of Census 1981i:620, 621).

Technological developments relating to travel through the air have been even more impressive. A mere sixty-six years—around the length of the average American life span—separated the twelve-second Wright brothers flight at Kill Devil Hill in Kitty Hawk, North Carolina, from the *Apollo 11* landing in the Sea of Tranquility on the moon. Forty-four years separated Kitty

Hawk from the first supersonic flight in 1947; and twenty years later, the fixed-wing aircraft speed record rested at just under seven times the speed of sound.

Larger, faster passenger transports have reshaped many aspects of social life. Consider, for example, the effect of greater migration and travel on ethnocentric attitudes, as people from different cultures come into increased contact with each other.

In general, all developments in transportation have immeasurably enhanced the possibilities for communication between peoples. We'll turn to another set of technological developments that involve communication even more directly—the mass media—later in this chapter. Now let's look at the activity people most directly associate with technology: science.

Science

Not only have we humans automatically responded to our environment by developing routinized techniques for handling situations, but we have, in a potent phrase, "made a science of it." Indeed, **science** is the most fully developed form of technique, the clearest example of it.

The Development of Science

The beginnings of rational-empirical science in the West are often traced to the philosophers of ancient Greece. Although the inquiries into nature associated with such early Greek thinkers as Thales, Zeno, Parmenides, and Pythagoras were not separated from—nor did they contradict—religious views of the world, they added two concerns that were essential to the growth of science. On the one hand, the Greeks sought to discover a logical and rational harmony in things, as in the "magical," regular relations among the sides of a right triangle of the Pythagoreans and in the mathematical relations among musical tones. By the same token, it was important to the early Greeks that the "truth" about phenomena be substantiated by observations in the real world. Increasingly, the assertions of tradition alone were felt to be insufficient: they needed to be confirmed by empirical observations and precise measurements. These two aspects of what we call "science" have remained central for the past 2,500 years.

Chapter 3 described some of the methodological norms that have grown out of the development of science: norms of logic, generality, specificity, and so forth. In the next section of this chapter, I want to look briefly at some of the norms that have come to characterize science as a social institution, as a set of interrelated beliefs, values, and norms governing this sector of life.

The Norms of Scientific Discovery

In an important sense, science is a matter of discovery and creation—the production of "new" things—and this provides a good beginning for our look at science as an institution.

In a 1957 study, Robert Merton found what seemed to be an inordinate concern among scientists over the issue of who was the *first* to discover what. The reason for this preoccupation, he suggested, lay in the most fundamental norm of science as a profession. "On every side, the scientist is reminded that it is his role to advance knowledge and his happiest fulfillment of that role, to advance knowledge greatly" (1957c:639).

This norm of making a contribution to the advancement of science, however, is complicated by another norm of science: that scientific knowledge belongs to the public domain. Private ownership of knowledge is contrary to the institutional norms of science. It becomes important, therefore, that a scientist get *credit* for his or her discoveries, since the discovery will soon belong to everyone. As Merton continues (1957c:640):

> Recognition for originality becomes socially validated testimony that one has successfully lived up to the most exacting requirements of one's role as scientist. . . . Interest in recognition, therefore, [is] the motivational counterpart on the psychological plane to the emphasis upon originality on the institutional plane.

Does this mean that scientists openly compete for recognition? It's not quite that simple, Merton points out, since another norm of science is humility. It would be unseemly for a scientist to *claim* credit for achievement or to promote his or her own standing. The value of this norm, in Merton's view, is "to reduce the misbehavior of scientists below the rate that would occur if importance were assigned only to originality and the establishing of priority" (1957c:646). Even so, Merton notes that scientists sometimes engage in shady practices in pursuit of recognition.

A concrete illustration of the consequences of emphasizing recognition for original discoveries can be found in James Watson's research biography, *The Double Helix* (1968), which describes the events that led up to his sharing the 1962 Nobel Prize in physiology and medicine with his colleague Francis Crick.

Crick and Watson received the Nobel for uncovering the nature of the DNA molecule (the fundamental building block of life), but they were not alone in this line of inquiry. British researcher Maurice Wilkins ultimately shared the prize with them as an acknowledgment of his earlier, independent research on the subject. More important, however, was the effort being made by Linus Pauling, already a Nobel laureate in chemistry.

One day, Pauling's son Peter came to visit Crick and Watson. He brought with him his father's paper outlining the current research path being followed by the senior Pauling. Watson reports looking at the paper with foreboding.

Were they about to be eclipsed by Pauling? Would all their work be for naught? Then, Watson realized that Pauling had made a simple mistake that pointed his inquiry toward failure. Did Watson point the error out to young Pauling, so that the "cause of science" would be supported? Hardly. As Watson candidly reports, "I began to breathe slower. By then I knew we were still in the game" (1968:103).

Watson wasn't unusual in straying from the formal norm of science in this respect. The only thing unusual is his candor in admitting what happened. The Watson anecdote notwithstanding, scientists in general *are* committed to the public nature of knowledge and to the collective advancement of science—as compared to the other sectors of society. For example, the scientific and the military communities have clashed frequently in the United States, the latter insisting on the need for withholding scientific breakthroughs, whereas the former have opposed secrecy.

An implicit norm in the preceding discussions is that scientists *should* seek new discoveries, publishing their results in scientific journals. Yet, some scientists are more productive in this regard than others. Research on the productivity of biochemists by J. Scott Long and Robert McGinnis (1981) points to the importance of organizational contexts. While it is generally believed that scientific productivity is rewarded by appointments to positions in prestigious research organizations, such as university research centers, Long and McGinnis discovered the relationship to be just the other way around. Being productive did not necessarily result in research center appointments, but those who received such appointments— for whatever reason—became more productive afterward. In an earlier study, Long (1978) found the same to be true of scientific productivity and appointment to prestigious faculty positions. While these findings challenge the American norm linking hard work to rewards, they confirm the sociological view that individ-

Robert Merton
1910–
Philadelphia, Pennsylvania

Some Important Works
Social Theory and Social Structure (New York: Free Press, 1957).
Contemporary Social Problems, with Robert Nisbet (New York: Harcourt Brace Jovanovich, 1971).
Science, Technology and Society in Seventeenth Century England (Bruges, Belgium: Osiris, 1938).

With much of American sociology divided between grand theory, on the one hand, and concrete empirical studies on the other, Robert Merton is best known for both urging and producing "theories of the middle range," analyses bringing theoretical understanding to classes of real-world events and situations. Merton's own practice of middle-range sociology has covered a variety of substantive topics. Most notable are his studies of science and of the social-structural roots of anomie.

Taking a functionalist point of view, Merton has brought the social systems model to bear on a variety of social situations, fine-tuning the theoretical model in the process, such as his elaboration of manifest and latent functions. Where functionalists are often accused of losing sight of individuals, Merton has used the perspective in ways that reveal the links between individuals and societies rather than concealing them.

uals behave according to the norms prevalant in their social settings.

The Progress of Scientific Discovery

Scientific progress is often seen as a more or less steady advancement, with ignorance giving way to knowledge. In this view, scientific advancement is seen as "cumulative," consisting of the steady building up of contributions and the continual refinement of what is known scientifically. Recent studies in the history of science, most notably those of Thomas Kuhn (1970), suggest, however, that scientific knowledge advances in a rather different manner.

Rather than steady refinement and progress, Kuhn suggests that science advances through what he calls **paradigm shifts.** A paradigm is a conceptual model. In sociology, for instance, the main paradigms are the theoretical points of view we discussed in Chapter 2: functionalism, interactionism, and conflict.

Here's the way paradigm shifts occur, in Kuhn's view. A scientist creates a paradigm of some phenomenon. Others agree with the accuracy and utility of the model, and it becomes accepted as truth. The model does not totally accord with observed reality, but new generations of scientists offer refinements and subtle changes to the model to explain the discrepancies. Essentially, however, the model stays the same. Eventually, someone suggests a radically different paradigm. Other scientists, who are wedded to the old model, resist the new paradigm, and it may even become the focus of ridicule. After a while, however, if scientists find value in the new model, agreement within the scientific community shifts, sometimes dramatically, from the old paradigm to the new one. The new model then becomes accepted as true, and it becomes an impediment to future innovations.

The classic example used in this context is the rise of the "heliocentric" theory offered by Copernicus as an alternative to the Ptolemaic system of movement in the heavens. Ptolemy was a second-century astronomer and mathematician who argued that the sun and other heavenly bodies revolved around a stationary earth. Since this model didn't accord with observations, it was modified with the addition of "epicycles," a system of imaginary points, with the observable bodies revolving around those points. As observations became more precise, the Ptolemaic system was made more and more complex to accommodate those observations within the basic model.

Around 1530, Nicolaus Copernicus completed work on a radically different model, based on the idea that the earth and other bodies revolve around the sun (hence the term "heliocentric" theory). Copernicus was subjected to both political and religious pressure, and his book's printing was delayed. He and other scholars who supported his view were threatened. (Half a century later, Galileo was forced by the Inquisition to denounce the idea that the earth revolved around the sun.)

Eventually, the heliocentric theory won out. And when a theory wins in science, it wins big. Today, it is "truth" about the movement of heavenly bodies. If you were to suggest that the sun revolves around the earth, you would be considered a fool. The irony, of course, is that the movement of the spheres is relative. From the standpoint of the sun, the earth moves. From the standpoint of the moon, both the sun and the earth move. Thus, the heliocentric theory is no more "truthful" than the Ptolemaic one, but it is perhaps more useful.

Kuhn's theory of paradigm shifts allows us to see that scientific agreements are often handled in the same fashion as nonscientific ones. The agreements are created, established, taught, and reified. People break the agreements and are sometimes punished. And over the long haul, the agreements change. There are probably no scientific agreements existent in the world today that won't eventually be overturned and replaced. Now let's look at the problems this can create for society at large.

Science and Society

Earlier, I discussed the extent to which social life is riddled with technological responses to the environment. In a modern society, the same may be said about science. It is difficult to imagine anything approaching what we experience as modern society without science. As a quantitative measurement of the influence of science on society, in 1981 the Census Bureau counted 670,000 scientists and engineers employed in research and development in the United States. In 1978, the federal government alone spent over 40 billion dollars on research and development, and billions more were spent by state governments and by private industry (U.S. Bureau of Census 1981i:600, 602).

As the data indicate, Americans have placed a good portion of their financial and human resources in science. Moreover, there is a broadly shared agreement that such an investment is worthwhile. As we saw in Chapter 8, Americans have very high esteem for the occupation of scientist.

Everyone can point to benefits we have gained from our investments in science: medical cures, advances in communication and transportation, and "bigger and better" creature comforts. Most Americans look forward to more advances, especially with regard to the cure of diseases such as cancer and heart disease. At a time of serious environmental problems, many Americans hold the "utopian view" that science will give us the tools to remedy all ills.

For all their high regard for scientists, however, Americans have reservations. Scientists are popularly portrayed as single-mindedly scientific, impractical in the nonscientific aspects of life, and generally hard to understand. A mystique surrounds science that often makes nonscientists uncomfortable and sometimes troubled.

Periodically in recent years objections have been raised to science in America, often centering on the financial investment made in it. Recently, for instance, increased concern was expressed in regard to the research funding of the National Science Foundation, as indicated in the following report from *The Christian Science Monitor* (1975:21):

> "Why study the perspiration of Australian Aborigines?" was a typical complaint that pounced on seemingly trivial research and ignored the fact that the Department of Defense wanted to find out why American soldiers dehydrate in the desert while Aborigines don't. Many a congressman's constituents, hearing the criticism, have demanded that such "waste" be curbed.

Representative Joseph Gaydos of Pennsylvania probably voiced the troubled feelings of many public officials and voters when he said "I hope we can bring this elite egghead empire under control" (*Christian Science Monitor* 1975:21).

Many Americans regard science as not only wasteful but also dangerous. Like education, science can be a threat to society as a set of shared agreements, for science has the task of evaluating as well as perpetuating agreements. Science poses a threat to the beliefs, values, and norms that the members of a society share.

Although science does not declare itself on the matter of values, its activities often reflect on our values. This happens, of course, whenever the findings of science contradict a society's beliefs, since beliefs specify values. More to the point, however, scientists often *study* those things that societies value, often examining whether they "work" or not. Thus, a scientist, although not able to say *scientifically* whether capitalism is "better" or "worse" than socialism, can examine the strengths and weaknesses of each, showing whether they support or work against other social values.

Science can pose a threat to society's norms. This happens when scientists question the

Technology transforms all aspects of life, nowhere more so than in the area of communication. Telephone lines such as these allow people to converse with one another from points all over the globe. What people say and the consequences of their communications, however, are matters of social agreements.

of evolution. This so offended the local Christian community that Scopes was brought to trial—defended by Clarence Darrow and prosecuted by William Jennings Bryan, two of the most famous attorneys of the era. Scopes was convicted, but later released on a technicality. The Tennessee law against teaching evolution remained on the books until 1967.

During the early 1980s, the debate between Christian fundamentalism and evolution broke out once more, with demands that "Scientific Creationism" (representing the Biblical view of creation) be taught alongside evolution. While the scientific creationists lost their battle in court, there is little doubt that we will witness more clashes between science and nonscientific culture in the future, as we have in the past. This will happen whenever a society contains competing sources of truth.

Science creates even more dramatic threats to society, of course. Nuclear weapons are a good illustration, and even nuclear-power generators pose threats in the form of potential accidents—dramatized by the 1979 crisis at Three Mile Island in Pennsylvania—and the persistent problem of nuclear-waste elimination. Thus, science poses a threat to our physical well-being as well as to our social agreements and social structures.

As we'll see next, technological progress in the area of communications has also been a mixed blessing.

Technology and Mass Communication

Charles Wright (1975:5–7) has defined "mass communication" in terms of its audience, the communication experience, and the communicator, thereby distinguishing mass communication from, say, face-to-face conversations among individuals.

1. *Audience:* Mass communication is directed toward a relatively large, heterogeneous, and anonymous audience.

beliefs and values the norms are based on. Sometimes science is troublesome for people when scientists—such as sociologists—merely point to the existence of unstated norms, showing the de facto discrimination against women in pay rates, for example.

One of the more dramatic clashes between science and nonscientific culture in modern times came to a head in Dayton, Tennessee, in 1925. A young biology teacher, John Scopes, had been teaching his students Darwin's theory

2. *Experience:* Mass communication may be characterized as public, rapid, and transient.

3. *Communicator:* Mass communication is organized communication. Unlike the lone artist or writer, the "communicator" in mass media works through a complex organization embodying an extensive division of labor and an accompanying degree of expense.

Unlike direct, face-to-face communication, mass communication is typically a one-way process. The receivers of mass-media communications are, for the most part, unable either to acknowledge receipt of a message or to respond with messages of their own. Interactive communication is largely impossible, which produces frustration on both ends of the mass-communication process.

A good deal has been said about the frustrations of consumers of mass media. When you hear a point of view you disagree with, you are nearly precluded from responding to it. The communicators are also frustrated, however, because they get no feedback. There is the feeling of emptiness experienced by the radio announcer, for example, whose rip-roaring joke is met with the unamused silence of the broadcast booth. Indeed, the media try to reduce the artificiality and strangeness of unacknowledged communications by using television "laugh tracks" and by filming shows before an audience.

Development of the Mass Media

Let's look a little more closely at the development of no-feedback communication in mass society—the printed media, radio, film, and television.

Printed Matter   Mass communication is a relatively recent development in human history. It is customarily traced to Gutenberg's inven-tion of movable type some five hundred years ago, which made possible the mass production of printed matter.

The volume of book production has grown immensely since Gutenberg first printed 600 pages a day on his press, and literacy has grown apace. In 1980, American publishers brought out 34,030 new books and 8,347 revisions of old books. One-sixth of those books were in the fields of sociology and economics (U.S. Bureau of Census 1981i:569, 570).

Newspapers first appeared in Europe shortly after the invention of movable type (DeFleur 1966). In America, newspapers began during the colonial period, but it was not until the 1830s and 1840s that the so-called penny press created mass consumption of daily newspapers. Daily circulation grew steadily from 758,000 in 1850 (U.S. Bureau of Census 1960:500) to 62,202,000 in 1980 (U.S. Bureau of Census 1981i:568). In terms of circulation per household, however, the trend has been curvilinear. Newspaper circulation in 1850 amounted to 0.21 copies per household, a figure that rose to 1.38 per household in 1919, a peak not subsequently matched (DeFleur 1966). In 1980, newspaper circulation in America was 0.79 copies per household (U.S. Bureau of Census 1981i:42, 568). This relative decline in newspaper circulation coincided with the arrival of radio and then television.

Elsewhere in the world, newspapers are still a more central mode of communication. India's 875 daily and 3,800 weekly newspapers, for example, provide information to the nation's multilingual population (Winsbury 1981:60). In Indonesia, a government-sponsored "Newspapers for Villages" program aims at bringing together a nation of rural villages scattered across several islands (*Asiaweek* 1980:63).

Radio   Unlike the telephone and telegraph, which are characterized by person-to-person communication, radio may be regarded as the first electronic *mass* medium—it beams its messages to anyone who cares to receive them.

The basic radio technology was developed during the latter part of the nineteenth century. Guglielmo Marconi's transmission of "wireless" telegraph messages set the stage for the transmission of voice and music. This new technology might never have formed a new mass medium except for the brainstorm of a young engineer, David Sarnoff. In 1916, Sarnoff wrote to his superiors at the American Marconi Company:

> I have in mind a plan of development which would make radio a "household utility" in the same sense as the piano or phonograph. The idea is to bring music into the house by wireless. . . .
>
> The same principle can be extended to numerous other fields as, for example, receiving lectures at home which can be made perfectly audible; also events of national importance can be simultaneously announced and received. Baseball scores can be transmitted in the air by the use of [a transmitter] installed at the Polo Grounds. (quoted in DeFleur 1966:56)

In 1920, the Westinghouse Company became the first company to establish a station, in East Pittsburgh, to support their manufacture and sale of receivers. Radio as a mass medium then became very popular. Between the last half of 1921 and the first half of 1922 alone, the number of licenses for new stations grew eightfold, from 32 to 254, as DeFleur (1966:59) reports.

Radio became a central medium for the transmission of information and entertainment. Family social life centered on the "music box." Americans from Maine to California could listen to the same national events as they occurred. Radio enhanced the stature of political and cultural heroes and created many of its own.

Today, radio is a nearly universal fact of American life. In 1980, the Census Bureau (1981i:559) estimated that 99 percent of all American households had at least one radio. The average household had 5.5—for a national total of nearly half a billion radios.

Film   Practical film technology has a longer "prehistory" than radio, but it, like radio, was developed in the late nineteenth century. Moving through silent films, talkies, technicolor, drive-ins, 3-D, and the wide screen, the film as a mass medium reached a peak in America during the 1940s. It has declined in popularity somewhat since then, though the 1970s and 1980s have seen a slight upsurge. Still, 1949 remains the "top" year for American film in at least two respects. Tickets sold each week numbered 90 million, and over 400 new films were released.

Television   Combining the visual appeal of film with the immediacy of radio, television is, in many respects, the most important mass medium in America today. It started as a vehicle for mass communication on the eve of World War II. It grew little during the war, but its use has skyrocketed since then. The number of television sets in America rose from some 8,000 in 1946 to well over 100 million at present (U.S. Bureau of Census 1960:491, 1981i:559). In 1981, according to the A. C. Nielsen Company, 98 percent of American homes have a television set—half have more than one—and 85 percent own a color television (*Public Opinion* 1981g:35).

Throughout this section, I've presented data on exposure to the mass media in terms of the numbers of radios, television sets, and newspapers that people buy. As regards the *use* of these, the best data available relate to television. Public-opinion polls indicate that the average adult American watches about three hours of television a day, a fairly constant average over the past ten years (*Public Opinion* 1981g:35).

An analyis of *who* is watching shows produces various results over the course of the day. The daytime audience is made up predominantly of women and children; the whole family watches during "prime time" (3 P.M. to 10 P.M.). As a national profile, Schramm and Alexander (1975:30) indicate, "In ten representative homes, we should expect in prime evening time to find about six sets in use, about thirteen people viewing, of whom four would be men, five women, one or two teen-agers, and perhaps two or three children."

Data are harder to come by for radio exposure, though it is usually estimated to be about half as many hours as television. More *people* are likely to listen to the radio in a given day or week even though more time is spent with television (Schramm and Alexander 1975).

Because they communicate messages to so many people, the mass media have become an important agent of cultural transmission (as we saw in Chapter 5). They also have become an important source of agreements in mass society. To the extent that people reify the messages received from television, radio, newspapers, and so forth, the media becomes a source of reality. You might say that the mass media are in the business of creating reality.

Mass Media and
the Creation of Reality

Recall from Chapter 1 that what we regard as "reality" is actually a function of agreements that we have with one another, agreements that take the form of beliefs, values, and norms. Such agreements take on the appearance of "reality" through reification. Reification, moreover, is a function of our awareness of the extent of agreement. If you learn that just about everyone around you agrees that the Dallas Cowboys are a better football team than the San Francisco Forty-Niners, you are likely to believe that it's "really true." Finally, the awareness of agreement is a function of communication. We discover that our points of view agree by communicating them.

The mass media have a special power for creating the appearance of agreement because they communicate the same point of view to millions of people at the same time. They have the capacity to plant the same point of view in millions of individuals who may then discover

agreements among themselves. This potential has not escaped the attention of those people who have an interest in consciously creating reality.

Propaganda   During World War II, for instance, Hitler and his minister of propaganda, Joseph Goebbels, operated on a principle later called the "big lie": people would believe anything that was repeated often enough. They used this principle to create unity and solidarity within Germany and to create divisions among people elsewhere. The Jews were the primary focus of the Nazi "big lie." The German people were told repeatedly that Jews were traitors to the fatherland, that they had been responsible for Germany's defeat in World War I, and that their greed had produced the economic troubles that followed the war. All "good and true" Germans were urged to unite in support of the fatherland and in opposition to the Jews.

Beaming the same message abroad, they sought to turn gentiles against Jews in America, Britain, and elsewhere. They sought to pit workers against "Wall Street" and to create national divisions and hatred among the Allies. Americans were told they were being dragged into the war by British trickery and treachery.

Propaganda is not limited, of course, to wartime. Quite possibly, it is inherent in all politics. Those who seek to gain and hold power do so, at least in part, by creating a view of reality that is favorable to their holding power and unfavorable to their opponents' gaining power. The technological developments of the mass media give them an extremely potent weapon in this regard.

In America, political campaigns provide a clear example of the political use of propaganda, typically called "public relations." The Census Bureau (1978a:525, 526) reports that 112.8 million dollars was spent in 1975–1976 for the presidential campaigns alone. Another 100 million dollars was spent on congressional races.

Political candidates are now "packaged" and "sold" in the same fashion as drugs, detergents, and dog food. Most campaigners consider a candidate's "image" to be far more important than political philosophy or points of view on specific issues (see, for example, Schwartz 1974).

Commercial advertising is another form of propaganda, one deeply embedded in the mass media. The extent of advertising on radio and television in America today is simply staggering. In 1980, over 11 billion dollars was spent on television advertising; another 3.8 billion was spent on radio. Newspaper advertising, nonetheless, was greater than television and radio combined: over 15 billion dollars. Another 3 billion was spent on magazine advertising. Nearly two-thirds of the 54.6 billion dollars spent on advertising in 1980 was channeled through these four media (U.S. Bureau of Census 1981i:572).

Commercials tell us that we will live richer, fuller, more satisfying lives if we have clean shirt collars, don't sweat, and avoid bad breath. They assure us that brand X is better, faster, more effective, longer lasting, softer, stronger, and better smelling than brand Y.

In Chapter 5, we examined some of the social stereotypes fostered by commercials, such as the undomestic male and unmechanical female. Eli Rubinstein (1978:207) reports on an unintended consequence of television advertising:

> While a vast majority of the advertisements adhere to the guidelines that attempt to protect children against exploitative practices, a number of studies show that, over time, children begin to distrust the accuracy of the commercial message. By the sixth grade, children are generally cynical about the truthfulness of the ads.

Sex and Violence   It is estimated that the average American child under five watches nearly twenty-four hours of television every week (*Newsweek* February 21, 1977). Parents jokingly refer to television as a new babysitter, but it's hardly a joke. For many children growing up, it is a babysitter, a source of knowledge about the world. What is the message that television passes on to children? It is mixed. In its time, television has perpetuated ethnic, racial, and sex stereotypes, and it has also been a force for breaking them down. It has sometimes presented an overly sanitized view of American life (in "Happy Days," for example) and it has also presented us as worse than we are ("Kojak").

The real and imagined impact of television on young children has produced many hot controversies in recent years, chiefly revolving around the issues of sex and violence. As we saw in Chapter 5, two major government studies address these issues. The National Commission on Obscenity and Pornography reported that sex in the media had no adverse effect on sex crimes. The U.S. Surgeon General's three-year study of violence on television concluded that it *did* have an adverse effect. TV violence was found to encourage violent acts and to make people more accepting of the violent acts of others.

More recent studies have pointed to a different impact of violence on television. Gerbner et al. (1980:712) found that among both adults and children, exposure to violence-laden TV "generates a pervasive and exaggerated sense of danger and mistrust." When asked the likelihood of being involved in violence during any given week, heavy watchers thought it more likely than light watchers. Similarly, heavy watchers gave higher estimates of the percentage of crimes that involved violence. Even when television doesn't affect behavior directly, then, it can affect people's views of the world around them.

Clearly, there are still disagreements about television's portrayal of fictional social life. But what about its reporting of the "real" reality?

Reporting the "News"   One of the chief functions of the mass media—and of communication more generally—is the transmission of information. The editorial function of the mass media is recognized as involving a point of view; the "news" function, however, has generally been regarded as different. As Richard Salant, president of CBS News, has indicated: "Our reporters do not cover stories from *their* point of view. They are presenting them from *nobody's* point of view" (quoted in Epstein 1974:i). The assumption, then, is that "facts are facts," "reality is reality," and that "news" is merely a statement of reality as it *is*.

Many, however, have come to a view more akin to the title of a 1975 newspaper-subscription advertisement: "The World You See Depends on the News You Get" (*Christian Science Monitor*, June 24, 1975). Even if you could assume that a purely objective reality of situations and events existed in the world, the simple *volume* of messages that would be required to report it in its entirety would make the reporting impossible. Inevitably, the course of day-to-day events must be sifted and filtered in what Edward Epstein (1975) has aptly called "the selection of reality."

Salant's disclaimer notwithstanding, the news media do report through points of view. The *New York Times's* promise "All the News That's Fit to Print" implies a point of view on "fitness." When news people discuss this issue, moreover, they often speak of "newsworthiness," "significance," "interest," and "balance"—none of which can be defined or measured scientifically. Each requires the exercise of a point of view. In the interest of "balance," for example, a television newscast may devote ten seconds to an excerpt from a sixty-minute political speech and another ten seconds to a one-minute protest that interrupted the speech. The suggestion is that the speech was continually heckled. But should the heckling have been ignored altogether, creating the impression that everyone loved the speech?

Given the limitations of time, space, and cost, the mass media have no choice but to *create* "reality" in their reporting of the "news." Whatever they do represents a point of view—implicit, explicit, or accidental—and forms the basis for agreement as to what's "really so." While some media people may consciously seek to "slant"

the news to reflect their personal biases, not even the most honest and honorable can avoid having an impact on what the remainder of mass society will come to regard as "facts."

In a major study of news creation, Herbert Gans (1979) spent several years examining two network news broadcasts, CBS and NBC, and two major newsmagazines, *Time* and *Newsweek*. He concluded that a clear set of implicit values could be found in what these media chose to report and how they reported it:

1. *Ethnocentrism:* For the most part, the American media report news about, or relevant to, our own nation. Reporting of the war in Vietnam, for example, was implicitly a matter of "us" versus "them," and reporters seeking to report on American atrocities—such as the My Lai massacre—had difficulty selling their stories.

2. *Altruistic democracy:* Democracy is clearly favored over dictatorship in foreign reporting, but domestic political values are also evident. Gans (1979:44) says "the news seems to imply that the democratic ideal against which it measures reality is that of the rural town meeting—or rather, of a romanticized version of it."

3. *Responsible capitalism:* While capitalism is clearly favored over socialism or communism, the ideal is a restrained capitalism in which "businessmen and women will compete with each other in order to create increased prosperity for all, but that they will refrain from unreasonable profits and gross exploitation of workers or customers" (Gans 1979:46).

4. *Small-town pastoralism:* Although cities were once idealized, the media today present them primarily as the scene of trying problems: crime, race riots, fiscal crises, pollution, and so forth. Suburbs are largely ignored, and the small town, reminiscent of our agrarian past, is today

ideal. Gans cites Charles Kuralt's "On the Road" series as an example.

5. *Individualism:* Like the small town, the "rugged individual" is idealized by the media. Struggling against adversity—especially against the forces of bureaucracy and urban life—the plucky individual goes hand in hand with the media's view of capitalism.

6. *Moderatism:* In a modern reflection of Aristotle's "golden mean," the media oppose extremism and excess on all sides. "For example, the news treats atheists as extremists and uses the same approach, if more gingerly, with religious fanatics" (Gans 1979:51).

7. *Social order:* Media coverage of social disorders—riots, protests, and so on—clearly favor the side of order. This is especially important to note at a time when substantial segments of the population have felt they could only gain justice through protest. As Gans concludes, "order" for the media is a middle-aged, upper-middle-class, white, male social order: "the news prefers women and blacks who move into the existing social order to separatists who want to alter it" (1979:61).

8. *Leadership:* Finally, the media stress the need for competent and moral leadership in order to achieve social order. In this regard, they shape the view that strong leadership is what makes things happen. Where organizations and movements lack leaders, the media create them. Gans reports (1979:62) that "in the 1960s, radical and black organizations functioning on the basis of participatory democracy sometimes complained that journalists would pick out one spokesperson on whom they would lavish most of their attention, thereby making a leader out of him or her."

The box entitled "Who and What is 'News' " presents more of Gans's findings.

Gans's final point regarding leadership in radical organizations is echoed in a detailed study by Todd Gitlin (1980) subtitled "Mass media in the making and unmaking of the new left."

In the late twentieth century, political movements feel called upon to rely on large-scale communications in order to *matter,* to say who they are and what they intend to publics they want to sway; but in the process they become "newsworthy" only by submitting to the implicit rules of newsmaking, by conforming to journalistic notions (themselves imbedded in history) of what a "story" is, what an "event" is, what a "protest" is. The processed image then tends to *become* "the movement" for wider publics and institutions who have few alternative sources of information.

As you'll recall from Chapter 7, institutions are inherently conservative—protecting established patterns. As you can see from the list of media values detailed above, the major news organizations in America clearly reflect established values of American society as a whole. Without having to disagree with any of those values, you should make a special note of how our sources of "what is" are aligned with our predominant views of "what should be." This fact makes it difficult for us to recognize changes going on around us.

Against this backdrop, note that most Americans get their "news" from television. When a 1980 Roper poll (*Public Opinion* 1981g:36) asked people "where you get most of your news about what's going on in the world today," here's what they said:

Television	64%
Newspapers	44
Radio	18
Magazines	5

Who and What Is "News"?

There's a traditional newspaper saying that if a dog bites a man, that's not news, but if a man bites a dog, *that's news.* An important part of the mass media's "creation" of the news involves the selection of what to report.

In his study, *Deciding What's News* (1979), Herbert Gans found that 70 to 85 percent of all domestic news is about well-known figures:

1. Incumbent presidents
2. Presidential candidates
3. Leading federal officials
4. State and local officials
5. Alleged and actual violators of the laws and mores (some of whom are known before getting into trouble—Spiro Agnew—and others who become known as a result—Charles Manson)

The main activities reported in the mass media are:

1. Government conflicts and disagreements
2. Government decisions, proposals, and ceremonies
3. Government personnel changes
4. Protests, violent and nonviolent
5. Crimes, scandals, and investigations
6. Disasters, actual and averted
7. Innovations and tradition
8. National ceremonies

Gans's research shows that *race* has been a featured topic in the media's coverage of the news, but *class,* so closely associated with race, has not. Thus, strikes by labor unions are covered "as incidents soon to be resolved rather than as permanent conflicts of interest." In particular, the media have shunned references to the "working class" because, Gans suggests, of its Marxist connotations.

Source: Herbert J. Gans, *Deciding What's News,* New York: Pantheon Books, 1979:8–28.

Not only are Americans more likely to get their news from television, they also trust it more than they do the other media. Fifty-one percent said television was the "most believable," well ahead of newspapers (22 percent), radio (18 percent), and magazines (9 percent). Overall, 61 percent said they had a "fairly good opinion of television and newspaper reporters." Similar results were found in a 1981 survey which asked how accurate people thought the major news media were. Fourteen percent said they were "almost always" accurate, and another 57 percent said "most of the time" (*Public Opinion* 1981g:37). However the news is created, then, most people tend to believe it.

We'll return to communication technology in the concluding essay of this chapter. At this point, let's examine the impact of technology on another social institution: medicine.

Technology and Medicine

The impact of science and technology is perhaps nowhere greater than in relation to health and illness. Medical technology has revolutionized our chances for long life and physical comfort. It has also led to the development of medicine as an institution, involving medical roles and relations, hospitals, clinics, health insurance, and so forth.

In this concluding section, we are going to look at several related topics. First, we'll examine the notions of "sickness" and "health," paying special attention to the extent to which those notions are determined and defined by cultural agreements. Next, we'll turn to the organization of medical care and to the impact of science and technology on health in this country and elsewhere. Finally, we'll look at some of the current controversies stirred by new developments in medical technology.

Science and Health

You might imagine that health and illness are fairly clear and unambiguous concepts, more in the realm of medicine than sociology. Not so. We have already talked about the social definition of mental illness earlier in the book. Physical illness is also a matter of social agreement, involving expectations and social roles.

Defining Health and Illness John Clausen (1963:139–40) has clearly stated the case for considering health and illness as social agreements:

> Health and disease are often conceived exclusively as states of the organism, but they represent social definitions as well. What one does in the presence of a given symptom or discomfort depends on whether one regards the symptom as an inevitable consequence of being alive or as a condition remediable by a professional healer or by a regime of care. This is true both at the societal level and at the family or individual level.

The social definition of illness that Clausen spoke of is susceptible to subcultural variations within a given society.

The Sick Role From a sociological point of view, being ill is the basis for a special social status, as Talcott Parsons (1951), among other sociologists, has noted. To begin, being labeled as sick exempts you from other responsibilities that you would normally be expected to carry. You're not expected to take exams when you have a fever of 103°F, for example. At the same time, sickness is regarded as a form of deviance that disrupts social relations. (Don't tell your instructor you're glad you got the flu.) Sick people are usually not blamed for being sick. (Remind your instructor that there's a lot of flu going around.) Finally, the sick person *is*

expected to seek recovery, especially through cooperating with medical professionals. (Take two aspirins every four hours, drink lots of liquids, and rest.) Failure to seek recovery (or to *appear* to seek recovery) cancels out the agreement about not blaming sick people for being sick.

Our social agreements about sickness and health are closely tied to the functions that have grown up around the practice of medicine. Let's look now at the changing functions of the physician.

There have been medical "professionals" around throughout human history, since they are mentioned in the earliest written records. Probably medical professionals extend well back into human prehistory as well, as some of the earliest human skulls show evidence of "trephination," a puncturing of the skull to relieve pressure.

Whatever the prehistoric roots of medicine, the profession has had one particular goal throughout most of its history in the West: to cure illness. The physician's function has been to restore human bodies (and later, minds) to proper working order once they have begun malfunctioning. We might call this medicine's *healing* function.

With the development of public health programs—including such diverse aspects as nutrition, sanitation, and inoculation—we have seen a new goal pursued by medicine: the prevention of illness. Thus, instead of repairing people when they become ill, the focus shifted to the avoidance of illness. We might call this medicine's *preventive* function.

More recently, Western medicine has begun paying attention to a quite different goal, sometimes associated with the term "positive health." Traditionally, people have thought of health as the lack of disease, and, by this definition, the best we can hope for is a total lack of aches and pains. In recent years, however, beyond feeling a lack of serious disease and injury, some people have begun demanding they they feel alive, vigorous, vital, and "healthy." This shift in interest among some has been reflected in a variety of behaviors, such as purchases of health foods, jogging, and reduced use of cigarettes, alcohol, caffeine, and other drugs.

These, then, are three major functions to be served by professional medicine. Let's take a look now at how the service has been organized.

Social Organization of Health Care

Every society has special statuses for healers, though they may be combined with other statuses. In many primitive societies, for example, religious and healing functions are linked. This makes a great deal of sense, of course, from a point of view in which illness has a supernatural component. Among the Navaho Indians, steeped in witchcraft, the same people are believed both to cure and cause disease. (This belief has the latent function of facilitating "one-stop shopping.")

Contemporary developed countries have done more than differentiate the healing function from religious and other functions. Indeed, specialization *within* the healing function is one of its more striking characteristics. The country doctor of America's romantically recalled past is virtually gone. This development has been a mixed blessing.

On one side, medical specialization has meant greater effectiveness in treatment. By devoting an entire career to the understanding of a particular disease, part of the body, or medical technique, a specialist can know more about what lies within his or her specialty than can someone attempting to deal with many diseases and techniques and with the whole body.

On the other side, medical specialization has been a source of concern and unhappiness. The traditional family physician is remembered for his breadth of concern for the whole patient. In contrast, specialists sometimes are charged with narrowly probing into their special area while forgetting other aspects of the whole person.

The narrowness of specialized points of view has been seen to have two different kinds of dysfunctions: one technical and one more generally human. Some fear that specialists will seek specialized success only: taking pride in repairing the ruptured aorta even though the patient dies. There is also considerable concern that, as medicine has become scientifically specialized, physicians have become more impersonal and detached in caring for patients. Both physicians and patients have complained about "assembly-line" medicine in which sick people are processed like television sets or automobiles in need of repair.

Medical care may or may not be getting more impersonal and dehumanized. But the question does not seem to be directly linked to scientific orientations of physicians. In a national survey of medical-school faculty members in departments of medicine and pediatrics (Babbie 1970), I found—as expected—that physicians varied in styles of patient care. Some seemed to exhibit more compassion toward patients than others did. Some maintained a direct responsibility for patients assigned to them, while others were more inclined to turn over responsibility to their assistants. Yet none of these differences appeared to reflect different degrees of "scientific" orientations. ("Scientific orientations" were measured in terms of what most interested them—science or patient care.) The "scientists" were no more or less compassionate or responsible than the "nonscientists."

Even the image of the "mad scientist" in medicine appears unfounded. When I asked respondents whether they felt that medical experimenters themselves should participate in experiments that might be dangerous to subjects, the scientists were as likely as the non-

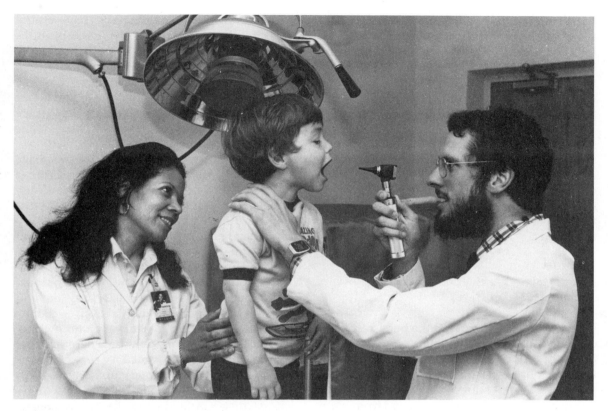

The relationship between patient and family physician has been a treasured one in American society. Many people now complain, however, that medicine has become more impersonal and uncaring.

scientists to feel morally obliged to take the same risks they would ask of others.

Scientifically inclined specialists may be no less compassionate than general practitioners, but the danger that specialists will overlook matters that lie outside their specialties remains. One solution to this problem has been sought in "comprehensive-care" programs aimed at training medical students to see the whole patient (see Merton et al. 1957). Another solution is medical "teamwork." Typically, the team is headed by a general "attending physician" who requests and coordinates the work of specialists. While retaining responsibility for the overall well-being of the patient as a whole person, the attending physician takes advantage

of the greater depth of knowledge and insight that specialists have within their particular specialties. The main dysfunction of this approach appears to be its astronomical cost.

Lying behind these matters of compassion and responsibility is the traditional view of the physician as an altruistic healer. Becker and associates (1961), in intensive participant-observations among medical-school students, suggested that medical education dampened "idealism," or altruism. In the students' view, they came to medical school motivated to help others and left, four years later, more intent on being personally and professionally successful. In the course of their training, for example, they tended to give up plans to become general practitioners who would care for the multifaceted needs of whole patients and to move in the direction of lucrative and less demanding specialties.

The view of physicians as altruistic, while traditional in America and elsewhere, is a complex matter. The code of ethics of the American Medical Association, for example, devotes considerably more attention to the obligations of physicians to one another than to their obligations to patients (Babbie 1970). Nowhere has the issue of altruism been more hotly debated, however, than in the question of who deserves to receive medical care and under what conditions.

Health Care—Right or Privilege?

Modern medicine has faced the persistent philosophical question of whether physical health is a right deserved by all people or a privilege to be bought and sold in the economic marketplace like other scarce goods and services. Agreements in this area have varied from place to place and time to time.

Throughout much of American history, medicine has operated on a "fee-for-service" basis. Physicians have offered the benefits of their training and experience in return for payments from those receiving the benefits. There have always been exceptions, however, and American physicians have traditionally offered free care to other physicians and their families and to the clergy. On a more discretionary basis, they have given free care to the poor, although American codes of medical ethics have warned doctors against taking potential fees out of the marketplace in this fashion.

Early American medicine, as elsewhere, sometimes was funded on a "capitation" basis. Members of a community would agree to contribute a certain amount apiece to pay for having a physician serve in their community. Modern health-insurance programs, both private and governmental, are an extension of this system.

Government health programs have clearly reflected the point of view that good health is a *right* rather than a privilege. Socialized medicine—in the socialist bloc, England, Sweden, Canada, and most Western nations with the exception of the United States—is the fullest implementation of this agreement. Health care is based on medical need rather than on the ability to pay for it.

By and large, American physicians have opposed any program approaching socialized medicine. Their opposition has been most clearly seen, perhaps, in the American Medical Association's opposition to Medicare. Many physicians have also opposed private, prepayment health programs such as those established by the late Henry Kaiser.

The Kaiser-Permanente program of prepaid health care had its roots in the Depression, and at first it had nothing to do with Kaiser. Sidney Garfield, a young physician, set up his medical practice in the southern California desert in 1933 with a plan of providing medical services to the many construction workers building a water system from the Colorado River to Los Angeles. At first, Garfield's practice was a failure. The contractors and their insurance agents were inclined to have serious, on-the-job injuries handled by the established hospitals in Los Angeles, and the workers were not inclined to spend their earnings on nonserious medical problems.

Garfield had an idea that he presented to one of the insurance company executives. If the companies would pay Garfield five cents per day per worker, and if each worker would voluntarily contribute the same, Garfield and his small staff would provide medical care that would include nonindustrial problems. The certainty of income that this arrangement provided allowed Garfield to plan ahead, and he eventually established two more hospitals and a good system of health care for the community.

Five years later, the Kaiser construction company began constructing Grand Coulee Dam in Washington State, in an area lacking proper medical facilities. Edgar F. Kaiser, son of industrialist Henry J. Kaiser, asked Garfield to establish the same type of prepayment system he had created in California, and the die was cast. Henry J. Kaiser was so pleased with the arrangement that he created new programs at other construction sites—such as World War II shipyard operations—and then began creating community health programs unrelated to his construction projects. As of 1976, more than 3 million members participated in Kaiser-Permanente Medical Care programs in six states, from Ohio to Hawaii (Moffat 1977).

Agreements on health care as a right or as a privilege reflect more general points of view concerning individual responsibility. Those who emphasize the concept of "free will" and regard each person as the master of his or her destiny tend to consider medical care a privilege to be earned. This point of view also produces opposition to welfare programs and regards deviance as something to be punished. The more "deterministic" point of view suggests that individuals are largely a product of their environments: that poor people are the victims of the economic system, that juveniles become delinquent because of social conditions, and that people should not be held personally responsible for either getting sick or being unable to pay for medical care. These conflicting points of view underlie countless disagreements in society, especially concerning matters of "social legislation" (see Babbie 1970).

Other controversies in medicine have been generated more directly by the effects, actual or feared, of new developments in medical technology on social life. Let's look now at some of these developments and the controversies they've raised.

Medical Technology and Society

The most significant medical developments over the course of human history might be classified as follows:

1. Drugs for curing illness, such as penicillin
2. Inoculations for preventing illness, such as smallpox vaccinations
3. Surgical remedies for illness, such as appendectomies
4. Public health measures, such as sanitation
5. Other preventive medical developments for avoiding onset or seriousness of illness, such as knowledge of nutrition

These technological developments in medicine have combined with increases in food production to decrease death rates and extend our life expectancies.

The extension of life expectancies, in turn, has brought about many changes in social life. The potentially productive life spans of individuals have been lengthened, permitting greater contributions to society. At the same time, an overabundance of workers has been created at times, which complicates economic systems. And, as we saw in Chapter 10, it has also produced a class of people who live in society without being capable of contributing in proportion to their needs: the very elderly have become like the very young in this respect.

Medical developments also have both permitted and, to an extent, encouraged people to live in ever denser populations in cities. Large cities were nearly wiped out in the plagues of the Middle Ages, for instance, but modern sanitation methods in concert with modern medicines make such plagues unlikely in developed nations.

The technological advances brought about through medical science even during this generation are legion. Organ transplants, for example, let some live who otherwise would die. New medicines for preventing or curing diseases are still being discovered each year, and surgical techniques have become so sophisticated that the performing surgeons must observe their own work under extreme magnification.

The technological advances of medical science, however, have also created new problems. The most advanced intensive-care equipment, for instance, now makes it possible to keep human bodies physiologically alive long after the bodies themselves have lost the ability to be self-sustaining, long after any hope of recovery has passed. Machines can keep hearts beating and blood coursing through the body, and they can keep up the flow of life-sustaining oxygen. But is "life" being sustained? What is life? What is death? These are the types of questions being forced upon us by medical science. At the present, we are still debating who should appropriately give the answers; we haven't reached agreement on the answers themselves.

Earlier in this chapter, I described some of the events surrounding the discovery of the structure and nature of the DNA molecule, often called the "fundamental building block of life." Arthur Snider (1978:507) has summed up the momentous next step in DNA research:

> Not since the 1940s, when significant advances in physics stimulated warnings that technology was outrunning man's ability to control it, has there been as much public and political concern over a new development in science. Three decades ago the issue was nuclear energy, a development with great potential for good or evil. In 1977 the debate centered on the capability of transplanting genetic material of one cell into a cell of a wholly different species, thereby creating a new organism; again the potential for good or evil appeared to be great.
>
> The "gene splicing" technique consists of cutting into small pieces the long, threadlike molecules of DNA (deoxyribonucleic acid), the transmitter of genetic information, then recombining these segments with the DNA of a suitable carrier molecule and inserting the combination into an appropriate host cell, such as a bacterium. The recombinant DNA changes and controls the hereditary characteristics of the host bacteria.
>
> Thus, recombinant DNA technology places in human hands the capability of redesigning living organisms that have evolved over millions of years.*

*Reprinted with permission from the 1978 *Britannica Book of the Year,* copyright 1978 by Encyclopedia Britannica, Inc., Chicago, Ill., p. 507.

Many have been quick to point out the possible advantages of this latest DNA research: the elimination of certain diseases, the improvement of nutrition, even the expansion of agriculture. Others have been just as quick to point out the dangers, even the potential horrors of the research. Monsters could be produced as easily as saints, deadly germs as easily as healing drugs.

With much of the most advanced DNA research being undertaken at Harvard and M.I.T., the Cambridge City Council organized a series of public hearings in 1977 that resulted in temporary suspension of the research—resumed later under carefully controlled conditions.

No less a controversy has been generated by the advent of "cloning": the exact duplication of organisms as an alternative to the merging of male and female genes. Again, both pros and cons have been pointed out. How great it would be to have hundreds of exact copies of Albert Einstein or of Picasso. Or on the other hand, as the popular book and movie *Boys from Brazil* dramatized, it would be just as easy to duplicate a battalion of Adolf Hitlers.

These scientific vignettes demonstrate some of the ways in which medical science is continually generating new sociomoral dilemmas for us to cope with. Fantastic new breakthroughs continually demonstrate the need to reconsider and restructure the agreements by which we seek to run our lives together.

The Computer Revolution

Certainly one of the most significant developments of recent years has been the proliferation of computers both in large organizations and in homes. The first large electronic computers, developed just before World War II, were huge. The ENIAC at the University of Pennsylvania, for example, contained 18,000 vacuum tubes, filled an entire room, and needed 140,000 watts of electricity to operate. Clearly, the vacuum tube put a limitation on the feasibility of computers. That limitation was transcended in 1947, when three Bell Laboratory scientists invented the transistor—for which they later received the Nobel Prize.

The transistor had two major advantages over the vacuum tube: energy requirement and size. Both are evidenced in the small pocket calculator which has become commonplace in American society. A nine-volt battery provides sufficient power for quite complex mathematical operations. The size factor is perhaps the more astounding. Through increasing miniaturization of transistors and circuitry on tiny silicon chips, thousands of transistors, diodes, and capacitators can be contained in an area about the size of a capital 'M' in this book. Also, realize that the preceding sentence will be woefully outdated by the time this book reaches your hands. At present, the finest lines for transmitting electricity within these chips are about $3/50$ the size of a human hair. Further miniaturization will soon run up against what the researchers call "the granularity of atoms." When the transmission lines are only a few atoms wide, the lines begin acting like atoms rather than like solid lines.

The impact of computers on your daily life is immense, and it's not always obvious. When you pick up the telephone to call a friend in another city, the entire process is moved along by a variety of computers. Computers keep track of the cost of your call and print out your bill at the end of the month. Computers facilitated your registering at college, and computers will keep track of and report how well you do. You deal with computers when you buy an item at the supermarket, cash a check at the bank, or drive along a city street. The truth is that you're interacting with computers every day, even when you're not aware of it.

A newer, and in some ways more exciting, development has been the *microcomputer.* You're probably familiar with them and may even have used one. These machines are small, complete computers not much larger than a typewriter.

Operations are displayed on a cathode-ray tube (usually you can use a standard television set). The early systems used standard tape cassettes to store data between uses, though these have now been generally replaced by "floppy disks"— round sheets of magnetic tape about five inches in diameter. A small printer for producing permanent copies of results completes the basic system.

Microcomputers have already proven effective in a variety of tasks. This book, for example, was written on a microcomputer. In addition, I use the same machine for all my correspondence; it schedules my time and prints daily appointments and to-do lists, maintains my checkbook, handles my personal telephone directory, and performs other tasks too numerous to list. When I want a break from writing, I play chess with the computer or save the world from alien invaders.

Microcomputers are just starting to blossom in the arena of social science research. The main drawback is their small *memory* size. Presently, microcomputers are not able to read, remember, and manipulate the massive data sets typically involved in social research. Smaller data sets are easily analyzed, however.

In the next few years, we are certain to see significant advances in the memory capacities of microcomputers, along with the expansions of other social science uses, including the use of microcomputers as "smart" terminals for time-sharing. Introducing a special issue of *Sociological Methods & Research* on "Microcomputers and Social Research," David R. Heise (1981:395) says:

> Microcomputers are cheap, reliable, portable, computationally powerful, and easy to use. This profile makes them significantly different from mainframe computers and guarantees wide diffusion. By the end of the decade, microcomputers will have changed the way social scientists do research, the way they teach courses, and the way they work in applied settings. Microcomputers also will create new topics for social analysis as the microcomputer revolution reaches diverse sectors of society.

Like all our inventions, computers can be used to improve the quality of our life or to make it miserable. In practice, both kinds of consequences result. The same kinds of computers that allow you to fly safely and quickly across the country also make it possible to send intercontinental ballistic missiles from one country to another. The same computers that can speed up your getting and using a credit card can also invade your privacy and blackball you as a consumer. The essential recognition is that computers, by themselves, are neither good nor bad in these respects. They are merely tools that we can use wisely or unwisely.

We have now seen—at some length—a few of the ways in which technology is woven through and through the fabric of modern social life. Clearly, such a discussion could go on endlessly, so thoroughly technological have we become. I suspect the foregoing will have been sufficient, however, to illustrate the human tendency to develop "techniques" as our response to the environment, in the terms presented by Jacques Ellul earlier in the chapter. And the discussions of mass communication have provided some dramatic illustrations of some of the dysfunctions of technique as well as the benefits.

Summary

In this chapter, we have taken a progressively deeper look into the institutional structure of society. The focus has been technology, growing out of what Jacques Ellul says is a fundamental human response to the environment: the development of standardized techniques for handling whatever we confront. Rather than merely taking care of the immediate situation, we develop systems and procedures for dealing with such situations whenever they appear. This tendency has both positive and negative sides, with the most negative aspects appearing when we grow unconscious of what we are doing and become the slaves of our techniques rather than their masters.

Technology pervades all aspects of our society, and people have taken different views of it. Some have regarded it as our salvation, others as our greatest enemy, and still others condition their judgments of technology on the political system that surrounds it. Value judgments aside, no one disputes the extent to which we have adopted technology: in food production, manufacturing, transportation, communication, and all other aspects of life. In looking into some of the concrete details of technological developments in all these areas, we have seen the impact they have had on all other aspects of life. Thus, the automobile transformed more than transportation, television transformed more than communication, and so forth.

Science is in many ways the clearest illustration of technology in a modern society. Science, we saw, can be examined as a social institution in its own right, made up of established agreements governing the behaviors of scientists and those who come in contact with science. At the same time, science is a part of the larger society, and we saw that—like technology generally—it has both positive and negative consequences. In particular, we saw that scientific discovery and innovation can seriously challenge and even overthrow established social agreements and structures. Depending on your view of the status quo, that can be seen as a benefit or a cost of science.

We have focused on medical science as a more specific illustration of technology at work in society. We've seen both the glory and the agony of medical "progress." Although medical science has made it possible for us to live longer, we are not necessarily happier. Indeed, the extension of life has created its own special problems, as the discussion of the elderly in Chapter 10 indicated.

Finally, we have seen some of the ways in which the "computer revolution" affects your day-to-day life. Perhaps more than any other example, the development of computers demonstrates the impact of technology on society.

Important Terms

technology
science
paradigm shifts

Suggested Readings

Bell, Daniel
1973   *The Coming of the Post-Industrial Society.* New York: Basic Books.
Presents the post-industrial society thesis concerning the world trends.

Ellul, Jacques
1964   *The Technological Society,* trans. John Wilkinson. New York: Knopf.
An insightful and stimulating examination of "technique" as a fundamental human response to the environment, and the implications of that response. Though not blindly opposed to technology, Ellul is critical of many things we tend to accept unconsciously.

Evans, Christopher
1979   *The Micro Millennium.* New York: Viking.
Reading like a novel, here's a fascinating history of the "computer revolution," beginning with its earliest roots and ending well into the future.

Gendron, Bernard
1977   *Technology and the Human Condition.* New York: St. Martin's.
An analysis of three major views of technology: utopian, dystopian, and socialist. You may or may not agree with Gendron's choice among the views, but you'll get a useful view of the interrelations of technology and social structure in any event.

Kuhn, Thomas
1970   *The Structure of Scientific Revolution.* Chicago: University of Chicago Press.
This is a modern classic. Kuhn discusses and illustrates at length the notion of *paradigm shifts*—those jumps in frame of reference that Kuhn says characterize scientific progress more accurately than gradual shifts.

Martin, James
1981   *Telematic Society: A Challenge for Tomorrow.* Englewood Cliffs, N.J.: Prentice-Hall.
Here's a fascinating and readable look at the telecommunications revolution. Packed with up-to-date information, the book examines the wide range of life situations which are already being impacted by computerized communications.

Merton, Robert K.
1957   "Priorities in Scientific Discovery: A Chapter in the Sociology of Science." *American Sociological Review* 22, no. 6: 635–59.
An older classic. Merton uses the question of scientific priority to reveal some of the structure of agreements composing science as a social institution.

Schumacher, E. F.
1976   *Small is Beautiful.* New York: Harper & Row.
Critiques the growth push and argues for alternatives to present course of technological development.

Wallerstein, Immanuel
1976   *The Modern World System.* New York: Academic Press.
Uses idea of single world system underlying economies of individual nations through their development over the past several centuries.

Watson, James
1968   *The Double Helix.* New York: New American Library.
A popular, readable, and revealing account of the discovery of the DNA molecule that produced the Nobel Prize for Watson and his colleagues. In contrast to sometimes pious statements of altruism and dedication in science, Watson gives an honest account of the jealousies, ambitions, and other motives that were involved in the search for scientific understanding.

In this chapter, we've discussed the impact of technology on communications, and we've also looked at the "computer revolution." In this concluding essay, we're going to see how those two topics have been linked.

James Martin, writing of the *Telematic Society* (1981:43), suggests there have been three great communication media in history: (1) printed matter, (2) film and television, and (3) computers. As we'll see in this discussion, computers—originally designed for data manipulation and mechanical control—have proven to be powerful communication devices. Let's see how this came about.

To begin, communication has been inseparable from computer technology from the start. The first communication issue was: *how do you communicate with a computer?* While you may be able to tell your family dog to "heel," computers have been a little slow in that regard. (They are excellent with "sit," however.) The most fundamental method of "communicating" with a computer is through its *wiring*. Some computers are simply wired to do a particular job; you push the "start" button and they do what they're supposed to do. Early in computer development, rewiring the machine was a common method of "telling" it to do something else.

Punched cards provided an early improvement for communicating with computers. The machine could be wired in such a way that it could receive instructions. The instructions would be punched on cards, and a *card-reader* would receive those instructions and transmit them to the computer proper. In this fashion, computers became more flexible.

Initially, however, computers could only understand instructions that were written in an obscure language based on the fundamental principle of "on/off." Thus, the computer would receive a series of 0s and 1s: telling it to turn certain switches on and others off. Soon, *programming languages* were being written which allowed computers to understand less cryptic instructions. For example, you might punch the instruction "5*6" in a card, and the computer would "interpret" that as an instruction to multiply 5 times 6. Over the years, numerous languages have been created, such as FORTRAN, BASIC, PASCAL, APL, COBOL, PL/1, and so on. Each of these languages offers a different way of communicating with computers. Here, for example, are some of the ways of instructing a computer (assuming it contains the language in question) to print the word "hello."

BASIC	PRINT"HELLO"
APL	'HELLO'
PASCAL	WRITE('HELLO')

As programming languages got more sophisticated, it was possible to give computers more and more complex tasks to perform. Sociologists, for example, could instruct the university computer to undertake extensive analyses of questionnaire data collected from thousands of respondents, printing out the results as tables, graphs, and the like. The power and speed of the computer, moreover, led to the development of analytical techniques too complicated to be performed by hand.

Until ten or fifteen years ago, the only way most researchers could "communicate" with computers was as follows. If you wanted to analyze a set of survey data, you would punch cards instructing the computer. Then you'd take those cards, plus your data (stored on cards or magnetic tapes) to the campus computer center and give them to a computer operator. As soon as the computer was free—since other people's jobs were also being run—the operator would feed your instructions and data into the computer. Once the analyses were completed, the operator would give you the printout results. The "turn-around time" would be minutes, hours, or days, depending on the machine's workload.

Two communication developments improved the process described above. *Remote job entry* systems placed card readers and printers near the researchers and allowed them to submit jobs and receive their results at locations some distance from the computer center. Communications to and from the computer center traveled over coaxial cables.

Time-sharing was a further advance. In a sense, computers have always operated on a time-sharing basis—several users sharing the same computer. Initially, however, computer facilities were shared in a serial fashion: the computer would run your job, then mine, then someone else's. The current, more sophisticated computers, however, can perform several different tasks simultaneously. It can read my request, analyze yours, and print out someone else's all at the same time. In fact, the tremendous speed of computers makes it possible to sandwich small operations (which may take only thousandths of a second) in the middle of larger jobs. This capacity has made it possible for computers to handle requests from hundreds of users simultaneously, often giving the impression that each has the computer's complete attention. Such interactions with the computer typically use *computer terminals*—typewriter devices that either print on paper or display their operations on CRT (cathode-ray tube) video monitors that look like television screens.

Time-sharing through the use of computer terminals supports a variety of uses. Text-editing programs allow users to write, edit, and print out reports. Or, if your computer center supports a time-sharing system, you'll probably find a variety of videogames stored somewhere in the system.

Making this process even more convenient, there are now a variety of portable computer terminals no larger than small, portable typewriters. Such terminals communicate with the computer over standard telephone lines. Thus, you can take a portable terminal home or on a trip around the world. To use it, you dial a special number on your regular phone. The computer answers—usually with a shrill tone. Then you fit the telephone handset into two rubber cups—called an *acoustical coupler*—on the terminal. Now anything you type on the terminal is transmitted over telephone lines to the computer. It does what you ask and sends the results back to your terminal. In the years to come, such communications may very well be accomplished by radio signals bounced off satellites.

Time-sharing systems can also connect you with nationwide computer *networks*. The possible uses of such networks are mind-boggling, and presently available services only scratch the surface of their potential. You can, for example, dial a special number and connect with a computer that will allow you to search rapidly through past editions of the *New York Times* and locate articles on some topic of interest to you. If you wish, you can have the articles printed out on your terminal.

The speed with which information can be communicated by computer is simply amazing. In computer language, a *bit* refers to a single on/off command. Normal television transmissions require a transmission capacity of 94 million bits per second. That same capacity, however, would permit a computer to transmit the entire Bible 1,000 times in an hour. Moreover, some of the newer transmission lines in use today transmit at a rate of 274 million bits per second (Martin 1981:29,30).

Data storage and transmission capacities are growing in leaps and bounds, often drawing on existing technology. Whereas most remote computer communications today are sent over telephone lines, television channels have a thousand times the capacity (Martin 1981:36). The 12-inch videodisc currently used to store a color movie could also hold the entire *Encyclopedia Britannica*, offering computer access to any single page.

Thus far, I've been talking about the development of methods for humans communicating with computers. But what's the implication of all this for humans communicating with other humans?

With the advent of time-sharing, it was possible for two people to communicate with one another through the computer. If you and I were using the computer at the same time, I could type a message that would be printed on your terminal; you'd then send your response back in the same manner in an electronic version of passing notes back and forth in class.

Today, this communication facility has far outstripped its "primitive" forebears. Computer networks such as TELEMAIL, TYMNET, and THE SOURCE allow subscribers to leave lengthy messages in the "electronic mailboxes" of a central computer, to be picked up later by other subscribers. (One of the unintended consequences of this capacity, however, has been the problem of electronic "junk mail"—it's so easy to send a copy of everything to everyone.) While this system offers an alternative to the telephone, telegraph, and mail, it only scratches the surface of the communication potential. Consider this possibility.

Computer networks make it possible for a researcher sitting at home in California to get a copy of a data set maintained on a computer in Massachusetts and to analyze those data using a program maintained on a computer in Texas.

The results of the analysis would be returned to the user in California, and the results could also be stored for examination by a colleague in Michigan. I don't mean to suggest that the procedure described above is commonplace today, but it is already possible.

James Martin (1981:6) envisions such uses of the computer becoming an ordinary fact of life for people in the years to come:

> Pocket terminals mushroom in sales and drop in cost as fast as pocket calculators did a decade earlier. Most people who carried a pocket calculator now have a pocket terminal. The pocket terminal, however, has an almost endless range of applications. It can access many computers and data banks via the public data networks. The pocket terminal becomes a consumer product (as opposed to a product for businesspeople) on sale at supermarkets, with human factoring that is simple and often amusing. The public regard it as a companion which enables them to find good restaurants, display jokes on any subject, book airline and theater seats, contact medical programs, check what their stockbroker computer has to say, send messages, and access their electronic mailbox.

Clearly the new telecommunication technology will affect virtually all aspects of life. Consider for a moment the impact the automobile had on residential patterns, leisure activities, education, and countless other elements of social life. The impact of telecommunications is likely to be far more powerful.

Work is sure to be transformed. At present, hundreds and thousands of employees—of an insurance company, for example—need to commute to their place of business every workday. In the future, they will be able to stay at home, doing more work more effectively, by computer. Already, sales representatives on the road return to their motel rooms at night, type up their daily reports on microcomputers, and transmit those reports over phone lines to the home office computer.

As you consider these possibilities, however, you should recall some of our earlier discussions of groups and organizations. We've seen how people establish interpersonal relations within formal organizations, for example. What will happen when co-workers seldom or never see each other? New forms of interpersonal relations will undoubtedly emerge.

The new telecommunication technology is likely to require a thorough rethinking of the "work" involved in organizations. Fernando Flores, a Chilean philosopher, has already begun adapting for computer the communication technology of John Searle, an American philosopher. Some of the key elements of communication, they suggest, are "assertions," "promises," and "requests." If you and I were working together in an office, we might have a long, somewhat indirect conversation that would boil down to: I *assert* that the office needs a new procedure for purchasing equipment; I *request* that you relieve me of my regular duties for three days; and I *promise* to draft the procedure. Flores is developing computer communication systems which will force people to get to the meat of their communications, eliminating the extraneous and often ambiguous materials that can get in the way of effective communications.

The ways in which computers will affect our communications and other aspects of our lives are virtually endless. Linking computers with cable television opens up another vista. In 1972, the United States government required cable television systems to provide the capacity for two-way communication. This capacity is now being exploited. The Warner Brothers' Qube system in Columbus, Ohio, for example, allows viewers—using pushbutton devices—to indicate their approval or disapproval of what is being broadcast. The political potential of this capacity is staggering. It would be possible for a whole community to discuss a local bond issue and cast ballots at the end of the discussion without ever leaving home. By extension, one day a whole nation could possibly debate and resolve issues of national and international significance.

These are but a few of the ways in which computers are already affecting our communications with one another. Ten years from now, you will look back on this discussion and probably regard it as primitive and short-sighted.

PRACTICING SOCIOLOGY

Concerns over the impact of television on young people were fueled by a 1982 report from the California Department of Education that indicated that sixth-graders who watched a lot of television achieved lower test scores in reading, writing, and math than did those who watched less television. The table below shows the basic data.

Hours of TV per weekday	Average test scores		
	Reading	Writing	Math
None	73	71	64
0–½	75	74	69
½–1	74	72	65
1–2	73	72	65
2–3	73	70	65
3–4	72	70	63
4–5	71	68	63
5–6	70	68	62
6+	66	64	58

More puzzling, the researchers found that whereas watching the "Dukes of Hazzard" (and other shows) was related to low test scores, watching "M*A*S*H" was related to *higher* scores, as indicated below.

Show and frequency of watching	Average test scores		
	Reading	Writing	Math
"Dukes of Hazzard"			
Regularly	69	67	62
Sometimes	75	72	66
Seldom/ never	74	74	66
"M*A*S*H"			
Regularly	72	70	64
Sometimes	71	69	63
Seldom/ never	68	68	61

Suggest possible explanations in answer to the following questions and describe how you might go about testing whether your explanations were accurate.

1. In the first table, why do students who watch no television have consistently lower scores than those who watch up to half an hour a day?

2. How do you account for the findings of the second table, comparing the two television programs?

3. *Why* is there apparently a significant connection between (a) amount and type of television watched, and (b) achievement test scores?

Source: William Grant, "M*A*S*H Achievers," *San Francisco Chronicle*, July 21, 1982, pp. 1, 4.

20

Social Change

It is especially appropriate that this book end with a chapter on the topic of social change. In the preceding chapters of Part Five, we have already seen some of the ways in which social life is changing as a consequence of population growth, environmental changes, and technology. In this concluding chapter, we'll examine social change per se.

Social change is a constant in social life. Society and social relations are continually changing. Such changes may occur with regard to beliefs, values, or norms. Thus, for example, secularization, which Max Weber regarded as one of the most significant changes taking place in modern societies, represents a shift from religious to nonreligious beliefs.

The emancipation of blacks and of women in America represents social change relating to norms. Other American examples include the great increase in the educational levels people achieve; the increasing number of supermarkets, which supplant family-run stores; and countless other shifts in the way we do things.

Social change, of course, has been taking place since human societies began. Many changes were related to technological developments, such as the invention of the wheel, the forging of metals, and the establishment of agriculture. Of special interest to contemporary sociologists, however, is the increased *rate* of social change. Societies are changing faster than ever, and the pace is likely to accelerate.

Alvin Toffler (1970:13–14) quotes the economist Kenneth Boulding as saying "I was born in the middle of human history, to date, roughly. Almost as much has happened since I was born as happened before." Toffler continues:

> This startling statement can be illustrated in a number of ways. It has been observed, for example, that if the last 50,000 years of man's existence were divided into lifetimes of approximately sixty-two years each, there have been about 800 such lifetimes. Of these 800, fully 650 were spent in caves.
>
> Only during the last seventy lifetimes has it been possible to communicate effectively from one

lifetime to another—as writing made it possible to do. Only during the last six lifetimes did masses of men ever see a printed word. Only during the last four has it been possible to measure time with any precision. Only in the last two has anyone anywhere used an electric motor. And the overwhelming majority of all the material goods we use in daily life today have been developed within the present, the 800th, lifetime.

The increasing rapidity of technological and social change led Toffler to formulate a concept he called "future shock." In much the same way that persons first confronting the agreements of a strange culture experience "culture shock," Toffler suggests that our own society will, in the years to come, seem equally strange and "shocking."

In this chapter, we're going to look at some of the ways social change comes about and some of the theories sociologists have put forward to make sense of those changes. We'll see that some social change results from external forces operating on a social system and others are generated by the internal dynamics of the system itself. Then, we'll look at the process of **modernization:** an increasingly rapid process in which societies around the globe are shifting from established, rural traditions to modern, urbanized forms.

To start, then, let's begin with some sociological theories of social change.

Theories of Social Change

In this section, I want to begin with the primary implications of social change from a conflict theory point of view and from a functionalist point of view. Both of these theoretical perspectives acknowledge the importance of innovations and natural events in bringing about social change. The proponents of both points of view would surely recognize the inevitability of change as a practical matter. Nonetheless,

there are significant differences between these perspectives.

Conflict Perspective

As I suggested earlier in the book, the conflict-theory perspective sees social change as an inevitable consequence of the way we structure society. This was clearest, perhaps, in the discussion of Dahrendorf in Chapter 2. If societies are held together by dominance—by one group holding another down—then it seems reasonable that there will be a constant tension in the direction of change. The "have-nots" will continually lean in the direction of replacing the "haves." Sometimes they will lean gently, sometimes violently in bloody revolution.

From the standpoint of social values, moreover, most proponents of the conflict perspective would probably hold the struggle of the have-nots against the haves to be morally just. In practice, this has been the struggle of workers, for example, against factory owners, the struggle of black slaves against white masters, or—more recently—a nonslave but disadvantaged black minority against a white majority.

This issue—the morality of struggle for social change—touches the same events and issues discussed earlier in the chapters on stratification, race and ethnic relations, inequalities of age and sex, and deviance. Let's now see what social change tends to look like from a functionalist point of view.

Functionalist Perspective

You'll recall from the discussion of social systems theory in Chapter 2 that the notion of "equilibrium" was central. The "balancing" of elements in a system leads to the persistence of the system as a whole. Early functionalists often likened society to the human body, which—biologically—maintains a state of equilibrium through self-regulating mechanisms. In

For much of this century, people have believed that all technological progress was a step forward for humankind. Beginning in the 1960s, however, many people began questioning the relative costs and benefits of some technological developments.

the body, such mechanisms keep body temperature from rising too high or dropping too low, for example; in society, a set of functionally interrelated beliefs, values, and norms maintains social harmony. From this point of view, social change, particularly social conflict—as well as deviance—is seen as "pathological" in the same sense that an irreversible fever in the body is pathological. Conflict threatens the survival of society just as a fever threatens the survival of the human body.

Contemporary functionalists, such as Talcott Parsons, do not speak of conflict and change as

pathological, although they regard it as a threat to the equilibrium of the system. The American Revolution was an example of social change that, while not evil in the eyes of contemporary Americans, clearly disrupted the political equilibrium of the British Empire.

Functionalists have come increasingly to speak of a "moving" equilibrium as distinguished from a "static" equilibrium. In this view, it is possible for a social system to undergo change continually all the while maintaining its equilibrium. A factory could grow in size and in the specification of functions and still main-

Table 20-1

Some Concepts of Linear Social Change

Year	Writer	Concepts
1855	Auguste Comte	Theology → Metaphysics → Science
1867	Karl Marx	Capitalism → Socialism → Communism
1876	Herbert Spencer	Simple forms → Complex forms
1887	Lewis Morgan	Savagery → Barbarism → Civilization
1887	Ferdinand Toennies	Gemeinschaft → Gesellschaft
1893	Emile Durkheim	Mechanical solidarity → Organic solidarity
1909	Charles H. Cooley	Primary groups → Secondary groups
1922	Max Weber	Charisma → Tradition → Rational bureauracy
1941	Robert Redfield	Folk society → Urban society
1950	David Riesman	Tradition-directed → Inner-directed → Other-directed
1951	Talcott Parsons	Particularism → Universalism
		Ascription → Achievement
		Affectivity → Affective neutrality
		Functional diffuseness → Specificity
		Collectivity orientation → Individual orientation

Note: Year refers to year of major publication discussing the concepts.

tain integration and cooperation among the multiplying specialists. That would be an illustration of "moving equilibrium."

Recall from Chapter 2 that the System Dynamics modeling system offers a method of diagramming and understanding such systems of equilibrium and disequilibrium. We'll look at some diagrams of social change a little later in the chapter.

The differences of view toward social change that are found in the conflict and functionalist perspectives are only the beginning of differences sociologists have had with one another on this topic. Let's step back a couple of paces and return to social change from a different direction.

In most of the examples of social change given in the discussion up to this point it has been implicitly assumed that social change has a direction, that the change is headed toward something. As we'll see now, the linear view of

social change is only a part of what sociologists have seen. Indeed, there are several different versions of linear change.

Linear Theories of Change

A number of social thinkers have suggested that, through social change, societies develop toward some goal. The trend from small, primitive societies to large, complex civilizations is commonly put forth as an example of linear development.

Table 20–1 illustrates the linear developments various important sociologists have detected in their examinations of human social life. Many of the names and terms in the table will be familiar to you from earlier discussions. Implicit in the views of these theorists is the idea that social forms evolve over the course of history. Indeed, the idea of "social evolution,"

Herbert Spencer
1820–1903
Derby, England

Some Important Works

The Principles of Sociology, 3 vols. (New York: Appleton, 1876–1896).

The Study of Sociology (Ann Arbor, Mich.: University of Michigan Press, 1873).

Descriptive Sociology: Or, Groups of Sociological Facts, Classified and Arranged by Herbert Spencer, 17 vols., comp., abst. David Duncan et al. (London: Williams and Norgate, 1873–1934).

Herbert Spencer was, in his time and by his self-assessment, an expert on virtually everything, publishing extensively in the fields of psychology, biology, education, law, physiology, philosophy, politics, administration, ethics, and others. Two "others" are the most relevant for sociologists: evolution and sociology.

In his own lifetime, Spencer intended to write the definitive volumes on society, and he surely wrote more volumes than anyone before or since. Most of his work has passed into obscurity. He was, however, the chief proponent for a recurrent view in sociology: the evolutionist perspective. Spencer saw a linear evolution of society from simple to complex and from poor to good, akin to the biological evolution described by his contemporary, Charles Darwin. Spencer was and is known as the chief "social Darwinist."

akin to Darwin's notion of biological evolution, has been popular in sociology from time to time, particularly in the late nineteenth century. Herbert Spencer (1820–1903), for example, argued

that societies evolve over time through "natural selection" and "survival of the fittest."

During much of the twentieth century, however, the notion of social evolution has not been very popular in sociology. Its critics generally consider it to be naive, a judgment partly in reaction to the zealous optimism of the early evolutionists, who felt that things were getting better and better as societies evolved. Faced with growing social problems, overpopulation, environmental pollution, alienation, and the threat of thermonuclear war, twentieth-century sociologists have been less willing to regard "progress" as automatically good.

Gerhard Lenski (1966) has offered one of the more useful recent analyses of social evolution. In particular, Lenski has traced the development of social inequality as societies have evolved from simple to complex structures. Whereas all people in the simplest societies are essentially equal, with the creation of surpluses through agriculture and other social innovations, inequality becomes possible—even inevitable. Unlike earlier proponents of social evolution, Lenski points to both benefits and drawbacks.

Sociologists also have recognized that social change does not occur smoothly. Progress, even in a given direction, often occurs in leaps and bounds. Sometimes there is forward development, and sometimes there is none. Sometimes things even seem to be going backward.

Wilbert Moore (1963) has diagrammed various models of social change that sociologists use. Figure 20–1 presents four of Moore's diagrams.

Model 1 represents the most simplistic view of linear, evolutionary social change. It suggests that societies steadily and smoothly get more and more "civilized," for example. No sociologist today would defend such a model.

Model 2, though also simplistic, is a more accurate picture of long-term social change. We might, for example, see hunting and gathering as the first stage of development, followed by

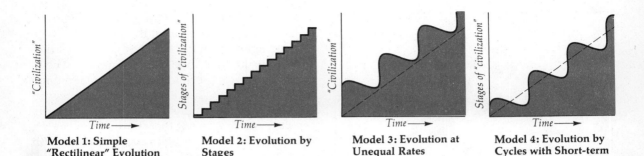

Figure 20-1 Some models of social change. Source: Figure adapted from Wilbert Moore, Social Change (Englewood Cliffs, N.J.: Prentice-Hall, 1963), Figure 1, page 38.

a step up occasioned by the development of agriculture. Later steps might be based on subsequent technological and economic developments.

Model 3 represents social change as a succession of spurts in which societies move forward, stay the same for a time, then move forward again. Model 4 is a modification of model 3, allowing for periodic retrogressions. The history of black equality in America might be described by model 4 because it is characterized by gains, setbacks, more gains, and more setbacks, all taking place within an overall framework of movement toward equality with whites.

None of these models is intended to be a precise and accurate picture of social change. To begin, the dimension of "civilization" is too ambiguous to permit the mathematical graphing of social change. And if measurable social changes were to be graphed, it is unlikely that any would be as smooth and regular as shown. These models are nonetheless useful in suggesting the variety of patterns in which social change occurs.

Notice that each model suggests a movement toward some final condition. Some writers have been optimistic about the final states. Comte and Marx, for example, foresaw science and communism, respectively, as being the goals toward which history was progressing. All the thinkers shown in Table 20–1, however, have

generally seen social change as going in a given, and possibly irreversible, direction. The implication is that technology will become increasingly complex rather than simpler and that roles will continue becoming more specialized and interdependent rather than more general and independent.

Cyclical Theories of Change

Several students of social change have suggested that it is not linear but cyclical. The German historian Oswald Spengler (1880–1936), for one, suggested that societies were like people: they were born, grew rapidly, reached full maturity—which he called the "Golden Age"—declined, and died. Spengler (1932) applied this theory to the West, arguing that Western civilization was in the process of dying and that nothing could be done to halt its decline.

The British historian Arnold Toynbee (1889–1975) has suggested that societies pass through cycles of "challenge" and "response": as each challenge is met by society's response, a new challenge arises. More optimistic than Spengler, Toynbee sees societies progressing toward perfection, or at least sees perfection as possible, in contrast to a prediction of sure decline (Toynbee 1962–1964).

The sociologist most associated with the cyclical view of social change is Pitirim Sorokin

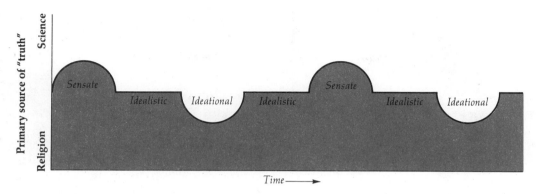

Figure 20-2 Sorokin's cyclical model of social change. Source: Figure adapted from Wibert Moore, Social Change (Englewood Cliffs, N.J.: Prentice-Hall, 1963), Figure 13, page 43.

(1889–1968), an immigrant to America following the Russian Revolution. Sorokin thought that three points of view characterized societies from time to time. The "sensate" point of view defines reality in terms of sense experiences. Science is important in such a point of view. The "ideational" point of view, by contrast, places greater emphasis on spiritual and religious factors. Unlike Comte and others, who saw a linear evolution from religion to science, Sorokin suggested that these two points of view alternated cyclically in societies. Finally, Sorokin's third point of view, the "idealistic," combined elements of the sensate and ideational in an integrated, rational view of the world (Sorokin 1937–1940).

Figure 20–2 presents Moore's diagram of Sorokin's cyclical model of social change. Notice that this model does not imply a long-term direction of social change. There is no implied final condition, such as civilization, science, or utopia.

To review, then, there are two major points of view on long-term social change. One of these sees a linear progression from one type of society or characteristic of social life to another. Some of the theories representing this point of view have been evolutionary in that they suggest that "higher" social forms (such as civilization) evolve from "lower" ones (such as barbarism). These

theories have typically been optimistic about the future. The other major point of view suggests that social change is cyclical, representing alternations among types of societies, for example, rather than proceeding in a given direction.

Neither the cyclical nor the linear theory of social change seems to describe adequately the whole course of history. Nevertheless, as models of the way particular changes occur, these theories can be useful. Some phenomena make more sense when viewed linearly. Other phenomena make more sense when viewed cyclically.

Moore (1963:34–35) cites "average increase in productivity (output per man-hour of work) over an entire economy such as the United States" as an example of social change that appears to approximate closely the linear model (model 1 in Figure 20–1). As an empirically observable example of cyclical change (Figure 20–2), he cites (1963:43) "the short-term course of marriage rates and birth rates in contemporary western societies." Observations of social change indicate that no single model encompasses all, and sociologists seek to discover the particular models that best represent specific aspects of social change.

Despite their differences in describing the long-term patterns of social change, there is no

Pitirim A. Sorokin
1889–1968
Turya, Russia

Some Important Works

Social and Cultural Mobility (Glencoe, Ill.: Free Press, 1959 [1927–1941]).

Contemporary Sociological Theories (New York: Harper, 1928).

Social and Cultural Dynamics (Englewood Cliffs, N.J.: Bedminster Press, 1962 [1937–1941]).

Born in humble circumstances in rural Russia, Sorokin became active in student political circles, participating in the Russian Revolution of 1917. He served as a member of the Constituent Assembly and was secretary to the prime minister, Kerensky. His opposition to the Bolsheviks, however, led to his expulsion from the Soviet Union in 1922. He then began his second career—as an American sociologist.

Like Parsons, Sorokin was a "grand theorist," intent on capturing all the phenomena of society at once. There the similarity ends, however, as the two men brought very different theoretical views to the task. Where Parsons emphasized the social-structural nature of society, Sorokin's approach was sweepingly historical, and he focused more on process than structure. Because of his experiences in the Russian Revolution, perhaps, he saw the flow of social history as more circular than "progressively" linear. More specifically, he saw societies moving through a cycle of stages emphasizing sensory, spritual, and rational bases of reality.

disagreement among these theorists as to the fact and significance of social change. Let's look now at some of its sources.

The Sources of Social Change

In Chapter 18, we looked at some important sources of social change: population growth and environmental impacts. In this section, we'll be looking at some of the many other sources of change in society. We'll begin with the part played by conflict. Though we discussed conflict theory in Chapter 2, we're now going to give special attention to the ways that conflict becomes a stimulus for change. Having considered conflict, we'll look at other important sources of social change. Then we'll conclude the chapter with an examination of modernization.

Social Conflict

Social conflict is a matter of disagreement. When people have different points of view, they often engage in activities aimed at gaining agreement for their point of view over others. Thus, for example, two children (of any age) may have different points of view regarding who is the stronger and will start a fistfight in an effort to gain agreement on one or the other point of view. Nations (of all ages) engage in the same sort of activity. When a new view gains dominance, social change occurs.

Put more formally, "social conflict" is an activity engaged in by two or more parties with differing points of view, each attempting to gain agreement for its point of view. The forms of social conflict vary greatly, ranging from debates, economic competition, and political campaigns to revolutions and thermonuclear wars. Let's look at some of the levels at which social conflict occurs in society and see how such conflicts can be a source of social change.

Within-Group Conflict Social conflict often occurs within groups, as the members disagree on matters relating to the group itself. Factions may form around different points of view relating to policies, actions, leadership, or the like. Family disputes and civil wars are both examples of within-group conflict. The influence of civil wars like that in the United States on changing agreements is obvious. But family conflicts when added one to another can effect large-scale changes in, for instance, the status of women.

Conflict is likely to be most hostile within groups normally characterized by close, intense ties among members. As Lewis Coser (1956:68) has observed:

> Individuals who participate intensely in the life of such groups are concerned with the group's continuance. If they witness the breaking away of one with whom they have shared cares and responsibilities of group life, they are likely to react in a more violent way against such "disloyalty" than less involved members.

As Coser (and Georg Simmel before him) observed, conflict within a group threatens the definition of the group and its boundaries. It can threaten the very survival of the group, whether it is a small clique or a nation. Consider, for example, the reaction to domestic communism within the United States and its many effects. For many Americans, the "enemy within" has been more feared than Russian or Chinese military divisions and has led to massive hunts for "un-Americans." Emotion-charged terms such as "turncoat" and "traitor" are used in reference to those group members who once agreed with "us" and now disagree. Thus, Benedict Arnold is regarded as more despicable than King George III in American history. In contemporary Communist nations, "revisionists" are similarly despised.

Between-Group Conflict In contrast to conflict within a group, which threatens its solidarity and survival, conflict between groups can strengthen each. (Recall the discussion in Chapter 6 of in-groups and out-groups.) A Democratic primary, for instance, may weaken the Democratic party as a group but strengthen both the conservative and liberal factions within it as factions. Thus, between-group conflict can be both a force for change and a force for stability.

The hostility of intergroup conflict is greater when the conflicting points of view have been reified, when the individuals involved believe they are fighting on behalf of "truth." As Coser (1956:113) notes:

> It appears . . . that conflict pursued with a "good conscience" . . . is generally more radical and merciless than where such inner support is lacking. For example, one reason for the apparently decreased combativeness of American management in labor struggles today, as compared with fifty years ago, can perhaps be found in a decreased belief in the absolute righteousness of maximizing profits both in the society at large and in the business community itself.

The perceived "righteousness," the "rightness" of your point of view, increases the viciousness with which you seek to gain agreement for it. It has been observed that religious wars are the bloodiest wars.

Class Conflict One type of between-group conflict that sociologists have studied extensively as a source of social change is the conflict that takes place between social classes. As you'll recall from Chapter 2, Karl Marx thought that class struggle was the moving force of history. During his own lifetime, he saw unfettered capitalism create two major classes of people: the "bourgeoisie" (the owners of the means of production) and the "proletariat" (the workers). He felt that the oppression of workers would drive them to realize their true class interests, to organize politically, and eventually to overthrow capitalism itself.

With the benefit of clear-eyed hindsight, we may now regard Marx's views of historical

"Narcissism" and Cultural Change

Talk of social and cultural change in the United States today often centers on what is perceived to be an erosion of basic values, a lack of concern for others, and a decline of authority—perceptions that often are accompanied by vague feelings of uneasiness about the future of our society. In-depth analyses of these modern currents, however, are sparse.

One social critic who has recently made a serious attempt to analyze what is happening to modern American culture and society is Christopher Lasch. Lasch characterizes our age as one of "narcissism," or self-absorption, the term deriving from the Greek myth of Narcissus, a boy who became enamored of his own image. Modern narcissists, as Lasch draws them, are wrapped up in themselves, uninterested in the past or future, fearful of death yet never feeling really alive, possessed by feelings of purposelessness, and unable either to develop lasting relationships with others or to subordinate their own personal desires to projects outside themselves. One might imagine that narcissists are simply self-indulgent, but pleasure is not their lot. Instead, the restless search for comfort masks a lack of self-esteem, an anxious search for approval from others, particularly those of a higher social status.

Lasch sees narcissistic tendencies, which he believes are coming into increasing prominence in modern American life, as attempts by individuals to defend themselves against the competitive social relations of modern capitalism. These tendencies are encouraged by our mass-consumption economy, which places the emphasis on people as consumers rather than producers. The development of the camera, television, and other electronic media, Lasch

---

change (and of the future) as somewhat simplistic. Nowhere did he anticipate the development of corporations, which spread economic ownership more broadly across populations. Neither did he anticipate the union movement that would result in better pay for skilled workers than for, say, teachers. Despite Marx's lack of "foresight" many sociologists still find value in his basic concept of a struggle between different social classes, even if they don't see such a struggle as being the dramatic engine of social change that Marx did. The box, "Narcissism and Cultural Change," suggests that narcissistic tendencies are attempts by individuals to defend themselves against the competitive social relations of modern capitalism.

Ralf Dahrendorf, a contemporary sociologist, has attempted to update and systematize Marx's concept of **class struggle.** Dahrendorf has often had to reflect a Marxian generalization and substitute specifics. Where, for example, Marx saw violence and civil war as inevitable, Dahrendorf (1959:136) concludes that the empirical hypothesis is false that insists that this class conflict must always assume the form of violent civil war and "class struggle." Indeed, it seems plausible that under certain conditions (which it is possible to determine) class antagonism becomes latent or is reactivated from a state of latency.

Dahrendorf (1959) goes on to construct a formal theory describing the conditions under which the intensity and violence of class conflict will be heated or cooled. He suggests that when different aspects of the class conflict are separated from one another, the intensity will be less than when they coincide. A closed class system will produce a more intense class conflict than an open class system. In Dahrendorf's theory, separating authority from economic rewards will also lessen the intensity of the conflict and the likelihood of explosive social change occurring in this way.

War   War is the most dramatic example of social conflict producing social change. Through war,

argues, also encourages narcissistic traits because these media lead people to think that they really exist only when they see their reflections.

The current emphasis on psychotherapy, Lasch believes, also encourages concentration on the self. In addition, the ethos of psychotherapy undermines the sense of moral responsibility by transforming moral questions into therapeutic ones concerning our state of mental fitness, and it disguises social relations of domination and hierarchy in the corporation, for instance, under the paternalistic guise of "teamwork" and "participation." The emphasis on professionalism and the growth of bureaucracy—by which Lasch means not just the growth of government, but the growth of corporate bureaucracy as well—encourage narcissistic traits by encouraging dependence on institutions and eroding personal feelings of competence. Thus, mothers often rush to books by "experts" to bring up their children, and citizens often don't recognize their own knowledge and good judgment unless these are certified by a professional.

The corporations and the state now control so much of the necessary know-how that Durkheim's image of society as the "nourishing mother," from whom all blessings flow, more and more coincides with the citizen's everyday experience. The new paternalism has replaced personal dependence not with bureaucratic rationality, as theorists of modernization (beginning with Max Weber) have almost unanimously assumed, but with a new form of bureaucratic dependence. What appears to social scientists as a seamless web of "interdependence" represents in fact the dependence of the individual on the organization, the citizen on the state, the worker on the manager, and the parent on the "helping professions." (p. 229)

Source: Christopher Lasch, *The Culture of Narcissism: American Life in an Age of Diminishing Expectations* (New York: Norton, 1978).

whole societies can be overturned in a few years. The German military strategist Clausewitz defined war as "the pursuit of politics by other means." As offensive as this definition may seem, it illustrates the fact that war is, ultimately, only another way of trying to gain agreement for your particular point of view. The "noble" end is permitted to justify any means.

The agreement that "war is terrible, but . . ." appears to be broadly shared. Few Americans today would quarrel with the "justice" of the American Revolution of 1776 or our fight against fascism in World War II, even though many Americans opposed both of those wars at the time. Yet many who regard the American Revolution as unquestionably "just" find no justice in the "wars of national liberation" now occurring in Asia and other parts of the globe.

Wars do not necessarily grow out of disagreements between total populations of nations. Throughout world history, bloody wars have been fought and enormous changes brought about in order to settle the disagreements of a few kings, dictators, and ruling elites. In *The Causes of World War Three* (1958), C. Wright Mills suggested that this pattern is still with us. Mills's analysis is relevant to our investigation for other reasons as well. In this book, he shows how just the threat of war can force domestic social changes and how social changes—in this case, militarization—can trigger changes that ripple through the whole society and have consequences that were never intended by their original promoters. Mills, for example, was especially concerned over how preparations for war had helped fuel the rise of an American ruling elite—the "military-industrial complex":

The top of modern America is increasingly unified and often seems willfully co-ordinated . . .

The power of decision is now seated in military, political, and economic institutions. Other institutions are increasingly shaped and used by these three. By them the push and pull of a fabulous technology is now guided, even as it paces and shapes their own development. (1958:21)

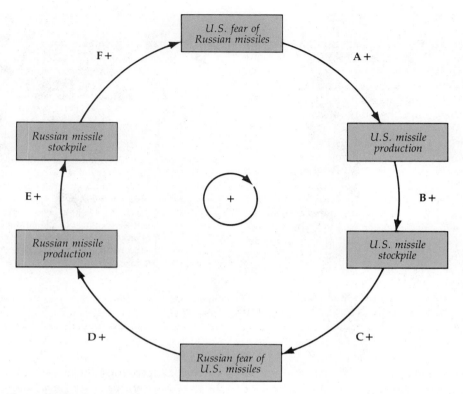

Figure 20–3 The nuclear arms race. Source: Understanding Sociology.

Mills stressed the fact that the "fabulous technology" paced and shaped the power elite: the growth of a war-oriented economy developed imperatives of its own. In the interest of military preparedness, great amounts of capital had to be invested in industries that could develop and produce the weapons of war, and that very investment made it necessary that more and more weapons be developed and produced continually. Halting war production in times of peace would, presumably, have serious economic consequences.

As political, business, and military leaders cooperate with one another in the interest of military preparedness, Mills argued, they develop a militaristic point of view, one that they have the power to act on at a national level.

Mills's fear was that this "power elite" (see Chapter 13) would act "in good faith" from its point of view of military preparedness. He wrote (1958:47): "The immediate cause of World War III is the military preparation of it."

Figure 20–3 presents a simple diagrammatic model of the positive feedback loop represented by the nuclear-arms race. Notice how the structure of the system causes a never-ending increase of missiles in both America and Russia.

Here are the individual steps in the model:

A.   The American fear of Russian missiles leads America to increase missile production.

B. Increased missile production increases America's missile stockpile.

C. The increased American missile stockpile, however, produces an increased Russian fear of American missiles.

D. So what do you suppose the Russians do? Their fear of American missiles leads to an increase in Russian missile production.

E. Russia's missile stockpile increases as a consequence.

F. The increased Russian threat heightens American fears. . . .

The plus sign in the center of the model indicates that it represents a positive feedback loop. The nature of the relationships composing the system will result in unending escalation. Only something external to this system can change it.

The point made by Mills and by the diagram is that systems have a dynamic of their own, quite aside from what the individuals involved consciously desire. Wars, thus, need not be caused by people who want war. As a footnote to Mills's study, it might be noted that the controversial "Pentagon Papers," made familiar by virtue of the competing attempts to publish or suppress them, were originally commissioned by Robert McNamara, then secretary of defense, to find out how an intellectual, peace-loving administration could have blundered into a war in Vietnam, while trying to avoid just that.

Conflict, though a major source of social change, is not the only one, however. Innovations of various sorts also have a powerful impact.

Innovations

New ideas, discoveries, and inventions are all important sources of social change. Thus, Max Weber argued that the Calvinist notion of religious predestination lay at the root of capital-ism. Whatever its source, the idea of capitalism made a significant difference in people's lives. Similarly, the idea of corporations, unions, and multinationals are among the ideas that have importantly shaped the economic aspect of modern social life.

Or consider the impact of Karl Marx's ideas. Without question, innovative ideas can substantially restructure social systems and the lives of those who live in them.

Discoveries and Inventions   As I've already suggested, discoveries and inventions are an important source of social change. From a sociological point of view, for example, Columbus discovered America, regardless of whether he was the first European to arrive in the New World. It was his **discovery** that spurred the vast social change that followed the subsequent waves of European migration. Similarly, the **invention** of television radically changed most aspects of social life—family activities, entertainment, information transmission, politics, economics, and so forth. In Chapter 19, we examined in detail one of the most important inventions of this century: the computer.

From the standpoint of social change, the actual discoveries and inventions are less important than are their adoption and use. Accordingly, sociologists have been especially interested in the manner in which such innovations gain widespread agreeement.

Diffusion   Ideas, discoveries, and inventions do not stay at the point of their origin. They spread. Thus two Americans flew the first motorized airplane, a German developed the first jet plane, the Russians orbited the first satellite, and the Americans first put people on the moon.

Diffusion refers to the spread of agreements, artifacts, and agreements about artifacts from one place to others. Donald Schon (1971) has described two models of diffusion. These are presented in Figure 20–4. The "center-periphery model" is characterized by one source

No recent technological development has had a greater impact on social life than the computer. Moreover, we are still at the very beginning of the computer revolution. Literally, no one can accurately predict the long-term consequences of this invention.

of innovations and several receivers of innovations; the "proliferation of centers model" describes the case in which the receivers of innovations become innovators in their own right.

We'll return to this process of diffusion in the discussion of modernization later in the chapter.

Natural Changes

Some social change has a cause seemingly beyond human control altogether. Natural events

such as earthquakes, volcanic eruptions, droughts, tidal waves, and the like can create sudden disruptions that have immediate and/or long-term impacts on social relations. At the extreme, some natural disasters are so colossal as to bring an end to change altogether. On August 24, 79 A.D., for example, Mount Vesuvius erupted, killing 20,000 to 30,000 people and destroying the two great cities of Pompeii and Herculaneum.

Less severe disasters produce changes that live on after them. The San Francisco earthquake of 1906, for example, killed some 600, left 300,000 homeless, and did about half a billion dollars damage (in 1906 dollars). Unlike Pompeii, however, San Francisco was rebuilt. This time, architectural design took account of the earthquake hazard, and the earthquake became a part of the city's heritage that will probably never disappear. Seventy years later, northern California faced a severe drought, which again changed social patterns. People began learning ways of conserving water, and water consciousness became a part of life, lasting beyond the end of the drought. In 1982, water-conscious northern Californians voted heavily (92 percent) against a proposal to construct a peripheral canal that would send water to southern California.

We will never know how many preliterate societies created religions or systems of magic based on similar, dramatic natural events. A solar eclipse, a tidal wave, a forest fire, or a severe thunderstorm could produce a system of beliefs and practices lasting a very long time.

On a longer time scale, we can guess what must have happened to humankind with the onset of the Ice Age, with glaciers forcing people farther and farther south. Similarly, we can imagine the return north as the ice receded and warm weather returned. Changes of that order may have been imperceptible to any of the individuals during their lifetimes, yet there is no questioning the incredible impact of the natural event on human life.

We could go on and on discussing historical

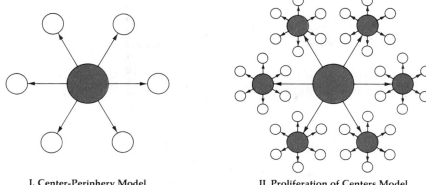

I. Center-Periphery Model   II. Proliferation of Centers Model

Figure 20-4 Two models of diffusion. Source: Figure from Donald Schon, Beyond the Stable State *(New York: Random House, 1971).*

events that have had an impact on social life. Certainly the pressures of population growth, already discussed in Chapter 18, deserve mention here. The same should be said for pollution and the depletion of resources. Although we are the cause of the changes in the natural environment, those changes are already doubling back on the societies that created them. By the same token, humans are involved in the spread of disease epidemics and in famines, but we experience them as coming from nature, and they produce important social changes. The Black Death of the Middle Ages, for example, is said to have killed one-fourth of the human population on the planet. Though we appear to have protected ourselves from such colossal plagues today, an outbreak of a new strain of flu in the United States can cause an immediate disruption of social relations, and concern over diseases such as polio a few decades ago and cancer today can bring about more lasting changes.

We've now seen some of the many sources of social change that operate in the world. As we'll see now, many of those factors have contributed to a particular kind of change, have pushed the evolution of society in a particular direction. Around the globe, social change has meant one thing above all others: modernization.

Modernization

In a general way, **modernization** refers to the process of social change that characterizes the development of simple, agrarian societies into complex, industrial ones. Economic changes are typically the most visible aspect of modernization, and they may also be the first changes to occur, but modernization eventually touches all aspects of social life—all the society's agreements.

While it makes sense to talk of the modernization of the United States (Lipset 1963) or of Britain, the term is more specifically used in reference to the current process through which the poorer countries of Asia, Africa, the Middle East, and Latin America are attempting to "catch up" with the wealthy, "developed" nations of the world. India's development of nuclear power plants and the development of oil-rich Arab states are examples of "modernization," as sociologists customarily use the term.

Economic Change

For the most part today, modernization comes about as a result of economic diffusion. The economic and technological developments of

Table 20-2

Selected Economic Indicators for Five Nations

Indicator	United States	Japan	Greece	Ecuador	India
a. 1980 energy consumption in the equivalent of kilograms of coal per capita	10,410	3,494	2,137	598	191
b. 1977 steel consumption in kilograms per capita	618	512	176	46	16
c. Telephones per 100 population in 1978	77.0	42.4	26.6	3.0	0.3
d. Radio receivers per 1,000 population in 1977	2,048	571	296	279	33
e. Television sets per 1,000 population in 1977	623	242	127	45	1

Source: U.S. Bureau of Census, *Statistical Abstract of the United States,* 1981, pp. 884–91.

wealthy, industrial countries are exported to poorer, less developed ones. All this occurs as part of a global drama in which poor—typically Third World—nations of the world attempt to catch up with the rich ones.

Despite the worldwide trend toward modernization, there are still enormous differences in the economic statuses of different nations. Table 20–2 shows the current level of economic development in five nations of the world: United States, Japan, Greece, Ecuador, and India.

The data shown in Table 20–2 reveal the gap separating the developed from the undeveloped nations of the world. Comparing the United States and India, for example, on a per capita basis, we find that the United States consumes 55 times as much energy and 39 times as much steel, has 257 times as many telephones, 62 times as many radios, and 623 times as many television sets. This is the gap that the underdeveloped nations of the world are seeking to close; this is modernization as such countries see it.

Modernization per se relates less to the gap than to its closing. Consider the performance of Japan. Almost destroyed by World War II, Japan has "risen from the ashes" to become one of the world's leading industrial nations. India, on the other hand, has had a much harder time modernizing. Figure 20–5 illustrates the rela-

tive economic growth experienced by Japan and India in comparison with the United States between 1967 and 1976 (more recent comparisons are not available).

The graphs in Figure 20–5 tell a number of stories. First, the United States is more industrially developed in each of the indicators shown than is either India or Japan. In each case, Japan is more developed than India.

Japan's rate of economic growth was also uniformly greater than India's. Thus, if the trends shown were to continue, the gap between Japan and India would increase rather than decrease.

In cement, steel, and motor-vehicle production, Japan has clearly been closing the gap with the United States. It had a greater rate of growth than the United States in each of those industries during the period shown. In cement production, in fact, Japan surpassed the United States in 1976.

Social Change

Economic change is only a part of modernization. Many of a society's agreements change in the process. Some change as a result of economic development; others must change to permit it. Table 20–3 summarizes some of the changes typically occurring in noneconomic institutions during the modernization process.

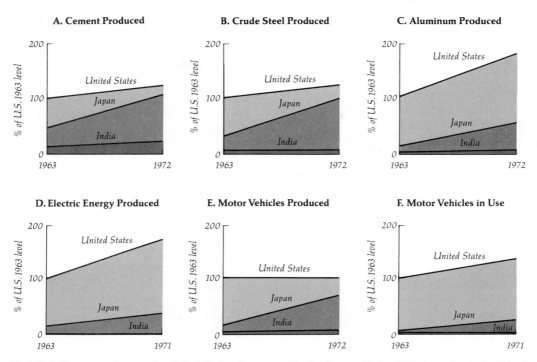

Figure 20-5 Relative economic growth: United States, Japan, and India. Source: United Nations Statistical Yearbook, *1977, pp. 327–31, 346, 401–402, 539–41.*

Modernization produces frequent conflict between economic development and cultural patterns. Consider, for example, what happens to agreements on sex roles. Japan traditionally has been a male-oriented society, where women have been restricted largely to family roles. With economic development, this situation has changed drastically. Japanese women have become actively engaged in various occupations, in offices, factories, and stores, thereby transforming the sex-role agreements.

The transition from a traditional society to a modern one is often painful for those involved in it, as Daniel Lerner (1964) has amply documented in the case of Turkey. For the Turks that Lerner called the "traditionals," national modernization has meant the need to think about societywide problems and to consider other areas of the world and strange people; in short,

it has meant the need to give up much of what was comfortable and familiar. When Lerner sought to tap such broader viewpoints, many of his Turk respondents refused to engage in "modern" thinking. When they were asked where they would like to live other than Turkey, half the "traditionals" could not imagine doing that, many of them saying that they would rather die.

For many people around the world, modernization—and the economic benefits it brings—means giving up a variety of accustomed beliefs, values, and norms. It may mean moving from the farm to the city, breaking up families, weakening religious ties, assuming unaccustomed occupational roles. Some may seem to gain, and others may seem to lose. All will probably feel somewhat uncomfortable.

Clearly, economic development in a poor

Table 20-3

Summary of Noneconomic Institutional Changes Associated with Modernization

Family

1. Family changes from economic production unit to economic consumption unit.
2. Women freed from family functions for participation in the market economy.
3. Birth rate declines.
4. More families reside in urban centers.
5. Family consumption patterns reflect mass production of goods.

Religion

1. Greater secularization in society.
2. Religious status becomes less significant than economic status in general social stratification.
3. Religious values and norms modified to support economic development.
4. Religions become more bureaucratically organized.

Education

1. Education becomes more open to women and dispossessed minorities.
2. Scientific, technical education strengthened.
3. Education becomes more formalized.
4. Volume of book publishing increases.
5. General literacy rate increases.

Government

1. Greater government support and regulation of industry.
2. Government becomes larger.
3. Government becomes increasingly bureaucratized.
4. Greater national unity.
5. Relations with other nations become more significant.

country does not necessarily bring broad-based social change with it. In several oil-rich Arab countries, for example, the billions of petro-dollars are concentrated in the hands of relatively few families. By way of illustration, Saudi Arabia has about the same Gross National Product (GNP) per capita ($11,260) as the United States ($11,360) in 1982. Its infant mortality rate (114), however, is about the same as the average for Africa (121), where the GNP per capita is only $770 (Population Reference Bureau 1982). Neville de Silva (1980:39), writing in the *Ceylon Daily News* summarizes the situation:

> The modernism of these essentially feudal societies is a sign of wealth without development. Moreover, their indigenous population is lacking in technical and professional skills, so they must import labor. But there is an inherent danger in this. Coming from more "progressive" societies, the imported workers could be the agents of socio-political change.

Often, the onset of the modernization process produces resistance to it—in varying degrees. American religious splinter groups such as the Amish and the Hutterites have resisted modernization by withdrawing into secluded communities. While they have not attempted to stop the modernization of America in general, they have chosen not to participate in it. More dramatic has been the desperate attempt by the Iranian clergy, personified in the Ayatollah Khomeini, to restore fundamentalist Islamic forms to a nation well on the way to modernization as a result of its vast petroleum wealth. In a remarkable move in July 1980, for example, Tehran's mullahs launched a campaign to eradicate music in Iran.

While social change is a continuing process, then, it is not smooth and steady. Often it moves in leaps and bounds.

Culture Lag

In 1922, sociologist William Ogburn coined a term to represent the pattern we have been observing throughout the discussion of modernization: **culture lag.** Ogburn was particularly interested in the impact of technological developments on a society, and the consequent

When societies modernize, some culture elements change faster than others. This creates a situation called "culture lag."

changes required in the structure of agreements—changes required in social relations, religion, education, and all other sectors of society. At the same time, he noted there tended to be a period of time that occurred between the change in the material culture and the consequent changes in the society's agreements, and it was this delay that he summarized as "culture lag."

Culture lag, more generally, refers to elements of culture—material or nonmaterial—being out of phase with one another. We have already discussed the process that occurs in connection with birth and death rates as societies develop economically. As we saw, nonindustrialized societies typically survive by matching their high death rates with equally

high birth rates. Improved public health and other medical care dramatically reduces death rates—but birth rates remain high for a time, producing severe population growth and aggravating other social problems.

Periods of culture lag are generally times of uncertainty, ambiguity, and unrest. People find themselves caught between conflicting sets of agreements, caught between beliefs, values, and norms that conflict with their physical circumstances. We have been looking at situations like that throughout this book. We've seen that such situations can produce self-destruction, mental illness, crime, rebellion.

In a sense, however, we are destined to live always in a period of culture lag. You've seen that we seem intent on structuring our systems of agreements for persistence, whereas we always find ourselves in the midst of change.

What's Ahead
for the Third World?

At several points in the book, we have paid special attention to the problems of the poor countries composing the "Third World" or the "South." As we've seen most recently, the issue of social change is relevant to them, as they seek to rise out of poverty.

Writing in *South* magazine, futurist Arthur C. Clarke (1981) suggests that communications technology will be central to progress in the Third World in the future. He suggests (1981:13) several types of communication that need to be developed.

> A reliable telephone system must surely have the first priority: it affects every aspect of life—personal, business and government. We have also belatedly realised that it can be a major energy saver, making countless journeys unnecessary. It is also the greatest life saver ever invented, though often it requires a tragedy to bring that point home. A few years ago, thousands died when a dam burst in an Asian country. The telephone that should have warned them was out of order.

The proliferation of radio and television is also important in Clarke's view. He notes the impact of transistors in making radios smaller and cheaper, and he foresees a similar impact from two prospective developments: solar cells to generate electricity for radios and direct satellite broadcasts that will bring perfect reception to even the most remote areas of the world.

Clarke also sees a need for Third World countries to develop Telex and computer communication networks, so they can begin managing and communicating the masses of data necessary for the development and management of societies. Recognizing that these latter resources are still quite expensive, Clarke antic-

ipates that they will not be developed for awhile. Of more immediate importance, he urges the development of "electronic tutors"—pocket-calculator-sized teaching machines that could trigger an educational revolution.

While these development needs in the Third World may seem to describe an enormous game of "catch up" with the developed nations of the North, Clarke also points out that the South can actually "leapfrog" a lot of obsolescent technologies. A few years ago, for instance, good calculators cost hundreds, even thousands of dollars. Today, the same power can be had for under ten dollars. By the same token, small home computers today have the same power as earlier computers costing hundreds of thousands of dollars.

There is an obstacle to this leapfrogging, however. In the past, the developed nations of the North have often used the South as a dumping ground for obsolete equipment. Thus, "progress" in the poor countries has often brought them to where the rich countries used to be, not where they are. Clarke (1981:14) quotes the comments of the late Dr. Vikram Sarabhai of India in this regard:

> The administrative structure of governments in many nations is dominated at the top not by technocrats but by professional administrators, lawyers, or soldiers, who are hardly likely to provide the insights, experience and the first-hand knowledge of science and technology which are necessary at the decision making level. Moreover, advanced nations often play a negative role in their interaction with the developing countries. There is seduction by their political and commercial salesmen who dangle new gimmicks which they suggest should be imported.

Many factors will affect these issues in the future. Parallel to the North/South dialogue are increased attempts to generate more cooperation among the nations of the South. In part, the aim is to cease more local control over resources needed in the North. In the recent past, the emergence of OPEC is an example of what is intended, and we may see more such developments in the future. At the same time, the slowing of population growth, recession, and other conditions in the North make the South more important as a market for manufactured goods.

As we have seen throughout this chapter, economic changes ripple out to all aspects of a society. Economic development in the societies of the South will bring about numerous social changes as well. Some will be generally beneficial to the people, others will not.

Until recently, it was generally believed that economic development in the Western model was the path to happiness for the Third World. Today, there is less agreement on that point. As we've seen repeatedly, an increased GNP does not necessarily produce improved living conditions for the citizens of a country. Where a nation's living standard was previously measured in terms of GNP per capita, scholars and policy-makers today increasingly pay more attention to the *physical quality of life index:* a combination of the literacy rate, life expectancy, and the infant mortality rate.

At the same time, it has become apparent that global limits to the resources required for industrialization make it impossible for all nations to achieve economic development equal to that of the United States. Still it is clear that the Third World countries are no longer willing to accept the economic disparities that divide the world today.

Summary

Although life changed little throughout most of human history, social change is a constant for today's societies. Indeed, the pace of social change is still increasing, leading Alvin Toffler to speak of "future shock."

From the perspective of conflict theory, social change is an inevitable consequence of the inequality built into the structure of society. As long as there are "haves" and "have-nots," there will be social change.

From a functionalist perspective, social change can be regarded as a threat to equilibrium—ultimately a threat to the survival of a society. Functionalists often speak of "moving equilibrium" in which societies change but maintain "balance" all the while.

Early scholars tended to see social change in fairly simplistic "linear" terms. Societies were seen as evolving from simple to complex forms, from the primitive to the civilized. More recent scholars have recognized that social change is not that neat. Sometimes, change occurs in leaps and bounds, and it may reverse at points.

Pitirim Sorokin and others have argued that social change is actually cyclical. In Sorokin's view, societies moved through a cycle of three phases: sensate, ideational, and idealistic.

There are many sources of social change. Social conflict—either within-group or between-group—is one source. Class conflict is a special case of this source of social change. So is war.

Innovations—inventions and discoveries—are another important source of social change. As we saw in Chapter 19, technological developments can bring about changes in all aspects of society.

The chapter has concluded with a discussion of modernization—the process in which the poorer, less developed societies of the world adopt the economic and social patterns of the richer, developed countries. We have seen that this is no simple process. Modernization is difficult to achieve, and it brings with it both benefits and costs.

Important Terms

modernization
social conflict
class struggle
discovery

invention
diffusion
culture lag

Suggested Readings

Case, John, and Rosemary C. R. Taylor, eds.
1979 *Co-ops, Communes, and Collectives: Experiments in Social Change in the 1960's and 1970's.* New York: Pantheon Books, 1979.
Analyzes the patterns of alternative organizations and why many are fading.

Coser, Lewis
1956 *The Functions of Social Conflict.* New York: Free Press.
Building on the earlier work of Georg Simmel, Coser elaborates the many ways in which social conflict strengthens group life rather than weakens it. Coser's attempt to develop formal, theoretical propositions regarding conflict are instructive from the standpoints of both sociological theory and conflict theory.

Gouldner, Alvin
1973 *The Coming Crisis of Western Sociology.* New York: Avon.
Discusses the possibility of reconciling functional and conflict theories and argues for a "socially committed" sociology.

Lenksi, Gerhard, and Jean Lenski
1974 *Human Societies.* 2nd ed. New York: McGraw-Hill.
Here's the big picture, as Lenski traces the evolution of societies from the simplest to the most complex. An excellent resource for the study of social change, Lenski focuses his attention on the development of social institutions and their interrelations with one another. The examination is filled with cross-cultural data drawn from important anthropological sources.

Lipset, Seymour Martin, ed.
1979 *The Third Century: America as a Post-Industrial Society.* Stanford, Calif.: Hoover Institution Press.
Presents projections of social scientists into future of United States in its 3rd century.

Moore, Wilbert
1963 *Social Change.* Englewood Cliffs, N.J.: Prentice-Hall.
In this small, readable book, Moore has summarized all the major theoretical points of view regarding social change, both linear and cyclical. He carefully examines small-scale and global change, and the final chapter on modernization is likely to be a useful introduction to the topic for many years to come.

Roszak, Theodore
1977 *Person/Planet: The Creative Disintegration of Industrial Society.* New York: Anchor Press.
Sequel to *Making of a Counterculture*, arguing 1970s brought desire for personal change, or "personalism."

South: The Third World Magazine
Published in London, *South* is the *Time* or *Newsweek* of the Third World. Not only is the magazine *about* the countries of the South, it is also written from the South's *point of view*. In addition to news reporting, it contains a great volume of up-to-date statistical data regarding social and economic development.

Toffler, Alvin
1980 *The Third Wave.* New York: Morrow Press.
Describes society as it is changing and predictions for the future.

Van den Berghe, Pierre
1975 *Man in Society.* New York: Elsevier.
Subtitled "a biosocial view," this provocative book examines human beings as animals—in both the biological and pejorative senses of the term. In large part, Van den Berghe finds out that technological developments have canceled out the natural, biological checks against human aggressiveness, leading to the creation of inhumane social institutions. This is not the jolliest of views, and Van den Berghe summarizes the tone when he concludes (p. 278): "If I leave my readers with a gnawing and lingering dissatisfaction with their society, their place in it, and my own irreverent and impertinent remarks about it, I shall consider that I have accomplished my purpose."

In the essay that concluded Chapter 1 of this book I suggested that sociology has a powerful contribution to make to the quality of life on this planet. In this final essay, I want to pick up and complete that discussion. The answer lies in the domain of social change—with special reference to some of the major social problems we've examined at various points in this book.

In examining some of the problems that plague life on this planet—war, hunger, discrimination, overpopulation, to name a few— we have seen that people often look to technology for solutions. Yet, as we've seen, technology has produced as many problems as it has produced solutions. Indeed, the solution to one problem (DDT to kill insects) often turns into a problem (residual poisons showing up in milk) later on.

At the same time, some of the social change experienced on this planet has actually eliminated major problems, even problems that seemed inevitable to people beforehand. The elimination of slavery is a good example.

At the beginning of the nineteenth century, an airtight case could have been made for the inevitability of slavery. After all, some people would always be more powerful than others, and slavery was an obvious outcome, as history documented. In the United States, it was obvious to many people that the nation's economy would collapse without slavery. Furthermore, the institution was 300 years old in America; something like that couldn't be changed.

It could be argued, moreover, that the slaves themselves depended on the institution of slavery. If they were set free, they wouldn't know how to care for themselves. Even the Bible seemed to suggest that God intended that some people live out their worldly existence as slaves. Many well-meaning people argued that the goal should be to make slavery more humane.

Despite all these powerful reasons for the inevitability of slavery, it essentially vanished from the earth during the nineteenth century. When we look back on the elimination of slavery on the planet, we often explain its passing as "an idea whose time had come." And as Victor Hugo observed, nothing is so powerful as an idea whose time has come.

Probably the same will be said about the elimination of other major problems sometime in the future. People have been aware of the problem of overpopulation at least since the time of Malthus. Awareness of the problem reached a new high during the 1960s and 1970s, though the problem was not solved. Even though people still debate the current seriousness of the problem, no one denies that population growth must end sometime. At some point the mass of human bodies would cause the planet to collapse into itself. Well in advance of that, however, the life-support systems of the planet will be exhausted. Clearly, population growth will cease eventually. When it does, moreover, we will say that it finally became an idea whose time had come. The same will be said about the eventual elimination of world hunger.

It seems clear to me that eventually men and women will enjoy truly equal opportunity in America. We are currently in the midst of the process that will lead to sexual equality. Whenever true equality is finally achieved, people will look back on these times and say it was an idea whose time had come. These observations point directly at sociology's most powerful, potential contribution to the world.

For all our technological developments, technology has not taught us how to cause an idea's time to come. Until we learn how, we are fated to continue suffering our major social problems until circumstances seemingly beyond our control do away with them.

Realize that it *is possible* to consciously cause an idea's time come. Perhaps the best recent example is the eradication of smallpox. Contemporary Americans have little awareness of this age-old killer, but the editors of *Science* (June 17, 1977) summed it up as follows:

Some experts contend that smallpox, by some measures, has been the most fearsome scourge in human experience, causing more harm over a longer period and in more geographic areas than such other forms of pestilence as bubonic plague, cholera, and yellow fever. The devastation it once caused was illustrated by an epidemic that killed 31 percent of the population of Iceland in 1707. As recently as 1926 an international conference was told that smallpox could be found in virtually every country.

In 1967, the World Health Organization launched a worldwide campaign to eradicate the disease. Its objective was the total annihilation of the virus on the planet. On August 9, 1977, the last known case of smallpox was recorded in Somalia. During the two years that followed, the United Nations offered a reward of $1,000 to anyone who reported another case. No one collected the reward, and smallpox was officially declared to be eradicated in 1979. This result had been achieved through the efforts of 600 health officials and some 150,000 to 200,000 health workers.

In 1967, an airtight case could have been made for the inevitability of smallpox. After all, there were over 4 billion people on the planet, most of them living in abominable poverty in faraway corners of the earth. How could all of them be protected from the disease?

In some areas, the people had superstitious fears of inoculation. Others had established religious prohibitions against it. In some countries, dictatorial rulers were not willing to have

United Nations workers roaming the countryside.

Once the commitment was made to eradicate smallpox, however, a powerful shift of context occurred. What was once a reason which smallpox couldn't be eradicated now became an obstacle on the road to success. The many obstacles were overcome in many ways, just as slavery was eliminated through a variety of methods.

Those World Health Organization officials who gathered in 1967 to make a commitment to the eradication of smallpox clearly were responsible for creating an idea whose time had come. What they created was far more powerful than any technological breakthroughs in medicine. In fact, although some advances were made in the storing and administration of the vaccine, smallpox was finally eradicated through the use of a vaccine invented 150 years ago.

Despite these demonstrations that it is possible to cause an idea's time to come, we do not now know exactly how to do that. One thing does seem clear to me. The answer will not come from technology; neither physicists nor biologists, engineers nor chemists will discover how to cause an idea's time to come. If we ever learn the answer to that question, it will come from sociology.

Rather than end this essay with an answer, I want to leave you with the question: how can we cause an idea's time to come? I will, however, suggest some of the places we might look for the answer.

1. Under what conditions and by what processes do people come to regard themselves as deterministically controlled by their environments—and under what conditions and by what processes do they regard themselves as capable of shaping their individual and

collective destiny? No one understands the deterministic side of human behavior, since our all our explanatory research is grounded in a deterministic model. At the same time, we have observed individuals and groups behaving in ways contrary to deterministic expectations. By and large the major social problems we suffer today are held by most people as well beyond their control. We must learn where that view comes from and what it takes for people to rise above such self-imposed limitations. Otherwise, we shall all remain helpless in the face of our problems.

2. What is the nature of responsibility in complex society? The division of labor can also be regarded as a division of responsibility. As an organized society, we assign responsibility for law enforcement to the police and courts, responsibility for lawmaking to legislatures, responsibility for medicine to physicians, and so forth. In the process, individuals give up any sense of responsibility for those things assigned to someone else. When the system breaks down, most of our attention is directed to finding out who is to blame, and usually we are unable to find out. Unless a critical mass of individuals is willing to operate from a sense of personal responsibility for the elimination of social problems, we have no hope of being successful.

3. In both of the above regards, what can we learn from the history of voluntary associations, especially in America? What led Ralph Nader to take on the public problem of automobile safety (and later consumer rights) and thousands of others to join with him in that crusade? A similar question could be asked with regard to Paul Ehrlich and Zero Population Growth. We need to understand the Guardian Angels and the countless other groups of individuals who have organized to take on public problems.

4. Where can we find a radically new model of social movements? Traditionally, social movements have been organized through the imposition of agreements. Individuals have been persuaded to accept and act on particular points of view. In such cases, however, it is necessary for a leader to continue reinforcing the agreements, keeping the troops in line. Some movements, however, have succeeded in uncovering a natural alignment of commitment. It has been my experience in The Hunger Project, for example, that all people are fundamentally opposed to starvation in the world. Their failure to act on that feeling, however, is a function of their having accepted the view that they can do nothing. Once people rediscover their own feelings in the matter, they can be counted on to act appropriately on their own initiative. An alignment of such individuals is surely an important element in an idea's time coming.

5. Much of what is needed can be found in the traditional sense of community that has been all but lost in modern, urban societies. Without reverting to an agrarian lifestyle, how can we recapture those elements of community that once led citizens to experience and act on responsibility for the whole, in contrast to the narrow self-interest of atomistic individuals more common today?

These are a few of the questions we need to address for sociology to help human beings take charge of their destiny and create a humane world. I invite you to join us in taking on that challenge.

PRACTICING SOCIOLOGY

The preceding discussion of "Sociology and Social Change" concluded with five sets of questions that might be addressed in learning what it takes to cause an idea's time to come. For this final "Practicing Sociology" exercise, I want you to look at how you might begin addressing some of those questions.

Pick one of the five sets of questions from the essay. Then look back through the textbook and identify some of the concepts and findings presented in any of the twenty chapters that would be useful to you in searching for the answers to the set of questions you selected.

Glossary

achieved status Social position gained through your actions, such as college graduate. Contrasted with *ascribed status*.*

adult resocialization The process wherein a change of social *status* requires that previously learned *roles* be unlearned and replaced by new ones.

affirmative action The public policy of actively seeking *minority-group* members in connection with employment, education, and so on, as a means to correcting existing imbalances due to past *discrimination*.

age grading The association of certain social *statuses* and *roles* with particular age groups, as in the assignment of fighting in wars to the youth.

age-sex composition The numbers (or proportions) of males and females in various age groups that make up a *population;* often presented by demographers in the form of an age-sex pyramid.

aggregation A gathering of people in the same physical location, such as a theater audience or people gathered to watch a fire.

agreement reality Your picture of the way things are, based on your acceptance of the agreements you share with those around you. Contrasted with *experiential reality*.

agribusiness Agriculture as big business, operated by giant corporations.

alienation A feeling of being outside of or unattached to the mainstream of *society;* a feeling of powerlessness in regard to the operation of society.

annihilation The eradication of a *category* of people: the most extreme form of *discrimination*. As an example, the Nazis attempted to annihilate the Jews during World War II, just as the white settlers in America sometimes attempted to annihilate the native American Indians.

anticipatory socialization The learning of behaviors that will be appropriate to a *status* you may occupy later in life, as in a young girl pretending to be a mother.

artifacts Physical elements of culture; such as paintings, totem poles, and beer cans.

ascribed status Social position established at birth, such as sex or *race*. Contrasted with *achieved status*.

assimilation The process through which members of a *minority group* blend into the mainstream *culture* of a *society,* taking on characteristics of that culture and—to a degree—contributing to it.

association A type of *secondary group,* organized around a shared interest or view; for example, the American Sociological Association.

attributes Characteristics, such as young, Republican, Oriental, female, unprejudiced, and so forth.

authority *Legitimated power;* power granted to social positions such as political or religious office. When the U.S.

---

*Italicized words appear elsewhere in the Glossary.

Constitution, for example, speaks of powers granted to various offices, these are examples of authority.

autocracy A political system vesting all power in one person, based on tradition.

automation The process through which jobs—especially those in manufacturing—are adapted to being done by machines instead of people.

autopoiesis a process in which a thing creates itself; e.g., society creates society.

belief An agreement about what's so, what's real or true.

bilateral descent See *lineage*.

bureaucracy A form of *social structure* epitomizing formal, *secondary relations*, especially characterized by specialization, hierarchy, and explicit rules governing interactions and specifying *authority*.

capitalism An economic system based on the private ownership of the means of production: factories, materials, and so forth.

caste A stratification *category* to which one is assigned by birth and from which there is no escape. The Indian caste system is a commonly cited example.

category A set of people who share a characteristic, such as women, tall people, or Chevrolet owners. They don't necessarily know each other or interact with one another.

census The enumeration or counting of a *population*. For example, the U.S. Bureau of the Census undertakes this in America every ten years (every five years beginning in 1980).

charisma The powerful, though indefinable, personal quality that gives one person sway over his or her fellows. Meaning literally a "gift of grace," Weber used this term to describe one of three forms of *authority*. (The other two were: *traditional* and *rational-bureaucratic*.) Charismatic authority is especially common in *religion*, particularly during a religion's founding.

charismatic authority The ability to exercise power on the basis of *charisma*.

church An established and "respectable" religion, characterized by generally less emotional fervor than *cults* and *sects*. Membership is likely to be inherited from one generation to the next, whereas cults and sects gain their members through conversion.

city A large *aggregation* of people residing in a densely populated geographical area, organized by some form of political structure.

civil disobedience A nonviolent refusal to be bound by agreements one feels are inappropriate—associated particularly with Henry David Thoreau, Mahatma Gandhi, and Martin Luther King, Jr.

civil religion A term coined by Robert Bellah in reference to the religious blend he feels characterizes the mainstream of American society. Nondenominational in content, it includes references to God on our money and public buildings, prayers and solemn oaths within political rituals, and so forth.

class For Marx, a class was a subset of society that shared an economic position and economic interests. Thus, "workers" composed a class, as did the capitalist owners. Marx saw all human history as the history of *class struggle*.

class consciousness For Marx, class consciousness was one's identification with one's economic class and the holding of a worldview in support of one's class interests. Thus, workers who believed that they were being exploited by the bosses and that the capitalist economic system should be overturned would be demonstrating their class consciousness in Marx's eyes.

class struggle The conflict rising out of the contradictory interests of different economic classes in society. Thus, the workers struggled to rise out of poverty, and the owners fought to keep them down.

closed-ended Questionnaire items in which the respondent chooses from among a set of answers provided by the researcher.

coalition A partnership formed in order to dominate others or to avoid domination by them.

coercive compliance The condition in which members of an organization behave in ways appropriate to the success of the organization because they are forced to—either physically or under threat of punishment.

collective behavior A general term referring to relatively spontaneous and unstructured social behavior such as found in rallies, panics, and mobs, and also in such things as *rumors, fads*, and fashions.

communication Process of transferring points of view from one person to another. Wilbur Schramm described it as an attempt to establish a "commonness" with someone else.

communism An economic system based on group ownership of all material goods, with little or no provision for private property.

community elites *Power elites* of specific, local communities.

compensatory education Special education programs designed to make up for the disadvantages suffered by minorities.

competency testing Testing students' progress in order to determine whether teachers have gotten their jobs done.

complex organization Often used interchangeably with *formal organization*, though carrying additional connotations of size and intricacy.

conceptualization The process of refining and specifying what is meant by the concepts to be examined in a research project. What observations will be taken as an instance of a concept (e.g., *prejudice*) and what observations will not? What range of variation is important? Ultimately, once the conceptualization process is complete, the researcher should be able to communicate clearly what will be meant by the concept, and the stage will be set for the development of concrete methods of observation and measurement—see *operationalization*.

conflict functionalism A sociological point of view, advanced by Georg Simmel and Lewis Coser, that focuses on the positive functions served by conflict within a social system. Hostile outbursts, for example, may "let off steam" and pass quickly, preventing the building up to a point of greater violence.

conflict theory The sociological point of view that addresses the structure of disagreements and the *social structures* and processes that generate disagreement.

conglomerate A term used loosely in reference to large corporations having significant activities in several economic sectors.

conservative movements Social movements whose main purpose is to maintain the *status quo,* to resist prospective *social change.*

content analysis A method of observation involving the careful examination and categorizing of human communications: written, spoken, or other. Thus, you might examine the editorial positions of northern and southern newspapers over time to determine shifts in regional attitudes toward, say, race relations.

control group Group of subjects in an *experiment* who are not exposed to the *experimental stimulus* under study; used to isolate the effects of the stimulus per se.

correlation A coincidence or correspondence between the *attributes* composing different *variables.* If, for example, educated people are typically unprejudiced and uneducated people are typically prejudiced (or educated people are less prejudiced than uneducated ones), we would say the education and prejudice are correlated (negatively) with each other.

crime Behavior that breaks the agreements that are officially established by law.

crime without victims Behavior regarded as a crime although it is not committed against anyone except—arguably—the "offender." Homosexuality (where illegal), prostitution, and smoking marijuana are common examples.

crowd Gathering of people sharing a common interest or purpose, such as a crowd gathered to hear a streetcorner orator. Crowds hold the potential for *collective behavior.*

crude birth rate The number of babies born during a year, divided by the *population* size and expressed as births per 1,000 population.

crude death rate The number of deaths during a year, divided by the size of the *population* and expressed as deaths per 1,000.

cult A small, loosely organized religious group—typically organized around the powerful personality of a *charismatic* leader or around a particular religious practice such as snake handling.

cultural lag The gap between the adoption of a technological innovation and the adjustment of other cultural agreements to it.

cultural relativity The opposite of *ethnocentrism*—the recognition that different groups have different sets of agreements without feeling that one set is superior to another.

culture The collection of *norms, values, beliefs, symbols,* and meanings shared by the members of a *society.*

deductive logic An approach to knowing and understanding that proceeds from general principles to *hypotheses* about specific cases. We reason, for example, that economic competition produces antiblack prejudice, hence prejudice should be higher among those in occupations employing a high percentage of blacks. We then proceed to measure antiblack prejudice among whites in various occupations, testing our hypothesis.

de facto Actual state of affairs, regardless of how things are supposed to be. De facto *segregation* refers to the existence of racial segregation even in the face of laws prohibiting it.

deferred gratification The delaying of gratification and the investment of resources in future success. Instead of buying the new stereo you have your eye on, you could make do with your old one and invest your money in pork-belly futures, become a Wall Street tycoon, and buy a *conglomerate* that makes stereos.

democracy Form of government in which political *authority* is derived from the consent of the governed.

demography The *science of population.* A subfield of sociology, demography addresses the size and characteristics of human populations, including the study of why they are the way they are.

dependent variable That variable whose observed variations are taken as being dependent upon or caused by something else—that is, caused by the *independent variable*(s). In the cause-effect model, the dependent variable is the effect.

descriptive analysis Data analysis aimed at answering the question "what." Thus, a study to determine the level of unemployment in a city would be an example of a descriptive analysis. Contrasted with *explanatory analysis,* which has the purpose of answering "why."

determinism Point of view implicitly assumed in *science,* holding that every event has a set of prior causes that determine it. In the context of *social science,* this view conflicts with the notion of individual freedom and choice (see also *free will*). All your thoughts and actions are seen as being caused by forces over which you have no control.

deviance The breaking of agreements held by a *group,* especially established *norms.* Thus, *crimes* such as murder, burglary, and rape are all examples of deviance, but much deviance does not involve breaking the law—for example, wearing your hair "too long" (or "too short") is also an instance of deviance.

dialectical The process of contradictions clashing and being resolved in compromise. Hegel said that was the way social thought progressed. An idea (thesis) was followed by the appearance of its opposite (antithesis) and a compromise (synthesis) would be generated out of the conflict between the two.

dialectical materialism Marx transformed Hegel's dialectical process by saying that the history of society could be seen as the conflict among material (especially economic) forces (not just ideas) that resolved their struggle in the rise of compromise.

differential association An explanation of *deviance* that depends on people learning subcultural agreements that deviate from the agreements of the larger society.

diffusion Spread of cultural elements from one *group* to another.

discovery The uncovering of something previously unknown—as in the discovery of the New World or the discovery of penicillin.

discrimination Actions taken on the basis of *prejudice* and *stereotypes*.

distributive justice In *exchange theory*, this is the guiding principle of relative equality between the costs and benefits of a particular line of action.

doubling time The length of time required for a *population* to double in size. At recent growth rates, the world population will double in about forty-one years.

downward mobility Movement from one social *class* or *strata* to a lower one—as in moving from upper to middle class.

dyad Two-person *group*.

ecclesia An established, officially recognized *church*, such as the Church of England.

economic determinism Karl Marx's theoretical point of view, suggesting that all aspects of social life are a result of economic forces.

economic institutions Sets of established, persistent agreements governing the production, distribution, and consumption of goods and services. Sometimes we speak of "the economy" as the totality of economic institutions.

educational institutions Social institutions dealing with the transmission and transformation of knowledge.

egalitarian A pattern of *power* relations within the *family* in which men and women share more or less equally.

emergent norms A view of *collective behavior* as the process of generating agreements in the face of ambiguous situations.

emissary prophet A religious leader who instructs others on how to behave, providing a system of morality to govern the "righteous" life on earth.

empirical Based in real-world observations and experiences involving our five senses.

empirical verification The testing of expectations through the observation of real-life events. You may think you did well on your final exam, but your grade is a means of empirical verification.

endogamy A mate-selection pattern requiring that one marry someone within the same kinship group.

equal opportunity The public policy of granting *minority-group* members equal treatment with regard to such matters as employment, education, and so on.

equilibrium A condition of checks and balances among the interdependent parts of a system, such that the survival of the system is maintained. "Static equilibrium" means that the system maintains or always returns to the same state, as in the case of the human body's temperature of 98.6°F. "Moving equilibrium" means that sufficient balance is maintained for the survival of the system, but that the system is changing over time, as in the case of inflation. Although the cost of living keeps getting higher each year, the overall balance of costs, income, and other elements is more or less maintained. When things get sufficiently out of balance to threaten the survival of the system, it is called "disequilibrium."

ethnic minority Social *category*—based on racial, religious, or national-origin similarities—whose members are denied proportionate shares of *power*, wealth, and opportunities within a *society*.

ethnocentrism The feeling that the agreements of your own *group* are superior to those of others, the feeling that your group's agreements are the "truth."

ethnomethodology A sociological point of view addressed to the discovery and understanding of the most fundamental, unspoken agreements lying at the base of everyday life. Often controversial for breaking agreements as a way of drawing them out for analysis.

evaluation research Scientific research undertaken for the purpose of determining the consequences of social interventions; e.g., studies to determine whether a prison rehabilitation does the job it was intended to do.

exchange theory A sociological point of view drawing on the analogy of economic exchange, in which individuals evaluate the worth of items to be exchanged and seek to maximize their profits. In contrast to the relative immediacy of economic exchange (cash and carry), social exchange largely involves the amassing of obligations and debts to be called in and used at some later date.

exemplary prophet A religious leader who guides others by his or her example, inspiring others to follow that example.

exogamy A mate-selection pattern requiring that one marry someone outside the kinship group.

experiential reality Your picture of the ways things are, based on your own personal experiences. Contrasted with *agreement reality*.

experiment A method of observation involving the manipulation of *variables*, typically under controlled conditions such as in a laboratory. If we wanted to find out whether oral or written instructions worked best in teaching people how to use a computer, for example, we could select groups of subjects, give oral instructions to one group, written instructions to another, and perhaps even give both kinds of instructions to a third group, and see which group was the most successful in using the computer.

experimental group   That group of experimental subjects to whom an *experimental stimulus* is administered. To determine the consequences of the stimulus, it is withheld from a *control group*, similar to the experimental group in all respects except in terms of the stimulus.

experimental stimulus   In an *experiment*, the experimental stimulus is that object or event whose consequences are the main focus of study. It is an *independent variable* whose effects are under study. In medical experiments, it might be a drug or a special therapy. In the study of, say, learning disabilities, it might be a new teaching technique. In the experiment, the stimulus is given to one group of subjects (the *experimental group*) and withheld from another (the *control group*).

explanatory analysis   Manipulation and interpretation of data for the purpose of discovering associations among *variables* and explaining how people come to be the way they are. Contrasts with *descriptive analysis.*

expressive functions   Those tasks involving *relationships*, emotions, and similar personal expressions. Parsons and Bales said that in most societies women have had the primary responsibility for expressive functions required by families.

expressive movements   Social movements whose primary function appears to be the expression of feelings—whether joyous or hateful.

expulsion   A form of *discrimination* in which the members of a social *category* are removed from the society—forced to leave or be imprisoned—as in the case of Japanese-Americans taken from the West Coast during World War II.

extended family   A *family* unit composed of at least three generations.

fad   Form of *collective behavior* that is very popular for a short period of time and involves something generally regarded as trivial—for example, goldfish swallowing, Hula-hooping, flagpole sitting.

false consciousness   For Marx, false consciousness was the world-view that supported the interests of a *class* that one did not belong to, a worldview that worked against one's own interests. Workers who shared the view that owners deserved to live better than workers suffered from false consciousness in Marx's view.

family   Social *institution* dealing with the group need for the replacement of members through reproduction and nurturance. The term is also used to refer to specific social organizations operating within the institution, such as "your family" and "my family."

fecundity   The biological ability of women to bear children.

fertility   The bearing of children.

fertility rate   Birth rate.

field research   That method of observation in which the researcher goes to the natural setting in which whatever he or she wants to study is happening. To study political rallies using this method, for example, you would go to a political rally and watch what happens.

formal organization   An explicitly structured social *group*, having formal rules, *roles*, and objectives.

free will   Point of view that holds individual actions to be the product of free, personal choice. This view conflicts with the *deterministic* view that is assumed by science.

function   As used in sociology, the consequences or impact of something, especially for the system within which it exists; the part it plays within the total operation of that system. Thus, a function of the police is to maintain order in society, to enforce the agreements. A function of the schools is to educate. Note: It is not necessary that the function served be intended by anyone; indeed "unintended consequences" are often significant, positively and negatively. Thus, Durkheim pointed out that a function of crime was to draw the rest of society together and actually to reinforce the agreements broken by the criminal. "Manifest functions" are overt, open, up-front, and often formalized; the manifest function of the schools is to educate. "Latent functions" are covert, hidden, and often unintended; a latent function of the schools is to keep young people out of the labor force.

functionalism   Theoretical point of view aimed at understanding the elements in a system in terms of their contributions to the whole.

functionally illiterate   Unable to read and write at a level of proficiency required for normal participation in society. "Functional literacy" would reflect such abilities as reading, signs, voting, writing letters, completing forms, and so forth.

game theory   a social scientific point of view that explains social behavior in terms of individuals devising strategies and weighing the pros and cons of alternative courses of action.

gemeinschaft   The term used by Ferdinand Toennies meaning "community" and implying a preponderance of *primary relations*. Contrasted with *gesellschaft.*

generalized other   A term developed by George Herbert Mead in reference to the hypothetical composite/average of all those around you. Whereas individuals differ in their views of things, the "generalized other" represents the generally prevailing views of the community. Thus, one person might feel you are the most beautiful thing to walk the earth, another might regard you as an ugly-duckling reject, but most people might feel you are so-so.

gesellschaft   Term used by Ferdinand Toennies meaning "society" and implying a preponderance of *secondary relations*. Contrasted with *gemeinschaft.*

group   A plurality or collectivity of people who share common interests, interact with one another, have a sense of identity with one another, and have some degree of structure.

homeostasis   A balance process in which the elements in a system keep each other in check, always returning the system to its earlier state.

homogamy   An observed pattern of mate-selection in which people tend to pick marriage partners who are very similar to themselves in terms of such things as age, social *class, race* and ethnicity, *religion,* and even geographical location.

human ecology   The study of human societies in relation to their environment, including the manner in which parts of society are distributed across the geographical space available to them.

human relations movement   An approach to organizational management that takes account of workers' psychological makeup: their goals, aspirations, fears, and so forth. This came as a replacement for the strictly economic view that regarded workers as purely rational beings.

hypothesis   A logically derived expectation, based on theoretical deductions and/or past empirical observations. The hypothesis becomes the basis for further observations, a check to see if things are as they are expected to be.

hypothesis testing   Mode of research in which empirical observations are used to verify or disconfirm the expectations derived from a *theory.*

ideal type   A term used by Max Weber in reference to an abstract model created to represent the essential characteristics of some class of empirical entities, events, or processes, for the purpose of clarifying the nature of the real-world referents. Thus, an ideal type for bureaucracy clarifies how bureaucracies operate in general and makes it possible to understand aspects of, say, a college administration that might otherwise make no sense.

imperatively coordinated association (ICA)   In Dahrendorf's view, a social unit exhibiting social order and stability by virtue of one person or group dominating others. People behave in an orderly fashion because they are forced to, not because they want to or because it comes naturally.

incest taboo   A virtually universal prohibition against having sexual relations with close family members, such as between parents and children or between brothers and sisters.

independent variable   That variable whose observed variations are taken as given, as the starting point in the cause-effect process under study. The independent variable is the cause in that process.

inductive logic   An approach to knowing and understanding that proceeds from many empirical observations to the development of generalized conclusions about the nature of things. For example, we notice that antiblack prejudice is highest among whites employed in various occupations that have large proportions of blacks. To make sense of these several observations, we conclude that the factor of economic competition holds the answer.

infant mortality rate   The number of children per thousand who die during their first year of life.

in-group   A group to which you belong, one you share an identity with. This, then, represents a *point of view* since others would see your in-group as an *out-group*—one they do not belong to. Kipling nicely summarized in-group as "we" and out-group as "they."

institution   A set of interrelated agreements dealing with some fairly broad segment of social life. Examples are family, government, religion, economics, education. Institutions prescribe the ways in which the needs for group survival will be handled and simultaneously prescribe how individuals will express their drives and desires.

institutionalization   Process whereby agreements are established and perpetuated. Institutions are sets of interrelated, institutionalized agreements.

institutionalized behavior   Actions that follow patterns established as appropriate by institutionalized agreements. Listening attentively to your sociology instructor's lecture is an example. Throwing rotten eggs and apples is not an example. See *collective behavior.*

institutional racism   A form of *racism* that is a function of the structure of agreements in the society rather than of individual racists. As a result, it is harder to uncover, understand, and solve.

instrumental functions   Those tasks involving concrete achievements, such as growing food, earning a living, building things. Parsons and Bales said that in most societies, men have had the primary responsibility for instrumental functions required by families.

integration   The harmonious intermeshing of parts within a system; in the case of a social system, the harmonious linking of agreements and institutions in support of one another.

interaction process analysis   A *small-group* research technique created by Robert Bales for the purpose of observing, coding, and analyzing different forms of participation in group interactions.

internalization   The process of putting the enforcement of agreements inside yourself, such that you keep the agreements because it "feels right"—even if no one would know whether you kept the agreements or broke them. Even if you could get away with the "perfect murder," you probably still just wouldn't "feel right" doing it. That's because you have internalized the agreement against murder.

invention   The creation of something new, usually a technological development—such as the invention of the clock, the airplane, or the laser.

iron law of oligarchy   A view put forward by German sociologist Robert Michels, suggesting that large-scale organization is ultimately incompatible with *democracy,* as follows: (1) the mass cannot actually administer a large organization—*bureaucracy* with officeholders is required: (2) the officeholders, thus, will be in a position to wield greater *power* within the organization than will the rank and file: and (3) the officeholders will use their power within the organization to maintain themselves in power, and they'll create cliques of faithful supporters. Thus, the tendency in any large organization is toward the creation of a ruling clique (oligarchy) dedicated to the perpetuation of its own rule.

labeling   The process whereby an individual is assigned a *status* by the *group*, whether warranted by the facts or not. For example, you might be labeled a "thief" if everyone thought you had stolen something, and your experience of group life from then on would reflect your being labeled a thief more than whether or not you ever stole anything.

latent function   See *function*.

legitimacy   A condition of agreement as to the appropriateness of something, especially regarding the exercise of *power*. *Authority* is legitimate power, and there are three major sources of authority: *charismatic, traditional,* and *rational-bureaucratic.*

legitimation   Process through which certain actions or *relationships* are made legitimate by agreement. Sociologists most frequently talk of this in terms of power relationships in a group.

lineage   Those people across the generations who make up your "family tree"—those people from whom you take your own identity. Some societies, like American society, are characterized by a pattern of "bilateral descent," in which you trace your lineage back through both your mother's and father's ancestors. Other societies have a pattern of "matrilineal descent," meaning that your lineage is limited to your mother, her mother, her mother, and so forth, through your female ancestors. Still other societies are characterized by a pattern of "patrilineal descent," in which lineage is traced through male ancestors only.

literacy rate   The percentage of people about a specified age (e.g., 15) in a population who are judged able to read and write.

Lombrosian view   Outdated theoretical point of view on *deviance* put forward by Cesare Lombroso holding that (1) deviance is biologically determined, and (2) it is possible to identify criminals by the way they look.

looking-glass self   Charles Horton Cooley's term for the image of yourself that you see reflected in the "mirror" provided by those around you.

manifest function   See *function*.

mass communication   The system of *communication* in which a message originates with a sender and is transmitted to a mass audience who can only receive and not effectively respond. It is one-way communication on a massive scale. Television advertising is a perfect example, as is television in general.

mass media   Communication agencies such as radio, television, and newspapers. They are very powerful in a mass society in that they address vast audiences, permitting little or no response from the members of that audience.

matriarchal   A pattern of *power* relations within the family in which the wife/mother predominates.

matrilineal descent   See *lineage*.

matrilocal residence   A residence pattern in which a newly married couple takes up residence at the home of the woman's parents.

mechanical   An artificially contrived system of solidarity, imposed on the members of a group to keep them working together and supporting the whole. Toennies said this was most typical of modern, complex society, whereas Durkheim said it characterized preliterate societies.

megalopolis   A term coined in reference to the joining of large cities into nearly uninterrupted urban ribbons, such as "BOSNYWASH."

meritocracy   A system in which rewards are presumably based entirely on merit, worth, achievement. Though it may seem undebatable, this idea is often criticized for implicitly reinforcing conventional *beliefs, values,* and *norms* and maintaining the *status quo.*

migration   Movement into or out of a *society,* also affecting *population* size and growth rates.

minority group   A *group* or *category* of people in a *society* who are denied *power,* opportunities, and/or scarce commodities—either totally or partially. Examples include racial and ethnic minorities, women, and groups based on age levels.

mixed economy   An economic system drawing elements from more than one model of economic organization. The U.S. economy, for example, has elements of both *capitalism* and *socialism.*

modernization   A process of *social change* that involves economic development along the lines of the Western experience—plus the changes in social attitudes and practices that tend to accompany economic development.

monogamy   A pattern of marriage involving one husband and one wife.

mortality   Death; used by demographers in reference to death rates.

multinational corporation   A large corporation operating actively in several countries: buying raw materials in one, processing them in another, and selling the finished product in a third, for example.

natural experiments   A method of observation in which natural events (e.g., earthquakes, sports victories) are treated by researchers as though they were *experimental stimuli.* Thus, the researcher may be able to study the consequences of an earthquake on a town without being able to cause one at will.

natural increase   That portion of *population* growth attributable to an excess of births over deaths—excluding *migration.*

negative feedback loop   In system dynamics, a feedback process among a set of variables which produces stability; e.g., supply and demand in economic systems.

neolocal residence   A residence pattern in which a newly married couple establish a new residence for themselves and for the family they create.

norm   An agreement about what's expected. Norms take the form of "prescriptions" (what you must do), "proscriptions" (what you can't do), or "permissions" (what you are allowed to do).

normative compliance   The condition in which members of an organization behave in ways appropriate to the success of the organization because of their acceptance of normative agreements as to what's appropriate.

nuclear family   A family unit composed of a husband, a wife, and their unmarried children, if any.

open-ended   Questionnaire items in which the respondent supplies his or her own answer.

operational definition   Concrete and specific definition of the operations by which observations are to be categorized in relation to a concept. The operational definition of "earning an A in this course" might be getting 90 percent of the final exam items right.

operationalization   An extension of the *conceptualization* process in which concrete methods for observing and measuring *variables* are devised. Thus, we might conceptualize the variable "education" as the number of years of formal schooling completed, and we might operationalize it as "the answer people give when we ask them: 'How many years of school have you completed?' "

organic   A form of solidarity growing naturally out of the wholeness of a social *group* as a single organism. Being parts of a whole, the parts of a society are naturally interwoven with one another and support each other and the whole. Toennies said this was mainly typical of the family and community, what Cooley was to call *primary relations.* Durkheim, in stark contrast, said it was more typical of modern, complex society.

out-group   Those people who are excluded from a particular *in-group* or from the rest of society.

paradigm   A fundamental *point of view* or frame of reference that determines what will be considered relevant in the development of explanations and understandings for things. A religious paradigm, for example, would point us toward supernatural answers to puzzles, whereas a scientific one would point us away from such answers.

paradigm shifts   Thomas Kuhn's view of most scientific advancement, not as gradual progress but as radical jumps from one fundamental view of things to another. In sociology, shifting from a view of social life as interaction to a view of *social systems* would be an example, as would a shift from *functionalism* to *conflict theory.*

parsimony   Getting the most for the least. Sometimes, people refer to this as Ockham's razor—the position that simple, uncomplicated explanations are best. Thus, a research conclusion that offered a powerful explanation for, say, voting behavior and involved only a few explanatory factors would illustrate the goal of parsimony in science.

participant-observation   A mode of observation in *field research* in which the researcher participates somewhat in whatever is being observed.

patriarchal   A pattern of *power* relationships within the *family* in which the husband/father predominates.

patrilineal descent   See *lineage.*

patrilocal residence   A residence pattern in which a newly married couple takes up residence in the home of the man's parents.

peers   People like you; your equals.

pluralism   A social pattern that provides the coexistence of different *subcultures* within the same *society.* Though one group may predominate, others are permitted to maintain their patterns across the generations.

pluralistic power   Exercise of *power* by a variety of groups within a society, such as by business, labor unions, the professions, the military, and consumer groups.

point of view   Way of seeing things; literally, a place from which to view. People occupying different social statuses typically have different points of view.

political ideology   A set of reified *beliefs, values,* and *norms* regarding the exercise of *power* in a society.

polygamy   Agreement permitting people more than one spouse at a time. Contrasted with *monogamy.*

population   In research, that *group* or *category* of people about whom we want to draw conclusions. For example, we might want to learn something about American voters in general, students at State University, or left-handed sharpshooters.

positive feedback loop   In system dynamics, a feedback process among a set of variables which produces ever-greater growth or decline; e.g., wage-price spiral, arms race.

positivism   A philosophical position developed by Auguste Comte that links knowledge to observation through the five senses, thereby ruling out intuition, theology, or metaphysics as legitimate sources of knowledge.

postindustrial society   A term used in reference to recent economic developments in societies like the United States. Whereas the focus of the economy in the past was on manufacturing goods, today's economy is more and more centered on the provision of services. For example, instead of building automobiles, you may end up selling insurance.

posttesting   Measurement made among *experimental* and *control groups* following administration of the *experimental stimulus,* compared with the results of *pretesting.*

power   The ability of an individual or group to have its desires carried out, with other people contributing to that whether they want to or not.

power elite   The ruling group in a society. C. Wright Mills, for example, said the United States was ruled by the heads of large corporations, the military, and the government.

prejudice   Prejudgments and expectations (usually negative) regarding some *category* of people (such as a racial, ethnic, or religious group), based on *stereotypes;* also the (usually negative) feelings such expectations foster about members of the category.

pretesting   The step in an *experiment* in which a *dependent variable* is measured among members of both the *experimental* and *control groups* prior to administering the *experimental stimulus* to members of the experimental group. Ideally, both groups should be about the same at the time of pretesting.

primary deviance   The breaking of agreements, prior to any response from others: for example, you take off your clothes at a party.

primary group   As first used by Charles Horton Cooley, this refers to those "characterized by intimate face-to-face association and cooperation." These are the groups—such as family and friendship cliques—with whom we feel the strongest sense of "we"-ness.

primary relations   Close, intimate *relationships,* such as those among friends; characterized by a "we feeling."

probability sampling   The primary model of social scientific sample selection, in which every member of a population has a known, nonzero probability (usually the same probability) of selection into the sample. This is accomplished through the use of *random numbers.*

public opinion   General pattern of attitudes that the members of a society have regarding a particular issue, such as public opinion on equal employment opportunities for women; sometimes used more specifically to refer to the dominant attitude in the society.

quota sampling   A social scientific sampling technique in which subjects are selected on the basis of their characteristics and the frequency of those characteristics in the larger population.

race   Human *category* based on biological and genetic similarities. Although there is little scientific agreement on the value of such categories, the caucasoid, negroid, and mongoloid are sometimes cited as the three main racial types. The social *labeling* of races seems to have more significant consequences than biological factors.

racism   An interrelated set of *stereotypes, prejudice,* and *discrimination* directed against a racial *group,* relegating the group to a generally inferior position within the society.

random selection   A selection process based on chance, used by researchers as a protection against the conscious or unconscious biases they might have in selecting subjects for study. Flipping a coin, tossing dice, and generating tables of random numbers by means of a computer all illustrate random selection. Random selection is an important method for achieving *representative samples.*

rational-bureaucratic authority   Ability to legitimately exercise *power* on the basis of bureaucratic organizational rules.

reactionary movements   Social movements whose main purpose is to restore prior agreements that have faded away or been overturned.

recidivism   Return to prison by those who have previously served time and have been released.

reference groups   Those groups that serve as a standard for us in judging how well we are doing. They may be groups we belong to or those whose judgments we value.

reformist movements   Social movements whose main purpose is the revision of agreements, modifying existing *social structures* without destroying the whole system.

reification   Regarding as real that which is not real; esp. assuming that certain social agreements reflect reality.

relationship   A system of *statuses* and *roles* linking two people to each other and laying out the rules by which they are to interact with one another. For example, the professor-student relationship describes the normal, expected interactions between professors and students. Notice that a relationship joins individuals together into a social unit.

relative deprivation   The experience of doing poorly because those we compare ourselves to are doing better. If you received an A − on an exam, you might feel it was a failure if everyone else got an A + .

religion   Social *institution* dealing with people's ultimate concerns, often—but not always—involving agreements about supernatural beings and forces. The term is also used to refer to specific social organizations operating within the institution, such as Roman Catholicism.

religiosity   Religiousness.

replication   The process of repeating a research project, using identical procedures to the extent possible, to see if the results produced in the original study are repeated in the subsequent one(s). Replication increases our confidence that a genuine discovery has been made, rather than something resulting from chance.

representative sample   A subgroup sample drawn from a *population* so that it has essentially the same distribution of characteristics as the population at large. It allows us to generalize discoveries from the sample to the population.

research methods   Modes of empirical observation and interpretation used in scientific inquiry. See also *content analysis, experiment, participant-observation, survey research.*

resocialization   Learning a new set of agreements to replace those previously learned in connection with an earlier *status.* Soldiers are being resocialized, for example, when they learn military agreements that may conflict with civilian ones.

revolutionary movements   Social movements aimed at substantial *social change,* often including the overthrow of rulers and even of the system of rule.

riot Form of *collective behavior*, involving mass violence and mob action.

role The dynamic aspect of *status*: the things you are expected to do because of the status you occupy. Thus, for example, students are expected to study, professors are expected to teach, police officers are expected to enforce the law, and so forth.

role conflict The situation in which the demands of your several *statuses* clash with one another, thrusting you into what Gregory Bateson called a "double bind." For example, your status as student may require you to spend this weekend studying for an exam, whereas your status as daughter or son may require you to spend the weekend with your parents, celebrating their anniversary. No matter what you do, you will have violated some role expectation.

role strain The situation in which the various demands of a *status* seem beyond your ability. If you were to become president of the United States and experience all the demands for time and attention that accompany that office, you might feel pressed to and beyond the limits of your resources. Many experience the same role strain in the status of "student."

role taking Behaving in ways appropriate to a *status* you do not occupy, as in children playing doctor or cops and robbers.

role theory A sociological point of view that draws on the analogy of the theater, regarding the established *norms* as analogous to a dramatic script, parts in the play as analogous to *statuses* in society, and so forth.

routinization The process of making patterns or processes regular and habitual.

rumors Unconfirmed stories purporting to be true accounts of events—Shibutani called rumors "improvised news."

sample The subgroup we select from a *population* for the purpose of observation leading to conclusions about the larger population. Thus, for example, we may want to talk about the voting intentions of all Americans in 1984, so we carefully select a sample of, say, 2,000 voters for interviewing—selecting them in such a way as to ensure that what we learn about the sample will also be true of the population.

sanctions Rewards (positive sanctions) and punishments (negative sanctions) used to enforce the agreements of the group.

scapegoating The practice of identifying someone else (individual, group, or category) to bear the blame for problems. Thus, the Nazis blamed Germany's pre-World War II economic woes on the Jews; American racists blamed the black civil rights movement on Communists.

science An approach to knowing and understanding that is based on (1) careful, empirical observations and (2) rational logic. Science often—though not necessarily—involves a manipulation of those things studied. Alter-

natives to science would include intuition, speculation, religion, mysticism.

secondary analysis The reanalysis of data previously collected by some other researcher.

secondary deviance A breaking of agreements that flows from your being labeled a "deviant"; for example, once you get a reputation for disrobing at parties and everyone expects you to, you live up to their expectations.

secondary groups In contrast to *primary groups*, these are characterized by more superficial, casual, and specialized relations. Thus, you and I may work for the same large corporation, but we may know each other only in terms of the jobs we perform there.

secondary relations Casual, impersonal relationships as contrasted to *primary relations*; usually aimed at accomplishing a specific purpose.

sect A religious form that is larger and somewhat more established than a *cult*. Characterized by religious fervor, Christian sects tend to be theologically fundamentalist.

secularization The decline of religion and/or religious influence.

segregation A form of *discrimination* in which members of a social *category* are forced to live a separate existence from the mainstream of society, although still living within it. An example is the segregation of black Americans during most of their history in the United States.

self A term variously used by social scientists, usually referring to a person's experience of who he or she is. George Herbert Mead wisely separated this into two aspects: the "me" was essentially your sense of who you are as derived from and reflected in the ideas others have of you—that is, your "social" self: the "I," on the other hand, referred to that sense of who you are that lies outside what others think of you.

small group A face-to-face group in close interaction with one another. Sociologists often create such groups in the laboratory in order to study group interactions. This is called "small-group research."

social change The process of modification to the agreements of society—its *beliefs*, *values*, *norms*, and organization.

social class A broad *category* of people sharing the same economic position—for example, "workers" in an industrial society—plus similar *values*, life-style, and so on. Whereas people with quite different characteristics can occupy the same *stratum* in a continuous ranking of *social stratification*, social classes are more discrete categories having a great deal in common.

social conflict Process of noncooperative interaction between individuals or groups based on disagreements; a struggle to gain dominance for competing points of view. It can occur between individuals (microconflict), within groups, between groups, between large social classes, and between societies in the form of war.

social control Enforcement of a group's agreements, accomplished by a variety of mechanisms and agencies.

social disorganization A condition of disruption, chaos, and conflict in society—involving a poor integration among various agreements and also extensive *deviance*.

social evolution Theoretical point of view that regards the development of society over time as moving in a particular direction, typically involving a shift from simple to complex structures. Reflecting the Darwinian view in biology, it was popularized in sociology by Herbert Spencer.

social indicators Statistical measures that reflect general social conditions in a society, such as crime rates, quality of schools, and physicians per capita. Similar to economic indicators that reflect the health of the economy.

social interaction The process in which one person directs a *communication* and evokes a response from the other that is conditioned by the initial communication. Realize in this that "communication" includes physical actions as well as words. Typically, it goes back and forth, back and forth, like a windshield wiper. Also, any number can play.

socialism An economic system based on state ownership of the means of production.

socialization The process through which social agreements of a particular group are learned and taught. The two major purposes of socialization are: (1) to pass the agreements from generation to generation, and (2) to give each individual a social identity within the group.

social mobility Movement from one social *class* or *strata* to another.

social movements Organized attempts to change some aspect of society—either reactionary or progressive. The women's liberation movement is an example.

social relationships The structure of links between social *statuses*, as specified by the *roles* associated with each. For example, a social relationship exists between the statuses "mother" and "son" in that we have agreements about the behavior of each toward the other.

social science An approach to knowing and understanding the nature of our social life based on the use of scientific methods, that is: (1) careful, empirical observation and (2) rational logic. The social sciences typically include sociology, political science, anthropology, psychology, geography, economics, and sometimes other fields as well.

social stratification The organization of inequality in society; the ranking of people in terms of things scarce and sought after—such as money, *power*, prestige, and so forth.

social structure The persistent network of *statuses* and *roles*, the *relationships* among statuses, and the interactions expected within those relationships that make up the organized framework for social life. For example, the statuses (professors, students, administrators, security guards, secretaries, etc.) making up a university, plus all the relationships and interactions among those statuses, constitute the social structure of the university.

social system A complex network of social agreements linking social *statuses* to one another in such a way as to satisfy the survival needs of a social group, all the while addressing the various needs and desires of individuals.

social systems theory The sociological *point of view* that addresses the network of agreements that provide the grounding for organized social life. It is also called *structural-functionalism* or simply *functionalism*.

societal disengagement The process in which old people are divested of the roles they have played in society, moving toward having no purpose or function.

society A *social system* with people living in it, usually associated with a definable geographical territory.

socioeconomic status (SES) A person's overall ranking within a system of stratification, reflecting his or her relative standing on the different dimensions making up that system. Referring to overall standing within a spectrum of continuous rankings from high to low, SES is analogous to *social class* within systems based on discrete groups such as "upper class," "middle class," and so on.

sociology The study of human group life.

status A social location that people occupy for the purpose of interacting with others. Examples include: professor, student, mother, barber, Republican. How you see the world is largely a function of the status(es) you are occupying, and how you interact with others is largely a function of the status(es) they are occupying.

status crime A behavior regarded as a *crime* only for those occupying certain social *statuses*, especially applying to minors. Thus, a young person is guilty of a crime when drinking alcohol, but an adult is not.

status inconsistency The condition of ranking high on some dimensions of stratification and low on others: for example, being highly educated but having little money.

status quo Current state of affairs. Those benefiting most from a particular set of social agreements tend to want to maintain the status quo.

stereotypes Mental pictures generalizing the characteristics of members of a social *category*. Walter Lippmann coined this term—meaning "pictures cast in metal"—to indicate the persistence of such mental pictures.

strata Levels or layers in a social stratification system; each stratum comprises those individuals having approximately the same rank in the stratification system.

structural-functionalism See *functionalism*.

subculture The collection of *symbols, beliefs, values, norms,* and meanings shared by the members of a subgroup within a larger society—for example, an ethnic or religious subculture. It is also used in reference to the subgroup itself, those who share a common identity related to the subcultural agreements.

survey research Research method utilizing questionnaires, either self-administered or administered by interviewers.

symbol   Representation of something else; a flag is a symbol of a nation.

symbolic interactionism   The sociological point of view that addresses the process of *social interaction* through which agreements and disagreements are created and shared meanings are established for the symbolic aspects of social life.

system imperatives   The conditions that must be satisfied for a system to survive. Parsons cited four: adaptation, goal attainment, integration, and latent pattern maintenance. Other sociologists have created different lists, though they have addressed similar concerns.

technology   That segment of culture made up of standardized techniques for handling aspects of life, including tools developed for that purpose. Thus, for example, medical scientific knowledge and medical instruments are an example of technology.

theory   A comprehensive explanation for some sector of existence, including (1) definitions of the elements making up that to be explained, (2) a set of assumptions and axioms that will be taken as the starting point for the theory, and (3) a set of interrelated statements about relationships among the elements.

theory of demographic transition   A theory explaining the process whereby small, undeveloped societies—with high birth and death rates and low rates of net growth—begin industrialization with the consequence of drastically reduced death rates and an equally drastic growth in population; this produces *urbanization*. Eventually birth rates decrease, and the society returns to a slow rate of net growth—although it is now a large, industrialized, and urbanized society.

totalitarianism   A form of government in which the state has *authority* over all aspects of life.

totemism   Preliterate form of religion in which the socioreligious group identifies itself with some animal or object (the totem).

tracking systems   Student-flow systems within schools, usually established on the basis of student ability, in which "bright" students are grouped together in advanced classes whereas "slow" students are put together in less demanding classes. Even when the same topic (e.g., algebra) is covered for the different groups, the level of difficulty is varied. The system is often criticized for trapping students into a status of low ability.

traditional authority   Agreement that the exercise of *power* by certain people is legitimate by virtue of its "always having been that way."

traditional autocratic   Form of government in which a single ruler, supported by a small elite, runs things on the basis of *traditional authority;* more common among small, underdeveloped countries.

transformation function   Primary function of economic institutions: to transform the physical environment so it provides for human needs and desires. People are also transformed into *roles* within the economy.

triad   A *group* comprising three or more members. Significantly different from a *dyad* in that someone can leave and a group still survives.

trial marriages   An emerging American pattern, still practiced by a minority only, in which couples live together as though they were married—but without actually marrying—in order to find out firsthand whether they want to commit themselves fully to marriage.

true believer   A term coined by Eric Hoffer in reference to a person who is totally and uncritically committed to an ideology.

upward mobility   Movement from one *social class* or *strata* to a higher one—as in moving from middle to upper class.

urbanism   The style of life associated with city life.

urbanization   Concentration of *populations* into *cities*, as opposed to rural patterns of social organization.

urban renewal   A general term referring to the process of upgrading distressed and deteriorated urban areas. Often carried out with little concern for social patterns, it has become something of a dirty term among the urban poor.

utilitarian compliance   The condition in which members of an organization behave in ways appropriate to the success of the organization because that also results in rewards for them as individuals.

value   An agreement about what's better than something else.

value-added   Analytical model for the study of social processes; "something" is charged by stages as a series of new elements are added. Marx introduced this model in studying economic production (workers added the value of their labor to raw materials), and Smelser adapted the model to the study of developing *collective behavior*.

variables   Logical sets of attributes representing the variations of characteristics among people, events, or objects. Thus, "sex" is a variable, composed of attributes "male" and "female." Each person should be describable in terms of one and only one attribute of a given variable.

voluntary association   *Secondary group* formed around a shared interest, ranging from hobby clubs to social reform movements.

voucher systems   Educational systems in which parents are given educational credits for their school-age children, and those credits can be used to educate the children in public schools or go toward the costs of private school education.

white-collar crime   Crimes committed in connection with white-collar occupations, such as embezzlement, price fixing, stock fraud, and so on.

zero population growth   A condition in which *population* size remains the same year after year.

Bibliography

Aberle, David F., et al.
  1950 "The Functional Prerequisites of a Society." *Ethics* 9(January):100–111.
Agarwal, Anil
  1980 "The Struggle for Clean Water." *Earthscan* (London), reprinted in *World Press Review,* December, pp. 34–36.
Allen, Brandt
  1975 "Embezzler's Guide to the Computer." *Harvard Business Review* 53(4):79–89.
Allen, Irving
  1975 "Social Relations and the Two-Step Flow: A Defense of the Tradition." In *Mass Media and Society,* ed. Alan Wells. Palo Alto, Calif.: Mayfield.
Alpern, David R.
  1982 "A New Outcry over Nukes." *Newsweek,* March 29, pp. 18–20.
Amir, Manachem
  1971 "Forcible Rape." *Federal Probation* 31(March):51–58.
Anderson, Walt, Ed.
  1970 *Politics and Environment.* Pacific Palisades, Calif.: Goodyear.
Andrain, Charles
  1974 *Political Life and Social Change.* Belmont, Calif.: Wadsworth.
Andrews, Lori B.
  1982 "Mind Control in the Courtroom." *Psychology Today,* March, pp. 66–73.
Ares, Charles, et al.
  1963 "The Manhattan Bail Project." *New York University Law Review* 38(January):66–92.
Aries, Philippe
  1962 *Centuries of Childhood: A Social History of Family Life,* trans. Robert Baldick. New York: Knopf.
Arnold, David
  1967 "The Meaning of the Laguardia Report: The Effects of Marijuana." In *Marijuana: Myths and Realities,* ed. J. L. Simmons. North Hollywood, Calif.: Brandon.
Aronoff, Joel, and William Crano
  1975 "A Re-Examination of the Cross-Cultural Principles of Task Segregation and Sex Role Differentiation in the Family." *American Sociological Review* 40:12–20.
Aronoff, J., and L. A. Messe
  1971 "Motivational Determinants of Small-Group Structure." *Journal of Personality and Social Psychology* 17:319–24.
Asch, Solomon, E.
  1955 "Effects of Group Pressure upon the Modifications and Distortion of Judgments." Reprinted in *Readings in Social Psychology,* 3rd ed., ed. Eleanor E. Maccoby et al. New York: Holt, Rinehart and Winston, 1958, pp. 174–83.

Asiaweek
1980 "Newspapers for the Villages." Reprinted in *World Press Review,* October, p. 63.
1981 "China Cracks Down." Reprinted in *World Press Review,* February, p. 58.

Asimov, Isaac
1975 "Violence–As Human as Thumbs." *TV Guide,* June 14.

Atchley, Robert C.
1977 *The Social Forces in Later Life.* Belmont, Calif.: Wadsworth.

Atchley, Robert, and Mildred Seltzer
1976 *The Sociology of Aging.* Belmont, Calif.: Wadsworth.

Babbie, Earl
1966 "The Third Civilization." *Review of Religious Research* 7:101–21.
1970 *Science and Morality in Medicine.* Berkeley: University of California Press.
1982 *Social Research for Consumers.* Belmont, Calif.: Wadsworth.
1983 *The Practice of Social Research.* Belmont, Calif.: Wadsworth.

Baca, Reynaldo, and Dexter Bryan
1982 "The 'Assimilation' of Unauthorized Mexican Workers: Another Social Science Fiction." Presented to the meetings of the Pacific Sociological Association.

Bales, Robert
1950 *Interaction Process Analysis: A Method for Study of Small Groups.* Reading, Mass.: Addison-Wesley.

Bales, Robert F., and Stephen P. Cohen
1979 *SYMLOG: A System for the Multiple Level Observation of Groups.* New York: The Free Press.

Balkan, Sheila, Ronald J. Berger, and Janet Schmidt
1980 *Crime and Deviance in America.* Belmont, Calif.: Wadsworth.

Ball, Samuel, and Gerry Bogatz
1970 *A Summary of the Major Findings in "The First Year of Sesame Street: An Evaluation."* Princeton, N.J.: Educational Testing Service.
1971 *The Second Year of Sesame Street.* Princeton, N.J.: Educational Testing Service.

Baltzell, E. Digby
1964 *The Protestant Establishment.* New York: Random House.

Bandura, A.
1969 "Social Learning Theory of Identificatory Processes." In *Handbook of Socialization Theory and Research,* ed. D. A. Goslin. Chicago: Rand McNally, chap. 3.

Banfield, Edward
1961 *Political Influence.* New York: Free Press.

Barnard, Chester
1938 *The Functions of the Executive.* Cambridge, Mass.: Harvard University Press.

Barry, Herbert III, Margaret K. Bacon, and Irvin L. Child
1955 "A Cross-Cultural Survey of Some Sex Differences in Socialization." *Journal of Abnormal and Social Psychology* 55:327–32.

Barton, Allen H.
1980 "A Diagnosis of Bureaucratic Maladies." In *Making Bureaucracies Work,* ed. Carol H. Weiss and Allen H. Barton. Beverly Hills: Sage, pp. 27–36.

Barzun, Jacques
1981 "The Wasteland of American Education." *The New York Review of Books,* November 5, pp. 34–36.

Beale, Calvin
1975 "Renewed Growth in Rural Communities." *The Futurist* 9(4):196–98.

Beauvoir, Simone de
1972 *The Coming of Age.* New York: Putnam.

Becker, Howard
1963 *Outsiders: Studies in the Sociology of Deviance.* New York: Free Press.

Becker, Howard, et al.
1961 *Boys in White.* Chicago: University of Chicago Press.

Becker, Jay J.
1980 *The Investigation of Computer Crime.* Washington, D.C.: Department of Justice.

Bellah, Robert N.
1967 "Civil Religion in America." *Daedalus* 96:1–2.
1975 *The Broken Covenant: American Civil Religion in Time of Trial.* New York: Seabury.
1978 "The Role of Preaching in a Corrupt Republic." *Christianity and Crisis,* December 25, pp. 317–22.

Bem, Sandra, and Daryl Bem
1971 "Training the Woman to Know Her Place: The Power of a Nonconscious Ideology." In *Understanding American Society,* ed. Robert Atchley. Belmont, Calif.: Wadsworth.

Bendix, Reinhard
1956 *Work and Authority in Industry.* New York: Wiley.

Benedict, Ruth
1946 *The Chrysanthemum and the Sword.* Boston: Houghton Mifflin.

Bennett, William, and Terry Eastland
1978 "Why Bakke Won't End Reverse Discrimination: 1." *Commentary* 66(3):29–35.

Benson, John M.
1981 "A Rebirth of Religion?" *Public Opinion Quarterly* 45:575–85.

Benson, Paul R.
1981 "Political Alienation and Public Satisfaction with Police Service," *Pacific Sociological Review,* Col. 24 No. 1 (January), 45–64.

Berelson, Bernard, Paul Lazarsfeld, and William McPhee
1954 *Voting: A Study of Opinion Formation in a Presidential Campaign.* Chicago: University of Chicago Press.

Berger, Peter L., and Thomas Luckmann
1967   *The Social Construction of Reality.* Garden City, N.Y.: Doubleday.

Berk, Richard A.
1974   "A Gaming Approach to Crowd Behavior." *American Sociological Review* 39:355–73.
1981   "On the Compatibility of Applied and Basic Sociological Research: An Effort in Marriage Counseling." *The American Sociologist,* November, pp. 204–211.

Berk, Richard A., William P. Bridges, and Anthony Shih
1981   "Does IQ Really Matter? A Study of the Use of IQ Scores for the Tracking of the Mentally Retarded." *American Sociological Review,* February, pp. 58–71.

Berle, A. A.
1958   *Economic Power and the Free Society.* New York: Fund for the Republic.

Bernard, Jessie
1972   *The Future of Marriage.* New York: Bantam.

Berry, Brian, and John Kasarda
1977   *Contemporary Urban Ecology.* New York: Macmillan.

Biddle, Bruce, and Edwin Thomas
1966   *Role Theory: Concepts and Research.* New York: Wiley.

Blau, Judith R., and Peter M. Blau
1982   "The Cost of Inequality: Metropolitan Structure and Violent Crime." *American Sociological Review,* February, pp. 114–29.

Blau, Peter M.
1964   *Exchange and Power in Social Life.* New York: Wiley.
1966   "The Structure of Small Bureaucracies." *American Sociological Review* 31:179–91.
1968   "The Hierarchy of Authority in Organizations." *American Journal of Sociology* 73:453–67.

Blau, Peter, and Otis Dudley Duncan
1967   *The American Occupational Structure.* New York: Wiley.

Blauner, Robert
1964   *Alienation and Freedom.* Chicago: University of Chicago Press.

Blood, Robert, and Donald Wolfe
1960   *Husbands and Wives: The Dynamics of Married Living.* New York: Free Press.

Blumer, Herbert
[1939]*   "Collective Behavior." *In Principles of Sociology,* ed. Alfred McClung Lee. New York: Barnes & Noble.
1946
1966   "The Mass, the Public, and Public Opinion." In *Reader in Public Opinion and Mass Communication,* ed. Bernard Berelson and Morris Janowitz. New York: Free Press.
1969   *Symbolic Interactionism: Perspective and Method.* Englewood Cliffs, N.J.: Prentice-Hall.

*Brackets indicate original publication date.

Boer, Connie de
1978   "Attitudes Toward Work." *Public Opinion Quarterly,* Fall, pp. 414–23.

Bollen, Kenneth A., and Burke D. Grandjean
1981   "The Dimension(s) of Democracy: Further Issues in the Measurement and Effects of Political Democracy." *American Sociological Review,* October, pp. 651–59.

Bottomore, T. B., and Maximilien Rubel, Eds.
1956   *Selected Writings in Sociology and Social Philosophy of Karl Marx,* trans. T. B. Bottomore. New York: McGraw-Hill.

Boorman, Howard L., and Scott A. Boorman
1967   "Strategy and National Psychology in China." *The Annals of the American Academy of Political and Social Science* 370(March):143–55.

Boorstin, Daniel J.
1978   *The Republic of Technology.* New York: Harper & Row.

Boserup, Ester
1970   *Woman's Role in Economic Development.* London: Allen and Unwin.

Bouvier, Leon
1976   "The Elderly Population: Its Relationship to Society." In *Population Profiles.* Washington, Conn.: Center for Information on America.

Bradbury, Wilbur
1975   *The Adult Years.* New York: Time-Life.

Braithwaite, John
1981   "The Myth of Social Class and Criminality Reconsidered." *American Sociological Review,* February, pp. 36–57.

Brecher, Jeremy
1972   *Strike.* San Francisco: Straight Arrow.

Bronfenbrenner, Urie
1970   *Two Worlds of Childhood: U.S. and U.S.S.R.* New York: Russell Sage.

Brown, Lester
1978   Interviewed in "The Plowboy Interview." *Mother Earth News,* March/April, pp. 17–23.

Bruner, Jerome
1982   "Schooling Children in a Nasty Climate." *Psychology Today,* January, pp. 57–63.

Burgess, Ernest
1925   "The Growth of the City." In *The City,* ed. Robert Park et al. Chicago: University of Chicago Press.

Bushman, Richard L.
1981   "Family Security in the Transition from Farm to City, 1750–1850." *Journal of Family History,* Fall, pp. 238–56.

Cahalan, Don
1970   *Problem Drinkers.* San Francisco: Jossey-Bass.

Cameron, William
1966   *Modern Social Movements.* New York: Random House.

Campbell, Angus, Gerald Gurin, and W. E. Miller
1954 *The Voter Decides.* Evanston, Ill.: Row, Peterson.

Caplovitz, David
1967 *The Poor Pay More: Consumer Practices of Low Income Families.* New York: Free Press.
1978 "Making Ends Meet: How Families Cope with Inflation and Recession." *Public Opinion*, May/June, pp. 52–54.

Caplow, Theodore
1959 "Further Development of a Theory of Coalitions in Triads." *American Journal of Sociology* 64:488–93.
1969 *Two Against One: Coalitions in Triads.* Englewood Cliffs, N.J.: Prentice-Hall.

Carlsson, Gösta
1967 "Swedish Character in the Twentieth Century." *The Annals of the American Academy of Political and Social Science* 370(March):93–98.

Carr-Saunders, A. M.
1936 *World Population.* Oxford: Clarendon Press.

Carson, Rachel
1962 *Silent Spring.* Boston: Houghton Mifflin.

Castaneda, Carlos
1969 *The Teachings of Don Juan.* New York: Bantam.
1971 *A Separate Reality.* New York: Simon and Schuster.
1972 *Journey to Ixtlan.* New York: Simon and Schuster.
1974 *Tales of Power.* New York: Simon and Schuster.

Cavender, Chris
1972 "A Critical Examination of Textbooks on Indians." In *Minority Problems*, ed. Arnold Rose and Caroline Rose. New York: Harper & Row.

Chaffee, Steven, and Michael Petrick
1975 *Using the Media: Communication Problems in American Society.* New York: McGraw-Hill.

Chambliss, William J.
1973 "The Saints and the Roughnecks." *Society* 11:24–31.

Child, John
1972 "Organization Structure and Strategies of Control: A Replication of the Aston Study." *Administrative Science Quarterly* 17:163–77.

Chomsky, Noam
1957 *Syntactic Structures.* The Hague: Mouton.
1972 *Language and Mind.* New York: Harcourt Brace Jovanovich

Christian Science Monitor
1975 April 30, p. 21.

Churchill, Ward, and Norbert S. Hill, Jr.
1979 "An Historical Survey of Tendencies in Indian Education: Higher Education." *The Indian Historian*, Winter, pp. 37–46.

Clarke, Arthur C.
1981 "Third World 2001." *South*, November, pp. 13–15.

Clausen, John
1963 "Social Factors in Disease." *The Annals of the American Academy of Political and Social Science* 346:138–48.

Clayton, Richard R., and Janet L. Bokemeier
1968 "Premarital Sex in the Seventies." *Journal of Marriage and the Family*, November, pp. 759–75.

Clinard, Marshall B., and Richard Quinney, Eds.
1967 *Criminal Behavior Systems: A Typology.* New York: Holt, Rinehart and Winston.

Coleman, James S., et al.
1966 *Equality of Educational Opportunity.* Washington, D.C.: U.S. National Center for Educational Statistics.

Coleman, James William, and Donald R. Cressey
1980 *Social Problems.* New York: Harper & Row.

Cooley, Charles Horton
[1902] *Human Nature and the Social Order.* New York:
1964 Schocken Books.
1909 *Social Organization.* New York: Scribner.

Cooper, David
1974 "The Death of the Family." In *Social Problems: The Contemporary Debates*, ed. John Williamson et al. Boston: Little, Brown.

Coser, Lewis
1956 *The Functions of Social Conflict.* New York: Free Press.

Cragg, Kenneth
1975 *The House of Islam.* Belmont, Calif.: Wadsworth.

Creme, Benjamin
1980 *The Reappearance of the Christ and the Masters of Wisdom.* London: The Tara Press.

Cressey, Donald
1953 *Other People's Money.* New York: Free Press.
1969 *Theft of the Nation.* New York: Harper & Row.

Dahl, Robert
1961 *Who Governs.* New Haven, Conn.: Yale University Press.

Dahrendorf, Ralf
1959 *Class and Class Conflict in Industrial Society.* Stanford, Calif.: Stanford University Press.

Davies, James
1962 "A Theory of Revolution." *American Sociological Review* 27:5–19.

Davis, Kingsley
1955 "The Origin and Growth of Urbanization in the World." *American Journal of Sociology* 60:429–39.

Davis, Kingsley, and Wilbert Moore
1945 "Some Principles of Stratification." *American Sociological Review* 10:242–49.

Davis, Thomas
1971 "A Technique for the Identification of Negative Black Stereotype Biases in Elementary School Children." M.A. thesis, University of Hawaii.

DeFleur, Lois
1973 "Biasing Influences on Drug Arrest Records: Implications for Deviance Research." *American Sociological Review* 40:88–103.

DeFleur, Melvin
1966 *Theories of Mass Communication.* New York: McKay.

DeLamater, J. D., and B. MacCorquodale
1979 *Premarital Sexuality: Attitudes, Relationships, Behavior.* Madison, Wisc.: University of Wisconsin Press.

Dellums, Ronald V.
1982 "Report to the 8th District [California]." Winter.

DeMott, Benjamin
1980 "The Pro-Incest Lobby." *Psychology Today,* March, pp. 11–16.

Dobash, Russell P., and R. Emerson Dobash
1981 "Community Response to Violence against Wives: Charivari, Abstract Justice and Patriarchy." *Social Problems,* June, pp. 563–81.

Dollard, John
1937 *Caste and Class in a Southern Town.* New Haven, Conn.: Yale University Press.

Domhoff, G. William
1967 *Who Rules America?* Englewood Cliffs, N.J.: Prentice-Hall.

Drucker, Peter F.
1974 *Management: Tasks, Responsibilities, Practices.* New York: Harper & Row.

Dulles, Foster
1959 *"The Indian Menace," The United States since 1865.* Ann Arbor, Mich.: University of Michigan Press.

Durand, John
1968 "The Modern Expansion of World Population." In *Population and Society,* ed. Charles Nam. New York: Houghton Mifflin, pp. 108–120.

Durkheim, Emile
[1889] "A Review of Ferdinand Toennies's *Gemeinschaft*
1972 *und Gesellschaft." Revue Philosophique* 27:416–22. In "An Exchange between Durkheim and Toennies on the Nature of Social Relations, with an Introduction by Joan Aldous. *American Journal of Sociology* 77:1191–1200.
[1893] *The Division of Labor in Society,* trans. George
1964 Simpson. New York: Free Press.
[1897] *Suicide: A Study in Sociology.* Glencoe, Ill.: Free
1951 Press
[1915] *The Elementary Forms of Religious Life,* trans. Joseph
1954 Swain. Glencoe, Ill.: Free Press.

Dye, Thomas, and L. Harmon Ziegler
1975 *The Irony of Democracy.* North Scituate, Mass.: Duxbury.

Dynes, Russell R.
1981 "The View from Inside." *The American Sociologist,* May, 97–100.

Easton, Carol
1975 "A Survey of Sex Surveys—1900–1975." In *The People's Almanac,* ed. David Wallechinsky and Irving Wallace, pp. 976–91. Garden City, N.Y.: Doubleday.

Eckstein, Susan
1981 "The Socialist Transformation of Cuban Agriculture: Domestic and International Constraints." *Social Problems,* December, pp. 178–96.

Edmiston, Susan
1973 "How to Write Your Own Marriage Contract." In *This Is a Sociology Reader,* ed. Angela Lask et al. San Francisco: Rinehart Press.

Efron, Edith
1975 "Does TV Violence Affect Our Society? NO." *TV Guide,* June 14.

Ehrlich, Paul
1971 *The Population Bomb.* New York: Ballantine.

Ehrlich, Paul, and Anne Ehrlich
1972 *Population, Resources, Environment: Issues in Human Ecology.* San Francisco: Freeman.

Ehrlich, Paul R., and S. Shirley Feldman
1977 *The Race Bomb.* New York: Quadrangle.

Einstein, Liz
1980 "Stepfamily: Chaotic, Complex, Challenging." *Stepfamily Bulletin,* Fall, pp. 1–3.

Eisenstadt, S. N.
1967 "Israeli Identity: Problems in the Development of the Collective Identity of an Ideological Society." *The Annals of the American Academy of Political and Social Science* 370(March):116–23.

Ellis, Dean
1967 "Speech and Social Status in America." *Social Problems* 45:431–37.

Ellul, Jacques
1964 *The Technological Society,* trans. John Wilkinson. New York: Knopf.

Emery, Edwin, et al.
1973 *Introduction to Mass Communications.* New York: Dodd, Mead.

Encyclopedia Britannica
1976 *Britannica Book of the Year.* Chicago: Encyclopedia
1978 Britannica.
1979
1982

Epstein, Edward
1974 *News from Nowhere.* New York: Vintage Books.
1975 "The Selection of Reality." In *Issues in Broadcasting,* ed. Ted Smythe and George Mastroianni. Palo Alto, Calif.: Mayfield.

Erikson, Erik
1963 *Childhood and Society.* New York: Norton.

Erlenmeyer-Kimling, L., and L. F. Jarvik
1963 "Genetics and Intelligence." *Science* 142:1477–78.

Ervin-Tripp, S.
1964   "An Analysis of the Interaction of Language, Topic and Listener." *American Anthropologist* 66:94–100.
Eskin, Marian
1980   *Child Abuse and Neglect: A Literature Review and Selected Bibliography.* Washington, D.C.: U.S. Department of Justice.
Etzioni, Amitai
1975   *A Comparative Analysis of Complex Organizations.* New York: Free Press.
Farley, Reynolds
1977   "Trends in Racial Inequalities: Have the Gains of the 1960s Disappeared in the 1970s?" *American Sociological Review* 42:189–208.
Federal Bureau of Investigation
1975   *Uniform Crime Report of the United States.* Wash-
1978   ington, D.C.: U.S. Government Printing Office.
1981   *Crime in the United States.* Washington, D.C.: U.S. Government Printing Office.
Ferleger, David
1977   "The Battle Over Children's Rights." *Psychology Today,* July, pp. 89–91.
Festinger, Leon, Henry Riecken, and Stanley Schacter
1956   *When Prophecy Fails.* Minneapolis: University of Minnesota Press.
Fiedler, Fred E.
1981   "Leadership Effectiveness." *American Behavioral Scientist,* May/June, pp. 619–32.
Field, Mervin D.
1982   "Majority Favors Nuclear Freeze." *San Francisco Chronicle,* April 21, p. 8.
Fischer, Claude, et al.
1974   "Crowding Studies and Urban Life: A Critical Review." Berkeley: Institute of Urban and Regional Development, University of California, working paper no. 242.
Foss, B. M.
1973   "Ability." In *The Seven Stages of Man,* ed. Robert Sears, S. Shirley Feldman. Los Altos, Calif.: Kaufmann, p. 19.
Foy, Eddie, and Alvin Harlow
[1928]   *Clowning Through Life.* Reprinted in part in *Col-*
1957   *lective Behavior,* ed. Ralph Turner and Lewis Killian. Englewood Cliffs, N.J.: Prentice-Hall.
Frazier, E. Franklin
1939   *The Negro Family in the United States.* Chicago: University of Chicago Press.
Freud, Sigmund
[1909]   "The Origin and Development of Psychoanaly-
1957   sis." In *A General Selection from the Works of Sigmund Freud,* ed. John Rickman. Garden City, N.Y.: Doubleday.
[1921]   "Group Psychology and the Analysis of the Ego."
1957   In *A General Selection from the Works of Sigmund*

Freud, ed. John Rickman. Garden City, N.Y.: Doubleday.
[1927]   *The Future of an Illusion,* trans. W. D. Robson-Scott.
1957   Garden City, N.Y.: Doubleday.
1930   *Civilization and Its Discontents,* trans. Joan Riviere. Garden City, N.Y.: Doubleday.
Freyre, Gilberto
1967   "Brazilian National Character in the Twentieth Century." *The Annals of the American Academy of Political and Social Science* 370(March):57–62.
Friedan, Betty
1981   *The Second Stage.* New York: Summit Books.
Friedman, Mickey
1982   "The Barter Circuit." *San Francisco Examiner* (Scene/Arts section), January 10, pp. 1–3.
Funkhouser, G. Ray
1973   "The Issues of the Sixties: An Exploratory Study of the Dynamics of Public Opinion." *Public Opinion Quarterly* 37:62–75.
Galbraith, John
1969   *How to Control the Military.* New York: New American Library.
Gall, John
1975   *Systemantics: How Systems Work and Especially How They Fail.* New York: Quadrangle.
Gallup, George
1972   *The Gallup Poll.* 3 vols. New York: Random House.
Gamson, William
1975   *The Strategy of Social Protest.* Homewood, Ill.: Dorsey Press.
Gans, Herbert J.
1971   "The Uses of Poverty: The Poor Pay All." *Social Policy,* July/August, pp. 20–24.
1979   *Deciding What's News: A Study of CBS Evening News, NBC Nightly News, Newsweek, and Time.* New York: Pantheon Books.
Gardner, Robert, and Eleanor Nordyke
1974   *The Demographic Situation in Hawaii.* Honolulu: East-West Population Institute.
Garfinkel, Harold
1967   *Studies in Ethnomethodology.* Englewood Cliffs, N.J.: Prentice-Hall.
Gaylin, Willard
1978   "Being Touched, Being Hurt." *Psychology Today,* December, pp. 117–21.
Gehrig, Gail
1981   "The American Civil Religion Debate: A Source for Theory Construction." *Journal for the Scientific Study of Religion,* March, pp. 51–63.
Geis, Gilbert
1967   "The Heavy Electrical Equipment Antitrust Cases of 1961." In *Criminal Behavior Systems,* ed. Marshall Clinard and Richard Quinney. New York: Holt, Rinehart and Winston, pp. 139–51.

Gendron, Bernard
1977   *Technology and the Human Condition.* New York: St. Martin's.
General Services Administration
1974   *Inventory Report on Real Property Owned by the United States throughout the World.* Washington, D.C.: U.S. Government Printing Office.
Gerbner, George, et al.
1980   "Television Violence, Victimization, and Power." *American Behavioral Scientist,* May/June, pp. 681–705.
Ginzberg, Eli
1982   "The Social Security System." *Scientific American,* January, pp. 51–57.
Gitlin, Todd
1980   *The Whole World is Watching.* Berkeley, Calif.: University of California Press.
Gittings, John
1981   "China Reassesses Its Moscow Links." *South,* June, pp. 19–22.
Glazer, Nathan
1978   "Why Bakke Won't End Reverse Discrimination: 2." *Commentary* 66(3):36–41.
Glenn, Norval D., and Charles N. Weaver
1981   "The Contribution of Marital Happiness to Global Happiness." *Journal of Marriage and the Family,* February, pp. 161–68.
Glock, Charles
1964   "The Role of Deprivation in the Origin and Evolution of Religious Groups." In *Religion and Social Conflict,* ed. Robert Lee. New York: Oxford University Press.
Glock, Charles, and Rodney Stark
1965   *Religion and Society in Tension.* Chicago: Rand McNally.
1966   *Christian Beliefs and Anti-Semitism.* New York: Harper & Row.
Goffman, Erving
1961   *Asylums: Essays on the Social Situation of Mental Patients and Other Inmates.* Chicago: Aldine.
1963   *Stigma: Notes on the Management of a Spoiled Identity.* Englewood Cliffs, N.J.: Prentice-Hall.
Gold, Raymond
1969   "Roles in Sociological Field Observation." In *Issues in Participant Observation,* ed. George J. McCall and J. L. Simmons. Reading, Mass.: Addison-Wesley.
Goode, William
1961   "Family Disorganization." In *Contemporary Social Problems,* ed. Robert Merton and Robert Nisbet. New York: Harcourt, Brace.
Goody, J.
1971   "Class and Marriage in Africa and Eurasia." *American Journal of Sociology,* January, pp. 585–603.
1973   "Polygyny, Economy, and the Role of Women." In *The Character of Kinship,* ed. J. Goody. London: Cambridge University Press, pp. 175–90.
1976   *Production and Reproduction: A Comparative Study of Domestic Domain.* New York: Cambridge University Press.
Gordon, Milton
1964   *Assimilation in American Life.* New York: Oxford University Press.
Gore, M. S.
1965   "The Traditional Indian Family." In *Comparative Family Systems,* ed. M. F. Nimkoff. Boston: Houghton Mifflin.
Gorer, Geoffrey
1967   "English Character in the Twentieth Century." *The Annals of the American Academy of Political and Social Science* 370(March):74–81.
Gough, E. K.
1971   "The Origin of the Family." *Journal of Marriage and the Family,* November, pp. 760–71.
Gould, Stephen Jay
1981   *The Mismeasure of Man.* New York: Norton.
Gouldner, Alvin
1954   *Patterns of Industrial Bureaucracy.* Glencoe, Ill.: Free Press.
1962   "Anti-Minotaur: The Myth of Value-Free Sociology." *Social Problems* 9:199–213.
Grant, William
1980   "Growing Rebellion by U.S. Catholics on Birth Control." *San Francisco Chronicle,* October 4.
Graubard, Allen
1973   "The Free School Movement." In *Education Yearbook.* New York: Macmillan Educational Corporation.
Greeley, Andrew
1979   *Crises in the Church.* Chicago, Ill.: Thomas More Press.
Greenstein, Fred
1963   *The American Party System and the American People.* Englewood Cliffs, N.J.: Prentice-Hall.
Greer, Scott
1966   *Urban Renewal and American Cities.* Indianapolis, Ind.: Bobbs-Merrill.
Gross, Kenneth
1976   "We Don't Want to Live in Fear Anymore." *San Francisco Examiner and Chronicle,* December 12.
Hadden, Jeffrey K., and Charles E. Swann
1981   *Prime Time Preachers: The Rising Power of Televangelism.* New York: Addison-Wesley.
Hall, Edward
1959   The Silent Language. Greenwich, Conn.: Fawcett.
Hall, Richard H.
1977   *Organizations: Structure and Process.* Englewood Cliffs, N.J.: Prentice-Hall.

Hamburger, Henry
  1979 *Games as Models of Social Phenomena.* San Francisco: Freeman.
Hammond, Philip, and Robert Mitchell
  1965 "Segmentation of Radicalism: The Case of the Protestant Campus Minister." *American Journal of Sociology* 71:133–43.
Hardin, Garrett
  1968 "The Tragedy of the Commons." *Science* 162:1243–48.
Hardin, Garrett, Ed.
  1969 *Population, Evolution, and Birth Control.* San Francisco: Freeman.
Hardy, Charles C.
  1982 "Teachers Who Can't Look." *San Francisco Examiner and Chronicle,* January 17, pp. A1, A20.
Hare, A. Paul
  1981 "Group Size." *American Behavioral Scientist,* May/June, pp. 695–708.
Hargrove, Barbara
  1980 "Evil Eyes and Religious Choices." *Society,* March/April, pp. 20–24.
Haring, Douglas Gilbert
  1967 "Japanese Character in the Twentieth Century." *The Annals of the American Academy of Political and Social Science* 370(March):133–42.
Harris, Chauncy D., and Edward L. Ullman
  1945 "The Nature of Cities." *The Annals of the American Academy of Political and Social Science* 242:12.
Harris, Marvin
  1977 *Cannibals and Kings: The Origins of Cultures.* New York: Random House.
Hartshorne, Thomas L.
  1971 "An Introduction to National Character." In *Forging American Character,* ed. James W. Hall. New York: Holt, Rinehart and Winston.
Hauser, Robert M., and David L. Featherman
  1977 *The Process of Stratification: Trends and Analyses.* New York: Academic.
Havighurst, Robert, and Bernice Neugarten
  1968 *Society and Education.* Boston: Allyn & Bacon.
Heer, David
  1966 "Economic Development and Fertility." *Demography* 3:423–44.
Heisse, David R.
  1981 "Foreword." *Sociological Methods & Research,* May, pp. 395–96.
Helfrich, Harold, Ed.
  1970 *The Environmental Crisis.* New Haven, Conn.: Yale University Press.
Hennessey, Bernard
  1975 *Public Opinion.* North Scituate, Mass.: Duxbury.
Higginbotham, A. Leon
  1978 *In the Matter of Color.* New York: Oxford University Press.

Hilst, Glenn
  1970 "Pollution: Another Dimension of Urbanization." In *Toward a National Urban Policy,* ed. Daniel P. Moynihan. New York: Basic Books.
Hirschi, Travis, and Hanan Selvin
  1967 *Delinquency Research.* Glencoe, Ill.: Free Press.
Hobbes, Thomas
  [1651] *Leviathan.* New York: Collier Books, Macmillan.
  1962
Hobsbawm, E. J.
  1967 *Laboring Men: Studies in the History of Labour.* Garden City, N.Y.: Doubleday.
Hochban, Jacquelyn
  1981 "Serving Public Needs through Nonprofit Organizations." *American Behavioral Scientist,* March/April, pp. 545–72.
Hodge, Robert, Paul Siegel, and Peter Rossi
  1964 "Occupational Prestige in the United States, 1925–63." *American Journal of Sociology* 60:286–302.
Hoffer, Eric
  1958 *The True Believer.* New York: New American Library.
Hollingshead, August
  1949 *Elmstown's Youth.* New York: Wiley.
Hollingshead, A. B., and F. C. Redlich
  1958 *Social Class and Mental Illness.* New York: Wiley.
Holmes, Thomas, and Richard Rahe
  1967 "The Social Readjustment Scale: A Comparative Study of Negro, Mexican, and White Americans." *Journal of Psychosomatic Research* 11:213–18.
Holsti, Ole
  1969 *Content Analysis for the Social Sciences and Humanities.* Reading, Mass.: Addison-Wesley.
Homans, George
  1961 *Social Behavior: Its Elementary Forms.* New York: Harcourt, Brace & World.
  1971 "Reply to Blain." *Sociological Inquiry* 41(Winter):19–25.
Hopson, Janet
  1976 "A Plea for a Mundane Mollusk." *New York Times Magazine,* November 14, pp. 58–74.
Horowitz, Irving Louis
  1967 *The Rise and Fall of Project Camelot.* Cambridge, Mass: M.I.T. Press.
Horton, Paul, and Gerald Leslie
  1974 *The Sociology of Social Problems.* 5th ed. Englewood Cliffs, N.J.: Prentice-Hall.
  1978 *The Sociology of Social Problems.* 6th ed. Englewood Cliffs, N.J.: Prentice-Hall.
Hoult, Thomas
  1974 *Sociology for a New Day.* New York: Random House.
Howell, Joseph
  1973 *Hard Living on Clay Street.* New York: Doubleday.

Humphreys, Laud
1970   *Tearoom Trade: Impersonal Sex in Public Places.* Chicago: Aldine.
Hunter, Albert
1980   "Why Chicago?" *American Behavioral Scientist,* December, pp. 215–27.
Hunter, Floyd
1953   *Community Power Structure.* Chapel Hill, N.C.: University of North Carolina Press.
Hyman, Herbert
1972   *Secondary Analysis of Sample Surveys: Principles, Procedures, and Potentialities.* New York: Wiley.
Hyman, Herbert, and John Reed
1969   "Black Matriarchy Reconsidered: Evidence from Secondary Analysis of Sample Surveys." *Public Opinion Quarterly* 33:346–54.
James, William
1890   *Principles of Psychology,* vol. 1. New York: Holt.
Jencks, Christopher, et al.
1973   *Inequality: A Reassessment of the Effect of Family and Schooling in America.* New York: Harper & Row.
Jennings, J. Kent, and Richard Niemi
1975   "Continuity and Change in Political Orientations: A Longitudinal Study of Two Generations." In *The Irony of Democracy,* ed. Thomas Dye and L. Harmon Ziegler. North Scituate, Mass.: Duxbury.
Jensen, Arthur
1969   "How Much Can We Boost IQ and Scholastic Achievement?" *Harvard Educational Review* 39:1–123.
Johnson, John M.
1981   "Program Enterprise and Official Cooptation in the Battered Women's Shelter Movement." *American Behavioral Scientist,* July/August, pp. 827–842.
Johnson, Norris, and William Feinberg
1977   "A Computer Simulation of the Emergence of Consensus in Crowds." *American Sociological Review* 42:505–521.
Jones, H. E.
1946   "Environmental Influences on Mental Development." In *Manual of Child Psychology,* ed. L. Carmichael. New York: Wiley, p. 622.
Kalven, Harry, Jr., and Hans Zeisel
1966   *The American Jury.* Boston: Little, Brown.
1976   "Jury." *Encyclopedia Britannica,* vol. 10, pp. 360–62.
Kamin, Leon J.
1974   *The Science and Politics of IQ.* New York: Wiley.
Karlins, Marvin, Thomas Coffman, and Gary Walters
1969   "On the Fading of Social Stereotypes: Studies in Three Generations of College Students." *Journal of Personality and Social Psychology* 19:1–16.
Kasarda, John D., and Robert L. Lineberry
1980   "People, Production, and Power." *American Behavioral Scientist,* December, pp. 157–76.

Kassebaum, Gene
1974   *Delinquency and Social Policy.* Englewood Cliffs, N.J.: Prentice-Hall.
Katz, D., and K. W. Braly
1933   "Racial Stereotypes of 100 College Students." *Journal of Abnormal and Social Psychology* 28:280–90.
Katz, Elihu, and Paul Lazarsfeld
1955   *Personal Influence.* New York: Free Press.
Kempe, C. H., et al.
1962   "The Battered Child Syndrome." *Journal of the American Medical Association,* p. 181.
Kilday, Gregg
1975   "Happy Endings—Have They All Vanished into the Sunset? In *Mass Media and Society,* ed. Alan Wells. Palo Alto, Calif.: Mayfield.
Killian, Lewis M.
1981   "The Sociologists Look at the Cuckoo's Nest: The Misuse of Ideal Types." *The American Sociologist,* November, pp. 230–239.
Kinsey, Alfred C., et al.
1948   *Sexual Behavior in the Human Male.* Philadelphia: Saunders.
1953   *Sexual Behavior in the Human Female.* Philadelphia: Saunders.
Kleck, Gary
1981   "Racial Discrimination in Criminal Sentencing: A Critical Evaluation of the Evidence with Additional Evidence of the Death Penalty." *American Sociological Review,* December, pp. 783–805.
Kluckhohn, Florence, and Fred Strodtbeck
1961   *Variations in Value Orientations.* Evanston, Ill.: Row, Peterson.
Kohlberg, Lawrence, and Card Gilligan
1971   "The Adolescent as a Philosopher: The Discovery of the Self in a Postconventional World." *Daedalus* 100:1051–86.
Kolbe, Richard, and Joseph C. LaVoie
1981   "Sex-Role Stereotyping in Preschool Children's Picture Books." *Social Psychology Quarterly,* December, pp. 369–74.
Kolko, Gabriel
1962   *Wealth and Power in America.* New York: Praeger.
Komarovsky, Mirra
1962   *Blue-Collar Marriage.* New York: Random House.
Kornhauser, William
1959   *The Politics of Mass Society.* Glencoe, Ill.: Free Press.
1966   " 'Power Elite' or 'Veto Groups'?" In *Class, Status, and Power,* ed. Reinhard Bendix and Seymour Martin Lipset. New York: Free Press.
Kottak, Conrad
1978   *Anthropology.* New York: Random House.
Kramer, Paul, and Frederick L. Holborn, Eds.
1970   *The City in American Life.* New York: Putnam.

Kuhn, M. H., and T. S. McPartland
1954 "An Empirical Investigation of Self-Attitudes." *American Sociological Review* 19:68–76.

Kuhn, Thomas
1970 *The Structure of Scientific Revolutions.* Chicago: University of Chicago Press.

Ladd, Everett
1978 "Left, Right, or Center: Which Way Are We Going?" *Public Opinion,* September/October, pp. 33–40.

Ladd, Everett C., and G. Donald Ferree
1981 "Were the Pollsters Really Wrong?" *Public Opinion,* January, pp. 13–20.

LaFree, Gary D.
1981 "Official Reactions to Social Problems: Police Decisions in Sexual Assault Cases." *Social Problems,* June, pp. 582–94.

Lamb, Rosemarie Wittman
1981 "The New Feminism." *San Francisco Chronicle,* December 22, pp. 17–19.

Lancashire, David
1981 "The Genie Escapes." *Toronto Globe and Mail,* reprinted in *World Press Review,* August, pp. 37–38.

Landau, N. J., and P. G. Rheingold
1971 *The Environmental Law Handbook.* New York: Ballantine.

Landecker, Werner S.
1964 "Group." In *A Dictionary of the Social Sciences,* ed. Julius Gould and William L. Kolb. New York: Free Press, pp. 295–97.

Lao Tzu
[c. 500 *The Way and Its Power,* trans. Arthur Waley. Lon-
B.C.] don: G. Allen; New York: Barnes & Noble.

Lapham, Lewis
1977 "The Energy Debacle," *Harper's,* August, pp. 58–74.

Lappé, Frances Moore, and Joseph Collins
1977 *Food First: Beyond the Myth of Scarcity.* Boston: Houghton Mifflin.

Lazarsfeld, Paul, Bernard Berelson, and Hazel Gaudet
1944 *The People's Choice.* New York: Columbia University Press.

Le Bon, Gustave
[1895] *The Crowd.* New York: Viking.
1960

Lee, Dinah
1981 "China Faces New Problems." *South,* June, pp. 17–19.

Lemert, Edwin
1951 *Social Pathology.* New York: McGraw-Hill.

Lenski, Gerhard
1966 *Power and Privilege.* New York: McGraw-Hill.

Lenski, Gerhard, and Jean Lenski
1978 *Human Societies: An Introduction to Macrosociology.* New York: McGraw-Hill.

Lenzer, Gertrud, Ed.
1975 *Auguste Comte and Positivism: The Essential Writing.* New York: Harper & Row.

Leon, Joseph, and Patricia Steinhoff
1975 "Catholics' Use of Abortion." *Sociological Analysis* 36:125–36.

Leonard, Jonathan A.
1980 "Danger: Nuclear War," *Harvard Magazine,* November/December, 21–25.

Lerner, Daniel
1964 *The Passing of Traditional Society: Modernizing the Middle East.* New York: Free Press.

Leslie, Gerald R.
1982 *The Family in Social Context.* New York: Oxford University Press.

Levinen, R. A., and D. T. Campbell
1972 *Ethnocentrism: Theories of Conflict, Ethnic Attitudes and Group Behavior.* New York: Wiley.

Levitin, Teresa, Robert Quinn, and Graham Staines
1971 "Sex Discrimination Against the American Working Woman." Report of the Institute for Social Research, University of Michigan.

Lieberman, Seymour
1963 "The Effects of Change in Roles on the Attitudes of Role Occupants." In *Personality and Social System,* ed. Neil Smelser and William Smelser. New York: Wiley, pp. 264–79.

Lightbourne, Robert, Jr., and Susheela Singh
1982 *The World Fertility Survey: Charting Global Childbearing.* Washington, D.C.: Population Reference Bureau.

Likert, Rensis
1961 *New Patterns of Management.* New York: McGraw-Hill
1967 *The Human Organization.* New York: McGraw-Hill.

Likert, Rensis, and Jane Likert
1976 *New Ways of Managing Conflict.* New York: McGraw-Hill.

Link, Bruce
1982 "Mental Patient Status, Work, and Income: An Examination of the Effects of a Psychiatric Label." *American Sociological Review,* April, pp. 202–215.

Linton, Ralph
1936 *The Study of Man.* New York: Appleton-Century.

Lipman-Blumen, Jean, and Ann R. Tickameyer
1975 "Sex-Roles in Transition: A Ten-Year Perspective." *Annual Review of Sociology,* pp. 297–337.

Lipset, Seymour M.
1963 *The First New Nation: The United States in Historical and Comparative Perspective.* New York: Basic Books.
1968 *Revolution and Counterrevolution: Change and Persistence in Social Structures.* New York: Basic Books.
1980 "Taking Stock of Business: Part Two." *Public Opinion,* June/July, pp. 22–29.

Literary Digest
    1936a "Landon, 1,292,669: Roosevelt, 972,897," October 31, p. 5–6.
    1936b "What Went Wrong with the Polls?" November 14, pp. 7–8.

Lofland, John
    1966 *Doomsday Cult.* Englewood Cliffs, N.J.: Prentice-Hall.

Lofland, John, and Rodney Stark
    1965 "On Becoming a World-Saver: A Theory of Conversion to a Deviant Perspective." *American Sociological Review* 30:862–75.

Lofton, Willis
    1957 "Northern Labor and the Negro during the Civil War." In *Collective Behavior*, ed. Ralph Turner and Lewis Killian. Englewood Cliffs, N.J.: Prentice-Hall.

Lombroso, Cesare
    1911 *Criminal Man*, ed. Gina Lombroso Ferrero. New York: Putnam.

Long, J. Scott
    1978 "Productivity and Academic Position in the Scientific Career." *American Sociological Review* 44:889–908.

Long, J. Scott, and Robert McGinnis
    1981 "Organizational Context and Scientific Productivity." *American Sociological Review*, August, pp. 422–442.

Lopez, Barry
    1978 "The American Indian Mind." *Quest* 2(5):109–124.

Loft, Joseph
    1969 *Of Human Interaction.* Palo Alto, Calif.: National.

Lundberg, Ferdinand
    1968 *The Rich and the Super-Rich.* Secaucus, N.J.: Lyle Stuart.

Lynd, Robert, and Helen Lynd
    1929 *Middletown.* New York: Harcourt, Brace.
    1937 *Middletown in Transition.* New York: Harcourt, Brace.

Maccoby, E. E., and C. N. Jacklin
    1972 "Sex Differences in Intellectual Functioning." Invitational Conference on Testing Problems, New York City, Fall.

Maccoby, Michael
    1967 "On Mexican National Character." *The Annals of the American Academy of Political and Social Science* 370(March):63–73.

Marcuse, Herbert
    1964 *One-Dimensional Man.* Boston: Beacon.

Marini, Margaret Mooney
    1981 "Effects of the Timing of Marriage and First Birth on Fertility." *Journal of Marriage and the Family.* February, pp. 27–46.

Marks, Stephen
    1977 "Multiple Roles and Role Strain: Some Notes on Human Energy, Time and Commitment." *American Sociological Review* 42:921–36.

Martin, James
    1981 *Telematic Society: A Challenge for Tomorrow.* Englewood Cliffs, N.J.: Prentice-Hall.

Martindale, Don
    1967 "The Sociology of National Character." *The Annals of the American Academy of Political and Social Science* 370(March):30–35.

Marty, Martin
    1980 "Fundamentalism Reborn." *Saturday Review,* May, pp. 290–293.

Marx, Karl
    [1843] *Selected Writings in Sociology and Social Philosophy*,
    1956 ed. T. B. Bottomore and Maximilien Rubel. New York: McGraw-Hill.

Masaoka, Mike
    1972 "The Evacuation of the Japanese Americans and Its Aftermath." In *Minority Problems*, ed. Arnold Rose and Caroline Rose. New York: Harper & Row.

Masters, William H., and Virginia E. Johnson
    1966 *Human Sexual Response.* Boston: Little, Brown.

Maturana, Humberto R.
    1980 *Autopoiesis and Cognition, The Realization of Living.* Dordricht, Holland: D. Reidel.

McCandless, Boyd R.
    1969 "Childhood Socialization." In *Handbook of Socialization Theory and Research*, ed. D. A. Goslin. Chicago: Rand McNally, chap. 19.

McCarthy, John, and Mayer Zald
    1973 *The Trend of Social Movements in America.* Morristown, N.J.: General Learning Press.

McClosky, Herbert, Paul Hoffman, and Rosemary O'Hara
    1960 "Issue Conflict and Consensus among Party Leaders and Followers." *American Political Science Review*, pp. 406–427.

McGregor, Douglas
    1960 *The Human Side of Enterprise.* New York: McGraw-Hill.

McLanahan, Sara S., Nancy V. Wedemeyer, and Tina Adelberg
    1981 "Network Structure, Social Support, and Psychological Well-Being in the Single-Parent Family." *Journal of Marriage and the Family*, August, pp. 601–612.

McVeigh, Frank (with Arthur Shostak)
    1978 *Modern Social Problems.* New York: Holt, Rinehart and Winston.

Mead, George Herbert
    1934 *Mind, Self, and Society*, ed. Charles Morris. Chicago: University of Chicago Press.

Mead, Margaret
    [1928] *Coming of Age in Samoa.* New York: New American
    1949 Library.

1935   *Sex and Temperament in Three Primitive Societies.* New York: Morrow.

Meadows, Dennis, et al.
[1973]   *The Dynamics of Growth in a Finite World.* Cam-
1978   bridge, Mass.: Wright-Allen.

Meadows, Donella, et al.
1972   *The Limits to Growth.* New York: Universe Books.

Merton, Robert K.
1957a   *Social Theory and Social Structure.* New York: Free Press.
1957b   "The Role Set: Problems in Sociological Theory." *British Journal of Sociology* 8:106–120.
1957c   "Priorities in Scientific Discovery: A Chapter in the Sociology of Science." *American Sociological Review* 22:635–59.
1968   *Social Theory and Social Structure.* New York: Free Press.
1976   "Discrimination and the American Creed." In *Sociological Ambivalence and Other Essays.* New York: Free Press, pp. 189–216.

Merton, Robert, et al.
1957   *The Student-Physician.* Cambridge, Mass.: Harvard University Press.

Michels, Robert
[1911]   *Political Parties.* New York: Free Press.
1967

Milgram, Stanley, Leonard Bickman, and Lawerence Berkowitz
1969   "Note on the Drawing Power of Crowds of Different Size." *Journal of Personality and Social Psychology* 13(2):79–82.

Mills, C. Wright
1956   *The Power Elite.* New York: Oxford University Press.
1958   *The Causes of World War Three.* New York: Simon and Schuster.
1959   *The Sociological Imagination.* London: Oxford University Press.

Miner, Horace
1956   "Body Ritual among the Nacirema." *American Anthropologist* 58:503–507.

Mintz, Beth, and Michael Schwartz
1981   "Interlocking Directorates and Interest Group Foundation." *American Sociological Review,* December, pp. 851–69.

Mitford, Jessica
1973   *Kind and Usual Punishment.* New York: Knopf.

Miyamoto, S. Frank, and Sanford Dornbusch
1956   "A Test of Interactionist Hypotheses of Self-Conception." *American Journal of Sociology* 61:399–403.

Moffat, Samuel
1977   "Kaiser-Permanente: Prepaid Care Comes of Age." *1978 Medical and Health Annual.* Chicago: Encyclopedia Britannica, pp. 125–137.

Mooney, J.
1939   *The 1870 Ghost Dance.* Berkeley: University of California Press.

Moore, Wilbert
1963   *Social Change.* Englewood Cliffs, N.J.: Prentice-Hall.

Morawetz, David
1977   *Twenty-Five Years of Economic Development,* 1950 to 1975. Baltimore, Md.: The Johns Hopkins University Press.

Morris, Charles, Ed.
1934   *Mind, Self, and Society.* Chicago: University of Chicago Press.

Moskowitz, Milton, Michael Katz, and Robert Levering, Eds.
1980   *Everybody's Business: An Almanac.* New York: Harper & Row.

Moursand, Janet
1973   *Evaluation: An Introduction to Research Design.* Monterey, Calif.: Brooks/Cole.

Murdock, George P.
1935   "Comparative Data on the Division of Labor by Sex." *Social Forces* 15:551–53.

Murstein, Bernard I.
1980   "Mate Selection in the 1970s." *Journal of Marriage and the Family,* November, pp. 777–92.

Mussen, Paul H., John J. Conger, and Jerome Kagan
1974   *Child Development and Personality.* New York: Harper & Row.

Nadkarni, Vithal C.
1981   "The Coming Water Crisis." *Illustrated Weekly* (Bombay), reprinted in *World Press Review,* September, p. 55.

Nakamura, Hajime
1974   *Ways of Thinking of Eastern Peoples.* Honolulu: University of Hawaii Press.

Nam, Charles, Ed.
1968   *Population and Society.* Boston: Houghton Mifflin.

Narain, Dhirendra
1967   "Indian National Character in the Twentieth Century." *The Annals of the American Academy of Political and Social Science* 370(March):124–32.

Nasatir, David
1967   "Social Science Data Libraries." *The American Sociologist* 2:207–212.

National Academy of Sciences
1977   *Supporting Papers: World Food and Nutrition Study.* 5 vols. Washington, D.C.

Niebuhr, H. Richard
1960   *The Social Sources of Denominationalism.* New York: Meridian.

Nyere, Julius
1979   "A Trade Union for the Poor," *Bulletin of Atomic Scientists,* July 17.

Ogburn, William
  1922   *Social Change*. New York: Viking.
Olsen, Lynn M.
  1974   *Women in Mathematics*. Cambridge, Mass.: M.I.T. Press.
Osmond, Marie Withers
  1980   "Cross-Societal Family Research: A Macrosociological Overview of the Seventies." *Journal of Marriage and the Family*, November, pp. 995–1016.
Otto, Herbert
  1974   "Communes: The Alternative Life-Style." *In Social Realities*, ed. George Witzer. Boston: Allyn & Bacon.
Ouchi, William G.
  1981   *Theory Z*. Reading, Mass.: Addison-Wesley.
Palazzolo, Charles S.
  1981   *Small Groups: An Introduction*. New York: D. Van Nostrand
Park, Robert
  1926   "The Urban Community as a Spatial Pattern and a Moral Order." In *The Urban Community*, ed. Ernest Burgess. Chicago: University of Chicago Press.
Parker, Marden G., Dennis G. Hogdson, and Terry L. McCoy
  1982   *Population in the Global Arena*. New York: Holt, Rinehart and Winston.
Parkinson, C. Northcote
  1957   *Parkinson's Law*. Boston: Houghton Mifflin.
Parsons, Talcott
  [1940]   "An Analytical Approach to the Theory of Social Stratification."
  1954   *American Journal of Sociology* 45:841–62. Reprinted in Talcott Parsons, *Essays in Sociological Theory*. Glencoe, Ill.: Free Press, chap. 4.
  1951   *The Social System*. New York: Free Press.
  1957   "The Distribution of Power in American Society." *World Politics* 10:123–43.
Parsons, Talcott, and Robert Bales
  1955   *Family, Socialization and Interaction Process*. Glencoe, Ill.: Free Press.
Perrow, Charles B.
  1970   *Organizational Analysis: A Sociological View*. Belmont, Calif.: Wadsworth.
  1979   *Complex Organizations*. Glenview, Ill.: Scott, Foresman.
Peter, Laurence, and Raymond Hull
  1969   *The Peter Principle*. New York: Morrow.
Petersen, Roger
  1980   "Social Class, Social Learning, and Wife Abuse." *Social Service Review*, September.
Piaget, Jean
  1954   *The Construction of Reality in the Child*, trans. Margaret Cook. New York: Basic Books.
  1965   *The Moral Judgment of the Child*, trans. Marjorie Gabain. New York: Free Press.

Pirsig, Robert
  1975   *Zen and the Art of Motorcycle Maintenance*. New York: Ballantine.
Piven, Frances Fox, and Richard A. Cloward
  1977   *Poor People's Movements: Why They Succeed, How They Fail*. New York: Pantheon.
Platt, John
  1973   "Social Traps." *American Psychologist* 28(8):641–51.
Plissner, Martin, and Warren Mitofsky
  1981   "Political Elites." *Public Opinion*, October/November, pp. 47–50.
Poloma, Margaret, and T. Neal Garland.
  1972   "The Married Professional Woman: A Study in the Tolerance of Domestication." In *Sociology, Students and Society*, ed. Jerome Rabow. Pacific Palisades, Calif.: Goodyear.
Ponsonby, Arthur
  1930   *Falsehood in Wartime*. London: G. Allen.
Population Reference Bureau
  1979   "World Population Data Sheet" (poster). Washington, D.C.
  1982   "World Population Data Sheet" (poster). Washington, D.C.
Porter, John
  1967   "Canadian Character in the Twentieth Century." *The Annals of the American Academy of Political and Social Science* 370(March):48–56.
President's Commission on Law Enforcement and Administration of Justice
  1967   *The Challenge of Crime in a Free Society*. Washington, D.C.
Price-Bonham, Sharon, and Jack O. Balswick
  1980   "The Noninstitutions: Divorce, Desertion, and Remarriage." *Journal of Marriage and the Family*, November, pp. 959–72.
Public Opinion
  1978a   "Homosexuality Today." July/August, p. 8
  1978b   "Left, Right, or Center: Which Way Are We Going?" September/October, pp. 33–39.
  1979a   "The Leisure Mass." August/September, pp. 24–27.
  1979b   "Religious Faith in America." March/May, pp. 32–39.
  1980a   "Women in the 70's." December/January, pp. 33–34.
  1980b   "Social Issues." August/September, pp. 37–39.
  1980c   "Families in the 70's." December/January, pp. 30–32.
  1980d   "The 70's: For Every Yes, A No." December/January, pp. 20–26.
  1981a   "Examining Elites." October/November, p. 29.
  1981b   "The State of Race Relations—1981." April/May, pp. 32–40.

1981c "Moments of Partisan Change." April/May, pp. 29–31.

1981d "Are Public Schools Making the Grade?" October/November, pp. 21–26.

1981e "America's Evangelicals: Genesis or Evolution?" April/May, pp. 22–27.

1981f "Politics from the Pulpit." April/May, p. 21

1981g "Looking at Television." October/November, pp. 35–38.

1982a "Americans Volunteer: A Profile." February/March, pp. 21–25.

1982b "Environmental Update." February/March, pp. 32–38.

Pugh, D. S., et al.
1968 "Dimensions of Organization Structure." *Administrative Science Quarterly* 13:65–105.

Queen, Stuart, Robert Habenstein, and John Adams
1974 *The Family in Various Cultures.* Philadelphia: Lippincott.

Quigg, Chaterine Thiel
1982 "The Nuclear Garbage Mess." *This World,* January 10, pp. 8–26.

Quinn, Bowden
1982 "Zimbabwe Turns to 'Practical' Schools to Keep Youths on the Farm." *Christian Science Monitor,* April 20, p. 12

Quinney, Richard
1974 *Criminology: Analysis and Critique of Crime in the United States.* Boston: Little, Brown.

Radelet, Michael L.
1981 "Racial Characteristic and the Imposition of the Death Penalty." American Sociological Review, vol. 46, December, pp. 918–27.

Rappaport, Roy
1969 "Ritual Regulation of Environmental Relations among a New Guinea People." In *Environmental and Cultural Behavior,* ed. Andrew Vayda. Garden City, N.Y.: Natural History Press.

Reid, Sue Titus
1982 *Crime and Criminology.* New York: Holt, Rinehart and Winston.

Reilly, Mary Ellen
1976 "The Family." In *Population Profiles.* Washington, Conn.: Center for Information on America.

Reinow, R., and L. T. Reinow
1967 *Moment in the Sun.* New York: Dial.

Reiss, Albert, Jr.
1971 *The Police and the Public.* New Haven, Conn.: Yale University Press.

Reiss, Albert, Jr., Otis Dudley Duncan, Paul Hatt, and Cecil North
1961 *Occupations and Social Status.* New York: Free Press.

Richey, Russell, and Donald Jones, Eds.
1974 *American Civil Religion.* New York: Harper & Row.

Richter, Maurice, Jr.
1972 *Science as a Cultural Process.* Cambridge, Mass.: Schenkman.

Riesman, David
1967 "Some Questions about the Study of American National Character in the Twentieth Century." *The Annals of the American Academy of Political and Social Science* 370(March):36–47.

Riesman, David, Nathan Glazer, and Reuel Denney
1953 *The Lonely Crowd: A Study of the Changing American Character.* Garden City, N.Y.: Doubleday.

Rifkin, Jeremy (with Ted Howard)
1980 *Entropy.* New York: Viking.

Ritzer, George, Ed.
1974 *Social Realities.* Boston: Allyn & Bacon.

Roethlisberger, F. J., and W. J. Dickson
1939 *Management and the Worker.* Cambridge, Mass.: Harvard University Press.

Rogoff, Natalie
1961 "Local Social Structure and Educational Selection." In *Education, Economy, and Society,* ed. A. H. Halsey et al. New York: Free Press.

Rokeach, Milton
1973 *The Nature of Human Values.* New York: Free Press.

Rose, Arnold, and Caroline Rose, Eds.
1972 *Minority Problems.* New York: Harper & Row.

Rosenberg, Morris
1965 *Society and the Adolescent Self-Image.* Princeton, N.J.: Princeton University Press.

Rosenthal, Robert, and Lenore Jacobson
1968 *Pygmalion in the Classroom.* New York: Holt, Rinehart and Winston.

Rousseau, Jean Jacques
[1750] "Discourse on the Origin and Foundation of
1964 Inequality of Mankind." In *The First and Second Discourses,* trans. Rodger Masters and Judith Masters. New York: St. Martin's.

[1762] *The Social Contract,* trans. Willmoore Kendall.
1954 Chicago: Regnery.

Rubinstein, Eli A.
1978 "Television and the Young Viewer." *American Scientist,* November, pp. 203–211.

Russell, Bertrand
1938 *Power: A New Social Analysis.* New York: Norton.

Sanderson, Dwight
1959 "Group." In *Dictionary of Sociology,* ed. Henry Pratt Fairchild. Ames, Iowa: Littlefield, Adams, p. 133.

Sanger, Margaret
1938 *An Autobiography.* New York: Norton.

Sapir, Edward
1960 *Culture, Language and Personality: Selected Essays.* Berkeley: University of California Press.

Scanzoni, Letha, and John Scanzoni
1976 *Men, Women, and Change.* New York: McGraw-Hill.

Schafer, Robert B., and Patricia M. Keith
  1981 "Equity in Marital Roles across the Family Life Cycle." *Journal of Marriage and the Family*, May, pp. 359–67.

Scheff, Thomas
  1966 *Being Mentally Ill: A Sociological Theory*. Chicago: Aldine.

Schell, Jonathan
  1982 *The Fate of the Earth*. New York: Knopf.

Schmitt, Robert
  1966 "Density, Health and Social Disorganization." *Journal of the American Institute of Planners* 32: 38–40.

Schmitt, Robert, Lynn Zane, and Sharon Nichi
  1978 "Density, Health, and Social Disorganization Revisited." *Journal of the American Institute of Planners*, April, pp. 209–211.

Schon, Donald
  1971 *Beyond the Stable State*. New York: Random House.

Schramm, Wilbur, and Janet Alexander
  1975 "Survey of Broadcasting: Structure, Control, Audience." In *Issues in Broadcasting*, ed. Ted Smythe and George Mastroianni, Palo Alto, Calif.: Mayfield.

Schulz, James H.
  1976 *The Economics of Aging*. Belmont, Calif.: Wadsworth.

Schur, Edwin
  1965 *Crimes without Victims*. Englewood Cliffs, N.J.: Prentice-Hall.

Schur, Edwin, and Hugo Adam Bedau
  1974 *Victimless Crimes: Two Sides of a Controversy*. Englewood Cliffs, N.J.: Prentice-Hall.

Schwartz, Tony
  1974 *The Response Chord*. Garden City, N.Y.: Anchor Books, Doubleday.

Sells, Lucy
  1982 "Leverage for Equal Opportunity." In *Women and Minorities in Science: Strategies for Increasing Participation*, ed. Sheila M. Humphreys. Washington, D.C.: American Association for the Advancement of Science.

Selznick, Gertrude Jaeger, and Stephen Steinberg
  1969 *The Tenacity of Prejudice*. New York: Harper & Row.

Selznick, Philip
  [1952] *The Organizational Weapon*. Glencoe, Ill.: Free Press.
  1960

Shaull, Richard
  1970 "Foreword." In Paulo Freire, *Pedagogy of the Oppressed*. New York: Seabury, pp. 9–15.

Shaw, Marvin E.
  1976 *Group Dynamics: The Psychology of Small Group Behavior*. New York: McGraw-Hill.

Sheley, Joseph F.
  1979 *Understanding Crime: Concepts, Issues, Decisions*, Belmont, Calif.: Wadsworth.

Sherif, Muzafer
  1936 *The Psychology of Social Norms*. New York: Harper & Row.

Shibutani, Tamotsu
  1966 *Improvised News: A Sociological Study of Rumor*. Indianapolis, Ind.: Bobbs-Merrill.

Shibutani, Tamotsu, and Kian Kwan
  1965 *Ethnic Stratification: A Comparative View*. New York: Macmillan.

Shils, Edward, and Morris Janowitz
  1948 "Cohesion and Disintegration in the Wehrmacht." *Public Opinion Quarterly* 12:280–94.

Shockley, William
  1967 *Proceedings of the National Academy of Sciences* 57:1771.

Silberman, Matthew
  1976 "Toward a Theory of Criminal Deterrence." *American Sociological Review* 41:442–61.

Silva, Neville de
  1980 "Alarms around the Gulf." *Ceylon Daily News*, reprinted in *World Press Review*, May, pp. 39–40.

Simmel, Georg
  [1908a] *Conflict and the Web of Group Affiliation*, trans, Kurt
  1955 Wolff. Glencoe, Ill.: Free Press.

  [1908b] *Sociology*, trans. and ed. Kurt Wolff. *The Sociology*
  1964 *of Georg Simmel*. New York: Free Press.

Simmons, J. L.
  1965 "Public Stereotypes of Deviants." *Social Problems* 13(Fall):223–32.
  1969 *Deviants*. Berkeley, Calif.: Glendessary.

Sjoberg, Gideon
  1965 "The Origin and Evolution of Cities." In *Cities*, ed. the Editors of *Scientific American*. New York: Knopf.

Skinner, B. F.
  1953 *Science and Human Behavior*. New York: Macmillan.

Smelser, Neil
  1962 *Theory of Collective Behavior*. New York: Free Press.

Smith, Douglas A., and Christy A. Visher
  1981 "Street-Level Justice: Situational Determinants of Police Arrest Decisions." *Social Problems*, December, pp. 167–77.

Smith, Huston
  1958 *The Religions of Man*. New York: Harper & Row.

Snider, Arthur J.
  1978 "DNA Research and the Law." Encyclopedia Britannica *Book of the Year*. Chicago: Encyclopedia Britannica, pp. 507–509.

Sorkin, Alan A.
  1978 "The Economic Basis of Indian Life." *The Annals of the American Academy of Political and Social Science*, March, pp. 1–39.

Sorokin, Pitirim
  [1937– *Social and Cultural Dynamics*. 4 vols. Englewood

1941]   Cliffs, N.J.: Bedminster Press.
1962
1967   "The Essential Characteristics of the Russian Nation in the Twentieth Century." *The Annals of the American Academy of Political and Social Science* 370(March):99–115.

Spengler, Oswald
1932   *The Decline of the West.* New York: Knopf.

Spitze, Glenna D., and Linda J. Waite
1981   "Wives' Employment: The Role of Husbands' Perceived Attitudes." *Journal of Marriage and the Family,* February, pp. 117–24.

Srole, Leo, et al.
1962   *Mental Health in the Metropolis.* New York: McGraw-Hill.

Stack, Carol B.
1974   *All Our Kin: Strategies for Survival in a Black Community.* New York: Harper & Row.

Stark, Rodney
1972   *Police Riots.* Belmont, Calif.: Wadsworth.

Stark, Rodney, William Sims Bainbridge, and Daniel P. Doyle
1979   "Cults of America: A Reconnaissance in Space and Time." *Sociological Analysis,* Winter, pp. 347–61.
1981   "Secularization and Cult Formation in the Jazz Age." *Journal for the Scientific Study of Religion,* December, pp. 360–73.

Stark, Rodney, and Charles Glock
1968   *American Piety: The Nature of Religious Commitment.* Berkeley: University of California Press.

Stark, Rodney, and Stephen Steinberg
1967   "It *Did* Happen Here: An Investigation of Political Anti-Semitism: Wayne, New Jersey, 1967." Berkeley: Survey Research Center, University of California.

Starr, Roger
1976   "Making New York Smaller." *New York Times Magazine,* November 14, pp. 32–33, 99–106.

Stouffer, Samuel
1962   *Social Research to Test Ideas.* New York: Free Press.

Stouffer, Samuel, et al.
1949   *The American Soldier,* vol. 1. Princeton, N.J.: Princeton University Press.

Strout, Richard
1978   "The Case of the Missing Half-Billion Earth People." *Christian Science Monitor,* October 31, p. 3.

Suczek, Barbara
1972   "The Curious Case of the 'Death' of Paul McCartney." *Urban Life and Culture* 1(1):61–76.

Sullerot, Evelyne
1974   *Women, Society and Change.* New York: McGraw-Hill.

Sullivan, Elizabeth.
1978   "Fading Forests." *The Inter-dependent* 5(September):3.

Sutherland, Edwin
1924   *Principles of Criminology.* Philadelphia: Lippincott.
1949   *White Collar Crime.* New York: Dryden.

Sykes, Gresham
1978   *Criminology.* New York: Harcourt Brace Jovanovich.

Szasz, Thomas
1961   *The Myth of Mental Illness.* New York: Hoeber-Harper.

Takeuchi, David
1974   "Grass in Hawaii: A Structural Constraints Approach." M.A. thesis, University of Hawaii.

Tanner, N., and A. Zihlman
1976   "Women in Evolution (Part 1): Innovation and Selection in Human Origins." *Signs,* Winter, pp. 585–608.

Taylor, Craig
1971   "The 'Battered Child': Individual Victim of Family Brutality." In *Social Problems Today: Dilemmas and Dissensus,* ed. Clifton Bryant. Philadelphia: Lippincott, pp. 210–16.

Theodorson, George A., and Achilles G. Theodorson
1969   *A Modern Dictionary of Sociology.* New York: Crowell.

Thomlinson, Ralph
1967   *Demographic Problems.* Belmont, Calif.: Dickenson.

Thompson, E. P.
1963   *The Making of the English Working Class.* New York: Vintage.

Thompson, George
[1886]   "The Evaluation of Public Opinion." In *Reader in*
1966   *Public Opinion and Communication,* ed. Bernard Berelson and Morris Janowitz. New York: Free Press.

Tillich, Paul
1952   *The Courage To Be.* New Haven, Conn.: Yale University Press.

Tilly, Charles, Louise Tilly, and Richard Tilly
1975   *The Rebellious Century.* Cambridge, Mass.: Harvard University Press.

Timberlake, Lloyd
1982   "Poland's Pollution Crisis." *New Scientist,* reprinted in *World Press Review,* January, p. 56.

Tobias, Sheila
1978   *Overcoming Math Anxiety.* New York: Norton.

Tocqueville, Alexis de
[1835,   *Democracy in America.* New York: Vintage Books.
1840]   Originally published in 2 vols.
1945

Toennies, Ferdinand
[1887]   *Community and Society,* trans. Charles Loomis. East
1957   Lansing: Michigan State University Press.
[1909]   *Custom: An Essay on Social Codes.* New York: Free
1961   Press.

Toffler, Alvin
1970   *Future Shock.* New York: Random House.

Toynbee, Arnold
1962–   *A Study of History.* 12 vols. New York: Oxford
1964   University Press.

Troeltsch, Ernst
[1931]   *The Social Teachings of the Christian Churches,* vols.
1960   1 and 2, trans. O. Wyon. New York: Harper &
Row.

Turner, John
1981   *The Ku Klux Klan: A History of Racism and Violence.*
Montgomery, Alabama: The Southern Poverty
Law Center.

Turner, Jonathan H.
1974   *The Structure of Sociological Theory.* Homewood,
Ill.: Dorsey.

Turner, Ralph, and Lewis Killian, Eds.
1972   *Collective Behavior.* Englewood Cliffs, N.J.: Prentice-Hall.

Tyler, Humphrey
1980   "Apartheid Switch: South African Call for 'Whites
Only' Homeland." *Christian Science Monitor,* July
14.

United Nations
1956   "The Past and Future Population of the World
and Its Continents." In *Demographic Analysis:
Selected Readings,* ed. Joseph Spengler and Otis
Dudley Duncan. Glencoe, Ill.: Free Press.
1974   *Demographic Yearbook, 1973.* New York: United
Nations.

U.S. Bureau of Census
1960   *Historical Statistics of the United States: Colonial Times
to 1957.* Washington, D.C.: U.S. Government
Printing Office.
1973   *Census of the Population. Vol. 1, Characteristics of the
Population. Pt. 1, United States Summary.* Washington, D.C.: U.S. Government Printing Office.
1975   *Statistical Abstract of the United States.* Washington, D.C.: U.S. Government Printing Office.
1976   *Bicentennial Statistics.* Washington, D.C.: U.S.
Government Printing Office.
1978a   *Statistical Abstract of the United States.* Washington, D.C.: U.S. Government Printing Office.
1978b   *Voting and Registration in the Election of November
1978.* Washington, D.C.: U.S. Government Printing Office, Series P–20, No. 332.
1979a   *Statistical Abstract of the United States.* Washington, D.C.: U.S. Government Printing Office.
1979b   *Money Income in 1977 of Families and Persons in the
United States.* Washington, D.C.: U.S. Government Printing Office, Series P–60, No. 118.
1979c   *Population Profile of the United States: 1978.* Washington, D.C.: U.S. Government Printing Office,
Series P–20, No. 336.
1979d   *Persons of Spanish Origin in the United States: March
1978.* Washington, D.C.: U.S. Government Print-
ing Office, Series P–20, No. 339.

1979e   *Educational Attainment in the United States: March
1977 and 1976.* Washington, D.C.: U.S. Government Printing Office, Series P–20, No. 314.
1979f   *The Social and Economic Status of the Black Population in the United States: An Historical View 1790–
1978.* Washington, D.C.: U.S. Government Printing Office, Series P–23, No. 80.
1980a   *Statistical Abstract of the United States.* Washington, D.C.: U.S. Government Printing Office.
1980b   *Selected Characteristics of Persons in Physical Science.*
Washington, D.C.: U.S. Government Printing
Office, Series P–23, No. 108.
1980c   *Social Indicators III.* Washington, D.C.: U.S. Government Printing Office.
1980d   *Persons of Spanish Origin in the United States: March
1979.* Washington, D.C.: U.S. Government Print-
ing Office, Series P–20, No. 354.
1981a   *Population of the United States: 1980.* Washington,
D.C.: U.S. Government Printing Office, Series
P–20, No. 363.
1981b   *Selected Characteristics of Persons in Life Science: 1978.*
Washington, D.C.: U.S. Government Printing
Office, Series P–23, No. 113.
1981c   *Population Profile of the United States, 1980.* Washington, D.C.: U.S. Government Printing Office,
Series P–20, No. 363.
1981d   *Money Income and Poverty Status of Families and Per-
sons in the United States: 1980.* Washington, D.C.:
U.S. Government Printing Office, Series P–60,
No. 127.
1981e   *Marital Status and Living Arrangements: March 1980.*
Washington, D.C.: U.S. Government Printing
Office, Series P–20, No. 365.
1981f   *Household and Family Characteristics: March 1980.*
Washington, D.C.: U.S. Government Printing
Office, Series P–20, No. 366.
1981g   *Farm Population in the United States: 1980.* Washington, D.C.: U.S. Government Printing Office,
Series P–27, No. 54.
1981h   *Money Income and Poverty Status of Families in the
United States: 1980.* Washington, D.C.: U.S. Government Printing Office, Series P–60, No. 127.
1981i   *Statistical Abstract of the United States.* Washington, D.C.: U.S. Government Printing Office (102d
edition).
1982a   *Voting and Registration in the Election of November
1980.* Washington, D.C.: U.S. Government Printing Office, Series P–20, No. 370.
1982b   *Characteristics of American Children and Youth: 1980.*
Washington, D.C.: U.S. Government Printing
Office, Series P–23, No. 114.

U.S. Bureau of Labor Statistics
1973   *Manpower Report to the President.* Washington, D.C.:
U.S. Government Printing Office.

1975a "Employment and Unemployment in 1974." *Monthly Labor Review*, February, pp. 3–14.
1975b "Educational Attainment of Workers, March 1974." *Monthly Labor Review*, February, pp. 64–69.
1975c *Directory of National Unions and Employee Associations*. Washington, D.C.: U.S. Government Printing Office.
1976 *Employment and Earnings*. Washington, D.C.: U.S. Government Printing Office, January, vol. 22, no. 7.
1979 *Employment and Earnings*. Washington, D.C.: U.S. Government Printing Office, June, vol. 26, no. 6.
1981a "Half the Nation's Children Have Working Mothers." USDL 81–522.
1981b *Monthly Labor Review*, July.
1981c *Monthly Labor Review*, April.
1982 *Monthly Labor Review*, January.

Vander Zanden, James
1972 *American Minority Problems*. New York: Ronald.
Van Dyke, Jon M.
1977 *Jury Selection Procedures*. Cambridge, Mass.: Ballinger.
Vanek, Joann
1980 "Work, Leisure, and Family Roles: Farm Households in the United States, 1920–1955." *Journal of Family History*, Winter, pp. 422–31.
Virtanen, Reino
1967 "French National Character in the Twentieth Century." *The Annals of the American Academy of Political and Social Science* 370(March)82–92.
Von Neumann, John, and Oskar Morgenstern
1947 *Theory of Games and Economic Behavior*. Princeton, N.J.: Princeton University Press.
Waegel, William B.
1981 "Case Routinization in Investigative Police Work." *Social Problems*, February, pp. 263–75.
Walbert, D. F.
1971 "The Effect of Jury Size on the Probability of Conviction: An Evaluation of *Williams v. Florida*." Ph.D. dissertation, University of Alabama.
Wallace, Walter
1971 *The Logic of Science in Sociology*. Chicago: Aldine-Atherton.
Wallechinsky, David, and Irving Wallace
1975 *The People's Almanac*. New York: Doubleday.
Wallerstein, Immanuel
1974 *The Modern World System*, New York: Academic Press.
1979 *The Capitalist World-Economy*, Cambridge: Cambridge University Press.
Ward, Russell
1977 "Aging Group Consciousness: Implications in an Older Sample." *Sociology and Social Research* 61:496–519.

Warren, Roland L.
1970 "The Good Community—What Would It Be?" *Journal of the Community Development Society* 1(1):14,23. Reprinted in *Sociology: Readings on Human Society*, ed. John E. Owen. Glenview, Ill.: Scott, Foresman, pp. 111–21.
Warner, W. Lloyd, and Paul Lunt
1941 *The Social Life of a Modern Community*. New Haven, Conn.: Yale University Press.
Warner W. Lloyd, et al.
1949 *Democracy in Jonesville*. New York: Harper & Row.
Watson, James
1968 *The Double Helix*. New York: New American Library.
Weber, Max
1951 *The Religion of China*, trans. Hans H. Gerth. Glencoe, Ill.: Free Press.
1952 *Ancient Judaism*. Glencoe, Ill.: Free Press.
1958 The Religion of India. Glencoe, Ill.: Free Press.
[1905] *The Protestant Ethic and the Spirit of Capitalism*, trans.
1958 Talcott Parsons. New York: Scribner.
[1922] *The Sociology of Religion*. Boston: Beacon.
1963
[1925a] *From Max Weber: Essays in Sociology*, trans. and ed.
1946 Hans Gerth and C. Wright Mills. New York: Oxford University Press.
[1925b] *The Theory of Social and Economic Organization*, ed.
1964 Talcott Parsons. New York: Free Press.
Webster, Murray J., and J. E. Driskell, Jr.
1978 "Status Generalization: A Review and Some New Data." *American Sociological Review* 43:220–36.
Weinberg, S. Kirson
1974 *Deviant Behavior and Social Control*. Dubuque, Iowa: Brown.
Weis, David, and Michael Slosnerick
1981 "Attitudes toward Sexual and Nonsexual Extramarital Involvements among a Sample of College Students." *Journal of Marriage and the Family*, May, pp. 349–58.
Weiss, Melford
1967 "Rebirth in the Airborne." *Transactions*, May. Reprinted in *Sociological Realities*, ed. Irving Louis Horowitz and Mary Symons Strong, pp. 195–97. New York: Harper & Row.
Weitzman, L. J., D. Eifler, E. Hokada, and C. Ross
1972 "Sex-role Socialization in Picture-books for Preschool Children." *American Journal of Sociology* 77:1125–50.
Welch, Charles E. III, and Paul C. Glick
1981 "The Incidence of Polygamy in Contemporary Africa: A Research Note." *Journal of Marriage and the Family*, February, pp. 191–93.
Wellborn, Stanley N.
1982 "Why More Americans Can't Cope." *This World*, May 23, pp. 12–14.

Wellman, Barry
  1979 "The Community Question: The Intimate Networks of East Yorkers." *American Journal of Sociology* 84:1201–31.
Wells, H. G.
  [1920] *The Outline of History.* Garden City, N.Y.:
  1961 Doubleday.
Wells, Richard H., and J. Steven Picou
  1981 *American Sociology: Theoretical and Methodological Structure.* Washington, D.C.: University Press of America.
Wernicke, Robert
  1974 *Human Behavior—The Family.* New York: Time-Life Books.
Westoff, Charles
  1972 "The Modernization of U.S. Contraceptive Practice." *Family Planning in Perspective* 4:9–12.
Weyr, Thomas
  1982 "Japanese Management: The Quick Fix?" *Working Woman*, April, pp. 28–29.
Whyte, William H.
  1956 *The Organization Man.* Garden City, N.Y.: Doubleday.
Wildavsky, Aaron
  1964 *Leadership in a Small Town.* Totowa, N.J.: Bedminster.
Wilkie, Jane Riblett
  1981 "The Trend toward Delayed Parenthood." *Journal of Marriage and the Family*, August, pp. 583–91.
Williams, Robin
  1959 *American Society: A Sociological Interpretation.* New York: Knopf.
Williams, Roger
  1977a "Alimony: The Short Goodbye." *Psychology Today*, July, pp. 70–77.
  1977b "The New Urban Pioneers: Homesteading in the Slums." *Saturday Review*, July 23, 9–16.
Wilson, Bryan
  1959 "An Analysis of Sect Development." *American Sociological Review* 24:3–15.
Wilson, Edward.
  1978a *On Human Nature.* Cambridge, Mass.: Harvard University Press.
  1978b "What is Sociobiology?" In *Sociobiology and Human Nature*, ed. Michael Gregory, Anita Silvers, Diane Sutch. San Francisco: Jossey-Bass, pp. 1–12.
Winch, Robert
  1971 *The Modern Family.* New York: Holt, Rinehart and Winston.
Winsbury, Rex
  1981 "India's Technology Dilemma." *Financial Times* (London), reprinted in *World Press Review*, February, p. 60.
Wirth, Louis
  1957 "Types of Minority Movements." In *Collective Behavior*, ed. Ralph Turner and Lewis Killian. Englewood Cliffs, N.J.: Prentice-Hall.
Wolfgang, Marvin E.
  1957 "Victim-Precipitated Criminal Homicide." *Journal of Criminal Law, Criminology, and Police Science*, Northwestern University School of Law, 48(1):1–11.
Wolfgang, Marvin E., and Franco Ferracuti
  1967 *The Subculture of Violence: Towards an Integrated Theory in Criminology.* London: Tavistock.
Wolman, Abel
  1965 "The Metabolism of Cities." In *Cities*, ed. the Editors of *Scientific American*. New York: Knopf.
Woodward, Joan
  1965 *Industrial Organization: Theory and Practice.* London: Oxford University Press.
World Opinion Update
  1982 "The Polish People Speak." January/February, pp. 4–6.
Wright, Charles
  1975 *Mass Communication: A Sociological Perspective.* New York: Random House.
Wrong, Dennis
  1961 "The Oversocialized Conception of Man in Modern Society." *American Sociological Review* 26:183–93.
Wuthnow, Robert
  1976 "Recent Pattern of Secularization: A Problem of Generations?" *American Sociological Review*, October, pp. 850–67.
Wyman, Anne C.
  1982 "Does Sociology Do Anybody Any Good?" *San Francisco Sunday Examiner and Chronicle* (Scene), January 17, pp. 1–2.
X, Malcolm
  1965 *The Autobiography of Malcolm X.* New York: Grove.
Yankelovich, Daniel
  1981a *The New Rules: Searching for Self-Fulfillment in a World Turned Upside Down.* New York: Random House.
  1981b "Stepchildren of the Moral Majority." *Psychology Today*, November, pp. 5–10.
Yinger, J. Milton
  1963 *Religion, Society and the Individual.* New York: Macmillan.
Yinger, Milton, et al.
  1977 *Middle Start: An Experiment in the Educational Enrichment of Young Adolescents.* New York: Cambridge University Press.
Zeisel, Hans
  1971 ". . . and Then There Were None: The Diminution of the Federal Jury." *University of Chicago Law Review* 38:710–24.
Zerubavel, Eviatar
  1982 "Easter and Passover: On Calendars and Group

Identity." *American Sociological Review*, April, pp. 284–89.

Zihlman, A.
1976 "Women in Evolution (Part 2): Subsistence and Social Organization Among Early Hominids." *Signs*, Autumn, pp. 178–99.

Zurcher, Louis A.
1981 "Editor's Comments." *Applied Behavioral Science* 17(4):437–38.

Name Index

Subject
Index